Contents

Preface

TO THE STUDENT

This *Study Guide* was designed to help you master the material in *Psychology*, Fourth Edition, by Bernstein/Clarke-Stewart/Roy/Wickens. The *Study Guide* supplements the textbook but does not replace it. If used properly, the *Guide* should help you not merely to memorize but to *take command* of the key facts, concepts, and issues discussed in the text.

We, the authors, want you to succeed in your introductory psychology course. We also want to help you deepen your understanding of how psychological principles can illuminate and enrich your life. These two desires steered us as we created this *Guide*.

Each *Study Guide* chapter corresponds to a text chapter and is divided into eight sections: Chapter Outline, Key Terms, Fill-in-the-Blanks Key Terms, Learning Objectives, Concepts and Exercises, Critical Thinking, Personal Learning Activities, and Multiple-Choice Questions.

1. *Chapter Outline* The outline presents the major topics and ideas from the text chapter. It reveals in handy fashion the organizational logic underlying each chapter—that is, the way each chapter's components fit together. Reviewing the Chapter Outlines may prove especially useful before a quiz or an exam.

2. *Key Terms* Terms that are underlined in the Chapter Outlines are also defined in the Key Terms section. We have tried to help you fix these terms in your memory: For many of them, we provide an illustrative example. For others, we present an idea to help you remember the key term. You will also find a number in parentheses at the end of each definition to identify the page on which the term is first defined and explained in the *textbook*.

   NOTE: We urge you to create your own examples of key terms as part of your study program. If you do so successfully, you will have taken a giant step toward mastering the material.

3. *Fill-in-the-Blanks Key Terms* Following the Key Terms definition section in each chapter are fifteen fill-in-the-blanks questions. These exercises are designed to help you check your mastery of many of the key terms and to review this definitional information before going on to later sections. Reading the answer provided at the end of the section will reinforce your learning and deepen your

understanding of chapter material as you work through later sections of the *Guide*.

4. *Learning Objectives* The Chapter Outline and Key Terms sections provide a basic overview of the contents of your textbook. The next section of each *Study Guide* chapter, Learning Objectives, will further strengthen your command of textbook material by focusing your attention on its specific goals: to be able to describe, compare, and explain the important information in each chapter. To help you master these learning objectives, we have identified the textbook pages to which each objective corresponds.

5. *Concepts and Exercises* This section will help you achieve selected learning objectives stated in the preceding section. The exercises apply key psychological concepts to situations from everyday life. You are asked to identify the concepts being applied. At the end of the exercises, we provide the correct answer to each exercise, along with an explanation of why the answer is correct.

6. *Critical Thinking* This section will help you sharpen your critical thinking skills by asking you to answer the five critical thinking questions presented in your text in relation to a particular situation or scenario. The five questions and their answers are stated in the answer section. This section is introduced in Chapter 2, where critical thinking is first presented.

7. *Personal Learning Activities* Active involvement is an excellent way to improve your understanding of and memory for the psychological issues, principles, and concepts described in *Psychology*. We have included personal learning activities to help you practice using the new information contained in each chapter.

8. *Multiple-Choice Questions* Once you have carefully worked through the previous sections, you will be ready to test your comprehension of the material covered. Every *Study Guide* chapter contains two multiple-choice quizzes, each consisting of twenty questions. At the end of the chapter, the correct answers are given, along with an explanation of *why* each is correct and why the alternatives are incorrect. If multiple-choice exams are part of your course, the multiple-choice quizzes in the *Study Guide* will provide a valuable way to prepare for them.

We suggest that you begin by taking Quiz 1. Next, check your answers against the answer key and fill in the number of items you answered correctly. For any items you miss, turn to the text pages listed next to the answers and reread the relevant sections. Write down, in your own words, information that will help you to better understand the material. Also, review appropriate sections of the *Study Guide*'s Chapter Outline and the appropriate Key Terms. Then reread the questions you missed on Quiz 1 to be sure you understand why the correct answer is correct and why the others are not.

Then take Quiz 2 and score it, noting our explanations of right and wrong answers. Finally, restudy the textbook and *Study Guide* materials as necessary. By following this procedure, you will build incrementally toward mastery of the contents of the text.

Finally, turn to the table at the end of the *Study Guide* chapter and circle the item numbers that you answered correctly the first time through Quizzes 1 and 2. (Quiz 2 is shaded to help you distinguish between your first and second tries at mastering the material.) The table will provide you with valuable information to further guide your studying. Look for a pattern in your results. Are you answering most of the definitional items correctly, but not the comprehension or application questions? Is there a topic that you mastered and another for which no items are circled? Write in the number of items you answered correctly on the first and second quizzes. Did you improve?

In the shortened example on the next page, the student circled the item numbers of questions that she or he correctly answered. The resulting pattern indicates that the student did well on definitional items, but not as well on application items. The table also shows that the student correctly answered more of the questions on current approaches (in the lower half of the table) than on historical schools (in the top half of the table). In addition to recognizing the need to review the historical approaches, the student should note that out of twenty-two items, he or she answered only eleven correctly. Perhaps the student should take additional notes on the chapter, write examples of the key terms, and consult the course instructor before the first graded quiz or exam.

As you can see, we have designed each chapter of this *Guide* as a sequenced program of study, and each section builds on the one before it. However, if you believe that a different sequencing of sections will work better for you, feel free to give it a try.

Here's to your success!

TOPIC	TYPE OF QUESTION		
	DEFINITION	COMPREHENSION	APPLICATION
History			
Structuralism		2	
			3
Gestalt			
		4	
Psychoanalysis	(3)		
Functionalism		4	
Behaviorism			
			(5)
Approaches			
Eclectic		5	
Biological	(7)		
Ethology			
	(10)		
Evolutionary		8	
Psychodynamic		(9)	
			6
Behavioral		(6)	10
Cognitive	(11)		
		(11)	7
Humanistic		12	
			(8)

TOTAL CORRECT BY QUIZ:

QUIZ 1:	5
QUIZ 2:	4

Developing Your Critical Thinking Skills

If you were to memorize every fact in the textbook, you might still miss its essentials. Much as sports announcers often say that the statistics of a game don't begin to indicate the contribution of a certain player, so, too, the facts conveyed by a college textbook often represent only a small part of its message. Thus, even if you forget many pieces of information within a year or two, you may retain something far more valuable from your introductory course in psychology.

What is there beyond the facts? Psychology and other disciplines have certain methods for defining, uncovering, and interpreting facts; they have certain ways of thinking. More generally, psychology and other fields of study rely on the ability to think critically—to evaluate claims, ideas, and evidence. Learning these ways of thinking enriches your ability to understand the world long after you may have forgotten specific pieces of information.

At its simplest, thinking critically means evaluating information rather than merely accepting it because it is endorsed by some authority or because it flatters your prejudices. In 1986, for example, a U.S. government commission declared that pornography is dangerous; it linked pornography and crime. You might be inclined to accept this conclusion because of the authority behind the commission or because you find pornography repugnant. But if you think critically, neither reason will be sufficient. At a minimum, you will ask why the commission came to that conclusion. What was their evidence? Even beyond asking for the reasons behind a conclusion, however, critical thinking requires the ability to evaluate those reasons. (The reasons for the commission's conclusions regarding pornography can be faulted on several grounds; they are evaluated in Chapter 18 of the text.) Is the argument logical? What is the source of the evidence that backs up the argument? If it's an experiment, were the experimental methods sound? Learning how to ask and answer questions like these is a first step in becoming skillful at critical thinking.

Throughout the text, the authors' discussions provide examples of critical thinking, illustrating how to examine the assumptions underlying an assertion, to evaluate evidence for an assertion, and to draw reasonable conclusions. In addition, each chapter of the textbook includes a section, labeled "Thinking Critically," that is devoted to critical thinking about one specific topic or assertion. In each case, the section examines the issue by considering five questions:

1. What am I being asked to believe or accept?
2. What evidence is available to support the assertion?
3. Are there alternative ways of interpreting the evidence?
4. What additional evidence would help to evaluate the alternatives?
5. What conclusions are most reasonable?

These questions represent steps that you can apply in thinking about most assertions, as Chapter 2 of the textbook explains. You can think critically without using these specific steps, but they constitute one useful model for critical thinking. Take time to consider the "Thinking Critically" sections, not only for their content, but also as a model of a way of thinking.

For further practice at critical thinking, do the Critical Thinking exercises in each chapter of the *Study Guide*. These will help you understand the importance of the five critical thinking questions and how to apply them. When you come across an issue of particular interest in your reading of the text, try applying these five steps to the discussion. No textbook can examine every issue in depth; if some of the steps are not fully explored in the text, try doing further research to follow these steps yourself. Or take a very specific assertion implicit in the discussion and explore it further by applying the five steps to that assertion. Most of all, as you read, remember to think critically. Throughout the text, the authors have tried to stimulate your own thinking. Just as they examine the flaws in existing research and acknowledge the many psychological questions that remain unanswered, so too should you probe what the authors have written and ask your own questions about it.

Applying the authors' model of critical thinking during the course should bring you at least four benefits. First, it should reinforce the habit of thinking critically. Are you going to buy brand X based on the endorsement of Candice Bergen or Michael Jordan? Will you take melatonin because others claim it is good for you? We hope this course will help you strengthen the habit of questioning claims and evaluating arguments for yourself. Second, the practice gained by applying the text's model of critical thinking should sharpen your critical-thinking skills. These skills can help you in every phase of life—whether you are weighing a politician's promises or the advantages of taking a new job, or searching for a new car or a way to reorganize a department. Third, going through this sequence of steps should lead you to a better understanding of the material and to wiser conclusions. Finally, thinking critically is likely to improve your memory of the material. As discussed in Chapter 8 of the textbook, organizing and thinking about information makes that information easier to remember.

Studying Linkages

A first glance at your textbook might suggest that introductory psychology resembles a cafeteria, consisting of a series of unrelated topics. Here is a little chemistry of the brain, over there a little biology of reproductive systems, and for dessert, a description of social pressures. But unlike a cafeteria, the diversity of topics in the textbook reflects not an attempt to satisfy every taste, but an effort to analyze essential parts of a complex whole. The diversity is necessary because all of these topics are pieces of the puzzle of psychology. If you wanted to understand why a friend became addicted to alcohol, for example, you would want to explore not only the person's history but also his relationships and the effects of chemicals on his brain.

Obviously you cannot study all of these topics at once; you would examine them one at a time. So, too, the textbook focuses on one aspect of psychology at a time. Eventually, however, it helps to put the pieces together. Much as parts of a jigsaw puzzle may take on new meaning when you see where they fit, so too the pieces of psychology take on new dimensions once you see how they are related. For example, the chemical messengers used in the brain (introduced in Chapter 3) are interesting in their own right; but your knowledge about them takes on new significance when you consider how these chemicals can be affected by drugs (discussed in Chapter 6) and by certain treatments for psychological disorders (discussed in Chapter 16).

To help you see how the pieces of psychology fit together, the authors of *Psychology*, Fourth Edition, have paid special attention to the ties among the aspects of human psychology, among the different areas of psychological research, and among the chapters of the textbook. These ties are all forms of what the authors call *linkages*, and the text highlights them in several ways. First, photographs, cross-references, and discussions throughout the text point out how topics in one chapter are related to discussions that appear in other chapters. Second, near the beginning of each chapter, a Linkages diagram presents questions that illustrate a link between the current chapter and the topic of other chapters in the text. These questions are then repeated in the margin next to where they are explored. Finally, a Linkages section discusses in some depth one specific question from the Linkages diagram.

You could read the text profitably without paying special attention to the Linkage elements, but they can help you gain a clearer view of psychology as a whole, a deeper understanding of specific issues, and a framework on which you can build your knowledge of psychology. And when you organize your knowledge and relate one piece of information to another, you improve your ability to remember the information. The Linkages diagrams in particular can be used in many ways as tools for learning and remembering information. Here are some suggestions.

Before reading the chapter, read the questions in the Linkages diagram. They will give you a feeling for the topic of the chapter and for the broader significance of specific issues. In each diagram, some of the questions are discussed in the current chapter and some in other chapters. Can you answer any of the questions? Do any of them concern a topic you have already read about in the text? If so, what do you remember about it? You might go to the page number given after the question, look for the question in the margin on that page, and scan or read the discussion. This will refresh your memory for concepts or facts related to the material to be discussed in the current chapter.

After reading the chapter, you can use the diagram to check your memory and understanding of the chapter. Try writing answers to those questions in the diagram that were discussed in the chapter. Check your answers against the text discussions. (Again, the page numbers in the diagram indicate where the discussion occurs.)

The diagrams can also help you go beyond the textbook in gaining and organizing knowledge of psychology. Suppose you are studying for a final exam and want to check your understanding of the topic of learning. You might go first to the Linkages diagram in the Learning chapter and check whether you can answer the questions; then you might flip to the Linkages diagrams in other chapters, find questions tied to Learning, and try to answer those questions. Also, keep in mind that the diagrams in the text provide only a sampling of linkages; there are many others. Finding additional linkages on your own can further your understanding of psychological issues and improve your memory of the material in the text. Finally, the questions in the Linkages diagrams or linkages that you find yourself may provide interesting topics for term papers.

Reading a Textbook

Effective learners engage in a very deep level of processing. They are active learners, thinking of each new fact in relation to other material. As a result, they learn to see similarities and differences among facts and ideas, and they create a context in which many new facts can be organized effectively.

Based on what is known about memory, we suggest two specific guidelines for reading a textbook. First, make sure that you understand what you are reading before moving on. Second, use the *SQ3R method*, which is one of the most successful strategies for remembering textbook material (Anderson, 1978; Frase, 1975; Rickards, 1976; Thomas & Robinson, 1972). SQ3R stands for the five activities that should be followed when you read a chapter: survey, question, read, recite, and review. These activities are designed to increase the depth to which you process the information you read.

1. **Survey** One of the best ways to begin a new chapter is by *not* reading it. Instead, take a few minutes to skim the chapter. Look at the section headings and any boldface or italicized terms. Obtain a general idea of what material will be discussed, how it is organized, and how its topics relate to one another and to what you already know. Some people find it useful to survey the entire chapter once and then survey each major section in a little more detail before reading it.

2. **Question** Before reading each section, stop and ask yourself what content will be covered and what information should be extracted from it.

3. **Read** Read the text, but think about the material as you read. Are the questions you raised earlier being answered? Do you see the connections between the topics?

4. **Recite** At the end of each section, stop and recite the major points. Resist the temptation to be passive by mumbling something like, "Oh, I remember that." Put the ideas into your own words.

5. **Review** Finally, at the end of the chapter, review all the material. You should see connections not only within a section but also among the sections. The objective is to see how the author has organized the material. Once you grasp the organization, the individual facts will be far easier to remember.

At the end, take a break. Relax. Approach each chapter fresh. Following these procedures will not only allow you to learn and remember the material better but also save you considerable time.

Study Guide

PSYCHOLOGY

Chapter 1

Introducing Psychology

OUTLINE

I. THE WORLD OF PSYCHOLOGY: AN OVERVIEW (pp. 3–10)

Psychology is the scientific study of behavior and mental processes.

A. The Scope of Behavior and Mental Processes

Psychologists are interested in many aspects of behavior and mental processes.

° The behaviors they examine may range from the physiological to the social level. Our senses, thoughts, personalities, and interactions with other people are part of what makes us unique and, therefore, are important for psychologists to understand.

° Psychology also includes the study of memory, mental abilities, health, stress, coping, and psychological disorders. Many psychologists use the research findings to improve their service to clients and organizations.

B. Research: The Foundation of Psychology

Psychologists use empirical research to collect and analyze information, rather than relying on speculation.

C. A Brief History of Psychology

° *Wundt and Structuralism.* Wilhelm Wundt wanted to study consciousness using scientific methods. With his technique of introspection, he documented "quality" and "intensity" as elements of sensation. Edward Titchener further identified "clarity" as one of the dimensions of consciousness; his approach was called structuralism. Gestalt psychologists disagreed with Wundt's methods, and suggested analyzing the whole conscious experience, not its elements.

° *Freud and Psychoanalysis.* Sigmund Freud developed a theory of personality based on the assumption that the unconscious could influence people's behavior.

° *James and Functionalism.* William James investigated how consciousness works to help people adapt to their environments. Because James thought that the function of sensations, ideas, and memories was important, his view became known as functionalism.

° *Watson and Behaviorism.* According to John B. Watson, psychologists should not study mental events but instead should observe people's behavioral reaction to stimuli without making inferences about consciousness. Watson inspired many psychologists to adopt behaviorism as the method of choice for scientific research in psychology.

° *Psychology Today.* Advances in technology have made it possible for psychologists to study the biological bases of mental activity. The study of consciousness has become more precise and objective.

II. UNITY AND DIVERSITY IN PSYCHOLOGY (pp. 11–23)

A. Approaches to Psychology

Each theoretical approach makes different assumptions about the factors that cause, maintain, and alter behavior and mental processes. Psychologists who use more than one approach are known as eclectic.

1. *The Biological Approach.* According to the biological approach, physiological factors determine behavior and mental processes. A psychologist with this approach would note changes in brain activity during memory formation or decision-making.

2. *The Evolutionary Approach.* Psychologists taking the evolutionary approach believe that behavior results partly from evolution through natural selection. Researchers seek to understand the reasons a behavior has evolved. Why is it adaptive, how has it been shaped by environmental conditions, and what anatomical and biological mechanisms underlie the behavior?

3. *The Psychodynamic Approach.* Though less influential today, this approach states that behavior

reflects unconscious internal conflict between people's instincts and society's behavioral rules.

4. *The Behavioral Approach.* The behavioral approach emphasizes learning in explaining behavior. For example, how do rewards and punishments shape, maintain, and change behavior? The cognitive-behavioral approach examines how learning influences thoughts and opinions, and how such cognitions influence observable behaviors.

5. *The Cognitive Approach.* According to the cognitive approach, behavior is a result of information processing (for example, perception, memory, thought, judgment, and decision making). Cognitive scientists work with biologists, linguists, computer scientists, and engineers to identify the components of thought that interact to produce behaviors.

6. *The Humanistic Approach.* According to the humanistic approach, people choose how to behave based on their perceptions of the world, in order to grow toward their unique potential. The humanistic approach is less influential today because its ideas are difficult to test empirically.

B. Subfields of Psychology

1. Cognitive psychologists study processes underlying perception, motivation, emotion, memory, problem solving, and other aspects of human thought.

2. The biological factors underlying our behavior are the concern of biological or physiological psychologists. How genetics, brain structures, and hormones affect our behavior are topics addressed by biological psychologists.

3. Social and industrial-organizational psychology research focuses on how people affect others' behavior and thinking. Social psychologists are interested in such subjects as advertising, prejudice, and interpersonal attraction, while industrial-organizational psychologists are interested in factors affecting work productivity, such as leadership styles.

4. Personality psychologists study the qualities that make people unique and explore relationships among personality characteristics, behavior, and mental processes.

5. Developmental psychology explores the causes and effects of changes in behavior and mental processes over the life span. Developmental psychologists study children's friendships, parenting styles and outcomes, and changes in thinking abilities.

6. Clinical and counseling psychology seeks to understand the origins of behavior disorders and to help people deal with disorders. Community psychologists provide psychological services to people who often do not seek help and work to prevent disorders by trying to lessen stresses such as poverty.

7. Educational psychologists investigate ways to improve student learning. School psychologists assess students' abilities and provide assistance when needed.

8. Quantitative psychologists create statistical methods for analyzing data and gauging the validity of tests.

9. Other subfields include health psychology, sport psychology, and environmental psychology.

C. Linkages Within Psychology and Beyond

Many psychologists are interested in several psychological subfields and may use more than one approach to study behavior and mental processes. Psychological research contributes to other disciplines such as neuroscience and uses theories from other disciplines (for example, math and physics) to understand psychological phenomena.

D. Human Diversity and Psychology

Psychologists are increasingly considering the influence of culture and sociocultural variables such as gender, social class, and ethnicity in shaping human behavior and mental processes.

KEY TERMS

1. **Psychology** is the science of behavior and mental processes. (p. 3)

   Example: Behavior is any action an organism performs, including those you can and cannot see (for example, jogging, laughing, heart rate, and blood pressure). Mental processes are activities involved in thinking (for example, remembering, dreaming, and forming opinions).

2. **Empiricism** is the position that facts should come from scientific investigation rather than conjecture. (p. 5)

   Example: Instead of speculating about why a group may follow the advice of a poor leader, psychologists will interview group members or design an experiment to answer the question.

3. **Empirical research** uses tests, observations, and controlled experiments to gather information. (p. 5)

Example: To discover whether noise is a factor in why people often ignore others in need of help, psychologists conducted an experiment in which noise was controlled.

4. **Structuralism** sought to discover the components of sensation and perception contributing to our conscious experiences. Wundt trained people to introspect, or attend to and describe their sensations and feelings, in order to learn about immediate experiences. (p. 8)

Example: A structuralist might show a person a piece of fabric and have the person report on its color, brightness, texture, and so on.

5. **Gestalt psychologists** viewed consciousness as a whole experience that might be different from the combined elements of sensations. (p. 8)

Example: Perceptual illusions show that sensations are not simply combined to form conscious experience: People may interpret an image differently depending on their mood, its context, and their prior experiences.

6. **Psychoanalysis** is a theory of personality and a treatment of psychological disorders based on the idea that behavior is caused by unconscious conflicts. (p. 8)

Example: Freud believed that some people's physical illnesses were cured when they recalled a previously unconscious traumatic experience from their past.

7. **Functionalism** focused on the role of consciousness in people's adjustment to their surroundings. James wanted to know the function of sensations and cognitive activity in everyday life. (p. 8)

Example: A functionalist would be interested in what influences a person's learning. Unlike the structuralists who wanted to separate the parts of sensation, functionalists wanted to understand how the process usually works.

8. **Behaviorism** suggests that psychologists study only observable behavior to find what rewards and punishments shape a person's behavior. (p. 9)

Example: Watson thought that control over the consequences of children's behavior would enable him to shape them into whatever type of person he chose.

9. **Functional analysis of behavior** was the method used by behaviorist B. F. Skinner to document the rewards and punishments controlling a behavior. (p. 9)

Example: A psychologist might watch children on a school bus and note that throwing trash out of the window was immediately rewarded by cheers from other students. The later punishment received might not be powerful enough to negate the first reward.

10. The **biological approach** assumes that biological factors—such as genetics, brain activity, or hormonal activity—are the most important factors determining behavior and mental processes. (p. 12)

Example: People who are chronically depressed may have abnormal levels of certain chemicals important to mood.

11. **Ethologists** observe animal behavior to identify adaptive, species-specific behavior. (p. 12)

Example: The work of ethologists has shown that some newborn birds automatically follow any moving object. This species-specific behavior keeps the chicks close to their mother and out of danger.

12. The **evolutionary approach** assumes that human and animal behavior is the result of evolution through natural selection. (p. 12)

Example: Psychologists study the adaptive value of behavior (running away from threats), the anatomical and biological systems that make the behavior possible (muscular construction of limbs), and the environmental conditions that encourage or discourage it (a culture may not approve of people running away).

13. The **psychodynamic approach** assumes that our behavior results from our struggle to fulfill instinctive desires and wishes despite society's rules. (p. 13)

Example: Freud might have said that surgeons express aggressive instincts in a manner that is approved of by society (performing surgery in an operating room rather than stabbing a stranger in a dark alley).

14. The **behavioral approach** assumes that the rewards and punishments that each person experiences determine most behaviors and thoughts. (p. 13)

Example: Doctors become surgeons because they are rewarded by their salaries, by the respect their positions receive, or by the satisfaction they receive from healing.

15. The **cognitive approach** assumes that mental processes guide behavior. The brain takes in information; processes it through perception, memory, thought, judgment, and decision making; and generates integrated behavior patterns. (p. 14)

> *REMEMBER:* Cognition means "thinking." The cognitive approach assumes that thoughts guide behavior.

16. The **humanistic approach** assumes that people control their behavior. This approach is thus unlike other models, which assume that biology, instincts, or the presence of rewards and punishments in the environment control behavior. The humanistic approach also assumes that people have an inborn tendency to grow toward their unique potential. (p. 14)

> *Example:* The innate tendency to grow toward one's unique potential is analogous to the development of a flower that will bloom if it receives adequate light, water, and nourishment. People, too, will achieve their potential if their environments provide the correct psychological and physical nourishment.

17. **Cognitive psychology** involves studying perception, learning, memory, thinking, language, and phenomena related to these basic mental and behavioral processes. (p. 16)

> *Example:* Is the memory of how to tie shoes developed, stored, and retrieved in the same ways as the memory of a friend's telephone number?

18. **Biological** or **physiological psychology** is the study of the biological factors that underlie behavior and mental processes. (p. 16)

> *Example:* Eating certain foods changes the chemical interactions within and between nerve cells in your brain, thereby possibly inducing drowsiness.

19. **Social psychology** is the study of how people influence one another and of the interactions between people in groups. **Industrial-organizational psychologists** study social influences on job performance. (p. 16)

> *Example:* How is behavior influenced by the type of group or situation a person is in? In a crowd, an anonymous person may be boisterous; however, when recognized as an individual (for example, in a classroom), the same person may be quiet and obedient.

20. **Personality psychology**, the study of what makes one person different from others, looks at the relationships among personality characteristics, behavior, and mental processes. (p. 16)

> *Example:* Why are some people consistently optimistic and others pessimistic?

21. **Developmental psychology** is the study of the causes and effects of changes in behavior and mental processes over the life span. (p. 17)

> *Example:* How do people develop morals, social skills, and intellectual abilities?

22. **Clinical and counseling psychology** is the study of abnormal behavior and mental processes, what causes them, and how to treat them. Clinical psychologists also evaluate how well and why a treatment works. (p. 17)

> *Example:* Is schizophrenia hereditary? What therapy produces the best results with schizophrenic patients?

23. **Community psychology** attempts to prevent psychological disorders and to treat people in their own communities. (p. 17)

> *Example:* Some community psychologists examine the problems students have in making the transition from high school to college and design programs to lessen these problems.

24. **Educational and school psychologists** study learning and teaching methods. (p. 17)

> *Example:* Educational psychologists found that when students take notes in their own words, they recall the information better.

> *Example:* School psychologists identify students' academic strengths and problems and tailor programs to meet students' needs.

25. **Quantitative psychologists** use statistics to evaluate data and improve the validity of tests. (pp. 17–18)

> *Example:* Researchers may consult a quantitative psychologist about how to analyze the results of a study.

26. **Approaches to Psychology Versus Subfields of Psychology.** Approaches to psychological study reflect assumptions concerning the causes of behav-

ior and mental processes. Subfields are areas of specialization or interest in the study of behavior and mental processes. (pp. 11–18)

> *Example:* Social psychologists (social refers to the subfield) may specialize, for instance, in research on decision making in groups. They may use an evolutionary, behavioral, or cognitive approach depending on their beliefs about what factors cause behavior and mental processes (evolution, rewards and punishments, or thoughts).

> *REMEMBER:* Many psychologists use more than one approach in their research because they believe that no single approach can fully account for all aspects of every behavior or mental process.

27. A **culture** is the accumulation of values, rules of behavior, forms of expression, religious beliefs, occupational choice, and so on, for a group of people who share a common language and environment. (p. 21)

28. An **individualist culture** encourages people to achieve personal goals. (p. 21)

> *Example:* People in individualist cultures often take credit for their success and emphasize their individuality.

29. A **collectivist culture** values people who place the goals of the collective ahead of their own goals. (p. 21)

> *Example:* People in collectivist cultures often attribute their success to help from others and emphasize their place in a family or work group.

FILL-IN-THE-BLANKS KEY TERMS

This section will help you check your knowledge of the key terms introduced in this chapter. Fill in each blank with the appropriate term from the list of key terms above.

1. _____ is the study of behavior and mental processes.

2. A person who runs an experiment, tracks results, and then reports those results is using _____ rather than speculation.

3. Supporters of _____ trained subjects to report the sensations they experienced when, for example, their hands were immersed in cold water.

4. A psychologist who attempts to find unconscious conflicts that have caused a psychological disorder is using _____.

5. A researcher who studies the influences on reaction time and how it helps people learn has a focus most similar to _____.

6. A developmental psychologist studying the correlation between brain development and changes in learning ability over the life span would be using the _____ approach.

7. A psychologist studying the adaptive value of maternal behavior would be using the _____ approach.

8. A(n) _____ psychologist researches how rewards change people's actions.

9. The president of a campus student group interested in understanding how peer pressure affects student members' political views should consult a(n) _____ psychologist.

10. A(n) _____ psychologist would study the effect of a drug on brain activity and the resulting impact on emotional responses.

11. A teacher interested in understanding how students' individuality influences their behavior would consult a(n) _____ psychologist.

12. Trying to determine the best type of treatment for an alcoholic would be of interest to a(n) _____ psychologist.

13. You would expect a(n) _____ psychologist to compare and contrast changes in learning ability from infancy through childhood, adolescence, middle age, and old age.

14. A(n) _____ psychologist would be interested in studying thought patterns underlying decision making in stressful situations.

15. An undercover police officer portraying a gang member would have to understand the _____ in which he or she will be working in order to avoid being detected.

Total Correct (See answer key) _____

LEARNING OBJECTIVES

1. Define psychology. (p. 3)

2. Define empiricism and describe empirical research. (p. 5)

3. Compare the goals and beliefs of <u>structuralism</u>, <u>psychoanalysis</u>, <u>functionalism</u>, and <u>behaviorism</u>. Describe <u>introspection</u> and the <u>functional analysis of behavior</u>. (pp. 7–9)

4. Compare and contrast the basic assumptions that define the six approaches to psychological phenomena: <u>biological</u>, <u>evolutionary</u>, <u>psychodynamic</u>, <u>behavioral</u>, <u>cognitive</u>, and <u>humanistic</u>. Define eclectic. (pp. 11–14)

5. Name the psychological subfields. Give examples of the questions and issues associated with each subfield. (pp. 15–18)

6. Explain why the field of psychology is unified, despite its many areas of specialization. Describe the linkages between psychology and other fields. (pp. 18–20)

7. Explain why psychologists have become increasingly interested in the influence of <u>culture</u> on behavior and mental processes. Define and give examples of sociocultural variables. Compare and contrast <u>individualist</u> and <u>collectivist</u> cultures. (pp. 20–23)

CONCEPTS AND EXERCISES

Research in a High School

Completing these exercises should help you to achieve Learning Objective 4.

Imagine you are a psychologist conducting research on violence at a local high school.

Questions

Identify which approach would be most likely to focus on each of the following to understand the students' behavior.

1. Do negative consequences such as detentions and expulsions deter a person from acting in a violent way? _____

2. Are certain types of decision-making styles more common among the violent students than the nonviolent students? _____

3. Is violent behavior related to a student's inability to deny other impulses? _____

4. Are the hormones associated with stress reactions at higher levels among students involved in violence? _____

Approaches

Biological
Psychodynamic
Behavioral
Cognitive
Humanistic

The Problem of Obesity

Completing this exercise should help you to achieve Learning Objective 5.

Questions

Match the subfields below with each of the following questions.

1. What is the effect of peer pressure on the eating patterns of obese people? _____

2. Is there a common pattern of weight gain throughout the life span of an obese person? _____

3. Are most obese people introverts or extroverts? _____

4. Is obesity correlated with any other disorder, such as depression? _____

5. Do fat cells in obese people differ in number or size from those in normal-weight people? _____

Subfields

Biological
Personality
Developmental
Clinical
Social

PERSONAL LEARNING ACTIVITIES

1. In a recent newspaper or magazine find a report describing a psychological study. Does it give details of empirical research or does it primarily focus on opinions, assumptions, and unsupported generalizations? (Learning Objective 2)

2. Look at a sheet of plain white paper and attempt introspection. Rather than simply describing it as a "white paper," notice any shadows, flecks of other colors, texture, and so on. Did introspection change your perception? (Learning Objective 3)

3. How might psychology have been different if Freud hadn't presented his ideas about the unconscious? (Learning Objective 3)

4. Listen to a radio or television talk show and attend to the comments made about people's behaviors. Try to classify the statements under the approach they are most like. For example, do people say that hormones or feelings of which they are unaware caused someone's behavior? (Learning Objective 4)

5. Do you agree or disagree with this statement: "Personality is determined by genetics." Why?

MULTIPLE-CHOICE QUESTIONS

SAMPLE QUIZ 1

1. Psychology is the study of
   a. the development of cultures, religions, and societies.
   b. behaviors and mental processes.
   c. earth, nations, plant life, and animals.
   d. how people relate to each other.

2. Introspection is a research method used primarily by _____ to discover the elements of consciousness.
   a. structuralists
   b. behaviorists
   c. functionalists
   d. ethologists

3. A psychologist who thinks current behavior is caused by unconscious conflicts was most likely trained in
   a. behaviorism.
   b. functionalism.
   c. gestalt psychology.
   d. psychoanalysis.

4. Which of the following is NOT a modern approach to psychology?
   a. behavioral
   b. cognitive
   c. evolutionary
   d. functionalism

5. Sometimes Janessa treats her clients with drugs, but at other times she tries to change the patterns of rewards and punishments the person receives. Janessa's approach can best be described as
   a. behavioral.
   b. biological.
   c. eclectic.
   d. humanistic.

6. To understand what rewards a child receives for bullying other children, we would most likely use
   a. cognitive science.
   b. functional analysis of behavior.
   c. introspection.
   d. psychoanalysis.

7. Dr. Atilano says that behavior is caused by activity in the nervous system, genetic inheritance, and hormones. Dr. Atilano takes a _____ approach to psychological phenomena.
   a. biological
   b. psychodynamic
   c. behavioral
   d. cognitive

8. An instructor tells you that the evolutionary approach best characterizes her viewpoint. Which of the following statements is she most likely to agree with?
   a. Each person learns what behaviors are best.
   b. Over generations, maladaptive behaviors will become less and less common in a species.
   c. People do what makes them feel good.
   d. We inherit only adaptive behaviors.

9. Deon believes that his friend Tom drives too fast on the interstate because Tom is unconsciously wishing for death. Deon suggests that Tom can't admit he feels guilty about being independent from his family. Deon most likely has a _____ approach to psychology.
   a. behavioral
   b. biological
   c. cognitive
   d. psychodynamic

10. Mercedes often procrastinates when faced with a big assignment. A psychologist with a behavioral approach would be most likely to say that Mercedes procrastinates because she
    a. believes it helps her to get motivated later.
    b. perceives the assignment as unfair and overwhelming.
    c. is rewarded by the lighter workload during her early avoidance of the project.
    d. unconsciously desires to fail her assignment.

11. Psychologists who emphasize the role of mental processes in explaining behavior take a(n) _____ approach.
    a. evolutionary
    b. biological
    c. cognitive
    d. deterministic

12. Hassan believes his clients are basically good; therefore, he wants to see things from their point of view. Because Hassan also says that if he can understand a client's feelings and perceptions he will be better able to help them achieve their potential, Hassan is most likely a(n) _____ psychologist.
    a. developmental
    b. evolutionary
    c. humanistic
    d. social

13. Francis majors in education and wants to understand the processes involved in learning and memory. Which of the following courses would best help Francis reach his goal?
    a. Cognitive psychology
    b. Neuroscience
    c. Clinical psychology
    d. Social psychology

14. You are a biological psychologist interested in the emotional reactions of students to exams. Which of the following would be of the most interest to you?
    a. Hormone levels
    b. How much support the student has from peers
    c. The dreams a student has before an exam
    d. Attitudes toward learning

15. Maria watches people to discover what unwritten rules for behavior they are following. Maria sees that people tend not to sit next to another person on the bus unless empty seats are limited. Maria's interests are most like psychologists in the _____ subfield.
    a. clinical
    b. developmental
    c. personality
    d. social

16. Michelle studies how sociable, conscientious, and anxious children are at age 8. She intends to see if she can predict differences in the number of years of school they have completed by age 25. Michelle is most likely a _____ psychologist.
    a. community
    b. humanistic
    c. personality
    d. social

17. Which of the following is the best example of the work of a psychologist interested in the clinical subfield?
    a. Sadie observes how changes in playground equipment affect the interactions between children.
    b. Tad attempts to assist people who are extremely depressed.
    c. Val compares the IQ scores of sociable people with those of shy people.
    d. Vince wonders if people's hormones influence their thinking.

18. Dr. Li tests students at a grade school and makes recommendations about who may benefit from an accelerated program and who may need a specific type of tutoring. Dr. Li is most likely a(n) _____ psychologist.
    a. community
    b. industrial-organizational
    c. personality
    d. school

19. A quantitative psychologist would be most interested in which of the following questions?
    a. What mathematical methods can measure, describe, and predict intelligence?
    b. What type of management style would generate the highest productivity?
    c. What mental steps are involved in perception and decision making?
    d. How do social skills evolve from the preschool years through old age?

20. David doesn't get any laughs from the audience in response to his comedy monologue. If David is from a collectivist culture, he will be most likely to think,
    a. "It's my writers' fault I wasn't funny."
    b. "I know I am funnier than other comedians; I just had a bad night."
    c. "My sense of humor is too sophisticated for this crowd."
    d. "It's my fault I wasn't funny enough for my audience."

Total Correct (See answer key) _____

SAMPLE QUIZ 2

Use this quiz to reassess your learning after taking Quiz 1 and reviewing the chapter.

1. A psychologist may be concerned with which of the following questions:
   a. Do schizophrenics have biochemical processes different from those of normal individuals?
   b. Does urban crowding cause higher crime rates?
   c. Does the decision-making process vary with the number of factors involved in the decision?
   d. All of the above

2. After speculating that a noisy environment reduces helping behavior, a psychologist using empiricism will most likely
   a. describe to talk-show viewers how noise affects us.
   b. design research to test the idea.
   c. try to reduce noise in the environment.
   d. try to help someone in a noisy environment.

3. Ming's research involves presenting subjects with objects and asking them to report the sensations that they are experiencing. Ming is most likely a
   a. functionalist.
   b. structuralist.
   c. behaviorist.
   d. humanist.

4. Roberto studies what people enjoy about listening to classical music. Roberto claims that it would be useless to isolate and listen to only a rhythm, a violin part, or any other single aspect of music, because it is the perception of the complete piece that is important. Roberto's emphasis on not dividing music into parts is most similar to
   a. structuralism.
   b. behaviorism.
   c. gestalt psychology.
   d. psychoanalysis.

5. Larry says that people act the way they learned to act. Larry believes that if others stop rewarding a person's annoying behaviors, those behaviors will lessen. Larry most likely has a(n) _____ approach to psychology.
   a. behavioral
   b. cognitive
   c. evolutionary
   d. humanistic

6. Paul's aunt thinks that Paul acts aggressively because he wants immediate gratification, so she insists that he learn to control his natural impulses. The approach most similar to her views is
   a. evolutionary.
   b. psychodynamic.
   c. biological.
   d. functionalism.

7. A cognitive psychologist investigating why students study regularly would be most interested in
   a. the students' decisions about the advantages and disadvantages of putting off work.
   b. the students' hidden internal conflicts.
   c. how diet and exercise influence motivation level.
   d. how past rewards and punishments have maintained this behavior.

8. Marissa says that she often doesn't attend classes because she doesn't find her courses interesting. Her roommate, Leslie, claims that Marissa doesn't attend because her natural drive toward self-improvement has been blocked. Leslie's view is most similar to a psychologist with a _____ approach.
   a. humanistic
   b. psychodynamic
   c. biological
   d. cognitive

9. Helen, a first-year college student, wants to become a biological psychologist. Her counselor will probably tell her to take which of the following courses?
   a. Cognitive development
   b. Physiology of behavior
   c. The history of Freud
   d. Community medical prevention programs

10. Species-specific behaviors are
    a. instinctive.
    b. learned.
    c. probably not adaptive.
    d. all of the above.

11. Bill's therapist told him that his thought patterns cause his depression. Bill's therapist follows the _____ approach to psychological phenomena.
    a. biological
    b. psychodynamic
    c. cognitive
    d. behavioral

12. Brendan runs a diversity training program that allows people to discuss stereotypes and become more accepting of people with different backgrounds. Brendan is especially interested in the effect his training has on the ability of employees to work together. Brendan is most likely a(n) _____ psychologist.
    a. cognitive
    b. community
    c. industrial-organizational
    d. personality

13. Rajesh is very concerned about meeting his parents' expectations. Rajesh doesn't want to attract attention to himself; therefore, when he is successful, he will usually emphasize the role his family played in helping him to achieve. According to the description in your textbook, Rajesh is most likely from a _____ culture.
    a. collectivist
    b. communist
    c. democratic
    d. individualist

14. Alisha notices people in her classes becoming friends and wonders what attracts people to each other. Alisha's interests are most like those of psychologists in the _____ subfield.
    a. clinical
    b. developmental
    c. personality
    d. social

15. Jill wants to start a personal-service business offering nannies, an adolescent big-brother and big-sister program, and companions for the elderly. Jill must be able to teach her employees how to fulfill the psychological needs of every age group. Jill should study _____ psychology.
    a. biological
    b. psychodynamic
    c. developmental
    d. cognitive

16. On a bus you overhear a man talking to himself. The man appears to be getting angry and eventually starts pounding one fist into the other palm and shouting unintelligibly. Because he seems like he has a psychological disorder and may need help, you would want to recommend that someone call a _____ psychologist.
    a. clinical
    b. developmental
    c. personality
    d. social

17. A psychologist who wants to prevent disorders by ensuring children have proper nutrition and educational opportunities is most likely a(n) _____ psychologist.
    a. biological
    b. clinical
    c. community
    d. educational

18. Candace is a proficient computer programmer who is interested in psychology. She would like to use her skills to analyze data and evaluate tests. Candace's interests are most like those of a psychologist in which subfield?
    a. biological
    b. clinical
    c. cognitive
    d. quantitative

19. Kwasi wants to know which study techniques are most efficient for which types of tests; therefore, he should consult a(n) _____ psychologist.
    a. behavioral
    b. clinical
    c. educational
    d. school

20. Cultures in which personal goals are more important than group goals are termed
    a. multicultural.
    b. individualist.
    c. collectivist.
    d. subcultural.

Total Correct (See answer key) _____

ANSWERS TO FILL-IN-THE-BLANKS KEY TERMS

1. Psychology (p. 3)
2. empiricism (p. 5)
3. structuralism (pp. 7–8)
4. psychoanalysis (p. 8)
5. functionalism (p. 8)
6. biological (p. 12)
7. evolutionary (p. 12)
8. behavioral (p. 13)
9. social (p. 16)
10. biological (p. 16)
11. personality (p. 16)
12. clinical (p. 17)
13. developmental (p. 17)
14. cognitive (p. 16)
15. subculture (p. 21)

ANSWERS TO CONCEPTS AND EXERCISES

Research in a High School

1. The <u>behavioral</u> approach focuses on the consequences of behavior as an explanation for current behavior. (p. 13)

2. Psychologists with the <u>cognitive</u> approach would be most interested in knowing about beliefs, decision-making strategies, and perceptions. (p. 14)

3. The <u>psychodynamic</u> approach claims that people spend much of their energy trying to control their negative natural impulses. (p. 13)

4. A researcher with a <u>biological</u> approach would link behavior to hormone levels and other physiological differences such as brain activity, blood pressure, and muscle tension. (p. 12)

The Problem of Obesity

1. <u>Social</u> psychologists are interested in group behavior and how it influences individual group members. (p. 16)

2. <u>Developmental</u> psychologists are interested in people's physical, behavioral, and mental growth over the life span. (p. 17)

3. <u>Personality</u> psychologists are interested in the extroversion/introversion phenomenon. (p. 16)

4. <u>Clinical</u> psychologists would be interested in finding out whether depressed people tend to be obese. Further research would be done to understand the relationship between depression and obesity. (p. 17)

5. <u>Biological</u> psychologists study the physiological factors that guide or control our behavior. Having fat cells that are larger in size or number may cause altered eating patterns and possibly weight increase. (p. 16)

ANSWERS TO MULTIPLE-CHOICE QUESTIONS

Circle the question numbers you answered correctly.

Sample Quiz 1

1. *b* is the answer. Psychologists research the actions and thoughts of organisms. Psychologists also try to help people who have difficulty coping. (pp. 3–6)
   a. An anthropologist would probably study the development of societies.
   c. The focus of psychology is narrower; geography is the study of the earth and its many inhabitants.
   d. Psychology is much more than the study of human interaction; psychologists may study development, learning, memory, psychological disorders, and much more.

2. *a* is the answer. Structuralists used introspection to study the elements that made up the "structure" of consciousness. (pp. 7–8)
   b. Behaviorists do not study consciousness. Watson, the founder of behaviorism, thought that consciousness could not be studied scientifically.
   c. Functionalists were more interested in how our consciousness directed our behavior. They were not as interested in the structure of consciousness.
   d. Ethologists are interested in instinctive species-specific behaviors, not consciousness, and do not use introspection.

3. *d* is the answer. Psychoanalysis is a treatment strategy that assumes that people are influenced by conflicts of which they are unaware. (p. 8)
   a. Behaviorists emphasize that people learn from the consequences of their behavior. The behavioral approach does not recognize the unconscious as an influence on people's behavior.
   b. Functionalism wanted to understand how consciousness works, but did not study the unconscious.
   c. Gestalt psychology viewed consciousness as an experience that could not be divided into its parts; Gestalt psychologists did not concern themselves with the unconscious.

4. *d* is the answer. James' functionalism influenced modern psychologists to study memory, education, and intelligence, but it is not a modern approach. (p. 8)
   a, b, c. Current psychologists may use the behavioral, cognitive, or evolutionary approach, among others.

5. *c* is the answer. Many psychologists choose what they consider to be the best features of several approaches and use whatever feature or combination of features will be most helpful to a client. (p. 11)
   a. A person with a behavioral approach would try to change the pattern of rewards and punishments, but would not use drug therapy.

b. The biological approach would view drug treatment as a reasonable way to alter the chemical or hormonal imbalances that caused the problematic behavior, but would not agree with altering the reward and punishment patterns.

d. A humanistic psychologist would be interested in a person's unique perceptions; therefore, a humanistic psychologist would not prescribe drugs or change the consequences of a client's behavior.

6. *b* is the answer. A behaviorist using functional analysis of behavior would study the events following a child's actions to see what benefits the actions have. (p. 9)

a. Cognitive science is a multidisciplinary approach to the study of thought and mental abilities, not a method for analyzing a behavior's consequences.

c. Introspection is a method used by structuralists to investigate consciousness.

d. Psychoanalysis was begun by Freud as a means of uncovering unconscious struggles, not as a means of discovering the impact of overt behaviors.

7. *a* is the answer. Biological psychologists assume that nervous-system activity, hormones, and genetic inheritance cause behavior. (p. 12)

b. The psychodynamic approach assumes that behavior results from our struggle to fulfill instinctive desires despite society's restrictions.

c. The behavioral approach assumes that behavior is caused by people's past experiences of rewards and punishments.

d. The cognitive approach assumes that behavior is caused by the thoughts involved with that behavior.

8. *b* is the answer. The evolutionary approach looks for evidence that organisms improve over generations. Those behaviors that were not helpful would be replaced by behaviors that were. (pp. 12–13)

a. The behavioral approach would agree that people learn what is adaptive for them, but the evolutionary approach would go on to say that organisms that cannot adjust to their environment do not survive.

c. A Freudian might take the view that people do what feels good, especially if a person has not learned about the limits society places on behavior.

d. We do not inherit **only** adaptive behaviors.

9. *d* is the answer. The psychodynamic approach describes behavior as guilt-driven or unconsciously influenced. (p. 13)

a. The behavioral approach does not address unconscious motives.

b. To psychologists with the biological approach, the cause of behavior is physiological rather than intellectual.

c. The cognitive approach emphasizes conscious thoughts, memories, and decisions.

10. *c* is the answer. A psychologist with the behavioral approach would look to the consequences of procrastination for an explanation of why Mercedes waits to do an assignment. (p. 13)

a. Motivation is a cognitive factor not dealt with by the behavioral approach.

b. Beliefs and feelings are cognitive factors that would be addressed by the humanistic approach.

d. The unconscious is part of the psychodynamic approach.

11. *c* is the answer. Cognitive psychologists investigate thoughts and information-processing. (p. 14)

a. The evolutionary approach is in agreement with Darwin's theory that adaptive behaviors will survive in a species, but it does not study current mental processes.

b. Mental processes are influenced by physiology, according to biological psychologists; therefore, physiology would be emphasized by biological psychologists.

d. The deterministic approach is not one of the major approaches to psychology.

12. *c* is the answer. Humanistic psychologists are concerned with viewing things from their clients' perspective. (p. 14)

a. Developmental psychologists study people across the life span.

b. Psychologists with an evolutionary approach do not try to help clients improve. They believe that we inherit adaptive characteristics; therefore, they do not focus on a person's perceptions.

d. Social psychologists research how people interact.

13. *a* is the answer. Cognitive psychologists study the processes of learning and memory. (pp. 15–16)

b. Neuroscience research may include studies on the neurological changes accompanying learning. However, Francis would have difficulty directly applying such knowledge to the teaching of his students.

c. Although clinical psychologists may have patients whose learning problems result from disorders, they do not focus their research in this area.

d. Social psychologists study interactions between people. This information will help Francis understand students' social behaviors, but not the processes of learning and memory.

14. *a* is the answer. Psychologists who take a biological approach would emphasize the relationship between emotions and physiological factors such as nervous system and hormonal activity. (p. 16)

b. Support from peers would be a concern of social psychologists.

c. Dreams might be analyzed by a psychodynamic psychologist.

d. Attitudes toward learning would interest cognitive psychologists.

15. *d* is the answer. Social psychologists are interested in how people influence each other's behavior. (p. 16)

a. Clinical psychologists study disorders and find ways to assist people in coping with disorders.

b. A developmental psychologist researches the changes that take place in people as they age.

c. Personality psychology documents individual differences, but does not study how people are affected by others.

16. *c* is the answer. A personality psychologist conducts research on long-lasting differences between people much like Michelle's study of the association between a personality description and later behavior. (p. 16)

a. Community psychologists work to prevent psychological disorders.

b. A person with a humanistic approach would focus on immediate experience and current perceptions instead of looking for a relationship between early judgments and later behavior.

d. Social psychologists look for general rules about how people interact.

17. *b* is the answer. Clinical psychologists help people cope with stressors and psychological disorders. (p. 17)

a. Sadie is a social psychologist.

c. Val is a personality psychologist.

d. Vince is a biological psychologist.

18. *d* is the answer. School psychologists watch for learning disabilities and giftedness in order to arrange for special education if warranted. (p. 17)

a. A community psychologist might be interested in keeping problems in academic achievement from occurring, but would not be trained in educational testing and program placement.

b. Industrial-organizational psychology is the study of social behavior in the workplace.

c. Personality psychologists might research the influence of personality characteristics on student achievement, but do not specialize in educational testing and placement as school psychologists do.

19. *a* is the answer. Quantitative psychologists study and develop methods of measuring and analyzing behavior and mental processes such as intelligence. (pp. 17–18)

b. Industrial-organizational psychologists study social behavior, such as a supervisor's style of communication at work.

c. Cognitive psychologists study perception, learning, memory, judgment, and decision making.

d. Developmental psychologists research how and why behavior and mental processes change over the life span.

20. *d* is the answer. If Dave is from a collectivist culture he is likely to give others credit when he succeeds, but to blame himself when he fails. (p. 21)

a, c. A person from a collectivist culture would be unlikely to blame others for a failure.

b. People in collectivist cultures are unlikely to emphasize their unique qualities.

Now turn to the quiz analysis table at the end of this chapter to find which areas you know well and which areas you need to work on. Circle the numbers in the table for items on Quiz 1 that you answered correctly.

ANSWERS TO MULTIPLE-CHOICE QUESTIONS

Circle the question numbers you answered correctly.

Sample Quiz 2

1. *d* is the answer. Psychologists are concerned with all behaviors and mental processes. Aberrant biochemical processes are a possible cause of schizophrenic behavior. Crime is a behavior, and decision making is a mental process. (pp. 3–5)

2. *b* is the answer. After speculating that a noisy environment reduces helping behavior, Mathews and Canon designed research that indicated that stimulus overload makes people less likely to help. (p. 5)
   a. Before empiricists describe a phenomenon, they study it.
   c. Trying to reduce noise in the environment before we know if it is the true cause of reduced helping behavior might be a waste of effort; therefore, empiricists see if their hunches are correct.
   d. Helping someone in a noisy environment, while it is a nice thing to do, does not show whether noise influences most people's helping behavior.

3. b is the answer. Structuralists used the method of introspection to determine the elements of or the structure of consciousness. (pp. 7–8)
   a. Functionalists studied consciousness, but they used a more experimental approach rather than introspection.
   c. Behaviorists study behavior, not consciousness.
   d. Humanists are interested in people's natural tendency toward growth, not in identifying elements of sensation.

4. *c* is the answer. Gestalt psychologists criticized other approaches for splitting up experience into its components rather than studying consciousness as a whole experience. (p. 8)
   a. Structuralism tried to identify the elements of sensation through introspection. People using introspection would often divide their experience into parts such as quality, intensity, and clarity.
   b. A behaviorist studies behaviors and the rewards and punishments that follow.
   d. Psychoanalysis is a method for identifying hidden conflicts and memories that affect current behavior.

5. *a* is the answer. The behavioral approach emphasizes that people think and behave in ways that have been previously rewarded. (p. 9)
   b. The cognitive approach emphasizes what people *think* about a situation and the consequences of their behavior, and emphasizes the way people process incoming information.
   c. Evolutionists try to understand the environmental conditions that encourage (reward) behaviors; however, rather than trying to change the consequences, they emphasize that adaptive behaviors are passed on to future generations.
   d. The humanistic approach emphasizes the role of a person's view of the situation.

6. *b* is the answer. Psychodynamic theory suggests that there is a tension between natural impulses and society's rules. (p. 13)
   a. The evolutionary approach explains current behaviors as the result of natural selection.
   c. A person with a biological approach would look to the influence of drugs, chemical imbalances, and other physiological characteristics as the cause of current behaviors.
   d. Functionalism did not comment on impulses or societal control; instead, it documented how mental events were adaptive.

7. *a* is the answer. Cognitive psychologists are interested in conscious decision-making. (p. 14)
   b. Internal conflicts are in the realm of psychodynamic psychologists.
   c. Diet and exercise would most likely interest a biological psychologist.
   d. Behavioral psychologists want to know what rewards and punishments maintain a behavior.

8. *a* is the answer. The humanistic approach stresses that people are basically good and will work toward improving themselves unless stopped by something major. (p. 14)
   b. The psychodynamic approach downplays the role of positive impulses and plays up the role of unconscious conflicts and negative impulses.
   c. Biological psychology emphasizes the importance of body chemistry in everyday life.
   d. Cognitive psychology does not recognize a drive toward self-improvement.

9. *b* is the answer. Helen will learn which physiological processes affect behavior. (p. 16)
   a. Cognitive development is the study of the development of thinking.
   c. Clinical, personality, and developmental psychologists may be interested in discussing and testing Freud's ideas, but biological psychologists probably would not.
   d. Community psychologists develop and operate prevention programs.

10. *a* is the answer. Species-specific behaviors are instinctive; that is, they do not require that learning take place before the behaviors are performed correctly in their entirety. (p. 12)
    b. Species-specific behaviors are not learned. Animals usually perform them perfectly the first time they try, even if they have never seen the behavior performed by another animal.
    c. Evolutionists believe that the adaptive value of species-specific behavior explains why it

evolved and why it is genetically passed on to future generations.

d. Only *a* is the answer.

11. *c* is the answer. The cognitive approach assumes that behavior results from the thoughts involved in that behavior. (p. 14)
   a. The biological approach assumes that genetic inheritance, nervous-system activity, and hormones cause behaviors.
   b. The psychodynamic approach assumes that behavior is a result of our struggle to fulfill instinctive desires despite society's restrictions.
   d. The behavioral approach assumes that behavior is caused by the rewards and punishments experienced by individuals in response to their behaviors.

12. *c* is the answer. Industrial-organizational psychologists research the influence of employee interactions and management structures on employee productivity. (p. 16)
   a. Cognitive psychologists might study mental processes involved in prejudice; however, they would be unlikely to study the impact of diversity training on employee relations.
   b. Community psychology attempts to reach people in need by providing affordable mental health care in the community.
   d. Personality psychologists study how people differ from each other, but do not study employee interactions.

13. *a* is the answer. People in collectivist cultures tend to try not to attract attention to themselves and are likely to credit their family or work group if they are successful. (p. 21)
   a. A communist society may or may not be collectivist.
   b. A democratic society may or may not be collectivist.
   d. Individualist cultures emphasize individuality. If Rajesh is from an individualist culture, he will be likely to take credit for his success.

14. *d* is the answer. Interpersonal attraction is a topic of interest to social psychologists. (p. 16)
   a. Clinical psychology deals with psychological disorders.
   b. A developmental psychologist would study differences in people as they age.
   c. Personality psychology looks for similarities within an individual over time, but does not study interpersonal attraction.

15. *c* is the answer. Developmental psychologists are interested in understanding how and why behavior and mental processes change over the life span. (p. 17)
   a. Biological psychology would teach Jill the areas of the brain and the physiological processes that are involved in learning, but this knowledge would be difficult for her personnel to apply in their jobs.
   b. Psychodynamic psychology would teach Jill that behavior is determined by the combination of unconscious internal conflicts and external (parents', peers', or society's) reactions to those conflicts. However, this approach would not help Jill fulfill changing needs for different age groups.
   d. Cognitive psychology would help Jill understand certain useful principles of learning. However, she must understand how learning and many other behaviors and mental processes change over the life span in order to help people of all ages.

16. *a* is the answer. A clinical psychologist would be most qualified to work with a person who has a psychological disorder. (p. 17)
   b. Developmental psychologists study age differences and do not provide counseling.
   c. A personality psychologist might be interested in the person's unique personality, but would not be able to offer counseling.
   d. Social psychology is the study of how people influence one another; however, it does not study disorders or treatment.

17. *c* is the answer. Community psychology not only provides counseling service in the community, but also works to reduce the number of risks that contribute to the appearance of disorders. (p. 17)
   a. Biological psychology investigates the influence of physiological factors on behavior, but does not seek to prevent disorders.
   b. Clinical psychologists are trained to help people once they have a disorder.
   d. Educational psychology focuses on learning and teaching strategies, but would not address the prevention of disorders through nutrition.

18. *d* is the answer. Analyzing data is part of quantitative psychology. (pp. 17–18)
   a. Biological psychologists are more interested in the nervous system, immune system, and hormonal balance than in test evaluation.
   b. A person in clinical psychology researches disorders and designs treatments.

c. Cognitive psychology focuses on thought processes.

19. *c* is the answer. Educational psychologists research studying and teaching techniques. (p. 17)
    a. A psychologist with a behavioral approach would know about incentives, but could not advise Kwasi on specific study techniques.
    b. Clinical psychologists are concerned with psychological disorders, not study habits.
    d. School psychologists administer IQ tests, identify learning problems, and set up educational programs to assist students; however, they do not research general study strategies.

20. *b* is the answer. Individualist cultures emphasize and reward behavior that contributes to the success of the individual person even if it sometimes occurs at the group's expense. (p. 21)
    a. Multicultural refers to the existence of more than one culture within a given geographic boundary such as a country (Kenya) or a city (Los Angeles).
    b. Collectivist cultures emphasize and reward behaviors that contribute to the success of the group. Remember, collectivist cultures emphasize "collections" of people (groups) over the individual.
    d. Subcultures are part of a multicultural society.

Now turn to the quiz analysis table at the end of this chapter to find which areas you know well and which areas you need to work on. Circle the numbers in the table for items on Quiz 2 that you answered correctly.

For each question you answered correctly, circle its number. (Quiz 1 numbers are not shaded; Quiz 2 numbers are shaded.) Are there patterns in the types of questions or the topics you got wrong that could direct your further study? Did you improve from Quiz 1 to Quiz 2?

TOPIC	TYPE OF QUESTION		
	DEFINITION	COMPREHENSION	APPLICATION
Scope of psychology	1		1
Empiricism		2	
History			
Structuralism		2	3
Gestalt		4	
Psychoanalysis	3		
Functionalism		4	
Behaviorism			5
Approaches			
Eclectic		5	
Biological	7		
Ethology	10		
Evolutionary		8	
Psychodynamic		9	6
Behavioral		6	10
Cognitive	11	11	7
Humanistic		12	8

TOPIC	TYPE OF QUESTION		
	DEFINITION	COMPREHENSION	APPLICATION
Subfields			
Cognitive		13	
Biological			14
		9	
Social/Industrial-organizational			15
		14	12
Personality			16
Developmental			
			15
Clinical/Counseling			17
			16
Community			
		17	
Educational and school			18
			19
Quantitative		19	
			18
Culture			20
	20	13	

TOTAL CORRECT BY QUIZ:

QUIZ 1:
QUIZ 2:

Chapter 2

Research in Psychology

OUTLINE

I. THINKING CRITICALLY ABOUT PSYCHOLOGY (OR ANYTHING ELSE) (pp. 26–30)

Critical thinking is the process of assessing claims or assertions and making judgments about them on the basis of well-supported evidence. You can use the following set of questions to think critically about any topic:

1. What am I being asked to believe or accept? What is the hypothesis?

2. What evidence is available to support the assertion? Is it reliable and valid?

3. Are there alternative ways of interpreting the evidence?

4. What additional evidence would help to evaluate the alternatives?

5. What conclusions are most reasonable based on the evidence and the number of alternative explanations?

A. Critical Thinking and Scientific Research

Psychologists investigate phenomena they are curious about by formulating hypotheses, which are testable propositions. As critical thinkers, scientists look for reliable, valid evidence that either supports or contradicts their hypothesis. Operational definitions are used to describe the methods used and the behaviors studied (that is, the psychological variables) in the research.

B. The Role of Theories

A theory is an integrated set of tentative explanations of behavior and mental processes. The results of testing hypotheses are used to build or evaluate theories, which in turn create new hypotheses to be studied. As a result, theories are constantly being formulated, evaluated, revised, and evaluated again.

II. RESEARCH METHODS IN PSYCHOLOGY (pp. 30–37)

Psychologists strive to attain four goals when researching a psychological phenomenon:

° Describe the phenomenon by gathering information about it.

° Make predictions and formulate hypotheses about the phenomenon.

° Control variables to eliminate alternative hypotheses and establish cause and effect.

° Explain the phenomenon.

A. Naturalistic Observation

Psychologists use naturalistic observation when they observe a phenomenon, without interfering, as it occurs in its natural environment.

B. Case Studies

A case study is an intensive examination of a phenomenon in a particular individual, group, or situation, often combining observations, interviews, tests, and analyses of written records. Case studies are used to describe a phenomenon.

C. Surveys

Surveys involve asking people questions, in interviews or questionnaires, in order to obtain descriptions of behavior, attitudes, beliefs, opinions, and intentions.

D. Experiments

° Psychologists use experiments to establish cause-effect relationships between variables and to help them choose among alternative hypotheses to explain a given phenomenon.

° Experiments allow researchers to manipulate or control one variable to observe the effect of that manipulation on another variable, while holding all other variables constant. In an experiment, the variable manipulated or controlled by the researcher is called the independent variable. The measurement of the consequences is called the dependent variable.

° Experiments have at least two groups of subjects: the experimental group and the control group. The control group receives no treatment, thus providing a baseline against which to compare the experimental group. The experimental group experiences the independent variable. Any difference in the dependent variable between the control and experimental groups is caused by the independent variable.

° Flaws in experimental control can reduce the validity of an experiment. Confounding variables are uncontrolled factors that might have affected the dependent variable and confused interpretation of the experimental data.

1. *Random Variables.* Random variables are uncontrolled factors such as differences in subjects' backgrounds, personalities, health, and so on, that might confound research results. Psychologists assign subjects to experimental and control groups randomly to reduce the impact of random variables on the results.

2. *Placebo Effects.* A placebo is a treatment that contains no active ingredient but produces a change in the dependent variable because the experimental subject believes it will.

3. *Experimenter Bias.* This occurs when experimenters unintentionally affect the dependent variable based on their expectations of experimental results. To prevent experimenter bias, psychologists use a double-blind design in which neither the experimenter nor the participants know which group received the independent variable.

4. *Quasi-Experiments.* When setting up a true experiment is impossible, psychologists study behavior and mental processes in the closest approximation of experimental design that ethics will permit.

E. Selecting Human Participants for Research

Sampling is an important process used to select subjects for an experiment. Research results can be generalized (that is, said to be true of the entire population of interest) only if the sample of subjects studied represents that population accurately. When choosing a sample, psychologists must consider the possible impact that subject variables such as age, gender, race, ethnicity, cultural background, socioeconomic status, sexual orientation,

disability, and so on, can have on the behavior or mental process being studied.

If every population member has an *equal* chance of being chosen for study, the subjects selected make up a random sample; if all such chances are not equal, the sample is biased. When drawing a truly random sample is impossible, representative samples are used instead.

III. STATISTICAL ANALYSIS OF RESEARCH RESULTS (pp. 37–41)

Statistical analyses are used to interpret research results. Descriptive statistics describe data. Inferential statistics are used to draw conclusions and make inferences about what the data mean.

A. Descriptive Statistics

1. *Measures of Central Tendency.* Measures of central tendency are values that best describe a set of data. The mode is the most frequent score in a data set. The median score splits the data set in two; half the scores are above the median and half are below. The mean is the mathematical average. It is calculated by summing the values of all the scores and then dividing by the total number of scores.

2. *Measures of Variability.* Measures of variability indicate the dispersion or spread in a set of data. The range is calculated by subtracting the lowest score in a data set from the highest score. The standard deviation measures the average difference between each score and the mean of the data set.

3. *Correlation and Correlation Coefficients.* The correlation coefficient is a mathematical calculation that describes the direction and strength of the relationship between two variables.

° Correlations, even very strong ones, do not necessarily reflect cause-effect relationships between variables.

° The sign (+ or –) of r describes a correlation's direction. A positive correlation (where the sign is +) describes a relationship in which two variables change in the same direction: as x increases, so does y (and vice versa). A negative correlation (where the sign is –) describes a relationship in which two variables change in opposite directions: as x increases, y decreases (and vice versa).

° A correlation's numerical value (r) can vary from -1.00 to $+1.00$. The larger the absolute value of r (whether + or –), the stronger the relationship. In a perfect correlation, $r = +1.00$ or -1.00; knowing the value of one variable allows the exact prediction of the other variable.

B. Inferential Statistics

Inferential statistics are used to analyze research results. When inferential statistics demonstrate a high probability that research results are not due to chance, the results are said to be <u>statistically significant</u>.

IV. ETHICAL GUIDELINES FOR PSYCHOLOGISTS (pp. 41–42)

Ethical guidelines and regulations exist for psychologists' use in treating patients and conducting research. Scientists must accurately report their results, minimize subject discomfort, and prevent any long-term negative effects. Human subjects must be fully informed about their participation before a given study and must be debriefed when the research is concluded. The obligation of psychologists to protect subjects' welfare also extends to animals.

V. LINKAGES: PSYCHOLOGICAL RESEARCH AND BEHAVIORAL GENETICS (pp. 42–44)

Many psychologists, despite their subfield or area of interest, attempt to understand how nature (genetic makeup) and nurture (environment/experiences) interact to produce behavior and mental processes.

Researchers interested in <u>behavioral genetics</u> study the effect of heredity and the environment on behavioral tendencies in groups. Their work employs quasi-experimental methods such as family, adoption, and twin studies.

KEY TERMS

1. **Critical thinking** is the process of evaluating propositions or hypotheses and making judgments about them on the basis of well-supported evidence. (p. 27)

Example: Consider the five steps of critical thinking. (a) What am I being asked to believe or accept? What is the hypothesis? (b) What evidence is available to support the assertion? Is it reliable and valid? (c) Are there alternative ways of interpreting the evidence? (d) What additional evidence would help to evaluate the alternatives? (e) What conclusions are most reasonable based on the evidence and the number of alternative explanations?

REMEMBER: If you find this concept difficult to understand, consider what it means to think <u>uncritically</u>. (What thought processes might have been omitted? What thought processes have led to incorrect conclusions?) Then go back and review the five sets of questions in the example above.

2. A **hypothesis** is an assertion or prediction stated as a testable proposition, usually in the form of an if-then statement. (p. 28)

Example: If rats have access to toys, *then* they can practice behaviors similar to those used in running a maze and perform better than rats raised without access to toys.

3. An **operational definition** is a statement of the specific methods used to measure a variable. (p. 29)

Example: If we are conducting a study regarding the effects of caffeine on anxiety, we would have to decide exactly *how* we plan to measure anxiety. Our operational definition of anxiety might be changes in blood pressure or the subjects' answers to an anxiety questionnaire—whatever logically fits our research hypothesis.

4. **Variables** are specific factors or characteristics that can vary. Researchers examine relationships between variables when testing hypotheses. (p. 29)

Example: Moods, decision-making processes, emotions, eating behaviors, chemical activity in the brain, heart rate, and types of clothing worn are just some of the many variables of possible interest to psychologists.

5. A **theory** is a cohesive cluster of explanations of behavior and mental processes. Theories are not definitive; they are constantly amended as researchers collect and analyze new data. (p. 29)

Example: Finding that people under stress often overeat or drink more alcohol led to the theory that behaviors that appear self-destructive may be stress alleviators.

6. **Naturalistic observation**, a method of gathering descriptive information, involves watching behaviors of interest, without interfering, as they occur in their natural environments. (p. 31)

Example: A researcher interested in how much time children of different ages play alone could observe children at a playground.

REMEMBER: A researcher *observes* a phenomenon in its *natural* environment.

7. **Case studies** are used to collect descriptive data through the intensive examination of a phenomenon in a particular individual, group, or situation. Case studies are particularly useful for studying rare or complex phenomena. (pp. 31–32)

Example: Biological psychologists cannot alter a person's brain in the laboratory for the purposes of study; therefore, they are interested in people who have suffered brain injuries in accidents. Researchers examine these patients intensively over long periods of time.

8. **Surveys** are questionnaires or special interviews administered to a large group. Surveys are designed to obtain descriptions of people's attitudes, beliefs, opinions, or behavioral intentions. (p. 32)

Example: Social psychologists interested in learning what teenagers from families of varying income levels think of marriage can administer a questionnaire to a sample of teenagers.

9. An **experiment** allows a researcher to control the data-collection process. A random sample of subjects is selected and divided into a control group and an experimental group. Both groups are identical in every way except the administration of the independent variable to the experimental group. The dependent variable is then measured in both groups. Any difference in the dependent variable between the two groups is caused by the independent variable. Experiments show causation. (p. 33)

REMEMBER: An experiment is a trial or test of a hypothesis.

10. **Independent variables** are manipulated or controlled by the researcher in an experiment. They are administered to the experimental group. (p. 33)

Example: An experiment is conducted to test the effects of alcohol on reflex speed. Two groups of subjects are randomly selected. One group, the experimental group, is given alcohol (alcohol is the independent variable), and the other group, the control group, is given a nonalcoholic beverage.

11. **Dependent variables** are the behaviors or mental processes affected by the independent variable. They are observed and measured before and after the administration of the independent variable. (p. 33)

Example: In the experiment examining the effects of alcohol on reflex speed, the dependent variable is reflex speed.

REMEMBER: The measure or value of the dependent variable depends on the independent variable.

12. The **experimental group** receives the independent variable in an experiment. (p. 34)

Example: In the experiment examining the effects of alcohol on reflex speed, the group who receives alcohol (the independent variable) is the experimental group.

13. The **control group** provides a baseline for comparison to the experimental group and does not receive the independent variable. This group is identical to the experimental group in every way *except* that these subjects *do not* receive the independent variable. (p. 34)

Example: In the experiment examining the effects of alcohol on reflex speed, the group who received the nonalcoholic beverage is the control group.

REMEMBER: The control group provides the control in an experiment. Comparing the measure of the dependent variable in both the control and experimental groups indicates whether the independent variable is causing the changes in the dependent variable or whether these changes occurred by chance.

14. **Confounding variables** are factors affecting the dependent variable in an experiment instead of or along with the independent variable. Examples of confounding variables include random variables, experimenter bias, and the placebo effect. (p. 34)

15. **Random variables** are uncontrollable factors that could affect the dependent variable in an experiment instead of or along with the independent variable. (p. 34)

Example: An experimenter wishes to test the effects of a teaching technique on test performance. The subjects are assigned randomly to the control and experimental groups. The researcher doesn't know it, but most of the students in the experimental group are much brighter than the control group students. The data may suggest that the students who received the teaching technique scored higher than those who didn't. In this case, however, intelligence is a random variable that, instead of the independent variable, could be responsible for the results.

16. A **placebo** is a physical or psychological treatment that contains no active ingredient but produces an effect

on the dependent variable because the person receiving it believes it will. (p. 34)

Example: In an experiment on the effects of alcohol, a researcher may find that people who have been given a nonalcoholic beverage behave as though they're drunk only because they *believe* they have been given an alcoholic drink.

17. **Experimenter bias** occurs when a researcher inadvertently encourages subjects to respond in a way that supports her hypothesis. (p. 35)

Example: An experimenter hypothesizes that an expert will be able to persuade a group of people that decision A is better than decision B. After the expert has spoken to the subjects, the researcher asks them which decision they prefer. She can ask in several ways. Asking, Now, don't you think A is better than B? will bias her data more than if she asks, Which do you think is better, decision A or decision B?

18. In a **double-blind design** neither the experimenter nor the subjects know who has received the independent variable. (p. 35)

Example: The experiment studying the effects of alcohol on reflex speed (described in relation to Key Term 10) is repeated using a double-blind design. Neither the subjects nor the experimenter knows who has received alcohol and who hasn't. Thus subjects are prevented from changing their behavior simply because they think they have been given alcohol. At the same time, the experimenter is prevented from biasing observations of the subjects' behavior or mental processes.

19. **Quasi-experiments** are conducted when an experiment with adequate controls would be unethical or impossible. Because these designs are not completely controlled, the results are usually not as generalizable as true experimental results and must be tested repeatedly. (pp. 35–36)

Example: You wish to test the hypothesis that alcohol has an adverse effect on fetal development. As an ethical psychologist you cannot instruct your subjects (pregnant women) to drink alcohol. You can, however, compare the development of children whose mothers drank alcohol during pregnancy to the development of children whose mothers did not.

20. **Sampling** is a procedure used to choose subjects for research. Ideally, the subjects chosen should be representative of the population being studied. (p. 36)

Example: If you are studying the behavior of gifted children, your sample should be drawn exclusively from this group.

21. **Random samples** are groups of subjects selected from the population of interest. A sample is random if every person in the population has an equal chance of being selected. If a sample is not random, it is said to be biased. (p. 36)

Example: A social psychologist is interested in studying the influence of parents on the career choice of first-year college students in the United States. If the sample is to be random, every first year student must have an equal chance of being selected as a subject. The researcher thus draws the sample from lists of first-year college students in schools all over the United States, not just from the schools in one state.

22. A sample is **biased** if everyone in the population of interest does not have an equal chance of being selected to participate in a study. (p. 36)

REMEMBER: Experimental results obtained from a biased sample may not be generalizable to the population of interest. The results are biased by characteristics of the subjects, not by the independent variable.

23. **Data** are the numerical representations of research results. (p. 37)

24. **Descriptive statistics** summarize a set of data. Examples of descriptive statistics are measures of central tendency, measures of variability, and correlation coefficients. (p. 37)

25. **A measure of central tendency** summarizes a set of data by providing a representative number. Examples of measures of central tendency are the mode, median, and mean. (p. 38)

26. The **mode** is the most frequently occurring score in a data set. (p. 38)

Example: In the data set 3, 12, 14, 16, 17, 18, 19, 22, 22, 22, 22, the mode is 22.

27. The **median** is the score that divides a data set in two; half the scores are higher than the median, and half the scores are lower than the median. (p. 38)

Example: In the data set, 3, 12, 14, 16, 17, 18, 19, 22, 22, 22, 22, the median is 18.

REMEMBER: The *median* is "the score in the middle"—the score that divides the data set in half. When there is an even number of scores in a data set, the median is halfway between the *two* middle numbers.

28. The **mean** is the arithmetic average. To compute the mean, add the numerical values of all the scores in a data set and divide that sum by the number of scores in the data set. (p. 39)

Example: For the previous data set the mean is equal to $(3 + 12 + 14 + 16 + 17 + 18 + 19 + 22 + 22 + 22 + 22)/11 = 187/11 = 17$.

REMEMBER: This measure of central tendency takes into account all of the values of the scores in a data set. Therefore, even one extreme score can change the mean radically, possibly making it less representative of the data.

29. **Measures of variability** summarize the spread or dispersion of data points. (p. 39)

REMEMBER: Disperse means "to scatter." Variability measures will tell you if the scores are very different from one another (scattered) or if they cluster around the mean.

30. The **range** is a measure of variability computed by subtracting the lowest score from the highest score in a data set. The range is affected by extreme scores. (p. 39)

Example: In the data set 2, 3, 4, 5, 5, 5, 6, 7, 8, 100, the range is $100 - 2 = 98$. If the extreme score (100) is dropped, the range is $8 - 2 = 6$. Extreme scores can radically affect the range of a data set.

31. The **standard deviation** is a measure of variability. It reflects the average distance between each score and the mean of a data set. The standard deviation will tell you how different the scores are from the mean. (p. 39)

Example: Following are two data sets.

Data set 1: 1, 2, 3, 4, 5, 6, 7, 8, 9
Data set 2: 4, 4, 4, 4, 5, 6, 6, 6, 6

The mean of both data sets is 5. However, the scores in data set 1 are a greater distance from the mean. In other words, they are *more different* from the mean than the scores in data set 2. Therefore, the standard deviation (SD) in data set 1 is larger than the SD for data set 2.

REMEMBER: To *deviate* means to "differ." The standard deviation describes, overall, how *different* the scores in a data set are from the mean.

32. A **correlation** is an indication of the relationship between two variables (x and y). The correlation coefficient (r), a number between -1.00 and $+1.00$, is a mathematical representation of the strength and direction of a correlation. The higher the absolute value of r is, the stronger the relationship is. A perfect correlation, whether positive or negative (where r equals + or -1.00), describes a perfect relationship; knowing the value of x allows the certain prediction of y. A positive correlation (where r varies from 0 to $+1.00$) describes two variables that change in the same direction: as x increases, so does y (and vice versa). A negative correlation (where r varies from -1.00 to 0) describes an inverse relationship: as x increases, y decreases (and vice versa). (pp. 39–40)

Example: In a small English town, the seasonal appearance of a large number of storks is positively correlated with the number of human births; as x (the number of storks) increases, y (the number of births) increases. If correlations indicated causation, we could say that the storks cause babies to appear. But correlations *do not* imply causation, and storks do not bring babies.

REMEMBER: Correlations do not indicate causation.

33. **Inferential statistics** are used to judge the meaning of data. Inferential statistics assess how likely it is that group differences or correlations would exist in the population rather than occurring only due to variables associated with the chosen sample. (p. 40)

REMEMBER: Inferential statistics allow psychologists to *infer* what the data mean.

34. If a statistic is **statistically significant**, it is an indication that the group differences or correlation is larger than would occur by chance. (p. 40)

Example: If the difference between two group means is statistically significant, a researcher would conclude that the difference most likely exists in the population of interest. If the difference is not statistically significant, a researcher would conclude that the difference occurred by chance—possibly because of an unrepresentative sample or the presence of confounding variables.

35. **Ethical guidelines** are rules about research, counseling, and teaching that psychologists are required to follow. (p. 41)

Example: The *Ethical Principles of Psychologists and Code of Conduct* provide standards of behavior that protect the rights of research subjects, clients, and students.

36. **Behavioral genetics** explores the impact of genetics and environmental factors on differences in the behavioral tendencies of groups. (p. 42)

Example: A behavioral genetics study might look for similarities in behavior among relatives. The children of a person who experiences depression, for example, might be more likely to develop depression than distant relatives or unrelated people.

FILL-IN-THE-BLANKS KEY TERMS

This section will help you check your factual knowledge of the key terms introduced in this chapter. Fill in each blank with the appropriate term from the list of key terms above.

1. The process of evaluating propositions or hypotheses and making judgments about them based on well-supported evidence is called _____.

2. A(n) _____ is a testable proposition about the relationship between two variables.

3. A description of the methods that will be used to measure a variable is called a(n) _____.

4. _____ , _____ , and _____ are methods of gathering descriptive data.

5. In an experiment, the variable manipulated by the experimenter is called a(n) _____.

6. The _____ group receives the treatment, or independent variable, in an experiment.

7. The main function of the _____ group in an experiment is to provide a comparison of the effects of the independent variable on the dependent variable.

8. Neither the experimenters nor the subjects know who has received the independent variable in a _____.

9. _____ are any factors other than the independent variable that introduce variation in the dependent variable.

10. A treatment that contains no active ingredient but can produce results simply because of a person's belief in its power is a _____.

11. To summarize a set of data by providing a representative number, a _____ is used.

12. Given a _____, knowing the value of x allows you to predict the exact value of y.

13. Researchers must look at the _____ of their data to decide whether their results could have occurred by chance alone.

14. The rules that should guide a psychologist's decisions on moral issues are called _____.

15. _____ is the study of the contributions of genetics and environmental factors to differences in the behavioral tendencies of groups.

Total Correct (See answer key) _____

LEARNING OBJECTIVES

1. Define critical thinking. Be able to think critically about a hypothesis by using the five-step process presented in the text. (pp. 27–28)

2. Define hypothesis, operational definition, and variable. (pp. 28–29)

3. Describe the evolution of a theory. (pp. 29–30)

4. Name the four scientific goals of psychology. (p. 30)

5. Describe the three basic research methods used to describe and predict a phenomenon and give examples of each. Explain the advantages and disadvantages of each method. (pp. 31–33)

6. Describe the experimental research method and give an example of it. (pp. 33–35)

7. Explain why an experiment allows investigation of causation. (p. 33)

8. Define and explain the role of independent and dependent variables and of experimental and control groups in an experiment. (pp. 33–34)

9. Define confounding variables. Discuss the problems presented by confounding variables in the interpretation of experimental results. Define random variables, placebo effect, and experimenter bias. (pp. 34–35)

10. Describe the relationship between a double-blind experimental design and experimenter bias. (p. 35)

11. Define quasi-experiments. Explain why they are used as experimental designs. (pp. 35–36)

12. Define sampling, random sample, and biased sample. Discuss the importance of sampling in data collection. (p. 36)

13. Summarize the use of <u>descriptive</u> and <u>inferential</u> <u>statistics</u> in evaluating research results. (pp. 37–41)

14. Discuss the role of <u>measures of central tendency</u> in summarizing and describing research results. (pp. 38–39)

15. Discuss the role of <u>measures of variability</u> in summarizing and describing research results. (p. 39)

16. Define <u>correlation</u>. Describe how the absolute value and sign of a correlation coefficient are interpreted. (pp. 39–40)

17. Explain why correlations do not imply causation. Describe the role of alternative hypotheses in the interpretation of a correlation. (p. 40)

18. Define <u>statistical significance</u>. Describe the role of statistical significance in thinking critically about scientific research. (pp. 40–41)

19. Describe the <u>ethical guidelines</u> that psychologists must follow. (pp. 41–42)

20. Define <u>behavioral genetics</u>. (pp. 42–43)

21. Explain how family, twin, and adoption studies help to establish the relative roles of genetic and environmental variables. (pp. 43–44)

CONCEPTS AND EXERCISES

No. 1: Research Methods

Completing this exercise should help you to achieve Learning Objectives 2, 3, 5, 6, 8, 12, and 16.

As a study aid for her final exam in a research methods course, Susan has made note cards listing the steps to be followed for conducting an experiment and descriptive research. Sitting down to study, she knocked the cards to the floor and they scattered. Your job is to put the cards back in order. Ignore those cards that don't describe the steps in an experiment.

A. Create an operational definition, if needed.
B. Measure the dependent variable.
C. Observe subjects in their natural environment.
D. Calculate a correlation coefficient.
E. Identify the independent and dependent variables.
F. Compare the measures of the dependent variables between the two groups of subjects.
G. Manipulate the independent variable.
H. Administer a questionnaire.
I. Assign subjects randomly between two groups.
J. Form a hypothesis based on previous descriptive and/or correlational data.

K. Use inferential statistics to determine statistical significance.

1. _____   5. _____
2. _____   6. _____
3. _____   7. _____
4. _____   8. _____

No. 2: Choose Your Method

Completing this exercise should help you to achieve Learning Objectives 5, 6, and 11.

From the list below, choose the best research method for obtaining the answer to each of the following questions.

1. Does a lack of sleep cause changes in problem-solving ability? _____

2. Throughout history, very young children have occasionally been lost in the wild and found several years later. Recently another such child was discovered. Has growing up in the wild affected his cognitive development? _____

3. What is the average five-year-old's attention span at a playground? _____

4. How do people residing near nuclear reactors feel about the nuclear arms race? Are their opinions different from those of people living far from nuclear facilities? _____

A. surveys
B. experiments
C. naturalistic observation
D. case study

CRITICAL THINKING

Completing this exercise should help you to achieve Learning Objective 1.

Sam, a rookie police officer, has been assigned to Martina, an experienced detective who is going to show him the ropes. Martina smiled when Sam proudly told her that he had two college degrees and graduated with honors. "Sam," she said, "a college degree shows that you have learned many facts, but hopefully college has also helped you to think critically about those facts. The most important thing you need to do in this job is ask yourself five questions. If you know the answers, or at least how to go about finding the answers, you will solve most of your cases." Sam, doubting that a detective's entire method of crime solving could be distilled down to five questions, decided to humor Martina and play along. "O.K., what are they, these five questions I have to ask myself?"

Help Martina by listing the five critical thinking questions as they might be used in a criminal investigation.

1. _____

2. _____

3. _____

4. _____

5. _____

PERSONAL LEARNING ACTIVITIES

1. Take a survey and try asking the same questions in different ways. See if you can affect the results. (Learning Objective 5)

2. Develop a rating scale for room neatness. How will you operationally define the various levels of neatness? Next visit the homes of several friends and rate them using your neatness scale. Do you see a link between neatness level and personality? (Learning Objectives 2 and 5)

3. Design an experiment. To do so, you should outline your hypothesis, variables, operational definitions, and so on. For example, if your hypothesis is that rock music played during studying improves retention of material, then you should decide what rock music to play and what the control group(s) will hear during studying. You might operationally define memory improvement as a score increase of a certain size on a test of list learning or on a test of reading comprehension. (Learning Objectives 2, 6, 8, 9)

4. Record the statistics cited in a news report and give alternate interpretations. Would additional descriptive or inferential statistics be helpful in drawing conclusions? For instance, imagine a news report decrying the 3 percent increase in the number of violent crimes in City A. (Perhaps the number of crimes increased by 8 percent during the previous year.) If the report compares City A's increase to a 5 percent reduction in violent crime in City B, you might wonder if the cities' populations have remained stable. (Maybe a report of the crime *rate*

adjusted for population sizes would tell a different story or maybe the difference between the cities is not statistically significant.) Can you identify other possible variables that would influence your interpretation of this report? (Learning Objectives 9, 13, 14, 15, and 18)

5. What statistics would help a business to decide whether residents would be interested in a weight training/exercise facility? What other information might be important for them to know before they design their facility? (Learning Objectives 13, 14, and 15)

MULTIPLE-CHOICE QUESTIONS

SAMPLE QUIZ 1

1. Sue, having had no experience with the breed, has purchased what a breeder claims are two purebred Abyssinian cats: Chessie and Baby. She hypothesizes that Baby is not really pure in breed because she doesn't act like Chessie. According to the critical thinking steps in your text, what does Sue need to do?
   a. Restate her hypothesis.
   b. Reexamine the behavioral differences between her two cats.
   c. Compare the behavior of other Abyssinians to her cats' behavior.
   d. Conclude that one of her cats is not purebred.

2. A hypothesis is a
   a. method of control used in experiments.
   b. method of describing a psychological phenomenon.
   c. specific, testable proposition about a phenomenon.
   d. theory in its final form.

3. Methods for collecting descriptive data include
   a. naturalistic observations.
   b. experiments.
   c. descriptive statistics.
   d. correlations.

4. Dr. McMarty has collected data by doing case studies and naturalistic observation on a new phenomenon never studied before. Her next step will probably be to
   a. design an experiment.
   b. examine the data for patterns or relationships among the variables.
   c. check for statistical significance.
   d. form an explanation that will lead to a theory.

5. Studying individuals in their own environments to collect data is called
   a. experimentation.
   b. naturalistic observation.
   c. personal observation.
   d. statistical analysis.

6. Case studies are used to
   a. avoid a placebo effect.
   b. determine the effects of an independent variable on a dependent variable.
   c. collect descriptive data.
   d. provide control in an experiment.

7. In an experiment the _____ variable is manipulated and the _____ variable is measured.
   a. dependent, independent
   b. confounding, dependent
   c. independent, confounding
   d. independent, dependent

8. Before using survey results to support a hypothesis, one must be sure that
   a. the questions are properly worded.
   b. the sample used is representative of the population being studied.
   c. the responses are not biased by "socially acceptable" standards.
   d. all of the above.

9. The experimental design that prevents experimenter bias from confounding a study's results is
   a. operational definition.
   b. naturalistic observation.
   c. random.
   d. double-blind.

10. Akuba believes that growing up in an abusive family causes children to become physically violent. Akuba wants to make the strongest possible conclusions about causality with the fewest ethical concerns; therefore, she should use
    a. case studies.
    b. an experiment.
    c. a quasi-experiment.
    d. a survey.

11. Jeremy designed an experiment to test the effects of praise on the sharing behavior of children. Children in Group A will be praised after they share; children in Group B will only be observed. Group A is the _____ group.
    a. control
    b. experimental

c. operational
d. random

12. Part of the data comparing the number of sharing behaviors for the two groups are listed below.
    Group A: 35, 12, 11, 9, 8, 6, 5
    Group B: 9, 8, 7, 7, 6, 5, 4
    Which of the following statistics would best represent the amount of sharing for the children in Group A?
    a. mean
    b. median
    c. mode
    d. range

13. Based on the data in question 12, which of the following statements about variability is most likely correct?
    a. Group A has a smaller range than Group B.
    b. Group A does not have a standard deviation.
    c. Group B has a smaller standard deviation than Group A.
    d. Group B has the same range as Group A.

14. Detective Brown observed that when he and his coworkers drank caffeinated tea while working on cases, they solved them faster. Brown conducted an experiment in which one group received caffeine pills and the other received inert sugar pills. Each person received a set of cases to solve and Brown recorded the number of cases solved by people in the caffeine group versus people in the sugar pill group. The strongest evidence that caffeine pills improved the case solution rate would be
    a. a large caffeine group mean.
    b. a positive correlation between the number of cases solved by the caffeine and the sugar pill groups.
    c. a small range of scores in the sugar pill group.
    d. statistically different means for the caffeine and sugar pill groups.

15. Susan wants to study the effects of peer pressure on study habits in first-year students at her university. She needs to obtain a random sample. How should she choose the subjects for her experiment?
    a. Select one dormitory and ask all of the first-year students residing there to participate in the experiment.
    b. Randomly select names from the introductory psychology course roster.
    c. Randomly select names from the dormitory phone book.
    d. Randomly select names from a list of all first-year students at the university.

16. Choose the strongest correlation coefficient.
    a. +.75
    b. −.99
    c. +.01
    d. −.01

17. A measure of central tendency
    a. is the average distance of scores from the mean of a data set.
    b. describes the typical score in a data set.
    c. is the lowest score in a data set subtracted from the highest score.
    d. determines if a sample is random or biased.

18. Several states implemented laws requiring drivers and passengers to wear seat belts. Since the laws' implementation, the number of accident-related deaths has decreased. Therefore, a negative correlation exists, which indicates that
    a. wearing seat belts causes fewer car accidents.
    b. wearing seat belts prevents accident fatalities.
    c. when the number of people wearing seat belts increases, the number of accident-related deaths decreases.
    d. enforcing the law causes fewer accidents to occur.

19. Because experimenters follow the ethical guidelines for psychologists, participants in psychological research can expect to be
    a. informed about the study before they agree to participate.
    b. offered counseling.
    c. psychoanalyzed.
    d. sent home without knowing they were deceived.

20. The question that puzzles Marianne is why some psychological problems seem to run in families. Marianne would like to discover whether it is nature or nurture that more strongly influences certain behaviors; therefore, she has an interest in
    a. behavior genetics.
    b. genetic engineering.
    c. "pop" psychology.
    d. replicability.

Total Correct (See answer key) _____

SAMPLE QUIZ 2

Use this quiz to reassess your learning after taking Quiz 1 and reviewing the chapter.

1. On a television program many people give testimony that they have never felt better than they have since they began using the Run-O-Sizer treadmill. Each person who is interviewed shows "before" and "after" photos depicting incredible weight loss and increased muscle tone. According to the critical thinking steps in your text, what should you do?
    a. Look for alternative ways of interpreting the evidence that the Run-O-Sizer works.
    b. Draw your conclusion about the worth of the Run-O-Sizer based on the strong testimonials.
    c. Decide whether to order the treadmill based on the price.
    d. Order only if they offer a money-back guarantee.

2. The four scientific goals associated with research are
    a. measurement, prediction, control, and explanation.
    b. explanation, understanding, reasoning, and control.
    c. description, critical thinking, control, and explanation.
    d. description, prediction, control, and explanation.

3. To document how the average first-year college student behaves during an exam, a researcher should conduct a(n)
    a. case study.
    b. experiment.
    c. naturalistic observation.
    d. survey.

4. The Food and Drug Administration (FDA) has tested fluoxetine, a new drug thought to decrease depression without causing weight gain. The experiment consisted of a random sample of depressed patients split into two groups. The experimental group received the drug; the control group received no treatment. The results were clear: those patients receiving fluoxetine experienced a decrease in depression without weight gain; those in the control group reported no change in depression or weight. Based on these results, should the FDA allow marketing of fluoxetine?
    a. No, the results may have been due to the placebo effect.
    b. No, the study should be repeated using a case study.
    c. Yes, the experimental design is appropriate and the results are clear.
    d. No, the results may have been due to incorrect sampling.

5. In the experiment done by the FDA on fluoxetine, which variable needs an operational definition?
   a. The independent variable
   b. Fluoxetine
   c. Depression
   d. The placebo

6. In the experiment done by the FDA on fluoxetine, the drug was the
   a. independent variable.
   b. dependent variable.
   c. operational measure.
   d. random variable.

7. A psychologist interested in maximizing control of variables in her research would use which of the following methods?
   a. Naturalistic observation
   b. Surveys
   c. An experiment
   d. A case study

8. Questionnaires or special interviews designed to obtain descriptions of people's attitudes, beliefs, opinions, and behavioral intentions are known as
   a. experiments.
   b. surveys.
   c. case studies.
   d. naturalistic observations.

9. Which of the following hypotheses should be tested with a quasi-experiment?
   a. Thinking of examples of concepts while studying improves students' performance on tests.
   b. An unpleasant odor presented for one hour will cause a mild negative emotional reaction.
   c. The loss of a job in a two-income family has a negative impact on marital communications.
   d. All of the above

10. To discover what variables (such as how much control a subject has or how they perceive an event) may *cause* a person to react to a negative event with intense emotion, a researcher should use what research design?
    a. Case study
    b. Experiment
    c. Naturalistic observation
    d. Survey

11. Which of the following is a possible random variable?
    a. Level of intelligence
    b. State of health
    c. Prior experience with the independent variable
    d. All of the above

12. After being struck by lightning, Nicole often runs down the street singing while wearing her underwear on the outside of her clothes. Nicole cannot concentrate on her work for more than 10 minutes, nor can she understand the comics she used to enjoy so much. To understand Nicole's condition, a researcher should use a(n)
    a. case study.
    b. experiment.
    c. naturalistic observation.
    d. survey.

13. Drawing a purely random sample from which of the following populations would be feasible?
    a. The human race
    b. New York City rats
    c. U.S. presidents past and present
    d. None of the above

14. Statistical analyses provide a means to
    a. summarize and analyze research data.
    b. measure the dependent variable.
    c. measure the independent variable.
    d. examine correlations for cause-effect relationships.

15. Following is a data set: 10, 11, 12, 22, 12, 11, 10, 10, 10, 11, 13. The value of 10 is the
    a. mean.
    b. mode.
    c. median.
    d. range.

16. A positive correlation indicates the existence of a relationship between two variables such that
    a. one variable increases as the other decreases.
    b. one variable increases as the other increases.
    c. one variable causes an increase in the other.
    d. one variable causes a decrease in the other.

17. A recruiter has administered an intelligence test to a college graduating class. The test results are rather disappointing, however. The means, medians, and modes of all the classes are very similar and very low. The recruiter is determined to find the class with the brightest students to interview. What statistic could this recruiter look at to decide which one of the classes probably has the greatest number of high scores?
    a. The range
    b. The standard deviation
    c. A measure of central tendency
    d. An operational score definition

18. You are studying the effects of alcohol consumption on decision-making time. Your hypothesis states that as alcohol consumption increases, decision-making time will also increase. If your data describe a _____ correlation, your hypothesis will be supported.
    a. negative
    b. curvilinear
    c. positive
    d. statistically significant negative

19. Why do psychologists follow ethical guidelines?
    a. Psychologists would not want the cost of participating in an experiment to be too high in comparison to the information to be gained.
    b. The American Psychological Association has set standards for psychologists to follow when conducting research and treating patients.
    c. Stress and pain could act as confounding variables in an experiment.
    d. All of the above

20. A psychologist is planning to examine the contributions of heredity and environment to intelligence. Of the methods listed below, the psychologist is most likely to use a(n)
    a. adoption study.
    b. experiment.
    c. factor analysis.
    d. naturalistic observation.

Total Correct (See answer key) _____

ANSWERS TO FILL-IN-THE-BLANKS KEY TERMS

1. critical thinking (p. 27)
2. hypothesis (p. 28)
3. operational definition (p. 29)
4. Naturalistic observation, surveys, and case studies (pp. 31–33)
5. independent variable (p. 33)
6. experimental (p. 34)
7. control (p. 34)
8. double-blind design (p. 35)
9. confounding variables (p. 34)
10. placebo (p. 34)
11. measure of central tendency (p. 38)
12. perfect correlation (p. 39)
13. statistical significance (p. 40)
14. ethical guidelines (p. 41)
15. behavioral genetics (p. 42)

ANSWERS TO CONCEPTS AND EXERCISES

No. 1: Research Methods

1. *J* Experiments are usually tests of hypotheses based on descriptive and correlational data. Correlations, even very strong ones, do not demonstrate causation. Scientists do experiments to determine whether there is a causative relationship between strongly correlated variables. (p. 33)

2. *E* Once scientists decide to do an experiment, they must identify and define the independent and dependent variables. (p. 33)

3. *A* Sometimes an operational definition is needed to specify how one or more of the variables will be measured. (p. 29)

4. *I* Experiments have two groups: experimental and control. Subjects should be assigned randomly to these groups to reduce the effect of random variables. (p. 34)

5. *G* In an experiment, researchers systematically manipulate the independent variable. (p. 33)

6. *B* Then they measure the dependent variable. (p. 33)

7. *F* Measurements of the dependent variable are compared for the experimental and control groups. (pp. 33–34)

8. *K* Statistical methods determine whether the differences between the dependent variables in the control and experimental groups occurred by chance. (pp. 33–37)

No. 2: Choose Your Method

1. *B* Experiments indicate causation. The question here is whether sleep loss *causes* changes in problem-solving ability. None of the other methods listed shows causation. (p. 33)

2. *D* This is a rare phenomenon, examination of which requires that a great deal of information be gathered about one person (the child). Researchers would conduct a case study in such circumstances. (pp. 31–32)

3. *C* Naturalistic observation would provide the data necessary to answer this question. The researcher would *observe* the attention span of five-year-old children at the playground, rather than asking them about it. (p. 31)

4. *A* Surveys are used to find out people's opinions.
    (p. 32)

ANSWERS TO CRITICAL THINKING

Martina lists the five critical thinking questions for Sam. Each of her questions is followed by its parallel question from the text.

> What do I think happened?
> *What is my hypothesis?*
>
> Why do I believe my hypothesis?
> *What evidence is available to support my hypothesis?*
>
> Is there a solution to the crime that explains all the evidence?
> *Are there alternative ways of interpreting the evidence?*
>
> What more do we need to prove I'm right?
> *What additional evidence would help to evaluate the alternatives?*
>
> Can I be certain that I'm right?
> *What conclusions are reasonable based on the evidence?*

Throughout the remaining chapters, Sam and Martina have to solve a variety of cases. As you work through each case, sharpen your own critical thinking skills. Remember, critical thinking can be applied to every aspect of your life, not just to your psychology studies and exams.

ANSWERS TO MULTIPLE-CHOICE QUESTIONS

Circle the question numbers you answered correctly.

Sample Quiz 1

1. *c* is the answer. Because Sue has had no experience with the Abyssinian breed, she cannot assume that Baby isn't purebred because she doesn't act like Chessie. Baby's behavior may be *more* typical of Abyssinians. Sue must compare her cat's behavior with that of other Abyssinians before she can draw conclusions about the purity of *either* cat's breeding. (pp. 27–28)
    a. It is Sue's hypothesis that, if Baby doesn't act like Chessie, she may not be a pure Abyssinian. She needs to investigate alternative ways of interpreting her evidence, not change her hypothesis.
    b. Even if Sue checks the behavior of her cats again, she still needs to compare her cats with other Abyssinians before she can draw any conclusions.
    d. Before a conclusion is drawn, the evidence must support the hypothesis. Sue's evidence, the behavior of her two cats, is insufficient to draw a conclusion regarding their breeding.

2. *c* is the answer. A hypothesis is a specific, testable proposition about a phenomenon, usually based on patterns or relationships found in descriptive data. (p. 28)
    a. Control is obtained via the experimental method.
    b. Hypotheses, though formulated from descriptive information about psychological variables, are predictions or testable propositions. They are not *just* descriptions about the relationship between variables.
    d. Tested hypotheses can contribute information to the creation of a theory. However, theories contain broader, more general rules about categories of behavior than do hypotheses. Theories are never considered final; they are repeatedly tested in new ways and added to or amended as researchers collect new data.

3. *a* is the answer. Methods for collecting descriptive data include naturalistic observation, surveys, and case studies. (pp. 31–33)
    b. Experiments are used to conduct controlled research.
    c. Descriptive statistics are used to describe and summarize data once it has been collected. Statistics are not a method of data collection.
    d. Correlations are mathematical representations of the relationship between two variables. Correlations are usually based on descriptive data but are not a descriptive method of data collection.

4. *b* is the answer. Dr. McMarty should examine the data for patterns or relationships between variables. (pp. 30–33)
    a. To design an experiment, one must have a hypothesis to test. Hypotheses are usually based on descriptive data; Dr. McMarty must examine the data before forming a hypothesis.
    c. Statistics are used to test the significance of correlational and experimental data. Dr. McMarty must examine the data to find patterns or relationships between variables to form a

hypothesis. After she tests the hypothesis, she can check for statistical significance.

d. Explanations are based on descriptive *and* experimental data. Dr. McMarty has only descriptive data. She should form a hypothesis based on relationships between variables in the data set and complete an experiment; *then* she may have information that will contribute to a theory.

5. *b* is the answer. Studying (observing) individuals in their own (naturalistic) environments is called naturalistic observation. (p. 31)
   a. Experiments are often conducted in a laboratory, which is not a subject's natural environment.
   c. Personal observation is not a research method.
   d. Statistical analysis is a method of summarizing or analyzing collected data.

6. *c* is the answer. (p. 31)
   a. The placebo effect usually occurs in an experimental setting where subjects respond to a treatment that has no active ingredients.
   b. Independent and dependent variables are used in experiments.
   d. Case studies do not provide control; experiments do.

7. *d* is the answer. (p. 33)
   a. The independent variable is manipulated; the dependent variable is measured.
   b, c. A confounding variable is any aspect of the experiment that affects the dependent variable instead of or along with the independent variable. Researchers try to avoid the presence of confounding variables.

8. *d* is the answer. A subject may misinterpret an improperly worded question, thus biasing the data. If the question is embarrassing, the subject may lie, thus again biasing the data. Representative samples are important regardless of the research method used. A sample unrepresentative of the population of interest will diminish the usefulness of data in the formation of a theory regarding that population's behavior. (pp. 32–33)

9. *d* is the answer. In a double-blind experimental design, neither the subjects nor the experimenters know who has received the independent variable. The *experimenters cannot bias* the data in favor of their hypothesis, because they do not know which subjects received the independent variable. (p. 35)
   a. An operational definition is a statement of how a variable (for example, anxiety) is to be measured.

b. Naturalistic observation is a research method but not an experimental design.
   c. Random refers to the means by which the subjects were selected for a study. It is not an experimental method.

10. *c* is the answer. Akuba cannot ethically use an experiment to determine causality. However, she could measure differences in the violent tendencies of those who are in abusive homes versus those who are not. Her conclusions won't be as strong as those from an experiment might be, but if she does many studies and/or has many participants, Akuba can be more certain of her inferences. (pp. 35–36)
   a. A case study might be used if abuse were a rare phenomenon. Unfortunately, it isn't uncommon; therefore, getting information on as many people as possible would yield more generalizable results.
   b. Akuba cannot ethically use an experiment to determine causality, because experimental design includes randomly assigning subjects to conditions. Here, that would mean randomly assigning people to abusive or nonabusive families, which wouldn't be ethical.
   d. A survey might be one way for Akuba to begin her research, but it will not allow her to make strong conclusions about causality. She would have participants' views of their families and their ratings of their own level of violence, but this wouldn't tell her if the family violence caused the participants' behavior.

11. *b* is the answer. The experimental group receives the independent variable. (p. 34)
   a. The control group receives a placebo or no treatment.
   c, d. Operational groups and random groups are not part of experimental design; they do not exist.

12. *b* is the answer. The median is the middle score of a distribution and is a better description of a sample than the mean when the sample includes extreme scores. (pp. 38–39)
   a. The mean would be affected by the extreme score to give the impression that there was typically more sharing than there truly was. (With the high score of 35, the Group A mean is about 12.3; without it the Group A mean would be 8.5, which is closer to most of the numbers.)
   c. There is no mode in Group A since no scores were repeated.

d. The range is not a measure of central tendency; it would only tell the distance between the highest and lowest scores.

13. *c* is the answer. Group B scores are very close to one another; therefore, the standard deviation for Group B should be smaller than for Group A, which has an extreme score. (p. 39)
    a. The range for Group A would be 30; the range for Group B would be 5. Therefore, Group A's range is larger.
    b. A standard deviation could be calculated for Group A.
    d. Groups A and B do not have the same range.

14. *d* is the answer. Statistically different means would show that the differences were unlikely to occur due to chance; this would be an indication that the experiment had an effect. (p. 40)
    a. A large caffeine group mean would be a small amount of evidence for the hypothesis; however, the sugar pill group could also have a large mean.
    b. Correlations do not support a hypothesis that one group will be different from another; they would support a hypothesis that two variables are related.
    c. A small range only shows that the subjects had *similar* scores (number of cases solved), not that the control group had *lower* scores.

15. *d* is the answer. Following this procedure will ensure that every student in the population Susan wishes to study (first-year students at her university) will have an equal chance of being selected for participation in the experiment. (p. 36)
    a. The use of one dorm will not give every first-year student an equal chance of being selected. Also, a particular dorm might house a certain kind of student. For example, the majority of students living in a dorm located next to the College of Agriculture might be agriculture majors who live there because of the convenient location. But Susan is interested in *all* first-year students, not just agriculture students.
    b. Some first-year students may not take introductory psychology. Therefore, first-year students do not all have an equal chance of being selected for the study.
    c. Some first-year students may not have a phone or a listed phone number.

16. *b* is the answer. The strongest correlation coefficient possible is 1.00. No other coefficient listed is

closer to a perfect correlation than −.99. (pp. 39–40)
    a. The strength and direction of a correlation are independent of each other. The positive or negative sign indicates the direction, and the number indicates the strength: the closer to 1.00, the stronger the correlation. As −.99 is closer to −1.00 than +.75 is to +1.00, −.99 is the stronger correlation.
    c, d. You may have thought that a positive or negative .01 correlation coefficient represented a perfect correlation. However, a perfect correlation is +1.00 or −1.00.

17. *b* is the answer. Measures of central tendency—the mean, median, and mode—describe the typical value in a data set around which the scores have a <u>tendency</u> to <u>center</u>. (p. 38)
    a. The standard deviation, a measure of <u>variability</u>, describes the average distance of scores from the mean of a data set.
    c. The range, a measure of <u>variability</u>, is equal to the lowest score in a data set subtracted from the highest score.
    d. Measures of central tendency do not affect the nature of a sample.

18. *c* is the answer. A negative correlation tells us that as one variable (seat-belt use) increases, the other variable (accident-related deaths) decreases. (pp. 39–40)
    a. Correlations do not imply causation. Also, the variables here are the number of seat belts worn and the number of accident-related deaths, not the number of accidents.
    b. Correlations do not imply causation. The word <u>prevents</u> implies causation.
    d. Correlations do not imply causation. Also, the variable is the number of accident-related deaths, not the number of accidents.

19. *a* is the answer. The ethical guidelines followed by psychologists require that researchers describe the study well enough for potential participants to give their informed consent to be involved. (pp. 41–42)
    b. Participants should not expect a psychologist conducting research to give them counseling. Perhaps if it became clear that a participant was in distress the researcher could recommend that he or she see a clinical or counseling psychologist, but not all researchers are trained in counseling.
    c. Psychoanalysis would be the job of a psychodynamic therapist, not a researcher conducting a study.

d. If an experiment requires that participants be misled, the researcher is required to disclose fully the reasoning behind the study after it is completed.

20. *a* is the answer. Behavioral genetics is the study of how genes (nature) and the environment (nurture) influence behavior. (p. 42)
   b. Genetic engineering and the field of behavior genetics are not the same thing. A genetic engineer, while interested in the role of genes in behavior, would use the results of genetics research to alter the gene set.
   c. "Pop" psychology is short for popular psychology, which offers answers that are easy rather than well-supported by research. A "pop" psychologist would be more likely to write an advice book than to conduct genetic research.
   d. Replicability means consistent results over many experiments. Replicating or repeating an outcome would most likely interest any scientist, but it does not describe the interest in problems that run in families.

Now turn to the quiz analysis table at the end of this chapter to find which areas you know well and which areas you need to work on. Circle the numbers in the table for items on Quiz 1 that you answered correctly.

ANSWERS TO MULTIPLE-CHOICE QUESTIONS

Circle the question numbers you answered correctly.

Sample Quiz 2

1. *a* is the answer. To think critically about the product offered, we should ask ourselves if there are other ways of interpreting the evidence. For example, were the people giving their testimonials because they were paid rather than because they used and benefited from the Run-O-Sizer? Are there other methods for achieving the same results? Could the photos have been altered to make the results look more dramatic? (pp. 27–28)
   b. Making your decision based on the testimonials would mean ignoring sources of information such as consumer magazines and fitness experts.
   c. The price is important to consider, but it says very little about the product's effectiveness or safety, or the likelihood you would use it.
   d. A guarantee might seem to make the purchase risk-free, but if the product is not worthwhile,

you will have wasted time trying it and may still lose money. Therefore, a critical thinker will evaluate the claims made about the Run-O-Sizer before examining the guarantee.

2. *d* is the answer. (p. 30)
   a, b, c. Measurement, understanding, reasoning, and critical thinking are processes involved in pursuing scientific goals, but are not goals specific to research methods.

3. *c* is the answer. To record the behavior of people during their usual activities is naturalistic observation. (p. 31)
   a. A case study is used to describe a rare condition completely; therefore, it would not describe average behaviors.
   b. A researcher would be unlikely to use an experiment, because behavior during a laboratory-simulated exam may be different from behavior during an actual exam.
   d. Using a survey would be a good way to find out how students describe their behavior during an exam, but it would not show what they look like, the number of times they shifted in their seats, and so on. In addition, their description might not match their behavior.

4. *a* is the answer. The subjects in the experimental group may report less depression because they think fluoxetine has medicinal value. (p. 34)
   b. Before the FDA approves a drug, a clear cause-effect relationship between the drug and the desired effect (decreased depression) must be demonstrated with very few side effects. Case studies are not used to detect cause-effect relationships; they describe a phenomenon of interest.
   c. The experimental design is incorrect. Both the experimental and the control groups should have been given pills. The experiment should be repeated using a double-blind design.
   d. Random samples are excellent for use in experiments and other types of research.

5. *c* is the answer. An operational definition, which will describe how depression is measured, can help the FDA determine whether patients experienced a change in level of depression. To understand why an operational definition is necessary, consider the following scenario. Joe, a subject in the experiment, is very, very depressed. After receiving the drug, he scores higher on the test. His test results show that he is still depressed, but not as depressed as he was prior to taking the drug. By using the test

to operationally define depression, the FDA was able to measure a *change* in depression. If, however, the FDA had merely asked Joe how he felt, he might have responded that he was depressed both before and after taking the drug. (pp. 28–29)

a, b. The independent variable is fluoxetine. Measuring the amount of a drug administered to the subjects is easy. It doesn't require an operational definition.

d. There was no placebo.

6. *a* is the answer. The treatment administered to the experimental group is always the independent variable. (pp. 33–34)

b. The dependent variable is depression.

c. The operational definition of depression is a low score on a questionnaire.

d. Because the sample used was purely random, the presence of random variables has been controlled.

7. *c* is the answer. Experiments are used to conduct controlled research. Experimental and control groups are formed, and both groups are treated identically except the administration of the independent variable in the experimental group. At the end of the experiment, the dependent variable is measured in both groups. If there is a difference between the two groups on the dependent variable, that difference can only have been caused by the independent variable. (p. 33)

a, b, d. Naturalistic observation, surveys, and case studies are all descriptive data collection methods.

8. *b* is the answer. Surveys are used to collect descriptive data on people's attitudes, beliefs, opinions, and behavioral intentions. (p. 32)

a. Experiments are controlled methods of establishing a cause-effect relationship.

c. Case studies are used to collect descriptive information from a particular individual, group, or situation. Case studies usually combine several forms of data collection—observations, interviews, tests, and analyses of written records. Case studies provide a close-up, in-depth view of subjects, whereas surveys paint a broad portrait.

d. Naturalistic observation is used to collect behavioral information from the subjects' natural environment.

9. *c* is the answer. A hypothesis about the effect of job loss should be tested with a quasi-experiment to avoid long-term negative effects to the subjects.

Testing this with an experiment would require subjects to quit their jobs. Such an experiment would be considered highly unethical and therefore cannot be allowed to take place. (pp. 35–36)

a. Trying to improve students' study methods is not unethical.

b. Experiencing an unpleasant odor for a short time would not be harmful, and the negative emotional reaction could be counteracted by the researchers once the experimental session is over.

d. All of the above are not true.

10. *b* is the answer. Experiments are used to study cause-effect relationships. (p. 33)

a. Case studies focus on one person in depth to document the person's behavior fully, his or her physical and psychological state, and so forth. It cannot determine cause and effect.

c. Because naturalistic observation involves watching people in their usual environments, it cannot be used to find out what changes a person's reaction to a negative event. Not only would the researcher be unable to wait for at least two negative events to occur for each subject, but he or she also couldn't determine which variables might have caused a change (or lack of change) in the subject's behavior.

d. A survey does not allow variables to be controlled to look for the effect on other variables.

11. *d* is the answer. Suppose an experimenter finds significant differences between the experimental group and the control group. If random variables exist in the experimental group but not the control group, for example, the experimenter cannot be sure what caused his results—the independent or the random variables. Random variables are a problem because they are difficult to control; sometimes they cannot be controlled. All of the variables listed would be difficult or costly for an experimenter to quantify and control. (p. 34)

12. *a* is the answer. A person with a rare condition is best studied in depth through a case study. (pp. 31–32)

b. An experiment could not be conducted to see if lightning causes unusual behavior; it would be wrong.

c. A researcher wouldn't use naturalistic observation to gain understanding of a person with an unusual problem, because unobtrusively watching a person doesn't provide information about family background, health history, current physical condition, and so on.

d. To survey a person who is having trouble regulating her behavior and concentrating would be difficult, if not impossible. In addition, a survey includes more than one or a few participants because its purpose is to discover something about a group of people.

13. *d* is the answer. Having an equal chance of being selected for participation in a study would be impossible, or nearly so, for all the members of these populations. (p. 36)
  a. Contacting every human being on the face of the earth to solicit participation in the study would be impossible.
  b. The researcher probably wouldn't be able to find all the rats in New York City to ensure that each had an equal chance of being selected as a subject.
  c. Many past U.S. presidents are dead and therefore would not have an equal chance of participating in the study.

14. *a* is the answer. Two types of statistics are used: descriptive statistics are used to summarize data, and inferential statistics are used to analyze data in order to draw conclusions about research results. (p. 37)
  b. Measuring the dependent variable is part of an experimental procedure. Statistics are used to describe and analyze experimental *results*.
  c. Independent-variable manipulation is a part of experimental procedure. Statistics are used to describe and analyze experimental *results*.
  d. Correlations do not yield cause-effect relationships.

15. *b* is the answer. 10 is the most frequently occurring score. (p. 38)
  a. The mean of this data set is 12. It is calculated by summing the values of all the scores and dividing by the number of scores.
  c. The median of this data set is 11. It is the score that cuts the data set in half.
  d. The range is 12. It is calculated by subtracting the lowest score from the highest score.

16. *b* is the answer. In a positive correlation, both variables *vary* in the same direction together; as one increases so does the other (and vice versa). (p. 39)
  a. A negative correlation tells us that as one variable increases, the other decreases.
  c, d. Correlations do not imply causation. One can never conclude that one variable *causes* the other to change in any direction based on a correlation—regardless of its positive or negative value.

17. *b* is the answer. The average test scores were very low. Since the recruiter wants to find students with the highest scores, he needs the data set with the greatest number of scores that are very distant from the mean. The standard deviation is a measure of variability; it describes the average distance from the mean in a data set. If the standard deviation is large, then there will be a large number of extreme scores; this, in turn, means there is a large probability that some scores are very high. Therefore, the recruiter should look at the data sets that have the largest standard deviations to find students who scored very high on the intelligence test. (p. 39)
  a. The range is also a measure of variability. If the range is large then the recruiter knows that at least one score in the data set is very low or very high. But the standard deviation takes into account more than two test scores and is a better measure of the probability that more than one high score exists in a data set.
  c. The recruiter has already identified the mean, median, and mode—all measures of central tendency—for the data sets.
  d. Operational definitions are used to describe ways of measuring a given variable (for example, anxiety).

18. *c* is the answer. A positive correlation indicates that as one variable increases, the other variable increases. This type of relationship supports the data; as alcohol consumption increases, so does decision-making time. (pp. 39–40)
  a, d. A negative correlation indicates that as one variable increases, the other decreases. This relationship does not fit the data.
  b. There is no such thing as a curvilinear correlation. Curvilinear correlations do not exist.

19. *d* is the answer. Psychologists follow ethical guidelines because they want their studies to benefit society, because specific guidelines are set forth by several organizations, and because undue stress and pain might become confounding variables in an experiment. (p. 41)

20. *a* is the answer. The quasi-experimental studies used in such behavioral genetics research include adoption, family, and twin studies. (pp. 43–44)
  b. An experiment would be a controlled study in which, for example, subjects were assigned to families; therefore, it would not be ethical.
  c. Factor analysis is a correlational method used to identify variables, such as personality traits, that tend to occur together. Factor analysis would not help in determining what relative

effect environment and genetics have on a variable.

   d. A psychologist using naturalistic observation would watch and record behaviors, but could make no conclusions about the impact of heredity or environment on something like intelligence.

Now turn to the quiz analysis table at the end of this chapter to find which areas you know well and which areas you need to work on. Circle the numbers in the table for items on Quiz 2 that you answered correctly.

For each question you answered correctly, circle its number. (Quiz 1 numbers are not shaded; Quiz 2 numbers are shaded.) Are there patterns in the types of questions or the topics you got wrong that could direct your further study? Did you improve from Quiz 1 to Quiz 2?

TOPIC	DEFINITION	COMPREHENSION	APPLICATION
	TYPE OF QUESTION		
Critical thinking			1
(Quiz 2)			1
Research	2		
(Quiz 2)			5
Research Methods			
Goals		3	4
(Quiz 2)	2	7	
Naturalistic observation	5		
(Quiz 2)			3
Case studies		6	
(Quiz 2)			12
Surveys		8	
(Quiz 2)	8		
Experiments			10
(Quiz 2)			10
Variables	7		
(Quiz 2)			6
Groups			11
(Quiz 2)			
Flaws		9	
(Quiz 2)			4, 9, 11
Sampling			15
(Quiz 2)			13
Statistics			
Central tendency	17		12
(Quiz 2)	14		15
Variability			13
(Quiz 2)			17
Correlation		16	18
(Quiz 2)	16		18
Inferential			14
(Quiz 2)			

TOPIC	TYPE OF QUESTION		
	DEFINITION	COMPREHENSION	APPLICATION
Ethics			19
		19	
Genetics		20	
	20		

TOTAL CORRECT BY QUIZ:

QUIZ 1:
QUIZ 2:

Chapter 3

Biological Aspects of Psychology

Biological psychology is the study of the physical and chemical factors that, either alone or through interaction with the environment, influence behavior and mental processes. The nervous system, one of the most important biological factors involved in behavior, receives input about the environment, processes it, and orchestrates outputs such as motor behavior and thought.

OUTLINE

I. THE NERVOUS SYSTEM (pp. 48–56)

A. Cells of the Nervous System

° Cells of the nervous system share many characteristics with other cells in the body.

° Many cells communicate with one another in a process whereby the internal activity of one cell changes in response to external stimuli (such as chemicals) released by another cell.

° Nervous system cells, like other body cells, each have an outer membrane, a cell body, and a nucleus. Neurons respond to environmental changes by means of three special features: structures called axons and dendrites, "excitable" surface membranes, and synapses. Axons carry signals away from the neuron to points where communication occurs with other neurons, whereas dendrites detect and carry information from other nerve cells to the cell body. Other nervous-system cells, called glial cells, hold neurons in place, direct their growth and repair, and keep their chemical environment stable.

B. Action Potentials

° The selective permeability of the neuronal membrane keeps positively charged sodium and calcium ions from freely entering the axon through the gates or channels. As a result, the membrane becomes electrically polarized, such that the inside of the cell is more negatively charged than the outside. When an action potential occurs, some part of the axon membrane becomes depolarized, causing a sodium or calcium gate to open. Sodium rushes into the axon, causing the neighboring sodium gates to open as well, and more sodium rushes in. This chain of events occurs along the entire length of the axon.

° The neuron either fires or does not fire in an all-or-none type of signal. The speed of the action potential is constant as it travels down the axon. If a neuron is larger or is coated with myelin, action potentials will be faster. The length of the pause between action potentials is known as the refractory period and determines the rate or number of action potentials that occur within a given time unit. Messages in the nervous system are coded by the speed and rate of action potentials.

C. Synapses and Communication Between Neurons

Communication between neurons occurs at the synapse.

1. *Neurotransmitters.* Communication at the synapse is chemical in nature. Neurotransmitters are chemicals that carry the signal across the synapse to the postsynaptic cell (usually a dendrite). When neurotransmitters bind to receptors in the postsynaptic cell, a membrane potential is created.

2. *Excitatory and Inhibitory Signals.* When a postsynaptic cell is reached by a neurotransmitter, the postsynaptic membrane becomes depolarized or hyperpolarized, creating a postsynaptic potential, and the signal once again becomes electric in nature. A depolarized membrane will cause an excitatory postsynaptic potential (EPSP), and a hyperpolarized membrane will cause an inhibitory postsynaptic potential (IPSP). The combined impact of the many EPSPs and IPSPs will determine whether or not an action potential will occur.

D. Organization and Functions of the Nervous System

° Neurons in the brain and spinal cord are organized into groups called networks. The sensory system provides input about the environment via the five senses. The motor system directs the response to the environment by influencing the muscles and other organs.

° The peripheral nervous system is made up of the sensory and motor systems. The central nervous system (CNS) processes information and is encased in bone. The CNS is made up of the brain and spinal cord.

II. THE PERIPHERAL NERVOUS SYSTEM: KEEPING IN TOUCH WITH THE WORLD (pp. 56–57)

The peripheral nervous system has two components: the somatic and autonomic systems.

A. The Somatic Nervous System

The somatic system carries information from the senses to the CNS and sends movement instructions back to the muscles.

B. The Autonomic Nervous System

The autonomic system, via the parasympathetic and sympathetic branches, transmits messages between the CNS and the body's organs and glands. The sympathetic branch prepares the body for action through the "fight-or-flight" response. The parasympathetic branch does the opposite: it slows organ and gland activity to conserve the body's energy.

III. THE CENTRAL NERVOUS SYSTEM: MAKING SENSE OF THE WORLD (pp. 58–74)

The central nervous system (CNS) is made up of collections of neuronal cell bodies called nuclei and the fiber tracts that connect them.

A. The Spinal Cord

° The spinal cord carries messages to and from the brain. Reflexes—quick, involuntary muscular responses (through efferent neurons) that are initiated on the basis of incoming sensory information (through afferent neurons)—occur in the spinal cord without instruction from the brain. The brain is informed of each reflex after it occurs.

° The spinal cord is an example of a feedback system, a process in which information about an action's results are conveyed back to the source of the action

so that further adjustments to the activity can be made.

B. The Brain

1. *The Hindbrain.* Hindbrain structures such as the medulla control vital functions (for example, blood pressure, heart rate, and breathing). The reticular formation is a network of cells running throughout the hindbrain that alters the activity of other brain structures. For example, the locus coeruleus, an area thought to be involved in the state of vigilance, is activated by the reticular formation. The cerebellum controls finely coordinated movements, including speech.

2. *The Midbrain.* Located between the hindbrain and forebrain, the midbrain controls certain automatic behaviors. The substantia nigra is a midbrain structure that, together with the striatum, is involved in initiating smooth movement.

3. *The Forebrain.* The forebrain is the most highly developed part of the human brain. The diencephalon includes the thalamus, which relays sensory signals, and the hypothalamus, which regulates basic drives. The suprachiasmatic nuclei, part of the hypothalamus, determines our biological rhythms. The cerebrum includes the amygdala and hippocampus. The limbic system plays an important role in regulating emotion and is involved in memory and other thought processes.

C. Focus on Research Methods: Manipulating Genes

To test hypotheses about the cause of Alzheimer's disease, experimenters implanted a gene into mice and found that it created brain damage similar to Alzheimer's. If the damage creates similar memory impairments, scientists may have succeeded in making an animal model of the disease that will allow more specific research on Alzheimer's.

D. Thinking Critically: Are There Drugs That Can Make You Smarter?

What am I being asked to believe or accept?
Certain drugs, called nootropics, improve cognitive functioning.

What evidence is available to support the assertion?
Some research results are positive; subjects showed significant improvement on memory and general cognitive tasks.

Are there alternative ways of interpreting the evidence?

Research studies using a double-blind design show weak and temporary results in a limited number of cognitive areas.

What additional evidence would help to evaluate the alternatives?
Much research remains to be done to determine which drugs have positive effects and on what type of cognitive functions with little or no side effects.

What conclusions are most reasonable?
Eventually, drugs that improve memory and other cognitive functions will be found, but those currently on the market have very limited effect.

E. The Cerebral Cortex

The cerebral cortex is the outer surface of the cerebrum or cerebral hemispheres. The frontal, parietal, occipital, and temporal lobes are used as physical landmarks for describing the cortex. The functional areas of the cortex include the sensory, motor, and association cortex.

1. *Sensory and Motor Cortex.* The sensory cortex receives sensory information. The motor cortex neurons control the onset of voluntary movement.

2. *Association Cortex.* The association cortex receives information from more than one sense and combines sensory and motor information. Aphasia, a deficit in understanding and producing language, is caused by damage to Broca's area or Wernicke's area. Many areas of the brain are related to language; several are associated with specific semantic abilities.

F. The Divided Brain in a Unified Self

1. *Split-Brain Studies.* Split-brain (severed corpus callosum) data demonstrate that each hemisphere is superior in certain abilities. The left hemisphere controls spoken language, and the right controls recognition of faces and tasks dealing with spatial relations, such as drawing three-dimensional shapes. In addition, the left hemisphere controls the right side of the body and the right hemisphere controls the left side.

2. *Lateralization of Normal Brains.* Data collected from people with intact brains demonstrate the superiority of the left hemisphere in logical thinking and language abilities. The right hemisphere exhibits better spatial, artistic, and musical abilities. But keep in mind that, while the two halves of the brain may have lateralized abilities, the cerebral hemispheres work closely together.

G. Plasticity in the Brain

° Synaptic plasticity is the brain's ability to strengthen neural connections and establish new connections. Unfortunately, synaptic plasticity is somewhat limited. New neurons cannot be generated, and exact replication of the many synaptic connections prior to brain damage is almost impossible. However, old neurons do produce new axons and dendrites, which make new connections.

° Scientists are continually trying new methods to reproduce and grow nerve cells. Several methods for enhancing brain-damage recovery are under study, such as tissue transplants into the damaged area from another brain, nerve growth factor for stimulation, and guidance of axon growth.

IV. LINKAGES: HUMAN DEVELOPMENT AND THE CHANGING BRAIN (pp. 74–76)

Patterns of behavioral development in infants are correlated with plastic changes in activity and structure in the developing brain. During development, the brain overproduces neural connections and, based on experience, establishes which connections are needed and then eliminates the extras. Even in adulthood, the number of connections is affected by experience: stimulating environments produce greater numbers of connections.

V. THE CHEMISTRY OF PSYCHOLOGY (pp. 76–79)

A group of neurons that communicates with the same neurotransmitter is called a neurotransmitter system. Some neurotransmitter systems are responsible for certain behaviors or problems. The suffix -*ergic* is added to a neurotransmitter name to make it an adjective.

A. Seven Major Neurotransmitters

1. *Acetylcholine.* Acetylcholine controls the contraction of muscles and is used by neurons in the parasympathetic nervous system. In the brain, cholinergic neurons are involved in movement and memory. A loss of cholinergic neurons is linked to Alzheimer's disease.

2. *Norepinephrine.* Arousal is the main task of norepinephrine, which is also known as noradrenaline. Noradrenaline is used by neurons in the sympathetic nervous system and in the locus coeruleus.

3. *Serotonin.* Sleep, moods, and appetite are influenced by serotonin.

4. *Dopamine.* Problems with the dopamine system in the substantia nigra and striatum contribute to Parkinson's disease, which leads to difficulty in the initiation of movement. Dopamine is also involved in the experience of pleasure. Malfunctioning dopaminergic neurons may be partly responsible for schizophrenia, a psychological disorder characterized by distorted perception, emotion, and thought.

5. *GABA.* Gamma-amino butyric acid or GABA is the major inhibitory transmitter of the central nervous system. Huntington's disease causes a loss of GABA-using neurons and results in uncontrollable movement of the arms and legs.

6. *Glutamate.* The major excitatory neurotransmitter in the CNS is glutamate. Glutamate helps strengthen synaptic connections, which may be the origin of learning and memory.

7. *Endorphins.* Endorphins, natural opiate-like compounds, can reduce pain and cause sleep.

VI. THE ENDOCRINE SYSTEM: COORDINATING THE INTERNAL WORLD (pp. 80–81)

The endocrine system, like the nervous system, influences a wide variety of behaviors. Glands secrete hormones, which travel via the bloodstream and affect coordinated systems of target tissues and organs, producing such responses as the fight-or-flight syndrome. A negative feedback system involving the brain regulates the amount of hormone released.

VII. THE IMMUNE SYSTEM: LINKING THE BRAIN AND THE BODY'S DEFENSE SYSTEM (pp. 81–83)

° The immune system is very similar to the nervous and endocrine systems: all three systems are capable of responding to their environment, and all have cells that communicate with one another. The function of the immune system is to monitor the internal body for the presence of foreign or harmful material and to eliminate it. In autoimmune disorders the immune system attacks normal body cells.

° Four lines of evidence demonstrate the interaction of the immune, nervous, and endocrine systems.

1. Stress has a negative impact on the functioning of the immune system.

2. Immune responses can be learned. Learning involves the nervous system.

3. Stimulating or damaging certain parts of the nervous system, such as the hypothalamus and portions of the cortex and brainstem, cause changes in the ways in which the immune system functions.

4. Immune system activity causes changes in neurotransmitter activity, hormonal secretion, and behavior.

KEY TERMS

1. **Biological psychology** is the study of the role of physical and chemical factors in behavior and mental processes. (p. 47)

Example: Changes in brain biochemicals are associated with depression.

REMEMBER: Biological psychology is the study of the biological factors that influence psychological phenomena.

2. The **nervous system** is a complex combination of cells that has three basic functions: to receive information, to integrate it with previous information to generate choices and decisions, and to guide actions and output based on those decisions. (p. 48)

Example: When we stand at the curb of a busy street, our nervous system receives sensory information about oncoming traffic, makes a decision to cross the street at a particular moment, and controls the movement (output) of stepping off the curb and crossing the street.

3. **Neurons** are the cells that make up the nervous system. Neurons can communicate with one another by receiving and sending signals. Three structures allow neurons to communicate: synapses, "excitable" (electrically polarized) membranes, and long thin fibers that extend outward from the cell called axons and dendrites. (See Figure 3.2 in your text.) (p. 49)

REMEMBER: A neuron is similar to a computer in that information comes in, is processed, and is sent out.

4. **Glial cells** hold neurons in place and help to sustain them. (pp. 49–50)

REMEMBER: Glial means "glue"; part of the glial cells' job is to "glue" neurons together.

Example: A glial cell may secrete chemicals to stabilize a neuron's environment or to help repair a damaged neuron.

5. **Axons** usually carry signals from the neuronal cell body out to the synapse, where communication with other nerve cells takes place. Generally, each neuron has only one axon. (p. 50)

REMEMBER: Axons create action potentials. Most of the time, the action potential travels from the cell body to the end of the axon. (See Key Term 9.)

6. **Dendrites** are branches of the neuron that usually receive signals from the axons of other neurons and carry those signals to the neuron's cell body. Each neuron can have many dendrites. (p. 50)

REMEMBER: Dendrites detect signals from other neurons.

7. A **synapse** is the very small gap between the presynaptic cell sending a message and the postsynaptic cell receiving that message. Typically, the axon is the presynaptic cell and the dendrite is the postsynaptic cell. Neurotransmitters released from the presynaptic cell cross the synapse and fit snugly into the receptors on the postsynaptic cell. (p. 50)

REMEMBER: Pre means "before." The presynaptic cell comes before the synapse. Post means "after." The postsynaptic cell comes after the synapse. (See Figure 3.4 in your text.)

8. **Ions** are small molecules that have a positive or negative electrical charge. (p. 50)

Example: Sodium (NA$^+$), an ion active in nervous-system communication, is positively charged and heavily concentrated outside the neuron. Though attracted to negative ions inside the membrane, it cannot enter the sodium channels until the neuron's membrane becomes depolarized.

9. **Action potentials** occur when the neuron becomes depolarized and sodium rushes into the axon. Opening one sodium gate causes the gate next to it to open, which causes the next one to open, and so forth, all the way down the length of the axon. Action potentials are all-or-nothing activities; the cell either fires at full strength or does not fire at all. (p. 50)

REMEMBER: Electrical potentials occur when there is a difference in charge between the outside and inside of the cell. When an active change occurs in

the electrical potential such as depolarization, sodium rushes into the axon and makes the inside less negative, causing an action potential.

10. **Myelin** is a fatty substance that wraps around some axons. It speeds an action potential's travel down the length of the axon. (p. 51)

Example: When a stray object flies toward your face, the sensory nerves must quickly transmit this information to your brain, and the motor nerves must carry the signal to your muscles to move very rapidly. These sensory and motor nerves are covered with myelin.

11. A **refractory period** is a rest period between action potentials. Following one action potential, the axon must repolarize before another action potential can occur. The time required for the axon to repolarize is called a refractory period. (p. 51)

REMEMBER: An axon refrains from firing an action potential during a refractory period.

12. **Neurotransmitters** are chemicals that carry a signal from the presynaptic cell across the synapse to the receptors on the postsynaptic cell. (p. 52)

REMEMBER: *Neuro* refers to neuron. *Transmit* means to send something across space. Neurotransmitters *send* the signal or message *across* the space of the synapse to the postsynaptic *neuron*.

13. **Receptors**, usually located on the dendrites of the postsynaptic cell, are stimulated when neurotransmitters fit into them, like a key fits a lock. (p. 53)

REMEMBER: A receptor is something that receives. Receptors receive neurotransmitters.

14. **Postsynaptic potential** occurs when the membrane potential of the postsynaptic cell is changed. (See Key Terms 15 and 16.) (p. 53)

15. An **excitatory postsynaptic potential (EPSP)** causes the postsynaptic membrane to become depolarized, thus increasing the probability that a neuron will fire an action potential. The strength of an EPSP weakens as it travels down the dendrite. (p. 54)

REMEMBER: An *excitatory* postsynaptic potential *excites* the neuron that will cause it to fire. But also note that all the EPSPs and IPSPs that a dendrite receives combine to determine whether or not the axon of the postsynaptic cell will fire an action potential. If there are more EPSPs than IPSPs, the neuron will fire an action potential.

16. An **inhibitory postsynaptic potential (IPSP)** causes the postsynaptic membrane to become hyperpolarized, thus <u>decreasing</u> the chances a neuron will fire an action potential. The strength of an IPSP weakens as it travels down the dendrite. (p. 54)

REMEMBER: An *inhibitory* postsynaptic potential *inhibits* or prevents the neuron from firing. But also note that all the EPSPs and IPSPs that a dendrite receives combine to determine whether or not the axon of the postsynaptic cell will fire an action potential. If there are more IPSPs than EPSPs, the neuron will not fire an action potential.

17. **Sensory systems**, which include vision, hearing, touch, taste, and smell, provide us with input about the environment. (p. 56)

Example: When you walk into a friend's house for a dinner party, your nose provides information about the food she or he has prepared.

18. **Motor systems** influence muscles and other organs to respond to the environment in some way. (p. 56)

Example: After you have smelled the food prepared for the dinner party (see Key Term 17) and have decided that you want to eat it, your motor system allows you to walk to the table, sit down, and manipulate the fork, knife, and spoon.

19. The **peripheral nervous system** is the major division of the nervous system that is not encased in bone. It has two major subdivisions, the <u>somatic</u> and <u>autonomic</u> nervous systems. (p. 56)

REMEMBER: Peri means "around." The peripheral nervous system is located *around* the center of your body. (See Figure 3.9 in your text.)

20. The **central nervous system (CNS)** is the major division of the nervous system that is encased in bone and includes the brain and spinal cord. Its primary function is to process the information provided by the sensory systems and to decide on appropriate courses of action for the motor system. (p. 56)

REMEMBER: The brain and spinal cord are *centrally* located. Your spinal cord is in the *center* of your torso; the brain is *centered* over your shoulders. Therefore, the brain and spinal cord make up the *central* nervous system. (See Figure 3.9 in your text.)

21. The **somatic nervous system**, which is part of the peripheral nervous system, transmits information from the senses to the CNS and carries signals from the CNS to the muscles that move the skeleton. (p. 56)

Example: When you dance, the somatic nervous system transmits the sound of the music to your brain and carries the signals from your brain to the muscles that move your arms and legs.

REMEMBER: Soma means "body." The somatic nervous system is involved with taking sensory information from the body parts, such as the ears, and sending signals back to the body, such as movement instructions to coordinate dance steps.

22. The **autonomic nervous system**, which is part of the peripheral nervous system, carries messages back and forth between the CNS and the organs and glands. (p. 57)

Example: While you dance, your peripheral nervous system may alter the expansion of your lungs so that you can inhale more oxygen. Also, your heartbeat increases so that more blood reaches your muscles.

REMEMBER: The *autonomic* nervous system regulates the *automatic* functions of your body, such as breathing and blood pressure. You do not normally think about these functions.

23. **Nuclei** are collections of cell bodies. (p. 58)

REMEMBER: If you think of the CNS as a map of Boston, nuclei would represent "neighborhoods" on the map.

24. **Fiber tracts** (pathways or nerves) are collections of axons that travel together in bundles. (p. 58)

REMEMBER: Again, if you think of the CNS as a map of Boston, fiber tracts would represent the large "superhighways" on the map.

25. The **spinal cord**, part of the central nervous system, receives signals from the somatic system in the periphery, such as vision, and relays them to the brain via fiber tracts within the spinal cord. The brain then relays signals to the muscles via fiber tracts in the spinal cord. (p. 58)

Example: The sensory information from feeling the fur on a kitten travels through the spinal cord's fiber tracts on its way to the brain. When your brain makes the decision to pick up the kitten, it sends signals through the fiber tracts in the spinal cord on the way to the muscles in your hands and arms.

26. **Reflexes** are quick, involuntary responses to incoming sensory information (along afferent neurons). The reflexive movement exits the nervous system and contacts the muscles along efferent (or motor) neurons. (p. 58)

Example: If you accidentally step on a pin embedded in your carpet, a withdrawal reflex occurs. The afferent sensory neurons will take the information from your foot to the spinal cord, and the efferent motor neurons will send the signal back to the foot to make it withdraw from the floor.

27. The **hindbrain**, a major subdivision of the brain, includes the medulla, reticular formation, and cerebellum. The hindbrain, an extension of the spinal cord, is housed in the skull and involved in controlling vital functions. (p. 59)

28. The **medulla** is located in the hindbrain. It helps to regulate blood pressure, heart rate, and breathing. (p. 59)

Example: A person with damage to her medulla would most likely need artificial life support to maintain breathing and perhaps would not survive the injury.

29. The **reticular formation** is not a well-defined area of brain tissue but a collection of nuclei and fibers that form a network of cells throughout the hindbrain and midbrain. The reticular formation is involved in arousal and attention. (p. 59)

REMEMBER: Reticular means "net-like." The cells of the reticular formation are not arranged in any distinct structure but, rather, thread throughout the hindbrain.

30. The **locus coeruleus** is a small group of cells that may be involved in the state of vigilance. Activity in the reticular formation stimulates the locus coeruleus. (p. 60)

Example: The numerous branches of axons from the locus coeruleus contact other cells, perhaps causing a state of attention or change in mood.

31. The **cerebellum** is located in the hindbrain. It controls fine motor coordination. (p. 60)

Example: Performing brain surgery requires delicate precision of movement so as to avoid damaging fragile tissue. A surgeon's cerebellum would be very active during an operation.

32. The **midbrain**, which includes the substantia nigra, is located between the hindbrain and the forebrain. Sensory information is integrated in the midbrain to produce the smooth initiation of movement. (p. 62)

33. The **substantia nigra** is part of the midbrain and assists in the smooth initiation of movement. (p. 62)

Example: Phil, a person with damage to his substantia nigra, is unable to reach out his arm to shake hands with a neighbor.

34. The **striatum** is part of the cerebrum and interacts with the substantia nigra to control the smooth initiation of movement. (p. 62)

35. The **forebrain**, which is composed of the diencephalon and the cerebrum, is the most highly developed brain structure. It is responsible for the most complex aspects of behavior and mental processes. (p. 62)

Example: Many years ago a surgical procedure called lobotomy was used to treat several types of mental disorders. The surgery involved destroying large parts of the forebrain. Patients on whom this surgery was performed were often unable to perform complex cognitive tasks afterward.

36. The **thalamus** is located in the forebrain. This region processes and relays sensory information on its way to higher centers of the brain. (p. 62)

Example: Jane has damage to her thalamus. She has normal processing of visual images with her eyes, but is unable to send that information on to be acted upon further by the brain. In fact, Jane reports being totally unable to see.

37. The **hypothalamus** is located in the forebrain. It regulates hunger, thirst, and sex drives, and is involved in emotion. (p. 62)

Example: Destroying certain parts of the hypothalamus causes an animal to cease eating and drinking. It will eventually die if not force-fed.

38. The **suprachiasmatic nuclei**, part of the hypothalamus, determines our biological rhythms, acting much like an internal alarm clock. (p. 62)

Example: Bob is used to getting up at 10:00 A.M. and working until about 2:00 A.M. Bob's suprachiasmatic nuclei have probably influenced him to be a "night person."

39. The **cerebrum** is part of the forebrain. Located within the cerebrum are the amygdala and the hippocampus. (p. 63)

40. The **amygdala**, part of the limbic system, plays an important role in combining the features of stimuli from two sensory modalities. (p. 63)

Example: When you eat ice cream, your amygdala is involved in your perception that the ice cream is both cold and sweet.

41. The **hippocampus**, also part of the limbic system, is involved in learning and storing new pieces of information or new memories. (p. 63)

Example: Going to class every day would be a waste of time if your hippocampus was damaged. Although you'd be able to understand everything the instructor said, you wouldn't be able to form a memory for the new information.

42. The **limbic system** is contained in several brain areas and is involved in emotion, memory, and some thought processes. Severe degeneration of limbic system structures is found in Alzheimer's patients. (p. 63)

Example: Grace has Alzheimer's disease, which causes not only memory lapses, but also emotional outbursts in which she falsely claims family members have taken advantage of her.

43. The **cerebral hemispheres** constitute the outermost part of the cerebrum. Each hemisphere makes up one half of the top of the brain. To understand how the cerebrum is split into hemispheres, do the following: place your finger right between your eyes, lift it straight over your forehead, and trace an imaginary part in the middle of your hair to the back of your head. The line that you have just traced is the dividing line of the two cerebral hemispheres. (For an illustration of this division, see Figure 3.17 in your text.) (pp. 66–67)

REMEMBER: Hemi means "half." Cerebral hemisphere refers to half of the cerebrum, which is round like a sphere.

44. The **cerebral cortex**, the outer surface of the cerebral hemispheres, is divided into four lobes: frontal, parietal, occipital, and temporal. The cortex is also divided into three functional areas: the sensory cortex, the motor cortex, and the association cortex. (p. 66)

45. The **sensory cortex**, located in the parietal, occipital, and temporal lobes, receives information from different senses, including touch, vision, and hearing. (p. 67)

Example: If you were to take a walk on the beach, your sensory cortex would be receiving various types of information in your lobes: occipital (the color of the water); parietal (the sandy feeling on your skin and the salt water on your face); and temporal (the sound of the surf).

46. The **motor cortex**, located in the frontal lobe, controls all voluntary movement. (p. 67)

Example: During that walk on the beach, your motor cortex would be sending information to your muscles to help you walk in the sand in a particular direction.

47. The **association cortex** pertains to *all* lobes of the cortex. These regions of cortex receive information from more than one sense or combine sensory and motor information. These are the areas that perform such complex cognitive tasks as associating words with images and other abstract thinking. (pp. 68–69)

REMEMBER: Think of the *association* cortex as forming an *association* between many types of sensory and motor information.

48. The **corpus callosum** connects the two cerebral hemispheres. Without the corpus callosum, the two hemispheres could not communicate regarding their respective activities. (p. 70)

REMEMBER: Corpus callosum begins with two c's. The corpus callosum connects the cerebral hemispheres.

49. A **lateralized task** is one that is performed more efficiently by one hemisphere than by the other. The left hemisphere is better at logical reasoning and language skills, while the right hemisphere is superior in musical and artistic abilities and spatial reasoning. (p. 71)

Example: When Lynne reads, her left hemisphere is more activated than her right.

50. **Synaptic plasticity** is the brain's ability to strengthen neural connections at synapses and to establish new synapses. (p. 72)

Example: New synapses are formed in your brain when you learn new material.

51. A **neurotransmitter system** is a set of neurons that communicates with the same neurotransmitter. A neurotransmitter system may control an aspect of behavior such as memory. (p. 76)

Example: The symptoms Grace experiences from Alzheimer's disease occur due to its effects on her acetylcholine neurotransmitter system.

52. **Acetylcholine**, the neurotransmitter found in the cholinergic system, is used by neurons in the peripheral and central nervous systems. It assists in the contraction of muscles and the formation of new memories. (p. 77)

Example: Grace's memory lapses are linked to a loss of cholinergic neurons in areas of her brain that store memories.

53. The neurotransmitter **norepinephrine** is used in the adrenergic system. It is involved in arousal, learning, and moods. (pp. 77–78)

Example: Miguel's sympathetic nervous system has activated the fight-or-flight response by releasing norepinephrine to allow him to jump out of the way of an inexperienced cyclist.

54. **Serotonin** is a neurotransmitter that regulates sleep, moods, and appetite. (p. 78)

Example: Joyce finished a high-carbohydrate meal of macaroni and cheese; therefore, her desire for carbohydrates is being reduced by the release of serotonin.

55. The neurotransmitter **dopamine** is used in the substantia nigra and striatum to control movement. Dopaminergic neurons also play a role in the experience of pleasure. (p. 78)

Example: Nelson has Parkinson's disease, which is associated with a deterioration of dopamine cells. Nelson finds it increasingly difficult to move from a sitting to a standing position and is discouraged by his increasingly noticeable hand tremors.

56. **GABA** is an inhibitory neurotransmitter that is involved in a variety of behaviors and mental processes. Malfunctioning GABA systems are associated with severe anxiety, Huntington's disease, and epilepsy. (p. 78)

Example: Huntington's disease has reduced the number of GABA-containing neurons in Victoria's striatum. Because her dopamine system is no longer inhibited by GABA, Victoria experiences uncontrollable movements of her arms and legs.

57. **Glutamate** is an excitatory neurotransmitter that helps signals cross the synapse more efficiently. (p. 79)

Example: Craig believes he will one day be able to show evidence of learning through the tracking of glutamate's effects on synaptic connections.

58. **Endorphins** are naturally occurring opiate-like neurotransmitters that modify pain signals being sent to the brain such that perceived pain is reduced. (p. 79)

Example: "Runner's high," or the absence of pain and the euphoric feeling that many runners report after covering long distances, may be caused by the release of endorphins.

59. The **endocrine system** is made up of cells that can communicate with one another. A wide variety of behaviors and mental processes are influenced by this system. Hormones, traveling via the bloodstream, affect coordinated systems of target tissues and organs by producing such responses as the fight-or-flight syndrome. (p. 80)

60. **Glands**, the structures that make up the endocrine system, secrete hormones. (p. 80)

Example: The pituitary, adrenals, testes, ovaries, pancreas, and thyroid are all glands of the endocrine system.

61. **Hormones** are chemicals that, when released by the glands of the endocrine system, travel via the bloodstream and communicate with other cells, thus influencing behavior and mental processes. (p. 80)

Example: A woman's menstrual cycle is governed by the timed release of several different hormones from the pituitary and ovary glands.

62. The **fight-or-flight syndrome**, caused by the release of hormones, is a coordinated set of responses to danger that prepares the organism for action. The heart beats faster, the liver releases glucose to be used as energy, and the organism is placed in a state of high arousal. In short, the organism is prepared to stay and *fight* or to *flee* very quickly. (p. 81)

Example: Any scary experience will induce the fight-or-flight syndrome. Hearing strange noises at night, giving your first speech in college, or almost being hit by a car can be very frightening. If you have been in any of these situations, you may recall how your heart suddenly thudded.

63. **Negative feedback systems** are designed to monitor and adjust the level of activity in your physiological systems. (p. 81)

Example: Think of the hormones that are released from pituitary glands. Negative feedback systems provide a way for your body to maintain the correct amount of pituitary hormone in your system—not too much and not too little. Your pituitary releases hormone X. Certain levels of circulating hormone X cause chemical Y to be secreted from another place in your body. Your pituitary can "read" the level of chemical Y in the bloodstream. When the Y level gets too high, the pituitary *stops* releasing hormone X.

REMEMBER: Negative feedback means providing feedback to a system and saying *"No more—Stop!"* to that activity (for example, releasing hormones).

64. The **immune system** monitors the internal state of the body, detects foreign and harmful substances, and eliminates them. (p. 81)

Example: A virus will be surrounded by immune system cells and destroyed if the system is working properly.

65. **Autoimmune disorders** are diseases in which the body literally attacks itself and kills normal cells. (p. 82)

REMEMBER: Auto means "self" (think of autobiography). In an autoimmune disorder the immune system attacks the "self."

FILL-IN-THE-BLANKS KEY TERMS

1. In most cases, _____ carry signals away from the cell body and _____ carry signals toward the cell body.

2. _____ occur when neurons become depolarized.

3. A neuron with a slow rate of firing would have a long _____.

4. An _____ postsynaptic potential will cause a cell to become depolarized, while an _____ postsynaptic potential will cause a cell to become hyperpolarized.

5. The _____ nervous system is part of the peripheral nervous system and regulates "automatic" activity.

6. The medulla, reticular formation, and cerebellum are all part of the _____.

7. Very fine motor coordination is controlled by the _____.

8. The _____ is part of the forebrain and helps regulate hunger, thirst, and sex drives.

9. The _____ plays a significant role in forming new memories.

10. The brain cannot create new _____ but is constantly creating and pruning _____.

11. The _____ and _____ are part of the limbic system and are located in the cerebrum.

12. The _____ connects the two cerebral hemispheres.

13. Neurotransmitters are to the nervous system what _____ are to the endocrine system.

14. _____ work like thermostats; they are designed to monitor and adjust levels of activity in your body.

15. _____ are diseases in which the body attacks and kills its own cells.

Total Correct (See answer key) _____

LEARNING OBJECTIVES

1. State the definition of biological psychology. (p. 47)

2. Define the nervous system. Describe the three main components of information processing that the nervous system performs. (p. 48)

3. Compare and contrast neurons and glial cells with other body cells. (pp. 49–50)

4. Name and describe the functions of the neuronal parts that allow them to communicate with one another. (p. 50)

5. Describe the electrical and chemical changes that lead to an action potential. Define myelin and discuss its effects. (pp. 50–51)

6. Explain how polarization and refractory periods affect signal transduction in the nervous system. (pp. 50–51)

7. Define neurotransmitter and describe its role in nervous-system activity. (p. 52)

8. Describe the role of receptors in the communication process between neurons. (p. 53)

9. Define excitatory and inhibitory postsynaptic potentials. Describe their role in the creation of an action potential in the postsynaptic cell. (pp. 53–54)

10. Compare and contrast action potentials and postsynaptic potentials. (pp. 50–54)

11. Define sensory system and motor system. Describe their roles in two components of information processing: input and output. (p. 56)

12. Name the two major divisions of the nervous system. (p. 56)

13. Name the two components of the peripheral nervous system and describe their functions. (pp. 56–57)

14. Name the two components of the autonomic nervous system and describe their functions. (p. 57)

15. Define nuclei and fiber tracts. (p. 58)

16. Name the type of neurons found in the spinal cord and describe their function. Define reflex. (pp. 58–59)

17. Name and define the three major subdivisions of the brain and describe their functions. (pp. 59–62)

18. Name and define the structures in the hindbrain. Describe their functions. (pp. 59–61)

19. Name and define the structures in the midbrain. Describe their functions. (p. 62)

20. Name and define the structures in the forebrain. Describe their functions. (pp. 62–64)

21. Describe the experimental methods used by scientists in their study of Alzheimer's disease. (pp. 64–65)

22. Describe the effects of nootropic drugs and the conclusions that are most reasonable about their use as "smart drugs." (pp. 65–66)

23. Define cerebral cortex. Name the four lobes that make up the cortex and state their locations. (pp. 66–67)

24. Name the three functional divisions of the cortex and describe their functions. (pp. 67–68)

25. Name and describe the role of the areas in the association cortex involved in understanding and producing language. (pp. 68–70)

26. Describe split brain studies and explain the function of the corpus callosum. (p. 70)

27. Describe the lateralization of the cerebral hemispheres. (pp. 70–72)

28. Define synaptic plasticity. Explain why it is impossible for the brain to heal damaged neurons. Describe the methods used to help people recover from brain damage today. (pp. 72–74)

29. Describe the changes that occur in the nervous system throughout development. (pp. 74–76)

30. Define neurotransmitter systems. Name and describe the location of the seven major neurotransmitters. Discuss the behaviors and mental processes associated with each of them. (pp. 76–79)

31. Define endocrine system, glands, and hormones. Compare and contrast the differences between the communication processes of the nervous and endocrine systems. (pp. 80–81)

32. Define the fight-or-flight syndrome. (p. 81)

33. Define negative feedback systems. (p. 81)

34. Compare and contrast the functionality of the immune system to the nervous and endocrine systems. Define autoimmune disorder. (pp. 81–82)

35. Describe the interaction of the immune, nervous, and endocrine systems. (pp. 82–83)

CONCEPTS AND EXERCISES

No. 1: The Organization of the Nervous System

Completing this exercise should help you to achieve Learning Objectives 12, 13, and 14.

The organizational chart on page 52 is all mixed up. Correct the mistakes.

No. 2: The Functions of the Brain

Completing this exercise should help you to achieve Learning Objectives 17, 18, 19, 20, 23, 24, 25, and 27.

In the year 3000, parents can decide what kinds of special talents their children will have by requesting changes in the genetic coding for the children's brain structures. Below are instructions from several sets of parents. Pick the part of the brain (from the list below) that the doctor must manipulate. Answers may be used more than once or not at all.

1. Victor and Cynthia want their child to be a dancer who can move across the floor as smoothly and easily as Fred Astaire once did. _____

2. Rob and Laura want their son to have the very fine hand dexterity necessary to become a world-class pianist. _____

3. Frank and Jean want their daughter to be a translator for the United Nations. This career will require her to understand the subtle inflections of many languages. _____

4. Stewart and Lori want their daughter to have enough artistic ability to become a great painter. _____

5. Joanna and Richard want their daughter to become a rock star. She will need extensive musical abilities. _____

6. Colleen and Tim want their son to have the mathematical ability required of an accountant. _____

    A. striatum and substantia nigra
    B. left cerebral hemisphere
    C. right cerebral hemisphere
    D. cerebellum
    E. Wernicke's area

CRITICAL THINKING

Sam and Martina are working on a murder case. The victim, a thirty-year-old male by the name of Jerry, was found dead in his office by his partner at 6:00 A.M. Jerry had multiple stab wounds. His girlfriend, Lisa, told Sam and Martina that she and Jerry had gone out to dinner. Jerry dropped her off at her apartment early, saying that he and his partner had to go back to the office and finish a presentation for the following day.

Lisa did have an alibi. She lived with her sister Susan in a high rise in the city. Susan said that she heard Lisa come in and go straight to bed at around 9:00 P.M.

The partner, Stephen, did not have an alibi. He said that Jerry was supposed to call and let him know whether the meeting was still on. If it was, then they were going to meet at 9:30 at the office. Stephen said he didn't receive a phone call and assumed the meeting and presentation were called off. He stayed home and read until 10:00 P.M. and then went to bed.

Meanwhile, back at the office . . . Sam, with youthful enthusiasm, called the pathologist before the doctor could possibly have been done with his report. Exasperated by Sam's impatience, the doctor told Sam what he knew so far. The cause of death was indeed the stabbing. Also, the man had a stomach full of undigested Chinese food.

Sam hung up the phone and grinned. "That's it," he said. "If the guy's stomach is still full, then he had to have been killed right after dinner. Let's say they get to the restaurant at 7:30. Let's say dinner takes an hour, they drive fifteen minutes to his office, and she kills him and takes a train home to the 'burbs."

Martina laughs to herself. She remembers that she made the same mistake that Sam was making today when she first started on the force. (They just didn't teach

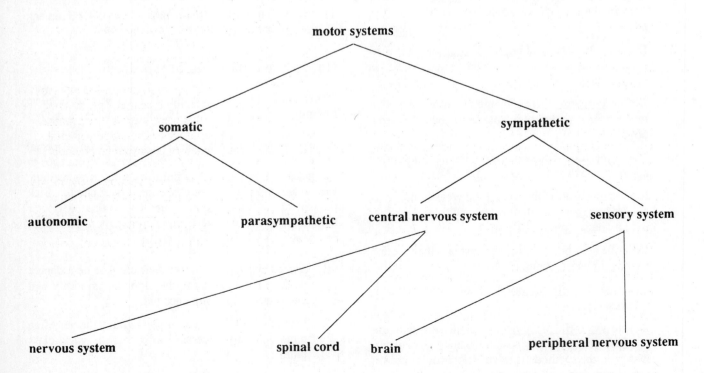

enough biology in school!) Martina knows that once the sympathetic nervous system is activated, as it is when an individual is really scared, the parasympathetic system ceases its activity.

Using the five critical thinking questions in your text, state Sam's original hypothesis and his evidence. Based on the clues in the story, what do you think Martina's alternative hypothesis is?

1. What is Sam's hypothesis?

2. What evidence does he have?

3. What is Martina's probable alternative hypothesis?

4. What is the evidence that supports her hypothesis? What else would you want to know if you were Martina?

5. What conclusion can be drawn?

PERSONAL LEARNING ACTIVITIES

1. To learn the structures of a neuron, come up with an activity to illustrate their functions. For example, you could line up with several friends and have them hold a wadded-up piece of paper in their left hands. Imagine that your right arm is a dendrite, your body is a cell body, and your left arm is an axon. Have everyone hold their arms out to their sides with the left hand holding the paper over the neighbor's cupped right hand. Have the person on the far right begin by dropping the piece of paper into the neighbor's hand. As soon as a paper ball is dropped in your hand, visualize a signal travelling across your right arm, across your body, and causing your left hand to release your paper. Explain what the ball of paper and right hand represent. Can you think of a way to show the role of ions in an action potential or to show how neurotransmitters bind with receptors? (Learning Objectives 4, 7, and 8)

2. Write a letter to a friend explaining the nervous system branch or brain structure responsible for a behavior you exhibited during high school. For instance, you could explain that the sympathetic nervous system was responsible for your sweaty palms and racing heart during a first date. (Learning Objectives 13, 14, and 23)

3. Draw a conceptual map of the brain. Position the most primitive, vital functions at the bottom and the most advanced functions at the top. How could

evolution have influenced brain development? (Learning Objectives 18, 19, 20)

4. List the things you are good at doing. Does the list suggest that one cerebral hemisphere is dominant? (Learning Objective 27)

5. Over the next month, keep track of the days you feel ill with a cold, flu, indigestion, allergy, or anything else. Can you see a link to your level of stress? (Learning Objective 35)

MULTIPLE-CHOICE QUESTIONS

SAMPLE QUIZ 1

1. Which of the following characteristics distinguishes neurons from other cells?
   a. Mitochondria, which turn oxygen and glucose into usable energy
   b. A nucleus that houses genetic information
   c. A cell body
   d. Axons and dendrites

2. This is a story from the neuron kingdom. The king of the neurons wanted to be able to create action potentials at his will, so he decreed that certain substances would be under his control. When he wants action potentials to occur *immediately,* he should allow
   a. neurotransmitters to flood into vesicles.
   b. neurotransmitters to flood into dendrites.
   c. sodium ions to rush into axons.
   d. sodium ions to rush into synapses.

3. Myelin serves what purpose in the nervous system?
   a. It accelerates an action potential's movement.
   b. It is a chemical that travels across the synapse.
   c. It causes an inhibitory postsynaptic potential.
   d. It causes an excitatory postsynaptic potential.

4. Walt Disney has made a new version of the movie *Fantastic Voyage.* The main characters are stuck in an axon with a short _____. If they do not find their way back to the cell body quickly, they will soon be hit with a lethal shower of positive ions.
   a. nucleus
   b. synapse
   c. refractory period
   d. sodium gate

5. While you are spying on a neuron neighbor, you see an equal number of excitatory and inhibitory postsynaptic potentials reach the cell body near the axon. You know this will
   a. cause an action potential.
   b. cause neurotransmitters to be released.
   c. keep the neuron from sending a message.
   d. keep the neuron from receiving a message.

6. A woman was rushed into an emergency room with severely burned hands. She had picked up an iron because she couldn't tell it was hot and she currently doesn't feel pain from the burns. The neurologist who examined her concluded that the woman's _____ system was malfunctioning.
   a. sensory
   b. motor
   c. autonomic
   d. parasympathetic

7. Dr. Frankenstein has given up on creating a human and is trying to build King Kong's cousin. He forgot to install the motor nerves of the somatic system. What will Kong's kin be unable to do?
   a. Lift skyscrapers
   b. Hear people scream
   c. Digest skyscrapers
   d. See people run from him

8. Kalli finishes her exam and hurries home. When she arrives home, she slumps down on her bed to relax. As Kalli relaxes, her _____ nervous system becomes less active while her _____ nervous system becomes more active.
   a. central; somatic
   b. somatic; central
   c. parasympathetic; sympathetic
   d. sympathetic; parasympathetic

9. You are setting the table for a romantic dinner. While lighting the candles, you begin to daydream and the match burns your fingers. What path would the information about your singed fingers follow first?
   a. Sensory system, sensory cortex, thalamus, motor cortex, and motor system
   b. Sensory system, sensory cortex, motor cortex, and motor system
   c. Efferent spinal neuron, afferent spinal neuron
   d. Afferent spinal neuron, efferent spinal neuron

10. The _____ is located in the hindbrain and helps to regulate blood pressure, breathing, and heart rate.

   a. medulla
   b. hypothalamus
   c. thalamus
   d. cerebellum

11. Kwan Li's auto accident caused her to have difficulty with her piano playing. She could no longer play even pieces that she knew well. When the doctors tested her, she also had difficulty tracking with her eyes the movement of a finger held in front of her face and difficulty in tracing drawings with a pen. Damage to Kwan Li's _____ would most likely cause such motor skill difficulties.
   a. cerebellum
   b. diencephalon
   c. parietal lobe
   d. occipital lobe

12. Broca's area and Wernicke's area are located in the _____ cerebral hemisphere and are involved in _____.
   a. right, language
   b. left, language
   c. right, movement
   d. left, biological rhythms

13. Derek has a tingling sensation in his left foot. Which area of the brain has most likely been affected?
   a. left temporal lobe
   b. left striatum
   c. right frontal lobe
   d. right parietal lobe

14. Which of the following is *not* a characteristic of our brains that would make complete recovery from brain damage difficult?
   a. Adult brains cannot generate new neurons.
   b. The brain, prior to damage, has millions of neural connections.
   c. Glial cells eliminate damaged neurons.
   d. Neurons cannot change their functions.

15. Your younger sister has asked you for help with her history homework. She must be able to recognize and name famous people. Which cerebral hemisphere is most likely activated while she does her homework?
   a. Right
   b. Left
   c. Both
   d. Cannot be determined

16. When her vision is blocked by a screen, Sue cannot name objects by using only the sense of touch with her left hand, but she can do so with her right hand. Sue can use the sense of touch to retrieve a previously held object from among several choices using the left hand only or the right hand only. Which part of Sue's brain was most likely damaged?
    a. hippocampus
    b. substantia nigra
    c. parietal lobe
    d. corpus callosum

17. Anne Marie is about one month old. Which part of her brain shows the most activity?
    a. Thalamus
    b. Striatum
    c. Cerebellum
    d. Frontal cortex

18. A nurse has mixed up some test results on neurotransmitter function in several patients at the hospital where you work. To help her out, you tell her that the Alzheimer patient's chart will show too little _____ and the Parkinsonian patient's chart will show too little _____.
    a. dopamine, norepinephrine
    b. dopamine, acetylcholine
    c. acetylcholine, dopamine
    d. acetylcholine, norepinephrine

19. Ted is trying to make a study sheet to help him learn the differences between neurotransmitters and hormones. Which of the following statements on his list is *not* correct?
    a. Neurotransmitters travel via the bloodstream and hormones travel across synapses.
    b. Both hormones and neurotransmitters stimulate only those cells and organs that have receptors for them.
    c. Hormones and neurotransmitters regulate complex behaviors and mental processes.
    d. All of the above are correct.

20. A cold virus entered Isaac's body. A team of cells surrounded the unwanted virus cells like a S.W.A.T team and destroyed them. Which of the following play the role of a S.W.A.T. team for our bodies?
    a. central nervous system
    b. endocrine system
    c. immune system
    d. reflexes

Total Correct (See answer key) _____

SAMPLE QUIZ 2

Use this quiz to reassess your learning after taking Quiz 1 and reviewing the chapter.

1. Veronica Neuron is bragging to Velma Cell. "You're not as special as I am," says Veronica, "because you and the other regular body cells don't have
   a. mitochondria, which create energy."
   b. an outer membrane with selective permeability."
   c. a nucleus with genetic information stored in DNA."
   d. an outer membrane with an excitable surface."

2. Following is a conversation between two axons. Fill in the blanks. *Axon No. 1:* "Life is so dull. I have not been _____ all day." *Axon No. 2:* "Don't complain. I have it rough, too. Even with all of this (these) _____ wrapped around me, I can't seem to get my signals to the synapse fast enough for the boss."
   a. depolarized, myelin
   b. depolarized, receptors
   c. polarized, sodium gates
   d. polarized, vesicles

3. Pretend your class is demonstrating the roles of various cells and structures of a neuron. If you are playing the role of a positive ion participating in an action potential, you should
   a. go in through an open gate in the axon.
   b. run from the cell body to the end of the axon.
   c. begin running from the cell body, but start slowing down at the end of the dendrite.
   d. float across the synapse and bind with a receptor.

4. Scientists have discovered a virus that binds to postsynaptic receptors and prevents the reception of neurotransmitter signals. On which parts of nerve cells could this virus be found?
   a. Dendrites
   b. Axons
   c. Cell bodies
   d. All of the above

5. Bernie the neurotransmitter is speeding across a synapse. Once he lands, he will cause the postsynaptic membrane to hyperpolarize. To what kind of postsynaptic potential will Bernie contribute?
   a. Excitatory
   b. Inhibitory
   c. Myelinated
   d. Refracted

6. The spinal cord is part of the _____ system.
   a. peripheral nervous
   b. somatic
   c. autonomic
   d. central nervous

7. You are watching your favorite soap opera. A doctor charges through the emergency room doors and tells a worried spouse that her husband has a neurological problem. The nerves that carry signals to the muscles are not functioning. The _____ system has been damaged.
   a. central
   b. autonomic
   c. somatic
   d. sympathetic

8. Sarah is playing volleyball. She is running, hitting the ball, and shouting encouragement to her teammates. As a consequence, her heart rate is high, her breathing is rapid, and she is sweating. Which subdivision of her autonomic nervous system is activated?
   a. parasympathetic
   b. peripheral
   c. somatic
   d. sympathetic

9. A reflex
   a. occurs without assistance from the brain.
   b. involves the activity of afferent and efferent neurons.
   c. is involuntary.
   d. all of the above

10. People with severed spinal cords cannot receive sensory information from, or send signals to, the muscles below the level of damage because
    a. the brain can no longer decipher incoming sensory information.
    b. the information going to and from the brain must travel through the spinal cord.
    c. the thalamus's relay station for sensory information always degenerates after spinal cord injuries.
    d. None of the above are true.

11. Latifah had surgery on her hindbrain, and swelling in that area has caused her to lapse into a coma. The swelling most likely occurred in the
    a. cerebellum.
    b. hippocampus.
    c. hypothalamus.
    d. reticular formation.

12. Conchita can meet a person or read the same story over and over for months but will never recall either. Which part of Conchita's brain was most likely damaged?
    a. cerebellum
    b. hippocampus
    c. medulla
    d. striatum

13. The occipital lobe receives sensory information concerning
    a. pain.
    b. body movement.
    c. vision.
    d. body temperature.

14. Almyra has a tumor in one of her lobes which has caused her to be unable to move her left leg. Her _____ lobe on the _____ side of the brain is the one most likely affected.
    a. frontal; left
    b. frontal; right
    c. parietal; left
    d. parietal; right

15. Robert is recovering in the hospital following a freak accident on the set of his latest movie. During an interview he says, "Noise . . . acting . . . ouch . . . hurts," and the interviewer comments that previously Robert was able to construct grammatical sentences and speak fluently. The area of his brain most likely causing this type of speech problem is
    a. Broca's.
    b. Sperry's.
    c. Wernicke's.
    d. Sylvia's.

16. Which of the following is *not* true? The corpus callosum
    a. connects the two cerebral hemispheres.
    b. contains many fibers.
    c. is enlarged in cases of severe epilepsy.
    d. allows the brain to function as a whole.

17. You have found an injured cat that cannot move the right side of its body very well. What kind of brain damage might explain the cat's condition?
    a. A severed corpus callosum
    b. Impaired functioning of the motor cortex in the left cerebral hemisphere
    c. A dysfunctional hypothalamus
    d. Impaired functioning of the somatosensory cortex in the right cerebral hemisphere

18. Dysfunctional cholinergic cells are associated with which problem?
    a. Parkinson's disease
    b. Alzheimer's disease
    c. Depression
    d. Eating disorders

19. When Mitch saw the woman who appeared to be drowning, he grabbed his life preserver ring and ran to save her. To prepare his body to run, Mitch's _____ released cortisol and other chemicals into his bloodstream.
    a. glands
    b. neurotransmitter systems
    c. synapses
    d. target organs

20. Terry has an autoimmune disorder; therefore, the cells of Terry's immune system
    a. are attacking normal body cells.
    b. are creating antibodies for viruses Terry hasn't encountered.
    c. automatically create tumors.
    d. automatically destroy tumors.

Total Correct (See answer key) _____

ANSWERS TO FILL-IN-THE-BLANKS KEY TERMS

1. axons, dendrites (p. 50)
2. Action potentials (p. 50)
3. refractory period (p. 51)
4. excitatory, inhibitory (p. 54)
5. autonomic (p. 57)
6. hindbrain (pp. 59–60)
7. cerebellum (p. 60)
8. hypothalamus (p. 62)
9. hippocampus (p. 63)
10. neurons, synapses or connections (pp. 74–75)
11. amygdala, hippocampus (p. 63)
12. corpus callosum (p. 70)
13. hormones (p. 80)
14. Feedback systems (p. 81)
15. Autoimmune disorders (p. 82)

ANSWERS TO CONCEPTS AND EXERCISES

No. 1: The Organization of the Nervous System

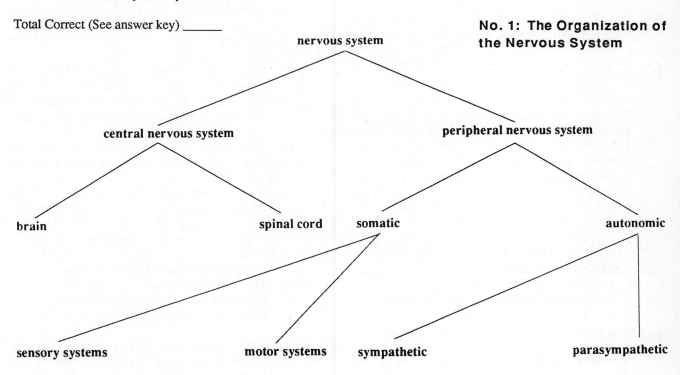

No. 2: The Functions of the Brain

1. *A* The substantia nigra and striatum are responsible for the smooth initiation of movement. (p. 62)

2. *D* The cerebellum is involved in fine motor movement. (p. 60)

3. *E* Wernicke's area is responsible for understanding language. (p. 69)

4. *C* The right cerebral hemisphere is superior at artistic tasks. (p. 71)

5. *C* The right cerebral hemisphere is superior at musical tasks. (p. 71)

6. *B* The left cerebral hemisphere is superior at mathematical tasks. (p. 71)

ANSWERS TO CRITICAL THINKING

1. Sam's hypothesis is that Lisa killed Jerry.

2. The fact that Jerry's stomach is still full of Chinese food leads Sam to believe that the murder was committed right after dinner.

3. Martina knows that digestion (controlled by the parasympathetic nervous system) stops if the sympathetic nervous system is stimulated for any reason, such as onset of fear. She probably thinks that Stephen showed up at the office later that evening and killed Jerry.

4. If you were Martina, you would probably want to get the complete pathology report, which would include the time of death. Most likely, it was after 9:00 P.M. when Susan, Lisa's sister, heard Lisa come home and go to bed. (Martina might also want to check out Jerry and Stephen's relationship at the office.)

5. If the answer to Martina's continued investigation turns out the way she thinks it will, she will probably be able to conclude that Stephen killed Jerry. *NOTE:* Critical thinking is a constant process of hypothesizing, examining evidence, rehypothesizing, collecting more evidence, and so on. Martina may not be correct. Can you think of any other hypotheses that could explain this data?

ANSWERS TO MULTIPLE-CHOICE QUESTIONS

Circle the question numbers you answered correctly.

Sample Quiz 1

1. *d* is the answer. A neuron has axons and dendrites. The sodium and calcium channels in axons and dendrites allow signals to travel their length—this is one special feature that allows neurons to communicate. (p. 50)
   a, b, c. All cells have a nucleus and a cell body as well as mitochondria, which turn oxygen and glucose into energy.

2. *c* is the answer. Action potentials in axons begin when gates open to admit positive ions, such as sodium. (pp. 50–51)
   a. Neurotransmitters are stored in vesicles; therefore, they could not flood in.
   b. Neurotransmitters bind with receptors on the postsynaptic cell, which could be a dendrite, but they don't flood into the dendrite. In addition, they may not eventually create an action potential because they could cause an inhibitory postsynaptic potential (IPSP).
   d. Sodium does not rush into the synapse; neurotransmitters do.

3. *a* is the answer. (p. x)
   b. A neurotransmitter travels across the synapse and fits into postsynaptic receptors.
   c, d. Myelin doesn't influence the nature of the postsynaptic potential.

4. *c* is the answer. An axon with a very short refractory period has very little time between action potentials. During the next action potential, positive ions like sodium and calcium will rush into the cell. If the refractory period were longer, the characters in the axon would have more time to make an escape. (p. 51)
   a. Axons do not have a nucleus.
   b. The size of a synapse does not affect the rate of action potentials.
   d. The length of a sodium gate will not affect the length of time between action potentials.

5. *c* is the answer. An equal number of excitatory and inhibitory signals will cancel each other out. (p. 54)
   a. An action potential will occur if enough excitatory signals reach the cell body. In this situation, not enough have reached the cell body to override the number of inhibitory signals.
   b. Neurotransmitters are not released until an action potential occurs.
   d. The neuron *is* receiving messages in the form of excitatory and inhibitory postsynaptic potentials.

6. *a* is the answer. The sensory systems, such as vision, touch, pain, taste, hearing, and smell, provide information about the environment. (p. 56)
   b. The motor system causes muscle movement.
   c. The autonomic system carries messages back and forth between the central nervous system and the body's organs and glands.
   d. The parasympathetic system is part of the autonomic system.

7. *a* is the answer. Without motor nerves to move the skeletal muscles, King Kong's cousin will not be able to move or pick up a rock, let alone lift a skyscraper. (p. 56)
   b. The somatic system's sensory nerves will be able to carry auditory information to the brain.
   c. The autonomic nervous system will allow King Kong's cousin to digest skyscrapers. The autonomic system carries messages to the organs of the body, such as the stomach.
   d. The somatic system's sensory nerves will be able to carry visual information to the brain.

8. *d* is the answer. The sympathetic nervous system is becoming less active now that Kalli is not hurrying or worrying. The parasympathetic system is responsible for conserving energy and relaxing a person, so it is becoming more active. (p. 57)
   a, b. The central nervous system is no more activated when a person is relaxing than it is when the person is aroused. The somatic nervous system takes care of receiving information from the senses and sending instructions to the muscles.
   c. The parasympathetic system is the part of the autonomic nervous system that calms a person, so it is becoming more active. The sympathetic system activates the person as in the fight-or-flight response.

9. *d* is the answer. When you burn your hand, a withdrawal reflex causes your hand to jerk away from the heat source. The information will travel to the spinal cord through an afferent sensory neuron and back down to the muscles that will withdraw your hand via efferent motor neurons. (pp. 58–59)
   a, b. Both of these answers involve brain structures. A reflex pathway does not involve the brain. The brain receives information about the occurrence of the reflex when you are already in motion.
   c. The order of neurons is mixed up. The information will go from an afferent neuron to the spinal cord and back to the muscle via an efferent neuron.

10. *a* is the answer. The medulla, located in the hindbrain, helps to regulate breathing and blood pressure. (p. 59)
    b, c. The hypothalamus and the thalamus are in the diencephalon, which is located in the forebrain.
    d. The cerebellum is located in the hindbrain, but it controls fine movement coordination.

11. *a* is the answer. The cerebellum controls well-rehearsed movements like piano playing and assists the eyes in tracking a moving object. (p. 60)
    b. The diencephalon is made up of the thalamus, which relays sensory information, and the hypothalamus, which regulates drives.
    c. The parietal lobe receives information from the skin senses, but would not account for difficulty in memories of rehearsed movements or difficulty in tracking.
    d. The occipital lobe receives information from the eyes, but would not account for difficulty in movement.

12. *b* is the answer. Broca's area and Wernicke's area, in the left cerebral hemisphere, are responsible for the mental organization, production, and comprehension of language. (p. 69)
    a. For most people the right side of the brain is less effective at tasks involving language.
    c. The motor cortex, found in the frontal lobe in *both* hemispheres, is involved in movement.
    d. The left hemisphere does include Broca's area and Wernicke's areas, but they are not involved in biological rhythms. The suprachiasmatic nuclei in the hypothalamus control biological rhythms.

13. *d* is the answer. The right parietal lobe receives skin sense information from the body's left side. (pp. 67–68, 70)
    a. The left temporal lobe is the location of Wernicke's area. It is involved in hearing and language.
    b. The striatum is part of the midbrain. Along with the substantia nigra, it is responsible for beginning a movement.
    c. The right frontal lobe would control the muscles for the left side of the body.

14. *d* is the answer. Neurons *can* change their functions and make new connections with other neurons; therefore, this is not a characteristic that would make recovery from brain damage difficult. (pp. 72–73)
    a, b, c. It is true that adult brain cells cannot divide and generate new brain cells and that the brain has so many neural connections that exact replication following brain damage would be highly unlikely. Finally, glial cells do eliminate damaged brain cells before they have a chance to regenerate. Therefore, each of these *is* a characteristic making recovery from brain damage difficult.

15. *c* is the answer. (p. 71)

   a, b, d. The right hemisphere would help your younger sister recognize the famous people's faces, and the left hemisphere would enable her to recite their names.

16. *d* is the answer. When the corpus callosum is cut, the two hemispheres are no longer joined. Without the corpus callosum, the information coming to the right side of Sue's brain (from her left hand) cannot reach the language centers on the left side of the brain. Sue can recognize the feel of the object because that task doesn't require help from the left hemisphere. (p. 70)

   a. The hippocampus is responsible for helping to store new memories. Sue could remember what the object was, as evidenced by her ability to choose it by touch.

   b. The substantia nigra works with the striatum to help a person start moving. Sue doesn't have a problem with starting to move.

   c. If Sue's parietal lobe were damaged, she would have trouble sensing touch, pressure, and temperature on her skin. Because she can choose the object, she must not have trouble with this lobe.

17. *a* is the answer. Newborns have relatively high neural activity in the thalamus. (p. 74)

   b, c. The striatum is not very active in newborns, a fact that may explain their uncoordinated movement.

   d. The frontal cortex begins to show increased activity at eight or nine months, when an infant's cognitive abilities start to appear.

18. *c* is the answer. Degenerating acetylcholine neurons are associated with Alzheimer's disease, and low levels of dopamine are associated with Parkinson's disease. (pp. 77–78)

   a, b, d. Decreased levels of dopamine are associated with Parkinson's disease; abnormal levels of norepinephrine are associated with depression; and degenerating cholinergic neurons are associated with Alzheimer's disease.

19. *a* is the answer. Neurotransmitters travel across synapses, and hormones travel via the bloodstream; therefore, statement *a* is incorrect. (p. 80)

   b, c. Both are true.

   d. *a* is incorrect.

20. *c* is the answer. The immune system oversees the condition of the body. If it detects foreign cells, immune system cells surround and destroy them. (pp. 81–82)

   a. The central nervous system guides all activity, but neurons in the CNS do not directly monitor or eradicate harmful invaders.

   b. The endocrine system monitors levels of hormones in the bloodstream, but its cells do not find and eliminate foreign cells.

   d. Although we do not have to consciously control our immune system in order for it to work, it is not a reflex. In a reflex, the spinal cord signals muscles to react to a stimulus; in immune system functioning, the cells locate and combat foreign cells.

Now turn to the quiz analysis table at the end of this chapter to find which areas you know well and which areas you need to work on. Circle the numbers in the table for items on Quiz 1 that you answered correctly.

ANSWERS TO MULTIPLE-CHOICE QUESTIONS

Circle the question numbers you answered correctly.

Sample Quiz 2

1. *d* is the answer. An excitable surface membrane allows a signal to be sent from one end of the axon to the other. While cells outside the nervous system can communicate with each other, they do not have an excitable surface membrane. (p. 50)

   a, b, c. All our body cells have mitochondria for providing energy, a selectively permeable membrane, and a nucleus in the cell body that determines the type of cell it is.

2. *a* is the answer. When an axon is at rest, it is polarized. Depolarization leads to action potentials. The bored axon with no action is polarized. Myelin speeds the action potential on its way. The second neuron, despite the myelin wrapped around its axon, cannot seem to get action potentials down the length of the axon to the synapse fast enough for the boss. (p. 50)

   b. Axons have receptors, but they do not affect conduction speed.

   c. An axon at rest is polarized. All axons have sodium gates. They do not affect the speed at which the action potential travels down the axon.

d. An axon at rest is polarized. Vesicles are located at the very tip of the axon and do not influence the speed of an action potential.

3. *a* is the answer. Positive ions depolarize an axon by entering through gates in a chain reaction from one end of the axon to the other. (pp. 50–51)

   b. The sodium and calcium ions do not rush down the axon. Instead, like a line of dominoes pushed over, positive ions coming through one open gate cause the next gate to open (and the next, and the next) until one segment after another has been depolarized.

   c. The postsynaptic potential does dissipate as it reaches the cell body, but an action potential starts and finishes at the same rate.

   d. After an action potential has reached it, a neurotransmitter floats across a synapse to bind with a receptor.

4. *d* is the answer. Axons release neurotransmitters at synapses, and the most common arrangement is to have postsynaptic receptors on dendrites. However, postsynaptic receptors are also found on cell bodies and on axons (the axon of a second neuron can be postsynaptic to a presynaptic axon). (p. 52)

5. *b* is the answer. An inhibitory postsynaptic potential (IPSP) makes it less likely the cell will fire. By making the cell more negative (hyperpolarized), more positive ions have to enter to cause an action potential. The first ions will only polarize it, or reset it, the next ions will build toward depolarizing it. (p. 54)

   a. A neurotransmitter that causes a postsynaptic cell to be depolarized causes an excitatory potential.

   c, d. Myelinated and refracted are not terms associated with postsynaptic potentials. Myelin is an insulator that allows axons to send messages faster; refractory periods are the pauses between firings.

6. *d* is the answer. The central nervous system includes the brain and the spinal cord. (p. 56)

   a, b, c. The peripheral system includes the somatic and autonomic systems.

7. *c* is the answer. The somatic system carries information from the senses to the central nervous system and carries signals from the central nervous system to the muscles that move the skeleton. (p. 56)

   a. The central nervous system includes the brain and spinal cord. The brain makes decisions about how to move, but the somatic nervous system (part of the peripheral nervous system) carries these signals to the muscles.

   b. The autonomic system (part of the peripheral nervous system) carries messages back and forth between the central nervous system and the body's organs and glands.

   d. The sympathetic system is part of the autonomic system (it controls the automatic functions of the body, not voluntary skeletal muscle movement).

8. *d* is the answer. The sympathetic system of the autonomic nervous system activates the body. (p. 57)

   a. The parasympathetic system of the autonomic nervous system calms the body.

   b. The peripheral nervous system has two branches: the somatic and autonomic. It is not a subdivision of the autonomic.

   c. The somatic nervous system is the branch of the peripheral nervous system controlling voluntary movement and receiving sensory information. It is not a subdivision of the autonomic.

9. *d* is the answer. A reflex can occur entirely within the spinal cord; it involves afferent and efferent neurons; and it is involuntary. (pp. 58–59)

10. *b* is the answer. Information about the environment travels through the spinal cord on its way to the brain. In addition, any directions that the brain sends to the skeletal muscles must pass through the spinal cord. If the spinal cord is severed, information cannot travel between the brain and any destination below the severed section of the spinal cord. (p. 58)

    a, c. Damage to the spinal cord will not injure the brain. The brain may not be as active because it does not receive as much information as it did prior to the spinal cord's injury, but it would still be capable of handling that information.

    d. *b* is the answer.

11. *d* is the answer. The reticular formation runs from the hindbrain through the midbrain and controls activation of the rest of the brain. If its fibers were disconnected, the person would go into a permanent coma. (p. 59)

    a. The cerebellum is part of the hindbrain but is in control of precise movements like threading a needle.

b. Hippocampal damage would cause the inability to form new memories. The hippocampus is part of the forebrain.

c. The hypothalamus is the part of the forebrain responsible for hunger, thirst, and sex drives.

12. *b* is the answer. Damage to the hippocampus causes the inability to form new memories. Conchita cannot form new memories for people or stories. (p. 63)
   a. The cerebellum controls movement, not memory.
   c. The medulla regulates vital functions like heart rate and breathing.
   d. The striatum controls movement, not memory.

13. *c* is the answer. The sensory cortex found in the occipital lobe receives information concerning vision. (p. 67)
   a. The thalamus, found in the forebrain, relays pain signals from the spinal cord and the senses to upper levels in the brain.
   b. The motor cortex, found in the frontal lobe, is involved in movement.
   d. The parietal lobe receives information about temperature from the skin.

14. *b* is the answer. The frontal lobe contains the motor cortex. The right side of the brain controls the left side of the body. (pp. 67, 70)
   a. The left leg is controlled by the *right* frontal lobe.
   c, d. The parietal lobe receives sensory information from the skin.

15. *a* is the answer. Damage to Broca's area creates difficulties in speaking. Its location is in the left frontal lobe near the motor cortex, and people with Broca's aphasia speak haltingly. (p. 69)
   b, d. Sperry and Sylvia's areas are made-up names not related to speech.
   c. Wernicke's area is in the left temporal lobe. It receives information from the auditory and visual cortices. Damage creates problems in understanding the meaning of words, but leaves speech fluency intact.

16. *c* is the answer. The corpus callosum, a massive bundle of fibers, connects the two cerebral hemispheres. It has been surgically severed, not enlarged,

in cases of severe epilepsy to decrease the spread of electrical seizures. (p. 70)
   a, b, d. All are true.

17. *b* is the answer. The motor cortex in the left hemisphere controls the movement of the body's right side. (pp. 67, 70)
   a. A severed corpus callosum will only prevent the right hemisphere from communicating with the left hemisphere.
   c. A damaged hypothalamus causes malfunction in eating, drinking, sex drives, and, possibly, emotional responses.
   d. The right somatosensory cortex receives sensory information from the body's left side. Thus, motor functioning will not be impaired.

18. *b* is the answer. People with Alzheimer's disease have degenerating acetylcholine neurons in the forebrain. (p. 77)
   a. In Parkinson's patients, dopamine cells in the substantia nigra degenerate.
   c. Malfunctioning norepinephrine systems are associated with depression.
   d. Damage to particular sections of the hypothalamus cause an irresistible urge to eat.

19. *a* is the answer. Glands release hormones such as cortisol into the bloodstream. (p. 80)
   b. Neurotransmitter systems are groups of neurons using the same neurotransmitter.
   c. Synapses are the gaps between neurons; they do not release hormones into the bloodstream.
   d. Target organs have cells with receptors for hormones. They receive, not send, the hormones.

20. *a* is the answer. (p. 82)
   b. Antibodies would not be created if a virus hadn't entered the body.
   c. The immune system does not create tumors.
   d. When the immune system is working properly, it will attack tumor cells. In an autoimmune disorder, the immune system is attacking the regular cells of the body, including brain cells.

Now turn to the quiz analysis table at the end of this chapter to find which areas you know well and which areas you need to work on. Circle the numbers in the table for items on Quiz 2 that you answered correctly.

For each question you answered correctly, circle its number. (Quiz 1 numbers are not shaded; Quiz 2 numbers are shaded.) Are there patterns in the types of questions or the topics you got wrong that could direct your further study? Did you improve from Quiz 1 to Quiz 2?

TOPIC	TYPE OF QUESTION		
	DEFINITION	COMPREHENSION	APPLICATION
Cells		1	
		1	
Action potentials			2, 3, 4
			2, 3
Synapses and communication			5
			4, 5
Organization			6
		6	
Peripheral nervous system			7, 8
			7, 8
Central Nervous System			
Spinal cord			9
	9		10
Brain	10		11
			11
Cerebral cortex	12		13
	13		12, 14, 15
Lateralization and plasticity		14	15, 16
	16		17
Development			17
Chemistry			18
		18	
Endocrine system		19	
			19
Immune system			20
	20		

TOTAL CORRECT BY QUIZ:

QUIZ 1:

QUIZ 2:

Chapter 4

Sensation

Our knowledge of the world comes through our senses; our senses translate information about the world into neural activity for interpretation by the brain. Messages received by the brain are called sensations.

OUTLINE

I. SENSORY SYSTEMS (pp. 87–90)

The first step in some systems occurs when the stimulus is modified by an accessory structure (the lens of the eye or the outer ear). Transduction, the transformation of incoming energy into neural activity, takes place at the receptors. Changes in stimuli produce the greatest receptor response; stimuli that remain at a constant level cause receptors to adapt. Receptors stimulate sensory neuron activity, which carries messages (except smell) to the thalamus and then to the cerebral cortex.

A. The Problem of Coding

Coding is the transformation of an object's distinguishing physical characteristics into a pattern of neural activity that precisely identifies those physical characteristics. According to the doctrine of specific nerve energies, each sensory system will produce codes for only that one sense. For example, any stimulation of the receptors in the eye, whether from light or eye pressure, will produce only the sensation of light. Codes for the physical attributes of an object can take different forms. Temporal codes cause changes in neural activity rates or timing; spatial codes are represented by the physical location of neural activity.

B. Linkages Sensation and Biological Aspects of Psychology

Visual, auditory, and tactile information travels through the thalamus to a primary area of sensory cortex. The information is contralaterally represented, and is mapped out in topographical representation. The density of neurons in the sense organ determines the extent of its representation in the brain. Regions of primary sensory cortex are divided into columns of cells that respond to similar stimuli in the environment. More complex processing of sensory information occurs in the association cortex.

II. HEARING (pp. 90–96)

Sound is a repetitive fluctuation in the pressure of a medium like air. Vibrating objects create the fluctuations in air pressure that create sound. A repetitive fluctuation or change in pressure is a wave.

A. Sound

1. *The Physical Characteristics of Sound.* Waves have three important characteristics: amplitude, wavelength, and frequency (frequency is described in units called hertz).

2. *Psychological Dimensions of Sound.* The amplitude of the sound wave determines loudness; loudness is described in units called decibels. The frequency of the sound wave determines pitch, how high or low a tone is. Complex waveforms added to the fundamental frequency that make up a sound wave produce timbre, a sound's quality.

B. The Ear

1. *Auditory Accessory Structures.* The pinna collects the sound waves, which then strike the tympanic membrane, which in turn produces a vibration that causes the malleus (hammer), incus (anvil), and stapes (stirrup) to vibrate.

2. *Auditory Transduction.* Vibrations pass through the oval window and the fluid in the cochlea to move the basilar membrane, which stretches along the floor of the cochlea. Movement of the basilar membrane causes tiny hair cells that touch it to move. Hair-cell movement causes neuron activity in the auditory nerve, which carries auditory information to the brain. This process is known as auditory transduction.

3. *Deafness.* Deafness can be caused by problems with the bones in the inner ear (conduction deafness) or by problems with the auditory nerve or hair cells (nerve deafness).

C. Coding Intensity and Frequency

The firing rate of neurons within the auditory nerve increases as sound intensity increases. Frequency is coded in one of two ways:

1. *Place Theory.* Hair cells at a particular place on the basilar membrane respond most to the wave peak associated with a particular frequency of sound. High frequencies are coded exclusively by the place where the wave peaks.

2. *Frequency Matching.* The firing rate of a neuron in the auditory nerve matches the frequency of a sound wave. The lowest frequencies are coded by frequency matching. Low to moderate frequencies are coded both by frequency matching and by the place on the basilar membrane where the traveling wave peaks. The volley theory is another name for the frequency-matching theory.

D. Auditory Pathways and Representations

Information from the right auditory nerve crosses to the left side of the brain and passes through the thalamus on its way to the primary auditory cortex. Cells in the primary auditory cortex have preferred frequencies; they respond maximally to sounds of particular frequencies. A temporal code is used to localize sounds.

III. VISION (pp. 96–111)

A. Light

Visible light is electromagnetic radiation that has a wavelength from about 400 to 750 nanometers. We cannot see electromagnetic radiation or light wavelengths that are outside of this range. Our sensation depends on light intensity and light wavelength.

B. Focusing Light

Light waves pass through the cornea, the pupil, and the lens, before being focused on the retina. The iris adjusts the size of the pupil opening. The cornea and the muscles that hold the lens in place focus the light on the retina through a process called accommodation.

C. Converting Light into Images

Visual transduction, the conversion of light energy into neural activity, takes place in the photoreceptors of the retina.

1. *Photoreceptors.* The photoreceptors contain photopigments that break down in reaction to light and cause changes in photoreceptor membrane potentials. Dark adaptation, the gradually increasing ability to see in the dark, occurs as new photopigments are synthesized. Rods, one photoreceptor, contain a photopigment called rhodopsin and are more sensitive to light but cannot discriminate between colors. Cones are the other type of photoreceptor and contain three varieties of iodopsin, which can detect color and are more active in bright light. Cones are highly concentrated in the fovea, where acuity is greatest.

2. *Interactions in the Retina.* (Examination of Figure 4.10 in your text will greatly facilitate your understanding of this section.) Activity in the eye actually enhances the visual image. Light energy stimulates photoreceptor cells, which stimulate bipolar cells. Many photoreceptors converge on one bipolar cell. Photoreceptors also stimulate interneurons, which signal (usually in an inhibitory manner) surrounding bipolar cells. As a result, the photoreceptor that receives the greatest light energy stimulus will stimulate one bipolar cell and, through lateral inhibition (involving interneurons), decrease the stimulation of surrounding bipolar cells. As a result, the brain receives messages of light contrasts or comparisons from two bipolar cells that represent neighboring points in the visual field.

3. *Ganglion Cells and Their Receptive Fields.* Bipolar cells stimulate ganglion cells, whose axons form the optic nerve that extends into the brain. Most ganglion cells have center-surround receptive fields. Stimulation of ganglion cells enhances the sensation of variations, such as edges and small spots of light or dark.

D. Seeing Color

1. *Wavelengths and Color Sensation.* Hue, saturation, and brightness are three psychological aspects of color sensation. Additive color mixing, the mixing of different wavelengths of light, always produces a lighter color. In subtractive color mixing, continued combinations of color (as in paints) will produce black.

2. *The Trichromatic Theory of Color Vision.* According to the trichromatic theory, there are three types of cones, each of which responds best to a different color (red, green, or blue) or wavelength.

3. *The Opponent-Process Theory of Color Vision.* The opponent-process theory states that the visual elements sensitive to color occur in three pairs and that the members of each pair inhibit each other.

Each element signals one or the other color in a pair, but never both. The three element pairs, which contain underlined complementary colors, are red-green, blue-yellow, and black-white.

4. *A Synthesis and an Update*. Together, the two theories of color vision can explain color vision. The existence of three types of cones that pick up information about red, green, and blue color conforms to trichromatic theory. And the center-surround receptive fields of the ganglion cells are color-coded in pairs, which correspond to the three-element pairs of the opponent-process theory.

5. *Colorblindness*. People who are colorblind discriminate fewer colors than other people. Their cones lack the color-sensitive pigments for red, green, or blue.

E. Visual Pathways

The axons of all the ganglion cells combine to form the optic nerve, which travels to the brain. There are no photoreceptors at the point where the optic nerve leaves the eye, creating a blind spot. At the optic chiasm, fibers carrying information about the right side of the visual field cross over to the left side of the brain (see Figure 4.21 in your text). Beyond the optic chiasm the fibers synapse in the lateral geniculate nucleus (LGN); from the LGN, fibers go to the primary visual cortex, located in the occipital lobe. The cells in the cortex, arranged in columns, form topographical maps of the visual world. Larger areas of the cortex are devoted to areas of the retina that have many photoreceptors.

F. Visual Representations

1. *Parallel Processing of Visual Properties*. The LGN is organized into multiple layers of neurons; each layer contains a complete map of the retina. Each also responds to different aspects of visual stimuli: form, color, movement, and distance. There is no place in the cortex at which all of this information merges. Instead, each layer processes information in parallel (simultaneously) and communicates with the other layers.

2. *Hierarchical Processing of Visual Information*. Cells in the cortex that respond to specific features of objects are called feature detectors. Complex feature detectors are built out of simpler feature detectors.

3. *Spatial Frequency Analysis*. According to the spatial frequency filter model, the brain evaluates patterns by analyzing changes in brightness as sine waves.

IV. THE CHEMICAL SENSES: SMELL AND TASTE (pp. 112–116)

A. Olfaction

Olfaction occurs when airborne chemicals are detected by receptor cells in the upper part of the nose. Axons from the nose travel to the olfactory bulb, and from there axons spread to many areas of the brain, especially to the amygdala. Chemicals called pheromones can shape the behavior and physiology of animals. For instance, mammals lick the pheromones of others of their kind and pass them into a specialized portion of the olfactory system called the vomeronasal organ. Although no solid evidence exists to suggest the action of pheromones in humans, it is known that people learn to associate smells with sexual activity or certain people.

B. Gustation

Papillae contain receptors for taste, which can detect only sweet, sour, bitter, and salty flavors. Each taste bud in the papillae responds best to one or two of these categories but weakly to the other categories. This is how gustation, our sense of taste, operates.

C. Smell, Taste, and Flavor

Flavor is a combination of smell and taste. The temperature and texture of food, along with human nutritional states, can enhance flavor.

V. SOMATIC SENSES AND THE VESTIBULAR SYSTEM (pp. 115–122)

The somatic senses, also known as the somatosensory systems, include the skin senses of touch, temperature, and pain. They also include kinesthesia, the sense that tells the brain where the parts of the body are relative to one another. The vestibular system tells the brain about the position of the head in space.

A. Touch and Temperature

Survival would be extremely difficult without a sense of touch.

1. *Stimulus and Receptors for Touch*. There are many types of receptors in or somewhere near the skin that respond to mechanical deformation of the skin. The fingers, which have many receptors for touch, are the primary sensory apparatus for exploring by touch.

2. *Adaptation of Touch Receptors*. We are most sensitive to changes in touch. When in constant contact with a stimulus, the touch receptors show adaptation by decreasing the rate at which they fire.

3. *Coding and Representation of Touch Information*. Information about the weight and vibration of a stimulus is coded by the number of nerves stimulated and the frequency at which individual nerves fire. Location is coded by the organization of the information, which is topographical and contralateralized; it tells the brain where you have been touched.

4. *Temperature*. Some skin receptors are sensitive to warmth and cold. Many receptors that respond to temperature also respond to touch.

B. Pain

1. *Pain as an Information Sense*. Painful stimuli cause the release of chemicals, causing pain nerves to fire. A-delta fibers and C fibers carry information about different types of pain to the spinal cord, where they synapse with neurons that carry the pain signals to the thalamus and other brain areas.

2. *Emotional Aspects of Pain*. Specific pathways carry an emotional component of the painful stimulus to areas of the hindbrain and reticular formation, activating emotional responses. Our expectations of the onset and intensity of pain affect our evaluation of it.

3. *Modulation of Pain: The Gate Control Theory*. According to the gate control theory, pain can be blocked in several ways at the spinal cord. Other sensory information, aside from pain, can compete and take over pain pathways. The brain can produce analgesia by sending signals down the spinal cord.

4. *Natural Analgesics*. Serotonin and endorphins are naturally occurring substances that block synapses in fibers carrying pain signals. The body releases endorphins in painful situations: when experiencing labor pains during childbirth, when eating very hot, spicy food, and when people believe they are receiving a painkiller.

C. Thinking Critically: Does Acupuncture Relieve Pain?

What am I being asked to believe or accept?
Acupuncturists assert that twirling a needle in the skin can relieve pain caused by just about any stimulus.

What evidence is available to support the assertion?
Well-controlled studies are surprisingly rare overall, and the results are contradictory. However, acupuncture does stimulate the release of endorphins, which are naturally occurring pain relievers.

Are there alternative ways of interpreting the evidence?
Endorphins can be activated by placebos, thus suggesting that acupuncture may not have an entirely physical basis for pain relief.

What additional evidence would be helpful to evaluate the alternatives?
Researchers need to study the relationship between internal painkilling systems and external methods for stimulating them. In addition, an understanding of the types of pain for which acupuncture is most effective may lead to a better understanding of the possible physical effects of acupuncture.

What conclusions are reasonable?
Acupuncture does relieve certain types of pain, but it is not a panacea.

D. Proprioception

We know where we are and what each part of our body is doing through information provided by the proprioceptive sensory system.

1. *Kinesthesia*. The ability to know where the parts of your body are with respect to one another is called kinesthesia. It operates through information sent from joint and muscle-fiber receptors to the thalamus and then to the somatosensory cortex and the cerebellum.

2. *Focus on Research Methods: A Case Study of Kinesthesia Lost*. Christina was studied by neurologist Oliver Sacks after she experienced difficulty holding onto objects. Sacks discovered that Christina's sensory neurons carrying kinesthetic information had degenerated. Without her kinesthetic sense Christina had to watch her limbs in order to have control over their movement.

3. *Vestibular Sense*. Often called balance, the vestibular sense tells the brain about the head and body's position in space as well as about general movement. Fluid and otoliths within the vestibular sacs and fluid within the semicircular canals located near the inner ear shift as our position changes; the resulting movement of hair cells stimulates neurons. The vestibular system has connections to the cerebellum, parts of the autonomic nervous system, and the eyes.

KEY TERMS

1. A **sense** is a system that translates information from outside the nervous system into neural activity, which provides the brain with information about the environment. (p. 87)

Examples: Vision, hearing, olfaction, touch, and taste

2. **Sensations** are messages from the senses that provide a link between the self and the world outside the brain. (p. 87)

Example: Feeling a touch on your mouth is a sensation. Knowing that you have been kissed—instead of, say, scratched—and by whom is a perception.

REMEMBER: Sensation is the message that is sent to the brain about an object's characteristics. Perception is the brain's interpretation of what is sensed. For example, your senses may tell your brain that there is a bright light filling the top half of your visual system and that the light energy has many different wavelengths. Your brain interprets these messages and perceives a sunset.

3. **Accessory structures** modify sensory stimuli prior to transduction. (p. 88)

Example: The lens in the eye bends light before it is picked up by photoreceptors in the retina and transduced into neural activity.

4. **Transduction** is the process whereby receptors translate stimulus energy into neural energy that the brain can interpret. (p. 88)

Example: Photoreceptors in the eye pick up information about light and change it into neural energy, which tells the brain about what is in the visual field.

5. **Receptors** are specialized cells that detect certain types of energy (such as light or sound) and convert it into neural energy through transduction. (p. 88)

REMEMBER: Just as a receptionist *receives* people, the receptors in the sensory systems *receive* information about the world.

6. **Adaptation** occurs when a constant stimulus is applied to the body. Initially, the receptors in the skin fire rapidly, but their activity decreases over time. (pp. 88–89)

Example: Try to feel your underwear. You probably had to concentrate to feel it against your skin, if you felt it at all. The reason is that the skin receptors in contact with your underwear may have fired rapidly when you got dressed this morning, but now have decreased their activity.

7. **Coding** is the conversion of an item's physical features into a specific pattern of neural activity, which represents those features in the brain. See Key Terms 9 and 10 for examples of different types of coding. (p. 89)

Example: Someone has just touched your cheek. How do the neurons communicate to the brain that your face has been caressed and not slapped? Coding must convey the intensity of the stimulus to your brain so that it can interpret the touch as a caress or a slap.

REMEMBER: Your brain interprets messages or sensations as if they were a type of Morse *code.*

8. **Specific nerve energies** is a doctrine stating that each sensory nerve has a specific sensation associated with it, and that these specific sensations will occur no matter how the nerve is stimulated. (p. 89)

Example: Putting pressure on your eyeballs, thereby stimulating sensory nerves with touch, generates the sensation of light. This happens because the receptors in the eye will always transmit a message about light, no matter what type of stimulus is experienced.

9. **Temporal codes** are based on the timing of neural activity. The speed with which neurons fire becomes a code. (p. 89)

Example: In the example given for Key Term 7, your brain was looking for information about the intensity of a touch on your cheek. The rate at which the neurons fire is a code that tells the brain about the intensity of the touch. The faster the neurons fire, the harder you have been hit.

10. **Spatial codes** are based on the location of neural activity. Two messages that are sent in neurons that are next to each other tell the brain that both stimuli occurred very close to each other. (p. 89)

Example: You know that you were touched on your toe and your ankle, not your toe and your ear, because of spatial codes. The neurons from your toe and your ankle are located very close to each other whereas the neurons from your ear are not next to your toe.

11. **Topographical representation** means that two points that are next to each other in many stimuli are represented next to each other in the brain. (p. 90)

Example: The cells in the brain that receive information about your thumb are right next to the cells that receive information about your index finger. The cells in the brain that represent your nose are close to the cells that represent your mouth. The cells that represent your knees are much farther away.

12. The **primary cortex** is the particular area of the brain that receives a type of sensory input directly from the thalamus. The primary cortex for visual information is not the same as for auditory information. (p. 90)

13. **Sound** is a repetitive change in the pressure of a medium like air. This activity can be represented in wave form. (p. 90)

Example: When an object (such as a violin string) vibrates, molecules in the air move, causing temporary changes in air pressure that stimulate the ear.

14. **Amplitude** is the difference in air pressure between the top of the wave and the baseline of the wave. Loudness is determined by the amplitude of a sound wave. (p. 91)

REMEMBER: When you amplify something, you make it greater. The greater the amplitude of the sound wave, the greater the loudness of the sound.

15. **Wavelength** is the distance from one peak to the next in the wave. Wavelength is related to frequency; the longer the wavelength, the lower the frequency or pitch of the sound. (p. 91)

REMEMBER: Long Wavelength and Low Pitch: they both begin with L.

16. **Frequency** is the number of complete waves that pass a given point in space in one second. As the wave's frequency increases, so does the sound's pitch. Frequency is described in a unit called hertz. (p. 91)

REMEMBER: Frequency means "how often." The frequency of a sound wave tells you how often a complete wave or cycle passes a given point in one second.

17. The **loudness** of a sound is determined by the amplitude of sound waves and is measured in decibels. (p. 92)

Example: People using a sound system in an auditorium control the loudness of the sound coming from the speakers by adjusting the amplitude of the sound waves with their equipment.

18. **Pitch**—how high or low a sound is perceived to be—is determined by the frequency of sound waves. (p. 92)

Example: Spanky sang a note of the wrong pitch, so his friend told him to sing a slightly higher note. When the frequency of the sound waves coming from Spanky's mouth increased, his friend sensed a higher note.

19. **Timbre** is the quality of a sound that distinguishes it from other sounds. The mixture of frequencies and complex wave forms that make up a sound determine timbre. (p. 92)

Example: The next time you listen to music, try to identify the instruments that you hear. The sound of each instrument has a unique timbre. A note played on the piano has a much different sound than the same note played on the cello.

20. The **pinna**, an accessory structure of the ear, collects sound waves and channels the sound down through the ear canal. It is the part of the ear that you can see. (p. 92)

REMEMBER: Make a visual image to help yourself remember the name of this structure. You have heard of the game "Pin a tail on the donkey." Simply change the name and the picture in your mind to "Pin a ear on the donkey."

21. The **tympanic membrane**, located at the bottom of the ear canal, vibrates when struck by sound waves. (p. 92)

REMEMBER: The tympanic membrane is stretched tightly across the end of the ear canal, just like the skin stretched tightly across the head of a drum. The tympanic membrane is also called the eardrum.

22. The **cochlea** is a spiral structure in the inner ear where transduction occurs. (p. 92)

REMEMBER: The cochlea is like a coiled hose; it contains fluid that moves when sound waves come in.

23. The **basilar membrane** is inside the cochlea. When vibrations come through the oval window and into the cochlea, the basilar membrane moves. As this membrane

moves, it moves the hair cells that touch it. The hair cells, in turn, stimulate neural activity in the auditory nerve. (p. 93)

REMEMBER: The basilar membrane, which runs along the base of the cochlea, moves the hair cells to create a neural signal. Imagine placing your thumb over the bristles on a toothbrush. The bristles bend when you press on them, much like the hair cells are moved when the basilar membrane reacts to the sound wave going through the fluid. Your thumb represents the pressure from the basilar membrane, and each bristle represents a hair cell that will now translate the pressure into neural activity.

24. The **auditory nerve** is a bundle of axons that run from the inner ear to the brain. (p. 93)

REMEMBER: The auditory nerve receives signals from the hair cells and carries them to the thalamus. From the thalamus, the signals are relayed to the primary auditory cortex in the temporal lobe of the brain.

25. The **place theory** helps explain the coding of auditory stimuli. It states that a particular <u>place</u> on the basilar membrane responds most to a particular frequency of sound, determining the pitch of a sound. (p. 94)

REMEMBER: In your mind, create an image of the basilar membrane all curled up inside the cochlea. Along the length of the membrane, mentally write the names of musical notes. Each place on the membrane is associated with one note or pitch.

26. The **frequency-matching theory** (also called the **volley theory**) helps explain the coding of auditory stimuli. It states that the firing rate of a neuron (how many times a neuron fires per second) matches the <u>frequency</u> of a sound wave (how many cycles or complete waves occur in a second). (p. 95)

REMEMBER: The frequency of the neuron's firing <u>matches</u> the frequency of the sound wave.

27. **Primary auditory cortex** is the area of the cortex within the temporal lobe that receives auditory input directly from the thalamus. (p. 95)

28. **Visible light** is electromagnetic radiation that has a wavelength of 400 to 750 nanometers. (p. 97)

29. **Light intensity** is a physical dimension of light waves that refers to how much energy the light contains; it determines the brightness of light. (p. 97)

REMEMBER: Just as a higher-amplitude sound wave is experienced as a louder sound, a higher light intensity is experienced as a brighter light.

30. **Light wavelength** is the main determinant of what color you perceive. (p. 97)

Example: A light wavelength of about 500 nanometers is perceived as green.

31. The **cornea** is the curved, transparent, protective layer on the outside of the eye. (p. 97)

REMEMBER: Like a plastic wrap covers a bowl, your cornea covers the opening to your eye, yet it allows light to pass through.

32. The **pupil** is an opening, located behind the cornea, that looks like a black spot in the middle of your eye. Light passes through it to get to the retina at the back of the eye. (p. 97)

33. The **iris** is the colored part of the eye that controls the amount of light that passes into the eye by dilating or constricting the pupil. (p. 97)

34. The **lens** bends light rays, thereby helping to focus them on the retina at the back of the eye. (p. 97)

35. Transduction takes place in the **retina**, a network of several different types of cells. (p. 97)

REMEMBER: Transduction is the process of converting incoming energy (wavelengths of light) into neural activity.

36. **Accommodation** is the process whereby the muscles holding the lens in place either tighten or loosen to change the curvature of the lens, thereby focusing the visual image. The degree to which the muscles pull the lens is related to the distance of the object being viewed. (p. 98)

REMEMBER: Think of the muscles (when they change the curvature of the lens) as helping the eyes to <u>accommodate</u> to the distance of the object they are looking at.

37. The **photoreceptors** in the retina code light energy into neural energy. The photoreceptors of the eye are called <u>rods</u> and <u>cones</u>: rods code light and cones code color. (p. 98)

REMEMBER: <u>Photo</u> means "light," and <u>receptors</u> "receive." Photoreceptors receive light from the visual environment.

38. **Photopigments** are chemicals inside the photoreceptors. When light strikes a photoreceptor, these chemicals break apart and cause changes in the photoreceptor's membrane potential. Photopigments are necessary to the transduction process. (p. 98)

39. **Dark adaptation** is the adjustment made by our eyes when the amount of light in our environment decreases. In the dark, photoreceptors synthesize more photopigments, and people can begin to see more and more clearly. The cones adapt to dark more quickly than the rods do (complete adaptation occurs in about forty-five minutes) and allow us to see with greater acuity in dim light. (p. 99)

Example: When Rakesh first sat in the darkened auditorium to watch the school play, he could not read the title on the program. After about a half hour he had no trouble seeing the title.

40. **Rods** are photoreceptors that are located in the retina. They are very sensitive to light but cannot distinguish color. (p. 99)

Example: The program for Rakesh's school play had pages of different colors, but while in the dark Rakesh couldn't tell the difference.

41. **Cones** are photoreceptors located in the retina that can detect color. It is because cones are less sensitive to light that we have difficulty seeing color in the dark. (p. 99)

REMEMBER: Cones are photoreceptors that can detect color. The C in cones reminds us of color.

REMEMBER: Cones, as compared to rods, are less sensitive to light. Thus they need more light to be stimulated. When you are in the dark, the lack of light decreases cone stimulation, which, in turn, decreases your ability to see color.

42. The **fovea** is located in the center of the retina. A very high concentration of cones in the fovea makes spatial discrimination or acuity (visual accuracy) greatest in the fovea. (p. 99)

REMEMBER: Use the following sentence to help you remember the definition of fovea: FOcusing Very Easy in this Area.

43. **Acuity** is a term that refers to the quality of vision—specifically, to the eye's ability to make spatial discriminations. (p. 99)

Example: When you take a vision test, your acuity is being assessed.

44. **Bipolar cells**, which are located in the retina, receive information from many rods and cones. Bipolar cells also receive information from interneurons, which have also been stimulated by rods and cones. Bipolar cells stimulate ganglion cells. (p. 100)

45. **Convergence** is the reception of information by one bipolar cell from many photoreceptors. Convergence enhances the contrast of visual stimuli. (See Figure 4.11 in your text.) (p. 100)

46. **Interneurons** are cells that make connections between bipolar cells and photoreceptors. Interneurons usually inhibit bipolar cells. (p. 100)

47. **Lateral inhibition** occurs when the greater activity in one cell suppresses the activity in neighboring cells. Lateral inhibition exaggerates the sense of contrast that occurs when light hits the photoreceptors. (Again, be sure to look at Figure 4.11 in your text.) (pp. 100–101)

Example: The photoreceptor that receives the greatest amount of light stimulates both a bipolar cell (A) and an interneuron. The interneuron inhibits the bipolar cells that are *next to* bipolar cell A, thereby sharpening the contrast between the message from the photoreceptor that receives the greatest amount of light and the surrounding inhibited photoreceptors.

REMEMBER: Lateral means "next to."

48. **Ganglion cells** are the cells in the retina whose axons extend out of the retina; their function is to generate action potentials that will reach the brain. (p. 101)

REMEMBER: Rods and cones transduce light and send the information to bipolar cells and interneurons, which send their information to ganglion cells, which send their information to the brain.

REMEMBER: A gang of ganglion cell axons reach from the retina to the brain.

49. A ganglion's **receptive field** is that part of the retina and the corresponding part of the visual world to which the cell responds. (p. 101)

50. **Hue**, the essential "color" of an object, is determined by the dominant wavelength of light. (p. 102)

Example: Red and green are two different hues with two different wavelengths. (See also Key Term 51.)

REMEMBER: Black, white, and gray are not considered colors because they do not have their own dominant wavelengths.

51. **Saturation** is the purity of a color. If many waves of the same length are present, the color is more pure or saturated. (p. 102)

Example: The next time you go to a fast-food restaurant, compare the pictures of food on the wall with the actual food you buy. The colors or hues are the same. However, the pictures appear to be more vibrant. The reason is that the pictures are saturated with wavelengths of similar lengths, whereas the food reflects a broad variety of wavelengths.

52. The **brightness** of colors corresponds to the overall intensity of the wavelengths making up light. (p. 102)

53. The **trichromatic theory** states that because any color can be made by combining red, green, and blue light, there must be three types of visual elements, each of which is most sensitive to one of these three colors. Indeed, there are three types of cones that are most sensitive to red, green, and blue wavelengths. (p. 104)

REMEMBER: Tri means "three" and chromo means "color." The trichromatic theory is concerned with the sensation of three colors.

54. The **opponent-process theory** states that visual elements sensitive to color are grouped into three pairs, and that each pair member opposes or inhibits the other. The pairs are red-green, blue-yellow, and black-white. Each element signals one color or the other, but not both. The ganglion cells in the retina have color-coded center-surround receptive fields. (p. 104)

Example: One ganglion cell may have a red-green center-surround receptive field. If red light causes the center to be stimulated, the surround is inhibited. If green light causes the surround to be stimulated, the center is inhibited. If both the center and the surround are stimulated, we see gray because the opponent colors cancel each other out.

REMEMBER: The color in the center and the color in the surround of a ganglion cell receptive field are opponents; they are competing.

55. Two colors are considered to be **complementary colors** when gray is the result of mixing the lights of the two colors together. Each color has a complementary color. Complementary colors are opponent colors in opponent-process theory and stimulate the same visual element. (p. 105)

56. The axons of all the ganglion cells come together at one point in the back of the retina to make up the **optic nerve**. There are no photoreceptor cells at the point where this nerve leaves the eye, creating a blind spot. (p. 106)

57. A **blind spot** is located at the exit point of the optic nerve from the retina. It is termed "blind" because it has no photoreceptors and is therefore insensitive to light. (pp. 106–107)

58. The **optic chiasm** is a structure in which fibers of the optic nerve coming from the inside half of both retinas cross over to the opposite side of the brain to provide the brain with complete visual representation. (p. 107)

REMEMBER: Chiasm means "cross."

59. The **lateral geniculate nucleus (LGN)** is a region of the thalamus in which ganglion cells in the retina end and form synapses. The neurons are organized into layers that respond to particular aspects of visual stimuli. (p. 107)

Example: When Jenny looks at a red cube, one layer of cells in the LGN may code which area of the visual field is red and what the background colors are. Another layer of cells may be firing in response to the horizontal and vertical orientations of the lines in the cube.

60. The **primary visual cortex** is in the occipital lobe and receives visual input directly from the thalamus. Within it is the same topographical representation of the visual field as that found in the retina. (p. 107)

61. **Feature detector** is another name for cells in the visual cortex. Visual cortical cells respond best to particular types of features. (p. 109)

REMEMBER: Cortical cells detect features, so they are called feature detectors.

62. **Olfaction** is our sense of smell. Receptors in the upper part of the nose detect chemicals in the air. (p. 112)

REMEMBER: Olere means "to smell" and facere means "to make." Olfaction literally means "to make a smell." If you prefer, you can use the following story to help you remember this word. My grandfather worked in a paper mill that was very old and produced an incredibly awful smell. Just remember that the OL' FACTory smells.

63. The **olfactory bulb** is a structure in the brain that receives information from nerves in the nose. Neural

connections from the olfactory bulb travel to many parts of the brain, especially the amygdala. (p. 113)

Example: The axons that synapse in Tyrone's olfactory bulb signaled that a flowery odor was being experienced. The information went on to Tyrone's amygdala, where memories of a friend who wore the same flower-scented perfume were activated.

64. **Pheromones** are chemicals that animals release into the air. Other animals may experience behavioral and physiological changes as a result of smelling the pheromones. However, there is no evidence that people give off or can smell pheromones. (p. 113)

Example: Female pigs immediately assume a mating stance after smelling a pheromone called "androsterone" in a boar's saliva.

65. The **vomeronasal organ** is a specialized portion of the olfactory system that detects pheromones. (p. 113)

66. **Gustation** refers to our sense of taste. Receptors in the taste buds pick up chemical information from substances inside the mouth. (p. 113)

REMEMBER: The first letters of the words in the following sentence spell gustation: Gus's Uncle Sam Tasted All The Indian's ONions.

67. **Papillae** are groups of taste buds. Each taste bud responds to all four categories: sweet, sour, bitter, and salty. However, each responds best to only one or two of them. (p. 113)

Example: The combination of signals from Maggie's papillae results in a salty and sweet taste, which Maggie perceives as caramel corn.

68. The **somatic senses**, also known as the **somatosensory systems**, are distributed throughout the body instead of residing in a single structure. The senses include touch, temperature, pain, and kinesthesia. (p. 115)

REMEMBER: Soma means "body." The somatosensory system senses what happens to the body in terms of touch, temperature, pain, and kinesthesia.

69. The **gate control theory** states that the nervous system has two methods of preventing pain information from reaching the brain. Other sensory information from the skin may take over the pathways the pain impulses would use to travel up the spinal cord to the brain. Alternatively, the brain can send signals down the spinal cord and prevent pain signals from ascending the spinal cord and entering the brain. (pp. 118–119)

REMEMBER: The nervous system can use the spinal cord as a gate that will allow only so much information to go through it in either direction. To better understand this concept, think of what happens when a movie lets out. There are so many people coming *out* the doors that nobody can get *into* the theater for a few minutes. Similarly, to prevent pain information from reaching its destination, the brain sends information *down* the spinal cord that blocks the pain signals from *ascending* the spinal cord.

70. **Analgesia** is the absence of pain sensation in the presence of painful stimuli. (p. 119)

Example: Aspirin is an analgesic drug. Our bodies make chemicals, called natural analgesics, that can reduce pain sensation. Endorphins are natural analgesics. Serotonin, a neurotransmitter, also plays a role in blocking pain sensation.

71. The **proprioceptive sensory system** provides us with the ability to know where we are in space and what each of our body parts is doing relative to all other body parts. Kinesthesia, which is part of the somatosensory system, and the vestibular system provide proprioceptive information to the brain. (pp. 121–122)

72. **Kinesthesia** is the sense that tells you where your body parts are in relation to one another. (p. 121)

Example: You must know where your head is in relation to your hands to be able to touch the tip of your finger to your nose while your eyes are shut.

73. The **vestibular senses** tell the brain about the position of the body in space and its general movements. The vestibular sacs and the semicircular canals in the inner ear provide vestibular information. (p. 122)

Example: Doing something as simple as a handstand requires vestibular information. If your vestibular senses were not working, you would not know if you were upside-down or right-side-up.

74. **Vestibular sacs** are part of the inner ear. They are filled with fluid and contain small crystals called otoliths, which rest on hair endings. When you move your head, the otoliths shift and activate neurons that travel with the auditory nerve, signaling the brain about the amount and direction of head movement. (p. 122)

75. **Otoliths**, also called **ear stones**, are located inside the vestibular sacs in the inner ear and function as part of the vestibular system. When you move your head, the otoliths shift and activate neurons that travel with the

auditory nerve, signaling the brain about the amount and direction of head movement. (p. 122)

76. Semicircular canals are fluid-filled, arc-shaped tubes located inside the inner ear that function as part of the vestibular system. When you move your head, the fluid also moves, activating neurons traveling with the auditory nerve and, in turn, signaling the brain about the amount and direction of the head movement. (p. 122)

FILL-IN-THE-BLANKS KEY TERMS

1. The sensory process in which physical energy is converted into neural energy is _____.

2. In the _____ process, neurons fire at different rates to translate and represent specific sensations to the brain.

3. When examining a sound waveform, one can determine loudness by measuring the _____ of the wave.

4. Regions of the cortex that do complex processing of single or multiple sensory representations are called _____.

5. The quality of a sound by which you can tell it apart from other sounds of the same pitch is called _____.

6. The part of the ear that physically vibrates in response to sound waves is the _____.

7. The hair cells in the ear send neural signals to the brain via the _____.

8. The _____ receives auditory sensory information directly from the thalamus.

9. The color that one perceives is a function of _____.

10. The ability to change the shape of the lens in order to focus images on the retina is called _____.

11. Photoreceptors in the retina that detect color are called _____.

12. The senses of touch, temperature, pain, and kinesthesia are called _____.

13. When sensory receptors decrease their firing in response to a constant stimulus, _____ is said to have occurred.

14. When a person feels no pain in the presence of pain-producing stimuli, they are experiencing _____.

15. The sense that tells you where your body parts are in relation to one another is called _____.

Total Correct (See answer key) _____

LEARNING OBJECTIVES

1. Define sense and sensation. Be able to explain the differences between sensation and perception. (p. 87)

2. Define accessory structure, transduction, and receptor. (p. 88)

3. Define adaptation and give an example. (pp. 88–89)

4. Define coding, temporal coding, and spatial coding. Explain why sensory information must be coded before it reaches the brain. (p. 89)

5. Define the doctrine of specific nerve energies. (p. 89)

6. Describe the six characteristics of sensory representation for vision, hearing, and the skin senses. Define topographical representation and primary cortex. (p. 90)

7. Define sound. Describe the physical characteristics of sound, including amplitude, wavelength, and frequency. (pp. 90–91)

8. Describe the psychological characteristics of sound, including loudness, pitch, and timbre. Discuss the relationship among pitch, frequency, and wavelength as well as that between amplitude and loudness. (p. 92)

9. Name and describe the accessory structures of the ear. (p. 92)

10. Describe the roles of the cochlea, basilar membrane, hair cells, and auditory nerve in the process of auditory transduction. Name and describe the types of deafness. (pp. 92–93)

11. Describe the process of coding auditory information. Discuss the relationship between place theory and the frequency-matching theory in frequency coding. (pp. 94–95)

12. Describe how information is relayed to the primary auditory cortex and how the cortex codes the frequency and location of sounds. (pp. 95–96)

13. Define visible light. (p. 97)

14. Define light intensity and wavelength. Describe how both are related to what you sense. (p. 97)

15. Define and describe the accessory structures of the eye, including the cornea, pupil, iris, and lens. (p. 97)

16. Define retina and explain how accommodation affects the image on the retina. (pp. 97–98)

17. Define photoreceptors and photopigments. Describe how these structures are involved in transduction and dark adaptation. (pp. 98–99)

18. Define rods, cones, and fovea. Explain why acuity is greatest in the fovea. (p. 99)

19. Define convergence and lateral inhibition. Describe the role of the bipolar and interneuron cells in convergence and lateral inhibition. (pp. 100–101)

20. Describe the center-surround receptive field of ganglion cells. (p. 101)

21. Define hue, saturation, and brightness. (p. 102)

22. Describe the trichromatic and opponent-process theories of color vision. Discuss the phenomena each explains, including complementary colors. (pp. 104–105)

23. Describe the physical problem that causes color-blindness. (p. 106)

24. Describe the path that visual information follows on its way to the brain, including the roles of the optic nerve, the optic chiasm, the lateral geniculate nucleus, and the primary visual cortex. Know what creates the blind spot. (pp. 106–108)

25. Describe parallel processing of visual properties, hierarchical processing of visual information using feature detectors, and spatial frequency analysis. (pp. 108–111)

26. Define olfaction. Describe the transduction process in the olfactory system. Discuss the path that olfactory information follows to the brain. Define pheromones and vomeronasal organ. (pp. 112–113)

27. Define gustation and papillae. Describe the relationship among taste, smell, and flavor. (pp. 112–115)

28. Define somatic sense or somatosensory system. Describe the transduction process in the skin senses, including touch, pain, and temperature. (pp. 115–118)

29. Describe the gate-control theory of pain sensation. Define analgesia. Know the names of the body's natural analgesics. (pp. 118–119)

30. Describe the evidence concerning acupuncture and the conclusions that are most reasonable. (pp. 119–121)

31. Define proprioception and kinesthesia. Name the source of kinesthetic information and explain what went wrong with Christina, who was the subject of a case study. (pp. 121–122)

32. Describe the types of information that the vestibular sense provides. Discuss the role of the vestibular sacs, otoliths, and semicircular canals in the sensation of vestibular information. (p. 122)

CONCEPTS AND EXERCISES

No. 1: Frankenstein's Senses

Completing this exercise should help you to achieve Learning Objectives 10, 15, 17, 26, 27, 28, and 31.

Dr. Frankenstein is constructing the senses in his monster. But he has forgotten to include several features. Describe the deficits that would occur in sensation without the following physical structures:

Iodopsin
Hair cells on the basilar membrane
Spinal cord
Papillae
Amygdala

No. 2: Processes in Sensation

Completing this exercise should help you to achieve Learning Objectives 4, 19, 22, and 28.

Name the sensory process demonstrated in each of the following incidents.

1. Lori has just stepped into the shower with her watch on. She did not realize the watch was on her arm until it got wet. _____

2. Dr. Malpeli is recording the activity of interneurons and bipolar cells in the retinas of cats. Whenever he places a figure with many contrasting features in the cat's visual field, the recordings show a large increase in neuronal firing. _____

3. In general, the faster a neuron fires, the more intense the stimulus is. _____

4. Jill is six years old. She awakens with a bad dream in the middle of the night. She decides to play with her crayons and coloring book. She becomes frustrated, however, because she cannot see the colors in the dim light. _____

CRITICAL THINKING

Sam and Martina have been called to Marsh Landing, a resort-like residential neighborhood. Recently, several jewelry robberies have occurred in this area. The thief apparently knows his trade very well. He steals only the "good stuff." Mr. and Mrs. Fletcher, who live in Marsh Landing, reported a robbery last night—the seventh in the past two weeks.

Sam and Martina talk to the Fletchers about what happened. They gave Sam and Martina a list of the items that were stolen: a ring, a bracelet, several pairs of cuff links, and a brooch.

Martina continues to ask questions. "Did you see the thief, Mr. Fletcher?"

"Oh, yeah, he woke me up when he came into the room. I was too scared to say anything, though. I didn't know if he was dangerous. Besides, it took him all of five minutes to locate our jewelry box and take our things. He tiptoed out of the bedroom and I think he went out through the back door."

"Well, what did he look like?" Martina asked.

"He was about six feet tall, and he was wearing a pink T-shirt and olive-green khakis. I think he had black hair. I also noticed that he stood very straight; he had great posture."

"Is the jewelry insured, Mr. Fletcher?"

Mrs. Fletcher piped up, "Oh yes—my goodness, dear, that jewelry was quite expensive. We took out a special policy on it last year."

Sam turns to Martina and says, "This has to be the same guy. Only the *valuable* jewelry is gone. And, as in every other hit, nothing but jewelry has been taken."

Martina just shakes her head. Sam was jumping to conclusions again.

"Mr. Fletcher, do you have a night-light in your room? And if so, is it located near the jewelry box?"

"No, Martina, we don't," Mr. Fletcher replied.

Using the five critical thinking questions in your text, state Sam's original hypothesis and describe his evidence. Based on the clues in the story, what do you think Martina's alternative hypothesis is?

1. What is Sam's original hypothesis?

2. What evidence does he have?

3. What is Martina's probable alternative hypothesis?

4. What is the evidence that supports her hypothesis? What else would you want to know if you were Martina?

5. What conclusions can Martina draw?

PERSONAL LEARNING ACTIVITIES

1. One by one, pretend that each of your sensory systems has stopped working. Now think of ten activities that you would no longer be able to do without each sensory system.

2. Take a survey of the people you know to find out how many of them have corrected vision or other aids to sensation.

3. Prepare additional analogies for how parts of sensory systems work. The action of the hair cells on the organ of corti in hearing, for example, might be likened to the action of reeds that move when a wave washes over them in a river.

4. Test your gustatory sense by having someone prepare foods for you to taste without the help of your senses of smell or vision. Without olfactory or visual cues, can you tell the difference between an apple and a potato or between mixtures of salt water and sugar water? Will gustation alone distinguish between tapioca pudding and cottage cheese? (Learning Objective 27)

5. Experiment on the cues you use to maintain your balance. In a place with room to move, stand without touching anything, close your eyes, and then lift one foot. Lead a blindfolded friend around a building, being careful to indicate obstacles, steps, and turns. Have the friend report on the experience of moving without benefit of sight. (Learning Objective 32)

MULTIPLE-CHOICE QUESTIONS

SAMPLE QUIZ 1

1. An accessory structure
    a. is where transduction occurs.
    b. functions as a receptor.
    c. modifies incoming stimuli prior to transduction.
    d. changes stimulus energy into neural energy.

2. The frequency of a waveform determines
    a. pitch.
    b. loudness.
    c. the wavelength of sound.
    d. amplitude.

3. Ashanti cannot hear. All of the structures in his hearing system work, except for those that transduce the sound waves. Ashanti's _____ do not work; therefore, he has _____ deafness.
   a. hair cells; nerve
   b. hammer, anvil, and stapes bones; conduction
   c. semicircular canals; conduction
   d. tympanic membranes; nerve

4. If the place theory is true, which of the following would cause the *least* amount of auditory impairment?
   a. Sitting in front of the speakers at a rock concert
   b. Hearing a pure tone with a very high amplitude
   c. Working in a factory where there are many noisy machines
   d. Listening to Bach at full volume over your headphones

5. As Bart plays the drums, his auditory system is translating the sound information into neural impulses. Which of the following is the order the information follows?
   a. Auditory nerve, basilar membrane, primary auditory cortex, thalamus
   b. Tympanic membrane, ear canal, auditory nerve, cochlea
   c. Outer ear, cochlea, tympanic membrane, basilar membrane
   d. Pinnas, tympanic membrane, basilar membrane, auditory nerve

6. Which of the following structures is *not* necessary for the transduction of light energy?
   a. Photoreceptors
   b. Rods and cones
   c. Visual cortical cells
   d. Photopigments

7. A villain is trying to obliterate the visual system of his opponent. If he destroys _____, the opponent will be unable to see color.
   a. rhodopsin
   b. rods
   c. iodopsin
   d. photoreceptors outside the fovea

8. Which of the following would cause the least amount of lateral inhibition to occur?
   a. Looking at a spider web covered with dew in the morning sun
   b. Looking at a zebra's black and white stripes
   c. Looking at a green refrigerator's surface
   d. Looking at the pattern of light coming through window blinds

9. While Becky watched a basketball game on TV, Cindy asked her, "Is this OK for dinner?" Becky didn't look away from the game, and thought, based on her peripheral vision, that Cindy held up a TV dinner, so she said, "Sure." Only when Cindy served Becky a plate of brussel sprouts did Becky realize that her visual acuity wasn't very good because she was relying primarily on
   a. bipolar cells.
   b. cones.
   c. ganglion cells.
   d. rods.

10. Which of these lights would be sensed as the most saturated color?
    a. Wavelengths ranging from 400 to 700 nanometers
    b. Wavelengths that have a very high intensity
    c. Wavelengths that are all 600 nanometers
    d. Wavelengths ranging from 600 to 700 nanometers

11. A projection-screen TV has a separate box which aims green, red, and blue lights at the screen. Because the TV shows a full range of colors by combining the green, red, and blue lights in differing amounts, it fits best with the _____ theory of color vision.
    a. convergence
    b. frequency-matching
    c. opponent-process
    d. trichromatic

12. Roxanne is responsible for teaching a new student how to do the stage lighting for their school's play. What should Roxanne tell the student?
    a. Mixing colors for lights is identical to the process used for mixing paint.
    b. Mixing two different colors of light produces a darker color.
    c. Mixing two different colors of light is called subtractive color mixing.
    d. Mixing all possible colors of lights produces a white light.

13. Which of the following is true?
    a. Fibers from the inside half of each retina cross to the right side of the brain.
    b. Fibers from the outside half of each retina cross to the right side of the brain.
    c. Fibers from the inside half of each retina cross to the opposite side of the brain.
    d. Fibers from the outside half of each retina cross to the opposite side of the brain.

14. Which sense does not send information through the thalamus on its way to the cortex?
    a. Hearing
    b. Vision
    c. Olfaction
    d. Somatosensory

15. Which of the following can alter the flavor of food?
    a. Texture
    b. Smell
    c. Temperature
    d. All of the above

16. In a biology class, Samantha rated solutions on how salty, sweet, or sour each was. Samantha most likely has taken a test of
    a. analgesia.
    b. gustation.
    c. kinesthesia.
    d. vestibulation.

17. The nerves that signal what is touching Gary's face are firing very, very rapidly. Which of the following most likely happened?
    a. He was just punched in the mouth.
    b. He was just kissed on the cheek.
    c. He just took a drink of water.
    d. A fly just landed on his nose.

18. Marina hit her elbow on the doorway. According to the gate control theory, in order to reduce the amount of pain she is feeling, Marina should
    a. use the image of a closing gate to give herself the expectation that the pain will end.
    b. rub the sore area.
    c. think about anything other than the pain.
    d. do any of the above.

19. Ally has lost her kinesthetic sense. Ally will most likely be unable to
    a. be sure her hand is raised without looking at it.
    b. detect the flavor of her ice cream cone.
    c. feel the warmth of the sun on her face.
    d. respond to pain.

20. Kareem has overstimulated his vestibular sense. Which of the following is the most likely result of this overstimulation?
    a. Difficulty judging distances
    b. Dizziness
    c. Incorrect feedback from joints and tendons
    d. Overarousal of the autonomic nervous system

Total Correct (See answer key) _____

SAMPLE QUIZ 2

Use this quiz to reassess your learning after taking Quiz 1 and reviewing the chapter.

1. Ben is undergoing an experimental treatment that electrically stimulates the hair cells on the organ of Corti. According to the doctrine of specific nerve energies,
   a. Ben's auditory neurons will fire at one specific rate.
   b. Ben's proprioceptive nerves will be activated.
   c. Ben will feel a touch.
   d. Ben will hear sounds.

2. The pitch of a dog whistle is so high that humans cannot hear it. What physical dimension of sound would describe such a high pitch?
   a. A waveform with a very high frequency
   b. A waveform with a very low frequency
   c. A waveform with a very high amplitude
   d. A waveform with a very low amplitude

3. When Adriana pushes forward on the backs of her pinnas near her scalp, she notices that she can no longer tell where a high-pitched sound is coming from. Adriana's action has directly affected her
   a. accessory structures.
   b. cochlea.
   c. timbre.
   d. transduction mechanisms.

4. Conduction deafness is related to problems with
   a. the hair cells of the basilar membrane.
   b. the auditory nerve.
   c. the malleus (hammer), incus (anvil), and stapes (stirrup).
   d. the pinna.

5. Which theory suggests that pitch is determined by the location of movement along the basilar membrane?
   a. The place theory
   b. The characteristic-frequency theory
   c. The frequency-matching theory
   d. The volley theory

6. It is too dim for Carly to see what she is reading; therefore, she should _____ by turning on a lamp.
   a. increase the light intensity
   b. increase the light wavelength
   c. decrease the light intensity
   d. decrease the light wavelength

7. Rhoda, who is visiting her sister, just turned out the bathroom light and has to grope along the wall to feel her way back to the bedroom. After being in bed again for about forty-five minutes, she realizes that she can see well. Why?
   a. Ganglion cells have been activated.
   b. Enough photopigments in her rods have been synthesized.
   c. The muscles that control her lenses have adapted to the dark.
   d. The dendrites in her optic nerve have finally resynthesized.

8. A receptive field is
   a. the area in which receptors are located.
   b. an area in the environment to which a neuron responds.
   c. the area in which transduction occurs.
   d. the part of a neuron that is sensitive to stimulation.

9. The process of lateral inhibition allows the brain to see
   a. color.
   b. black and white.
   c. more distinct contrasts in stimuli.
   d. movement.

10. A villain is working feverishly in his laboratory to devise a way of preventing visual transduction. Which of the following methods would work?
    a. Destroy all the photopigments in a person's eye.
    b. Remove the lateral geniculate nucleus.
    c. Uncross the optic nerve at the optic chiasm.
    d. All of the above will prevent transduction.

11. Evelyn tried on a pair of sunglasses with red lenses. After wearing them for a few minutes, Evelyn took them off and realized that everything she looked at now had a green tint. The cells directly responsible for this afterimage were Evelyn's
    a. cones.
    b. bipolar cells.
    c. ganglion cells.
    d. rods.

12. The theory that best explains the afterimage seen by Evelyn is the _____ theory.
    a. computational
    b. opponent-process
    c. trichromatic
    d. volley

13. Michelle is an advertising executive. She wants her staff to create purer colors in the print ad they are working on. What will they have to do?
    a. Alter the ad's hue.
    b. Saturate the ad's colors.
    c. Increase the ad's brightness.
    d. Add a red tint to all green objects in the ad.

14. Your right visual cortex can "see" a mosquito biting one of your hands. If your right hand is in only your right visual field and the left is in only the left visual field, which hand will swat the mosquito?
    a. The right
    b. The left
    c. Cannot be determined

15. Neural activity concerning an object that Maria has in her visual field has reached her lateral geniculate nucleus (LGN). A neuron in her LGN is most likely responding to the incoming information by
    a. sending a different message to indicate which side of the visual field the object is in.
    b. sending information to ganglion cells.
    c. combining information about types of lines, colors, and the distance of the object into one message.
    d. sending information about one aspect of the object, such as its depth.

16. When Pete bought a hot dog and fries at a street festival, the smell suddenly brought back memories of playing baseball for his adoring fans. The memory was most likely activated because his nose
    a. sends its messages to the thalamus, which is connected to the olfactory network.
    b. sends its messages to the olfactory bulb, which is connected to the amygdala.
    c. causes papillae to become activated.
    d. causes the basilar membrane to become activated.

17. Andre's papillae do not work. Which of the following statements is Andre most likely to make?
    a. "I miss the feeling of a hot shower on my skin."
    b. "Green and red both look gray to me."
    c. "I couldn't smell the toast burning."
    d. "Nothing tastes right any more."

18. Jim's girlfriend has informed him that he must buy her a ring that is heavy with gold. Jim has bought a phony ring but wants to convince his girlfriend that it is heavy. What can he do just before she comes over to get the ring?

a. Keep the ring in the refrigerator until just before giving it to her.
b. Keep the ring wrapped in a very warm heating pad until just before giving it to her.
c. There is nothing that Jim can do.
d. Both (a) and (b) will work.

19. At a track and field competition, Paige pulls a muscle on her best discus throw of the season, but in all the excitement of her school's win, she does not experience much pain from the injury. Paige's lessened pain could be due to
a. activated A-delta fibers.
b. activated C fibers.
c. a higher-than-usual naloxone level.
d. a higher-than-usual endorphin level.

20. Excellent proprioception would be required for which of the following careers?
a. Chef
b. Wine taster
c. Acrobat
d. Musician

Total Correct (See answer key) _____

ANSWERS TO FILL-IN-THE-BLANKS KEY TERMS

1. transduction (p. 88)
2. coding (p. 89)
3. amplitude (p. 91)
4. association cortex (p. 90)
5. timbre (p. 92)
6. tympanic membrane (p. 92)
7. auditory nerve (p. 93)
8. primary auditory cortex (p. 95)
9. light wavelength (p. 97)
10. accommodation (p. 98)
11. cones (p. 99)
12. somatic senses (p. 115)
13. adaptation (pp. 88–89)
14. analgesia (p. 119)
15. kinesthesia (p. 121)

ANSWERS TO CONCEPTS AND EXERCISES

No. 1: Frankenstein's Senses

1. Iodopsin is the photopigment in the cones that allows transduction to occur. Without it, you would not be able to see color. Also, the fovea has many cones and very few rods. If iodopsin were missing, your cones would not work and the fovea would no longer have a high degree of acuity. (p. 99)

2. The hair cells on the basilar membrane cause changes in auditory-nerve activity. This is the point where transduction occurs. If sound could not be converted to neural energy, you would be deaf. (p. 93)

3. The information from all of the skin senses, including touch, pain, and temperature, reaches the brain after ascending the spinal cord. Without a spinal cord, you would not be able to detect touch, pain, and temperature. (pp. 115–119)

4. The taste buds are located in the papillae, which consist of bumps on the tongue. Transduction takes place in these structures. Without them, you would not be able to taste anything. (p. 113)

5. The amygdala, which plays a large role in emotion, receives olfactory information. Without your amygdala, smells would probably not have any emotional meaning for you. (p. 113)

No. 2: Processes in Sensation

1. Your inability to feel a watch on your wrist is due to the adaptation process. When you put on your watch, the cells in the skin begin to fire rapidly and then decrease their activity back to a baseline rate. When Lori stepped into the shower, the cells that would detect the presence of her watch had long ago returned to a baseline firing rate. If you think about it, you will realize that the process of adaptation is very necessary. For just a moment, make yourself notice everything that is touching you. Without adaptation, all of the information would feel as though it were new—as if you had just put on all of your clothes, had just sat down, and had just put on your makeup and jewelry. Without adaptation, we would be overloaded with sensory information. (pp. 88–89)

2. Stimuli with contrasting features—light, dark, edges, or lines—cause bipolar cells and interneurons to engage in lateral inhibition so that the brain receives exaggerated information regarding these contrasts. The exaggerated information makes it easier for the brain to "see." (pp. 100–101)

3. A neuron's firing rate tells the brain how intense a stimulus is. This process is an example of temporal coding. (p. 89)

4. Jill is experiencing dark adaptation. Her cone and rod cells have adapted so that she can see shapes and images. However, the rods, which work best in dim light, cannot pick up color information. That is why Jill cannot see the colors of her crayons. (p. 99)

ANSWERS TO CRITICAL THINKING

1. Sam hypothesizes that the same jewelry thief who has been in the neighborhood for the past several weeks is also the culprit in the Fletcher burglary.

2. The fact that the Fletchers live in Marsh Landing and that the thief took only the good jewelry supports Sam's hypothesis.

3. Martina believes that the Fletchers made the whole thing up so they could claim the insurance money.

4. Martina knows that because rods are more active in the dark, Mr. Fletcher wouldn't be able to tell what colors the thief was wearing (hence the night-light question).

   Martina should also find out if the Fletchers are having money troubles. Financial problems may have been their motive for faking the crime.

5. Martina probably can't conclude anything just yet, but she is well on her way to supporting her hypothesis. *NOTE:* Critical thinking is a constant process of hypothesizing, examining evidence, rehypothesizing, collecting more evidence, and so on. Martina may not be correct. Can you think of any other hypotheses that could explain the data?

ANSWERS TO MULTIPLE-CHOICE QUESTIONS

Circle the question numbers you answered correctly.

Sample Quiz 1

1. *c* is the answer. An accessory structure modifies the stimulus in some way prior to transduction. For example, the pinna of the ear collects sounds to be funneled into the ear canal. (p. 88)
   a. Transduction takes place in the receptors.
   b. Receptors are involved in transduction. Accessory structures modify a stimulus in some way prior to transduction.
   d. Transduction is the process of changing stimulus energy into neural energy. Transduction takes place at the receptors.

2. *a* is the answer. The frequency of a waveform determines pitch. (p. 92)
   b. The amplitude of a waveform determines loudness.
   c. The wavelength is the distance from one peak to the next in a waveform. Wavelength and frequency are related: Longer wavelengths are lower frequencies, but either could be described as causing the other.
   d. The amplitude of a waveform determines loudness.

3. *a* is the answer. Hair cells are the transduction mechanisms for hearing; if they or the auditory nerve malfunction, nerve deafness results (p. 93)
   b. The hammer (malleus), anvil (incus), and stirrup (stapes) are accessory structures. If these middle-ear bones are fused, conduction deafness results.
   c. The semicircular canals are the parts of the inner ear used for the vestibular sense.
   d. Tympanic membranes (eardrums) send vibrations to the bones of the middle ear; they do not transduce sound waves.

4. *b* is the answer. A very pure tone has only one frequency. According to the place theory, a specific frequency will cause a specific place on the basilar membrane to move. A damaging pure tone would therefore cause damage to only one location. (pp. 94–95)
   a, d. Both rock and orchestral music would be made up of many frequencies, thus causing damage all along the basilar membrane.
   c. Machinery noise consists of many frequencies, thus causing damage all along the basilar membrane.

5. *d* is the answer. It is an abbreviated version of the complete path, which follows. The sound waves are collected by the pinna (funneled down the ear canal), strike the tympanic membrane (vibrate the middle-ear bones), move the fluid along the basilar membrane (which deforms the hair cells), and send a message to the auditory nerve. (pp. 92–93)

6. *c* is the answer. Transduction is the conversion of stimulus energy into neural energy. This process occurs before information reaches the central nervous system. Therefore, the visual cortical cells in the brain receive already transduced information about the world. (pp. 98–107)
   a, b, d. Visual transduction takes place at the photoreceptors (rods and cones) in the retina. Photopigments in the rods and cones break apart when

stimulated by light, causing changes in membrane potential. A change in membrane potential is the first step toward neural activity.

7. *c* is the answer. Iodopsin is the photopigment in cones that initiates the transduction process. If this substance were destroyed, transduction would not occur and color vision would be impossible. (p. 99)
   a, b. Rods contain the photopigment rhodopsin. Rods detect black and white. Destroying rhodopsin would not destroy color vision.
   d. The photoreceptors outside of the fovea are rods, which detect black and white.

8. *c* is the answer. Lateral inhibition occurs when there are many contrasts in visual stimuli, such as stripes or patterns of light and dark. The surface of a refrigerator does not feature much contrast. (pp. 100–101)
   a. The edges of the lines in the web would be seen as differences between light and dark, causing a great deal of lateral inhibition.
   b. The edges of a zebra's stripes would be seen as differences between light and dark, causing a great deal of lateral inhibition.
   d. The pattern of light coming through the blinds would create strips of dark next to strips of light. The contrast would cause a great deal of lateral inhibition.

9. *d* is the answer. Rods are predominant in the periphery of the retina. If Becky uses peripheral vision, her acuity will be poorer. (p. 99)
   a, c. Bipolar and ganglion cells receive information from the rods and cones; the lack of information from the cones causes the poor vision.
   b. Cones are located primarily in the fovea, or center, of the retina and are responsible for its high visual acuity.

10. *c* is the answer. Saturation refers to the purity of a color. If a light contains a single wavelength that is relatively more dominant than other wavelengths, the color is saturated and will appear to be pure and vibrant. Since there is only one wavelength in *c*, it is clearly dominant. Therefore, the light is sensed as saturated. (p. 102)
    a. Waves of visible light range from 400 to 700 nanometers in length. If all the waves of visible light were present, you would see white.
    b. Waves that have a very high intensity would appear to be very bright.
    d. Waves that range from 600 to 700 nanometers in length would be a reddish brown.

11. *d* is the answer. The trichromatic theory proposes that combining three colors of light will produce any other color. (pp. 103–104)
    a. Convergence is the arrangement whereby bipolar cells receive information from many photoreceptors; it isn't a theory of color vision.
    b. Frequency-matching theory is a theory of hearing which states that the firing rate of a neuron will match the frequency of a sound wave.
    c. The opponent-process theory of color vision proposes that colors in pairs inhibit each other. Therefore, if red is activated in one pair, green will be inhibited in that pair.

12. *d* is the answer. Mixing lights is called additive color mixing. The more colors of light you add, the closer the resulting color is to white. (pp. 102–103)
    a. Mixing paint is called subtractive color mixing. The more colors of paint you add, the darker the color becomes. This occurs because the two paints absorb, or subtract, more wavelengths of light than either color can alone.
    b. Mixing two colors of light will always produce a lighter, not a darker, color.
    c. Mixing paint, not light, is called subtractive color mixing.

13. *c* is the answer. Fibers from the inside half of each retina cross to the opposite side of the brain at the optic chiasm. (p. 107)
    a. Only fibers from the inside half of the left retina cross to the right side of the brain.
    b, d. Fibers from the outside half of the retinas never cross to the opposite side of the brain.

14. *c* is the answer. Nerves that carry information about smell leave the nose and travel to the olfactory bulb. Axons leaving the olfactory bulb travel to many parts of the brain, especially to the amygdala. (p. 113)
    a, b, d. Nerves carrying information about hearing, vision, and touch do travel through the thalamus.

15. *d* is the answer. Texture, smell, and temperature all contribute to food's flavor. (pp. 114–115)

16. *b* is the answer. Gustation is the sense of taste. (pp. 112–113)
    a. Analgesia is the lack of a pain sensation in response to a usually painful stimulus.
    c. Kinesthesia is our sense of where our body parts are in relation to one another.
    d. Vestibulation is not a term. You may have been thinking of the vestibular sense, but that sense

provides information about our head position, not taste.

17. *a* is the answer. The intensity or heaviness of an object touching the skin is coded by the number of active neurons as well as by the speed with which they are firing. Many of Gary's neurons are firing rapidly, so the touch must be heavy. Getting punched in the mouth is the heaviest touch among the choices. (p. 116)

b, c, d. A kiss on the cheek, the feel of a glass against one's lips, and the feel of a fly on one's nose would cause only a few neurons to be active, and they would not fire very rapidly.

18. *b* is the answer. According to the gate control theory of pain, other sensations can compete with the pain sensations for the pathways to the brain. If Marina rubs her elbow, the rubbing may overpower some of the pain sensations and thereby reduce her pain. (pp. 118–119)

a. An image of a closing gate might help Marina reduce her pain, but visualizations are not covered in the gate control theory. The gate control theory states that signals coming up the spinal cord or down from the brain may block the pain sensations.

c. Thinking about something else may reduce Marina's pain, but the gate control theory does not address this.

d. Only *b* is correct.

19. *a* is the answer. Kinesthesia gives us knowledge of the position of our body parts by sending information from our muscles and joints. (p. 121)

b. Gustation and olfaction would allow Ally to detect ice cream flavors.

c, d. The feeling of warmth on skin and responding to pain are part of the somatosensory systems, but are not kinesthetic senses.

20. *b* is the answer. The vestibular sense informs us about the position of our head. If Kareem has over-stimulated this sense, perhaps by spinning around in a circle, he will most likely be dizzy. (p. 122)

a. Difficulty judging distances might occur if the visual system were affected.

c. Incorrect feedback from joints and tendons would indicate that the kinesthetic sense is malfunctioning.

d. Overarousal of the autonomic nervous system would not result from vestibular stimulation. The autonomic nervous system activates or calms the automatic processes in the body like heart rate and digestion. Overstimulation might result in some arousal, but not overarousal.

Now turn to the quiz analysis table at the end of this chapter to find which areas you know well and which areas you need to work on. Circle the numbers in the table for items on Quiz 1 that you answered correctly.

ANSWERS TO MULTIPLE-CHOICE QUESTIONS

Circle the question numbers you answered correctly.

Sample Quiz 2

1. *d* is the answer. The doctrine of specific nerve energies states that a sensory nerve can only code information for that sense. The hair cells on the organ of Corti transduce sound waves; therefore, any stimulation will be perceived as sounds. (p. 93)

a. The auditory neurons might fire at different rates, depending on how much stimulation they are receiving.

b, c. The proprioceptive and touch senses are unrelated to the hair cells on the organ of Corti.

2. *a* is the answer. A very high frequency will produce a very high-pitched sound. (p. 92)

b. A very low frequency will produce a very low-pitched sound.

c. A very high amplitude will produce a very loud sound.

d. A very low amplitude will produce a very soft sound.

3. *a* is the answer. The pinnas (outer ears) are accessory structures; they modify the sound waves entering the ears. (p. 92)

b. The cochlea is in the inner ear and would not be directly affected by Adriana's action.

c. Timbre is a quality of sound not related to the pinnas.

d. The transduction mechanisms for hearing are in the cochlea and would not be directly affected by movement of the pinnas.

4. *c* is the answer. Conduction deafness is caused by improper vibration in the malleus (hammer), incus (anvil), and stapes (stirrup). Onset usually occurs with increasing age when the bones begin to fuse together, preventing their movement. (p. 93)

a. Damage to the hair cells of the basilar membrane results in nerve deafness.

b. Damage to the auditory nerve results in nerve deafness.

d. Depending on its severity, damage to the pinna may not harm hearing.

5. *a* is the answer. According to the place theory, the location of movement along the basilar membrane determines the pitch that we hear. (pp. 94–95)

  b. There is no such thing as the characteristic-frequency theory.

  c, d. The frequency-matching or volley theory suggests that the rate of neuronal firing in the auditory nerve matches the frequency of the sound.

6. *a* is the answer. Light intensity determines brightness. Carly should increase intensity to increase brightness. (p. 97)

  b, d. Wavelength determines color.

  c. Decreasing light intensity would dim the light.

7. *b* is the answer. The rods, which are photoreceptors in the retina, allow us to see well in the dark. When the lights are first turned out, the rods must synthesize photopigments. This process takes between a half-hour and forty-five minutes. (p. 99)

  a. Ganglion cells receive information from both rods and cones, but it is the rods that are responsible for dark adaptation.

  c. The muscles of the lens do help us to focus on objects in the environment. However, the level of light in the environment does not affect the efficiency of these muscles.

  d. Dendrites are fibers that are permanent fixtures. They do not have to be resynthesized in any way.

8. *b* is the answer. Every neuron that carries sensory information responds to a particular area of that sense's environment. In vision, the receptive field is some small part of the world that you see. (p. 101)

  a. There is no general name for all locations of receptors.

  c. Not necessarily. Whereas a ganglion cell's receptive field is in the retina (where transduction occurs) as well as in the environment, the receptive field of a rod is only in the environment, not where transduction occurs.

  d. The part of a neuron that is sensitive to stimulation is the dendrite (or perhaps the axon and cell body).

9. *c* is the answer. Lateral inhibition occurs when a cell with the greatest stimulation (cell number one) causes a reduction in activity in the surrounding cells (cells two through five). This will cause the brain to receive information indicating that the receptive field of cell one contains much more light than the receptive fields of cells two through five—

in other words, that there is a light region next to a dark region. Therefore, lateral inhibition codes for contrast in the environment. (pp. 100–101)

  a. Cones detect color information.

  b. Rods detect black-and-white information.

  d. Specialized cells in the cortex detect movement.

10. *a* is the answer. Visual transduction occurs at the retina's receptors, called rods and cones. Photopigments in the rods and cones break apart when stimulated by light and cause changes in membrane potential. (pp. 98–99)

  b. Removal of the lateral geniculate nucleus would impair vision but not the transduction process.

  c. Uncrossing the optic nerve at the optic chiasm would change the way we see the world, but it would not impair transduction.

  d. Only *a* is the answer.

11. *c* is the answer. Ganglion cells have a center-surround receptive field that responds to opponent colors. Red or green, blue or yellow, and white or black are the opposing colors, only one of which can be signaled at a time. After one stops being stimulated, the other is activated, which creates afterimages. (pp. 105–106)

  a. Cones are responsible for color vision, but are not set up in opposing pairs to create afterimages.

  b. Bipolar cells receive information from rods and cones, but do not have receptive fields responding to opponent colors.

  d. Rods are responsible for black and white differentiation and cannot create afterimages.

12. *b* is the answer. The opponent-process theory explains afterimages. When one color in a pair has been inhibited, it will "overreact" and become activated when the other color is no longer stimulated. (pp. 104–105)

  a. There is no such thing as a computational theory of color vision.

  c. Trichromatic theory cannot explain afterimages; it describes how three colors can be combined to create all colors.

  d. Volley theory is another term for the frequency-matching theory of hearing.

13. *b* is the answer. A saturated color will appear pure and vibrant. (p. 102)

  a. If Michelle changes the hues, she will change the colors but not necessarily their pureness.

  c. Increasing the ad's brightness will not increase the colors' pureness.

  d. Adding two opponent colors will produce grey.

14. *a* is the answer. Your right hand will swat the mosquito. Information in the right visual cortex comes from the right sides of both eyes after coming from the left environment. Therefore, the mosquito is on your left hand and the right hand will swat it. (pp. 97–98, 106–108)

   b. If the mosquito were on your right hand, then the left visual cortex, not the right, would receive the information.

   c. It can be determined that *a* is the answer.

15. *d* is the answer. The LGN consists of layers of neurons that respond to different types of stimuli. Separate aspects of visual information are handled by parallel processing systems. Therefore, one neuron is responsible for depth information, another is responsible for color, and so on, and all work simultaneously. (p. 108)

   a. The LGN has a complete map of the retina, and hence, the visual field. Neighboring cells respond to neighboring areas of the retina; therefore, they do not need to send another type of signal to indicate the area to which they are responding.

   b. The ganglion cells send information to the thalamus, specifically the region known as the LGN.

   c. There does not appear to be a place in the LGN or elsewhere in the brain where all streams of visual information are combined.

16. *b* is the answer. Axons from the nose synapse in the olfactory bulb, which makes connections to the amygdala and many other brain areas. The amygdala is involved in emotion, which may explain why some smells activate memories. (p. 113)

   a. Olfaction does not relay signals through the thalamus.

   c. Papillae are the structures containing taste buds; they are not activated by smells.

   d. The basilar membrane is in the cochlea of the inner ear.

17. *d* is the answer. Papillae contain taste buds. (p. 113)

   a. Feeling a hot shower is the responsibility of the somatosensory system.

   b. If green and red appear the same, one type of iodopsin, the photopigment in cones, may be missing.

   c. Olfaction does not receive information from taste buds.

18. *d* is the answer. Objects that are warm or cold feel heavier than those that are thermally neutral. (p. 116)

   a. This will work but so does (b).

   b. This will work but so does (a).

   c. Jim can either heat or cool the ring so that it will feel heavier.

19. *d* is the answer. Endorphins can reduce a person's sense of pain. (pp. 117–119)

   a, b. Activated A-delta fibers indicate sharp pain; activated C fibers indicate dull aches.

   c. Naloxone is a drug that can block the pain-reducing effects of endorphins.

20. *c* is the answer. Proprioception, which includes kinesthesia and the vestibular sense, is the ability to know where the body parts are in space and in relation to each other. An acrobat would need excellent proprioception. (p. 121)

   a, b. A chef would need very discriminating taste buds, as would a wine taster.

   d. A musician would require an ability to discriminate sounds.

Now turn to the quiz analysis table at the end of this chapter to find which areas you know well and which areas you need to work on. Circle the numbers in the table for items on Quiz 2 that you answered correctly.

For each question you answered correctly, circle its number. (Quiz 1 numbers are not shaded; Quiz 2 numbers are shaded.) Are there patterns in the types of questions or the topics you got wrong that could direct your further study? Did you improve from Quiz 1 to Quiz 2?

TOPIC	TYPE OF QUESTION		
	DEFINITION	COMPREHENSION	APPLICATION
Sensory systems	1		
			1
Hearing			
Sound		2	
			2
Ear		3	
		4	3
Coding and pathways		5	4
	5		
Vision			
Light			
			6
Eye		6	7, 8, 9
	8	9	7, 10, 11
Theories		10	11, 12
			12, 13
Pathways and representations		13	
		15	14
Chemical Senses			
Olfaction		14	
			16
Gustation		15	16
			17
Somatic Senses and Vestibular System			
Touch and temperature			17
			18
Pain			18
			19
Proprioception			19, 20
			20

TOTAL CORRECT BY QUIZ:

QUIZ 1:
QUIZ 2:

Chapter 5

Perception

Perception is the process by which we take raw sensations from the environment and interpret them, using knowledge and understanding of the world, so that they become meaningful experiences.

OUTLINE

I. THREE VIEWS OF PERCEPTION (pp. 127–128)

According to the ecological view of perception, we perceive most clues from the environment directly, without interpretation. Constructionists argue that the perceptual system must often make a reality out of bits of sensory information. Computationalists believe that neural activity transforms sensory stimulation into our experience of reality.

II. PSYCHOPHYSICS (pp. 128–133)

Psychophysics is the study of the relationship between the physical energy of the environmental stimuli and the psychological experience that those stimuli produce.

A. Absolute Thresholds: Is Something Out There?

Absolute threshold is the minimum amount of energy that can be detected 50 percent of the time. During experiments to determine absolute thresholds, subjects sometimes perceive internal noise (spontaneous neural firing) as environmental stimuli even when no stimuli are present. A person's willingness or reluctance to respond, called the response criterion, also affects absolute threshold measurements.

B. Overcoming the Threshold Problem: Signal-Detection Theory

Signal-detection theory is a mathematical model that describes what determines whether a person perceives a near-threshold stimulus. This model assumes that sensitivity—the physical ability to detect a stimulus—and the response criterion determine perception. If a person expects a stimuli to be present, then his or her response criterion will be lowered. In other words, as expectations of stimuli increase, the amount of stimulus energy necessary to trigger perception is lowered. Signal-detection theory has led to improvement in the accuracy of people who are responsible for signal-detection tasks.

C. Judging Differences Between Stimuli

° Weber's law states that the amount of stimulus you must add to detect a change in the stimulus is proportional to the original amount of the stimulus. The just-noticeable difference (JND) is the smallest difference in stimulus energy that can be detected. $JND = KI$, where K is the constant fraction and I is the intensity of the stimulus.

° According to Fechner's law, constant increases in physical energy will produce progressively smaller increases in perceived stimulus size. Stevens's power law describes the relative changes in perception of size for stimuli that Fechner's law doesn't cover.

D. Thinking Critically: Can People Perceive What Cannot Normally Be Sensed?

Some people claim to have extrasensory perception (ESP). They claim to perceive stimuli from the past, present, and future through a mechanism beyond vision, hearing, touch, taste, and smell. The study of ESP is called parapsychology.

What am I being asked to believe or accept?
Those who believe in ESP think it is possible to transmit information from the outside world to the brain and back again without using traditional sensory receptors.

What evidence is available to support the assertion?
Several studies have demonstrated that people can "know" what color an object is or influence the movement of objects with greater accuracy than chance alone would predict.

Are there alternative ways of interpreting the evidence?
Some research suggests that those who can identify color with no visual cues are extrasensitive to the heat radiated by color. Some scientists argue that the use of "random" stimuli (such as computer-generated lists of random

numbers) is not really random. Finally, several ESP experiments have been fraudulent.

What evidence would help to evaluate the alternatives? Understanding what stimuli energy forms and what human receptor/transmitter systems for sending information to and from the brain are at work in ESP phenomena would further the understanding and believability of ESP.

What conclusions are most reasonable? A strong case for ESP cannot be made.

III. ORGANIZING THE PERCEPTUAL WORLD (pp. 133–143)

A. Principles of Perceptual Organization

1. *Figure and Ground.* Our perceptual processes actively try to assign some stimuli to the foreground (figure) and some to the meaningless background (ground).

2. *Grouping.* According to Gestalt psychologists, we see a figure via principles of grouping. These principles are proximity, similarity, continuity, closure, texture, simplicity, common fate, and common region.

3. *Auditory Scene Analysis.* Grouping principles are applied to sounds to categorize sounds with similar characteristics into auditory streams.

B. Perception of Depth and Distance

Depth perception allows people to experience the world in three dimensions.

1. *Stimulus Cues.* Relative size, height in the visual field, interposition, linear perspective, reduced clarity, light and shadow, textural gradients, and movement gradients all provide depth cues.

2. *Cues Based on Properties of the Visual System.* To help determine distance, the brain receives and processes information from the eyes: how much the lens muscles must tighten (accommodation) and how much the eyeballs must rotate inward (convergence) in order to help focus an image on the retina. The brain can evaluate binocular disparity, the difference between what each eye sees, to determine an object's distance. Also, the brain processes information about the difference in timing of sounds reaching the right and left ears and about the intensity of sound to determine the distance of the sound source.

C. Perception of Motion

Our brains decide if something is moving by evaluating movement cues in the retinal image (such as those produced by looming), eye and head movement, and vestibular and tactile cues.

D. Perceptual Constancy

Perceptual constancy is the ability to perceive sameness even when the image on the retina changes.

1. *Size Constancy.* Our perception of an object's size is based on the size of our retinal image and how far away we think the object is. We interpret the retinal image in relation to its perceived distance.

2. *Shape Constancy.* The brain automatically puts together information about retinal images and distance as movement occurs. Take a square object, turn it in all different directions (movement and distance cues), and see if you perceive anything other than a square.

3. *Brightness Constancy.* How bright we perceive an object to be is based on real-world knowledge and on the brightness of that object relative to its background.

E. Perceptual Illusions

An illusion is a distortion of reality. The Ponzo illusion seems to be due to a misinterpretation of size constancy and depth cues. The Müller-Lyer illusion, which is multiply determined, combines a misinterpretation of depth (linear perspective) cues and other sensation cues.

F. Culture, Experience, and Perception

People's cultural experience shapes their perceptions of reality.

IV. RECOGNIZING THE PERCEPTUAL WORLD (pp. 144–150)

Perception is a result of top-down processing and bottom-up processing.

A. Bottom-up Processing

We can recognize an object because we perform feature analysis, meaning that our sensory systems analyze stimuli into basic features before higher centers of the brain recombine them to create a full perceptual experience. Color, motion, spatial orientation, and patterns of light and darkness are some of the features that our visual systems analyze.

B. Top-down Processing

In top-down processing, our knowledge, motivations, and expectations influence perception. Schemas are mental representations of our knowledge and expectations and can create a perceptual set, which is a predisposition to perceive a stimulus in a certain way. Such expectancies are influenced by context and past experience. Motivation—that is, the way we want to perceive—can also alter perceptions.

C. Top-down and Bottom-up Processing Together

These two types of processing information interact to produce perception. When one kind of processing is impaired, the other "fills in" and completes the perception.

D. Network Processing

° Network processing is the extensive interaction and communication among the various feature analyzers detecting and sending sensation messages to the brain. Network processing has characteristics of both bottom-up and top-down processing.

° According to parallel distribution processing (PDP) models, recognition occurs as a result of simultaneous (parallel) operation of connected units in the brain that are activated by stimulus features. Other units are excited or inhibited by the connections that exist between units.

V. LINKAGES: PERCEPTION AND HUMAN DEVELOPMENT (pp. 150–151)

Since much of perception grows out of knowledge and past experiences, the study of newborns has helped psychologists identify innate perceptual processes such as feature analysis. At two months, infants begin to scan object perimeters as they learn to recognize patterns and shapes. At three months, infants begin to use binocular disparity and relative motion depth cues. They also possess the ability to use accommodation and convergence as depth cues.

VI. ATTENTION (pp. 151–156)

Attention is the process of directing and focusing certain psychological resources, usually by voluntary control, to enhance perception, performance, and mental experience. Attention improves mental processing, is associated with a sense of effort, and has limited resources. Attention may be directed overtly or covertly.

A. Focus on Research Methods: An Experiment on "Mind Reading"

Psychologists wondered whether perceptual systems might become more sensitive to stimuli where people have covertly shifted their attention. Volunteers watched a fixation point on a computer screen where a symbol indicated the likely location of the target. When the fixation point cue gave correct information about the location of the stimulus, the participants covertly directed their attention to that area and detected the target significantly faster.

B. Allocating Attention

Selective attention is the tendency to focus on some stimuli in the environment while ignoring others. Attention can be voluntarily guided by motivation and a knowledge of what sources of information are critical to the task at hand. A feature of the environment may attract our attention involuntarily.

Divided Attention. Although attention resources are limited, people can sometimes divide their attention between two tasks. It is easier to divide attention between two practiced or automatic tasks (for example, tying a shoe while chewing gum) or between tasks that are automatically processed at lower levels of the nervous system. Attention can also be divided when different sensory systems are utilized to accomplish each task (such as listening and using both hands).

C. Attention and Automatic Processing

Automatic processing suggests that features are analyzed prior to the point where attention is required. Parallel processing is the ability to search a number of locations rapidly and automatically for targets.

D. Attention and the Brain

There is no single area of the brain responsible for attention. Tasks requiring attention to multiple stimuli produce activity in more than one part of the brain. Thus, damage to specific regions of the brain produce specific types of attention deficits.

VII. APPLICATIONS OF RESEARCH ON PERCEPTION (pp. 156–157)

A. Aviation Psychology

Some landing scenarios decrease a pilot's ability to rely on top-down and bottom-up processing. At night, bottom-up processing cues are decreased, and not being familiar with a particular airstrip reduces the pilot's ability to use top-down processing. To compensate, engineers have developed cockpit displays that represent a realistic three-dimensional image of the flight environment. In addition, visual displays have been developed that minimize reliance on auditory cues.

B. Human-Computer Interaction

Engineering psychologists employ perception principles in designing computer displays. The displays use depth perception cues, attention-getting stimuli, and simple visual images to make computers easier to operate.

KEY TERMS

1. **Perception** is the process by which we take raw sensations from the environment and interpret them, using our knowledge and understanding of the world, so that they become meaningful experiences. (p. 126)

Example: After being in school for years, you will recognize the sign +. You know what it is and what it is used for. However, at your first birthday, you would have been unable to understand this sign.

2. The **ecological view** of perception argues that the environment holds many clues that allow us to perceive our surroundings. (p. 127)

Example: As Margie walks across the street she only needs to look around to perceive the visual and auditory cues that traffic is coming.

3. The **constructionist view** of perception holds that we construct reality by putting together raw bits of sensory information. Our expectations of reality influence our perceptions. (p. 127)

Example: Many children's books contain connect-the-dot tasks. On the page are a series of dots and some features, such as eyes, ears, or a mouth. A constructionist would say that we can make good guesses as to what the picture is going to be by putting together all the bits of information from the dots and the features. Since eyes and ears go with a face, the completed drawing will probably have a person in it.

4. The **computational view** of perception holds that perception is the result of nervous system activity that modifies and processes raw sensations into reality. (p. 127)

Example: To identify an object as a red ball, the neurons in our visual cortex each respond to one aspect, such as the color, curved edges, or texture, and other neurons join the information to create our perception.

5. **Psychophysics** is the study of the relationship between the physical characteristics of environmental stimuli and the conscious psychological experiences that those stimuli produce. (p. 128)

REMEMBER: Psych is part of the word psychological, and physics is part of the word physical. Psychophysics is the study of the relationship between perception's psychological and physical aspects.

6. **Absolute threshold** is the amount of stimulus energy necessary for a stimulus to be detected 50 percent of the time. (p. 129)

7. **Internal noise** is the spontaneous, random firing of nerve cells. Sometimes, when internal noise is "loud" enough, we perceive a nonexistent stimulus. This can cause variation in the amount of stimulus energy necessary for an absolute threshold. (p. 129)

Example: The noise of the nervous system resembles that of static on a radio. It is meaningless, background activity that is internal to the nervous system.

8. The **response criterion** is a person's willingness or reluctance to respond to a stimulus. A bias in either direction is created by changes in expectancy and motivation. (p. 129)

Example: Dr. Charles, a cancer specialist, sees cancer patients who have been referred to him by other physicians. Therefore, when he looks at patients' x-rays for the first time, he expects to perceive cancerous shadows. Therefore, he is likely to perceive even faint shadows as cancer when, in reality, none may exist.

9. **Signal-detection theory** is a mathematical model that can help explain why a person does or doesn't detect

a stimulus. This model attributes perception to stimulus sensitivity and response criterion. (p. 129)

10. **Sensitivity** is the ability to detect a stimulus. This capacity is influenced by internal neural noise, the intensity of the stimulus, and how well a person's nervous system is working. (p. 129)

> *Example:* In the chapter on sensation, you learned how age can affect the ability of the three bones in the inner ear to conduct sound. A person with a decrease in bone conductivity would be less sensitive to external auditory stimuli.
>
> *REMEMBER:* In contrast to the response criterion (influenced by a person's motivation and expectancies), sensitivity reflects physical changes in the nervous system, sensory system, or stimulus.

11. **Weber's law** states that the amount of stimulus that you have to add before you just notice a difference or change in that stimulus depends on and is proportional to the original amount of the stimulus. (p. 130)

> *Example:* Imagine that a book weighing ten pounds is in your knapsack. You notice a change in the weight of your knapsack after adding two pounds of books. According to Weber's law, if you started out with twenty pounds of books, you would need to add four pounds of books before you would notice a difference. The proportion of 2 to 10 is the same as the proportion of 4 to 20.

12. A **just-noticeable difference (JND)** (or **difference threshold**) is the smallest difference in stimulus energy that can be detected. (pp. 130–131)

> *Example:* During a power outage, your roommate lights twenty candles while you are in the basement coping with the fuse box. When you get back, you tell her that the room is still too dark and ask her to light another candle. She replies that she will have to light several more candles before you can "just notice the difference" in the light in the room.

13. **Figure-ground** is a principle of perceptual organization. The figure is that part of the visual field that has meaning and stands out from the rest of the stimulus. The rest of the visual field is the ground. The perception of what is figure and what is ground is influenced by grouping. (p. 133)

14. **Gestalt psychologists** believe that our perception of a whole object is more than just the sum of that object's various parts. (p. 134)

> *Example:* What do you see at the end of this sentence? •
>
> Now what do you see below this sentence?
>
> • • • • • • • • • • • • • • • • •
>
> Like most people, you probably "saw" a dot at the end of the first sentence and a line below the second. A Gestalt psychologist would argue that there is nothing about a dot that tells you about the characteristics of the line. Therefore, perception of the line must be something more than just the sum of the properties of many dots.

15. **Proximity** is a Gestalt principle of perception stating that objects that are close together are perceived as a whole. (p. 134)

> *Example:* You would be more likely to call the dots in (a) a line than you would be to call the dots in (b) a line.
>
> a. • • • • • • • • • • • • • •
>
> b. •   •   •

16. **Similarity** is a Gestalt principle of perception stating that similar objects are perceived as part of the same group. (p. 134)

> *Example:* When you watch basketball or some other sports game on television, you perceive the players on one team as similar because they are all dressed the same way.

17. **Continuity** is a Gestalt principle of perception stating that sensations appearing to create a continuous form are perceived as belonging together. (p. 134)

> *Example:* The long, vertical brackets on Jerry's wall each support one end of the boards Jerry uses for bookshelves. Although the shelves cross in front of the brackets, Jerry does not perceive the shelf/bracket unit as sets of T's. The brackets still appear to be continuous forms and are grouped together.

18. **Closure** is a Gestalt principle of perception stating that people tend to fill in missing contours to form a complete object. (p. 134)

> *Example:* Sally saw a fence with many slats missing, but she nevertheless perceived the fence as complete.

19. **Texture** is a Gestalt principle of perception stating that when basic features have the same texture, they will be perceived as a group. (p. 134)

Example: The curtains hanging on either side of the mini-blinds are seen as a group, although they are separated. The horizontal slats of the mini-blinds and the vertical fabric of the curtains are different textures.

20. **Simplicity** is a Gestalt principle of perception stating that we tend to group stimulus features in a way that provides the simplest interpretation of the world. (pp. 134–135)

Example: When you look at a picture of a structure in which you grew up, you probably perceive a house. You do not perceive a collection of separate objects, such as the door, windows, chimney, and front steps. It is much simpler for you to group these sensations into one object, the house.

21. **Common fate** is a Gestalt principle of perception stating that objects moving together at the same rate are perceived as a group. (p. 135)

Example: Cars going south on the highway are perceived as a group.

22. **Common region** is a Gestalt principle of perception stating that objects within a border are grouped together. (p. 135)

Example: Although there is a row of plates and utensils placed on each side of the table, the placemats beneath each set cause them to be perceived as separate groups.

23. **Auditory scene analysis** is the method of representing and interpreting sounds. Sounds are divided based on pitch, loudness, and location into separate streams, which are sounds perceived as coming from the same source. (p. 135)

Example: Earl hears children's voices, people shifting in their seats, vehicles passing by outside, and the lecturer. He is able to listen to the speaker by attending to that stream of sounds and ignoring the other types of sounds coming from other locations.

24. **Depth perception** is the perception of distance and allows people to experience the world in three dimensions. (p. 135)

25. **Relative size** is stimulus cue for depth perception. Objects that are larger are perceived as being nearer. (p. 135)

Example: Monica and her twin daughters, Jackie and Mary, are in the backyard. When Monica looks up

from the book she is reading, her retinal image of Jackie is much larger than her image of Mary. She knows that Jackie is closer because she seems bigger. Mary, who is playing at the farthest end of the yard, seems farther away, not tiny.

26. **Height in the visual field** is a stimulus cue for depth perception. Distant objects are higher in the visual field than close objects. (p. 135)

Example: When you are standing in the end zone of a football field, the goal post at the opposite end will be higher than the fifty-yard line in your visual field.

27. **Interposition** is a stimulus cue for depth perception. Objects that are closer block a complete view of objects farther away. (p. 135)

Example: Stand in your driveway and look at your residence. You know that the bushes in front of your house, dorm, or apartment are closer to you than the building is because they block your complete view of the building.

28. **Linear perspective** is a stimulus cue for depth perception. Parallel lines that stretch out into the distance seem to converge, or come together, at a point. A stimulus is farther away as it approaches the point of convergence. (p. 136)

Example: Stand in the middle of railroad tracks and look far into the distance. The tracks seem to come together to make a point. Objects that are close to that point appear far away.

29. **Reduced clarity** is a stimulus cue for depth perception. Objects that are blurry appear to be far away. (p. 136)

Example: A view of a city through smog will make the city appear farther away than it appears when the sky is clear.

30. **Light and shadow** provide our perceptual system with cues for perceiving three dimensions. (p. 136)

Example: Shadows and bright spots on a building at night help us judge which building parts are close and which are farther away.

31. **Textural gradients** are stimulus cues for depth perception. A graduated change in the texture, or "grain," of the visual field indicates distance. (p. 136)

Example: Try to find the biggest, steepest classroom on campus. Go to the front of the class and look up at the empty seats. Your view should form a texture. As you look toward the back of the classroom, you will notice that the texture is gradually changing as the chairs get smaller and smaller. The amount of change in texture indicates how far away the chairs are.

32. **Movement gradients** are stimulus cues for depth perception. The rate of an object's movement tells you how close or far away the object is. (pp. 136–137)

Example: The next time you ride in a car, notice that objects close to you whiz by but that those farther away seem to move more slowly.

33. **Convergence** is a depth perception cue. The closer an object is, the more your eyes must turn inward to focus on it. Your brain uses information from the muscles that move your eyes inward to perceive depth. (p. 138)

Example: Try to focus on the end of your nose. You will feel your eyes strain as they attempt to "find" your nose. Slowly shift your focus to an object across the room, and you will feel your muscles relax.

34. **Binocular disparity** is the difference between the two retinal images and tells the brain about depth. The greater the difference is between the two images, the closer an object is. (p. 138)

Example: Hold your arm straight out in front of your face, and focus on the tip of one finger. To see the disparity in the two images that your eyes see, look at your finger first with one eye and then with the other. Now focus on an object at the far end of the room. Again, shut one eye and then the other. There should be a greater difference between the images your eyes saw when you focused on your finger than between those your eyes saw when you focused on the object far away from you.

35. **Looming** is a motion cue. Objects that enlarge quickly are perceived as moving toward the viewer instead of just growing in size. (p. 138)

Example: Ted is in a fight on the playground. He knows that the fist that is quickly getting bigger and bigger is moving toward his face. He doesn't perceive the fist as simply growing in size.

36. **Perceptual constancy** is the ability to perceive sameness even when the object on the retina changes. We have perceptual constancy for size, shape, and brightness. (p. 139)

Example: At a concert, you end up sitting very far from the stage. As you look at the members of the band, you perceive them as being adults rather than children, because of the constancy of their size.

37. **Bottom-up processing** refers to aspects of recognition that depend primarily on the brain's reception of stimulus information from sensory receptors. (pp. 144–145)

Example: When presented with an image of the letter "A", feature detectors for "/", "–", and "\" are activated, and then the features are recombined to create the perception of "A."

38. **Top-down processing** refers to aspects of recognition that begin at the "top" (the brain), guided by higher-level cognitive processes and by psychological factors such as expectations and motivation. (pp. 144, 146–147)

Example: Jill's friend says that the cloud looks like a soda can with a straw sticking out of it. When Jill first looks at it, she sees a soda can and straw, although the cloud looks as much like a candle, cup, or piece of candy as it does a can.

39. **Schemas** are mental models of what we know, which are created based on experience. Schemas create perceptual sets, which affect our top-down processing. (p. 147)

Example: Claude's schema for nurse includes characteristics like "wears white" and "is a woman." When a man dressed in regular clothes called his name in the doctor's office, Claude didn't respond at first, because the man didn't fit his schema of a nurse.

40. **Parallel distributed processing (PDP) models** suggest that recognition of objects is based on the simultaneous operation of connected neural units that are activated when matched by features in the stimulus. (p. 148)

REMEMBER: A stimulus activates a network of feature detectors that work concurrently (in parallel) in various areas of the brain (distributed) to identify the object.

41. **Attention** is the process of directing psychological resources to enhance information processing. (p. 151)

Example: Sonia leans forward and listens intently to the speaker.

FILL-IN-THE-BLANKS KEY TERMS

This section will help you check your factual knowledge of the key terms introduced in this chapter. Fill in each blank with the appropriate term from the list of key terms above.

1. The _____ view of perception holds that we combine all the pieces of sensory information to create an understanding of reality.

2. Increased expectations of perceiving a stimulus will lower the _____.

3. The smallest difference in stimulus energy that can be detected is called the _____.

4. People's ability to perceive the world in three dimensions is based on _____.

5. The amount of stimulus energy required for a person to perceive a stimulus 50 percent of the time is called the _____.

6. The principle that objects within a border are grouped together is called _____.

7. The brain uses information from muscles that control the inward turning of the eyes, a cue called _____, to judge the distance of a visual stimulus.

8. _____ is a depth cue in which the brain compares the differing retinal images from the eyes to create a three-dimensional image.

9. _____ calculates the amount of stimulus change required for a person to perceive a change.

10. People who hold the _____ view argue that perception is an automatic process based on information found in the environment.

11. _____ is a stimulus cue for depth perception in which objects that block a complete view of another object are perceived as closer.

12. Our ability to perceive objects as remaining the same even though the image on our retina varies is explained by the principle of _____.

13. The recognition of stimuli that is guided by knowledge, expectations, and motivation is referred to as _____.

14. The process of directing psychological resources to enhance information processing is called _____.

15. When the brain recognizes a stimulus based first on incoming sensory information, it is said to be employing _____.

Total Correct (See answer key) _____

LEARNING OBJECTIVES

1. Define perception. Compare and contrast perception and sensation. (p. 126)

2. Discuss the debate among the constructionist, computational, and ecological viewpoints as to how perception works. (p. 127)

3. Define psychophysics and absolute threshold. Explain the influence of internal noise and response criterion on perception. (pp. 128–129)

4. Define and describe signal-detection theory. Be sure to include sensitivity to stimuli and response criterion in your answer. Describe how information can change the response criterion. (pp. 129–130)

5. Describe Weber's law. Define just-noticeable difference (JND). Explain the equation JND = KI. (pp. 130–131)

6. Describe Fechner's law. (p. 131)

7. Describe parapsychology and extrasensory perception (ESP). Explain what conclusions are most reasonable about ESP. (pp. 131–133)

8. Describe the two basic principles of perceptual organization: figure-ground and grouping. Define and give examples of proximity, similarity, continuity, closure, texture, simplicity, common fate, and common region. (pp. 133–135)

9. Discuss how auditory scene analysis organizes our perception of sounds. (p. 135)

10. Define and describe depth perception. (p. 135)

11. Describe the stimulus cues that influence depth perception. Your answer should include relative size, height in the visual field, interposition, linear perspective, reduced clarity, light and shadow, textural gradient, and movement gradient. (pp. 135–137)

12. Describe the cues to depth provided by accommodation, convergence, and binocular disparity. (pp. 137–138)

13. Describe the cues used to perceive motion. Your answer should include looming and the brain's ability to sense the position of the eyes and head. (p. 138)

14. Define perceptual, size, shape, and brightness constancy. (pp. 139–140)

15. Explain the basis of the Ponzo and Müller-Lyer illusions. (pp. 140–143)

16. Describe the impact of culture on perception. (p. 143)

17. Explain how feature analysis works. (pp. 144–146)

18. Compare and contrast <u>bottom-up processing</u> and <u>top-down processing</u>. (pp. 144–147)

19. Discuss the influences on top-down processing. Your answer should include expectancy, motivation, and <u>schemas</u>. (pp. 146–147)

20. Describe how top-down processing and bottom-up processing work together. (pp. 147–148)

21. Define <u>network processing</u>. Explain the <u>parallel distributed processing models</u> of pattern recognition. (pp. 148–150)

22. Describe an infant's perceptual abilities. (pp. 150–151)

23. Define <u>attention</u>. Describe the research on the covert shifting of attention. (pp. 151–153)

24. Describe the influences that determine the ease of directing or dividing our attention. Explain parallel processing. (pp. 153–156)

25. Describe the influence of perceptual studies on the development of aviation and computer displays. (pp. 156–157)

CONCEPTS AND EXERCISES

No. 1: James Bond's Psychological Secrets

Completing this exercise should help you to achieve Learning Objectives 3, 5, and 6.

James Bond needs to have some weapons and equipment made for a new assignment. He has hired you to make them. After reading the description of each, decide whether you will need to know the absolute threshold or difference threshold in order to make the device.

1. A lipstick with a deadly poison in it

2. A poison that can be added to spice

3. A pen that is really a silent gun

4. An alcoholic drink containing a powerful tranquilizer

5. A watch that is really a radio that beeps a little louder than usual when Bond's accomplices are trying to get in touch with him

No. 2: Perception on the Playground

Completing this exercise should help you to achieve Learning Objectives 8, 10, 11, 12, and 14.

Many childhood activities and games require the ability to perceive figure-ground, grouping, and depth. Match the grade-school activities listed below with the appropriate cues or principles of perception from the list that follows. Answers may be used once or not at all. Each problem may have more than one answer.

1. One hundred children are to participate in a spelling bee. Because the children sit down when they've made a mistake, the audience knows that only those children left standing are part of the group that has not misspelled a word. _____

2. As Alice runs to get in the line progressing back into the building, she sees a *line* of students instead of separate individuals. _____

3. Roy is playing softball. He knows that he has hit the ball very far because he can barely see it as it soars through the air. _____

4. Sally is calling to Penny and Ali, who are across the playground. She knows that Ali is closer because she is blocking part of Penny from Sally's view. _____

5. The fifth graders are performing a play in the gym. Mark, a fourth grader, wants to sit with his pals. As he looks for them among the sea of faces in the bleachers, the heads of people seem to be getting smaller and smaller, creating a difference in texture on his retina. _____

6. Children play a game called "Duck, Duck, Goose." Everyone stands in a circle. One or two people are chosen to leave the circle. They walk around the circle, touching each person as they go and saying "Duck." Eventually, they touch someone and say "Goose." The "goose" must chase the person all the way around the circle and try to catch him or her. Even though there are always two to four individuals missing from the circle, everyone still perceives a circle. _____

7. Consuela likes to ride on the merry-go-round. She loves to try looking at the objects that are close to the merry-go-round because they seem to move so fast. _____

   ° Similarity
   ° Reduced clarity
   ° Simplicity

° Proximity
° Textural gradient
° Orientation
° Linear perspective
° Movement gradient
° Interposition
° Relative size

CRITICAL THINKING

Sam and Martina are investigating a bomb that exploded at a rock concert. They are curious as to how this could have happened because the doors all have sensors that are extremely sensitive to any materials that could be used in any type of bomb or electronic weapon. None of the ushers or security guards at the theater noticed anything amiss that night. There were no clues that a bomb had either entered the theater or was going to explode while the theater was full.

Sam pulls in all the theater personnel for questioning. He is convinced that one of the sensor monitors (people who watch the sensors to see if anyone is carrying anything suspect into the theater) was a partner in the crime. He thinks that whoever carried the bomb in made an arrangement with a sensor monitor to let the bomb remain undetected.

Sam discovers that one of the sensor monitors knows the bomb suspect. Sam is sure he has found the guilty party.

Martina joins the questioning of Sam's suspects for about an hour. Finally she tells Sam to let the sensor monitor go home. Frustrated, Sam asks, "How can you do that? He is the only clue we have."

Martina replies, "Sam, just send him home. Then get me a list of all the employees who have worked there for a couple of years and anybody who was working a double shift that night."

Using the five critical thinking questions in your text, the clues in the story, and what you have just learned about perception, answer the following:

1. What is Sam's hypothesis?

2. What is the evidence in support of Sam's hypothesis?

3. What is Martina's alternative hypothesis?

4. What is the evidence in support of Martina's hypothesis?

PERSONAL LEARNING ACTIVITIES

1. Try to approximate your absolute threshold for tastes. You could have someone prepare several glasses, some of which are plain water, the rest of which have varying amounts of salt or sugar in them. How much must be there before you notice it? Does the amount change if you try the experiment at another time of day? (Learning Objective 3)

2. Conduct an experiment on judging differences between stimuli. For example, to test your perception of weight differences, you could close your eyes and have a friend place one magazine or notebook on your hand. How many sheets of paper can the friend add before you just notice a difference? How much must be added before you believe it is twice as heavy as it was originally? If you start with a textbook, how many magazines or notebooks are needed for you to notice a difference or to judge it to be twice as heavy? (Learning Objectives 5 and 6)

3. Examine the evidence given in commercials for psychic readings. Is the evidence personal testimony or is other corroboration of the accuracy given? Use the critical thinking steps outlined in your text to identify questions that should be answered before you make a conclusion. (Learning Objective 7)

4. What errors in perception have you made? Did the illusions in Figures 5.13 and 5.14 fool you? Have you experienced a situation like the error in depth perception that follows? Large rock formations or mountains may appear to be near to the inexperienced viewer, because it is hard to compare them to the surroundings. Although they could be a day's journey away on foot, people new to the area can't see that a tree at the base is a tiny dot on their retina, and that, therefore, the mountain must be far away. (Learning Objectives 11 and 15)

5. Use a computer program you know. As you run through the familiar steps of loading a program and working in it, identify the features that help or hinder your progress. Most programs, for instance, have highlighted either the cursor position or an outline of the cell you are editing to help draw your attention to it. Are the messages that appear on the screen in a convenient place, easy to read, understandable? (Learning Objective 25)

MULTIPLE-CHOICE QUESTIONS

SAMPLE QUIZ 1

1. A proponent of the computational view of perception would say,
   a. "The environment has enough cues for our sensory systems to detect and perceive reality."
   b. "Top-down processing is important in the perceptual process."
   c. "Bottom-up processing is important in the perceptual process."
   d. "Both (a) and (c) are true."

2. Vicki is sailing toward shore. Her expectation of seeing shore soon will _____ her response criterion for perceiving land.
   a. increase
   b. decrease
   c. have no effect on
   d. delay

3. Dante raises his hand each time he hears a tone over headphones in an experiment. The tone gets quieter and quieter until Dante misses hearing it half the time. After repeating the same procedure many times, the researcher concludes the experiment, because she has found Dante's
   a. absolute threshold.
   b. difference threshold.
   c. internal noise.
   d. response criterion.

4. Which of the following would *not* affect a person's sensitivity?
   a. The level of internal noise in the nervous system
   b. The person's motivation
   c. The condition of the person's sensory system
   d. The intensity of the stimulus

5. Subjects are watching a computer screen, which displays randomly appearing dots of different colors. Each time subjects see a red light, they are to press the "enter" key. When subjects are told they will be given $1 each time they correctly indicate they've seen a red light, their number of _____ will increase.
   a. thresholds
   b. correct rejections
   c. false alarms
   d. misses

6. The experimenters in the question above used money to alter subjects'
   a. difference threshold.
   b. internal noise.
   c. response criterion.
   d. sensitivity.

7. Paul and Javier love to sneak out of their houses at night. Paul shines a dim light when he cannot leave the house. When Javier sees a light twice as bright, he knows that he should meet Paul behind his garage. Which law will give a description of how much light is necessary for Javier to perceive it as being twice as bright?
   a. Weber's law
   b. Fechner's law
   c. Gestalt's law
   d. Ebbinghaus's law

8. Luna claims to know what is happening in places where she is not present. For example, when a friend was in a wreck she claimed that she could see the car heading for danger at the time of the crash. Luna's ability is called _____ and is, according to the Thinking Critically section in your text, _____.
   a. clairvoyance; not supported by research
   b. clairvoyance; well-supported by research
   c. telepathy; the only true parapsychological phenomenon
   d. telepathy; not a true parapsychological phenomenon

9. Four swimmers practicing their synchronized swimming routine are perceived as a group, because they are performing the same movements at the same speed. This is an example of the grouping principle
   a. closure.
   b. common fate.
   c. orientation.
   d. interposition.

10. Harriet Greene is going to take her Brownie troop on a field trip to Chicago. She wants all the children to wear the same T-shirt. That way, a stray child will still be recognized as part of the troop. This demonstrates the principle of
    a. similarity.
    b. proximity.
    c. orientation.
    d. textural gradients.

11. Knowing that an object is closer to you because it blocks out part of the background is called
    a. linear perspective.
    b. reduced clarity.
    c. interposition.
    d. movement gradient.

12. A Cyclops has only one eye. What depth cue based on the properties of her visual system would a Cyclops *not* have?
    a. Linear perspective
    b. Movement gradient
    c. Convergence
    d. Reduced clarity

13. As Cliff exits his front door using a garbage can lid as a shield, he sees a snowball coming straight for him. Although the size of the snowball on his retina is enlarging, he realizes the snowball is approaching, not getting larger, because of
    a. induced motion.
    b. looming.
    c. the movement gradient.
    d. reduced clarity.

14. When Jean sees her cat from one angle, she has no difficulty identifying her, but from another angle Jean isn't even sure that what she's seeing is a cat. Jean is having difficulty with
    a. closure.
    b. interposition.
    c. proximity.
    d. shape constancy.

15. "Look at this picture of me!" exclaimed Jake. "I don't like the way that tiny chair and all those tall, thin people around me make me appear flabby." In order to appear fit enough to sell his aerobic work-out videotape, Jake asks that his chair be widened and that shorter, heavier models pose for the cover photo. By trying to appear thin in contrast to his surroundings, Jake is using
    a. an illusion.
    b. a difference threshold.
    c. the common region principle.
    d. the proximity principle.

16. As soon as Jocelyn stepped on a tack, she reflexively pulled her foot up from its sharp point. Jocelyn primarily used _____ processing to sense and react reflexively.
    a. bottom-up
    b. parallel
    c. serial
    d. top-down

17. Which of the following does not contribute to the creation of a perceptual set?
    a. Context
    b. Expectancy
    c. Past experience
    d. Sensitivity

18. When Frieda first looked at an advertisement, she noticed only that it showed a glass of cola on a tray. After her friend Cal told her that he saw two cows kissing in the blur on the left ice cube, Frieda instantly noticed the cows. "You're right; I can see them," said Frieda, "but I think I see them mostly due to _____, since you made me expect them to be there."
    a. bottom-up processing
    b. top-down processing
    c. common fate
    d. similarity

19. As strings of letters were flashed on the screen, Carrie recognized the letter "t" more quickly in the word "met" than in the nonsense letter string "lgt." Carrie's brain was faster at recognizing the "t" in "met" because its features, "m," "e," and "t," have more connections due to Carrie's experience. _____ processing was most responsible for the differences in recognition speed.
    a. Bottom-up
    b. Network
    c. Relative
    d. Serial

20. Ron needs to find the section of his physics text that lists general thermodynamics equations. Luckily he marked the top edge of the pages with a bright pink highlighter pen, so the important pages automatically grab his attention when he scans. Ron used _____ processing to locate the target pages.
    a. absolute threshold
    b. network
    c. parallel
    d. schema

Total Correct (See answer key) _____

SAMPLE QUIZ 2

Use this quiz to reassess your learning after taking Quiz 1 and reviewing the chapter.

1. The _____ viewpoint is best at explaining our use of the grouping principle, closure.
   a. computational
   b. constructionist
   c. ecological
   d. signal detection

2. Expecting to see a stimulus will _____ the response criterion.
   a. increase
   b. decrease
   c. not influence
   d. be influenced by

3. Shari studies the factors that will affect whether a cheese lab technologist will notice white curd specks in a loaf of yellow processed cheese. Specifically, Shari needs to know how to decrease false alarms and increase hits; therefore, Shari should study
   a. signal detection theory.
   b. extrasensory perception.
   c. optical acuity theory.
   d. Weber's law.

4. LaKisha has an ear infection that muffles the sounds presented to her during a signal detection experiment. Because LaKisha's hearing is poor, she responds to very few of the tones. Her lowered _____ is causing an increase in _____.
   a. absolute threshold; false alarms
   b. difference threshold; misses
   c. response criterion; false alarms
   d. sensitivity; misses

5. JND = KI. The I stands for
   a. absolute threshold.
   b. a constant that varies among different senses.
   c. the intensity of the stimulus.
   d. difference threshold.

6. With which of the following types of stimuli does Fechner's law not work?
   a. Pain
   b. Light
   c. Sound
   d. All of the above

7. Jake is a detective. He is usually very good at his job but has been making mistakes lately. Last night, he was on a stakeout and let Benny slip away. Which of the following explanations would point to inadequate sensitivity as the reason for Jake's mistake?
   a. Jake was sure that Benny was going to sleep that night instead of making a break for it.
   b. Jake fell asleep in the car at about 5:00 A.M.
   c. Jake knew that Benny's partner was across the street aiming a gun at Jake. If Jake had made a move, he would have been shot.
   d. Jake knows that he is going to retire soon; a few mistakes will not mar his record.

8. When you arrive at a party, you are distressed to discover that people have already paired off. Although couples are just talking while sitting near to each other, you think that no one is available to talk to. The perceptual grouping principle most likely causing your perception of the party attenders as several pairs of people rather than as individuals is
   a. closure.
   b. continuity.
   c. figure-ground.
   d. proximity.

9. A burglar will paint her face black and wear dark clothing in order to keep people from using which principle of perceptual organization or grouping?
   a. Proximity
   b. Figure-ground
   c. Closure
   d. Similarity

10. Which of the following is *not* a clue for depth perception?
    a. Interposition
    b. Orientation
    c. Linear perspective
    d. Reduced clarity

11. Pretty Boy, a Persian cat, bounds across the yard after a mouse, only to watch it crawl under the fence. Pretty Boy steps up to the fence and peers through a hole with one eye. He realizes that the mouse is already far away because it looks very small. This is an example of
    a. convergence.
    b. binocular disparity.
    c. relative size.
    d. looming.

12. At football games, people in the stands hold up colored cards. The fans on the other side of the stadium see these cards as spelling a word because of which of the following?
    a. Proximity
    b. Similarity
    c. Interposition
    d. Both (a) and (b)

13. _____ allow(s) us to perceive an object as being the same size despite a change in the size of the retinal image.
    a. Looming
    b. Proximity
    c. Size constancy
    d. Movement gradients

14. After tying 100 yellow ribbons into bows for party decorations, Aparna saw blue afterimages. "I had no idea that would happen," says Aparna. "Therefore, my _____ processing must have been most active in creating the perception."
    a. bottom-up
    b. constructionist
    c. network
    d. top-down

15. A group of Pygmies living in a very thick forest in a preindustrial country probably would not understand perceptual
    a. size constancy.
    b. brightness constancy.
    c. shape constancy.
    d. complexity.

16. Which perceptual process is affected by expectations and motivation?
    a. Bottom-up processing
    b. Internal noise
    c. Top-down processing
    d. Sensitivity

17. When Lou looks at a lily, her brain matches its features (stem, petals, fragrance, and color) to the perceptual category "flower." Such feature analysis is characteristic of _____ processing.
    a. bottom-up
    b. ecological
    c. illusory
    d. top-down

18. John, a newlywed, is expecting his wife home from work in ten minutes. Suddenly, her footsteps are on the stairs. He jumps up and runs out the door, ready to scoop up his wife. To his embarrassment, he almost kisses the landlord. What type of processing caused John's close call?
    a. Feature analysis
    b. Bottom-up processing
    c. Perceptual set
    d. Auditory gradients

19. Although Alan appears to be listening as Rich talks about his new clothes, vacation plans, and exercise routine, Alan is thinking through his list of errands to run. Alan has
    a. covertly shifted attention.
    b. overtly shifted attention.
    c. used parallel distributed processing.
    d. used serial processing.

20. Engineering psychologists used the outcome of perception research to suggest that the cursor on computer screens should blink to attract attention. The flashing light on the screen allows the operator to use _____ processing to locate the cursor.
    a. absolute threshold
    b. network
    c. parallel
    d. serial

Total Correct (See answer key) _____

ANSWERS TO FILL-IN-THE-BLANKS KEY TERMS

1. constructionist (p. 127)
2. response criterion (p. 129)
3. just-noticeable difference (pp. 130–131)
4. depth perception (p. 135)
5. absolute threshold (p. 129)
6. common region (pp. 134–135)
7. convergence (p. 138)
8. Binocular disparity (p. 138)
9. Weber's law (p. 130)
10. ecological (p. 127)
11. Interposition (p. 135)
12. perceptual constancy (p. 139)
13. top-down processing (p. 144)
14. attention (p. 151)
15. bottom-up processing (p. 144)

ANSWERS TO CONCEPTS AND EXERCISES

No. 1: James Bond's Psychological Secrets

1. *Absolute threshold.* You would need to know the absolute threshold for the taste of the poison so that the person using the lipstick would not be able to taste the poison. (p. 129)

2. *Difference threshold.* Spices already have a flavor. Therefore, you would need to know how much poison you could add before someone just noticed a difference in the taste. (pp. 130–131)

3. *Absolute threshold.* You would have to know the absolute threshold for the sound of the gunshot. The amount of auditory stimulus that the gunshot would make would have to be *below* the absolute threshold so that nobody could hear it. (p. 129)

4. *Difference threshold.* Most alcohol already has a taste. You would have to find out what amount of tranquilizer you could add before someone would just notice a difference. (pp. 130–131)

5. *Difference threshold.* Bond would have to be able to just notice a difference in the amplitude of the beep of the watch/radio. (pp. 130–131)

No. 2: Perception on the Playground

1. *Orientation.* This is a grouping principle. Those children who are standing all have the same orientation. This will tell the audience which children belong to the group of disqualified people and which children are still in the spelling bee. (p. 134)

2. *Simplicity.* This is a grouping principle. We perceive the most simple pattern in an object. Seeing many individual students would be much more complicated than just seeing a line of people. Continuity would be an equally good answer. We perceive sensations that appear to create a continuous form (a line) as belonging together. (pp. 134–135)

3. *Reduced clarity.* This is a depth cue. The clarity with which Roy can see the ball is reduced as it gets farther and farther away. Relative size, also a depth cue, would be an equally good answer. As the size of the ball gets smaller, Roy perceives it as being farther away. (pp. 135–136)

4. *Interposition.* This is a depth cue. Objects that block the view of other objects are closer to us. Ali is blocking the view of Penny; therefore, Ali is closer to Sally. (p. 135)

5. *Textural gradient.* This is a depth cue. Mark knows that the objects that create a smaller image and different texture on his retina are farther away. (p. 136)

6. *Closure.* This is a grouping principle. Even though parts of the circle are missing, the children still perceive the group as a circle. Their perceptual abilities allow them to fill in the gaps. (p. 134)

7. *Movement gradient.* This is a depth cue. Consuela knows that the objects that are closer to her seem to be moving much faster than those objects that are farther away. (pp. 136–137)

ANSWERS TO CRITICAL THINKING

1. Sam's hypothesis is that one of the sensor monitors is the bomb suspect's partner.

2. Sam believes his hypothesis because the sensor monitor knows the bomb suspect.

3. Martina hypothesizes that someone missed the sensor's signal, probably because of an altered response criterion or inadequate sensitivity.

4. In asking Sam to get a list of employees, Martina suspects the culprit to be someone who has worked on the job for a long time. Working at the theater for several years and never seeing a monitor get tripped might have increased that person's response criterion. (*NOTE:* A new employee would probably have a very low response criterion and have several false alarms.) Someone working there for a long time would have probably thought that night was going to be like every other boring night and would not have expected to see a bomb. This would have resulted in the monitor missing the alerting sensor signal. Martina also wants to know who had a double shift; anyone who was very tired might not have been sensitive enough to detect the stimulus.

ANSWERS TO MULTIPLE-CHOICE QUESTIONS

Circle the question numbers you answered correctly.

Sample Quiz 1

1. *c* is the answer. Proponents of the computational view think that perception is the result of neurological and sensory system activity. (pp. 127–128)
   a. Someone with an ecological view would say this.
   b. Constructionists believe that we use top-down processing to construct our environment.
   d. Only *c* is correct.

2. *b* is the answer. Vicki's expectations of seeing a light on shore soon will decrease her response criterion. This means she will need less stimulus (light) to perceive that she is seeing a shore light. (p. 129)
   a. Increasing Vicki's response criterion means that she will be less likely to perceive a stimulus.
   c. *b* is the answer.
   d. The response criterion is the willingness or reluctance to respond to a stimulus; therefore, it is not something that can be delayed.

3. *a* is the answer. The absolute threshold is the point at which you perceive a stimulus half the time. (p. 129)
   b. The difference threshold is the amount of change required before a person will just notice a difference in a stimulus.
   c. Internal noise is not something that can be seen or heard by a researcher, but it can interfere with a person's perception if it is too high. Internal noise is the automatic, random firing of cells in the nervous system.
   d. Expectancies and motivation affect our response criterion, which is our willingness or hesitancy to react to a stimulus.

4. *b* is the answer. Sensitivity is the ability to detect a stimulus. Motivation affects whether we do perceive a stimulus, but it does not affect our ability to perceive a stimulus. (p. 129)
   a. A very high level of internal noise may be mistaken for a very faint stimulus. This will alter sensitivity.
   c. The sensory system's physical health can affect its ability to perceive a stimulus. For example, a person with burned finger tips will be unable to detect slight pressure very well.
   d. The intensity of a stimulus will affect our ability to detect it. If the stimulus is below absolute threshold, it will be undetectable.

5. *c* is the answer. Because the participants have something to gain from seeing a stimulus, they are more likely to say they've seen one when it didn't actually appear. (pp. 129–130)
   a. You may have been thinking of a change in the level of absolute or difference thresholds, but the number of these wouldn't change.
   b. The participants will not increase their number of correct rejections, because they are more motivated to see the light than not to see it.
   d. Misses will decrease, because participants are motivated by money to watch carefully.

6. *c* is the answer. The criterion was lowered by the chance to gain money. (pp. 129–130)
   a. Difference thresholds are the smallest noticeable change in a stimulus and depend on the intensity of the stimulus, not factors in the subjects.
   b. Internal noise is the random firing of neurons and is not affected by motivation.
   d. Sensitivity is related to the abilities of the sensory systems and the amount of internal noise.

7. *b* is the answer. Fechner's law describes how much stimulus must be added for Javier to perceive the light as twice as bright. (p. 131)
   a. Weber's law describes the amount of stimulus required before a just-noticeable difference is perceived.
   c. There is no such thing as Gestalt's law.
   d. There is no such thing as Ebbinghaus's law.

8. *a* is the answer. Clairvoyance is a term used for the alleged ability to perceive objects or events through extrasensory perception (ESP) rather than usual sensory perception. So far no well-controlled studies support the notion that some people have ESP. (pp. 131–133)
   b. Clairvoyance is not an ability supported with empirical evidence.
   c, d. Telepathy is the alleged ability to read someone's mind and is not supported by research.

9. *b* is the answer. Objects (or people) moving at the same rate and in the same direction are perceived as a group. (p. 135)
   a. Closure would be filling in the gaps of a still object.
   c. Orientation is one aspect of a stimulus that relates to texture, not movement.
   d. Interposition is a depth perception cue.

10. *a* is the answer. Harriet Greene wants to be sure that all her Brownies look alike so that people will perceive them all as members of the same group. (p. 134)
    b. If one child wanders away from the rest of the Brownies, she will *not* be close enough to be perceived as part of the group.
    c. Even if one child strays from the group, she will still be in the same orientation (standing up) as everyone else in the museum. Her orientation will not distinguish her as one of Harriet Greene's Brownies.
    d. Textural gradients are a depth cue, not a principle of grouping.

11. *c* is the answer. Interposition is a depth perception cue. (p. 135)
    a. Linear perspective is a depth cue. As parallel lines get farther and farther away, they seem to converge at a point.
    b. Reduced clarity is a depth cue. As objects get very far away, we see them less clearly.
    d. Movement gradient is a depth cue. As you move forward—for example, in a car—the objects that are close to you seem to go by more quickly than those that are far away.

12. *c* is the answer. The brain receives and processes information from the eye muscles about the amount of muscular activity. The eyes must converge, or rotate inward, to project the image of an object on each retina. The closer the object is, the greater the convergence is, and thus the greater is the muscular activity reported to the brain. The brain of a Cyclops would receive no information about the convergence since a Cyclops has only one eye. (p. 138)
    a. Linear perspective is a depth cue that can be seen with one eye.
    b. A movement gradient is a depth cue that can be seen with one eye.
    d. Reduced clarity is a depth cue that can be seen with one eye.

13. *b* is the answer. (p. 138)
    a. Induced motion is not a term used in your text, but it is the feeling that we are moving when something on either side of us moves. For example, when sitting in a car in a parking lot, if both cars next to you back out, you may feel for a moment as if you are moving forward although your car is still.
    c. the movement gradient is the difference in the *apparent* movement of objects, which occurs as we move by them.
    d. Reduced clarity is the depth cue in which less clear images are perceived as farther away.

14. *d* is the answer. (p. 140)
    a, b. Both the grouping principle closure and the depth cue interposition would require that something was blocking Jean's view of the cat.
    c. Proximity is a grouping principle that automatically organizes objects that are close together into a group.

15. *a* is the answer. Jake is using an illusion, specifically the Ebbinghaus illusion. Illusions use context to fool the eye. See Figure 5.13 to see how the size of circles in the outer ring (in the Ebbinghaus illusion) influences our perception of the circle in the middle. (pp. 140–141)
    b. A difference threshold would be important if someone were trying to detect a small difference between two stimuli. Jake is trying to look thinner through the use of illusions, not to use his photo to test judgment of differences.
    c. Common region is a grouping principle that states that items within a boundary are automatically grouped together.

    d. Proximity is a grouping principle that automatically organizes objects that are close together into a group.

16. *a* is the answer. Bottom-up processing is the reaction of cells in the nervous system to aspects of a stimulus. The cells each process one characteristic, and eventually the characteristics are combined to make a whole stimulus perception. In a reflexive action, sensory neurons send the pain information to the spinal cord, which sends a "pull away" message to the muscles. (pp. 144–145)
    b, c. Parallel and serial processing are used when a person is scanning the environment for a stimulus.
    d. Top-down processing is influenced by motivation and expectation.

17. *d* is the answer. A perceptual set is a readiness to perceive a stimulus in a certain way. Sensitivity is the ability to perceive an object *at all,* not an indication of *how* we perceive it. (pp. 129, 147)
    a. Context can change the way we perceive an object. For example, the sound of "reed" means two different things depending on the context of the sentence. "The oboe contains a reed." "I like to read."
    b. Our expectations, based on past experience and context, can create a perceptual set.
    c. Our past experiences can create perceptual sets. A person who does not have children may take some time to realize that children's bloodcurdling screams may not always signify pain. Anyone who has been around children for any length of time knows that they sometimes scream while they play and that alarm is not always the necessary response.

18. *b* is the answer. Frieda's bottom-up processing sent on information about the features of the objects in the advertisement, but it was Cal's suggestion that caused her to see the cows. (pp. 146–147)
    a. The expectation of what was in the picture influenced the perception. Frieda *did* use bottom-up processing, but it doesn't explain the difference between her two impressions.
    c. Common fate is the grouping principle that uses similar movement to place objects into a group.
    d. Similarity is the grouping principle that states that the more resemblance there is between items, the more likely they will be grouped.

19. *b* is the answer. Network processing causes the word superiority effect that Carrie experienced. The

neural links between letters previously seen together in a word are stronger than those between letters not previously shown together as a word. (p. 148)

a. Perception cannot occur without bottom-up processing, the reaction of nervous system cells to features of the stimulus, but the effect Carrie experienced was related to the networks of information in Carrie's brain.

c. Relative is not a processing type.

d. Serial processing is when a person must scan the environment carefully, examining several characteristics before deciding if the target has been found.

20. *c* is the answer. When a person can quickly and automatically pick out a target by examining all locations at once, it is parallel processing. Ron can examine the whole edge of the book to rapidly locate the highlighted page edges. (pp. 154–155)

a. Absolute threshold deals with sensing the presence of a stimulus, not finding a specific object from among an array of stimuli.

b. Network processing emphasizes the links between features of objects, meanings, and so on.

d. Schemas are mental representations created based on experience and are used in top-down processing, but an actual visual marker was used in this example.

Now turn to the quiz analysis table at the end of this chapter to find which areas you know well and which areas you need to work on. Circle the numbers in the table for items on Quiz 1 that you answered correctly.

ANSWERS TO MULTIPLE-CHOICE QUESTIONS

Circle the question numbers you answered correctly.

Sample Quiz 2

1. *b* is the answer. The constructionist viewpoint is that we piece together a perception from fragmented parts of sensory information by using our experience and knowledge. In closure, missing gaps are filled in to create a perception of a whole, based on our experience of how the whole perception should appear. (p. 127)

a. A computational view is one that explains that features of the environment are formed into complete perceptions through the actions of nervous system structures and mechanisms.

c. The ecological view asserts that everything needed for perception is present in the environment; we only have to attend to the important aspects.

d. Signal-detection theory does not address why someone would use the grouping principle of closure.

2. *b* is the answer. Response criterion determines the amount of physical energy needed for a person to justify reporting that a stimulus is present. Expecting to see a stimulus decreases, or lowers, the response criterion. (p. 129)

a. Expecting to see the stimulus does not increase, or raise, the response criterion. In other words, when the response criterion is decreased, we are more likely to report seeing a stimulus because we know it is coming.

c, d. Expectations do influence the response criterion, and the response criterion does not influence expectations.

3. *a* is the answer. Signal detection theory addresses the factors that influence whether we will perceive a stimulus. (p. 129)

b. Some people claim that extrasensory perception (ESP) exists. It is defined as the ability to perceive stimuli without the use of the five ordinary senses.

c. Optical acuity theory is not a term.

d. Weber's law addresses the perception of differences between stimuli, not stimulus detection itself.

4. *d* is the answer. An ear infection muffling sounds has affected the capacity of LaKisha's sensory systems, one influence on sensitivity. LaKisha doesn't hear many of the tones, or, in other words, she misses them. (p. 129)

a. Absolute threshold is the point at which a stimulus is perceived on half of its presentations; false alarms are saying stimuli were presented when they weren't.

b. The experiment is not testing whether LaKisha can notice a difference between two stimuli, and her difference threshold is not affected.

c. Nothing is said about LaKisha's response criterion; therefore, we don't know if she lowered it; she did not have any false alarms since she was barely responding to any tones.

5. *c* is the answer. *I* stands for the stimulus intensity. (p. 131)

a. This formula indicates the amount of stimulus that must be added before a just-noticeable difference is detected. An absolute threshold is the amount of stimulus necessary before a stimulus can be detected.

b. *K* is the constant that varies with each sensory system.

d. The entire formula demonstrates the amount of stimulus that must be added before a just-noticeable difference is detected. *I*, representing stimulus intensity, is only part of the formula.

6. *a* is the answer. Fechner's law predicts that one must add more stimulus to produce the psychological effect of a threefold change in stimulus intensity than that required to produce the psychological effect of a twofold change in intensity. However, for painful stimuli, less and less of an increase is necessary to detect psychologically more and more of a stimulus. (p. 131)

b, c. Fechner's law will work with light and sound.

d. Only *a* is the answer.

7. *b* is the answer. Changes in internal noise, stimulus intensity, or the workings of the sensory system alter sensitivity. If Jake is asleep, his visual sensory system is not working. Jake's eyes must be open before he can see Benny creep by the car. (p. 129)

a. If Jake thought that Benny was in for the night, then his expectations of activity would decrease. This would increase the necessary response criterion but would not affect sensitivity.

c. If Jake thought that Benny's partner was aiming a gun at him, then his motivation to grab Benny might have been lowered. Jake may think he is too close to retirement to take chances. This would affect Jake's motivation, not his sensitivity.

d. If Jake is not concerned about his record, he may not be as attentive at work. This would lower his response criterion (he is probably a bit reluctant to hear Benny) and increase his absolute threshold (the amount of noise required before Jake hears Benny).

8. *d* is the answer. The people closer to each other are seen as groups. (p. 134)

a. The grouping principle closure fills in gaps.

b. Continuity groups seemingly unbroken forms.

9. *b* is the answer. Burglars want to fade into the background. Painting their faces black and wearing dark clothing make it very difficult to see the burglars as separate from the background of the dark sky. (pp. 133–134)

a. Proximity is the tendency to perceive objects that are close together as part of a group.

c. Closure is the ability to fill in the gaps when sensory stimulation is missing. The black paint and dark clothing do not cause a lack of stimuli but do affect our ability to distinguish background and foreground.

d. Things that are similar are perceived as part of the same group. This question deals with just one burglar, not groups of burglars.

10. *b* is the answer. Orientation is a grouping principle. Objects that have the same orientation are perceived as members of the same group. (pp. 135–136)

a. Interposition is a depth cue. Closer objects block the view of objects that are farther away.

c. Linear perspective is a depth cue. Parallel lines seem to converge at a point in the distance.

d. Reduced clarity is a depth cue. Objects that are far away are less clear and therefore more difficult to see.

11. *c* is the answer. Although several of the alternatives are depth cues, the reduced or relative size of the mouse tells Pretty Boy that his quarry is far away. (p. 135)

a. Convergence is a depth cue, but it requires a visual image from both eyes. The cat is peering through the fence with only one eye.

b. Binocular disparity is a depth cue, but it requires a visual image from both eyes. The cat is peering through the fence with only one eye.

d. Looming is a motion cue. Objects are perceived as moving closer as they take up more and more of our retinal space.

12. *d* is the answer. Both similarity (color of the cards) and proximity (people sitting next to each other having the same color) are responsible for fans perceiving the individual cards as a group spelling a word. (p. 134)

a. *b* is one part of the answer.

b. *a* is one part of the answer.

c. Interposition is a depth cue.

13. *c* is the answer. Due to size constancy, we perceive objects as retaining their same size despite changes in retinal size. (p. 139)

a. Looming is a motion cue. Objects fill the entire retinal space as they get closer and are perceived as moving.

b. Proximity is a grouping principle. The closer objects are, the more likely we are to perceive them as part of the same group.

d. Movement gradients help us perceive depth.

14. *a* is the answer. Aparna's sensory systems automatically reacted to create the afterimages. (p. 144)
   b. Constructionist is a view, not a processing type.
   c. Network processing involves accessing linked concepts.
   d. Top-down and bottom-up processing generally work together, but top-down processing is affected by expectation and motivation—neither of which was a factor in the creation of the afterimages.

15. *a* is the answer. The Pygmies live in a very dense forest; they have probably never seen something far away on the horizon. Therefore, they would not be able to watch a person or an animal approach from far away, and they perceive size as constant. (p. 139)
   b. The Pygmies are probably very good at perceptual brightness constancy. The pattern of sunlight that filters through the leaves creates patches of varying brightness. The Pygmies perceive objects that move through these patches of sunlight as being constant in brightness.
   c. To experience shape constancy, one merely needs to pick up an object and hold it at different angles. No matter what the angle, perception of the shape remains constant. The Pygmies are not prevented from doing this just because they live in a dense forest.
   d. There is no such thing as perceptual complexity.

16. *c* is the answer. (p. 144)
   a. The contribution of our sensory systems to the process of perception is called bottom-up processing. For example, lateral inhibition causes us to see edges and contrasts quite clearly. Our expectations and motivation do not alter lateral inhibition.
   b. Internal noise is the spontaneous, random firing of neurons and is unaffected by expectations and motivation.
   d. Sensitivity is influenced by internal noise, stimulus intensity, and the health of the sensory systems, not expectations or motivation.

17. *a* is the answer. Feature analysis is part of bottom-up processing. It is usually followed by top-down processing, but that is not described in the item. (pp. 144–145)

   b. There is no such thing as ecological processing; you may have been thinking of the ecological view of perception.
   c. Illusory processing is a made-up term.
   d. Top-down processing and bottom-up processing work together. Lou's top-down processing probably started as soon as the perceptual category "flower" was activated, but her inference that, for example, the flower was given to her by someone who likes her is not described in the question.

18. *c* is the answer. John has a perceptual set; he expects the footsteps on the stairs to be his wife's. (p. 147)
   a, b. Feature analysis is a type of bottom-up processing. If John had analyzed the features of the footsteps in order to determine if they were his wife's, he would not have almost kissed the landlord. John's expectations made him think that he heard his wife.
   d. There is no such thing as an auditory gradient.

19. *a* is the answer. Covert orienting is a shift of attention that isn't possible for the casual observer to see. (p. 152)
   b. An overt attention shift would be turning away from Rich to stare at a person approaching you.
   c, d. Parallel and serial processing are types of searches.

20. *c* is the answer. Parallel processing is observing all locations at once in a search. It is possible when the target stands out from the background. (p. 157)
   a. Absolute threshold is the point at which you can perceive an object 50 percent of the time; it is not a type of processing.
   b. Network processing deals more with links between stimuli than it does with searching for a target.
   d. Serial processing is necessary when people must examine more than one feature of an object before deciding if it is the target. It requires a slower, more careful search.

Now turn to the quiz analysis table at the end of this chapter to find which areas you know well and which areas you need to work on. Circle the numbers in the table for items on Quiz 2 that you answered correctly.

For each question you answered correctly, circle its number. (Quiz 1 numbers are not shaded; Quiz 2 numbers are shaded.) Are there patterns in the types of questions or the topics you got wrong that could direct your further study? Did you improve from Quiz 1 to Quiz 2?

TOPIC	TYPE OF QUESTION		
	DEFINITION	COMPREHENSION	APPLICATION
Views		1	
			1
Psychophysics			
Absolute threshold			2, 3
		2	
Signal detection		4	5, 6
			3, 4, 7
Differences			7
	5	6	
Extrasensory perception?			8
Organization			
Principles			9, 10
			8, 9, 12
Depth	11		12
	10		11
Motion			13
			13
Constancy			14
			15
Illusions, culture			15
Recognition			
Bottom-up			16
		17	14
Top-down		17	18
	16		18
Network			19
Attention			20
			19
Applications			
		20	

TOTAL CORRECT BY QUIZ:

| QUIZ 1: |
| QUIZ 2: |

Chapter 6

Consciousness

Consciousness is the awareness of both external stimuli and one's own mental activity.

OUTLINE

I. ANALYZING CONSCIOUSNESS (pp. 161–162)

The scientific study of consciousness began with Wilhelm Wundt. Today, three questions dominate the study of consciousness: What is the relationship between the mind and the body? What is the nature of consciousness? What is the relationship between mental activity and consciousness?

II. THE SCOPE OF CONSCIOUSNESS (pp. 162–170)

A. Mental Processing Without Awareness

Research on priming and the mere exposure effect indicate that many important mental operations, such as learning, can occur without awareness.

B. Focus on Research Methods: Presenting Stimuli Outside of Awareness

To investigate whether priming could have an influence if the subject was unaware of the priming, researchers used visual masking. A masking pattern was presented to one eye and a word to the other eye so that the person could not consciously see the priming word. Investigators found that the priming word still influenced later behavior; therefore, the stimuli affected people although they were unaware of it.

C. The Neuropsychology of Consciousness

Brain damage can impair consciousness. Documented cases include prosopagnosia, blindsight, and anterograde amnesia.

D. Levels of Consciousness

Mental activity that you are aware of occurs at the conscious level of experience. However, mental activity can occur outside of consciousness at the nonconscious or cognitive unconscious levels. At the nonconscious level, physiological processes that you cannot consciously monitor without the aid of biofeedback occur. The cognitive unconscious includes the preconscious, unconscious, and subconscious levels. The preconscious level contains everything that can easily be brought into consciousness. According to Sigmund Freud, at the unconscious level, sexual, aggressive, and other impulses occur, as do unacceptable thoughts and feelings that are kept out of consciousness. Those who reject Freud's view use the term subconscious to describe mental activity that is not usually accessible, such as the priming effect.

E. Thinking Critically: To What Extent Can You Be Influenced by Subliminal Perceptions?

What am I being asked to believe or accept?
Many people believe that humans can be persuaded by subliminal messages, which are detected, perceived, and overtly acted upon without conscious awareness.

What evidence is available to support the assertion?
Some research studies show that subliminal information can influence judgment and emotion.

Are there alternative ways of interpreting the evidence?
One alternative explanation of the supposed success of subliminal stimuli is the possibility that only research supporting the idea of subliminal perception has been reported. Another possibility is that people's positive expectations of subliminal stimuli (such as with self-help tapes) are more important than the subliminal message content; therefore, the findings may be due to the placebo effect.

What additional evidence would help to evaluate the alternatives?
Double-blind placebo-controlled experiments would provide empirical research results that could offer insight into the extent of the influence of subliminal perceptions.

What conclusions are most reasonable?
The evidence available to date suggests that subliminal perception does occur but that it has no potential for "mind control."

F. States of Consciousness

State of consciousness refers to the characteristics of consciousness at any particular moment. Possible states range from deep sleep to alert wakefulness, with many gradations in between. Significant changes in behavior and mental processes are characteristic of altered states of consciousness. The value of altered states of consciousness varies from culture to culture.

III. SLEEPING AND DREAMING (pp. 170–177)

Early researchers thought that sleep was a time of mental inactivity. Modern research shows, however, that sleep is actually a very active, complex state.

A. Stages of Sleep

1. *Stage 0 and Quiet Sleep.* In stage 0, you are relaxed with eyes closed but are still awake. Stages 1 through 4 are progressively deeper stages of quiet sleep. Each stage has an EEG pattern characterized by slow brain waves and accompanied by deep breathing; calm, regular heartbeat; and reduced blood pressure.

2. *REM Sleep.* REM (rapid eye movement) sleep, or active sleep, is a paradoxical state in which brain waves and other physiological functions resemble those of a person who is awake, but muscle tone resembles that of paralysis.

3. *A Night's Sleep.* We travel through the five stages of quiet and REM sleep four to six times each night. REM sleep is most frequent during the second half of the night. The amount of time spent in stages 1 to 4 and REM sleep varies with age.

B. Sleep Disorders

° Insomnia, fatigue resulting from little sleep or difficulty falling asleep, is the most common sleep disorder and is correlated with mental distress. Relaxation training, biofeedback, and sleep restriction therapy are all approaches that can decrease insomnia.

° People with narcolepsy fall, without warning, into REM sleep from an active waking state.

° Sleep apnea is a disorder in which people stop breathing momentarily while they sleep. Apnea episodes can occur hundreds of times per night, thus leaving the victim feeling tired during the day.

° Sudden infant death syndrome (SIDS) is a disorder, primarily affecting infants two to four months old, in which a baby stops breathing and dies. Doctors now recommend that babies sleep on their backs to keep them from accidentally suffocating in soft bedding.

° Nightmares are frightening dreams that can occur during REM sleep. Night terrors occur during stage 4 and are characterized by horrific images, screaming upon wakening, and difficulty in calming down afterwards.

° Sleepwalking, which is most common among children, is walking during non-REM sleep. REM behavior disorder, a condition similar to sleepwalking, occurs during REM sleep. In this condition, the normal paralysis that occurs during REM sleep is absent, and the person acts out his or her dreams.

C. Why Do People Sleep?

1. *Sleep as a Circadian Rhythm.* Humans have a built-in biological clock that is linked to light and dark environmental cues. Jet lag and its accompanying symptoms of fatigue and irritability are examples of what happens when the sleep-wake cycle is interrupted. Human circadian rhythms are "clocked" by a brain structure called the suprachiasmatic nucleus.

2. *The Functions of Sleep.* Sleep is necessary for resting and restoring the body. REM sleep may help maintain the activity of neurons that use norepinephrine. It may also be a time for developing, checking, and expanding the brain's nerve connections. Finally, REM sleep may help consolidate what has been learned during the day.

D. Dreams and Dreaming

Dreams are storylike sequences of images, sensations, and perceptions that occur during REM sleep. Lucid dreamers know when they are dreaming. Some theories suggest that dreaming helps mammals process and consolidate information of great personal significance or survival value. Psychodynamic theory suggests that dreams express unconscious wishes. The activation-synthesis theory suggests that dreams represent efforts to make sense of random signals sent to the cortex. Another theory is that dreams may help people solve problems while sleeping.

IV. HYPNOSIS (pp. 177–179)

Hypnosis is an altered state of consciousness brought on by special techniques and characterized by responsiveness to suggestions for changes in perceptions and behavior.

A. Experiencing Hypnosis

° Procedures for inducing <u>hypnosis</u> focus people's attention on a restricted, often monotonous set of stimuli while asking them to shut out everything else as they imagine certain feelings. <u>Hypnotically susceptible</u> people are more imaginative, have a tendency to fantasize, can focus their attention for long periods, and are able to process information quickly and effortlessly.

° Under hypnosis, people respond to suggestions and can appear to forget their names or even display <u>age regression</u>. <u>Posthypnotic suggestions</u> affect behavior after hypnosis has ended. Some people experience <u>posthypnotic amnesia</u>, which is an inability to remember what happened under hypnosis. Hypnotized people exhibit reduced planfulness (the ability to initiate action on their own), redistributed attention, increased ability to fantasize, reduced reality testing, and enhanced ability to role-play.

B. Explaining Hypnosis

Three major theories attempt to explain hypnosis. According to <u>role theory</u>, subjects under hypnosis merely act in accordance with the hypnotized role. They are not in a special state; they simply comply with the hypnotist. According to <u>state theory</u>, hypnotized people experience an altered state of consciousness. According to <u>dissociation theory</u>, hypnotized subjects dissociate, or split, various aspects of their behavior and perceptions from the "self" that normally controls these functions. When hypnotized, these subjects are sharing some of this control with the hypnotist.

C. Applications of Hypnosis

Hypnosis has been used to decrease pain from surgery, childbirth, headaches, and cancer. More controversially, it has been used in attempts to enhance memory.

V. LINKAGES: MEDITATION, HEALTH, AND STRESS (pp. 179–180)

<u>Meditation</u> is an altered state of consciousness characterized by inner peace, calmness, and tranquility. Most types of meditation share common characteristics, including a method for focusing, a quiet environment, a comfortable position, a mental device to organize attention, and a passive attitude. Physiological effects include decreases in respiration rate, heart rate, muscle tension, blood pressure, and oxygen consumption, along with the appearance of alpha-wave activity. People who meditate regularly report experiencing decreases in stress-related problems such as anxiety and high blood pressure.

VI. PSYCHOACTIVE DRUGS (pp. 180–188)

<u>Psychoactive drugs</u> cause psychological changes by altering the functioning of the brain. <u>Psychopharmacology</u> is the study of psychoactive drugs.

A. Psychopharmacology

Psychoactive drugs or substances influence the interaction between neurotransmitters and receptors. These drugs get into the brain through the blood supply when they pass the <u>blood-brain barrier</u>. Drugs that act as <u>agonists</u> mimic the effects of neurotransmitters, whereas those acting as <u>antagonists</u> prevent neurotransmitters from binding with receptors and inhibit neurotransmitter activity.

B. The Varying Effects of Drugs

<u>Substance abuse</u> is the self-administration of drugs in ways that deviate from either medical or social norms. <u>Psychological dependence</u> occurs when a person continues to use the drug to gain a sense of well-being even when the drug produces adverse consequences. <u>Physical dependence</u> or <u>addiction</u> exists when there is an altered physiological state in which continued use of the drug is required to prevent the onset of <u>withdrawal syndrome</u>. <u>Tolerance</u> may develop with prolonged use of a drug.

1. *Expectations and Drug Effects.* People who think they have taken a drug but really haven't sometimes act as though they have because they expect to be affected by the drug. The learned expectations regarding a drug's effect vary from culture to culture.

C. Depressants

<u>Depressants</u> reduce central nervous system activity. Many depressants increase GABA neurotransmitter activity.

1. *Alcohol.* Alcohol has an impact on the dopamine, norepinephrine, serotonin, endorphin, and GABA neurotransmitters. Genetics influences people's tendency toward alcohol dependency.

2. *Barbiturates.* Also called <u>downers</u> or sleeping pills, barbiturates cause relaxation, some euphoria, and diminished attention, among other effects.

3. *Anxiolytics.* Formerly known as <u>tranquilizers</u>, these widely prescribed drugs relieve anxiety.

D. Stimulants

<u>Stimulants</u> increase behavioral and mental activity.

1. *Amphetamines.* Commonly known as <u>uppers</u> or <u>speed</u>, amphetamines increase the release, and

decrease the removal, of norepinephrine and dopamine at synapses, resulting in increased receptor activity. Amphetamines stimulate the brain and sympathetic nervous system, raising heart rate and blood pressure and constricting blood vessels. In some extreme cases, abuse of these drugs produces symptoms very similar to paranoid schizophrenia.

2. *Cocaine*. This drug's effects are similar to but more rapid than those of amphetamines. Additionally, the effects of cocaine are short-lived, which may help explain why this drug is especially addictive both psychologically and physiologically.

3. *Caffeine*. This drug decreases drowsiness, makes thought more rapid, increases physical work capacity, and raises urine production. Caffeine can cause physical dependence.

4. *Nicotine*. This drug stimulates the autonomic nervous system. Whether regular nicotine use can cause psychological and/or physiological dependence is a controversial issue.

5. *MDMA*. Also called Ecstasy, MDMA is similar to both stimulants and psychedelics. It increases the activity of dopamine and serotonin neurons. Although MDMA doesn't appear to be physically addictive, it does cause permanent brain damage and can lead to panic disorder.

E. Opiates

Opiates, which include opium, morphine, heroin, and codeine cause sleep and pain relief. These drugs are quite addictive and act as agonists for endorphins.

F. Psychedelics

Psychedelics, sometimes referred to as hallucinogens or psychotomimetics, cause a loss of contact with reality and induce changes in emotion, perception, and thought. LSD, lysergic acid diethylamide, is one of the most powerful psychedelics. LSD is not addictive, but tolerance does develop. Marijuana, Cannabis sativa, may cause relaxation, but it disrupts memory formation and muscle coordination.

KEY TERMS

1. **Consciousness** is the awareness of both external stimuli and your own mental activity. (p. 161)

Example: At this moment, you are aware of the words printed on this page. You may also be aware of noises around you, such as a radio playing or a jet flying overhead.

2. The **conscious level** of consciousness holds the thoughts and mental processes that you are aware of from moment to moment. (p. 166)

Example: You are conscious of the words you are reading at this moment.

3. The **nonconscious level** of activity includes physiological processes that you are not conscious of. Training in techniques such as biofeedback can make you conscious of them indirectly. (p. 166)

Example: Your brain is sensing the amount of sugar in your blood, but you cannot consciously experience this activity, even if you try to attend to it.

4. The **preconscious level** of activity stores sensations, memories, inferences, and assumptions that are not at the conscious level but that can be easily brought into consciousness. (p. 167)

Example: Before reading this sentence, you probably did not feel your socks or your underwear on your skin. But now that you are attending to them, you can feel these physical sensations. They were at the preconscious level but were easily brought into consciousness, in this case by a shift in attention.

5. The **unconscious level** of activity, according to Freud, holds sexual, aggressive, and other impulses as well as once-conscious but unacceptable thoughts and feelings that would cause anxiety if they became conscious again. (p. 167)

Example: A wish to kill your sister is a thought that could cause you anxiety. According to Freud, this thought would be kept in the unconscious to prevent it from doing so.

6. The **subconscious level** of mental activity includes mental processes that are important but normally inaccessible. Unlike Freud's unconscious, subconscious material isn't necessarily negative. (p. 167)

Example: In studies of priming, people could not remember having seen certain words on a study list, but could solve anagrams of those words faster than words they had not seen. The influence of having studied the words was subconscious and inaccessible.

7. **State of consciousness** refers to the characteristics of consciousness at any particular moment. (p. 169)

8. **Altered states of consciousness** occur when changes in the stream of consciousness are noticeably different from normal waking experience. (pp. 169–170)

9. **Quiet sleep** is a term for the first four stages of sleep, when breathing is slow, heartbeat is regular, and blood pressure is reduced. Each stage of quiet sleep is differentiated by a change in the EEG. For example, K-complexes and sleep spindles appear in stages 2 and 3, and delta waves occur in stage 4 more than 50 percent of the time. (p. 170)

> *REMEMBER:* These four stages are called quiet sleep because, in comparison to REM sleep, body and brain activity are relatively calm and quiet.

10. **REM (Rapid eye movement) sleep**, or **active sleep**, is characterized by EEG and physiological measures (heart rate, respiration, blood pressure) that are similar to those that occur when the person is awake. During REM sleep, the eyes move rapidly back and forth, and muscle tone decreases to the point of near-paralysis. (p. 171)

> *REMEMBER:* This stage is called active because physiologically our bodies and brains are very active (except for the muscles).

11. **Insomnia** is the inability to fall or stay asleep. People with insomnia report feeling tired during the day. (p. 172)

> *REMEMBER:* The Latin word in means "no," "not," or "without." *Somnus* means "sleep." Therefore, insomnia means "without sleep."

12. **Narcolepsy** is a disorder in which people fall directly into REM sleep from an active, waking state. They experience all the physiological changes that occur during REM sleep, including reduced muscle tone. (p. 173)

13. **Sleep apnea** is a disorder in which people stop breathing momentarily while sleeping, up to hundreds of times per night. Apnea episodes wake the sleepers, and thus people suffering from this disorder feel unrested in the morning and tired throughout the day. (p. 173)

14. In **sudden infant death syndrome (SIDS)**, a sleeping baby stops breathing but does not awaken and therefore suffocates. (p. 173)

15. **Nightmares** are frightening dreams that occur during REM sleep. (p. 173)

16. **Night terrors**, which occur during stage 4 sleep, are frightening non-REM dreams that bring on intense fear after waking. These fearful episodes may last for as long as half an hour. (p. 173)

17. **Sleepwalking**, which occurs during non-REM sleep and is most common during childhood, is walking while asleep. Awakening a sleepwalker is not dangerous. (p. 173)

18. **REM behavior disorder** is similar to sleepwalking, but it occurs during REM sleep. The normal paralysis that accompanies REM sleep is absent, thus allowing a person to act out dreams. This can be especially dangerous when the dreams are of a violent nature. (p. 173)

19. **Circadian rhythm** is a term for the normal sleep-waking cycle that occurs during a twenty-four-hour period. These cycles are governed by an internal biological clock. (p. 173)

20. **Jet lag** is a disruption of the sleep-wake cycle. Physiologically, the body is ready to wake up or sleep at an inappropriate time of day for a particular time zone. Jet lag is common among travelers arriving in time zones very different from their own, especially when traveling from west to east. (p. 174)

21. **Dreams** are storylike sequences of images, sensations, and perceptions that occur during REM sleep. (p. 176)

22. **Lucid dreaming** is knowing during a dream that you are dreaming. (p. 176)

> *REMEMBER:* The word lucid means "clear" or "readily understood." Lucid dreamers clearly know while still asleep that they are dreaming.

23. **Hypnosis** is an altered state of consciousness brought on by special techniques and characterized by susceptibility to suggestions made by the hypnotist. (p. 177)

> *Example:* Maria, who is hypnotized, believes that she can see a cat sitting on her lap because the hypnotist has suggested to her that a cat is there.

24. **Hypnotic susceptibility** is the degree to which people can become hypnotized and follow a hypnotist's suggestions. (p. 177)

25. **Age regression** is a term used to describe the phenomenon exhibited by a hypnotized subject in which he or she behaves as if reliving experiences from childhood. The person is probably recalling early memories as well as imagining and acting out past actions. (p. 177)

26. **Posthypnotic amnesia** is the inability to remember what has happened during hypnosis. (p. 177)

REMEMBER: Posthypnotic amnesia is a loss of the memory of what happened under hypnosis. This does not mean a person has amnesia in general.

27. **Posthypnotic suggestions** are instructions that are given during hypnosis and that a person follows after the hypnotic state ends. These suggestions wear off in minutes, hours, or days. (p. 177)

Example: Eric, while hypnotized, was told that he would forget the number three. After he awoke, the hypnotist asked Eric to count the number of fingers on his hands. Eric counted eleven because he had skipped the number three.

REMEMBER: Post means "after." Posthypnotic suggestions are directions to be followed after a person is no longer hypnotized.

28. The **role theory** of hypnosis states that people only play the "role" of being hypnotized, which includes complying with the hypnotist's directions. (p. 178)

29. The **state theory** of hypnosis maintains that hypnosis is a special altered state of consciousness. Supporters of the state theory believe that real, significant changes in basic mental processes take place during hypnosis. (p. 178)

30. **Dissociation theory** contends that hypnosis is a splitting of the central control of thought processes and behavior. The hypnotized person agrees to give some of the control to the hypnotist. (p. 178)

31. **Psychoactive drugs** bring about psychological changes by affecting the physiological functioning of the brain. (p. 180)

Example: LSD, a psychedelic, changes the perception of sensory information and drastically alters thought processes.

32. **Psychopharmacology** is the study of psychoactive drugs. (p. 180)

33. A **neurotransmitter system** is a set of neurons that tend to use the same neurotransmitter. (p. 180)

Example: The cholinergic neurotransmitter system uses acetylcholine.

34. The **blood-brain barrier** is part of the structure of the blood vessels that supply the brain. Many chemicals cannot permeate the barrier, and thus do not have access to brain tissue. (p. 180)

35. **Agonists** are drugs that mimic the effects of a particular neurotransmitter by binding to its receptors. (p. 180)

Example: Agonists for endorphins stimulate endorphin receptors, resulting in the same mood-elevating response as an endorphin would cause.

36. **Antagonists** prevent neurotransmitters from having an effect by blocking receptors' ability to accept specific neurotransmitters. (p. 181)

Example: Naloxone, an endorphin antagonist, keeps endorphins from binding with receptors, thereby preventing a "high."

37. **Substance abuse** is the self-administration of drugs in ways that are disapproved of by one's culture. (p. 181)

38. **Psychological dependence** is the process whereby a person needs to continue taking a drug, despite its adverse effects, in order to maintain a sense of well-being. (p. 181)

39. **Physical dependence**, or **addiction**, is the process whereby the body has a physical need for a drug. Addicts who discontinue drug use typically experience very unpleasant, and often dangerous, withdrawal symptoms. (p. 181)

Example: Carol's addiction to a barbiturate became evident when, after attempting to quit using the drug, she experienced restlessness, violent outbursts, convulsions, and hallucinations.

40. **Tolerance**, a by-product of addiction, is the process whereby repeated use of an addictive substance results in the body's requiring ever-increasing amounts of the drug to achieve the same psychological and physical effects. (p. 181)

Example: After using cocaine daily for several weeks, Jesse began to need more and more of the drug to achieve the same "high" he had initially experienced.

41. A **withdrawal syndrome** is what occurs when a drug to which a person is physically addicted is removed. Symptoms vary from drug to drug but usually include an intense craving for the drug and its effects. (p. 181)

42. **Depressants**, which include alcohol, barbiturates, and anxiolytics, reduce activity in the central nervous system. (p. 182)

REMEMBER: Depressants usually make a person sedate or calm.

43. **Stimulants** increase behavioral activity. They include amphetamines, cocaine, nicotine, caffeine, and MDMA. Overdoses of cocaine, especially of crack cocaine, can be deadly. (p. 184)

44. **Opiates**, including opium, morphine, heroin, and codeine, produce sleep and pain relief. These substances are highly addictive, and overdoses can be fatal. (p. 186)

REMEMBER: In Chapter 3 you learned that your brain produces a class of neurotransmitters called <u>endorphins</u>, which have effects similar to those of morphine.

45. **Psychedelics**, such as LSD and marijuana, cause a loss of contact with reality and changes in thought, perception, and emotion. Because many of these changes are similar to symptoms of psychotic forms of mental illness, these drugs are sometimes referred to as <u>psychotomimetics</u>, meaning they mimic psychosis. (p. 186)

FILL-IN-THE-BLANKS KEY TERMS

This section will help you check your factual knowledge of the key terms introduced in this chapter. Fill in each blank with the appropriate key term from the list of key terms above.

1. When consciousness is characterized by changes from normal waking thought and behavior, a person is said to be in a(n) _____.

2. Physiological processes of which we are unaware, such as brain activity and blood pressure, occur at the _____ level of consciousness.

3. Stages of sleep characterized by slow brain waves are called _____.

4. People who report not being able to go to sleep have _____.

5. _____ occurs when infants die because they did not awaken from an accidental interruption of their breathing.

6. Acting out dreams during active sleep is characteristic of a person who suffers from _____.

7. The sleep-waking cycle that occurs in humans during a twenty-four-hour period is called a _____.

8. People who involuntarily fall directly into REM sleep even while engaging in activities suffer from _____.

9. The awareness of the fact that one is having a dream while it is occurring is called _____.

10. The instructions given during hypnosis that a person will follow while in a nonhypnotic state are called _____.

11. The theory that suggests that hypnotism is a phenomenon in which subjects voluntarily act as they believe hypnotized people should act is called _____.

12. A person with a physical need for a drug is experiencing _____.

13. _____ are drugs that reduce central nervous system activity.

14. Drugs that are highly addictive and produce pain relief belong to the class called _____.

15. _____ can cause hallucinations and changes in thought, perception, and emotion.

Total Correct (See answer key) _____

LEARNING OBJECTIVES

1. Define <u>consciousness</u>. (p. 161)

2. Describe the three main questions that dominate the psychological study of consciousness today. (*HINT:* Include dualism and materialism, the Cartesian theater versus the multiple drafts view of consciousness, and the link between mental activity and conscious awareness.) (pp. 161–162)

3. Describe priming and the mere exposure effect. (pp. 163–164)

4. Discuss the experiments that used visual masking to study the priming effect. (pp. 164–165)

5. Describe the effects of prosopagnosia, blindsight, and anterograde amnesia on consciousness. (p. 165)

6. Distinguish among the various levels of conscious activity: <u>conscious</u>, <u>nonconscious</u>, <u>preconscious</u>, <u>unconscious</u>, and <u>subconscious</u>. Give an example of each. (pp. 166–167)

7. Define subliminal perception. Discuss the debate about the degree to which people's behavior can be influenced by subliminal perception. (pp. 167–169)

8. Define <u>state of consciousness</u> and <u>altered state of consciousness</u>. (pp. 169–170)

9. Compare and contrast quiet and active sleep. List the stages of quiet sleep. (pp. 170–171)

10. Explain the differences among the EEGs of each sleep stage. Your answer should include descriptions of alpha waves, sleep spindles, K complexes, and delta waves. (pp. 170–171)

11. Define REM (rapid eye movement) sleep. Discuss the physiological changes that occur during this stage of sleep. Describe a night's sleep. (pp. 171–172)

12. Discuss the symptoms of insomnia, narcolepsy, sleep apnea, sudden infant death syndrome (SIDS), nightmares, night terrors, sleepwalking, and REM behavior disorder, and indicate during which stages of sleep they occur. (pp. 172–173)

13. Define circadian rhythm and explain its role in sleep patterns. Discuss jet lag and other effects of interfering with the human body clock. (pp. 173–174)

14. Define REM rebound. Discuss the various hypotheses on the reasons for quiet sleep and dreaming. (pp. 174–176)

15. Define dreams and lucid dreaming. (p. 176)

16. Discuss the various theories that explain why people dream, including wish fulfillment, activation-synthesis theory, and problem-solving theory. (pp. 176–177)

17. Define hypnosis and describe the process of becoming hypnotized. (p. 177)

18. Define hypnotic susceptibility, age regression, posthypnotic suggestions, and posthypnotic amnesia. Describe the changes people experience during hypnosis. (pp. 177–178)

19. Compare and contrast the role, state, and dissociation theories of hypnosis. (pp. 178–179)

20. List some of the applications of hypnosis. (p. 179)

21. Define meditation. List the common characteristics of meditation techniques, and describe their effects. (pp. 179–180)

22. Define psychoactive drugs and psychopharmacology. Explain the function of the blood-brain barrier and discuss how agonist and antagonist drugs work. (pp. 180–181)

23. Define substance abuse. (p. 181)

24. Define psychological dependence and physical dependence. Explain the mechanisms of withdrawal syndrome and tolerance. (p. 181)

25. Explain the role of expectations in the influence of drugs on behavior. (p. 182)

26. Define depressant. Describe the effects of alcohol, barbiturates, and anxiolytics on the nervous system and behavior. (pp. 182–184)

27. Define stimulant. Describe the effects of amphetamines, cocaine, caffeine, nicotine, and MDMA on the nervous system and behavior. (pp. 184–186)

28. Define opiates. Describe the effects of opium, morphine, codeine, and heroin on the nervous system. (p. 186)

29. Define psychedelic. Describe the effects of LSD and marijuana on the nervous system and behavior. (pp. 186–188)

CONCEPTS AND EXERCISES

No. 1: Types of Consciousness

Completing this exercise should help you to achieve Learning Objective 6.

Several types of activities are described in the following list. Decide whether these activities are conscious, preconscious, nonconscious, or unconscious. Answers may be used more than once or not at all.

1. Belinda, enjoying the taste of her favorite food, thanks her mother for preparing it. _____

2. Carmen is putting an adhesive bandage on a cut. She cannot feel the neural activity in her brain that is directing her hand movements. _____

3. Leslie Anne has been in a car accident. She is so busy helping people that she does not feel the pain from her broken collarbone. _____

No. 2: Stages of Sleep at a Slumber Party

Completing this exercise should help you to achieve Learning Objectives 11 and 12.

Joanna's daughter is having a slumber party. The noise died down about one hour ago. Joanna decides to see if everyone is asleep. Match the listed stages of sleep or sleep disorders with the description of what Joanna finds when she checks on the girls. Answers may be used more than once or not at all.

1. LaVonne is perfectly still except for a few twitches of her face and hands. Joanna notices that the girl's

eyes are moving rapidly back and forth even though they are closed. _____

2. Joanna spies Isabella in the corner of the room all curled up but clearly still awake. She tells Joanna that it is always hard for her to fall asleep no matter what the time. _____

3. Suddenly Brenda sits up in her sleeping bag. Staring straight ahead, she lets out a bloodcurdling scream. It takes Joanna half an hour to calm her. What has Brenda just experienced? _____

4. Joanna counts only six girls in the room. She knows that there should be seven. She makes a quick search of the house and finds Juliette stumbling around the living room, still asleep. _____

- ° Hypersomnia
- ° Insomnia
- ° Night terrors
- ° Nightmares
- ° REM sleep
- ° Stage 1 sleep
- ° Sleepwalking

CRITICAL THINKING

Sam and Martina have been put on a case involving a robbery at a house in the country. The thieves left no marks on any doors or windows. Sam assumes, given the rural location, that the owners didn't lock the house every night and so asks the husband what their habits are regarding the doors and windows. The owner, named Jack, says, "We used to live in the city where we locked our doors every night. When we moved out here, we just kept up the habit. I lock up every night while Leona is gettin' ready for bed. And, no, we haven't given a key to anyone else." Sam, however, is convinced that Jack must have given keys to someone else and then forgotten about it.

Meanwhile, Martina and Leona are chatting like long lost friends and eating pie in the kitchen. Leona is describing a hypnosis demonstration in which she has just participated. The hypnotist told her that for two weeks she would go outside and howl at the moon like a dog. She laughs and says, "For the first couple of nights, Jack came out just to see if I would do it, but now he sleeps right through the noise. I still don't believe it myself." Martina asks, "Who gets up first in the morning, you or Jack?" "Oh, I don't know; it varies, I guess," Leona replies.

Sam comes grumpily into the kitchen and motions Martina over to the door for a private consultation. "I'm sure these old folks just gave the wrong kind of neighbor a key. We should go question all the neighbors in the vicinity."

Martina shakes her head slowly and tells Sam to have some pie. She says that Jack and Leona didn't give a key to anyone and that even if they did, that person didn't rob the house.

Using the five critical thinking questions in your text, the clues in the story, and what you have learned in this chapter, answer the following:

1. What is Sam's hypothesis?

2. What evidence supports Sam's hypothesis?

3. What is Martina's alternative hypothesis?

4. What evidence supports Martina's hypothesis?

PERSONAL LEARNING ACTIVITIES

1. Examine your own behavior for habits that occur at the preconscious level of consciousness. For example, do you bite your nails or twist your hair without realizing it until someone brings it to your attention? (Learning Objective 6)

2. Evaluate your amount of sleep. Do you sleep more or less on weekends? Can you tell a difference in your motivation level on days after you have had less sleep? (Learning Objective 13)

3. Keep a note pad next to your bed to write down your dreams as soon as you awaken, and on a calendar record daily events. For example, if you have an exam, a date, or a major assignment due, write down how it went. After a week of jotting down the images from your dreams and the events from your waking life, try to see if there is a connection between the two. Do you see wish fulfillment or problem solving in your dreams? (Learning Objective 16)

4. Study your use of any psychoactive drugs you ordinarily ingest. For instance, do you have a caffeinated drink in the morning and find that you feel drowsy without one? Are there times when you are more likely to need a pain reliever, an allergy medication, or a sleep aid? (Learning Objective 22)

5. While you watch a few of your favorite television programs, note any statements or actions that relate to drug use. Are there misperceptions about the effects of any drugs? Do people casually mention that they "have" to get a cup of coffee or an alcoholic drink? What types of messages relate to legal and illegal drug use? (Learning Objectives 22, 25, 26, 27, 28, 29)

MULTIPLE-CHOICE QUESTIONS

SAMPLE QUIZ 1

1. Kelly and Juanita are having an argument. Kelly believes that consciousness is separate from the mind, while Juanita believes that consciousness and the mind are the same thing. Kelly believes in _____, and Juanita believes in _____.
   a. materialism; dualism
   b. dualism; materialism
   c. multiple drafts view; materialism
   d. dualism; multiple drafts view

2. According to Freud, unacceptable thoughts and sexual and aggressive impulses reside in the _____ level.
   a. nonconscious
   b. preconscious
   c. subconscious
   d. unconscious

3. Heather never really noticed the framed prints of famous Rembrandt paintings that lined the hallways of the English building. When Heather was in an art appreciation class the next semester, she found that she liked Rembrandt paintings more than those by other artists, although she had never had a preference for his work before. Heather has experienced
   a. the prosopagnosia effect.
   b. the mere-exposure effect.
   c. priming.
   d. visual masking.

4. The memories of the Rembrandt paintings that caused Heather's liking of them are stored at the _____ level of consciousness.
   a. nonconscious
   b. preconscious
   c. subconscious
   d. unconscious

5. Lisa can never seem to remember to take off her watch before she steps into the shower. This is probably because the sensation of the watch on her arm occurs at the _____ level.
   a. nonconscious
   b. preconscious
   c. subconscious
   d. unconscious

6. Karin has purchased a tape that is supposed to contain subliminal messages to help her lose weight. According to the "Thinking Critically" section in your text, Karin's success in losing weight will most likely depend on
   a. the content of the subliminal message.
   b. her expectation that the subliminal messages will help.
   c. how relaxed the subliminal messages make her feel.
   d. the number of times the subliminal message occurs.

7. Denise is not acting like her usual self. Because she's had too much alcohol to drink, she readily accepts her friends' suggestion that they use an alley as a restroom. Denise is not considering the consequences of her actions; therefore, Denise is most likely
   a. in an altered state.
   b. in a preconscious state.
   c. under the influence of priming.
   d. under the influence of a stimulant.

8. An EEG taken during REM sleep would most closely resemble which other stage of sleep?
   a. Stage 1
   b. Stage 2
   c. Stage 3
   d. Stage 4

9. Last night Sybil woke up screaming. She told her mother that she saw an image of someone repeatedly stabbing her. It took her mother almost thirty minutes to calm her down. Sybil was probably in what stage of sleep just before she awoke?
   a. Stage 0
   b. Stage 2
   c. Stage 4
   d. REM

10. REM sleep is most prevalent during
    a. infancy.
    b. puberty.
    c. young adulthood.
    d. old age.

11. Benjamin Franklin said, "Early to bed, early to rise, makes a man healthy, wealthy, and wise." A psychologist who knew about circadian rhythms would probably say which of the following?
    a. "Whenever you bed, whenever you rise, a change in your rhythm will be your demise."
    b. "Bed when you will, rise when you wish, it just doesn't make that big of a dif."
    c. "Early to bed, early to rise, makes a man grisly and grumpy, but wise."
    d. None of the above

12. Which of the following is *not* a current theory of why we dream?
    a. As we dream, our nerve connections are developing, checking, and expanding.
    b. We dream to satisfy unconscious urges.
    c. Dreaming allows us to solidify what we have learned the previous day.
    d. Dreaming reduces our level of mental activity, heart rate, and blood pressure.

13. Khalid's therapist suggests that they use hypnosis to help him to quit smoking. During hypnosis the therapist tells Khalid that his next sight of a cigarette will make him feel nauseous. The therapist most likely is using _____ to help Khalid.
    a. age regression
    b. posthypnotic amnesia
    c. posthypnotic suggestion
    d. reduced planfulness

14. Eli's hypnotist suggested that Eli saw a big fluffy cat sitting in the chair next to him. Although no cat was present, Eli said that he could see its tail swishing back and forth. This is characteristic of which type of hypnotic behavior?
    a. Reduced planfulness
    b. Role-playing
    c. Reduced reality testing
    d. Redistributed attention

15. If Eli is pretending that he sees a cat seated next to him only because the situation provided him with a socially acceptable reason for seeing things that do not exist, this would support the _____ theory of hypnosis.
    a. dissociation
    b. lucid
    c. role
    d. state

16. Norman has found himself a quiet spot, settled into a comfortable position, started using his mantra, and assumed a passive attitude. He is about to
    a. start meditating.
    b. be hypnotized.
    c. go to sleep.
    d. start daydreaming.

17. Tolerance is
    a. a need for larger and larger amounts of a drug to achieve the same effect.
    b. a physical need for a drug.
    c. dependence on a drug in order to function.
    d. a drug buildup that prevents overdosing.

18. Abel's endorphin receptors were activated by the drug he took to reduce the pain from his broken arm. Therefore, the drug can be described as a(n)
    a. agonist.
    b. antagonist.
    c. hypnogogic.
    d. psychotomimetic.

19. The drug Abel took is most likely a(n)
    a. depressant.
    b. opiate.
    c. psychedelic.
    d. stimulant.

20. Which of the following is true about the consumption of alcohol?
    a. Eating prior to excessive drinking will prevent you from getting drunk.
    b. It is impossible to overdose on alcohol.
    c. Alcohol is a stimulant.
    d. Alcohol can cause memory problems, poor motor coordination, and reduced inhibitions.

Total Correct (See answer key) _____

SAMPLE QUIZ 2

Use this quiz to reassess your learning after taking Quiz 1 and reviewing the chapter.

1. A person who agreed with the approach to the mind-body problem known as _____ would most likely believe that brain surgery would *not* affect a person's conscious mind.
    a. Cartesian theater
    b. dualism
    c. materialism
    d. multiple drafts

2. Miranda, following brain damage, states that she is blind. But when her doctors ask her to guess what she is facing, she can accurately name the object. Miranda's brain damage has caused
    a. anterograde amnesia.
    b. blindsight.
    c. implicit memories.
    d. prosopagnosia.

3. Material that can be easily brought into consciousness is at the _____ level.
    a. nonconscious
    b. preconscious
    c. subconscious
    d. unconscious

4. Lorena dreamed that her friends kept giving her their books to carry. Soon Lorena was crushed under the huge stack of books she carried. In describing the dream, Lorena said, "I don't know why I had this dream; my friends are the pest. Oops, I mean the best." Lorena's Freudian psychoanalyst suggests that she can't consciously admit that she is angry with her friends. Lorena's therapist would most likely say that those negative feelings are kept at the _____ level of consciousness.
   a. nonconscious
   b. preconscious
   c. subconscious
   d. unconscious

5. Which of the following is the best example of a process operating at the nonconscious level?
   a. Alice names all her teachers from kindergarten to the present.
   b. Brian accidentally calls his sister "creepy" instead of "sleepy" because he dislikes her, although he is not consciously aware of it.
   c. Chris now likes country music, but doesn't realize that it's due to hearing it at work.
   d. Derek uses biofeedback to help him control his blood pressure.

6. Your friend Jay suggests that to increase the sale of Chocomints at your next charity film festival you should insert the subliminal message "Eat Chocomints" in the film. According to the "Thinking Critically" section in the text, you should tell Jay that the "Eat Chocomints" message most likely would
   a. anger the audience.
   b. be more effective than a regular advertising campaign.
   c. have to appear more than once a minute to have an effect.
   d. not affect the audience.

7. Altered states of consciousness are characterized by
   a. increased reality testing.
   b. changes in perception.
   c. increased self-control.
   d. planfulness.

8. Sleep stages 2 and 3 are distinguished from other stages of sleep by the presence of
   a. reduced blood pressure.
   b. a regular heartbeat.
   c. sleep spindles.
   d. slow breathing.

9. Snookers the cat has decided that he wants a snack. However, his owner is taking a nap. Despite several minutes of tap-dancing on his owner's face, Snookers cannot wake her up. The cat's owner has most likely been asleep for
   a. no more than five minutes.
   b. no more than ten minutes.
   c. at least thirty minutes.
   d. This cannot be determined.

10. Delta just awakened from a very strange dream. She thought an evil butcher was chasing her with a knife and urging her to do aerobics. The dream became very scary, but because it took place in REM sleep, she often had the feeling that she couldn't move or scream. Delta's dream would be classified as a
   a. REM behavior disorder.
   b. narcoleptic vision.
   c. nightmare.
   d. night terror.

11. Ruby has had a terrible evening. Just as her boyfriend, Kato, started to propose to her, he fell asleep. Ruby would feel better if she knew that Kato has
   a. hypersomnia.
   b. narcolepsy.
   c. insomnia.
   d. night terrors.

12. Which of the following people would most likely have the greatest amount of REM sleep?
   a. A person who goes to bed and gets up at exactly the same time each day
   b. A ninety-year-old person on vacation
   c. A student who has been studying constantly for three days and three nights
   d. A person who has just recovered from hypersomnia

13. Hypnosis has been used to reduce
   a. nausea due to chemotherapy.
   b. surgical bleeding.
   c. pain.
   d. all of the above.

14. An example of a successful posthypnotic suggestion to Brendan is
   a. Brendan believes during hypnosis that he is unable to see.
   b. Brendan is instructed during hypnosis to cluck like a chicken whenever anyone says "Hi," and he does this when he is no longer hypnotized.
   c. Brendan cannot remember what happened while he was hypnotized.
   d. telling Brendan while he is no longer hypnotized that his pants are ripped and he checks them.

15. Brendan believes during hypnosis that he cannot see. Later, Brendan tells you that he felt like he was sharing control over his actions with the hypnotist. It was as if his ability to see was not part of him while he was hypnotized. Brendan's description of his experience agrees most with the _____ theory of hypnosis.
    a. dissociation
    b. lucid
    c. role
    d. state

16. A mantra is
    a. a person trained in meditation.
    b. the object or sound the meditator focuses on.
    c. the position a person assumes when meditating.
    d. a special form of meditation.

17. A molecule that fits into a receptor and blocks neurotransmitters from binding is a(n)
    a. agonist.
    b. antagonist.
    c. placebo.
    d. cytoblocker.

18. One night a young man experiencing hallucinations is brought to a hospital emergency room. Which of the following drugs could his doctor rule out as a possible cause of the hallucinations?
    a. PCP
    b. Cocaine
    c. Valium
    d. LSD

19. Which of the following is *not* an opiate?
    a. Cocaine
    b. Heroin
    c. Morphine
    d. Opium

20. Noel has just taken a drug that increases the activity of the neurotransmitter norepinephrine. Which of the following drugs has Noel taken?
    a. Alcohol
    b. LSD
    c. Cocaine
    d. Opium

Total Correct (See answer key) _____

ANSWERS TO FILL-IN-THE-BLANKS KEY TERMS

1. altered state of consciousness (pp. 169–170)
2. nonconscious (p. 166)

3. quiet sleep (p. 170)
4. insomnia (p. 172)
5. sudden infant death syndrome (p. 173)
6. REM behavior disorder (p. 173)
7. circadian rhythm (p. 173)
8. narcolepsy (p. 173)
9. lucid dreaming (p. 176)
10. posthypnotic suggestions (p. 177)
11. role theory (p. 178)
12. physical dependence or addiction (p. 181)
13. depressants (p. 182)
14. opiates (p. 186)
15. psychedelics (p. 186)

ANSWERS TO CONCEPTS AND EXERCISES

No. 1: Types of Consciousness

1. *Conscious.* Belinda is aware of the taste of the food in her mouth. (p. 166)

2. *Nonconscious.* Carmen is not and cannot become aware of the neural activity in her motor cortex. (p. 166)

3. *Preconscious.* Leslie Anne has her attention focused on the people who need her help. Once she attends to the pain in her collarbone, it will easily come into consciousness. (p. 167)

No. 2: Stages of Sleep at a Slumber Party

1. *REM sleep.* LaVonne is not moving because muscle tone decreases to near-paralysis during this stage. The eyes move rapidly back and forth. (p. 171)

2. *Insomnia.* This sleep disorder is characterized by an inability to fall asleep. (p. 172)

3. *Night terrors.* Night terrors are vivid and terrifying dreams that occur during stage 4 sleep. It often takes quite a while to calm people after they have a night terror experience. (p. 173)

4. *Sleepwalking.* Juliette is taking a tour of the house, but she is still asleep. This is sleepwalking. (p. 173)

ANSWERS TO CRITICAL THINKING

1. Sam's hypothesis is that someone used a key to get into the house.

2. The evidence in support of the hypothesis is that none of the doors or windows had marks on them typical of forcible entry. Sam also believes that Jack has just forgotten that he gave a key to someone.

3. Martina believes that Leona has probably gone out every night since her hypnosis escapade to "howl at the moon." She probably hasn't remembered to lock the doors when she comes back in because that has been Jack's responsibility for years. Therefore, any passing burglar could have just walked into the house.

4. The evidence supporting Martina's hypothesis is that if either Jack or Leona consistently got up first and left the house each morning, one of them would probably have noticed the unlocked door. However, if the first person up varied, then each probably assumed the other had unlocked the door on the way out of the house.

ANSWERS TO MULTIPLE-CHOICE QUESTIONS

Circle the question numbers you answered correctly.

Sample Quiz 1

1. *b* is the answer. (p. 162)
   a. Materialists believe that consciousness and the mind are the same thing, whereas dualists believe that consciousness is separate from the mind.
   c. A multiple drafts view of consciousness holds that conscious experience is made up of parallel streams of information.
   d. Juanita may take a multiple drafts view of consciousness, but this doesn't address her belief that the mind and consciousness are the same thing.

2. *d* is the answer. (p. 167)
   a. Nonconscious processes are those physiological activities that people cannot become directly aware of.
   b. Preconscious activities are those that are easily brought into consciousness.
   c. Priming and the mere-exposure effect are processes that take place at the subconscious level. The unconscious and subconscious are both difficult to access, but Freud believed that negative memories and desires are pushed into the unconscious.

3. *b* is the answer. Her exposure to the paintings, although not consciously noticed, caused her to like them more than other paintings. (pp. 163–164)
   a. Prosopagnosia is the inability to recognize faces. There is no such thing as the prosopagnosia effect.
   c. Priming causes people to react more quickly to stimuli they have seen before. It does not involve *liking* them more, however, as the mere-exposure effect does.
   d. Visual masking is a method used to present stimuli subliminally. The paintings were not subliminal, they just weren't noticed consciously.

4. *c* is the answer. Mere-exposure effects occur at the subconscious level. (p. 167)
   a. Nonconscious activities, such as level of brain activity are not accessible consciously.
   b. The preconscious level of consciousness contains memories that can easily become conscious.
   d. The unconscious is a Freudian term for memories and urges that cannot easily become conscious.

5. *b* is the answer. Physical sensations and memories that we can easily access are at the preconscious level of activity. When Lisa stepped into the shower, the sensation of her watch on her arm was at the preconscious level of activity. (p. 167)
   a. Nonconscious activities are those that cannot reach consciousness. Lisa did feel the watch on her arm, even if she was a bit late in doing so.
   c. Subconscious activity cannot be easily brought into consciousness. The feeling of water between watch and skin is very easy to bring into consciousness.
   d. Unconscious activity cannot be easily brought into consciousness. The unconscious is the level to which Freudians suggest our socially unacceptable desires, impulses, and wishes are banished.

6. *b* is the answer. (pp. 167–169)
   a, d. According to research, the content and number of subliminal messages will not influence a person as much as the person's belief in their effectiveness.
   c. Relaxation is not a factor known to influence the effectiveness of subliminal messages.

7. *a* is the answer. In an altered state, inhibitions are lessened and mental processing and perceptions are changed. (pp. 169–170)

b. Preconsciousness is a level of consciousness, not a state. In addition, memories at the preconscious level are easily brought to consciousness. Denise is under the influence of alcohol and may not be able to remember what occurred while she was intoxicated.

c. Priming has nothing to do with intoxication or relaxation of inhibitions.

d. Alcohol is not a stimulant.

8. *a* is the answer. The EEG during REM sleep looks similar to that of stage 1; it appears as though the person is awake. (p. 171)

b, c. The EEG shows sleep spindles and K complexes during stages 2 and 3.

d. The EEG shows delta waves during stage 4.

9. *c* is the answer. Sybil had a night terror. Night terrors, which occur in stage 4 sleep, are likely to cause a person to sit up in bed, scream, and then be difficult to calm down. (p. 173)

a. Stage 0 is the relaxed stage before falling asleep.

b. Night terrors do not occur in stage 2.

d. Nightmares are less frightening, more storylike dreams that happen mostly during REM sleep.

10. *a* is the answer. An average infant sleeps 16 hours a day; about 8 hours of that is spent in REM. (p. 172)

b, c, d. As people get older, they spend less and less time asleep. Most of the loss is a decrease in REM sleep.

11. *a* is the answer. Disrupting your circadian rhythm can make you grouchy and less productive and can cause difficulties getting to sleep. It does not really matter what times you choose to go to sleep and wake up as long as you are consistent. (pp. 173–174)

b. Your sleeping schedule does influence your productivity and happiness. If you go to bed and get up at different times every day, you will disrupt your circadian rhythm.

c. If you go to bed early and get up early on a consistent basis, your circadian rhythm will not be disrupted.

d is incorrect because *a* is a correct answer.

12. *d* is the answer. During dreaming, our mental activity, heart rate, and blood pressure are similar to those of a person who is awake. They are not decreased. (pp. 176–177)

a, b, c. These are all possible explanations of why people dream.

13. *c* is the answer. The therapist is giving a suggestion during hypnosis that will influence Khalid after he is no longer hypnotized. (p. 177)

a. In age regression, the person seemingly returns to childhood in thoughts or actions while hypnotized.

b. Posthypnotic amnesia is a person's inability to remember what happened while he or she was hypnotized.

d. A characteristic of people who are hypnotized is reduced planfulness. Khalid may tend not to initiate actions while hypnotized, but the therapist is trying to change his later behavior; therefore, this is not the best answer.

14. *c* is the answer. The ability to see things that are not there, or not to see things that are there, is the result of a reduction in reality testing. (p. 178)

a. Hypnotized people do not initiate plans on their own. They usually prefer to wait until the hypnotist tells them what to do. This is not, however, the reason Eli saw the cat when it was not there.

b. An example of role-playing would be acting like a cat or feeling as though you were someone else or a different age.

d. When attention is redistributed, one of the senses may seem to fill perceptions. For example, the hypnotist's voice may seem to be the only stimulus. Redistributed attention would not explain why Eli saw a cat that did not exist.

15. *c* is the answer. Eli is acting in accordance with the social role of being a hypnosis subject; therefore, he is not in a different state. (p. 178)

a. The dissociation theory states that people will experience changes in mental processes if enough control is relinquished to the hypnotist. (p. 178)

b. This is not a theory of hypnosis. You may have been thinking of lucid dreaming.

d. State theorists would argue that hypnosis causes an altered state of mental activity, not compliance with a social role.

16. *a* is the answer. Norman is about to start meditating. Finding a quiet spot, assuming a comfortable position, using a mantra, and taking a passive attitude are all elements of meditation methods. (p. 179)

b. Hypnotists do not normally use mantras.

c. Use of a mantra and a passive attitude is more likely to be a method of meditation than sleep inducement.

d. Daydreaming does not necessarily require a quiet spot; nor does it require a mantra.

17. *a* is the answer. (p. 181)
   b. When there is a physical need for a drug, the person is addicted or physically dependent. Physical dependence can lead to tolerance, but they are not the same phenomenon.
   c. Psychological dependence occurs when the drug user relies on a drug in order to function every day. Not taking the drug may cause psychological discomfort.
   d. No matter how long a person uses a drug, she or he can still overdose if the amount is large enough.

18. *a* is the answer. An agonist binds with a receptor and stimulates it as a usual neurotransmitter would. (p. 180)
   b. An antagonist blocks neurotransmitters from entering a receptor.
   c. Hypnogogic state is the transition from wakefulness into sleep, not a drug type.
   d. A psychotomimetic is another term for psychedelic.

19. *b* is the answer. Opiates relieve pain and cause sleep. (p. 186)
   a. A depressant reduces activity of the central nervous system, but is not used for pain relief.
   c. Psychedelics alter perceptions, but do not relieve pain.
   d. Stimulants increase activation and do not reduce pain.

20. *d* is the answer. (pp. 183–184)
   a. Eating prior to drinking may slightly delay the absorption of alcohol and therefore delay its effects, but it does not prevent them from occurring.
   b. It is possible to overdose on alcohol. The alcohol first affects the frontal cortex, then the midbrain, and finally the hindbrain.
   c. Alcohol is a depressant, which inhibits central nervous system activity.

Now turn to the quiz analysis table at the end of this chapter to find which areas you know well and which areas you need to work on. Circle the numbers in the table for items on Quiz 1 that you answered correctly.

ANSWERS TO MULTIPLE-CHOICE QUESTIONS

Circle the question numbers you answered correctly.

Sample Quiz 2

1. *b* is the answer. Dualism views the mind and brain as separate. Our consciousness can become aware of brain events but is not merely the sum of brain activity. (p. 162)
   a. The Cartesian theater view deals with the nature of consciousness, not the mind-body problem. It suggests that incoming information joins together to create one experience.
   c. Materialism views the mind and brain as one entity. Just as a piano's keys, strings, and sound board are structures that work together to create music, our brain cells create our consciousness. According to this view, therefore, a surgery that changes a person's brain would change a person's conscious mind.
   d. The multiple drafts view deals with the nature of consciousness, not the mind-body problem. It suggests that information of various sorts can be processed independently and simultaneously.

2. *b* is the answer. A person who is blind due to damage of the visual cortex may be able to process some visual information without awareness. The eyes may send on visual information to other areas, but without a functioning visual cortex the person cannot become aware of such information. People with blindsight may think they are guessing when they correctly identify the location of objects. (p. 165)
   a. Anterograde amnesia is the inability to form new memories.
   c. Implicit memories influence us without our awareness, but incoming information is not a memory.
   d. Prosopagnosia is characterized by an inability to recognize faces.

3. *b* is the answer. Preconscious memories can be recalled easily. (p. 167)
   a. Nonconscious processes are those physiological activities that people cannot become directly aware of.
   c. Subconscious activity includes thought processes that cannot easily be brought into consciousness, such as priming and mere-exposure. This label is used by those who disagree with Freud's theory about the unconscious.

d. Unconscious processes are also not easily brought into consciousness. Freud suggested that socially unacceptable urges are kept in the unconscious.

4. *d* is the answer. A Freudian would say that unacceptable thoughts and memories are kept in the unconscious to protect a person from anxiety. (p. 167)

a. Nonconscious activities are those biological activities that Lorena cannot become directly aware of.

b. The preconscious level of consciousness can be easily accessed. It includes memories that you are not aware of but could be.

c. The subconscious is similar to the unconscious, because neither is easily accessible, but Freudians did not use this term. In addition, the term subconscious is used for the level at which research-supported processes such as the mere-exposure effect and priming take place.

5. *d* is the answer. Nonconscious activity is not available to our conscious awareness. In biofeedback training, a machine would indicate Derek's blood pressure, but he could not feel it. (p. 166)

a. Alice is using her conscious memories to name her teachers.

b. Brian may have an unconscious dislike of his sister.

c. Chris may be experiencing the mere-exposure effect, which occurs at the subconscious level of consciousness.

6. *d* is the answer. Subliminal perception does not control our behavior. (pp. 168–169)

a. No evidence suggests that subliminals will anger people.

b. Regular advertising campaigns that are consciously perceived are more influential than something subliminal.

c. Presenting subliminal images more than once a minute will still not cause people to buy Chocomints.

7. *b* is the answer. People in an altered state of consciousness experience a change in mental processes significant enough for others to notice. Perceptions are altered and inhibitions are weakened. (pp. 169–170)

a. Reality testing is decreased in individuals who are in altered states of consciousness.

c. Self-control is decreased in altered states.

d. Planfulness, the ability to initiate action on one's own, is decreased in altered states.

8. *c* is the answer. Sleep spindles first appear in stage 2 sleep and last appear in stage 3 sleep. (p. 170)

a, b, d. Reduced blood pressure, regular heartbeat, and slow breathing are characteristics of all stages of quiet sleep (1 through 4).

9. *c* is the answer. During stage 4, a very deep sleep that occurs about thirty minutes after falling asleep, it is difficult to rouse someone. (pp. 170–171)

a. After five minutes the sleeper would be in stage 1 or just entering stage 2 (not deep sleep).

b. After ten minutes the sleeper would be in stage 2 or 3 (not deep sleep).

d. It can be determined. Snooker's owner is in a very deep sleep, and the timing of the first episode of stage 4 sleep can be determined from sleep-cycle research.

10. *c* is the answer. Nightmares are frightening dreams that take place during REM sleep. (p. 173)

a. REM behavior disorder is a sleep disorder characterized by lack of muscle paralysis during REM sleep. The fact that Delta couldn't move eliminates this option.

b. Narcolepsy is the abrupt switch from a waking state into REM sleep. Narcoleptic vision is not a term.

d. Night terrors occur during stage 4 sleep. They involve horrifying images that cause a person to become extremely frightened. The person may wake up with a scream and be difficult to soothe.

11. *b* is the answer. People who have narcolepsy often fall asleep in the middle of an active waking state. They immediately shift into REM sleep. Ruby would feel much better if she knew that Kato had fallen asleep because of narcolepsy, and not because he was bored with the thought of their engagement. (p. 173)

a. People with hypersomnia sleep longer than most people at night, feel tired during the day, and take one or more naps during the daytime. However, they do not fall asleep in the middle of an active waking state.

c. If Kato had insomnia, he would not be able to fall asleep at all.

d. Night terrors occur during stage 4. Ruby is worried about why Kato fell asleep, not about what happened while he was asleep.

12. *c* is the answer. When people go without REM sleep, they have more REM periods than usual when they finally do sleep. (pp. 174–176)

   a. People who go to sleep and get up at the same time every day will not have their REM periods interrupted. Therefore, their REM periods will not increase in number or length.

   b. The older people get, the less time they spend asleep. Most of the decrease is in REM sleep.

   d. People with hypersomnia have plenty of time to go through REM sleep. Upon recovery, they have no REM deficiency to correct.

13. *d* is the answer. Hypnosis has been used to help people reduce nausea from chemotherapy, surgical bleeding, and pain. (p. 179)

   a, b, c. These are all uses of hypnosis.

14. *b* is the answer. Posthypnotic suggestions are given during hypnosis but are followed after hypnosis. (p. 177)

   a. Brendan may believe he is unable to see during hypnosis due to reduced reality testing. This is not posthypnotic because it occurs during hypnosis.

   c. Not remembering what occurred while under hypnosis is posthypnotic amnesia.

   d. This sounds like a joke that could work on anyone—hypnotized or not.

15. *a* is the answer. The dissociation theory states that people will experience changes in mental processes if enough control is relinquished to the hypnotist. (pp. 178–179)

   b. This is not a theory of hypnosis. You may have been thinking of lucid dreaming.

   c. The role theory of hypnosis says that people are complying with a social role, and are not in a different state.

   d. State theorists would argue that hypnosis causes an altered state of mental activity, but they do not include releasing control to the therapist and a dissociation of abilities (like sight) from central control.

16. *b* is the answer. (p. 179)

   a. There is no special name for a person well versed in meditation.

   c. Many different types of positions have been used to meditate. Their only common characteristic is that they are comfortable.

   d. Several different techniques of meditation exist, but none of them is called a mantra.

17. *b* is the answer. Antagonists bind to a receptor but do not trigger action potentials. (p. 181)

   a. An agonist binds with a receptor, but activates it as the neurotransmitter would.

   c. A placebo is not a molecule.

   d. Cytoblocker is a made-up name. There is no such thing.

18. *c* is the answer. Valium is a tranquilizer, which does not cause hallucinations. (p. 184)

   a, b, d. PCP, prolonged cocaine use, and LSD can all cause hallucinations.

19. *a* is the answer. Cocaine is a stimulant. (p. 186)

   b, c, d. Heroin, morphine, and opium are all opiates.

20. *c* is the answer. Cocaine increases norepinephrine activity in the central nervous system. (p. 184)

   a. Alcohol is a central nervous system depressant.

   b. LSD alters activity in serotonergic neurons.

   d. Opium stimulates receptors that normally recognize endorphins, the brain's natural supply of opiate.

Now turn to the quiz analysis table at the end of this chapter to find which areas you know well and which areas you need to work on. Circle the numbers in the table for items on Quiz 2 that you answered correctly.

For each question you answered correctly, circle its number. (Quiz 1 numbers are not shaded; Quiz 2 numbers are shaded.) Are there patterns in the types of questions or the topics you got wrong that could direct your further study? Did you improve from Quiz 1 to Quiz 2?

TOPIC	TYPE OF QUESTION		
	DEFINITION	COMPREHENSION	APPLICATION
Analyzing consciousness		1	
			1
Scope of Consciousness			
Research			3
			2
Levels	2	4	5
	3		4, 5
Subliminal perception		6	
			6
States			7
	7		
Sleep and Dreams			
Sleep stages		8	
		8	9
Disorders			9
			10, 11
Reasons for sleep		10	11
			12
Dreams		12	
Hypnosis			
Experiencing			13, 14
			14
Theory			15
			15
Application			
		13	
Meditation			16
	16		
Psychoactive Drugs			
Psychopharmacology		18	
	17		

TOPIC	TYPE OF QUESTION		
	DEFINITION	COMPREHENSION	APPLICATION
Effects	17		
Classes		20	19
		19	18, 20

TOTAL CORRECT BY QUIZ:

QUIZ 1:
QUIZ 2:

Chapter 7

Learning

Learning is the modification through experience of pre-existing behavior and understanding.

OUTLINE

I. CLASSICAL CONDITIONING: LEARNING SIGNALS AND ASSOCIATIONS (pp. 198–198)

A. Pavlov's Discovery

° Ivan Pavlov's experiment was the first demonstration of classical conditioning. Pavlov's experiment had three phases. During the first phase, a natural reflex and a neutral stimulus were established. During the second phase, the neutral stimulus and the stimulus causing the natural reflex were repeatedly paired. During the third phase, the neutral stimulus alone caused some form of the natural reflex to occur.

° In classical conditioning, a neutral stimulus is paired with a stimulus that elicits a reflex or other response until the formerly neutral stimulus alone elicits a similar response. The stimulus that causes the natural reflex is called the unconditioned stimulus (UCS); the reflex itself is designated the unconditioned response (UCR). The neutral stimulus that is paired with the UCS is the conditioned stimulus (CS), and the learned response to the conditioned stimulus is the conditioned response (CR).

B. Conditioned Responses Over Time: Extinction and Spontaneous Recovery

The CS will continue to elicit a CR only if the UCS continues to appear at least some of the time. If the CS and UCS are unpaired (that is, the CS is not followed by the UCS), the CR gets weaker and weaker and undergoes extinction. However, the learned relationship between the CS and the UCS isn't completely forgotten, as is demonstrated by reconditioning and spontaneous recovery. In reconditioning, the relationship between the CS and the UCS is relearned as the stimuli are paired once again. This time the CS will elicit the CR much more quickly. Spontaneous recovery occurs when, after no presentation of either the CS or the UCS for a period of time, a single presentation of the CS elicits the CR.

C. Stimulus Generalization and Discrimination

Stimulus generalization occurs when a stimulus similar but not identical to the original stimulus also elicits a response. Stimulus discrimination is a complementary process through which organisms learn to differentiate between stimuli that are similar but not identical to the CS.

D. The Signaling of Significant Events

In classical conditioning, the CS acts as a signal that the UCS is about to appear. Situations that highlight and strengthen the CS-UCS relationship will produce stronger CRs.

1. *Timing*. Classical conditioning produces the strongest CRs when the CS precedes the UCS by about one-half second.

2. *Predictability*. A strong CR will be developed if a very noticeable CS is reliably followed by the UCS.

3. *Signal Strength*. The relationship between the CS and the UCS is learned faster as the salience or intensity of the CS and UCS increases.

4. *Attention*. Often, more than one CS is associated with a UCS. The CS that is most attended to will be the best predictor of the UCS.

5. *Second-Order Conditioning*. Second-order conditioning occurs when a second conditioned stimulus predicts the presence of the first conditioned stimulus, which predicts the presence of the UCS. For example, UCS causes UCR, CS1 predicts UCS, CS1 causes CR, CS1 causes CR, CS2 predicts CS1, and CS2 causes CR.

6. *Biopreparedness*. Humans and animals may be innately likely or biologically "prepared" to learn certain adaptive associations. Nausea is likely to be a conditioned response to an internal stimulus such as taste (conditioned taste aversion), and pain is likely to be a conditioned response to an external stimulus such as noise.

E. Some Applications of Classical Conditioning

1. *Learned Immune Responses.* Immune responses can be classically conditioned by pairing a neutral stimulus (CS) with a drug (UCS) that, for example, prevents or reduces an allergy attack or increases circulating natural killer cells. After conditioning, the CS alone will elicit a conditioned immune response.

2. *Phobias.* Phobias are fears of objects or situations that are not harmful. Classical conditioning can both produce (via stimulus generalization) and eliminate (through systematic desensitization) phobias.

3. *Predator Control.* Some ranchers have set out mutton laced with lithium for wolves and coyotes. The dizziness and severe nausea (UCR) caused by the lithium becomes associated with the smell and taste of mutton (CS), thus making sheep an undesirable meal.

II. LINKAGES: LEARNING AND CONSCIOUSNESS (pp. 198–200)

° Habituation is considered a simple form of adaptive learning; organisms stop paying attention to stimuli that are often repeated when they don't signal any important environmental events.

° According to the opponent-process theory, habituation to repeated stimuli causes two processes. The first, known as the A-Process, is an almost reflexive increase or decrease in some response. The second, called the B-Process, causes an opposite or opposing response. The opponent-process theory has been used to explain drug tolerance development (A-Process = drug effect; B-Process = coming down from high).

III. INSTRUMENTAL AND OPERANT CONDITIONING: LEARNING THE CONSEQUENCES OF BEHAVIOR (pp. 200–201)

People learn more than just an association between neutral and unconditioned stimuli. For many behaviors, the stimuli that follow an action are important. In other words, people learn to respond in a way that brings about positive consequences.

A. From the Puzzle Box to the Skinner Box

According to the law of effect, if a response made in the presence of a particular stimulus is followed by a reward, that response is more likely to be made the next time the stimulus is encountered. Responses that are "instrumental," meaning they help produce some rewarding or desired effect, are learned; therefore, Thorndike called this learning instrumental conditioning. Skinner's emphasis on how an organism learns to "operate on" its environment to produce a positive effect led him to rename instrumental conditioning to operant conditioning.

B. Basic Components of Operant Conditioning

1. *Operants and Reinforcers.* An operant is a behavioral response that has some effect on an organism's environment. In operant conditioning people learn the relationship between operants and their consequences. A reinforcer is a consequence that increases the probability that a behavioral response will occur again. Two types of reinforcers exist. Positive reinforcers are positive stimuli that act like rewards. Negative reinforcers are negative stimuli that, once removed, encourage or reinforce behavior.

2. *Escape and Avoidance Conditioning.* Negative reinforcements are used in escape and avoidance conditioning. In escape conditioning, an organism learns behaviors that lead to an escape from an unpleasant situation (negative reinforcement). In avoidance conditioning, an organism learns behaviors that allow it to completely avoid an unpleasant situation (negative reinforcement). Avoidance conditioning is very strong and may prevent an organism from learning new behaviors.

3. *Discriminative Stimuli and Stimulus Control.* Discriminative stimuli signal to an organism that reinforcement is available if a certain response is made. This response is said to be under stimulus control. Stimulus generalization, recognizing a stimulus similar to the original stimulus that signaled reinforcement, also occurs in operant conditioning.

C. Forming and Strengthening Operant Behavior

1. *Shaping.* Creation of new responses never before displayed can be accomplished through shaping, or reinforcing successive approximations (more and more like the desired response) of the desired behavior.

2. *Secondary Reinforcement.* Often, operant conditioning will begin with primary reinforcers—events or stimuli that are intrinsically rewarding, such as food. A secondary reinforcer is a previously neutral stimulus that, if paired with a stimulus that is al-

ready reinforcing, will itself take on reinforcing properties.

3. *Delay and Size of Reinforcement.* Operant conditioning is strongest when the delay in receiving a reinforcer is short and when the reinforcer is large.

4. *Schedules of Reinforcement.* On a continuous reinforcement schedule, every correct response receives a reward. On a partial, or intermittent, reinforcement schedule, reinforcement is received only some of the time.

    (a) Fixed-ratio (FR) schedules give a reward after a fixed number of responses.

    (b) Variable-ratio (VR) schedules give a reward after an average number of responses.

    (c) Fixed-interval (FI) schedules reward the first response displayed after a fixed time interval.

    (d) Variable-interval (VI) schedules reward the first response displayed after a varying time interval.

5. *Scheduling and Extinction.* Eliminating reinforcers for behavioral responses eventually causes the behavioral response to cease. The partial reinforcement extinction effect demonstrates that it is more difficult to extinguish an operant behavior learned under a partial rather than a continuous reinforcement schedule.

D. Why Reinforcers Work

Primary reinforcers are items that fulfill basic needs or are inherently rewarding experiences such as relief from pain. Behaviors that are high on an organism's preferred list of activities can be used to reinforce the organism to perform behaviors lower on the preferred activity list. Stimulating certain areas of the brain speeds up the learned relationship between stimuli and behaviors.

E. Punishment and Learning

° Punishment presents an aversive stimulus or removes a pleasant stimulus to decrease the frequency of a behavior. Punishment has several disadvantages. First, it doesn't eliminate learning; it merely suppresses an operant response. If an organism knows that punishment is unlikely, then the behavior is repeated. Second, punishment may be associated with the punisher. Eventually the punisher is feared. Third, punishment is not effective unless it immediately follows the undesired behavior. Fourth, the organism being punished may learn to relate to others in an aggressive manner. Fifth, punishment makes clear what behaviors are incorrect, but it doesn't provide any demonstration of desired behaviors.

° Punishment can work if used wisely. One should punish the behavior, not the person; punish immediately; use a severe enough punishment to eliminate the behavior; and explain and reinforce more appropriate behaviors.

F. Operant Conditioning of Human Behavior

Operant conditioning can be used to teach people the "rules" of social behavior and to eliminate problematic behavior and reinforce positive, desired behavior in people afflicted with mental retardation, autism, and other behavior disorders. Operant conditioning principles can also be used to help people understand the stimuli that trigger behaviors they want to eliminate (such as smoking or overeating). Understanding and avoiding discriminative stimuli can reduce the undesired behavior. However, humans and animals placed in situations that eliminate their control over the environment tend to give up any effort to exert control over their environment in new situations. They learn to be helpless.

IV. COGNITIVE PROCESSES IN LEARNING (pp. 212–221)

Cognitive processes, such as how people store, represent, and use information, can influence learning.

A. Learned Helplessness

Learned helplessness is a tendency to give up any effort to control the environment.

B. Focus on Research Methods: A Two-Factor Experiment on Human Helplessness

In this experiment the dependent variable—the degree to which subjects acted to control noise—could be affected by two independent variables: prior experience with noise and expectation about the ability to influence the noise. People tend to feel less able to control a situation if they previously could not control it or if they are told they are powerless.

C. Latent Learning and Cognitive Maps

Learning that is not immediately evident in an organism's behavior is known as latent learning. Cognitive maps are mental representations of the environment.

D. Insight and Learning

The cognitive process of insight involves understanding the global organization of a problem.

E. Observational Learning: Learning by Imitation

A series of experiments by Albert Bandura demonstrated that people learn by watching others, which is termed observational, or social, learning. In observational learning, a person learns new behaviors by watching others' behavior. In vicarious conditioning, a type of observational learning, a person learns new behaviors by observing the consequences (reinforcement or punishment) of someone else's behavior.

F. Thinking Critically: Does Watching Violence on Television Make People More Violent?

What am I being asked to believe or accept?
Watching violence on television causes violent behavior in viewers.

What evidence is available to support the assertion?
Anecdotes and case studies describe incidents of violence among children after watching violence on TV. Many studies show a positive correlation between watching and doing violence. Controlled studies show increases in violent behavior following violent visual stimulation.

Are there alternative ways of interpreting the evidence?
Anecdotal and correlational evidence do not prove causation. It may be possible that the dependent variables used in the controlled studies are not similar enough to violence in everyday life.

What additional evidence would help to evaluate the alternatives?
More controlled studies are needed to better understand the relationship between viewing violence and committing violent acts. However, ethical considerations prohibit these types of studies.

What conclusions are most reasonable?
The large number of studies done in this area make it reasonable to conclude that watching TV violence may be one cause of violent behavior.

G. Neural Networks

Learned associations are represented in multiple brain locations and are integrated through neural networks.

V. USING RESEARCH ON LEARNING TO HELP PEOPLE LEARN (pp. 221–224)

A. Classrooms Across Cultures

The formal discipline principle focused on improving mental abilities through practice with material in difficult courses. The identical elements approach, which emphasizes generalizability, is most prevalent in U.S. schools. The better math and reading scores of Asian students may be due to the classroom format. Japanese schools use more group work and provide more immediate feedback to students.

> *Teaching Machines.* B. F. Skinner's machine gave students immediate feedback on their answers to questions about course material presented in a window.

B. Active Learning

Active learning exercises improve memory of material and make classrooms more enjoyable. Active learning is a more elaborate processing in which students solve problems in groups, think about how material relates to what they know, and answer every question asked by the teacher.

C. Skill Learning

Repeated skill performance is the most critical component of skill learning. How much effort is put into practicing the skill, by working on a variety of difficult problems or movements, will be a critical factor in performance. Coaching is helpful in limited doses; the learner should be encouraged to try independent practice in addition to coaching.

Feedback lets the learner know if she or he is correct and may provide understanding of the cognitive and physical processes used in the skill. Feedback should be given after a learner is done practicing and should not be so detailed that the learner doesn't have to learn from his or her own mistakes.

KEY TERMS

1. **Learning** is the modification of preexisting behavior and understanding through experience. People learn primarily by identifying relationships between events and noting the regularity in the surrounding world. (p. 191)

2. **Classical conditioning** is a procedure in which a neutral stimulus is paired with a stimulus that elicits a reflex or other response until the neutral stimulus alone elicits a similar response. Organisms learn the relationships and associations between stimuli. (p. 193)

> *Example:* Cat owners who feed their cats canned food and use an electric can opener know that just the sound of the opener will cause the cat to come running into the kitchen and salivate. The sound of the

opener (an originally neutral stimulus) is paired with food (a stimulus that elicits a reflexive response such as salivation or other behavioral responses such as running into the kitchen) until the sound alone elicits the response. This occurs because the sound of the electric opener predicts the presence of food.

REMEMBER: Throughout the chapter, the word <u>response</u> is used. It is equivalent to a behavior or mental process. If you become confused by the use of this word, simply substitute the words <u>mental process</u> or <u>behavior</u>, and the sentence's meaning should become clear.

3. An **unconditioned stimulus (UCS)**, in classical conditioning, is the stimulus that elicits a response without conditioning or learning having to take place. (p. 193)

Example: In the cat example in Key Term 2, food is the unconditioned stimulus; it naturally causes the cat to salivate.

REMEMBER: <u>Unconditioned</u> means "unlearned." Cats do not have to learn about food every time in order to respond to food.

4. An **unconditioned response (UCR)**, in classical conditioning, is the automatic or reflexive response to the unconditioned stimulus. (p. 193)

Example: In the cat example in Key Term 2, salivation is an unconditioned response. This behavior or response is reflexive or unlearned and occurs in the presence of the unconditioned stimulus (food).

5. A **conditioned stimulus (CS)**, in classical conditioning, is the stimulus that, only *after* repeated pairings with the unconditioned stimulus, causes a conditioned response that is similar to the unconditioned response. (p. 193)

Example: In the cat example in Key Term 2, the sound of the can opener is the conditioned stimulus because it initially elicited no response from the cat (as a neutral stimulus). Only when the sound of the opener was paired with the presentation of food did the sound predict the presence of food (UCS) and cause the cat to run to the kitchen and salivate.

REMEMBER: <u>Conditioned</u> means "learned." The conditioned stimulus is originally neutral; the organism must learn that it predicts the presence of the UCS.

6. A **conditioned response (CR)**, in classical conditioning, is the learned response elicited by the conditioned stimulus. (p. 193)

Example: In the cat example in Key Term 2, the cat's response of running to the kitchen and salivating when it hears the can opener is the conditioned response.

7. **Extinction**, in classical conditioning, occurs when the conditioned stimulus, after being presented without the unconditioned stimulus, loses its predictive value. Eventually, the conditioned stimulus no longer elicits the conditioned response. In operant conditioning, a response is extinguished when it is no longer reinforced. (p. 194)

Example: The story "The Boy Who Cried Wolf" is an example of extinction in classical conditioning. Shepherds learned that hearing someone cry "Wolf!" (CS) meant that a wolf (UCS) had appeared, and consequently they would run (CR) for help. When one little boy repeatedly cried "Wolf!" for no reason, the other shepherds stopped responding (CR) to his cry (CS) because it no longer predicted the presence of a wolf (UCS).

REMEMBER: To become <u>extinct</u> means to "no longer exist." In the above example, the CR (running) no longer exists when the cry of "Wolf" (CS) is heard.

8. **Reconditioning**, in classical conditioning, refers to the repairing of the CS and the UCS after extinction has taken place. During reconditioning, an organism learns more quickly than it did the first time that the CS predicts the UCS. (p. 194)

REMEMBER: Conditioning involves the association of two stimuli such that one (CS) begins to predict the occurrence of the other (UCS). <u>Reconditioning</u> is simply <u>repeating</u> this process.

9. **Spontaneous recovery** is the reappearance of the conditioned response when the CS is presented after extinction in the absence of reconditioning. (p. 194)

Example: Pavlov's dogs were conditioned to salivate (CR) in response to the sound of a bell. After extinction (hearing the bell without receiving food), the dogs no longer responded. If, after a long time following extinction, the dogs heard the sound of the bell again, they would most likely salivate. The conditioned response would have spontaneously "recovered."

REMEMBER: <u>Spontaneously</u> means "suddenly" or "without planning." In spontaneous recovery, the CR occurs suddenly or immediately after only *one* presentation of the CS (bell).

10. **Stimulus generalization**, in classical conditioning, occurs when an organism displays a conditioned response to a stimulus that is similar but not identical to the conditioned stimulus. In operant conditioning, several different but similar stimuli can inform an organism that, if a particular response is made, a reinforcer or punishment will be presented. (p. 194)

> *Example:* Nguyen was very curious as a child. He had never seen a spider (CS) before the time he picked up a big reddish-brown one to investigate it closely. Eventually, the spider bit him (UCS), causing him to become ill (UCR) for several days. Nguyen is now an adult and avoids (CR) all spiders, not just reddish-brown ones. He is reacting to stimuli that are similar but not necessarily identical to the original conditioned stimulus (reddish-brown spiders).

11. **Stimulus discrimination** occurs when an organism learns that stimuli similar but not identical to the conditioned stimuli do not predict the occurrence of the unconditioned stimulus. (See Key Term 22 for more information about discrimination in operant conditioning.) (pp. 194–195)

> *Example:* Raoul the dog receives an injection (UCS) at the veterinarian's every four months. Raoul usually loves to ride in the car. However, whenever his owner drives Raoul to the veterinarian's (CS), Raoul whimpers (CR) for most of the ride. Raoul has learned to discriminate between the route to the veterinarian's and the route to other places.

12. **Second-order conditioning** occurs when a new neutral stimulus is associated with a conditioned stimulus and itself comes to produce the CR in the absence of the CS. (p. 196)

> *Example:* If Pavlov had turned on the light in the room before ringing the bell (CS) and the dogs eventually began to salivate (CR) as soon as he turned on the light, second-order conditioning would have occurred.
>
> *REMEMBER:* Second-order conditioning means that there is a second conditioned stimulus.

13. The **law of effect** holds that if a response made in the presence of a particular stimulus is followed by a reward, that same response is more likely to occur the next time the stimulus is encountered. Responses that are not rewarded are less and less likely to be performed again. (p. 201)

> *REMEMBER:* The law of effect means the law of being effective. If an organism learns that a behavior produces a desired effect, such as good grades or money, the organism will repeat the behavior. If the behavior is ineffective (it doesn't produce anything, or it produces bad effects, such as a scolding), it will not be repeated.

14. **Instrumental conditioning** is a procedure during which an organism learns that certain responses are instrumental in producing desired effects in the environment. (p. 201)

> *Example:* Most students have learned that studying (response) results in receiving good grades (desirable effects).

15. **Operant conditioning** is a synonym for instrumental conditioning. (p. 201)

16. **An operant** is a behavior that, in instrumental conditioning, brings about a consequence in an organism's environment. (p. 202)

> *REMEMBER:* Operant responses are behaviors that operate on the world in some way.

17. **A reinforcer** is anything that increases the likelihood that a behavior will be repeated. Reinforcers can be positive or negative. (p. 202)

18. **Positive reinforcers**, in operant conditioning, are like rewards. If presented following a behavior, they increase the likelihood of that behavior's future occurrence. (p. 202)

> *Example:* If Rover gets a bone (a positive reinforcer) every time he rolls over, he will probably roll over frequently.
>
> *REMEMBER:* A reinforcer always encourages the repetition of the behavior that it follows. A pleasant stimulus (+) is added (+) to the environment. You can remember this by thinking that a positive number times a positive number yields a positive number.

19. **Negative reinforcers**, in operant conditioning, are unpleasant stimuli that, if removed following a behavior or response, will increase the likelihood of that behavior's future occurrence. (p. 202)

> *Example:* Hunger pains are unpleasant stimuli. Eating causes them to go away. People learn the habit of eating when they experience hunger pains because the pains disappear (negative reinforcers).

REMEMBER: A reinforcer always encourages the repetition of the behavior that it follows. In negative reinforcement a negative stimulus (–) is subtracted from (–) the environment. You can remember this by thinking that a negative number times a negative number always yields a positive number.

20. **Escape conditioning** occurs when an organism learns that a particular response will terminate an aversive stimulus. (p. 202)

Example: Lydia has recently set up a computer at home and now does most of her work there. Her cat, Spooky, has begun to sit next to the terminal and cry until Lydia gets up to feed him. Lydia has learned that her response of feeding the cat will remove the distracting sound of his cries.

REMEMBER: Escape and avoidance conditioning are sometimes confused. In order for escape conditioning to occur, the organism must first be in trouble.

21. **Avoidance conditioning** occurs when an organism responds to a signal in a way that prevents exposure to an aversive stimulus. (p. 202)

Example: Leslie has learned that by accepting most men's invitations for dates she avoids the awkwardness of explaining that she is not interested in them.

REMEMBER: Escape and avoidance conditioning can be confused. In avoidance conditioning, the organism avoids ever getting into trouble. In escape conditioning, the organism learns how to get out of trouble.

22. **Discriminative stimuli,** in operant conditioning, are signals to an organism that, should a particular response be made, reinforcement is available. Such a response is said to be under stimulus control because the response is usually made when only the discriminative stimulus is present. (p. 203)

Example: Alicia knows that her business partner is in a good mood if she is smiling, is not wearing her suit jacket, and has opened the blinds. These discriminative stimuli inform Alicia that she can approach her partner with a new idea (Alicia's particular response) and expect her partner to be supportive (reinforcement). Alicia's behavior is under stimulus control because Alicia will not approach her partner unless the discriminative stimuli are present.

23. **Shaping** is an operant conditioning process in which successive approximations of a behavior are reinforced until the entire desired behavior pattern appears. (p. 205)

Example: Trainers at Sea World want to teach a whale to jump through a hoop. Since wild whales do not normally perform this behavior, the trainers must shape it. They might begin by rewarding the whale for jumping out of the water. Then they reward the whale for jumping toward a hoop and eventually for touching it. Each of these behaviors is a successive approximation of jumping through a hoop. Eventually, the entire behavior pattern will be learned and rewarded.

REMEMBER: To shape means to "mold into something." In shaping, the behavior must be gradually molded.

24. **Primary reinforcers** are inherent rewards. Thus, learning that the reinforcement is positive is not necessary. (p. 205)

Example: Food and water are primary reinforcers if you are hungry.

25. **Secondary reinforcers** are those rewards that have acquired meaning by their association with primary reinforcers. (p. 205)

Example: Before people used money in exchange for goods, they worked to produce or exchange life's basic necessities, such as food. Money, because it allows people to buy food and has therefore become associated with food, is a secondary reinforcer.

26. A **continuous reinforcement** schedule involves reinforcing a desired response every time it occurs. This is one type of fixed-ratio schedule. (p. 206)

Example: Denzel is a housekeeper. When he gets paid every time he cleans a house, he is experiencing continuous reinforcement.

REMEMBER: Continuous means "always." A desired behavior always receives a reinforcement.

27. **Partial,** or **intermittent, reinforcement** schedules are used when a desired response is reinforced only some of the time. (p. 206)

REMEMBER: Any reinforcement schedule other than a continuous one is an example of this.

28. **Fixed-ratio (FR)** schedules provide reinforcement after a fixed number of responses. (p. 206)

Example: Phil, a real estate broker, receives a bonus for every ten houses he sells.

REMEMBER: The word <u>fixed</u> in a schedule always means "set"; the word <u>ratio</u> always means "behavior." A fixed-ratio schedule indicates that a reward is given after a set number of behaviors.

29. **Variable-ratio (VR)** schedules call for reinforcement after a variable number of responses. (p. 206)

Example: Joycelyn's parents will reward her with a gift of her choice when she gets one to three good report cards.

REMEMBER: The word <u>variable</u> means "changing"; the word <u>ratio</u> means "behavior." A reward is presented after a varying number of behaviors—in other words, after some variable number of responses.

30. **Fixed-interval (FI)** schedules call for reinforcement for the first response that occurs after some fixed time has passed since the last reward. (p. 206)

Example: Levar, a graduate teaching assistant, gets paid once a month.

REMEMBER: The word <u>fixed</u> in a schedule means "set"; the word <u>interval</u> in a schedule means "time period." An organism is rewarded for the first behavior after a set time period.

31. **Variable-interval (VI)** schedules reinforce the first response after some period of time, but the amount of time varies. (p. 206)

Example: Students who study a little every day in order to be prepared for surprise quizzes given at various times throughout the semester are on a variable-interval schedule.

REMEMBER: The word <u>variable</u> in a schedule means "changing." The word <u>interval</u> means "time period." An organism is rewarded at changing periods of time.

32. The **partial reinforcement extinction effect** occurs when a partial reinforcement schedule has been used in the operant conditioning process. The more difficult it is for the organism to predict the occurrence of a reinforcement (meaning the behavior isn't rewarded every time), the harder the response is to extinguish. (p. 208)

REMEMBER: To extinguish an operant behavior, reinforcement is no longer given following a response. On a partial reinforcement schedule, an organism will have to perform a response more than once or wait for a period of time before realizing that responses are no longer being rewarded. An animal on a continuous reinforcement schedule can know after only one response that reinforcement has been withdrawn.

33. **Punishment** is the presentation of an aversive stimulus, which decreases the frequency of the immediately preceding response. (p. 209)

Example: For people who want to break their nail-biting habit, there is a fingernail polish with a bad taste. When people wearing this polish bite their nails, they are punished with an aversive stimulus (the taste of the polish). This is done to decrease the behavior (nail biting) immediately preceding the taste.

REMEMBER: Punishment has several side effects.

34. **Learned helplessness** occurs when an organism believes that behaviors are not related to consequences. (p. 212)

Example: Children may develop learned helplessness if they find that no matter how much or how little they try to learn, failing grades always result. At that point they may no longer feel that it is worth trying to achieve at school.

REMEMBER: Organisms learn to be helpless.

35. **Latent learning** is learning that is not demonstrated at the time that it occurs. (p. 214)

Example: You discover that you enjoy your psychology class. However, you do not demonstrate the knowledge that you learned during the first lecture until the first test several weeks later.

REMEMBER: <u>Latent</u> means "not visible." What you have learned is not visible until a later time.

36. **Cognitive maps** are mental representations of the environment. (p. 214)

Example: When he was at college, Dale lost his sight in a car accident. When he got out of the hospital, he still knew how to get around the campus because he had a mental representation (or cognitive map) of the campus.

37. **Insight** is the sudden grasp of new relationships that are necessary to solve a problem and that were not learned in the past. (p. 216)

38. **Observational learning** occurs when people learn by watching others' responses. Learning takes place even if others' responses are not rewarded. (p. 216)

Example: Suppose you found a being from another planet on your doorstep. Charlie the alien is intelligent and looks just like a human being. That night, Charlie watches you brush your teeth. Then he picks up the toothbrush and imitates your behavior. This is not because he knows you get great checkups at the dentist. He is merely learning a behavior by watching you do it.

39. **Vicarious conditioning** occurs when an organism learns the relationship between a response and its consequences (either reinforcement or punishment) by watching others. (p. 217)

Example: Tara is the youngest of six children. By watching her brothers and sisters, she learns which behaviors her parents reward and which behaviors they punish.

FILL-IN-THE-BLANKS KEY TERMS

This section will help you check your factual knowledge of the key terms introduced in this chapter. Fill in each blank with the appropriate term from the list of key terms above.

1. _____ is a phenomenon in which organisms respond to a stimulus that they have learned will predict the occurrence of another stimulus.

2. In classical conditioning, the stimulus that elicits a reflexive response is called the _____.

3. In classical conditioning, learned responses that are made to a once-neutral stimulus are called _____.

4. If a CS is repeatedly presented without the UCS, _____ is likely to occur.

5. During _____, an organism learns the relationship between the conditioned stimulus and the unconditioned stimulus more quickly.

6. When an organism responds to a stimulus that is similar to the conditioned stimulus, this is called _____.

7. Intense, inappropriate fears that may be learned through classical conditioning are called _____.

8. Something that increases the chances that a behavior will be repeated is called a _____.

9. _____ are unpleasant stimuli that, if removed following a behavior or response, will

increase the likelihood of that behavior's future occurrence.

10. When an organism learns that it can prevent certain consequences from occurring by behaving in a certain way, this is called _____.

11. Rewarding successive approximations of a behavior is called _____.

12. Operant responses that are rewarded every time they occur are on a _____ schedule of reinforcement.

13. Knowledge that comes through watching the behavior of others being reinforced or punished is called _____.

14. When an organism learns that its behavior has no bearing on the consequences of its actions, this is called _____.

15. _____ are mental representations of the environment.

Total Correct (See answer key) _____

LEARNING OBJECTIVES

1. Define learning. (p. 191)

2. Define classical conditioning, unconditioned stimulus, unconditioned response, conditioned stimulus, and conditioned response. Describe how classical conditioning works by using the stimuli and responses in an example. (p. 193)

3. Describe the processes of extinction, reconditioning, and spontaneous recovery. Give an example of each. Explain Figure 7.3 in your text. (p. 194)

4. Define and give an example of stimulus generalization and stimulus discrimination. Describe the adaptive balance between these two phenomena. (pp. 194–195)

5. Describe the role that timing, predictability, and strength of signals play in the speed and strength of conditioned response development. Indicate which type of conditioning produces the strongest type of conditioned response. (p. 195)

6. Discuss how attention influences which stimulus is linked to the unconditioned stimulus. Define and give an example of second-order conditioning. (p. 196)

7. Explain how biopreparedness influences taste-aversion learning. Explain why it is a special case of classical conditioning. (pp. 196–197)

8. Describe the relationship between classical conditioning and learned immune responses, phobias, and predator control. (pp. 197–198)

9. Describe the linkage between learning and consciousness. Define habituation and give an example. Explain the opponent-process theory of drug addiction. (pp. 198–200)

10. Define the law of effect. (p. 201)

11. Define instrumental conditioning, and explain how it differs from classical conditioning. (p. 201)

12. Define the components of operant conditioning: operants and reinforcers. (pp. 201–202)

13. Define positive reinforcers and negative reinforcers and give examples of each. (p. 202)

14. Define escape conditioning and avoidance conditioning. Give an example of each that demonstrates their similarities and differences. (pp. 202–203)

15. Define discriminative stimulus and stimulus control. Give an example of stimulus control. Explain how stimulus discrimination and stimulus generalization can work together. (pp. 203–204)

16. Define shaping. Explain when it is used in instrumental conditioning. (pp. 204–205)

17. Discuss the differences between primary and secondary reinforcers. (p. 205)

18. Define continuous and partial reinforcement schedules. Compare and contrast the fixed-ratio, variable-ratio, fixed-interval, and variable-interval reinforcement schedules; include a description of their effect on the intensity of operant responses and the partial reinforcement extinction effect. (pp. 206–208)

19. Explain why activity preference and physiological factors influence the efficiency of reinforcement. (pp. 208–209)

20. Define punishment and describe its role in operant conditioning. Discuss the disadvantages of and guidelines for using punishment. (pp. 209–210)

21. Discuss how operant conditioning can be used to treat problematic behavior and improve education. (pp. 210–211)

22. Define learned helplessness and give an example of it. Describe the experiments used to study learned helplessness and the results. (pp. 212–213)

23. Define and give an example of latent learning and a cognitive map. (pp. 213–214)

24. Define insight. Discuss the differences in what is learned in classical conditioning, instrumental conditioning, and insight. (pp. 193, 201, 215–216)

25. Define observational learning and vicarious conditioning. Discuss their similarities and differences. (pp. 216–217)

26. Describe the research on the effects of television violence. State what conclusions are most reasonable based on the evidence available. (pp. 217–219)

27. Describe the representation of learning in neural networks. (pp. 220–221)

28. Define the formal discipline principle and compare it to identical elements theory. Describe the potential causes of cultural differences in scholastic achievement. (pp. 221–222)

29. Describe teaching machines and the learning principle on which they are based. Define active learning and give an example (pp. 222–223)

30. Describe the roles of practice and feedback in skill learning. (pp. 223–224)

CONCEPTS AND EXERCISES

No. 1: Learning in Advertising

Completing this exercise should help you to achieve Learning Objectives 2, 3, 11, 13, 18, and 20.

Advertising is all around you: television, magazines, radio, billboards, pencils, the backs of cabs, matchbooks, just about anywhere you look. The people who create these ads often use learning principles to persuade you to buy their products. In the following exercise, you are the ads' creator. It is your job to tell your boss the learning principle behind each of the following ad descriptions. Choose from the list at the end of the exercise. Answers may be used more than once or not at all.

1. *Television spot, thirty seconds.* Scene: The counter at a Brand X dry cleaner. An anxious-looking woman enters carrying a yellow dress with chocolate stains on it.

   Customer: I need to have this dress cleaned by noon.

   Counter clerk: Don't worry; it'll be ready at noon.

   Customer: I hope so. I really have to have the dress by noon.

   Counter clerk: We'll have it by noon. No problem.

(Shift of scene: customer is at home, smiling as she talks on the phone.)

Customer: Hi. I dropped a dress off there earlier—to be ready at noon. Can I pick it up now?

(Pause. Customer's smile abruptly turns to a frown.)

Narrator: Why take chances? Speedy Dry Clean guarantees that your clothes will always be ready on time.

a. This is an example of _____ conditioning.

b. The dress failing to be ready illustrates the use of _____ for the behavioral response of using a dry-cleaning service other than Speedy.

c. The service guarantee that states, "Your clothes will always be ready on time" is an example of a _____ reinforcement schedule.

d. How many times do you think Speedy Dry Clean can break the service guarantee before its customers will go to another dry cleaner? _____

2. *Television spot, thirty seconds.* Scene: Mother checking on sleeping child. Mother speaks very quietly.

Mother: Jennifer went to the doctor today to get the stitches taken out of her knee. Before we went to the Stone Clinic, just mentioning the word *doctor* made her cry for fear of getting a shot. But the doctors and nurses at the Stone Clinic understand a child's needs; they're gentle, soothing, kind, and thoughtful. That makes Jennifer happy. I know that the Stone Clinic staff are experts in their fields, and as a mother (mother looks lovingly at Jennifer) that makes me very happy. (Mother leans over, smooths Jennifer's hair, kisses her on the forehead, and tiptoes out of room.)

a. This is an example of _____ conditioning.
b. The doctors are a(n) _____ _____ .
c. Jennifer's old fear of doctors is a(n) _____ _____ .
d. What conditioning process caused Jennifer to lose her fear of doctors? _____

° Instrumental
° Positive reinforcement
° Negative reinforcement
° Punishment
° Classical

° Conditioned stimulus
° Conditioned response
° Unconditioned stimulus
° Unconditioned response
° Extinction
° Continuous
° Fixed interval
° Once
° Ten times
° One hundred times

No. 2: Teaching an Alien

Completing this exercise should help you to achieve Learning Objectives 4, 7, 11, 13, 15, 17, 20, 23, and 25.

To discover the prevalence of learning in our everyday lives, read the following story of Sam and Gufla, an alien. You will find many of the basic learning principles embedded in the plot. Afterward, answer the questions using the list of terms at the end of the exercise. Answers may be used more than once.

One day while playing in the park, Sam met someone he thought was a boy his own age. Thinking the boy was human, Sam began a conversation. Even though the stranger spoke perfect English, Sam soon realized that he was from another planet and had landed here by accident. Eight-year-old Sam was more curious than afraid and invited the alien home for dinner.

The trip home was eventful. Sam, worried about being late, decided to take a shortcut that one of his pals had told him about earlier. As the two boys entered a backyard, a snarling German shepherd charged them. Sam quickly figured out that the dog's chain could not reach to the fence. He and the alien, whom he had named Gufla, ran along the fence until they were out of the yard. After slowing down and catching his breath, Sam realized that he would have to tell Gufla a few things about the family and how to behave so that Sam's mother would not suspect anything. Most important, Sam knew that he could not share his discovery with his sister, who would tell his mother. Gufla asked Sam what eating felt like. How would he recognize food? Sam replied that anything that smelled good was edible. Gufla promptly picked a rose from a garden they were passing and ate it. Sam laughed, but Gufla was holding his stomach because the rose, which had fertilizer on it, made him feel ill. Gufla vowed never to go near a rose again.

Sam told Gufla that anytime Sam nodded his head, Gufla could eat whatever his fork was touching. Anytime Sam shook his head, Gufla was not to eat whatever his fork was touching. Sam tried to explain that food, not napkins or salt and pepper shakers, tastes good, which is a pleasant feeling. By the time they reached Sam's driveway, Sam realized that there was not enough time to teach Gufla all the behaviors he would need to know, so Sam told Gufla to imitate Sam's behavior whenever he felt confused. Sam said that since it was Friday night, his mother might let them stay up and watch the late-night horror movie, a special treat, if all went well.

1. Sam's mother had probably successfully used _____ to decrease his tardiness.

2. Sam was using a _____ _____ to follow a shortcut home. This was also a case of _____ _____ since Sam had never taken this shortcut before, even though he had known about it before that day.

3. Sam decided not to tell his sister about his find. This illustrates a _____ _____. Sam did not want his sister to tell his mother about Gufla.

4. Gufla became ill after eating the rose, probably because it had fertilizer on it. This is an example of learning a _____ _____.

5. Gufla knew that the direction in which Sam moved his head would be a _____ _____ because this would let Gufla know if what he put in his mouth (the behavior) would taste good or bad. Good food in this case is a _____ _____.

6. Gufla will watch and imitate what Sam does even though he won't really understand why he is doing it or if it will bring him any sort of pleasure. This is an example of _____ _____.

7. Sam and Gufla may be allowed to watch a late-night movie if they behave well at dinner. This illustrates the use of a _____ _____.

° Primary
° Secondary
° Avoidance conditioning
° Escape conditioning
° Punishment
° Positive reinforcer
° Taste aversion
° Discriminative stimulus
° Observational learning
° Cognitive map
° Latent learning

CRITICAL THINKING

Sam and Martina have just dropped a teenager, Rose, off at juvenile hall. She has been in trouble on and off for the past two years. They are discussing the causes of her delinquency.

Sam fumes, "Do you realize that's the fifteenth time she's been hauled down there in the past two years?"

Martina mumbles, "Hmmm."

Sam continues, "And do you realize that every time she does something, it's the same old thing? She waits till her dad comes back from a business trip, she tells him what she has done, they have a huge fight, and he brings her to us."

Martina mumbles again, "Hmmm."

Sam finally decries, "She's just a bad apple. She probably has an antisocial personality disorder."

Martina finally says, "Nope, I think Rose is a good kid at heart. Based on the pattern you describe, I think she has just learned to be bad."

Using the five critical thinking questions in your text, the clues in the story, and what you have learned in this chapter, answer the following:

1. What is Sam's hypothesis?

2. What is the evidence in support of Sam's hypothesis?

3. What is Martina's alternative hypothesis?

4. What is the evidence in support of Martina's hypothesis?

PERSONAL LEARNING ACTIVITIES

1. Based on the text's description of classical conditioning, write down an example of an unconditioned stimulus. What natural (unconditioned) response does it cause? Below your example of an unconditioned stimulus and response, write how you could pair the unconditioned stimulus with a neutral stimulus to eventually classically condition yourself. If your unconditioned stimulus, for instance, was a loud noise, perhaps you could have someone flash a light just before making a loud noise until you respond to the light with the same jump you did to the loud noise. (Learning Objective 2)

2. Recall a time when someone tried to punish you. What emotional and behavioral reactions did you have? Did it, in fact, behave as a punishment and decrease your behavior or was it somehow reinforcing? (Learning Objectives 13 and 20)

3. Try to reinforce someone's behavior and watch for the effects. Perhaps a friend does a favor for you or a salesclerk is particularly helpful. You could show your appreciation immediately and see if the person is more likely to behave in the same manner again. (Learning Objective 13)

4. Have someone use observational learning to master a skill that you have. For instance, if you make a delicious casserole or know how to skate backwards, you could attempt to pass on those talents. What problems did you encounter? Was there a particular demonstration or explanation that made things clearer for your volunteer? Based on your first lesson, how much practice do you think will be required before the person masters the skill? What type of feedback was most helpful to the person? (Learning Objectives 25 and 30)

5. Use active learning when working with a classmate to understand material. For example, if you are studying with a psychology classmate, you could work on this chapter by comparing answers to Personal Learning Activity 1, which is an active learning exercise. (Learning Objective 29)

MULTIPLE-CHOICE QUESTIONS

SAMPLE QUIZ 1

1. In classical conditioning, an organism learns
   a. an association between the unconditioned stimulus and the conditioned response.
   b. that the conditioned stimulus is a substitute for the unconditioned stimulus.
   c. that the conditioned stimulus predicts the occurrence of the unconditioned stimulus.
   d. an association between the unconditioned response and the conditioned response.

2. Spontaneous recovery follows
   a. reconditioning.
   b. extinction.
   c. stimulus control.
   d. stimulus degradation.

3. Which of the following demonstrates the need for an adaptive balance between stimulus discrimination and stimulus generalization?
   a. Phobias
   b. Learned helplessness
   c. Extinction
   d. All of the above

4. Reconditioning refers to
   a. the appearance of a conditioned response following extinction.
   b. the elimination of the association between the conditioned stimulus and the unconditioned stimulus.
   c. the occurrence of spontaneous recovery.
   d. the repairing of the conditioned stimulus and the unconditioned stimulus after extinction.

5. Marsha reads aloud a list of words and shoots a puff of air at Kat's eye. It's only after Marsha says "nice" that she blasts Kat's eye with air to make her wink. Eventually Kat winks even when Marsha says "nice" and doesn't shoot the puff of air into her eye. If Kat undergoes extinction, she will
   a. be unable to wink at anything.
   b. feel she is being punished.
   c. wink when she hears the word "night."
   d. not wink when she hears the word "nice."

6. The fact that you didn't notice the feeling of your underwear until you read this sentence is an example of
   a. habituation.
   b. hypothalamic stimulation.
   c. stimulus discrimination.
   d. spontaneous recovery.

7. The optimal interval between the onset of the conditioned stimulus and the unconditioned stimulus is
   a. one-half to one second.
   b. one to two minutes.
   c. two to five minutes.
   d. thirty seconds to one minute.

8. Manuel has learned that every time he cleans his room, his mother makes his favorite dessert. This is an example of
   a. classical conditioning.
   b. negative reinforcement.
   c. instrumental conditioning.
   d. association of stimuli.

9. In instrumental conditioning, negative reinforcers are
   a. pleasant stimuli presented following a response.
   b. unpleasant stimuli that are removed following a response.
   c. methods of decreasing a response.
   d. rewards considered basic to survival, such as food and drink.

10. Ten minutes before a movie starts, the theater is filled with people who are talking or laughing. As soon as the lights go out, everyone becomes quiet. A few people, who continue to laugh out loud and prevent the audience from hearing the show, are booed and hissed until they are quiet. Turning off the lights serves as a _____ in this example of operant conditioning.
    a. positive reinforcer
    b. negative reinforcer
    c. punishment
    d. discriminative stimulus

11. Sometimes Amy hits her sister, Zoe, in the arm until Zoe says "I give," and then Amy stops. Because Amy stops hurting Zoe when she says "I give," Zoe says it whenever she is being hit. In this example of _____, the operant is _____.
    a. negative reinforcement; Zoe saying "I give"
    b. positive reinforcement; Amy stops hitting Zoe
    c. punishment; Zoe saying "I give"
    d. punishment; Amy stops hitting Zoe

12. In operant conditioning, a reinforcer is presented to an organism on a fixed-ratio schedule after a(n)
    a. fixed amount of time.
    b. fixed number of responses.
    c. average number of responses.
    d. average amount of time.

13. Which reinforcement schedule produces the fastest extinction rate?
    a. Fixed ratio
    b. Fixed interval
    c. Variable ratio
    d. Variable interval

14. Every fifth time Russell washes the dishes, his mom gives him a candy bar, and he now washes them every day. Susan's dad only gives her reinforcement for washing the dishes once a week, on average, and she also washes them every day. What schedules of reinforcement are Russell and Susan on, respectively?
    a. fixed interval, variable interval
    b. fixed ratio, variable interval
    c. variable ratio, fixed interval
    d. variable interval, fixed ratio

15. Julio and Carlos's mother asks them what they want for breakfast. Carlos replies, "I want some #$!@* corn flakes." His mother immediately yells, "Don't say that!" and repeats the question. Carlos replies, "Well okay, I'll have some #$!@* rice puffs." Carlos's mother becomes angry and sends Carlos to his room. She then looks at Julio and says, "What do you want for breakfast?" Julio replies, "I don't know, but you can be sure I don't want any #$!@* cereal." Julio's response illustrates
    a. the effectiveness of negative reinforcers.
    b. stimulus discrimination.
    c. the disadvantages of using punishment.
    d. all of the above.

16. In learned helplessness, an organism believes that
    a. behavior is unrelated to consequences.
    b. certain behaviors always result in negative consequences.
    c. positive consequences are rare.
    d. certain behaviors provide escape from negative stimuli.

17. Gertrude's grandfather came to visit her recently for the first time. In the middle of the night he got up to use the bathroom. Half asleep, he took a wrong turn and walked into a wall. This is an example of
    a. use of an incorrect cognitive map.
    b. reverse insight.
    c. latent learning.
    d. vicarious learning.

18. After being bitten by a dog at a young age, Cathy became fearful of all types of dogs. When Cathy sees a dog, her heart races and she feels like running away. From the list below, which is the conditioned stimulus (CS) for Cathy?
    a. dog bite
    b. fear
    c. running away
    d. seeing a dog

19. Later Cathy watches a number of people petting and playing with a dog and decides that dogs aren't just scary and mean. The next day at her neighbor's house she pets their dog. She has learned to pet a dog through
    a. classical conditioning.
    b. operant conditioning.
    c. vicarious classical conditioning.
    d. observational learning.

20. A person who believes in the formal discipline principle would be most likely to recommend that schools
    a. classify students based on ability.
    b. have strict rules about attendance and performance.
    c. provide students with information they can use in real life.
    d. strengthen students' minds through courses in Latin, literature, mathematics, physics, chemistry, and history.

Total Correct (See answer key) _____

SAMPLE QUIZ 2

Use this quiz to reassess your learning after taking Quiz 1 and reviewing the chapter.

1. In classical conditioning, a neutral stimulus
   a. is one that does not elicit a reflexive response.
   b. is synonymous with an unconditioned stimulus.
   c. causes an unconditioned response.
   d. predicts the presence of an unconditioned response.

2. Letitia's first experience at the dentist was a traumatic one. During that first visit, the dentist used no anesthetic before drilling her teeth. Now, just sitting in the waiting room and hearing the whirring sound of the drill make Letitia nauseous. This is an example of what kind of conditioning?
   a. Classical conditioning
   b. Negative reinforcement
   c. Instrumental conditioning
   d. Positive reinforcement

3. When Antonio rode the Ferris wheel at the amusement park for the first time, he became very dizzy. Now when Antonio sees an advertisement for amusement parks, he feels nauseous. In this case, the unconditioned stimulus is
   a. the Ferris wheel ride.
   b. the feeling of dizziness.
   c. nausea.
   d. the sight of an amusement park.

4. In this case of Antonio's feelings about Ferris wheels, the conditioned response is
   a. dizziness.
   b. the Ferris wheel ride.
   c. the sight of an amusement park.
   d. nausea.

5. In the case of Antonio's feelings about Ferris wheels, the conditioned stimulus is
   a. dizziness.
   b. the Ferris wheel ride.
   c. the sight of an amusement park.
   d. nausea.

6. Stimulus generalization involves responding to stimuli that
   a. had always occurred in the presence of the unconditioned stimulus.
   b. produce a reflexive response.
   c. are similar but not identical to the conditioned stimulus.
   d. are similar to the unconditioned stimulus but do not produce an unconditioned response.

7. On September 1, Jefferson High School's fire alarm sounded, and students ran from the building to escape the flames. For the next few weeks, the school experienced a rash of false alarms, and people began to ignore the sound. On December 15, a fire alarm sounded, and students ran from the building in panic. What phenomenon was responsible for the students' renewed fear?
   a. Reconditioning
   b. Spontaneous recovery
   c. Stimulus control
   d. Stimulus generalization

8. After Ernie the lab rat was exposed to repeated pairings of a dark blue light and electrical shock, he became very nervous whenever a turquoise light was flashed in his cage. This phenomenon is called stimulus
   a. generalization.
   b. discrimination.
   c. degradation.
   d. control.

9. Which of the following types of conditioning produces the strongest conditioned response?
   a. Spontaneous conditioning
   b. Forward conditioning
   c. Simultaneous conditioning
   d. Backward conditioning

10. When Tamya was given chemotherapy, she developed a conditioned response to the food that she ate just prior to feeling nauseous. Tamya developed an aversion to the food rather than to the song she heard on the radio due to
    a. biopreparedness.
    b. generalization.
    c. simultaneous conditioning.
    d. signal strength.

11. In operant conditioning, discriminative stimuli
    a. automatically trigger a conditioned response.
    b. indicate the presence of reinforcement if a response is made.
    c. are successive approximations of a desired response.
    d. are similar but not identical to the conditioned stimulus.

12. Punishment is
    a. the presentation of an aversive stimulus.
    b. the removal of a pleasant stimulus.
    c. a means to decrease the occurrence of an undesired response.
    d. all of the above.

13. Kent does not like to take drugs of any kind. When he goes to the dentist, he tries not to ask for any anesthesia. However, sometimes he cannot handle the pain of drilling, and so he lets the doctor give him a shot. This illustrates the use of
    a. a positive reinforcer.
    b. a negative reinforcer.
    c. punishment.
    d. all of the above.

14. Anne is angry at her boss and would like to tell him exactly how she feels about him. But the last time Anne did something similar, she was fired. Now she is afraid of losing her job as well as her temper. What kind of learning does this represent?
    a. Escape conditioning
    b. Classical conditioning
    c. Avoidance conditioning
    d. Discriminative stimuli

15. Shaping is used when the conditioned response
    a. is physically difficult to perform.
    b. is to be decreased.
    c. has never been displayed before.
    d. is reflexive.

16. Which reinforcement schedule produces the highest response rate?
    a. Fixed ratio
    b. Fixed interval
    c. Variable ratio
    d. Variable interval

17. If you reinforce participants in your experiment after their first response and every ten minutes thereafter, you are using a _____ schedule of reinforcement.
    a. fixed interval
    b. fixed ratio
    c. variable interval
    d. variable ratio

18. Advertisements for breath mints frequently involve a chance meeting of strangers who end up falling in love because they had great breath when they met. Advertisers are hoping that people who watch the commercial will learn by _____ that using breath mints will improve their love lives.
    a. vicarious conditioning
    b. observation
    c. classical conditioning
    d. stimulus control

19. The discovery of the advantage of immediate feedback on performance led to the development of
    a. identical elements theory.
    b. formal discipline theory.
    c. teaching machines.
    d. the typical class session in the U.S.

20. According to your text, to cause the most improvement in students' recall of material, teachers should
    a. lecture more slowly.
    b. give students lecture outlines as handouts before class begins.
    c. encourage students to recopy their notes.
    d. have students work in groups to solve problems.

Total Correct (See answer key) _____

ANSWERS TO FILL-IN-THE-BLANKS KEY TERMS

1. Classical conditioning (p. 193)
2. unconditioned stimulus (p. 193)
3. conditioned responses (p. 193)
4. extinction (p. 194)
5. reconditioning (p. 194)
6. stimulus generalization (p. 194)
7. phobias (p. 197)
8. reinforcer (p. 202)
9. negative reinforcers (p. 202)
10. avoidance conditioning (p. 202)
11. shaping (p. 205)
12. continuous (p. 206)
13. vicarious conditioning (p. 217)
14. learned helplessness (p. 212)
15. Cognitive maps (p. 214)

ANSWERS TO CONCEPTS AND EXERCISES

No. 1: Learning in Advertising

1a. *Instrumental*. The customer is learning a relationship between a behavior (using a dry cleaner other than Speedy) and its consequence (clothes that aren't cleaned on time). (p. 201)

1b. *Punishment*. The dress's not being ready will cause the customer problems and is therefore aversive. (p. 209)

1c. *Continuous*. Every time a behavior (going to Speedy Dry Clean versus any other dry cleaner) occurs, it is rewarded or reinforced (getting clothes back on time). (p. 206)

1d. *Once*. Behaviors learned on a continuous reinforcement schedule are very easy to extinguish. (pp. 207–208)

2a. *Classical*. Jennifer has learned that one stimulus (the doctor) predicts another (activities that cause pain). (p. 193)

2b. *Conditioned stimulus*. Jennifer was not always afraid of doctors; originally they were a neutral stimulus. When neutral stimuli begin to predict the presence of another stimulus, such as an injection, they become conditioned stimuli. (p. 193)

2c. *Conditioned response*. Since Jennifer had to learn to be afraid of doctors, this is a conditioned (or learned) response. (p. 193)

2d. *Extinction*. The association between the CS (doctors) and the UCS (activities that cause pain) has been eliminated or at least greatly diminished. The CR (fear of doctors) has also been eliminated. (p. 194)

No. 2: Teaching an Alien

1. *Punishment*. Sam has decreased his behavior of being late for dinner. Punishment decreases the occurrence of the behavior it follows. When Sam was late, he was probably punished. (p. 209)

2. *Cognitive map; latent learning*. Sam learned a shortcut by representing the information in his mind in the form of a map. We know that he learned the shortcut before he demonstrated his knowledge of it. (p. 214)

3. *Avoidance conditioning*. Sam learned to avoid having his sister inform his mother of his doings by simply not telling her what he did. (p. 202)

4. *Taste aversion*. Gufla learned that roses (CS) predict the presence of fertilizer (UCS). Fertilizer causes stomachaches (CR). Gufla will stay away from all roses (CS) in the future. (p. 196)

5. *Discriminative stimulus; primary positive reinforcer*. The direction in which Sam nodded his head would be a discriminative stimulus, or signal, that would let Gufla know when to make a response (eating whatever his fork touched) in order to receive the reinforcement of eating food. Food is a pleasant stimulus and basic to survival. Therefore, it is a primary positive reinforcer. (pp. 202–205)

6. *Observational learning*. Gufla will attend to what Sam is doing, retain the information, and reproduce it because Sam has told him to. Gufla is not performing each specific behavior to obtain a reward. (p. 216)

7. *Secondary positive reinforcer*. Watching a movie, although not basic to survival, is a pleasant stimulus. Therefore, this is an example of secondary positive reinforcement. (pp. 202–205)

ANSWERS TO CRITICAL THINKING

1. Sam hypothesizes that Rose has an antisocial personality.

2. Rose's history of being in trouble lends some support to his hypothesis.

3. Martina's probable hypothesis is that Rose has learned that she will be rewarded with her father's attention when she misbehaves. She probably has to go to extremes to get his attention since he is apparently so busy.

4. Martina will probably want to find out more about Rose's family situation.

ANSWERS TO MULTIPLE-CHOICE QUESTIONS

Circle the question numbers you answered correctly.

Sample Quiz 1

1. *c* is the answer. The conditioned stimulus predicts the occurrence of the unconditioned stimulus. (p. 193)

   a. There is no relationship between the UCS and the CR. The UCS causes a natural reflexive response (UCR); only the conditioned (learned) stimulus causes a conditioned (learned) response.

b. If the CS was merely a substitute for the UCS, the conditioned response would always be identical to the unconditioned response (UCR). This is not the case.

d. No relationship between the UCR and the CR is learned.

2. *b* is the answer. For a conditioned response to recover, it must first have undergone extinction. (p. 194)

    a. Reconditioning once again pairs the conditioned stimulus and the unconditioned stimulus. The conditioned response is relearned. Spontaneous recovery is just that, spontaneous. No relearning is necessary.

    c. Stimulus control is associated with instrumental or operant conditioning. Spontaneous recovery is a phenomenon in classical conditioning.

    d. There is no learning phenomenon called stimulus degradation.

3. *a* is the answer. Some phobias are learned after generalizing the conditioned stimulus in a classical conditioning scenario. For example, after one bad experience with a dog (CS = sight of dog, UCS = dog bite, UCR = pain, CR = fear and escape), a child may learn to fear all real dogs or even pictures of dogs. Although being able to generalize the conditioned stimulus is an adaptive response because the child will be wary of dogs, he or she should also be able to discriminate between large, menacing dogs that could really cause injury and a picture of a dog. (pp. 197–198)

    b. In operant conditioning, stimulus discrimination and generalization indicate that a reinforcement is available if the organism responds. In learned helplessness, an organism learns that no response it makes will bring about a reinforcement.

    c. Extinction is a deterioration of the relationship between the CS and the UCS (classical conditioning) or between a response and a reinforcing or punishing stimulus (operant conditioning). Stimulus generalization and discrimination require learned relationships to be intact; an organism won't respond at all if a stimulus no longer signals an important event or reward.

    d. *a* is the answer.

4. *d* is the answer. Reconditioning is a repetition of the conditioning process. This occurs after extinction; if extinction had not already occurred, there would be no need for reconditioning. (p. 194)

    a, c. The occurrence of a conditioned response after extinction is called spontaneous recovery.

b. The process of extinction removes the association between the CS and the UCS so that the CS no longer predicts the presence of the UCS. Reconditioning replaces the association between the CS and the UCS.

5. *d* is the answer. A person's conditioned response is extinguished when a long time passes without the unconditioned stimulus appearing with the conditioned stimulus. (p. 194)

    a. Kat will be able to wink at things if she undergoes extinction. She will just be less likely to wink at "nice" than she was before.

    b. A feeling of being punished wouldn't happen as a result of discontinuing the pairing of the CS and UCS.

    c. Winking upon hearing the word "night" is an example of generalization.

6. *a* is the answer. In habituation, an organism stops responding to repeated stimuli that do not signal a change in the environment. When you put your underwear on in the morning, you feel it. However, after a few minutes, your body begins to ignore the sensation (p. 199)

    b. Hypothalamic stimulation has nothing to do with stimulation.

    c. In classical conditioning, organisms discriminate among stimuli when they can make finer and finer distinctions among them. For example, if the CS is a red ball, an organism may not respond to a green ball. Stimulus discrimination doesn't play a role in the process of habituation.

    d. Spontaneous recovery occurs when a CS that has not been paired with a UCS for some time elicits a conditioned response.

7. *a* is the answer. It is usually best to allow an interval of one-half to one second to elapse between the conditioned stimulus and the unconditioned stimulus. (p. 195)

    b, c, d. The other options are much too long. Typically, intervals longer than several seconds will fail to produce a conditioned response.

8. *c* is the answer. Instrumental (or operant) conditioning involves learning that behaviors have consequences. When Manuel cleans his room (the operant), his mom makes his favorite dessert (the consequence). (p. 201)

    a, d. Classical conditioning involves making an association between stimuli such that one (CS) comes to predict the presence of the other (UCS). This example involves learning that a behavior (cleaning the room) will bring about a reinforcer (dessert) and is therefore an example of instrumental conditioning.

    b. A negative reinforcer is an unpleasant stimulus that is removed following a desired response. In this case, a positive reinforcer (a pleasant stimulus: dessert) is being presented following a desired behavior (cleaning the room).

9. *b* is the answer. In instrumental conditioning, reinforcers always produce a positive effect and work to increase a behavior. A negative reinforcer is a negative stimulus that is removed after the organism displays a desired response. (p. 202)

    a. Positive reinforcers are pleasant stimuli that are presented after an organism displays a desired response.

    c. Punishment and extinction are used to decrease the occurrence of a response. (You may be confusing punishment and negative reinforcers.) Remember, reinforcements (both positive and negative) increase the occurrence of a desired behavior.

    d. Rewards that are basic to survival are primary reinforcements.

10. *d* is the answer. A discriminative stimulus tells the people in the theater that if they are quiet (the response), they will be rewarded by seeing a movie (the reinforcement). Those who do not pay attention to the light (those who are not under the control of the light stimulus) are punished by being booed and hissed at. (p. 203)

    a. The lights are not turned off to reward the audience for its behavior.

    b. The turned-off lights do not represent the removal of an unpleasant stimulus following the display of a desired behavior. Lights that are on are not unpleasant, and the audience did not display any behaviors in order to get the lights to go out.

    c. Turning off the lights does cause a decrease in the behavior that preceded it, but turned-off lights are not aversive, so they cannot be considered punishment.

11. *a* is the answer. Zoe is being negatively reinforced for saying "I give." When she says it, Amy removes the unpleasant stimulus (hitting her arm). (p. 202)

    b. Amy is not rewarded for stopping her hitting.

    c. If Zoe were punished for saying "I give," she would be less likely to say it in the future.

    d. If Amy were punished for stopping her hitting, she would be less likely to stop hitting in the future.

12. *b* is the answer. (p. 206)

    a. This is called a fixed-interval schedule.

    c. This is called a variable-ratio schedule.

    d. This is called a variable-interval schedule.

13. *a* is the answer. A fixed-ratio schedule of reinforcement produces the fastest rate of extinction because the organism realizes very quickly that reinforcements have ceased to be presented and that after the appropriate number of responses has been made, the reinforcement should be there. A continuous schedule of reinforcement, which is a type of fixed-ratio schedule, produces the fastest rate of extinction possible. (pp. 206–208)

    b. Fixed intervals also produce a fast rate of extinction, but the organism must wait until the fixed interval elapses before it responds and finds no reinforcement.

    c, d. Organisms on a variable schedule of reinforcement cannot predict when the reinforcement will appear. They therefore take longer to realize that the reinforcement is missing once the extinction process has begun.

14. *b* is the answer. A fixed number of behaviors must be exhibited by Russell to receive reinforcement. Susan must wait a variable amount of time before receiving reinforcement for her actions. (p. 206)

    a. Russell doesn't have to wait a set amount of time before reinforcement. If he washed dishes twice a day while company was around he could have his reinforcement (after five operants) in a day and a half. If he skipped a day of washing dishes, he would still get rewarded after the fifth operant, but it might take six days.

    c, d. Russell is on a fixed ratio schedule and Susan is on a variable interval schedule.

15. *c* is the answer. Sometimes humans or animals do not understand what it is they are being punished for; this is one of the disadvantages of using punishment. Julio thought his mother was angry because Carlos wanted cereal, not because Carlos swore at her. (pp. 209–210)

    a. Negative reinforcers are the removal of negative stimuli following a desired behavior. The boy's mother did not remove a negative stimuli; she added one by yelling and sending Carlos to his room.

    b. Stimulus discrimination is found in classical conditioning scenarios. This is an example of operant conditioning.

    d. *c* is the answer.

16. *a* is the answer. In learned helplessness, an organism learns that its behaviors are unrelated to the consequences that occur. It learns that it is helpless or unable to control its circumstances. (p. 212)
   b. If an organism learns that certain behaviors always result in negative consequences, then it is not helpless; it can avoid doing those behaviors.
   c. Learning that positive consequences are rare is not learned helplessness. In learned helplessness an organism learns that its behaviors are unrelated to the consequences that occur.
   d. In learned helplessness an organism learns the opposite: that no behavior provides escape from negative stimuli or consequences.

17. *a* is the answer. Gertrude's grandfather used a cognitive map of his own house when he sleepily tried to find his way to the bathroom in hers. (p. 214)
   b. There is no such thing as reverse insight.
   c. Latent learning occurs when an organism learns something but does not overtly demonstrate this new knowledge until later. If Gertrude's grandfather had successfully learned a cognitive map and made it to the bathroom without walking into a wall, this would have been an example of latent learning.
   d. To learn a response vicariously, an organism must watch someone else display that response and be rewarded or punished for it.

18. *d* is the answer. Seeing a dog is enough to make Cathy fearful. (p. 193)
   a. The unconditioned stimulus is the dog bite.
   b, c. These are the likely conditioned responses.

19. *d* is the answer. Cathy watched others petting a dog and learned from it. (p. 216)
   a. Classical conditioning is the pairing of unconditioned stimuli with neutral stimuli.
   b. In operant conditioning a person's behavior is followed by a consequence. According to the story, Cathy only watched people; she wasn't rewarded.
   c. Vicarious is not a type of classical conditioning. You may have been thinking of vicarious conditioning, which is a type of observational learning in which a person sees someone reinforced or punished for his or her actions.

20. *d* is the answer. The formal discipline principle suggests the use of difficult material to give mental practice to students. (p. 221)

a, b. The principles and theories of education discussed in your text do not address classification of students or formation of rules.
c. The identical elements theory suggests that students should learn material that is generalizable.

Now turn to the quiz analysis table at the end of this chapter to find which areas you know well and which areas you need to work on. Circle the numbers in the table for items on Quiz 1 that you answered correctly.

ANSWERS TO MULTIPLE-CHOICE QUESTIONS

Circle the question numbers you answered correctly.

Sample Quiz 2

1. *a* is the answer. A neutral stimulus does not elicit a reflexive response. A neutral stimulus becomes a conditioned stimulus (CS) and elicits a conditioned response (CR) only after it is paired with an unconditioned stimulus (UCS). (pp. 192–193)
   b. An unconditioned stimulus elicits a reflexive response or an unlearned response that happens automatically. Therefore, a neutral stimulus is not synonymous with an unconditioned stimulus.
   c. A neutral stimulus does not elicit any response.
   d. A neutral stimulus does not elicit any response. A neutral stimulus becomes a conditioned stimulus and elicits a conditioned response only when it is paired with an unconditioned stimulus.

2. *a* is the answer. The conditioned stimulus is the sound of the drill. The unconditioned stimulus is the use of the drill on the teeth. The unconditioned response is the pain that the drill causes. The conditioned response is nausea, which is elicited by the CS, the sound of the drill. (p. 193)
   b, d. Reinforcement, both positive and negative, is used in instrumental conditioning.
   c. Instrumental conditioning involves learning an association between a behavior and its consequences. Letitia is learning an association between two stimuli: the sound of the drill and the feeling of the drill on her teeth.

3. *a* is the answer (see below).

4. *d* is the answer (see below).

5. *c* is the answer. Antonio's nausea in response to Ferris wheels is an example of classical conditioning. The conditioned stimulus is the sight of the amusement park. The unconditioned stimulus is the ride on the Ferris wheel. The unconditioned response is feeling dizzy. The conditioned response is feeling nauseous. (p. 193)

6. *c* is the answer. An organism will generalize by responding to stimuli that are similar to the conditioned stimulus. (p. 194)
   a. Stimulus generalization is not dependent on whether the CS has occurred in the presence of the UCS. The generalized stimulus just has to be similar to the conditioned stimulus.
   b. In stimulus generalization, stimuli that are similar to the CS elicit a CR. This response is *always learned;* it is never reflexive.
   d. Generalization refers to responses made to stimuli that are similar to the CS, not to the UCS.

7. *b* is the answer. Spontaneous recovery is the recurrence of a conditioned response following extinction in the absence of reconditioning. (p. 194)
   a. Reconditioning is the repairing of the CS and the UCS after extinction. The fire alarm (CS) would have to be paired repeatedly with fire (UCS) again for reconditioning to occur.
   c. Operant conditioned responses are under stimulus control. This is an example of classical conditioning. The CS is the fire alarm, and the UCS is the fire.
   d. If stimulus generalization had occurred, the students would have run out of the building in response to an alarm (CS) that was similar but not identical to the original fire alarm. The students heard the same fire alarm in December and September.

8. *a* is the answer. Ernie has been classically conditioned to a dark blue light. When he reacts to a turquoise light, he is generalizing his response to a different but similar stimulus. (p. 194)
   b. If Ernie had learned to discriminate between stimuli, then he would not react to any stimulus other than the one that originally predicted the electric shock.
   c. There is no stimulus degradation in this example.
   d. Stimulus control occurs with the use of instrumental conditioning.

9. *b* is the answer. Forward conditioning produces the strongest conditioned responses. The CS is pre-

sented prior to the UCS, so it becomes a good predictor of the UCS. (p. 195)
   a. There is no such thing as spontaneous conditioning per se. (You may be thinking of spontaneous recovery, where the conditioned response is elicited after extinction.) But remember, even the spontaneous conditioned response isn't very strong. (See Figure 7.3 in your text.)
   c. In simultaneous conditioning, the CS and the UCS are presented simultaneously. This is not the strongest conditioning scenario because the CS doesn't predict the UCS and the organism is probably paying more attention to the reflex-producing UCS.
   d. In backward conditioning, the CS is presented after the UCS. Again, this order of events doesn't allow the CS to become a good predictor of the UCS.

10. *a* is the answer. Biopreparedness is a natural tendency to make certain associations, such as between food and nausea rather than between a sound and nausea. (p. 196)
    b. Tamya did not generalize from one food to another; she associated the food with the nausea.
    c. In simultaneous conditioning the CS and UCS arrive at the same time. Tamya didn't experience chemotherapy and food at the same time.
    d. High signal strength causes more rapid learning, but doesn't explain why she had a conditioned response to the food rather than the song.

11. *b* is the answer. Discriminative stimuli allow the organism to discriminate between situations that will produce a consequence—a reinforcer or punishment—and those that will not. (p. 203)
    a. Discriminative stimuli let an organism know when to make a response; they do not cause a response. Conditioned stimuli elicit or cause a conditioned response. There are no conditioned stimuli in operant conditioning.
    c. Shaping involves rewarding successive approximations of a behavior (behaviors that come closer and closer to the desired response).
    d. Stimulus generalization in classical conditioning is when a conditioned response is made to a stimulus similar to the conditioned stimulus.

12. *d* is the answer. (p. 209)
    a, b, c. These are all true. Punishment is not pleasant for the organism. It is accomplished by presenting an aversive stimulus (getting fired) or taking away a positive stimulus (the privilege of going out on the weekend). Punishment is

used to decrease the occurrence of the behavior that precedes it.

13. *b* is the answer. The negative reinforcer is the removal of drilling pain by the anesthetic. The behavior (asking for a drug to deaden the pain) will increase because the negative reinforcer has removed a potentially aversive stimulus (drilling pain). (p. 202)
    a. A positive reinforcer is a pleasant stimulus that is added to the environment following a desired response. In this example, an unpleasant stimulus, pain, is being removed; a pleasant one is not being added.
    c. If Kent was being punished, his behavior would be followed by an aversive stimulus or the removal of a pleasant one. Being relieved of pain is the removal of an unpleasant stimulus.
    d. *b* is the answer.

14. *c* is the answer. Anne is not going to tell her boss how she feels about him because she wants to avoid being fired. (p. 202)
    a. Escape conditioning involves learning to respond in order to get away from an already present aversive stimulus. Anne does not decide to not tell her boss what she is feeling in order to escape anything. She is trying to avoid the possibility of an aversive stimulus (getting fired) in the future.
    b. This is an example of instrumental, not classical, conditioning. Anne avoids making a behavioral response because she has learned that the consequence of that response is getting fired. She has not learned that one stimulus (CS) predicts the occurrence of another (UCS).
    d. Discriminative stimuli let an organism know when to respond in order to avoid punishment or receive reinforcement. There are no stimuli in the environment that let Anne know when not to tell her boss that she is angry. She simply knows that she should not yell at her boss. A discriminative stimulus in this question would have been some clue that her boss was in a good mood and therefore more receptive to hearing what she had to say.

15. *c* is the answer. A behavior must occur before it can be reinforced. If an organism has never performed the desired behavior, behaviors that are successive approximations of the desired response are reinforced until the whole behavior appears. For an example of successive approximation, see the example of teaching your dog to "shake" in your text. (pp. 204–205)

    a. Behaviors that are shaped are not always difficult to perform. For example, it is not physically difficult for a dog to roll over, but if the dog has never done so, its behavior must be shaped.
    b. Shaping is the creation of a new behavior, not the decreasing of an existing behavior.
    d. Shaping allows an organism to learn a new behavior. Reflexive behaviors are not new. Also, conditioned responses are learned, not reflexive.

16. *a* is the answer. When the organism can predict how many responses are necessary for a reward, it will vigorously respond in expectation. (pp. 206–207)
    b. On a fixed-interval schedule, an organism will respond in order to receive a reinforcement, then wait until the next interval has passed before responding again.
    c. A variable-ratio schedule produces a high response rate but not as high a rate as that produced by a fixed-ratio schedule.
    d. A variable-interval schedule produces a slow, steady rate of response.

17. *a* is the answer. In a fixed interval schedule, reinforcement is given after a set amount of time. (p. 206)
    b. In a fixed ratio schedule, reinforcement is given after a set number of desired behaviors.
    c. Variable interval schedules give reinforcement after an average amount of time has passed. If you were using variable interval you would give reinforcement after an average of ten minutes had passed.
    d. In variable ratio schedules of reinforcement, an experimenter would wait for an average number of desired behaviors before giving reinforcement.

18. *a* is the answer. By watching the commercials, people learn that use of breath mints is rewarded or reinforced by meeting an attractive stranger with whom they will live happily ever after. This is called vicarious conditioning. (p. 217)
    b. Observation learning does involve learning by watching the behavior of others. But the people being observed do not have to receive a reward or punishment in order for the person watching them to learn. Advertisements, as in this example, usually depict people being rewarded for buying and using the advertised products. Therefore, *a* is the better answer.
    c. This is an example of instrumental, not classical, conditioning.

d. There is no stimulus mentioned in the question that lets a person know when to use breath mints. You may have thought that the presence of a stranger of the opposite sex was a discriminative stimulus, but this is not the case. The stranger is the reward or reinforcement in this example.

19. *c* is the answer. Teaching machines are based on the idea that immediate feedback will be most helpful. (p. 222)

   a. Identical elements theory proposes that students should be taught what will be most useful for them to know in later settings.

   b. Formal discipline theory proposes that the specific information learned is not important; it is the practice of working with material that improves the mind.

d. The typical class session in the United States does not provide immediate feedback.

20. *d* is the answer. Active learning is the key to remembering information. Working in groups causes people to use information, which makes it more meaningful. (p. 223)

   a, b, c. Slower lectures, lecture outlines, and recopying of notes all use passive learning. Although they may cause some improvement in retention, none of them are as effective as active learning is.

Now turn to the quiz analysis table at the end of this chapter to find which areas you know well and which areas you need to work on. Circle the numbers in the table for items on Quiz 2 that you answered correctly.

For each question you answered correctly, circle its number. (Quiz 1 numbers are not shaded; Quiz 2 numbers are shaded.) Are there patterns in the types of questions or the topics you got wrong that could direct your further study? Did you improve from Quiz 1 to Quiz 2?

TOPIC	TYPE OF QUESTION		
	DEFINITION	COMPREHENSION	APPLICATION
Classical Conditioning			
Pavlov's discovery	1		18
	1		2, 3, 4, 5
Responses, generalization, discrimination	2, 4		3, 5
	6		7, 8
Signaling and applications		7	6
		9	10
Instrumental and Operant Conditioning			
Components	9		8, 10, 11
	11, 12		13, 14
Forming and strenghtening behavior	12	13	14, 15
		15, 16	17
Cognitive processes in learning	16		17, 19
			18
Using research on learning		20	
		19	20

TOTAL CORRECT BY QUIZ:

QUIZ 1:
QUIZ 2:

Chapter 8

Memory

OUTLINE

I. THE NATURE OF MEMORY (pp. 228–235)

A. Basic Memory Processes

The process of putting information into memory is called encoding. Acoustic codes represent information as sequences of sounds. Visual codes represent information in the form of images. Semantic codes represent the meaning of information. Holding information in memory over time is called storage. Pulling information out of memory and into consciousness after it has been stored is called retrieval.

B. Types of Memory

There are at least three basic types of memory, each of which is named for the type of information it handles. Any memory of a specific event that happened while you were present is an episodic memory. Semantic memory contains generalized knowledge of the world that does not involve memory of a specific event. Procedural memory (skill memory) represents knowledge of how to perform physical tasks.

C. Explicit and Implicit Memory

Explicit memory is the process of deliberately trying to remember something; implicit memory is the unintentional influence of prior experiences. Explicit memory processes are much more negatively affected by the passing of time than are implicit memory processes.

D. Focus on Research Methods: Measuring Explicit vs. Implicit Memory

To document the difference between explicit and implicit memory, participants studied a word list and were tested on it an hour later and a week later. For the explicit memory test, participants picked which words on a new list had been on their study list. For the implicit memory test, they solved word fragment problems. Explicit memory decreased between the two tests, but implicit memory hardly changed. This research showed that time differentially affects explicit and implicit memory.

E. Models of Memory

Currently, there are four models of memory that attempt to explain what and how well items such as processes, episodes, and general information are remembered.

1. *Levels of Processing.* The levels-of-processing model suggests that what and how well we remember are a function of how deeply information is processed or rehearsed and encoded when first experienced. Maintenance rehearsal is simply repeating an item over and over. Elaborative rehearsal is building associations or linkages between new and old information. Elaborative rehearsal requires a deeper level of processing; hence these memories are stronger than those encoded with maintenance rehearsal.

2. *Transfer-Appropriate Processing.* This model suggests that the most important memory determinant is how well the encoding process matches what is retrieved.

3. *Parallel Distributed Processing (PDP).* PDP models suggest that new facts change our knowledge base by altering interconnected networks, facts, and associations. These networks allow us to quickly and efficiently draw inferences and generalizations about new and old information. (See Figure 8.12 in your text.)

4. *Information Processing.* This model states that there are three stages of mental processing required before information can be permanently stored in memory: sensory, short-term, and long-term memory.

II. ACQUIRING NEW MEMORIES (pp. 235–242)

A. Sensory Memory

Sensory memory holds information from all the senses in sensory registers for a fraction of a second.

B. Short-Term, or Working, Memory

Short-term memory (STM) receives the information that was perceived and selectively attended to in sensory memory or retrieved from long-term memory. If no further processing occurs, short-term memory disappears in twenty to thirty seconds. Working memory has two functions: to form and update a picture of our world on a minute-to-minute basis and to think and solve problems.

1. *Encoding*. Across cultures, people tend to use acoustic codes to encode information into short-term memory. Visual codes tend to decay faster than acoustic codes.

2. *Storage Capacity in STM*. The immediate memory span is the number of items you can recall perfectly after one presentation of a stimulus. It is usually seven plus or minus two chunks of information.

3. *The Power of Chunking*. Short-term memory can be noticeably improved by creating bigger and bigger chunks of information. Efficient chunking requires the interaction of short- and long-term memory.

4. *Duration of STM*. Brown-Peterson procedure research results indicate that, unless rehearsed, material stays in short-term memory for about twenty seconds.

C. Long-Term Memory

1. *Encoding*. Encoding information into long-term memory (LTM) is the result of a deep level of conscious processing and usually involves some form of semantic coding. Visual codes are also used to encode long-term memories. The dual coding theory states that information is remembered better if both semantic and visual codes are used.

2. *Storage Capacity in LTM*. Most theorists believe that there is no limit to the amount of information that can be stored in long-term memory.

D. Distinguishing Between Short-Term and Long-Term Memory

Psychologists disagree about the differences between short-term and long-term memory. Some believe that short-term and long-term memory are the same; what is referred to as short-term memory is the part of long-term memory that is being used at a particular moment in time.

1. *Experiments on Recall*. Serial position curves show a tendency to recall both the first and last parts of a list (primacy and recency effects) when memory is immediately tested. If subjects are distracted just prior to being asked to recall a list, the primacy effect remains, but the recency effect disappears. This suggests that the last words were stored in short-term memory, which quickly decays.

2. *Results of Brain Damage*. Hippocampal brain damage results in anterograde amnesia, a loss of memory for any event occurring after the injury. Patients cannot transfer new experiences from short-term memory to long-term memory. Retrograde amnesia is the loss of memory of events prior to an injury. Although many injury patients regain most of their memories, few can recall the events just prior to the injury. As a result of the injury, the short-term memories of what happened were never transferred to long-term memory. Memory deficits in several medical conditions support the theory that short-term memory and long-term memory are distinct storage systems.

III. RETRIEVING MEMORIES (pp. 243–251)

Retrieval is the ability to bring a memory into consciousness.

A. Retrieval Cues and Encoding Specificity

Retrieval cues help retrieve information from long-term memory. According to the encoding specificity principle, these cues are more efficient when they reflect the meaning of the originally encoded information.

B. Context and State Dependence

When people remember more material while in a physical location that is similar to the one where the material was originally learned, it is called context dependence. In state dependence, people remember better when their psychological state is the same as it was when the information was encoded. In the mood congruency effect, information processing is facilitated if a person's emotional state is similar in tone to the information being processed.

C. Retrieval from Semantic Memory

1. *Semantic Networks*. One theory states that semantic memories are represented in a dense network of hierarchical associations. Strong associations and/or those at the top of the hierarchy are quickly retrieved. Network theory suggests that information is retrieved through a spreading activation process; for example, thinking about concept A spreads neural activity to all other features, attributes, and concepts associated with concept A. (See Figure 8.11 in your text.)

2. *Retrieving Incomplete Knowledge.* In a phenomenon called incomplete knowledge (as when something is on the tip of the tongue), we often retrieve features and attributes of a concept but can't access the entire concept. For example, we may not remember the name of a place, but we can remember its physical features.

D. Constructing Memories

People construct memories from their existing knowledge to fill in gaps in new information that is being encoded.

1. *Relating Semantic and Episodic Memory: PDP Models.* PDP models allow us to increase our general knowledge of the world by accessing a network of facts and associations. A note of caution: PDP models can facilitate spontaneous generalizations of networks that are based on limited or biased information.

2. *Schemas.* According to PDP models, the generalized knowledge contained in schemas provides the basis for making inferences about incoming information during the encoding stage.

E. Thinking Critically: Can Traumatic Memories Be Repressed, Then Recovered?

What am I being asked to believe or accept?
Some people claim that subconscious processes such as repression could keep a person from recalling a memory.

What evidence is available to support the assertion?
Research supports that mental activity can occur outside of awareness, that implicit memories can influence people, and that the use of retrieval cues can allow people to access buried memories. In addition, people may be motivated to forget especially unpleasant events.

Are there alternative ways of interpreting the evidence?
Even vivid memories retrieved may have been constructed. A person might be led by books or therapists to construct false memories.

What additional evidence would help to evaluate the alternatives?
If we knew how frequently people repress traumatic memories, it would be easier to evaluate such reports. Knowledge of the process leading to repressed memories and a method for distinguishing between genuine memories and constructed memories would also help evaluate the alternatives.

What conclusions are most reasonable?
Although people do forget unpleasant events and remember them later, they also may distort their memories. For now, people should neither uncritically accept nor reject a report of a recovered memory, but should investigate the evidence for and against the claim.

IV. FORGETTING? (pp. 251–255)

A. The Course of Forgetting

Hermann Ebbinghaus's contributions to psychology included demonstration of the method of savings and the shape of the forgetting curve. The forgetting curve, which depicts how much and when people forget, stays relatively constant regardless of the type of information learned.

B. The Roles of Decay and Interference

Decay, the gradual erosion of a memory, is the most common culprit for short-term memory loss. Interference causes forgetting by interrupting the encoding or retrieval process through the presence of other information. In short-term memory, new information displaces old information because of the limited number of spaces available. However, in long-term memory, space is not the issue; rather, as the number of memories stored increases, it becomes more and more difficult to "find" one particular memory among the huge number of memories. Interference, the main cause of forgetting in long-term memory, can be retroactive or proactive.

V. LINKAGES: MEMORY AND PERCEPTION IN THE COURTROOM (pp. 255–256)

Witnesses can accurately report what they have seen or heard, but can be biased by the manner in which questions are asked and relevant occurrences are discussed. Jurors may rely too heavily on *how* witnesses present evidence, such as reporting a great deal of detail or appearing very confident of what they are reporting.

VI. BIOLOGICAL BASES OF MEMORY (pp. 256–258)

Brain cells change as memories are formed and stored.

A. Biochemical Mechanisms

Two types of synaptic changes occur during memory formation; new synapses are formed and communication at existing synapses is improved. Neurotransmitters, such as glutamate and acetylcholine, are involved in memory processes.

B. Brain Structures

The hippocampus and the thalamus are important in memory processes. Damage to the hippocampus impairs episodic memory but leaves procedural memory processes undisturbed. Both of these brain regions send nerve fibers to the cortex, where memories are probably stored. Many parts of the cortex (visual, auditory, motor, and so on) can store memories that are all aspects of one episode. Hence memories of one incident involve many brain systems.

VII. IMPROVING YOUR MEMORY (pp. 259–261)

A. Mnemonics

Mnemonics are strategies for remembering information. The method of loci associates well-known locations with information to be remembered.

B. Guidelines for More Effective Studying

Create a context, such as an outline, for organizing information. Elaborate the new information and associate it with related knowledge you already possess. Remember that distributed practice is more effective than massed practice.

> 1. *Reading a Textbook.* Make sure you understand what you are reading before you go on. Use the SQ3R method of survey, question, read, recite, and review.
>
> 2. *Lecture Notes.* Focus on creating a framework for facts (outline) and expressing major ideas in relatively few words. Finally, work to see and understand the relationship between facts and concepts. Review your notes as soon as possible after a lecture and fill in the gaps.

KEY TERMS

1. **Encoding** is the process of coding information so that it can be placed in sensory, short-term, or long-term memory. There are three types of codes: visual, acoustic, and semantic. (p. 229)

2. **Acoustic** codes are representations of the sounds we hear. (p. 229)

> *Example:* Think of your favorite song and hum it to yourself. The memory of how the melody sounds is an acoustic code in long-term memory.

3. **Visual** codes are representations of the images we see. (p. 229)

> *Example:* If you think of a Christmas tree or the car you would buy if you had enough money, you will most likely see images of these things in your mind. You do so because you have visual codes for them.

4. **Semantic** codes are representations of the meaning of experiences or factual information. (p. 229)

> *Example:* If you visit Israel, you may notice that the children can sing the top rock songs from the United States but that they do not know what the words mean. This is because they are using an acoustic code to remember a song and sing it, but they do not have a semantic code for the meaning of the words.

5. **Storage** is the process of maintaining or keeping a memory. (p. 229)

> *Example:* Memories of your kindergarten class, your second-grade teacher, or the first home you lived in are old memories. They have been stored for quite some time.

6. **Retrieval** is the process of transferring memories from storage to consciousness. (p. 229)

> *Example:* Whenever you remember anything, you are retrieving that memory from storage. Some memories are retrieved so quickly that you are unaware of the process. Answer the following questions: How old are you? How many people have been president of the United States? Both questions require you to retrieve information, but the retrieval process is much easier for the first question than for the second.

7. **Episodic memory** is any memory of a specific event that happened while you were present. (p. 230)

> *Example:* The memory of your first pony ride, a surprise birthday party that you held for a friend, or your first day of college is an episodic memory.
>
> *REMEMBER:* Episodic memories are episodes that involved you.

8. **Semantic memory** contains factual knowledge. This memory differs from episodic memory in that its contents are not associated with a specific event. (p. 230)

> *Example:* Knowing that the freezing point is 32 degrees Fahrenheit, that red lights mean stop, and that the capital of the United States is Washington, D.C., are all examples of semantic memory. You

probably cannot remember the specific time or episode during which you learned these facts.

9. **Procedural memory** (skill memory) holds "how-to" methods or processes that usually require some motor movement. (p. 230)

Example: Knowing how to waltz, do a somersault, tie a tie, and drive a car are all procedural memories.

10. **Explicit memory** is the process of purposely trying to remember something. (p. 230)

Example: While you are taking an exam, you are using explicit memory to retrieve information regarding the questions.

11. **Implicit memory** is the subconscious recall or influence of past experiences. (p. 230)

Example: Although you don't understand why, you are nervous whenever you wait for a bus on a specific corner. Stored subconsciously is the memory of a frightening event from your childhood in which a stranger approached you at that corner and you ran away.

12. The **levels-of-processing model** holds that differences in how well something is remembered reflect the degree or depth to which incoming information is mentally processed. (p. 232)

REMEMBER: Maintenance rehearsal does not require much processing and is effective for encoding information into short-term memory. Elaborative rehearsal requires a great deal of processing and is effective for encoding into long-term memory.

13. **Maintenance rehearsal**, repeating information over and over, keeps information in short-term memory. (p. 232)

Example: Kan arrives in New York to visit his cousin Zhou but loses Zhou's phone number. Kan calls directory assistance and the operator tells him the number. Kan repeats it over and over to himself while he inserts coins for the call.

REMEMBER: Maintenance rehearsal maintains information in short-term memory.

14. **Elaborative rehearsal** involves thinking about how new material is linked or related in some way to information already stored in long-term memory. It is an effective method of encoding information into long-term memory. (p. 232)

Example: Ursula is a world-class shopper. She has a mental image of all the major cities she has shopped in and images of the locations of all her favorite stores on each street. When Ursula wants to store information about a new store, she uses her mental image and places the new store on its street. She thinks about the new store in relationship to the stores surrounding it. Ursula is not just repeating the address of the new store but is also relating it to the addresses of all the other stores that she knows.

REMEMBER: New information is elaborated with information already in long-term memory. The new address is elaborated by relating its location to all the old addresses of stores already in long-term memory.

15. The **transfer-appropriate processing** model suggests that memory retrieval will be improved if the encoding method matches the retrieval method. (p. 233)

Example: Samantha studied for an auto mechanics test by spending many weekends with her head under the hood of a car. However, much to her surprise, when it came time to take the test, the professor handed out a multiple-choice exam. Samantha, who felt that she had really learned the material, scored poorly. According to the transfer-appropriate processing model, Samantha did not do well because she encoded the material by applying what she had learned from the text, but the exam asked her only to retrieve specific facts. Samantha's encoding process wasn't appropriate for the retrieval process required by the exam.

REMEMBER: Think of this model as stating that the encoding process that transfers information into long-term memory must be appropriate (match) for the retrieval cues.

16. **Parallel distributed processing** (or **PDP**) models of memory suggest that the connections between units of knowledge are strengthened with experience. Tapping into any connection (via a memory process) provides us with access to all the other connections in the network. (p. 233)

Example: Zoë's knowledge that the term *neonate* means "newborn" is linked to her memory of seeing a premature infant taken to a neonatal unit. Both neonate and neonatal are connected to her memory that *neo* means "new." When Zoë thinks of neonate, an image of her nephew as a newborn is also readily accessible. This background made it easier for her to understand that a *neofreudian* is a person who developed a new version of Freud's theory.

17. The **information-processing** model of memory has three stages: sensory memory; short-term, or working, memory; and long-term memory. (p. 234)

18. **Sensory memory** holds sensory information for a fraction of a second in sensory registers. If the information is attended to and recognized, perception takes place, and the information can enter short-term memory. (p. 235)

19. **Sensory registers** hold incoming sensory information until it is processed, recognized, and remembered. There is a sensory register for each sense. (p. 235)

20. **Selective attention** determines what information is held in sensory registers. Information that is not attended to decays and cannot be processed any further. (p. 236)

> *Example:* Imagine going to New York's Times Square for New Year's Eve. The crowd is immense. Suddenly, you see someone waving a sparkler in front of you. Even though your eyes and ears are being hit with a variety of stimuli, your sensory registers will retain information about the person with the sparkler because you "selected" that particular stimuli to "attend" to.

21. **Short-term memory** (or **working memory**) receives information that was perceived in sensory memory. Information in short-term memory is conscious but quite fragile and will be lost within seconds if not further processed. (p. 236)

> *Example:* If you look up a phone number and repeat it to yourself until you finish dialing, you will have kept it active in your short-term memory. However, it is likely that you will have forgotten it by the time you get off the phone, because you were using your working memory to process the new information coming in during the conversation.

22. An **immediate memory span** is the largest number of items or chunks of information that you can recall perfectly from short-term memory after one presentation of the stimuli. Most people have an immediate memory span of five to nine items. (p. 237)

> *Example:* Use a telephone book to help you test your own immediate memory span. Read the first two names at the top of the page, look away, and then try to recall them. Then read the next three names, look away, and try to recall them. Continue this process, using a longer list each time, until you cannot repeat the entire list of names. The number of names that

you can repeat perfectly is your immediate memory span.

23. **Chunks** are meaningful groupings of information that you place in short-term memory. The immediate memory span of short-term memory is probably between five and nine chunks of information. Each chunk contains bits of information grouped into a single unit. (p. 237)

> *Example:* During her first night as a waitress, Bridget needed all five to nine chunks in short-term memory to remember one order for one person. For example, a drink before dinner, a drink with dinner, a main dish, a type of salad dressing, a type of potato, and whether the customer wanted cream, sugar, or both with coffee made up five to nine chunks of information. After two years of waitressing, Bridget can easily hold in memory four to eight people's complete food and drink orders. Each person's order had become one chunk of information.
>
> *REMEMBER:* Chunks can be anything—letters, numbers, words, names, or locations—just to list a few. The more information you can condense or group into one chunk, the more information you can hold in short-term memory.

24. The **Brown-Peterson procedure** is a research method that prevents rehearsal. A person is presented with a group of three letters and then counts backward by threes from an arbitrarily selected number until a signal is given. The counting prevents the person from rehearsing the information. (p. 238)

25. **Long-term memory** is the stage of memory in which the capacity to store new information is believed to be unlimited. (p. 239)

26. The **primacy effect** occurs when we remember words at the beginning of a list better than those in the middle of the list. (p. 241)

> *REMEMBER:* Primacy means "being first." The primacy effect is the remembering of the first words in a list better than other words in the list.

27. The **recency effect** occurs when we remember the last few words on a list better than others on the list. The list's final items are in short-term memory at the time of recall. (p. 241)

> *Example:* After hearing all her students' names once, Leslie tries to recite them one by one. She remembers the names of students in the first two rows (primacy effect) and the names of the students in the last

two rows (recency effect), but she has difficulty recalling the names of students in the middle two rows.

REMEMBER: Recency means "that which occurred most recently." The last items of a list are presented most recently.

28. **Anterograde amnesia** is a loss of memory for events that occur after a brain injury. Memory for experiences prior to the trauma remains intact. (p. 241)

Example: People with anterograde amnesia will not be able to remember the new people they meet, because they are unable to form new memories.

REMEMBER: Anterograde amnesia is a loss of memory for the future, or after some point in time.

29. **Retrograde amnesia** is a loss of memory of events prior to a brain injury. Memories encoded days or years before the injury or trauma can be lost. Usually most memories return. (p. 242)

REMEMBER: Retro means "backward." The memory loss goes back in time.

30. **Retrieval cues** help us recognize information in long-term memory. In other words, they help you "jog" your memory. (p. 243)

Example: On a multiple-choice exam, the answer appears somewhere in the question. Some of the words in the correct answer should jog your memory and allow you to answer the question correctly.

31. The **encoding specificity principle** maintains that if the way information is encoded and the way it is retrieved are similar, remembering the information will be easier. (p. 243)

32. In **context-dependent** memory, the environment acts as a retrieval cue. This means that it is easier to remember information when you are in the location (context) where you originally learned that information. (p. 243)

Example: When taking his exam in his regular classroom, Leon's memory for lecture information is improved by glancing around at the chalkboard, peeling paint, and lecturer's desk. Although he doesn't realize it, he recalls the discussion of the opponent process color vision theory better because he is among familiar classmates and surroundings. Unfortunately, he does not remember as much of the information he studied in his room at home with the stereo blaring because there are fewer associated

retrieval cues there than in the quiet classroom environment.

33. In **state-dependent** memory, your psychological state acts as a retrieval cue. When you are trying to remember, if you are in the same psychological state you were in at the time of learning, you will retrieve more material. (p. 243)

Example: In the evening when she studied psychology, Lydia had several cups of coffee to keep her alert. The next morning, she did not do well on the quiz. Later, when drinking coffee with some friends, she was in the same state as when she studied for the quiz, and, to her amazement, she remembered some of the material that had escaped her during the quiz.

34. **Spreading activation** describes the way in which information is retrieved from long-term memory according to semantic network theories. Whenever a question is asked, neural activation spreads from those concepts contained in the question down all paths related to them. (p. 244)

Example: When Jane thinks about pizza, this activates other concepts such as food, delivery, cost, etc.

35. **Schemas** are summaries of knowledge about categories. We tend to automatically place people, objects, and events into classes. (p. 247)

Example: If your schema for a classroom is a square room filled with desks, upon seeing people seated on pillows in a round room you might be likely to classify it as a lounge.

36. The **method of savings** is a term introduced by Ebbinghaus to refer to the difference in the amount of time required to relearn material that has been forgotten and the amount of time it took to learn the material initially. (p. 251)

Example: If it took a subject twenty repetitions to learn a list of items but only five repetitions to relearn the list a semester later, there would be a savings of 75 percent.

37. **Decay** is a mechanism whereby information not used in long-term memory gradually fades until lost completely. (p. 252)

Example: Marissa learned Spanish, but has not tried to speak it in years. When Marissa tries to say, "Hello; how was your day?" to her roommate, she cannot remember the vocabulary necessary.

38. **Interference** is a mechanism whereby the retrieval or storage of information in long-term memory is impaired by other learning (retroactive and proactive interference). (p. 253)

39. **Retroactive interference** occurs when information in memory is displaced by new information. (p. 253)

> *REMEMBER:* <u>Retro</u> means "back." New information goes back and interferes with old information.

40. **Proactive interference** occurs when old information in long-term memory interferes with the remembering of new information. (p. 253)

> *Example:* If you have ever learned something incorrectly and then tried to correct it, you may have experienced proactive interference. Young children who take music lessons once a week experience this. They learn an incorrect note, and at their lesson the next week, their teacher points out the mistake. However, it is very difficult to play the correct note because the old memory of the wrong note interferes with the new memory of the correct note.
>
> *REMEMBER:* <u>Pro</u> means "forward." Old information goes forward and interferes with new information.

41. **Mnemonics** are encoding methods that increase the efficiency of your memory. (p. 259)

> *Example:* To remember the name "Hathaway," you might picture the person coming "half the way" to you.

FILL-IN-THE-BLANKS KEY TERMS

This section will help you check your factual knowledge of the key terms introduced in this chapter. Fill in each blank with the appropriate term from the list of key terms above.

1. Memories that contain general, factual knowledge are called _____ .

2. Sounds that we perceive are represented as _____ in memory.

3. Incoming stimuli from the world are held in _____ until they are processed or decay.

4. Information in _____ memory will be lost within twenty seconds if it is not further processed.

5. When new information interferes with the remembering of old information, this phenomenon is called _____ .

6. Repeating information over and over as a way to remember it is called _____ .

7. The difference in the amount of time it takes to relearn something compared to the amount of time it took to learn it originally is called _____ .

8. Methods that can improve your memory by increasing encoding efficiency are called _____ .

9. _____ is the phenomenon in which people's memory is enhanced if they are in the same situation as when they learned the material.

10. Immediate memory span refers to the capacity of _____ memory.

11. When a person remembers the last few items on a list better than others, this is called the _____ effect.

12. _____ rehearsal is an effective method for encoding information into long-term memory.

13. The _____ model holds that differences in remembering information are based on the degree to which the information is mentally analyzed.

14. Retrieval cues help us recall information from _____ memory.

15. The inability to remember any information before a certain point in time is called _____ .

Total Correct (See answer key) _____

LEARNING OBJECTIVES

1. Define and give an example of <u>encoding</u>, <u>acoustic codes</u>, <u>semantic codes</u>, <u>visual codes</u>, <u>storage</u>, and <u>retrieval</u>. Discuss the importance of encoding, storage, and retrieval in memory processes. (p. 229)

2. Define and give an example of <u>episodic</u>, <u>semantic</u>, and <u>procedural memories</u>. (p. 230)

3. Define and give an example of <u>explicit</u> and <u>implicit memories</u>. Discuss the series of experiments on explicit and implicit memory. (pp. 231–232)

4. Define the <u>levels-of-processing model</u> of memory. Describe the role of rehearsal in this memory model. Define <u>maintenance</u> and <u>elaborative rehearsal</u>. (p. 232)

5. Define <u>transfer-appropriate processing</u>. Describe the role of encoding and retrieval processes in this memory model. (p. 233)

6. Define the <u>parallel distributed processing (PDP) model</u> of memory. Describe the role of association

networks in drawing inferences and making generalizations. (p. 233)

7. Define the information-processing model of memory. Name the three stages of processing. (p. 234)

8. Define sensory memory and sensory registers. Discuss the amount of information and the length of time it stays in sensory memory. (pp. 235–236)

9. Explain why selective attention is important in determining which information is transferred to short-term memory from sensory memory. (p. 236)

10. Define short-term memory (STM). Explain why some psychologists refer to this as working memory. (p. 236)

11. Describe short-term memory encoding. (pp. 236–237)

12. Define immediate memory span and chunking. Discuss the role of long-term memory in the chunking process. (pp. 237–238)

13. Define the Brown-Peterson procedure. Describe the importance of rehearsal in maintaining information in short-term memory. (pp. 238–239)

14. Define long-term memory (LTM) and discuss the importance of semantic encoding in long-term memory. Describe the storage capacity of LTM. (pp. 239–240)

15. Describe the controversy over the differences between short-term and long-term memory. Define primacy and recency effects. (pp. 240–241)

16. Define anterograde and retrograde amnesia and discuss their relevance to the STM/LTM difference controversy. (pp. 241–242)

17. Define retrieval cue and explain why its use can increase memory efficiency. Define the encoding specificity principle. (p. 243)

18. Define context dependence and state dependence and give examples of each. Explain the mood congruency effect. (pp. 243–244)

19. Describe the semantic network theory of memory. Explain the process of spreading activation in memory. (p. 244)

20. Define the tip-of-the-tongue and the feeling-of-knowing phenomena. Explain how these are related to the semantic network theory of memory. (p. 245)

21. Define constructive memory. Describe how PDP memory models explain the integration of semantic

and episodic memories in memory construction. (pp. 245–246)

22. Explain how PDP models produce spontaneous generalization and why they help explain the operation of schemas. (pp. 246–249)

23. Discuss the controversy surrounding repressed memories. Describe motivated forgetting, false memories, and flashbulb memories. (pp. 249–251)

24. Define Ebbinghaus's method of savings. Explain his discoveries and why they are important memory research. (pp. 251–252)

25. Compare and contrast the decay and interference theories regarding forgetting information stored in long-term memory. Define retroactive interference and proactive interference. (pp. 252–255)

26. Discuss the use of eyewitness testimony in the courtroom. (pp. 255–256)

27. Describe the synaptic activity associated with forming new memories. Describe the role of the hippocampus in episodic and procedural memory formation. (pp. 257–258)

28. Define mnemonics and explain why they improve memory. Give an example of the method of loci. (p. 259)

29. Explain why distributed practice is more effective than massed practice. Describe the SQ3R method and its use. Describe the best method of taking notes in a lecture. (pp. 259–261)

CONCEPTS AND EXERCISES

No. 1: Memory Cues

Completing this exercise should help you to achieve Learning Objectives 1, 2, 12, 18, and 25.

There has been a robbery at a local bank. For questioning, the police have placed the witnesses in the locations they occupied during the robbery. Indicate what type of memory, code, or process is responsible for each statement. Draw your answers from the list following the exercise. Answers may be used more than once or not at all.

1. Police: We are questioning you here at the bank because we think it will improve your recall of the robbery. _____ What was the suspect wearing?

2. Teller 1: I know he had a coat on, but I don't remember the color. _____

3. Teller 2: I remember. It was green. _____

   Police (To teller 3): Where were you when the robbery took place?

4. Teller 3: I was standing in the manager's office when the man approached me and told me to unlock the door to the safe. _____

   Police: Did you have to look up the combination to the safe?

5. Teller 3: No, sir. The manager had just given me the new combination for the day ten seconds before the man approached me. I just grouped the numbers into a date so I'd remember them for the few minutes it would take me to walk from the office to the safe. Just as I'd finished thinking about the combination, the gunman was there ordering me to unlock the safe. _____

   Police: Did the man have any unusual speech characteristics?

6. Teller 2: Yes, he did. I remember hearing him slur his S's. _____

   Police (To teller 1): Please demonstrate the steps you follow in order to sound the alarm.

7. Teller 1: I have to step on this foot pedal like this. _____

   Police: Why did it take you so long to sound the alarm?

8. Teller 1: Well, sir, I've just started working at this bank. The alarm at my last job sounded at the push of a button. I guess I panicked a bit. I was looking for the button for a few seconds before I realized that here I have to push a foot pedal. _____

   Police: Thank you, everyone. That will be all for now.

   ° Acoustic code
   ° Procedural memory
   ° Context dependence
   ° Chunking
   ° Semantic code
   ° Visual code
   ° Episodic memory
   ° Proactive interference
   ° Retroactive interference

No. 2: Learning How to Study

Completing this exercise should help you to achieve Learning Objectives 4, 28, and 29.

Below are descriptions of study methods that need improvement. Use the information you have learned in this chapter to fill in the blanks following the descriptions.

1. Rodney is taking a vocabulary improvement class. He is learning to recognize the roots of words and their meanings. He tries to memorize the material by repeating it to himself over and over again. Instead of doing this, he should probably try using _____.

2. Ginny is a college freshman. She is taking a course in biology, a subject she never had in high school. When she takes notes, she desperately tries to write down every word the instructor says. Instead, she should _____ the information.

3. Carin hates to read. She wants to get it over with quickly, so she reads large amounts of material at a time. Then she complains that she can never remember what she has just read. She should try using the _____ method.

CRITICAL THINKING

Sam is very frustrated. He had to release a suspect that he was sure was guilty, because the only witness couldn't remember what happened.

Sam had found the witness next to the scene of the crime about fifteen minutes after it happened. The witness was an old man who lived on the corner at the scene of the crime. He spent most of his time drinking and was in pretty bad shape. Sam pulled the witness in and let him sleep in the jail, figuring that if the witness got a good, warm, and safe night's sleep, a hot meal, and a chance to sober up, he would be willing to talk. However, Sam's efforts were to no avail. The witness just couldn't remember what he had seen. In fact, all he wanted to do was get back to his corner so that he could get a drink.

Sam, crestfallen, tells Martina that he failed and had to let the witness go.

Martina says, "All may not be lost. Grab your coat and let's go."

"Where are we going?" asks Sam.

Martina replies. "First we are going to the liquor store, and then back to the scene of the crime."

Using the five critical thinking questions in your text, the clues in the story, and what you have just learned about memory, answer the following:

1. What is Sam's hypothesis?

2. What is the evidence in support of Sam's hypothesis?

3. What is Martina's alternative hypothesis?

4. What evidence must Martina gather to support her hypothesis?

5. What conclusions can Martina draw if the evidence she needs to collect supports her hypothesis?

PERSONAL LEARNING ACTIVITIES

1. Describe your earliest memories of several family members and see how well they match your relatives' recollections of the same events. (Learning Objectives 2 and 21)

2. Do an experiment to see the effects of maintenance versus elaborative rehearsal. One way to do this would be to read a list of about twenty words or names and repeat them to yourself several times. Then write down the time of day, your full name, address, and phone number (to clear the words from your short-term memory). Without looking at the list, write as many as you can. Next study a list of twenty words or names by associating an image with each, clear your short-term memory, and then write as many as you can. Was there a difference? Does the size of any difference depend upon what type of information you are trying to learn? (Learning Objective 4)

3. Do you think your memory has improved with increasing age? Why or why not? What factors do you think most influence whether you will recall a phone number, an appointment, someone's name, or lecture information? (Learning Objectives 9, 13, and 14)

4. To understand how context-dependent memory works, try two very different locations for learning and remembering. After learning new information, test yourself on it in the same location in which you learned it—a classroom, or wherever you do your homework. After learning some other new material, go to an equally quiet but different place—the shower, your car, or even your closet—and test yourself. Notice the difference in how much you remember in the original location as compared to the different location. (Learning Objective 18)

5. Try a new study method and use a sample quiz to test for memory improvement. For instance, you could use SQ3R for a chapter and see the effects of using the survey, question, read, recite, review method for learning from your textbook. (Learning Objective 29)

MULTIPLE-CHOICE QUESTIONS

SAMPLE QUIZ 1

1. Steven heard his instructor say, "Remember to read the short stories by Christie, Cheever, Porter, and Sayers for next week." Because Steven isn't familiar with the names, he remembers them as "Krissy, Cleever, Porter, and Savers." Steven most likely used _____ encoding.
   a. acoustic
   b. episodic
   c. semantic
   d. visual

2. The memory for how to perform a physical action is called _____ memory.
   a. episodic
   b. procedural
   c. semantic
   d. short-term

3. A murder investigation is going on at the resort where you are vacationing. The police are asking you for your alibi. What kind of memory do you need to provide an alibi?
   a. Episodic
   b. Procedural
   c. Semantic
   d. Short-term

4. Nathan doesn't consciously think about an incident from his childhood when a red-haired neighbor gave him candy and comforted him after he skinned his knee. Due to the subconscious influence of that memory, however, Nathan tends to react positively to any red-haired people he meets; therefore, he is being influenced by his _____ memory.
   a. episodic
   b. explicit
   c. implicit
   d. procedural

5. Raquel was still studying ten minutes before her test. As she entered the classroom, she kept repeating the last sentence she had read: "Henry VIII had six wives." This is an example of
   a. elaborative rehearsal.
   b. maintenance rehearsal.
   c. mnemonics.
   d. retrieval.

6. At the same time that Reepal is listening to her father tell about the party the family is planning, Reepal smells popcorn, hears her radio, sees lightning, and feels hot. Reepal is able to transfer the information about the party to her short-term memory primarily because of
   a. elaborative rehearsal.
   b. implicit memory cues.
   c. selective attention.
   d. transfer-appropriate processing.

7. An immediate memory span is the number of items that
   a. can be held in the sensory registers.
   b. are stored in long-term memory.
   c. can be held in semantic codes.
   d. can be recalled in perfect order following one presentation of a stimulus.

8. Unrehearsed information stays in short-term memory for no more than
   a. one second.
   b. three seconds.
   c. eighteen seconds.
   d. forever.

9. Which of the following sentences would require the most chunks in short-term memory if you only knew how to speak English?
   a. John has many friends.
   b. *Ich liebe dich.*
   c. *Je ne sais pas.*
   d. –.–.–.–..–..–..– (Morse code)

10. In order to chunk efficiently, you will need to
    a. use your long-term memory.
    b. group many items into one chunk.
    c. transfer information quickly from short-term to long-term memory.
    d. all of the above.

11. Vinnie is exasperated. He has gone to the library to look up a book for class. Even though he checked his class notes before he left, he cannot remember the name of the book. What could account for his memory lapse?
    a. Inefficient storage in sensory memory
    b. Information not getting transferred to long-term memory
    c. Problems with selective attention
    d. None of the above

12. Loss of memory for incidents following hippocampal damage is called _____ amnesia.
    a. retrograde
    b. anterograde
    c. proactive
    d. retroactive

13. Multiple-choice questions are easier to answer than essay questions because multiple-choice questions
    a. cause more interference.
    b. contain more retrieval cues.
    c. use only semantic memory.
    d. use only procedural memory.

14. Better recall of the first few words of a list from long-term memory is called the _____ effect.
    a. primacy
    b. recency
    c. fatigue
    d. parallel position

15. Alberta is a night owl. She loves to stay up late and study. However, she has so many classes this semester that she is forced to take her calculus class and study calculus in the morning when she is sluggish and a bit sleepy. Alberta's calculus teacher has given the class a take-home test. Alberta should take the test
    a. in the evening.
    b. in the afternoon.
    c. in the morning.
    d. whenever she feels like it.

16. To answer a question such as, "How many legs do spiders have?" a person will most likely use _____ memory.
    a. episodic
    b. semantic
    c. sensory
    d. short-term

17. An officer shows Sarah a box of office supplies believed to have been stolen from her store and then puts them at the back of the room. When Sarah is asked whether the staplers appear to be those stolen from her store, she thinks for a minute about the staplers she recalls seeing in the box and says they are like the ones stolen. To Sarah's surprise, the officer then shows her that there are no staplers in the box! Sarah must have used _____ memories to answer the question.
    a. constructive
    b. elaborative
    c. generalized
    d. implicit

18. Sudden short-term memory overload will most likely cause
    a. decay.
    b. proactive interference.
    c. displacement.
    d. all of the above.

19. Last week Sigrid had to memorize a poem to recite in front of the class. When she rehearsed at home, her mom told her that she had memorized an incorrect word and told her what to say instead. However, Sigrid had memorized the incorrect version so well that she had difficulty learning the correct word. This is an example of
    a. retroactive interference.
    b. proactive interference.
    c. anterograde amnesia.
    d. decay.

20. Kristi has memorized a list of names by imagining each person in a specific spot in her dorm room. One person is in the closet, another is under the bed, one is hanging upside down from the ceiling, and so on. She is using
    a. context dependence.
    b. distributed practice.
    c. the encoding specificity principle.
    d. the method of loci.

Total Correct (See answer key) _____

SAMPLE QUIZ 2

Use this quiz to reassess your learning after taking Quiz 1 and reviewing the chapter.

1. Al saw a movie called "Fight of the Kodiak" and immediately thought, "Kodiak is a bear, so this is going to have good scenery." Unfortunately, because Al only _____ encoded the name of the movie as "about a bear," he couldn't remember the actual name when someone asked him later what movie he saw.
    a. acoustically
    b. procedurally
    c. semantically
    d. visually

2. Colleen frequently loses her keys. To find them, she always has to sit and remember where she had them last. This is an example of
    a. semantic memory.
    b. procedural memory.
    c. episodic memory.
    d. acoustic coding.

3. As Kaliina completes a personal history questionnaire, she recalls her birthdate, names of schools she's attended, and relatives' names. Suddenly, she feels hot, flushed, and embarrassed, but doesn't know why. Kaliina's mom realizes that Kaliina subconsciously remembers the time she filled out a similar form and then fainted. When Kaliina tries to remember her personal information, she is using _____ memory; when she feels embarrassed, she is using _____ memory.
    a. episodic; semantic
    b. semantic; episodic
    c. implicit; explicit
    d. explicit; implicit

4. Which of the following would be most effective for encoding information into long-term memory?
    a. Chunking
    b. Maintenance rehearsal
    c. Elaborative rehearsal
    d. Serial rehearsal

5. As Laura reads her psychology textbook, the image of each word is stored long enough to be processed and understood. Laura's _____ memory holds the images just long enough to allow stimulus identification to begin.
    a. long-term
    b. semantic
    c. sensory
    d. short-term

6. Beck is bewildered. She has just spent an hour making a list of items to pack for her year of school abroad. She got up to take a look in her closet, came back to the desk, and now cannot find the list. With a sigh, she decides just to start packing. If she forgets an item, it will probably be from the _____ of the list.
    a. beginning
    b. middle
    c. end
    d. none of the above

7. Perception determines what information is transferred to
    a. sensory memory.
    b. short-term memory.
    c. long-term memory.
    d. sensory registers.

8. Ramona's mother has given her a grocery list, and she is off to the store. As she enters the parking lot, she realizes that she forgot to bring the list with her. However, she can recall the first ten items on the list and decides to buy just those. Her recollection of the first ten items on the list is an example of
   a. the recency effect.
   b. the primacy effect.
   c. interference.
   d. retroactive amnesia.

9. Remembering the phone number 217-1967 as your birthday, February 17, 1967, is an example of
   a. chunking.
   b. the Brown-Peterson procedure.
   c. the SQ3R method.
   d. the method of loci.

10. Ted showed his third-graders pictures of famous presidents. To quiz them, he gave them clues about what these people looked like. For example, "He wore a big black hat, enjoyed reading by the fireplace, was very, very tall, and had a black beard." These clues will function as
    a. retrieval cues.
    b. primacy cues.
    c. contextual codes.
    d. acoustic codes.

11. Context dependence means that information is easier to remember when
    a. it is organized, for example, in an outline.
    b. people are in the same place as they were when they learned the material.
    c. people are in the same psychological state of mind as they were when they learned the material.
    d. a mnemonic is used.

12. When Molly tried to remember the name of the actor who portrayed Dr. Eilam on her favorite TV program, she could see the first letters, but could not think of the name. Molly's experience of the tip-of-the-tongue phenomenon is caused by retrieval of incomplete information from her
    a. constructive memory.
    b. sensory memory.
    c. semantic networks.
    d. schemas.

13. If you lost the ability to retrieve any information from long-term memory, you would not be able to
    a. chunk information.
    b. recognize information in sensory memory.

    c. use the method of loci.
    d. all of the above

14. When Kris sees his son without clothes on after having his bath, Kris suddenly feels extremely worried. In a discussion of the incident during therapy, Kris recalls for the first time that he was sexually molested by a relative. Kris's therapist might describe this recollection as a(n) _____ memory.
    a. elaborative
    b. procedural
    c. repressed
    d. state-dependent

15. The memory that Kris has recovered should, according to the "Thinking Critically" section in your text, be
    a. considered a constructed memory.
    b. immediately accepted as an accurate memory.
    c. examined through the use of other evidence.
    d. recorded as a case of retroactive amnesia.

16. Retroactive interference occurs when
    a. new information interferes with the ability to recall old information.
    b. old information interferes with the learning of new material.
    c. old information decays.
    d. new information decays.

17. When Robin moved to a new state, her new teacher told her that the class was learning the names of all the presidents. Robin was horrified. She had painstakingly memorized all those names the year before and could not remember very many of them. To her surprise, however, learning them the second time took much less time than it had the first time. This is an example of
    a. mnemonics.
    b. release from proactive interference.
    c. savings.
    d. state dependence.

18. Jen has hippocampus damage; therefore, she has memory problems. Which of the following will she most likely be unable to do?
    a. Learn how to solve a puzzle
    b. Remember the names of new people she met ten minutes ago.
    c. Remember a childhood birthday party
    d. Remember how to ride a bike

19. Mentally placing objects in specific geographic locations in order to remember them more efficiently is called
    a. the method of loci.
    b. procedural memorization.
    c. use of retrieval cue.
    d. context dependence.

20. Jacques was so involved in his social life his first semester that he almost flunked out. At the beginning of second semester, he asked his friends for their advice. Which friend should he *not* listen to?
    a. Friend 1: "Read the material a second time."
    b. Friend 2: "Create an outline for your lecture notes. You need to mentally organize the material somehow."
    c. Friend 3: "Ask yourself questions about the material as you read, and then look for the answers in the text."
    d. Friend 4: "Try to relate the material to information you already know."

Total Correct (See answer key) _____

ANSWERS TO FILL-IN-THE-BLANKS KEY TERMS

1. semantic memories (p. 230)
2. acoustic codes (p. 229)
3. sensory registers (p. 235)
4. short-term or working (p. 236)
5. retroactive interference (p. 253)
6. maintenance rehearsal (p. 232)
7. savings (p. 251)
8. mnemonics (p. 259)
9. Context dependence (p. 243)
10. short-term or working (pp. 236–237)
11. recency (p. 241)
12. Elaborative (p. 232)
13. levels-of-processing (p. 232)
14. long-term (p. 243)
15. retrograde amnesia (p. 242)

ANSWERS TO CONCEPTS AND EXERCISES

No. 1: Memory Cues

1. *Context dependence.* The context, in this case the bank, acts as a retrieval cue and helps the witnesses remember as much as possible about the robbery. (p. 243)

2. *Semantic code.* Teller 1 remembers that the robber had a coat on but does not have a visual code containing the color of the coat. (p. 229)

3. *Visual code.* Teller 2 does have a visual code of the robber, which includes the color of the robber's coat. (p. 229)

4. *Episodic memory.* Teller 3 is remembering an event (or episode) in which he was a participant. (p. 230)

5. *Chunking.* Teller 3 has used chunking to remember the combination to the safe. He has grouped the numbers into one meaningful unit of information: a date. (p. 237)

6. *Acoustic code.* Teller 2 has an acoustic code for the sound of the robber's voice. (p. 229)

7. *Procedural memory.* Teller 1 has a procedural memory for how to sound the alarm. (p. 230)

8. *Proactive interference.* The old information, how to sound the alarm in the bank that Teller 1 used to work at, is interfering with her ability to remember how to sound the alarm at her present job. (p. 253)

No. 2: Learning How to Study

1. *Elaborative rehearsal.* Classical mnemonics are good tools for memorizing long lists of words, as Rodney has to do. Maintenance rehearsal is a good method for keeping information in short-term memory. However, it will not help Rodney place the information in long-term memory. (p. 232)

2. *Summarize.* Ginny should think about the lecture when she hears it in order to build a framework or overall organization for the material. She should write down only summaries of basic ideas. (p. 261)

3. *SQ3R method.* The SQ3R method is a series of five steps that will increase the amount of information Carin remembers from her reading assignments. (p. 260)

ANSWERS TO CRITICAL THINKING

1. Sam's hypothesis is that the witness simply cannot remember what happened.

2. The fact that after a hot meal, a good night's sleep, and the opportunity to sober up the witness can't remember supports Sam's hypothesis.

3. Martina remembers the concepts of context and state dependence. She hypothesizes that if the witness goes back to the corner where he lives

(same context) and has a drink (same state), he will be better able to remember.

4. Martina needs to carry out her hypothesis—that is, question the witness on his corner, after he has had a drink, and see if he can remember.

5. Martina can't really draw any conclusions even if the man does remember. He could lie just to ensure that he is allowed to drink. Therefore, Martina can only follow up the clues that the old man provides and hope that his memory is accurate and that he is telling the truth. (*NOTE:* Critical thinking is a constant process of hypothesizing, examining evidence, rehypothesizing, and collecting more evidence. Can you think of any other hypotheses to explain the situation?)

ANSWERS TO MULTIPLE-CHOICE QUESTIONS

Circle the question numbers you answered correctly.

Sample Quiz 1

1. *a* is the answer. When acoustic codes are used the errors likely to be made are errors in remembering the sound of the words. (p. 229)
   b. Episodic memories are those of events you witnessed, but episodic is not a type of coding.
   c. Semantic encoding represents the meaning of the information. If Steven had used a semantic code, he might have remembered something about the meaning of the names (assuming he was familiar with them, which he wasn't) such as the titles of the stories or the homelands of the authors.
   d. A visual code would require a visual stimulus, but the instructor just said the names.

2. *b* is the answer. Remembering how to do something is procedural memory. (p. 230)
   a. Episodic memories are memories of events that occurred while you were present, such as the memory of your first day at school.
   c. Semantic memories are memories of generalized knowledge, such as remembering the tribal names of the Plains Indians.
   d. Remembering how to do something isn't necessarily a short-term memory. It could be in long-term memory.

3. *a* is the answer. Where you were at the time of the murder would be a memory of an episode at which

you were present. This is episodic memory. (p. 230)
   b. Procedural memories involve how to do something or how to carry out a procedure.
   c. Semantic memories involve general knowledge.
   d. Short-term memory is where episodic, procedural, and semantic memories can be stored for about 20 seconds, but this wouldn't be long enough to use in answering questions about your whereabouts.

4. *c* is the answer. Implicit memories are not purposefully recalled but do influence behavior. (p. 230)
   a. Episodic memories are memories of events, but Nathan has not recalled the childhood event; therefore, it is not what is influencing him.
   b. Explicit memories are those we purposely try to remember. Nathan has not tried to remember the childhood incident, nor has he remembered it.
   d. Procedural memories are skill memories. Nathan is not recalling a skill like bike riding, he is being influenced by a subconscious childhood memory.

5. *b* is the answer. Maintenance rehearsal is a method of keeping information in short-term memory. Raquel is trying to keep in short-term memory the most recently read information. (p. 232)
   a. Elaborative rehearsal occurs when new information is related to old information in long-term memory. If Raquel tried to integrate the number of wives that Henry VIII had with other information about him, she would have been using elaborative rehearsal.
   c. Mnemonics are strategies for creating a new context for material in order to recall it later. Raquel was not doing anything other than repeating the information. She did not use mental imagery or the method of loci.
   d. Raquel was trying to keep the information in storage, not trying to retrieve it.

6. *c* is the answer. Selective attention allows the most important information processed by the sensory registers to be retained in short-term memory. (p. 236)
   a. Reepal is not described as having used elaborative rehearsal. Elaborative rehearsal would be relating new information to old information.
   b. Implicit memory is the unintentional recall and influence of prior experiences, but there is no such thing as an implicit memory cue.
   d. Transfer-appropriate processing is when encoding method matches retrieval method.

7. *d* is the answer. An immediate memory span or the capacity of short-term memory is that amount of information a person can remember after one presentation of a stimulus. (p. 237)

   a. An unlimited amount of information can be stored in sensory memory, but only for a short time.

   b. There is no span or limit on the amount of information that can be stored in long-term memory.

   c. Items in memory can take the form of a semantic code, but items are not stored *in* semantic code.

8. *c* is the answer. Unrehearsed information stays in short-term memory for about eighteen seconds. (p. 236)

   a, b. Information in the sensory registers is maintained for no more than a few seconds.

   d. Information may stay in long-term memory until death, unless it decays.

9. *d* is the answer. Morse code uses a different "alphabet" than English does. A person who does not know Morse code would not have any information in long-term memory that would help put more than one symbol into one chunk. Therefore, the Morse code statement (which translates as the one-word sentence "No") would require the greatest number of chunks in short-term memory. (pp. 237–238)

   a. The entire sentence could be one chunk for a native English speaker.

   b, c. Both French and German use the same alphabet as English. Therefore, each word would be a chunk because information stored in long-term memory would help recognize the letters as words. However, each dot or dash of a Morse code letter would be one unit of new information, causing that statement to require a greater number of chunks.

10. *d* is the answer. In order to chunk information efficiently, you must be able to use long-term memory to recognize the new information in short-term memory and create chunks, put as many items as possible into one chunk, and be able to transfer information quickly from short-term to long-term memory. (pp. 237–238)

11. *b* is the answer. When Vinnie remembered what it was he needed, he put that information into short-term memory. He then probably became distracted before the memory was transferred into long-term memory. (p. 239)

   a, c. If Vinnie checked his class notes before he left for the library, information had probably already been processed and transferred from sensory to short-term memory. Selective attention determines what is held in the sensory registers for further processing.

   d. *b* is the answer.

12. *b* is the answer. As described in the famous case of HM in your text, damage to the hippocampus results in anterograde amnesia—the inability to form new long-term memories. (pp. 241–242)

   a. Retrograde amnesia is the inability to remember what happened before damage or injury.

   c, d. There is no such thing as proactive or retroactive amnesia. (You are probably thinking of proactive and retroactive interference.)

13. *b* is the answer. The answer to a multiple-choice question is listed on the page. It will act as a retrieval cue by helping you recognize information stored in long-term memory. (p. 243)

   a. Answering multiple-choice questions actually creates less interference. Retrieval cues decrease the effect of interference.

   c. A good answer to an essay question would require more extensive semantic memory than would a multiple-choice answer.

   d. Neither multiple-choice questions nor essay questions use only procedural memories.

14. *a* is the answer. Better recall of the first few words of a list from long-term memory is called the primacy effect. (p. 241)

   b. Better recall of the last few words of a list from short-term memory is called the recency effect.

   c. There is no such thing as the fatigue effect.

   d. There is no such thing as the parallel position effect.

15. *c* is the answer. Taking the test in the morning lets Alberta's state of mind act as a retrieval cue (utilizes state-dependent memory). (p. 243)

   a, b, d. At any other time of the day, Alberta would not be in the same psychological state as she was when she learned the material.

16. *b* is the answer. Semantic memory contains general knowledge that isn't linked to a particular event. (p. 230)

   a. Episodic memory would not answer a question about facts that are not related to a personally experienced event.

   c. A person uses sensory memory to hear or read a question, but in order to answer the question the person must draw upon information in the semantic memory.

d. Short-term memory lasts only 20 seconds; therefore, it would be unlikely to contain the answer to a question of general knowledge.

17. *a* is the answer. Constructive memories can be very vivid. Sarah probably thought that staplers would be likely to be in the box of office supplies and accidentally created a memory of their image. (p. 245)

b. There is no such thing as elaborative memories. Elaborative rehearsal is the term for linking new information to old information. Sarah was probably not rehearsing the information about what was in the box.

c. Generalized memories is not a term. You may have been thinking of semantic memories, but Sarah was not using her semantic memory to create the memory of a stapler.

d. Implicit memories are actual memories that we have not tried to retrieve but that affect us anyway. Since there were no staplers in the box, Sarah couldn't have an implicit memory of them.

18. *c* is the answer. Overloading short-term memory causes interference with old information through displacement. Short-term memory can hold only a limited amount of information; new information literally squeezes out old information because of inadequate space. (p. 253)

a. Memories that decay disappear gradually. When short-term memory is suddenly overloaded, old information doesn't slowly decay; rather, it is quickly displaced.

b. Proactive interference occurs when old information prevents the learning of new information. When short-term memory is overloaded, the old information is lost, and the new information is stored.

d. Only c is the answer.

19. *b* is the answer. Proactive interference occurs when the process of remembering new information is disrupted by the presence of old information. The old, incorrect version of the poem that Sigrid had memorized kept getting in the way of her learning the correct word. (p. 253)

a. For retroactive interference to be the correct answer, learning the new word in the poem should have interfered with Sigrid's ability to remember the old, incorrect version of the poem. Retroactive interference refers to new

information disrupting the recall of old information.

c. Anterograde amnesia is the inability to form new memories after hippocampal damage. Sigrid's hippocampus was intact.

d. Decay is the gradual disappearance of a memory. Sigrid would have had to learn the new word and then forget it for this to be the right answer.

20. *d* is the answer. Kristi is using the method of loci to mentally place people in various spots in her dorm room. When she needs to remember these people, she will mentally look for them in her dorm room. (p. 259)

a. Kristi is using imagery, not her current environment (context), to recall information.

b. Distributed practice is taking a break between study sessions instead of "cramming." Kristi is not described as taking study breaks.

c. The encoding specificity principle refers to the similarity between information when it is learned and when it is retrieved. This is not a mnemonic.

Now turn to the quiz analysis table at the end of this chapter to find which areas you know well and which areas you need to work on. Circle the numbers in the table for items on Quiz 1 that you answered correctly.

ANSWERS TO MULTIPLE-CHOICE QUESTIONS

Circle the question numbers you answered correctly.

Sample Quiz 2

1. *c* is the answer. Semantic encoding is a meaning code, which makes it less likely that exact words (such as in a title) will be recalled, although the topic may be recalled. (p. 229)

a. Acoustic codes represent what something sounds like. If Al had acoustically encoded the movie title, he might have remembered the exact words, or words that sounded similar.

b. Procedural memory is the knowledge of how to do something; it is not a code.

d. Visual codes are images. Al coded the meaning of the title, not an image of it.

2. *c* is the answer. Colleen has to remember where she was when she last had her keys. This is episodic memory; she will be present in the remembered event. (p. 230)

a. Semantic memories are of general knowledge. Since Colleen is trying to remember an incident or episode that involves her presence, this cannot be the answer.

b. Procedural memories are of how to do something. Colleen is trying to remember an episode, not a procedure.

d. Acoustic memory is for sounds. Colleen is trying to remember where she left her keys, not what sound they made.

3. d is the answer. Trying to recall personal information is using explicit memory; accidentally being influenced by a subconscious memory is an effect of implicit memory. (p. 230)

a, b. Kaliina is not remembering an episode from her life nor general knowledge.

c. Implicit memories unintentionally influence us; they are not the intentional recall of personal information. (See d.)

4. c is the answer. Elaborative rehearsal, which is relating the new information to be remembered to information in long-term memory, is an effective way of encoding information into long-term memory. (p. 232)

a. Chunking is an effective method for storing information in short-term memory.

b. Maintenance rehearsal is an effective method for retaining information in short-term memory.

d. There is no such thing as serial rehearsal.

5. c is the answer. Sensory memory lasts about a second, then the information is transferred to short-term memory or lost. (p. 235)

a. Long-term memory can last for years; it is not a sensory register.

b. Semantic memory is part of long-term memory. A network links information.

d. Short-term memory is involved in reading, but it is not a sensory register.

6. b is the answer. Because of the primacy and recency effects, Beck will probably remember those items at the beginning and end of the list better than those in the middle. (p. 241)

a. The information at the beginning of the list has had a chance to enter long-term memory. She probably will not forget these items. This is called the primacy effect.

c. The information at the end of the list is in short-term memory. She probably will not forget these items. This is called the recency effect.

d. b is the answer. Beck will most likely forget information in the middle of the list.

7. b is the answer. Perception determines which information in sensory memory will be transferred to short-term memory. (p. 236)

a. Selective attention determines which information in sensory memory will be processed further. It does not determine which information goes into sensory memory.

c. Scientists are not sure what causes consolidation or transformation into long-term memory.

d. When the senses pick up information, it is automatically transferred to the sensory registers in sensory memory.

8. b is the answer. Remembering the beginning of a list but forgetting the middle constitutes the primacy effect. (p. 241)

a. If the question said that Ramona could remember the end of the list, recency effect would have been the correct response.

c. If Ramona's memory of something she learned just prior to or after reading the grocery list prevented her from remembering all the items, this would have been the correct answer.

d. There is no such thing as retroactive amnesia. (You may have been thinking of retrograde amnesia.)

9. a is the answer. Chunking is the ability to group information into a meaningful unit that can be stored in short-term memory. (p. 237)

b. The Brown-Peterson procedure is used to determine how long unrehearsed information remains in short-term memory.

c. The SQ3R method is a way to read a textbook by surveying, questioning, reading, reciting, and reviewing.

d. The method of loci is a mnemonic.

10. a is the answer. Ted has listed features that should help his students recognize the correct information stored in long-term memory: the name *Abraham Lincoln*. (p. 243)

b. Primacy cue is not a term. You may have been thinking of primacy effect.

c, d. When Ted's students hear his question, the clues will enter sensory memory as acoustic codes and then, after further processing, will enter short-term memory. However, the students will use the clues in short-term memory, not the acoustic codes, as retrieval cues to help them pull information out of long-term memory. There is no such thing as contextual coding. You may have been thinking of context dependence.

11. *b* is the answer. It is easier to remember material when you are in the place where you originally learned it. The surrounding environment acts as a retrieval cue. (p. 243)
    a. Organizing material in an outline is one way to remember it more easily later on, but context dependence doesn't refer to this.
    c. State dependence occurs when people find it easier to recall material when they are in the same psychological state of mind as they were when they learned the information. A psychological state acts as a retrieval cue.
    d. Using mnemonics can improve your memory, but this is not the same thing as context dependence.

12. *c* is the answer. Semantic networks are links of related information. When a person recalls information from one node of the network, it can feel as if the person is very close to accessing the information needed in the next node. (p. 245)
    a. Constructive memory is a fabricated, but seemingly real, recollection.
    b. Sensory memory lasts only a second or so; Molly is using her long-term memory.
    d. Schemas are mental representations of categories and do not explain the tip-of-the-tongue phenomenon.

13. *d* is the answer. In order to chunk, you must use the information in long-term memory to help you group items into one chunk in short-term memory. The ability to recognize something in sensory memory involves retrieving a similar pattern of information or material from long-term memory. In order to use the method of loci, you must retrieve knowledge about a specific location or loci stored in long-term memory. (pp. 235, 237, 259)

14. *c* is the answer. A repressed memory is described as one that cannot be easily accessed. (p. 249)
    a. Elaborative memory is not a term. You may have been thinking of elaborative rehearsal.
    b. Procedural memories are memories of skills, like piano playing. They are not traumatic memories.
    d. State-dependence of memory occurs when information is more easily retrieved when the person is in the same state as he was when the information was encoded.

15. *c* is the answer. Some apparently repressed memories may be accurate, but some may be inaccurate. Therefore, corroborating evidence should be sought in each case. (pp. 249–251)

    a. To assume that a recovered memory was constructed would not be wise, given that some recovered memories have been substantiated by other evidence.
    b. To assume that a recovered memory is accurate would not be wise, given that some recovered memories have been shown to be false.
    d. There is no such thing as retroactive amnesia. Retrograde amnesia would be the result of a brain injury. The person would most likely lose memory for more than one event prior to the injury.

16. *a* is the answer. The presence of new information displaces old information in short-term memory. (p. 253)
    b. Proactive interference occurs when old information disrupts the learning of new information.
    c, d. Decay is the gradual disappearance of memories.

17. *c* is the answer. Ebbinghaus discovered that relearning took much less time than learning. Savings is the difference between learning and relearning time. (p. 251)
    a. A mnemonic is a memory strategy that involves placing information in an organized context. In this question, Robin did not use any strategies or methods to relearn the names of the presidents.
    b. Release from proactive interference occurs when new information differs so greatly from old information that the old information interferes less with the learning of the new information. Robin is trying to relearn exactly the same information. There is no new information with which the old information can interfere.
    d. Because state dependence means that cues from your physical state help you to remember, Robin would have to be in the same state (mood, arousal level, etc.) as she was when she first learned the names of the presidents. Not only is this not mentioned specifically in the description of her situation, but it also is unlikely that a person would be in *one* state when learning such a large amount of information.

18. *b* is the answer. Hippocampal damage usually results in anterograde amnesia, which is the inability to form new memories. Procedural memory formation and recall appears to be affected, however. (p. 258)

a, d. Both of these are procedural memories. She could learn to solve a puzzle or could remember how to ride her bike.

c. Recall of a childhood event would be unaffected by anterograde amnesia.

19. *a* is the answer. The method of loci involves mentally placing objects in various spots in a familiar location (loci). (p. 259)

b. Procedural memorization is not a term. You may have been thinking of procedural memory, which is skill learning, but this is not the same as imagining items in locations.

c. Using a retrieval cue helps you recognize or retrieve material from long-term memory. Using mnemonics is a method of encoding by organizing information in a certain way.

d. Context dependence occurs when the environment (context) acts as a retrieval cue.

20. *a* is the answer. Just rereading the material is not an effective way to learn information from a text. (pp. 259–261)

b, c, d. These are all good study habits to adopt.

Now turn to the quiz analysis table at the end of this chapter to find which areas you know well and which areas you need to work on. Circle the numbers in the table for items on Quiz 2 that you answered correctly.

For each question you answered correctly, circle its number. (Quiz 1 numbers are not shaded; Quiz 2 numbers are shaded.) Are there patterns in the types of questions or the topics you got wrong that could direct your further study? Did you improve from Quiz 1 to Quiz 2?

TOPIC	TYPE OF QUESTION		
	DEFINITION	COMPREHENSION	APPLICATION
Nature of Memory			
Processes			1
			1
Types	2		3
			2
Explicit and implicit			4
			3
Models			5
		4	
Acquiring Memories			
Sensory			6
		5	
Short-term	7	8, 10	9
		7	9
Long-term			11
			13
Distinguishing	12, 14		
			6, 8
Retrieving Memories			
Cues and encoding		13	
			10
Dependence			15
	11		
Semantic memory			16
			12
Constructing			17
Repression			
		15	14
Forgetting		18	19
	16		17
Biological bases			
			18
Memory improvement			20
	19		20

TOTAL CORRECT BY QUIZ:

QUIZ 1:

QUIZ 2:

people feel worse about losing a certain amount than they feel good about gaining the same amount. Most people see large losses as disproportionately more serious than small losses. People assess the probability of a decision incorrectly because they tend to estimate incorrectly the probability of rare or frequent events, are operating from gambler's fallacy, or have too much confidence in their own predictions.

2. *How Biased Are We?* Psychologists are not sure how to answer this question. Do people make too many decision-making mistakes because they are attempting to satisfy criteria other than expected value?

VI. LINKAGES: GROUP PROCESSES IN PROBLEM SOLVING AND DECISION MAKING (pp. 287–288)

° Groups influence decision-making processes. The usual sequence of events in a group decision-making process is as follows: all options are identified, the option with minimum amounts of opposition is agreed to, and even if better options are presented later, the minimally agreed to solution usually wins. The outcomes of group decisions are often more extreme than individual decisions—a phenomenon called group polarization.

° Some groups perform better than the average member performance because the correct hypothesis has been identified, incorrect hypotheses have been rejected, and the information-processing load is shared. Several factors can improve or impair group performance. Improvement increases as the group number increases up to a limit. High-status group members (whether the status is deserved or not) can heavily influence a group's decisions.

VII. LANGUAGE (pp. 288–299)

A. The Elements of Language

A language has two basic elements: symbols and grammar.

1. *From Sounds to Sentences.* Phonemes are the smallest unit of sound with meaning. Morphemes are the smallest unit of language with meaning. Words are made of morphemes, which in turn consist of phonemes. Rules of syntax determine the ways in which words are combined to form sentences. Semantics are rules that govern the meanings of words and sentences.

2. *Surface Structure and Deep Structure.* The surface structure of a sentence (the string of words) may have more than one meaning, or deep structure.

B. Understanding Speech

1. *Perceiving Words and Sentences.* The gaps we hear between spoken words are not real but are perceived because of top-down processing. Syntax, memories, and knowledge of the world help us comprehend and remember verbal and written communication.

2. *Using Context and Scripts.* An understanding of language depends on constructing information based partly on the context in which the information is encoded. Context may be created by the situation and by personal factors such as education and culture.

3. *Conventions and Nonverbal Cues.* Conventions, built up over years of experience, often govern the meaning of conversations. Nonverbal cues also play a role in the understanding of conversations.

C. Learning to Speak: Stages of Language Development

1. *From Babbling to Words.* At about four months of age, babies begin repeating simple syllables, called babblings. At about nine months, babies stop uttering sounds that aren't part of the language to which they are exposed. At twelve to eighteen months, babies utter their first real words, which usually are proper names and object words. In the one-word stage, children tend to use one word at a time and overextend its use to mean more than one object.

2. *First Sentences.* These appear at about eighteen to twenty-four months of age as two-word pairs. These first sentences are telegraphic: brief and to the point. Next are three-word sentences that use subject-verb-object sequences. Word endings begin to appear, but at first are used incorrectly. Finally, adjectives and auxiliary verbs are added. By age five, children have acquired most of the syntax of their native language.

3. *Complex Sentences.* At about age three, children begin to use auxiliary verbs, question words, and clauses.

D. How Is Language Acquired?

1. *Conditioning, Imitation, and Rules.* Conditioning, imitation, and rules do not fully explain the development of language in children. However, when

adults provide correct revisions of a child's conversation, the learning process is enhanced.

2. *Biological Bases for Language Acquisition.* Noam Chomsky suggests that children possess an innate language acquisition device that helps them learn the complexities of language. There appears to be a critical period for language development.

3. *Bilingualism.* Children in a bilingual environment prior to the end of the critical period show enhanced language performance. Those children with similar mastery of two languages, or balanced bilinguals, may have more cognitive flexibility and creativity.

E. Thinking Critically: Can Nonhumans Use Language?

What am I being asked to believe or accept?
Some researchers believe that nonhumans can use language.

What evidence is available to support the assertion?
Research with chimpanzees suggests that animals can learn to use words and adopt a crude grammar.

Are there alternative ways of interpreting the evidence?
Other researchers argue that chimps' very short sentence structure and lack of spontaneous and creative use of language mean that they are incapable of language. In addition, experimenter bias may explain some of the "language learning" results seen in chimpanzees.

What additional evidence would help to evaluate the alternatives?
Studies in the area are few in number. More studies using more subjects need to be done. In addition, researchers need to examine the limiting capacity of nonhuman working memory and its effects on animals' use of language.

What conclusions are most reasonable?
Psychologists are still not in full agreement on this issue. The communication displayed by animals is much more limited than human children's language. And the level of language produced by chimps so far falls short of matching their very high levels of intelligence. But the evidence does suggest that under the right conditions, animals can learn language-like skills.

F. Knowledge, Language, and Culture

Does language determine perception? Experiments suggest that language does not always determine perception. We perceive subtle differences in objects and label them when necessary for survival.

VIII. FUTURE DIRECTIONS (pp. 299–300)

Researchers study the interaction between thought processes and the environment (situated cognition), and apply knowledge of thought processes to display designs (cognitive engineering).

KEY TERMS

1. An **information-processing system** receives information, represents information through symbols, and manipulates those symbols. (p. 265)

> *REMEMBER:* Psychologists consider people similar to information-processing systems in the way they take in information, pass it through several stages, and finally act on it.

2. **Thinking** can be described as part of an information-processing system in which mental representations are manipulated in order to form new information. (p. 265)

3. **Mental chronometry** is the timing of mental events. (p. 266)

> *REMEMBER:* Chrono means "time." Meter means "measure." Mental chronometry is the measure of the time that mental events take.

4. A **reaction time** is the amount of elapsed time between the presentation of a physical stimulus and an overt reaction to that stimulus. (p. 266)

> *Example:* Susan and several of her friends are standing in her office looking for her keys. Suddenly, Dave calls out, "Hey!" and throws her the keys. The reaction time is the time it takes Susan to look up and get ready to catch the keys after hearing Dave call out.

5. **Evoked brain potentials** are small temporary changes in voltage that occur in the brain in response to stimuli. Psychologists can study information processing and can look for abnormal functioning in the brain by examining evoked potentials. (p. 267)

> *REMEMBER:* Evoke means to "cause" or "produce." Stimuli evoke, or produce, small changes in the brain. Psychologists have instruments that allow them to record these changes for study.
>
> *Example:* About 300 milliseconds after a stimulus is presented, a large positive peak—the P300—occurs.

The timing can be affected by how long sensory processing and perception take.

6. Cognitive maps are mental representations of familiar parts of your world. (p. 268)

Example: Lashon's friend asks, "How do you get to the mall from here?" To answer the question, Lashon pictures the roads and crossroads between their location and the mall and is able to describe the route for his friend to travel.

7. Images are visual pictures represented in thought. Cognitive maps are one example. (p. 268)

8. Concepts are basic units of thought or categories with common properties. Artificial and natural concepts are examples. (p. 269)

9. Artificial concepts are concepts that are clearly defined by a set of rules or properties. Each member of the concept meets all the rules or has all the defining properties, and no nonmember does. (p. 269)

Example: A square is an artificial concept. All members of the concept are shapes with four equal sides and four right-angle corners. Nothing that is not a square shares these properties.

10. Natural concepts are defined by a *general* set of features, not all of which must be present for an object to be considered a member of the concept. (p. 269)

Example: The concept of vegetable is a natural concept. There are no rules or lists of features that describe every single vegetable. Many vegetables are difficult to recognize as such because this concept is so "fuzzy." Tomatoes are not vegetables, but most people think they are. Rhubarb is a vegetable, but most people think it is not.

11. A prototype is the best example of a natural concept. (p. 270)

Example: Try this trick on your friends. Have them sit down with a pencil and paper. Tell them to write down all the numbers that you will say and the answers to three questions that you will ask. Recite about fifteen numbers of at least three digits each, and then ask your friends to write down the name of a tool, a color, and a flower. About 60 to 80 percent of them will write down "hammer," "red," and "rose" because these are common prototypes of the concepts tool, color, and flower. Prototypes come to mind most easily when people try to think of a concept.

12. Schemas are generalizations about categories of objects, events, and people. (p. 270)

Example: Dana's schema for books is that they are a bound stack of paper with stories or other information written on each page. When her fifth-grade teacher suggests that each student read a book on the computer, Dana is confused until she sees that the same information could be presented on a computer screen. Dana has now revised her schema for books to include those presented through electronic media.

13. Scripts are mental representations of familiar sequences, usually involving activity. (p. 270)

Example: As a college student, you have a script of how events should transpire in the classroom: students enter the classroom, sit in seats facing the professor, and take out their notebooks. The professor lectures while students take notes, until the bell rings and they all leave.

14. Propositions are the smallest units of knowledge that can stand as separate assertions. Propositions are relationships between concepts or between a concept and a property of the concept. Propositions can be true or false. (p. 270)

Example: Carla (concept) likes to buy flowers (concept) is a proposition that shows a relationship between two concepts. Dogs bark is a proposition that shows a relationship between a concept (dog) and a property of that concept (bark).

15. Mental models are clusters of propositions that represent people's understanding of how things work. (p. 270)

Example: There is a toy that is a board with different types of latches, fasteners, and buttons on it. As children play with it, they form a mental model of how these things work. Then, when they see a button, perhaps a doorbell, they will have an understanding of how it works.

16. Reasoning is the process whereby people make evaluations, generate arguments, and reach conclusions. (p. 271)

17. Formal or logical reasoning is the collection of mental procedures that yield valid conclusions. An example is the use of an algorithm. (p. 272)

18. Algorithms are systematic procedures that always produce solutions to problems. In an algorithm, a specific sequence of thought or set of rules is followed to solve the problem. Algorithms can be very time-consuming. (p. 272)

Example: To solve the math problem 3,999,999 × 1,111,111 using an algorithm, you would multiply the numbers out:

$$\begin{array}{r} 3,999,999 \\ \times\ 1,111,111 \\ \hline 4,444,442,888,889 \end{array}$$

This computation takes a long time. You could, however, use a heuristic to solve the problem: round the numbers to 4,000,000 × 1,000,000, multiply 4 × 1, and add the appropriate number of zeros (000,000,000,000). Although simpler and faster, this heuristic approach yields a less accurate solution than that produced by the algorithmic approach.

19. **Syllogisms**, components of the reasoning process, are arguments made up of two propositions, called premises, and conclusions based on those premises. Syllogisms may be correct or incorrect. (p. 272)

Example: Here is an incorrect syllogism: All cats are mammals (premise), and all people are mammals (premise). Therefore, all cats are people (conclusion).

20. **Heuristics** are mental shortcuts or rules of thumb used to solve problems. (p. 274)

Example: You are trying to think of a four-letter word for "labor" to fill in a crossword puzzle. Instead of thinking of all possible four-letter combinations (an algorithmic approach), you think first of synonyms for labor—job, work, chore—and choose the one with four letters.

21. The **anchoring heuristic** is a biased method of estimating an event's probability by adjusting a preliminary estimate in light of new information rather than by starting again from scratch. Thus, the preliminary value biases the final estimate. (p. 275)

Example: Jean is getting ready to move to the city. Her parents lived there ten years ago and were familiar with the area that she wants to move into now. Ten years ago it was an exceedingly dangerous neighborhood. Since that time, however, many changes have taken place, and the area now has one of the lowest crime rates in the city. Jean's parents think that the crime rate may have improved a little, but, despite the lower crime rate, they just cannot believe that the area is all that safe.

22. The **representativeness heuristic** involves judging that an example belongs to a certain class of items by first focusing on the similarities between the example and the class and then determining whether the particular example has essential features of the class. However, many times people do not consider the frequency of occurrence of the class (the base-rate frequency), focusing instead on what is representative or typical of the available evidence. (p. 275)

Example: After examining a patient, Dr. White recognizes symptoms characteristic of a disease that has a base-rate frequency of 1 in 22 million people. Instead of looking for a more frequently occurring explanation of the symptoms, the doctor decides that the patient has this very rare disease. She makes this decision based on the similarity of this set of symptoms (example) to those of the rare disease (a larger class of events or items).

23. The **availability heuristic** involves judging the probability of an event by how easily examples of the event come to mind. This leads to biased judgments when the probability of the mentally available events does not equal the actual probability of their occurrence. (p. 275)

Example: A friend of yours has just moved to New York City. You cannot understand why he has moved there since the crime rate is so high. You hear from a mutual acquaintance that your friend is in the hospital. You assume that he was probably mugged because this is the most available information in your mind about New York City.

24. **Mental sets** occur when knowing the solution to an old problem interferes with recognizing a solution to a new problem. (p. 279)

Example: The last time his CD player door wouldn't open, Del tapped the front of it and it popped open. This time when it won't open, Del does the same thing—not noticing that the power isn't even on!

25. **Functional fixedness** occurs when a person fails to use a familiar object in a novel way in order to solve a problem. (p. 279)

Example: Lisa is very creative in her use of the objects in her environment. One day she dropped a fork down the drain of the kitchen sink. She took a small refrigerator magnet and tied it to a chopstick. She then put the chopstick down the drain, let the fork attach itself to the magnet, and carefully pulled the fork out of the drain. *If* Lisa had viewed the magnet as being capable only of holding material against the refrigerator, and the chopstick as being useful only for eating Chinese food, she would have experienced functional fixedness.

26. **Artificial intelligence (AI)** is the study of how to make computers "think" like humans, including how to program a computer to use heuristics in problem solving. (pp. 281–282)

Example: Lydia plays chess against a computer that has been programmed with rules, strategies, and outcome probabilities.

27. **Expert systems** are computer programs designed to solve specific types of problems. (p. 282)

Example: Doctors can use expert systems to help narrow down a specific diagnosis.

28. The **utility** of an attribute is its subjective, personal value. (p. 284)

Example: Andrew prefers large classes because he likes the stimulation of hearing many opposing viewpoints. In choosing courses, Andrew decides whether the positive utility of the preferred class size is greater than the negative utility of the inconvenient meeting time.

29. **Expected value** is the likely benefit a person will gain if he or she makes a particular decision several times. (p. 284)

Example: Jennifer doesn't have enough money for this month's rent. She knows that going on a shopping spree would be a wonderful stress-reliever in the short run, but the increase in her amount of debt would outweigh the enjoyment in the long run.

30. **Group polarization** is the tendency of groups to make extreme decisions. (p. 287)

Example: After the few people who suggested that a protest march was warranted were strongly criticized for being reactionary, the people in the majority decided that not only would they not protest, but they wouldn't even write a letter to the newspaper stating their view.

31. **Language** is comprised of two elements: symbols, such as words, and a grammar. (p. 288)

Example: The German and English languages use the same symbols (Roman characters), but each has a different set of rules for combining those symbols.

The Russian language has different symbols (Cyrillic characters) as well as different rules of grammar.

32. **Grammar** is the set of rules for combining symbols, or words, into sentences in a language. (p. 288)

33. **Phonemes** are the smallest units of sound that affect the meaning of speech. (p. 288)

Example: Phonemes are sounds that make a difference in the meaning of a word. By changing the beginning phoneme, the meanings of the following words are changed: bin, thin, win.
REMEMBER: Phono means "sound." Phonemes are sounds that change the meaning of a word.

34. **Morphemes** are the smallest units of language that have meaning. (p. 288)

Example: Any prefix or suffix has meaning. The suffix s means "plural," as in the words bats or flowers. The prefix un means "not," as in unhappy or unrest. S and un are morphemes for the words bat, flower, happy, and rest.

35. **Words** are made up of one or more morphemes. (p. 288)

Example: The word unwise is made up of two morphemes: un and wise.

36. **Syntax** is the set of rules that dictates how words are combined to make phrases and sentences. (p. 288)

REMEMBER: Syn means "together" (as in synchronized). Syntax is the set of rules that determines the order of words when they are put together.

37. **Semantics** is the set of rules that governs the meaning of words and sentences. (p. 289)

Example: The sentence, "Wild lamps fiddle with precision" has syntax, but incorrect semantics.

38. **Surface structures** of sentences are the order in which the words are arranged. (p. 289)

39. The **deep structure** of a sentence is an abstract representation of the relationships expressed in a sentence, or, in other words, its various meanings. (p. 289)

Example: The eating of the animal was grotesque. The surface structure of this sentence is the order of the words. The deep structure contains at least two meanings: The way the animal is eating could be grotesque, and the way people are eating an animal could be grotesque.

40. **Babblings** are the first sounds infants make that resemble speech. Babbling begins at about four months of age. (p. 292)

   Example: While Patrick plays, he says, "ba-ba-ba."

41. The **one-word stage** of speech is that period when children use one word to cover a number of objects and frequently make up new words. This stage lasts about six months. (p. 293)

   Example: Laura says "ba" to stand for bottle, ball, or anything else that starts with a <u>b</u>. Amy always asks for milk, even if she wants something else to drink, such as water or juice.

42. **Telegraphic** speech describes the nature of the early sentences formed by eighteen- to twenty-four-month-old children. Sentences are often only two words long and communicate the message with simple words. (p. 293)

   Example: Rick says, "Give ball" when he wants someone to give him a ball.

FILL-IN-THE-BLANKS KEY TERMS

This section will help you check your factual knowledge of the key terms introduced in this chapter. Fill in each blank with the appropriate term from the list of key terms above.

1. The most commonly given example of a natural concept is a(n) _____.

2. Concepts that are defined by a very specific set of properties are called _____.

3. Cognitive representations of how things work are called _____.

4. _____ are representations of familiar patterns of human activities.

5. An argument made up of two assertions and a conclusion is called a(n) _____.

6. A shortcut in problem solving is called a(n) _____.

7. The _____ is a method of estimating the probability of an outcome based on initial information without appropriate adjustment for later information.

8. The timing of mental events is called _____.

9. The set of rules that dictate the order in which words should be put together to form a sentence is called _____.

10. _____ is a term used to describe the two-word sentences of eighteen-month-olds.

11. _____ are the first speech-resembling sounds that infants make, starting at about four months of age.

12. The meaning of a sentence is expressed in its _____.

13. Even though a suffix isn't a word, because it carries meaning, a suffix is considered a _____.

14. When people are unable to solve a problem because they cannot recognize how they could use a familiar tool in a new way, this is called _____.

15. A _____ exists when old solutions interfere with a person's ability to solve a new problem.

Total Correct (See answer key) _____

LEARNING OBJECTIVES

1. Describe the core functions that form a circle of thought. (p. 265)

2. Define <u>information-processing system</u> and <u>thinking</u>. Discuss the relationship between information-processing systems and decision making in humans. (pp. 265–266)

3. Define <u>mental chronometry</u> and <u>reaction time</u>. Describe the factors that influence reaction time. (pp. 266–267)

4. Define <u>evoked brain potential</u>. Discuss the use of evoked brain potential in the study of mental chronometry. (p. 267)

5. Define <u>cognitive maps</u>, and discuss their use and the biases that distort them. Describe the manipulation of mental images. (p. 268)

6. Define <u>artificial</u> and <u>natural concepts</u> and <u>prototype</u>. Give an example of each. (pp. 269–270)

7. Define <u>schemas</u>, <u>scripts</u>, <u>propositions</u>, and <u>mental models</u> and describe their role in the thinking process. (pp. 270–271)

8. Define <u>reasoning</u>, <u>formal reasoning</u>, <u>algorithms</u>, and <u>syllogisms</u>. Discuss the causes of errors in logical

reasoning. Describe cultural differences in formal reasoning. (pp. 271–274)

9. Define informal reasoning and heuristics. Describe and give an example of the anchoring, representativeness, and availability heuristics. (pp. 274–276)

10. Describe the problem-solving strategies: decomposition, working backward, and analogies. (pp. 276–277)

11. Explain how the striking-feature syndrome and causal uncertainty may limit the usefulness of case studies. Describe the use of comparative case studies to document the techniques used by successful problem solvers. (pp. 277–278)

12. Explain why multiple hypotheses, mental sets, functional fixedness, confirmation bias, and lack of attention to negative evidence can hinder problem solving. Give an example of each. (pp. 278–280)

13. Explain why an "expert" is better at solving problems. Explain why experts use chunking more efficiently than novices do. Discuss the dangers of being an expert when solving problems. (pp. 280–281)

14. Define artificial intelligence, symbolic reasoning, and neural networks. Describe how expert systems can be used. (pp. 281–283)

15. Give an example of a multiattribute decision. Define utility and expected value, and explain their role in the decision-making process. (pp. 284–285)

16. Describe the sources of bias and flaws in decision making in regard to perceptions of utilities, losses, and probabilities. Be sure to include loss aversion and gambler's fallacy. (pp. 285–287)

17. Describe the impact of groups on decision making. Outline the typical discussion patterns in groups trying to make a decision. Define group polarization, and list the factors that improve or impair group decision making. (pp. 287–288)

18. List the components of language. Define grammar. (p. 288)

19. Define phoneme, morpheme, and words. Give an example of the phonemes and morphemes in a word. (p. 288)

20. Define syntax and semantics. Explain how syntax and semantics help us comprehend language. (pp. 288–289)

21. Define surface structure and deep structure. Describe the surface and deep structures of a particular sentence. (pp. 289–290)

22. Discuss the role of top-down processing, context, scripts, conventions, and nonverbal cues in the comprehension of language. (pp. 290–292)

23. Describe language development in children. Define babblings, the one-word stage, telegraphic speech, and complex sentences. (pp. 292–293)

24. Discuss the roles of conditioning, imitation, nature, and nurture in language development. (pp. 293–295)

25. Describe the impact of a bilingual environment on the development of language abilities. (p. 295)

26. Discuss the controversy surrounding the question, "Can nonhumans use language?" and describe what conclusions are reasonable given the evidence so far. (pp. 295–298)

27. Discuss the relationship among language, culture, and perception. (pp. 298–299)

CONCEPTS AND EXERCISES

No. 1: Approaches to Problem Solving

Completing this exercise should help you to achieve Learning Objectives 5, 8, 9, 10, and 12.

Below are several problems. Read the description of each problem, and answer the questions following it.

1. Viola's parents have just moved to a suburb of Chicago. She is home for a visit for the first time since they moved. To her embarrassment, she is always getting lost. The streets seem to be arranged in a triangular pattern instead of a square one.

   ° What is Viola trying to develop?

   ° What bias is causing her problems?

2. Trixy and her brother Peter are home by themselves, and the lights have all gone off. Both children are terrified of the dark. Trixy remembers that her dad once told her about a fuse box. She hypothesizes that this is the problem. But Trixy and her brother do not want to enter the dark basement.

   ° How can they decide whether going to the basement is necessary?

   ° What have they avoided if they do this?

   ° What kind of evidence about their hypothesis are they ignoring?

3. Al is lost somewhere in Paris. He wants to get to a museum that a friend told him to visit, but he has no idea where he is. He stops someone on the street and asks for directions. The Parisian says that she can give Al either a tricky shortcut or a very long set of directions that will be easy to follow. Al decides to take the long way since it will guarantee his arrival at the museum, even though it will take a bit longer.

   ° What two choices did the Parisian offer Al?

   ° Which one did Al choose?

4. Carlotta, a color analyst at a paper mill, is upset because something is wrong with the paper's color as it comes off the machine. She and the people who work with her have thought about all the previous color problems they have encountered, but they cannot find a solution. Carlotta decides to bring in a person who has just started to work in the paper room and ask him what he thinks.

   ° What might be preventing Carlotta from solving the problem?

No. 2: Structures of Language

Completing this exercise should help you to achieve Learning Objectives 18, 21, and 22.

Below are several sentences. Identify the structures of language as indicated. (HINT: When you look for morphemes, use a dictionary to discover the prefixes, suffixes, and roots of words.)

1. *The husband's dinner was terrible.* Underline all the morphemes, and identify at least two deep structures.

2. *My friend painted me in his backyard.* Underline all the morphemes, and identify at least two deep structures.

CRITICAL THINKING

Sam and Martina are just arriving at the scene of what promises to be a media event. Sylvia Star, a famous ninety-eight-year-old gossip columnist, has been found dead in her bed. Sylvia has a long list of enemies, and Sam, eager for action, immediately decides that she has been murdered. While Martina stands calmly in the bedroom doorway surveying the room, Sam scurries around looking for evidence of foul play.

In his search, Sam finds a glass of water on the bedstand. Smugly, he turns toward Martina and beckons her closer. "When I was in the academy," Sam said, "I read about this real rare drug case. The drug dissolves in water and can't be traced in the water or the body. I bet one of the people the old bird was writing about dumped some in this glass or paid off the maid to do it. No Sylvia, no bad press. Everybody knew she was an elderly woman with a heart problem. The murderer probably figured it would look like a heart attack. We should check her notes for her next column and find out who was here today! And we should check out the maid!"

Martina, looking slightly bemused, takes a drink from the glass of water and says, "I couldn't disagree with you more on this one!"

Using the five critical thinking questions in your text, the clues in the story, and what you have just learned in this chapter, answer the following.

1. What is Sam's hypothesis?

2. What evidence supports Sam's hypothesis?

3. What is Martina's alternative hypothesis?

4. What evidence supports Martina's hypothesis?

PERSONAL LEARNING ACTIVITIES

1. Make a list of the defining characteristics of a natural concept, choose a prototype, and then identify things that fit or don't fit your definition. For the natural concept "home," perhaps you might list "has walls, floors, a roof, doors, and an address." What is the prototypical home? Now find examples of homes that have fewer and fewer of the features you have listed and decide whether they still have enough characteristics to earn the "home" label. Are residence halls, apartments, small houses, motel rooms, an underpass, and a cardboard box homes? How did you decide? (Learning Objective 6)

2. Experiment with the problem-solving strategies—decomposition, working backward, analogies, and incubation—to see if they can help you. For instance, you might try decomposition with a research paper assignment or try to think of an analogy to help you remember a biological process. (Learning Objective 10)

3. Think of all the uses you can for a blanket (or some other item). Were you at first held back from creative uses by functional fixedness? (Learning Objective 12)

4. For a multiattribute decision you need to make, try listing all the characteristics you want to consider, ranking them, and then looking at the options to see where they fall on each characteristic. If, for example, you are deciding which portable stereo to buy, you might list whether you want a radio, a cassette tape player, a CD player, or all three. Is tape-to-tape dubbing important? Is cost the most important variable? Do you prefer buttons or slide controls, or does it matter? Once you have your list of stereo features, rank them in terms of importance. Now look at the available portable stereos and keep track of which ones meet the most important features on your list. (Learning Objective 15)

5. Watch a young relative or observe children in a day care center to see what early language use is like. Are the children at an age when babbling is most common, or are they forming words and/or sentences? If you hear errors, what sort are they? (Learning Objective 23)

MULTIPLE-CHOICE QUESTIONS

SAMPLE QUIZ 1

1. Shaniqua types on different word processors and computers. Because the keyboards have different layouts, Shaniqua often hits a slash key ("/") rather than the shift key when trying to capitalize a letter using the least familiar computer. Shaniqua reaches for the slash key because it is in the same location as the shift key on her other keyboards; therefore, Shaniqua's problem is that she has to make a(n)
   a. compatible response.
   b. incompatible response.
   c. fundamental attribution.
   d. multiattribute decision.

2. Halle watches mayonnaise jars going by on an assembly line and is supposed to grab any jars with crooked lids or two labels. Halle's reaction time will most likely decrease if she
   a. also has to look for underfilled jars or crooked labels.
   b. doesn't know when the defective jars come by.
   c. tries to be extremely careful not to grab a good jar.
   d. only has to watch for crooked lids.

3. Imposing a north-south-east-west orientation on cognitive maps is called
   a. rectangular bias.
   b. reconstructive memory.
   c. directional bias.
   d. none of the above.

4. Propositions
   a. are the basic components of words.
   b. show the relationships among concepts.
   c. are always true.
   d. show the relationship among mental models.

5. Try to figure out the name of the natural concept to which the following four items belong, and then choose the prototypical example of that concept.
   a. A fist
   b. A brick
   c. A gun
   d. Sharp fingernails

6. An algorithm
   a. is a shortcut to the solution of a problem.
   b. will sometimes yield a correct answer to a problem.
   c. will always yield a correct answer to a problem.
   d. is subject to bias from the availability heuristic.

7. "All monsters are ugly. The Creature from the Black Lagoon is a monster. Therefore, the Creature is ugly." The three statements together are an example of a
   a. premise.
   b. proposition.
   c. natural concept.
   d. syllogism.

8. Amy thinks the earth is about 10,000 years old. When a friend shows her reports of 12 million-year-old fossil remains, Amy then says, "OK. Maybe it's as much as 13,000 years old," which shows that Amy is most likely using the _____ heuristic.
   a. algorithmic
   b. anchoring
   c. availability
   d. representativeness

9. Thalia expects most rock-and-roll band members to wear black leather jackets, black jeans, and black t-shirts. She also believes that they will have long hair and wear at least one earring. When she sees a long-haired man dressed in the black clothes described above, Thalia assumes that the man is a band member because he fits her description of one. Thalia has used the _____ heuristic.
   a. anchoring
   b. availability
   c. confirmation
   d. representativeness

10. "An action potential fires 'all or none' like a gun," says Jamila. Jamila is using _____ to help her understand the concept of threshold.
    a. an analogy
    b. decomposition
    c. negative evidence
    d. a script

11. Functional fixedness occurs when a person
    a. uses old solutions to solve new problems.
    b. looks only for information that will confirm a hypothesis.
    c. ignores negative evidence.
    d. cannot think of novel uses for familiar objects in order to solve a problem.

12. While trying to balance equations in a chemistry assignment, Luna uses the same method of working through the first ten problems. On the eleventh problem, however, a completely different approach is necessary and Luna can't figure out what it is. Luna most likely developed
    a. an algorithm.
    b. functional fixedness.
    c. a mental model.
    d. a mental set.

13. Luna (see question 12 above) decides to forget about the problem for a while at dinner. When she returns to her room, she realizes how to solve the problem. Luna used _____ to solve the problem.
    a. deep structures
    b. expert systems
    c. incubation
    d. prototypes

14. Each time Lily pulls a card from the deck, she has a 1 in 52 chance of getting the queen of spades if she replaces the card before drawing again. After drawing a queen of spades five times in a row, she remarks, "I'm certain I won't draw the queen of spades next time!" Lily is being influenced by
    a. the gambler's fallacy.
    b. loss aversion.
    c. ignoring negative evidence.
    d. confirmation bias.

15. The utility of a choice in decision making refers to which of the following?
    a. The likelihood of that choice being the actual outcome
    b. The subjective perception of its value
    c. The perception of its risk
    d. All of the above

16. The deep structure of a sentence is
    a. the sequence of words in the sentence.
    b. the meaning of the sentence.
    c. the syntax of the sentence.
    d. a reflection of the complexity of the sentence.

17. The sentence "Singing mute horses watched deliciously while thin, dark, gloomy lights melted in the rodeo mound" follows _____ rules.
    a. schematic
    b. semantic
    c. syllogistic
    d. syntactic

18. Many advertising campaigns designed for foreign countries have failed because the words in the ads had the wrong meanings in other languages. For example, Nova, the name of a car, means "does not go" in Spanish. The advertisers did not consider the _____ of the Spanish language when creating the ad.
    a. syntax
    b. language acquisition device
    c. semantics
    d. surface structure

19. Context can alter the interpretation of a sentence. Which of the following would not be considered a part of context?
    a. A person's knowledge of the world based on experience
    b. The situation in which the communication is taking place
    c. The inflection of a person's voice when communicating
    d. All of the above contribute to the context of a situation.

20. Charlie is two years old. At the zoo with his father, he points to all the animals and says, "Dog." Patiently, his father tells him the names of all the animals he is seeing and that they are not all dogs. Charlie is probably at the _____ stage of language development.
    a. babblings
    b. one-word
    c. prototype-matching
    d. telegraphic

Total Correct (See answer key) _____

SAMPLE QUIZ 2

Use this quiz to reassess your learning after taking Quiz 1 and reviewing the chapter.

1. Reaction time is the
   a. time it takes to perceive a stimulus.
   b. time it takes to react to a stimulus after it has been perceived.
   c. time it takes to react to a stimulus after it has been presented.
   d. timing of mental events.

2. The specific evoked potential called the P300 is not sensitive to
   a. the complexity of a stimulus.
   b. how hard it is to detect a stimulus.
   c. changes in stimulus-response compatibility.
   d. stimulus presentation.

3. Cliff has just stopped his car at a red light when the light changes to green. Which of the following will affect his reaction time?
   a. Cliff is driving a stick shift for the first time.
   b. Cliff did not expect the light to change to green so quickly.
   c. Five roads intersect at this light. Cliff can turn onto one of these roads or go straight ahead.
   d. All of the above

4. The smallest segments of knowledge that can stand as individual assertions are called
   a. schemas.
   b. propositions.
   c. syllogisms.
   d. scripts.

5. Natural and artificial concepts differ in that
   a. artificial concepts provide a way to classify objects, whereas natural concepts do not.
   b. natural concepts provide a way to classify objects, whereas artificial concepts do not.
   c. artificial concepts are fuzzy and sometimes difficult to define, whereas natural concepts are rigidly defined.
   d. natural concepts are fuzzy and sometimes difficult to define, whereas artificial concepts are rigidly defined.

6. Which of the following alternatives is an example of a proposition?
   a. th
   b. Flowers
   c. ed
   d. Cats eat flowers.

7. You would use a _____ when thinking about how to record on a VCR.
   a. schema
   b. script

c. mental model
d. proposition

8. Clinton is really frustrated. His uncle has been beating him at checkers all night. He is going to play another game, but this time he is going to base his strategy on an algorithm, not a heuristic. What problem will this cause?
   a. Clinton still may not win the game.
   b. Clinton and his uncle may be playing the same game of checkers for a very long time.
   c. Clinton is ignoring overall probabilities.
   d. The representativeness heuristic will bias Clinton's choice of strategy.

9. Cindy is 100 percent positive of her ability to find an advertising job in New York City. When she gets to New York, she reads in the paper that jobs are extremely scarce because of the large number of recent corporate mergers. Despite this, she is still 90 percent sure that, with her qualifications, she will land a job. Which heuristic is responsible for her reasoning?
   a. The anchoring heuristic
   b. The availability heuristic
   c. The representativeness heuristic
   d. The base-rate information heuristic

10. Many companies are reporting an inability to staff their foreign offices in Europe. Employees previously interested in overseas work are frightened of the terrorist activity they keep hearing about in the news. They are sure that something disastrous will happen to their families if they move to Europe. Which heuristic are the employees using to assess the incidence of terrorist activities?
    a. The availability heuristic
    b. The representativeness heuristic
    c. The anchoring heuristic
    d. None of the above

11. What should the companies in the preceding question do to increase the willingness of their employees to work overseas?
    a. Have their public relations departments make frequent reports to the major news networks about the positive experiences their employees have had abroad.
    b. Publish reports on the number of fatalities from terrorism to show how small a threat it is.
    c. Reduce the minimum length of stay in a foreign country from two years to six months so that employees can have a trial period.
    d. None of the above will work.

12. The representativeness heuristic causes us to
    a. ignore overall probabilities.
    b. give improper weight to contradictory evidence when making a decision.
    c. focus on solutions that are easily brought to mind.
    d. consider only those hypotheses with which we are the most familiar.

13. Mike and Cal are marketing executives working as a team for a Fortune 500 company. They have been given an extremely difficult project: They are to design a new consumer product. Mike wants to review all the market research on consumer needs, identify what the product must do to solve those needs, and then see if his company can build it. Cal wants go to the library and look up case histories of other companies noted for developing brilliant new products. Mike wants to use a(n) _____ process to solve the problem, and Cal is trying to use a(n) _____ to solve the problem.
    a. analogy; decomposition
    b. working backward; analogy
    c. analogy; visual representation
    d. incubation; visual representation

14. Winnie, a teacher, has been told that the test scores of one of her new students, Nelson, suggest that he is very bright. The principal has asked her to keep an eye on Nelson and let him know what she thinks of Nelson's intelligence. All through the first six weeks of the semester, she finds examples that seem to show that Nelson is indeed very bright. However, during the seventh week, she finds out that the records have been mixed up. Nelson's actual test scores show him as being strictly average. What explains Winnie's observations?
    a. Confirmation bias
    b. Functional fixedness
    c. Mental set
    d. Decomposition

15. Emmeline works as a lab technician in a neurobiological laboratory. She has just received an announcement that must be posted in the lab immediately. Because she cannot find any thumbtacks, she uses the ends of hypodermic needles to attach the announcement to the bulletin board. What pitfall in problem solving has Emmeline just avoided?
    a. Functional fixedness
    b. Confirmation bias
    c. Ignoring of negative evidence
    d. Faulty hypothesis testing

16. Gambler's fallacy occurs when people
    a. overestimate the probability of very rare events.
    b. overestimate the probability of very common events.
    c. are overconfident about their predictions.
    d. believe that if they fail several times to get "heads" on a coin flip, their next attempt will probably be a success.

17. The newspaper headline reads, "Campus police start operation to run down jaywalkers." This statement has two
    a. deep structures.
    b. surface structures.
    c. morphemes.
    d. phonemes.

18. Which of the following is correct?
    a. Phonemes make up morphemes, which make up words.
    b. Morphemes make up phonemes, which make up words.
    c. Words make up morphemes, which make up sentences.
    d. Words make up phonemes, which make up morphemes.

19. Which of the following sentences would be the easiest to memorize? 1) A grickly aftla hicktored the bubla. 2) Oftla grick hickt bubla.
    a. The first sentence
    b. The second sentence
    c. Both will be equally easy to memorize.
    d. The answer cannot be determined.

20. In Tarzan movies, a husband, his wife, and their baby are shipwrecked. The baby survives and is raised by apes until a doctor finds him twenty years later. The doctor takes the wild man out of the jungle, teaches him to speak French and English, and introduces him to society. Although the wild man's accents are not perfect, he manages to live in England for some time before choosing to go back to the jungle. Why are these movies unrealistic?
    a. A language acquisition device needs to be learned.
    b. A critical period may exist for language acquisition.
    c. The wild man should have been able to learn proper French and English accents.
    d. All of the above

Total Correct (See answer key) _____

ANSWERS TO FILL-IN-THE-BLANKS KEY TERMS

1. prototype (p. 270)
2. artificial concepts (p. 269)
3. mental models (p. 270)
4. Scripts (p. 270)
5. syllogism (p. 272)
6. heuristic (p. 274)
7. anchoring heuristic (p. 275)
8. mental chronometry (p. 266)
9. syntax (p. 288)
10. Telegraphic speech (p. 293)
11. Babblings (p. 292)
12. deep structure (p. 289)
13. morpheme (p. 288)
14. functional fixedness (p. 279)
15. mental set (p. 279)

ANSWERS TO CONCEPTS AND EXERCISES

No. 1: Approaches to Problem Solving

1. Viola is trying to develop a cognitive map, and she is being affected by rectangular bias. The main roads are in the shape of a triangle, but the rectangular bias causes her to attempt to put them into a north-south-east-west square. (p. 268)

2. Trixy has hypothesized that the fuse box is the cause of the sudden loss of lights in her house. In order to avoid confirmation bias, she and Peter could look out the window to see if other houses are without lights. If that is the case, then the problem is not the fuse box but, rather, a major power failure in the neighborhood. When the problem is a blown fuse, only part of the house is dark. This is the symptom that Trixy and Peter are overlooking. They are ignoring negative evidence. (pp. 279–280)

3. The Parisian offered Al a choice between a heuristic (the shortcut) and an algorithm (the sure but longer way to get to the museum). Al chose the algorithm. (pp. 272, 274)

4. Carlotta has realized that being an expert has caused her to have a mental set. Therefore, she is bringing in someone who doesn't have old answers that will get in the way of thinking of new answers. (p. 279)

No. 2: Structures of Language

1. The morphemes (meaningful units) are as follows: the, husband, s (after an apostrophe means a posses-

sive), dinner, was, and terrible. Two possible deep structures are as follows: The dinner that the husband cooked was impossible to eat, and the meal that the husband was eating was prepared poorly. (pp. 288–289)

2. The morphemes are as follows: my, friend, paint, ed, me, in, his, back, and yard. Two possible deep structures are as follows: My friend created a painting depicting me in his backyard, and my friend and I were in his backyard, where he was painting my portrait. Can you think of others? (pp. 288–289)

ANSWERS TO CRITICAL THINKING

1. Sam hypothesizes that Sylvia Star was murdered by a rare drug.

2. The evidence includes the following facts: Sylvia had lots of enemies, old and current; a drug could have been slipped into her drink; Sam knows a crime like that has been committed before; and there could be a connection between Sylvia's visitors that day and her current writing subjects.

3. Martina hypothesizes that the woman died of old age.

4. The probability of a death resulting from natural causes is the evidence Martina uses to support her hypothesis.

ANSWERS TO MULTIPLE-CHOICE QUESTIONS

Circle the question numbers you answered correctly.

Sample Quiz 1

1. b is the answer. The response seems unnatural to Shaniqua. Usually when she sees a letter to capitalize, her response is compatible, but on the unfamiliar computer it is not; therefore, she types more slowly there. (p. 266)
   a. She is making an incompatible response.
   c. Fundamental attribution is not a term associated with reaction time differences.
   d. Multiattribute decisions are those in which each option has many characteristics to be considered.

2. d is the answer. If the task were less complex, Halle's reaction time would decrease. (pp. 266–267)

a. If she needed to look for two additional problems, Halle's reaction time would increase, or lengthen.

b. If Halle didn't know when to expect the jars, her reaction time would increase. People who anticipate stimuli can respond more quickly.

c. Halle would be making the speed-accuracy tradeoff if she tried to be very careful not to grab a good jar.

3. *a* is the answer. Rectangular bias is the tendency to make cognitive maps fit a north-south-east-west orientation. To remember this, think of a rectangle with the top as north, the bottom as south, and the right and left sides as east and west, respectively. (p. 268)

b. Reconstructive memory is the process of filling the gaps in our memories with information that has been stored in long-term memory.

c. There is no such thing as directional bias with regard to cognitive maps.

d. *a* is the answer.

4. *b* is the answer. (p. 270)

a. Propositions are made up of words. (You may be thinking of phonemes and morphemes.)

c. Propositions can be true or false.

d. Mental models are made up of propositions, not the other way around. Propositions show the relationship between concepts or the relationship between a property or characteristic and a concept.

5. *c* is the answer. The concept is weapons, and a gun is the best example of a weapon. (pp. 269–270)

6. *c* is the answer. (p. 272)

a. A heuristic, not an algorithm, is a shortcut to the solution of a problem.

b. An algorithm always produces a correct answer.

d. An algorithm is not subject to bias.

7. *d* is the answer. A syllogism is made of two or more premises and a conclusion. (p. 272)

a. "All monsters are ugly" is one premise. "The Creature from the Black Lagoon is a monster" is the second premise. The three statements together are a syllogism.

b. A premise may be a proposition, or a statement of a relationship, but the three statements together are not a single proposition.

c. A natural concept is one with fuzzy boundaries. A member of a natural concept must have most of a set of characteristic features, but need not have all of them.

8. *b* is the answer. Amy's first answer of 10,000 served as an anchor that kept her second estimate nearby. (p. 275)

a. An algorithm is a systematic method that always attains a result; a heuristic is a shortcut.

c. The availability heuristic uses how quickly the hypothesis or examples come to mind as an indicator of probability. Amy is adjusting an estimate, not thinking of which hypothesis seems more available.

d. People using the representativeness heuristic base their conclusions on how similar a stimulus is to category description.

9. *d* is the answer. Thalia concluded that the person looked similar enough to her category description of rock-and-roll band members. (p. 275)

a. The anchoring heuristic is a shortcut in which a first estimate is only slightly adjusted in the face of new information.

b. Availability heuristic users take the answers that are most easily accessed from their memory. Thalia wasn't necessarily thinking about rock and roll bands when she saw the man.

c. Confirmation is a tendency to find evidence for your hypothesis.

10. *a* is the answer. Jamila created an analogy for the problem of remembering how an action potential works. (p. 276)

b. Decomposition is breaking apart a problem into subproblems and working on each.

c. Ignoring negative evidence is an obstacle to problem solving.

d. A script is a description of how you expect an event to go.

11. *d* is the answer. Many objects designed for a particular purpose can be used to solve other types of problems. However, when people can think of an object as serving only its intended purpose, they are victims of functional fixedness. (p. 279)

a. A mental set causes people to use old solutions to solve new problems instead of looking for simpler solutions.

b. Confirmation bias occurs when people look only at information that will confirm a hypothesis.

c. Ignoring negative evidence means that people do not consider the lack of symptoms when testing a hypothesis.

12. *d* is the answer. Getting stuck in one way of solving a problem is a mental set. (p. 279)

a. An algorithm is a formal reasoning procedure that always results in a correct answer.

b. Functional fixedness is being unable to think of a novel use for an object.

c. A mental model is a description of how something works.

13. *c* is the answer. In incubation, the problem is set aside for awhile. (p. 277)

a. Deep structure is the meaning of a sentence.

b. Expert systems are computer programs that are capable of solving problems in a specific area.

d. Prototypes are the most typical example of a natural concept.

14. *a* is the answer. The gambler's fallacy is the belief that events in a random process will correct themselves. (p. 286)

b. People with loss aversion usually feel worse about losing an amount of money than they would feel good about gaining the same amount.

c. Ignoring negative evidence is the practice of overlooking absent symptoms that might eliminate a hypothesis.

d. People with a confirmation bias are likely to ignore information that is inconsistent with their hypothesis.

15. *b* is the answer. The utility of a choice refers to its personal, subjective value to the decision maker. (p. 284)

a. The likelihood of a choice being the outcome deals more with expected value, which takes into account the probability of an outcome and its perceived benefits and costs.

c. The perception of risk relates to the probability of an outcome.

d. *b* is the answer.

16. *b* is the answer. Deep structure is the underlying meaning of a string of words. (p. 289)

a. Surface structure is the sequence of the words.

c. The syntax of the sentence is the set of rules that govern the way the words are strung together.

d. Deep structure refers to the meaning of a sentence, not to its complexity.

17. *d* is the answer. The sentence follows rules for word order. (p. 288)

a. You may have been thinking of schemas; there is no such thing as a schematic rule.

b. Semantic rules are rules of meaning. The sentence does not make sense.

c. Syllogisms are logical arguments.

18. *c* is the answer. Semantics is the set of rules governing the meanings of words and sentences. The words no va have a particular meaning in Spanish, but this particular combination of letters has no meaning in English. (p. 289)

a. Syntax is a set of rules governing the way words are put together.

b. A language acquisition device is an innate ability to understand the regularities of speech and the fundamental relationships between words.

d. The surface structure is the sequence in which words are strung together.

19. *d* is the answer. (pp. 290–292)

a, b, c. Each option is only one part of the contextual information that will influence the interpretation of a sentence.

20. *b* is the answer. Children at the one-word stage of language development use one word for many different objects. (p. 293)

a. Babblings are the first language-like sounds that infants make.

c. Prototype matching does involve identifying a prototype and then adding less typical examples, but it is not a stage in language development.

d. Telegraphic speech consists of two- and three-word sentences. These sentences are brief and to the point, and they leave out words that are not essential to meaning.

Now turn to the quiz analysis table at the end of this chapter to find which areas you know well and which areas you need to work on. Circle the numbers in the table for items on Quiz 1 that you answered correctly.

ANSWERS TO MULTIPLE-CHOICE QUESTIONS

Circle the question numbers you answered correctly.

Sample Quiz 2

1. *c* is the answer. Reaction time is the time elapsed between the stimulus presentation and an overt response. (p. 266)

a. Perceiving a stimulus is only part of the activity that takes place between the presentation of a stimulus and the overt response to that stimulus.

b. The overt reaction to a stimulus is only part of the activity that takes place between the presentation of a stimulus and the overt response to that stimulus.

d. Mental chronometry is the timing of mental events. Making an overt response, which is one of the activities measured by reaction time, is not solely a mental event.

2. c is the answer. Changes in stimulus-response compatibility would cause an evoked potential associated with response and execution to change. The P300 is sensitive to stimulus presentation. (p. 267)

a, b, d. The P300 is a large positive evoked potential that occurs after a stimulus is presented. If the stimulus is difficult to detect or is very complex, the P300 will be changed.

3. d is the answer. Cliff will need more time to respond to the green light (the stimulus) since he is driving a stick shift for the first time, which requires a starting procedure different from that of an automatic. Also, the light turned green sooner than he expected, and unexpected stimuli lengthen reaction time. Finally, an increase in the complexity of the decision will lengthen reaction time. Cliff has more than the usual number of streets to choose from when the light turns green. (pp. 266–267)

4. b is the answer. (p. 270)

a. Schemas are collections of information about the world that influence how we remember and store information.

c. Syllogisms are basic arguments that consist of two premises.

d. Scripts contain knowledge about sequences of human activity.

5. d is the answer. (p. 269)

a, b. Both natural and artificial concepts provide a way to classify objects.

c. Artificial concepts have rigid definitions. If an object doesn't meet all the specifications, then it is not part of that particular artificial concept. Natural concepts are fuzzy. For example, an ostrich is a bird even though it doesn't meet all the criteria for "bird"—that is, it can't fly.

6. d is the answer. Cats eat flowers is a proposition because it relates two concepts, cats and flowers. (p. 270)

a. th is a phoneme.

b. Flowers is just a concept.

c. ed is a morpheme.

7. c is the answer. Mental models are clusters of propositions that represent people's understanding of how things (usually physical things) work. (p. 270)

a. Schemas serve as general representations of a large set of more specific examples that generate expectations of the world. Schemas are broader than mental models.

b. Scripts are mental representations of what is supposed to happen during sequences of events, such as weddings or parties. Mental models are clusters of propositions about how things or objects work.

d. A proposition is the smallest unit of knowledge that can stand alone. A mental model is made up of many propositions.

8. b is the answer. An algorithm will always produce the correct answer, which in this case is winning the game. However, Clinton and his uncle will be playing for a very long time. Clinton will have to evaluate the consequences of every possible move he can make each time it is his turn. (p. 272)

a. Algorithms always produce a correct answer.

c, d. People usually ignore overall probabilities when using a representativeness heuristic. Clinton is using an algorithm, not a heuristic.

9. a is the answer. Cindy starts out being 100 percent sure that she will get a job. After reading the paper, she should realize that her chances are very slim. Instead she is still very sure; she is anchored in her hypothesis that she will get a job. (p. 275)

b. People use the availability heuristic when they judge the probability of an event by how easily examples of that event come to mind. If Cindy had thought of all her many friends who had gotten jobs in the city, this would have been the correct answer.

c. If Cindy was using the representativeness heuristic, she would have focused on the representative information (the paper) instead of her original estimate.

d. There is no such thing as the base-rate heuristic. (You may be thinking of the representativeness heuristic. Ignoring base-rate frequencies results in the use of this heuristic.)

10. a is the answer. Employees are judging the probability of terrorism based on the information that is most available to them. This bias is due to the availability heuristic. (p. 275)

b. Employees are not trying to determine whether an example is part of a class of objects as they would do when using the representativeness heuristic.

c. Employees are not adjusting their hypothesis to match new information. They have made a decision about the degree of terrorist activity based on the information available to them.

d. Only *a* is the answer.

11. *a* is the answer. If employees are relying on the most easily available information in order to decide how safe living abroad is, companies should make positive information more available than the negative reports on terrorist activities. (p. 275)

b. By publishing the numbers of fatalities, the companies will simply be making the information on terrorist activities more available to their employees' minds.

c. The problem is employees' incorrect estimate of the probability of terrorism. Reducing the minimum length of stay in another country will do nothing to change employees' incorrect estimates.

d. Only *a* is the answer.

12. *a* is the answer. The representativeness heuristic leads us to look at an example and compare it to a larger class of items. We focus on the similar appearances of the example and the larger class of items, ignoring information on how often the larger class of items occurs (overall probability). (p. 275)

b. The anchoring heuristic causes us to give improper weight to contradictory evidence in making a decision.

c, d. The availability heuristic causes us to focus on the solutions that are most easily brought to mind and that are therefore most familiar. These are usually the hypotheses that have occurred most frequently in the past.

13. *b* is the answer. Mike wants to start with what the product has to do (an end point) and work backward to the solution of what the product will be. Cal wants to use an analogy: employing the same techniques that other companies employ in trying to solve the same kind of problem. (p. 276)

a. Cal, not Mike, wants to employ an analogy by looking at other companies' solutions to the same problem. Decomposition is breaking a problem into its subparts.

c. Mike is trying to develop his own strategy, not use a strategy that has worked for anyone else facing a similar problem.

d. Mike is not letting the problem incubate by laying it aside for awhile.

14. *a* is the answer. Winnie has a hypothesis that Nelson is very smart. She takes into consideration only the evidence that supports her hypothesis and ignores evidence that Nelson is only average. (p. 279)

b. Winnie is testing a hypothesis, not trying to find a solution involving the use of an object.

c. A mental set means using the solutions to old problems to try to solve new ones. Winnie is not using old solutions to test her hypothesis about Nelson's intelligence.

d. Decomposition is a way to simplify problem solving by breaking a problem into smaller subproblems. Winnie is not engaged in this activity.

15. *a* is the answer. If Emmeline had thought of the hypodermics as being useful only for giving injections, she would have experienced functional fixedness. Instead, she used them for something other than their traditional function and solved her problem. (p. 279)

b, d. Confirmation bias occurs because people always try to confirm, rather than refute, their hypotheses. Emmeline is not testing a hypothesis, so neither of these alternatives is correct.

c. People ignore negative evidence when looking for explanations of some event. Emmeline is not looking for an explanation but, rather, for a way to solve a problem.

16. *d* is the answer. Random events are independent of each other. For example, the result of the flip of a coin, whether for the first, second, third, or sixtieth time, is independent of the results of the previous flips. Each time the coin is flipped, there is a fifty-fifty chance of seeing heads. Gambler's fallacy occurs when someone thinks that because many heads have turned up, tails are soon due to appear. (p. 286)

a, b, c. Incorrectly estimating the probability of events is a bias in perception of probability, but neither this nor overconfidence in one's own predictions can be described as the gambler's fallacy.

17. *a* is the answer. The sentence has two meanings. The police are probably trying to catch jaywalkers, but it sounds as if they could be running them down with a vehicle! (p. 289)

b. The sentence only has one surface structure, since that is the string of words.

c. More than two morphemes make up the sentence. For example, <u>campus</u>, <u>police</u>, and <u>start</u> are all morphemes.

d. More than two phonemes make up the sentence. For example, campus has six: c̲, a̲, m̲, p̲, u̲, and s̲.

18. *a* is the answer. Phonemes (sounds that affect the meaning of a word) make up morphemes (the smallest units of meaning in a language), which make up words. (p. 288)

19. *a* is the answer. The words a̲ and the̲, as well as the ly̲ and ed̲ suffixes, make it easier for us to chunk the nonsense syllables in short-term memory, because of the similarity to English usage. The sentence also has syntax similar to English. (p. 290)
    b. There are no words or suffixes that help us chunk information in the second sentence. It is more difficult to remember, even though it is shorter than the first sentence.
    c. If one sentence is easier than the other, then both cannot be equally easy.

d. The answer can be determined.

20. *b* is the answer. Many cases support the idea that a critical period exists for language development. The wild man was found when he was in his twenties and was past the critical period for language development. Therefore, he should not have been able to learn any language. (p. 295)
    a. The language acquisition device Chomsky proposed is innate.
    c. When people learn a second language after the age of twelve to fifteen, they usually cannot speak with a flawless accent.
    d. Only *b* is the answer.

Now turn to the quiz analysis table at the end of this chapter to find which areas you know well and which areas you need to work on. Circle the numbers in the table for items on Quiz 2 that you answered correctly.

For each question you answered correctly, circle its number. (Quiz 1 numbers are not shaded; Quiz 2 numbers are shaded.) Are there patterns in the types of questions or the topics you got wrong that could direct your further study? Did you improve from Quiz 1 to Quiz 2?

TOPIC	TYPE OF QUESTION		
	DEFINITION	COMPREHENSION	APPLICATION
Basic functions			1, 2
	1	2	3
Mental representations	3	4	5
	4	5	6, 7
Thinking Strategies			
Formal reasoning	6		7
			8
Informal reasoning			8, 9
		12	9, 10, 11
Problem Solving			
Strategies			10, 13
			13
Obstacles	11		12
			14, 15
Decision making	15		14
	16		
Language			
Elements	16	19	17, 18
		18	17, 19
Development			20
			20

TOTAL CORRECT BY QUIZ:

QUIZ 1:
QUIZ 2:

Chapter 10

Mental Abilities

Mental ability is the capacity to reason, remember, understand, solve problems, and make decisions.

OUTLINE

I. TESTING FOR INTELLIGENCE (pp. 304–307)

Many psychologists agree with Robert Sternberg that three characteristics encompass intelligence: possession of knowledge, ability to efficiently use knowledge to reason, and ability to employ that reasoning adaptively in different environments.

A. A Brief History of IQ Tests

Alfred Binet's original test included a series of age-graded items that demonstrated differences among children in reasoning, judgment, and problem-solving abilities. Children who answered questions at their age level were considered of "regular" intelligence. Louis Terman developed the Stanford-Binet test, devised a scoring method known as the intelligence quotient (IQ), and created the IQ test, which included questions for adults. Despite cultural biases, IQ tests were given to screen immigrants and to place soldiers in appropriate assignments. David Wechsler developed a new test that was made up of several subtests. Wechsler's test reduced the extent to which answers depended on a certain culture and had some subtests that had little or no verbal content.

B. IQ Tests Today

° The Wechsler test, which is designed to be administered individually, includes the verbal scale and the performance scale.

° The average result obtained by people at each age level is assigned an intelligence quotient, or score, of 100. Each individual's score is compared to the average for his or her age level in order to compute an IQ. Therefore, an IQ score is a relative measurement.

II. MEASURING THE QUALITY OF TESTS (pp. 308–310)

Tests have three advantages over other means of evaluation: they are standardized, quantifiable (which allows the calculation of norms), and economical and efficient.

A. Reliability

If a test is reliable, a person will receive about the same score when tested on different occasions. There are three methods of checking the reliability of a test: test-retest, alternate-form, and split-half reliability. If the correlation coefficient between two scores is high and positive, the test is considered reliable.

B. Validity

A valid test measures what it is designed to measure. There are four measures of validity: content validity, construct validity, criterion validity, and predictive validity.

III. EVALUATING IQ TESTS (pp. 310–321)

A. The Reliability and Validity of IQ Tests

1. *How Reliable Are IQ Tests?* IQ tests usually provide consistent results. However, test-retest reliability can be low if the initial testing is done prior to seven years of age. The testing conditions and the person's motivation when taking the test can also affect results.

2. *How Valid Are IQ Tests?* The validity of IQ tests is difficult to measure, in part because intelligence itself is difficult to define. IQ tests do a reasonably good job of predicting academic and job success, but scores can be distorted by the response to the tester.

3. *How Fair Are IQ Tests?* Controversy about the fairness of IQ tests continues, especially in terms of cultural factors. Although many of the technical problems in IQ tests have been solved, the social consequences of testing should be evaluated.

B. Thinking Critically: Are IQ Tests Unfairly Biased Against Certain Groups?

What am I being asked to believe or accept?
Intelligence tests are biased against some minority groups.

What evidence is available to support the assertion?
Differences in IQ scores may reflect motivation and a person's trust in the test administrator. Some tests are not "culture fair." People may interpret the test questions intelligently but differently than the defined "right" answer.

Are there alternative ways of interpreting the evidence?
Intelligence tests may be biased in assessing general intelligence, but they may still be good predictors of who will do well in school or on the job.

What conclusions are most reasonable?
Current tests, while not completely culture fair, can be useful as predictors of success in the culture in which they are administered. Psychologists should also spend time developing alternative tests based on problem-solving skills and more open-ended questions.

C. IQ Scores as a Measure of Innate Ability

° The influences of heredity and the environment interact to produce intelligence. Correlational studies with twins suggest that heredity influences the development of IQ. However, the environment also exerts a strong influence on IQ. Previously underprivileged children placed in homes that provide an enriching intellectual environment have shown moderate but consistent increases in IQ. And children placed in enrichment programs show improved health, academic achievements, and intellectual skills.

D. Group Differences in IQ Scores

An examination of the differences among group means on IQ tests does not provide information about specific individuals in those groups. A person in the low score group may have an individual score that is much higher than a person from the high score group. In addition, inherited features may be influenced by the environment.

1. *Socioeconomic Differences.* A child's ability is influenced by genetic factors and perhaps by the effects of the parents' occupation and education on the home environment. Also, higher-income families may encourage a higher level of motivation to succeed.

2. *Ethnic Differences.* There is variation in average IQ scores between ethnic groups, but more variation within groups. Research indicates that differences in IQ among ethnic groups may be due to differences in socioeconomic environment, parental education, nutrition, health care, and schools. Also, people in some cultures may be more or less motivated during testing, depending on the value their cultures place on education or intelligence.

E. Conditions that Can Raise IQ Scores

Enrichment programs such as Head Start can cause at least temporary gains in IQ scores. Spending time in projects such as Head Start may cause a child to be more motivated and have a better attitude toward school.

F. IQ Scores in the Classroom

IQ scores may influence teachers' expectations about the abilities of their students. In turn, these expectancies may influence students' performance.

IV. UNDERSTANDING INTELLIGENCE (pp. 321–325)

A. The Psychometric Approach

The psychometric approach tries to describe the structure of intelligence by examining the correlations among scores on various tests. Charles Spearman postulated two factors that account for test scores: the g-factor, or general intelligence; and the s-factors, which are the specific skills and knowledge needed to answer the questions on a particular test. L. L. Thurstone disagreed. He used factor analysis, a statistical technique, to find several independent primary mental abilities, including numerical ability, reasoning, verbal fluency, spatial visualization, perceptual ability, memory, and verbal comprehension. Later, Raymond B. Cattell argued that a g-factor exists and that it consists of fluid intelligence and crystallized intelligence. Most psychologists agree that there is a g-factor. They just do not agree on what the g-factor is.

B. The Information-Processing Approach

Psychologists using the information-processing approach have tried to understand intelligence by examining the mental processes involved in intelligent behavior. Research suggests that those with greater intellectual ability have more attentional resources available when performing a task. Speed of basic processing plays only a small role in determining intelligent behavior.

C. The Triarchical Theory of Intelligence

Robert Sternberg proposed that intelligence is composed of internal components, the relation of components to the external world, and adaptation to the environment. The internal components are performance components, knowledge-acquisition components, and metacomponents. The first two components are the information-processing capacities of perceiving stimuli, holding information in working (short-term) memory, performing transformations on that information, and retrieving information from memory. Metacomponents are the processes involved in organizing and setting up a problem. The relationship between components and the external world is the ability to profit from experience. Adaptation to the environment can be thought of as "street smarts."

D. Multiple Intelligences

Howard Gardner proposed that certain abilities are relatively independent of one another and that individuals may develop some "intelligences" more highly than others. Gardner suggested six different intelligences: linguistic, logical-mathematical, spatial, musical, body-kinesthetic, and personal.

E. The Ecological Approach

This approach emphasizes the role of the environment in the development of intelligence. What is intelligent in one situation may not be intelligent in another situation.

V. LINKAGES: MENTAL ABILITIES AND THINKING (pp. 325–326)

Cognitive complexity and the ability to think multidimensionally are good predictors of problem-solving ability. IQ scores are not. Cognitive complexity abilities are usually domain-specific.

VI. DIVERSITY IN MENTAL ABILITIES (pp. 326–331)

A. Creativity

Creativity is often assessed by tests of divergent thinking, which measure the ability to generate many different but plausible responses to a problem. Expertise in the field, a set of creative skills, and intrinsic motivation are necessary for creativity. External rewards can deter creativity. The correlation between IQ scores and creativity is not very high. IQ tests measure convergent thinking, whereas creativity is characterized by divergent thinking.

B. Unusual Mental Ability

1. *Giftedness.* Those with extremely high IQs do not necessarily become creative geniuses. They do, however, usually become very successful in this society or culture.

2. *Mental Retardation.* This label is applied to people whose IQs are 70 or below and who fail at daily living skills. Mental retardation sometimes has very specific causes, such as Down's syndrome. In most cases of familial retardation, there is no specific cause. Psychologists believe familial retardation results from an interaction between heredity and the environment. Mildly retarded children differ from other children in three ways: they perform certain mental operations more slowly, they know fewer facts about the world, and they are not very good at using particular mental strategies in learning and problem solving. In general, retarded children are deficient in metacognition.

C. Learning Disabilities

People with learning disabilities have academic performance that doesn't measure up to their measured intelligence. People with dyslexia see letters as distorted or jumbled. Dysphasia is difficulty in understanding spoken words. In dysgraphia a person has trouble writing, while in dyscalculia a person has trouble with arithmetic.

VII. FOCUS ON RESEARCH METHODS: USING QUASI-EXPERIMENTS TO TRACK MENTAL ABILITIES OVER THE LIFE SPAN (pp. 331–333)

Age-related changes in mental abilities can be examined through cross-sectional and longitudinal studies. The cross-sequential with resampling design combines cross-sectional and longitudinal studies. Results show that crystallized intelligence may continue to grow into old age. Fluid intelligence remains stable in adulthood and then declines in late life. Specifically, problems in working memory, processing speed, problem-solving strategy organization, flexibility, and control of attention appear late in life.

KEY TERMS

1. **Mental ability** is the capacity to perform higher mental processes of reasoning, remembering, understanding, and problem solving. (p. 304)

2. **Intelligence**, according to Sternberg's working definition, is the combination of three characteristics: the possession of knowledge, the ability to use information processing to reason about the world, and the ability to employ that reasoning adaptively in different environments. Note, however, that psychologists do not agree on an exact definition of intelligence. (p. 304)

3. The **Stanford-Binet** test was a revised version of Binet's original test of mental abilities. Each set of age-graded questions could be answered correctly by a substantial majority of the children in that age group. Children were above average if they could correctly answer questions above their age grade. The score received, called mental age, was divided by chronological age and then multiplied by 100, resulting in an IQ. (p. 305)

> *Example:* Mark's IQ has been tested. Although he is only twelve, he answered questions designed for children up to fourteen years of age. The following steps are used to determine his IQ.
> a. Mark's mental age is fourteen.
> b. Mark's chronological age is twelve.
> c. $14/12 = 1.16$
> d. $1.16 \times 100 = 116$.
> e. Mark's IQ is 116.

4. **IQ tests** are any tests designed to measure intelligence on an objective, standardized scale. (p. 306)

5. A **verbal scale** in the Wechsler tests measures verbal skills. (p. 306)

> *Example:* These tests include remembering a series of digits, solving arithmetic problems, defining vocabulary words, and understanding and answering questions.

6. A **performance scale** in the Wechsler tests measures spatial ability and the ability to manipulate materials. (pp. 306–307)

> *Example:* One of the tasks on the performance scale is putting blocks together to match a given design. Another task requires a person to look at a picture and decide what is missing.

7. **Intelligence quotient** (or **IQ score**) reflects relative standing on a test within a population of the same age group. IQ values reflect how far each score deviates from the age-group average. (p. 307)

8. **Tests** are systematic procedures for observing behavior in a standard situation. Behavior is described with the help of a numerical scale or a category system. (p. 308)

Example: To give a test in a standard situation, the directions, setting, and scoring methods used are the same regardless of the people involved. An example of a numerical scale would be the calculation of an IQ.

9. **Norms** are descriptions of the frequency of particular scores. Norms provide information about how a certain person's test score compares to the population upon which the norms are based. (p. 308)

10. A **reliable** test is one whose results will be consistent or stable over repeated test occasions. (p. 308)

> *Example:* Each time Connie takes an intelligence test, she scores at the mean for her age group.

11. A **valid** test is one that measures exactly what it is designed to measure. (p. 309)

> *Example:* Defining a list of words is a valid test of vocabulary but may not be a valid test of intelligence.

12. The **psychometric approach** is a method for analyzing test scores in order to describe the structure of intelligence. Psychologists have examined correlations of test scores in order to find the skills and talents that define intelligence. (p. 321)

> *REMEMBER:* <u>Psych</u> means "mental." <u>Metric</u> means to "measure." Those who use the psychometric approach study measures (test scores) of mental functions (in this case, intelligence).

13. **G**, or the **g-factor**, is a representation of general mental ability or intelligence. (p. 321)

14. **S's**, or the **s-factors**, are a representation of special intelligences. Specific information and skills needed for a particular task are s-factors. (p. 321)

> *Example:* A person with a high level of g-factors might still answer a mathematics question incorrectly if the person lacked the necessary s-factors.

15. **Fluid intelligence** is the basic power of reasoning and problem solving. It produces deduction, induction, reasoning, and understanding of the relationships between different ideas. (p. 322)

> *Example:* To be a good detective, you must be able to look at all the available clues and deduce "who done it." The powers of deduction and reasoning represent fluid intelligence. (Read the example of

crystallized intelligence, Key Term 16, to understand the difference between the two types.)

16. **Crystallized intelligence** involves specific knowledge gained as a result of applying fluid intelligence. It produces verbal comprehension and skill at manipulating numbers. (p. 322)

Example: Detectives who have been working for a long time have gained specific knowledge about how to read clues and people. An experienced detective may be able to examine the scene of a crime and notice clues that tell her when the crime took place. This specific knowledge (crystallized intelligence) gained from previous experience (previous applications of fluid intelligence) will increase her overall chances of solving the crime.

17. The **information-processing approach** studies intelligence by examining the mental processes that underlie intelligent behavior. (p. 322)

Example: A psychologist using this approach to study intelligence would ask the following types of questions: What influence does effective chunking ability have on intelligent behavior? Does being able to rapidly access information in long-term memory increase the ability to behave intelligently? (Chunking and accessing long-term memory are ways of processing information.)

18. **Creativity** is the ability to generate novel but viable or workable solutions to a problem. (p. 326)

19. **Divergent thinking**, characteristic of creative people, is the ability to think along many alternative paths to generate many different solutions to a problem. (p. 327)

Example: Consider the following question: What can you use a newspaper for? Answers that relate to gaining information or news represent convergent thinking. Answers that are examples of divergent thinking include using newspapers to create a papier-mâché object, to light a fire, to pad a package, to cover oneself for warmth, to provide insulation from noise, to stuff shoes so that they keep their shape, to make a higher seat for a short child, to make a toy for a cat, to make an airplane, to wrap a box, to train a puppy, to humidify the air (by draping wet newspapers over a radiator), to make a ransom note (by cutting out letters from a newspaper), and to soak up water (by putting newspapers in wet shoes).

20. **Convergent thinking** is the ability to apply the rules of logic and knowledge about the world to reduce the number of possible solutions to a problem. (p. 328)

21. **Familial retardation** is mild retardation. It is called familial because most people in this group come from families of lower socioeconomic status and they are more likely than those suffering from a genetic defect to have a relative who is also retarded. Familial retardation results from a complex interaction between heredity and environment. (pp. 328–329)

22. **Metacognition** is the knowledge of what strategies to apply, when to apply them, and how to deploy them in new situations so that new specific knowledge can be gained and different, and new problems can be mastered. (p. 330)

23. **Cross-sectional studies** attempt to look at age-related differences by comparing data collected simultaneously from people of different ages. This type of study can be confounded by generational differences. (p. 331)

Example: Older people in such a study will have had different environments, including teaching methods, parental social norms, nutrition, culture, and medical experiences.

24. **Longitudinal studies** examine age-related variables by repeatedly testing a group of people as they age. Since some people drop out of longitudinal studies as a result of death or incapacitation, and the healthiest may have also retained better mental capacities, longitudinal studies tend to underestimate age-related changes in mental abilities. (p. 331)

REMEMBER: Longitudinal studies take place over a long time.

25. The **cross-sequential with resampling** design combines cross-sectional and longitudinal methods. This design allows for confounds to be identified and corrected. (p. 332)

Example: A set of volunteers of various ages is given an IQ test once to tentatively identify differences across ages, then is retested ten years later to compare the differences in the amount of change in their scores. In addition, a new sample from the same group is drawn and tested for the first time. Their test scores are compared to people of their age who were previously tested to identify a testing effect.

FILL-IN-THE-BLANKS KEY TERMS

This section will help you check your factual knowledge of the key terms introduced in this chapter. Fill in each blank with the appropriate term from the list of key terms above.

1. The capacity to perform processes such as reasoning is called _____.

2. Information necessary to decide how a person's test score compares to the scores of others comes from _____.

3. A _____ is a systematic procedure for observing behavior in a standard situation.

4. If a person achieves a high score on an IQ test the first time but a very low score the second time he or she takes it, the test has low _____.

5. A test that actually measures what it is designed to measure is said to be _____.

6. The _____ reflects relative standing on a test within a population of the same age group.

7. According to Cattell, the basic power of logical thought is _____.

8. Psychologists who seek to describe and understand intelligence by analyzing data from intelligence tests take the _____ approach.

9. A psychologist who takes the _____ approach examines intelligence by studying the mental operations that underlie intelligent behavior.

10. _____ is the ability to come up with new or unusual but viable solutions to a problem.

11. _____ studies examine age-related variables by repeatedly testing a group of people as they age.

12. A person adept at _____, or capable of thinking along many paths when generating problem solutions, is considered to be creative.

13. In _____ studies, data from different people representing a range of ages are compared to gain information about age-related differences.

14. Spatial ability is measured in the _____ scales in the Wechsler tests.

15. Cattell believed that intelligence involving specific knowledge gained through reasoning and problem solving is called _____.

Total Correct (See answer key) _____

LEARNING OBJECTIVES

1. Define mental ability. (p. 304)

2. Define intelligence. Discuss the reasons that intelligence is so difficult to define. (p. 304)

3. Discuss the history of intelligence test construction. Explain the scoring methods used in the Binet and Stanford-Binet intelligence tests. (pp. 304–306)

4. Discuss the use and abuse of intelligence testing in the United States in the early 1900s. (p. 306)

5. Describe Wechsler's intelligence test. Explain why it is different from tests that were used previously. Define verbal and performance scales. (pp. 306–307)

6. Describe the process of IQ test scoring used today. (p. 307)

7. Define test. Describe the advantages of tests over other evaluation methods. (p. 308)

8. Define norms. Describe their usefulness. (p. 308)

9. Define reliability. Describe the process of assessing reliability using test-retest, alternate-forms, and split-half correlations. Give an example of each. (pp. 308–309)

10. Define validity as well as content, construct, criterion, and predictive validity. (pp. 309–310)

11. Describe the results of checks on IQ test reliability. Describe studies of the validity of IQ tests. (pp. 310–311)

12. Discuss the evidence for and against the argument that IQ tests are culturally biased. Define culture-fair tests. (pp. 311–314)

13. Discuss the possible interpretations of evidence from correlational twin studies on the role of heredity and the environment in the development of intelligence. (pp. 314–315)

14. Explain why a group intelligence score tells you nothing about the individuals in the group. Discuss the variables that affect group intelligence scores. (pp. 316–318)

15. Describe the conditions that can raise IQ scores. Explain why a teacher's expectancies can affect students' classroom performance and improvement. (pp. 318–321)

16. Describe the psychometric approach to studying intelligence. Define g, s, group factors, primary mental abilities, fluid intelligence, and crystallized

<u>intelligence</u>. Give an example of each. (pp. 321–322)

17. Describe the <u>information-processing approach</u> to studying intelligence. Describe the role of attention in intelligent behavior. (pp. 322–323)

18. Describe the triarchical theory of intelligence. Define performance components, knowledge-acquisition components, and metacomponents. (p. 323)

19. Explain Gardner's theory of multiple intelligences. List the six types of intelligences he proposed. Describe the ecological approach. (pp. 323–325)

20. Discuss the relationship between <u>creativity</u> and intelligence. Define <u>divergent</u> and <u>convergent thinking</u>. (pp. 326–328)

21. Define cognitive complexity, and explain how it relates to problem-solving ability. (pp. 325–326)

22. Describe the correlation between giftedness and success in our society. Define mental retardation, <u>familial retardation</u>, and <u>metacognition</u>. (pp. 328–330)

23. Define <u>learning disability</u>. Describe the types of learning disabilities and their possible causes. (pp. 330–331)

24. Explain the differences between <u>cross-sectional</u> and <u>longitudinal studies</u> as tools for examining age-related changes in intelligence. Describe the <u>cross-sequential with resampling</u> design and the confounds for which it corrects. (pp. 331–332)

25. Describe the types of changes in intelligence that occur with aging. (pp. 332–333)

CONCEPTS AND EXERCISES

No. 1: Defining Intelligence

Completing this exercise should help you to achieve Learning Objectives 3, 5, 16, 17, 18, 19, and 20.

Following is a conversation among several professors who want to found a new university. They are arguing about what admission requirements would ensure that only the brightest students attended their school. Determine which approach each professor would use to study intelligence and who generated the original ideas behind those approaches. Choose your answers from the list following the conversations. Answers can be used more than once.

Pedro: I think we should have several tests: one for language, one for musical abilities including dancing, one for analytical skills, and one for personal knowledge. (Pedro would follow the _____ approach as suggested by _____.)

Pam: How many engineers do you know who can do the polka? I think we should give prospective students a general intelligence test and look at the correlations among the various subscales to see how high their g-factor is. (Pam would follow the _____ approach as suggested by _____.)

Steve: The g-factor theory doesn't explain all the available data. Besides, we could end up admitting someone with a high g-factor who doesn't have many of the primary mental abilities, such as reasoning, spatial visualization, perceptual ability, memory, and verbal fluency and comprehension. (Steve would follow the _____ approach as suggested by _____.)

Elena: <u>G</u>-factor, schmee-factor, and who cares about primary mental abilities? Let's get down to what counts. I want to know if someone can get information from short-term into long-term memory and get the stuff back out again. It's simple. Can the kids approach a problem correctly, and then do they have the component skills to solve the problem? (Elena would follow the _____ approach as suggested by _____.)

Leigh: We really need to find people who can think creatively. I know a ton of dull but brilliant people. Let's ask them to produce a film on what would happen if all higher-level education was banned by the government and decide on the basis of that. (Leigh wants to test for _____.)

- ° Sternberg
- ° Divergent thinking
- ° Gardner
- ° Psychometric theory
- ° Spearman
- ° Thurstone
- ° Multiple intelligences
- ° Triarchical theory

No. 2: The Testing Business

Completing this exercise should help you to achieve Learning Objectives 7, 9, 10, and 12.

Sean Dorgan has recently begun a testing service. Following are some descriptions of his activities. Fill in the blank with the correct term by either choosing from the list at the end of the exercise or recalling the appropriate information from your reading. Answers can be used more than once.

1. Dorgan has just received information on a new test on the market. He has ordered a sample copy of the test and plans to give it to the same group of people twice. Dorgan is using the _____ method to check for reliability.

2. Dorgan has just received a new achievement test. He knows that it has already been successfully tested for reliability. Since the test is reliable, does Dorgan have to test it for validity? _____

3. Dorgan wants to attract newcomers from foreign countries as clients. To do this, he will have to develop _____ tests.

4. Dorgan has just issued a memo to all his employees saying that all tests are to be administered in exactly the same way, given in the same room, and scored in exactly the same way. Dorgan wants to ensure that all of his tests are _____.

5. Dorgan has just received a new test of mathematical ability. He is confused because there are no math problems on the test. What kind of validity is he worried about? _____

   ° Standardized
   ° Culture-fair
   ° Achievement test
   ° Predictive validity
   ° Construct validity
   ° Content validity
   ° Reliability
   ° Test-retest
   ° Alternate forms
   ° Split half

CRITICAL THINKING

Sam and Martina, who work in New York, are trying out a new lie detector test that requires no equipment. The test was designed in South Carolina. Supposedly, if a suspect looks down when answering a question, she or he is lying. If the suspect looks up and to the right, she or he is considering all possible responses. If the suspect looks up and to the left, she or he is simply trying to pull information out of long-term memory.

Sam and Martina have tested quite a number of people in New York City and are not happy with the results. Some people who were innocent were unable to pass the test. Consequently, Sam has decided that the test has no validity. Martina, however, thinks she knows why some people couldn't pass the test.

Using the five critical thinking questions in your text, the clues in the story, and what you have learned about mental abilities and testing, answer the following.

1. What is Sam's hypothesis?

2. What evidence supports Sam's hypothesis?

3. What is Martina's alternative hypothesis?

4. What evidence would Martina need to collect to support her hypothesis?

PERSONAL LEARNING ACTIVITIES

1. List behaviors and abilities you consider to be intelligent. Now write your own definition of intelligence. What problems did you encounter in writing your definition? (Learning Objective 2)

2. Design a test that will measure intelligence as you have defined it. Create two or three sample tasks or items that could differentiate between people of varying levels of ability and give them to volunteers. How did your volunteers perform on your test? How culturally fair do you think your test is? (Learning Objectives 7, 9, 10, and 12)

3. Read the list, definition, and items you wrote for Personal Learning Activities 1 and 2 and identify the approach you took to intelligence. Was your theory more similar to the psychometric approach, information-processing approach, triarchical theory, multiple intelligences theory, or ecological approach? (Learning Objectives 10, 16, 17, 18, and 19)

4. Based on the information on the reliability, validity, and impact of IQ testing presented in your text, do you think the testing should continue? Why or why not? Describe the advantages and disadvantages of assigning people IQ scores. (Learning Objectives 7, 11, 12, and 14)

5. Imagine that you have a different level or type of mental ability than you do now. How would people react to you differently if they knew? How would your life change? For example, if you were extremely creative, how would it change your choice of a major or career? (Learning Objectives 20–23)

MULTIPLE-CHOICE QUESTIONS

SAMPLE QUIZ 1

1. Questions in the Binet and the original Stanford-Binet tests were age-graded. This means that questions for a particular age group could be answered by
   a. most of the children in that age group.
   b. children younger than that age but not children older than that age.
   c. adults but not children.
   d. children of a particular age but not adults.

2. Terman would calculate an intelligence quotient by dividing
   a. mental age by chronological age.
   b. chronological age by mental age.
   c. mental age by chronological age and multiplying the result by 100.
   d. chronological age by mental age and multiplying the result by 100.

3. Wechsler's test of intelligence differs from the original Stanford-Binet test in that
   a. Wechsler's test has two subscales: verbal and performance.
   b. Wechsler's test is more culturally biased.
   c. Wechsler's test requires greater familiarity with the English language.
   d. Wechsler's test is a group test.

4. Today, IQ scores are relative scores. This means that your IQ will tell you
   a. your g-factor.
   b. how many primary mental abilities you possess.
   c. how intelligent you are in comparison to other people your age.
   d. how creative you are.

5. Lonnie wants to design a test that will accurately measure mathematics aptitude. According to the text, what characteristics should Lonnie's test have?
   a. Standardized conditions
   b. Qualitative descriptions
   c. Written questions
   d. All of the above

6. A test is reliable if it
   a. measures what it is supposed to measure.
   b. predicts a person's success in some field.
   c. yields consistent and stable results.
   d. none of the above

7. The Dacmarth Massive Intelligence Measure was given to the same group of people twice. The large positive correlation between the two scores was significant; therefore, the test has
   a. test-retest reliability.
   b. split-half reliability.
   c. high construct validity.
   d. low predictive validity.

8. Which of the following is true with respect to reliability and validity?
   a. A reliable test is always valid.
   b. A valid test must have a substantial level of reliability.
   c. There is no relationship between reliability and validity.
   d. Reliability and validity are the products of standardization procedures.

9. What factors explain the inability of an IQ test to perfectly predict academic performance?
   a. Academic success is not wholly determined by intelligence.
   b. IQ tests may be culturally biased.
   c. IQ tests may measure factors other than intelligence that do not influence academic success.
   d. All of the above could explain the imperfect correlation between IQ and academic performance.

10. Randy's students are very upset with him. He told them that he was going to give a quiz on the principles of learning, but instead he asked about the principles of memory. The students told him that his quiz had no _____ validity.
    a. construct
    b. predictive
    c. content
    d. criterion

11. Comparing someone's job success with test scores received prior to employment results in an assessment of _____ validity.
    a. construct
    b. content
    c. predictive
    d. split-half

12. Janice has been given an assignment: She is to devise a way to test the validity of intelligence tests. Why is her task so difficult?
    a. She can't find a group of people to give the same test to twice.
    b. Some controversy still exists over the definition of intelligence.

c. Intelligence covers a narrow range of qualities and abilities, whereas most IQ tests test a broad range of abilities.

d. None of the above

13. Which of the following is true about how the interaction between heredity and environment affects intelligence?

a. A favorable environment can improve a child's performance, even if the inherited influences on that child's IQ are negative.

b. Inherited characteristics are fixed, but environmentally determined features are changeable.

c. The environment has very little impact on a person's intelligence.

d. Inherited characteristics have very little impact on a person's intelligence.

14. Devon is a ten-year-old from an inner-city culture. He is taking an IQ test that requires him to match patterns. Devon most probably

a. has mental retardation.

b. is taking a culture-fair test.

c. is taking a culture-free test.

d. is taking a mathematical achievement test.

15. According to Cattell, fluid intelligence

a. is the basic power of reasoning and problem solving.

b. is one dimension of cognitive style.

c. involves specific knowledge gained from experience.

d. none of the above

16. An educator who takes an information-processing approach would look to which of the following to explain a student's poor performance on an aptitude test?

a. The student's g-factor

b. The student's attentional skills

c. The student's IQ

d. The environment in which the student was raised

17. Chuck says that intelligence is a general characteristic, meaning that a person capable in one area is also capable in another area. Chuck believes that testing people will support his hypothesis; therefore, he has a(n) _____ approach to intelligence.

a. information-processing

b. multiple intelligences

c. psychometric

d. triarchical

18. Betsy's teacher evaluated her personal and body-kinesthetic intelligence, because the teacher believes that those are important skills *not* measured by standard intelligence tests. Betsy's teacher has the _____ approach to intelligence.

a. information-processing

b. multiple intelligences

c. psychometric

d. triarchical

19. Shlomo and Jaime are both twelve years old. They have been given identical boxes and are told to open them. Shlomo finds the latch and pushes it up, down, and then sideways. Even though he cannot get the latch to open, he persists in his efforts. Jaime realizes that the latch is not going to open the box, so he looks at it from many different angles, trying to find another way to open it. Shlomo is thinking _____, and Jaime is thinking _____.

a. convergently; divergently

b. divergently; convergently

c. convergently; convergently

d. divergently; divergently

20. Mary Beth has an IQ of 105, but cannot write a sentence without mixing up the letters in some words or mixing up the word order. Mary Beth most likely has

a. cognitive complexity.

b. dysphasia.

c. dysgraphia.

d. familial retardation.

Total Correct (See answer key) _____

SAMPLE QUIZ 2

Use this quiz to reassess your learning after taking Quiz 1 and reviewing the chapter.

1. The original mental abilities test created by Binet was designed to

a. assess intelligence in children.

b. determine which children would benefit from special education.

c. determine which immigrants should be allowed into the country.

d. determine the intelligence of army recruits.

2. If the gradual increase in intelligence tapers off during the mid-twenties, _____ method of calculating an IQ would make older people look very unintelligent.
   a. Binet's
   b. Spearman's
   c. Terman's
   d. Wechsler's

3. Which of the following would you *not* find on the performance scale of an intelligence test?
   a. Block design
   b. Maze solving
   c. Picture completion
   d. Mathematical word problems

4. Which of the following could jeopardize the standardization of a test?
   a. Individual variations in how the instructions are read to test takers
   b. Changes in the way the test is scored
   c. Variations in the environment in which the test is taken
   d. All of the above

5. Consuela is giving a test that she has devised to the same group of people twice. She is testing for
   a. reliability.
   b. validity.
   c. norms.
   d. none of the above.

6. Lola has written a test for her psychology class. She is not sure of the test's reliability, so she compares the scores on just the odd questions to the scores on just the even questions. Which method is she using to test for reliability?
   a. Test-retest
   b. Alternate forms
   c. Split half
   d. Criterion forms

7. A test is valid if it
   a. measures what it is supposed to measure.
   b. is standardized.
   c. yields consistent and stable results.
   d. none of the above

8. Joel theorizes that knowledge of introductory psychology material is positively related to general vocabulary size. Joel uses his students' combined midterm and final exam scores (called "exam total") as his measure of introductory psychology knowledge. To find out if his test has construct validity, Joel should compare the

   a. exam total to students' scores on a psychology graduate school entrance exam.
   b. exam total to students' scores on a vocabulary test.
   c. odd items on the combined exam to the even items on the combined exam.
   d. midterm scores to the final exam scores.

9. Joel shows his midterm and final exams to the other psychology instructors to find if the items fairly assess knowledge of introductory psychology material. By getting the other instructors' opinions, Joel is evaluating his tests'
   a. alternate-form reliability.
   b. split-half reliability.
   c. content validity.
   d. criterion validity.

10. In the interpretation of the differences between group scores of intelligence, _____ should be considered.
    a. socioeconomic status
    b. the range of scores within each group
    c. the test takers' level of motivation
    d. all of the above

11. The Mullis family has five children: Andy and Andrea are fraternal twins, Louise and Lanie are ten-year-old identical twins, and Adrian is six years old. The highest correlation should be between the IQ scores of
    a. Andy and Adrian, because they are the only male siblings.
    b. Andy and Andrea, because they are fraternal twins.
    c. Louise and Lanie, because they are identical twins.
    d. All of them should be equally correlated, because they are all siblings.

12. Following are questions from an intelligence test for adults. The instructions, test environment, and scoring are the same for all test takers.
    ° What color is the sun?
    ° How many fingers are on each hand?
    ° How many biological mothers do you have?
    ° The weather in summer is usually _____.
    What's wrong with this test?
    a. This test has no reliability.
    b. This test has no validity.
    c. This test is not standardized.
    d. What is wrong cannot be determined from the information given.

13. Ana has developed a new test for engineering students. She is delighted because people's scores on her new test correlate highly with their scores on other engineering tests used to successfully measure their skill in this area. This demonstrates that her test has _____ validity.
    a. construct
    b. predictive
    c. content
    d. criterion

14. Studying scores on intelligence tests in order to understand the structure of intelligence is using the _____ approach.
    a. psychometric
    b. information-processing
    c. triarchical
    d. divergent-convergent

15. A month after Hank bought his first calculator, it stopped working. Although he had no experience with fixing calculators, he figures that it might have a power supply problem. Hank looks for a battery compartment, but there isn't one. Hank notices a tiny screw at each corner of the case, so he opens the case, finds the batteries inside, and replaces them. Hank fixed his calculator without having experience to guide him; therefore, he used mostly _____ intelligence.
    a. crystallized
    b. fluid
    c. personal
    d. triarchical

16. Which of the following is the best example of a culture-fair test item?
    a. Define common words.
    b. Describe similarities between concepts like "truth" and "honor."
    c. Identify what's missing from a drawing of a grandfather clock.
    d. Outline geometric figures embedded in a pattern of dots.

17. Convergent thinking is
    a. typical of creative people.
    b. characterized by thinking of many alternative solutions to a problem.
    c. measured by intelligence tests.
    d. all of the above.

18. Corrina agrees with the multiple intelligences approach to mental abilities. *Unlike* people with any other approach, Corrina would be interested in hearing about a person's

    a. athletic ability.
    b. attention level.
    c. spatial visualization.
    d. vocabulary.

19. _____ refers to the abilities to set up a problem.
    a. Divergent thought
    b. Convergent thought
    c. Metacomponents
    d. Metacognition

20. If scientists ever capture an alien, they will want to check its creativity. Which of the following would be the best way to do that?
    a. See how fast it learns to speak English.
    b. Administer a verbal scale of the Wechsler.
    c. Administer a performance scale of the Wechsler.
    d. Administer a test of divergent thinking.

Total Correct (See answer key) _____

ANSWERS TO FILL-IN-THE-BLANKS KEY TERMS

1. mental ability (p. 304)
2. norms (p. 308)
3. test (p. 308)
4. reliability (p. 308)
5. valid (p. 309)
6. intelligence quotient (p. 307)
7. fluid intelligence (p. 322)
8. psychometric (p. 321)
9. information-processing (p. 322)
10. Creativity (p. 326)
11. Longitudinal (p. 331)
12. divergent thinking (p. 327)
13. cross-sectional (p. 331)
14. performance (p. 306)
15. crystallized intelligence (p. 322)

ANSWERS TO CONCEPTS AND EXERCISES

No. 1: Defining Intelligence

° Pedro would follow the multiple intelligences approach as suggested by Gardner. (pp. 323–324)

° Pam would follow the psychometric approach as suggested by Spearman. (p. 321)

° Steve would follow the psychometric approach as suggested by Thurstone. (p. 321)

° Elena would follow the <u>triarchical approach</u> as suggested by <u>Sternberg</u>. (p. 323)

° Leigh would test for <u>divergent thinking</u>. (p. 327)

No. 2: The Testing Business

1. *Test-retest.* (p. 309)

2. *Yes.* A test may be reliable but invalid because it does not test the correct abilities. (p. 309)

3. *Culture-fair.* In this way unfamiliarity with the English language or Western culture will not bias the results. (pp. 311–314)

4. *Standardized.* (p. 308)

5. *Content validity.* He is worried about whether the questions on the test are related to the skills that the test is supposed to assess. (p. 309)

ANSWERS TO CRITICAL THINKING

1. Sam hypothesizes that the test is not a good measure of whether someone is lying.

2. That not everyone they tested in New York could pass the test is evidence supporting his hypothesis.

3. Martina, realizing that the test was designed and tested in South Carolina, hypothesizes that the test is culturally biased. (In some cultures, for example, looking down when being asked a question is a demonstration of respect.)

4. Martina would have to discover the cultural impact on people's head movements of answering questions, especially when under stress or when questioned by the police.

ANSWERS TO MULTIPLE-CHOICE QUESTIONS

Circle the question numbers you answered correctly.

Sample Quiz 1

1. *a* is the answer. Questions for one age group could be answered correctly by most children that age, could not be answered by most children younger than that, and could be answered correctly by most children older than that. (pp. 304–305)
   b. Questions answered correctly by most children of one age should not be answered correctly by most children of a younger age. If this was the case, then the questions could not discriminate between the age groups.
   c, d. Binet's original test was designed for children, not adults.

2. *c* is the answer. The first intelligence quotient, developed by Terman, was calculated by dividing mental age by chronological age and multiplying the result by 100. (pp. 305–306)

3. *a* is the answer. Wechsler's test contained two subscales: a verbal scale and a performance scale. (p. 306)
   b. Wechsler developed the performance scale, which included items such as block design and spatial reasoning tasks, in order to avoid bias caused by lack of familiarity with the English language or Western culture.
   c. Performance scale items do not test language ability or cultural familiarity.
   d. Wechsler's test was designed for individual administration, not group testing.

4. *c* is the answer. An IQ score tells how smart you are <u>relative</u> to other people your age. If your IQ is 100, then you are average with respect to others your age. A higher IQ means you scored higher than others your age. (p. 307)
   a. Spearman suggested that intelligence is a general mental ability. However, your g-factor is not relative to the g-factors of others.
   b. Thurstone suggested that intelligence is made of primary mental abilities. An IQ score may tell you about these abilities, but more important, the score tells about them relative to other people.
   d. An IQ score will not tell you how creative you are. IQ scores are not highly correlated with creativity.

5. *a* is the answer. An advantage of using a test is that the administration, scoring, and interpretation are standardized. (p. 308)
   b. Quantifiable terms allow norms to be calculated. Qualitative descriptions would not be numerical.
   c. A test does not have to be written. Lonnie could have people listen to a problem and use tokens to show a number answer.
   d. Only *a* is correct.

6. *c* is the answer. Reliable tests yield consistent and stable scores over time. (p. 308)
   a. When a test measures what it is designed to measure, it has validity.

b. When a test can predict someone's success in a particular field, it has predictive validity.

d. *c* is the answer.

7. *a* is the answer. (p. 309)

b. Split-half reliability is checked by comparing answers on half of the items on a test to the other half.

c, d. Validity is not determined by administering the same test twice. Construct validity is based on a theory about the concept. Predictive validity compares scores on a test to a criterion later.

8. *b* is the answer. If a test is valid, it must be reliable. If a test produces scores that vary from one test occasion to another, there is no way that the test would correlate highly enough with a criterion to establish validity. (pp. 308–310)

a. A test that is reliable is not necessarily valid.

c. There is a relationship between reliability and validity, while a reliable test yields the same results repeatedly. A valid test must have a substantial level of reliability.

d. If a test is valid, it measures what it is supposed to measure. This is not dependent on standardization procedures. Standardization does not guarantee validity.

9. *d* is the answer. Cultural bias, other factors affecting academic success, and the fact that IQ tests may measure factors other than intelligence (such as motivation) all contribute to the imperfect correlation between IQ scores and academic success. (pp. 311–321)

10. *c* is the answer. The questions on the quiz did not assess the knowledge they were supposed to test. (p. 309)

a. When test scores correlate highly with the theoretical basis of the trait or construct of interest, then the test has high construct validity.

b. Using a test to predict the ability to carry out some later endeavor successfully, such as a job or major in school, requires the test to have predictive validity.

d. The correlation of a test score with some other measure of the ability tested is the test's criterion validity.

11. *c* is the answer. A test score should predict the future performance of the test taker on the job. This is predictive validity. (pp. 309–310)

a. When test scores correlate highly with the theoretical basis of the trait or construct of interest, then the test has high construct validity.

b. If a test measures what it is supposed to measure, it has high content validity.

d. There is no such thing as split-half validity. (You may have been thinking of split-half reliability.)

12. *b* is the answer. It is very difficult to tell if a test is measuring what it is supposed to measure when the tester can't define what is supposed to be measured. (pp. 304–305, 309)

a. This is an example of not being able to check test-retest reliability.

c. Intelligence covers a broad range of qualities and abilities, whereas most IQ tests test a narrow range of abilities.

d. *b* is the answer.

13. *a* is the answer. The quality of the environment can cause children's IQ scores to increase. (pp. 314–315)

b. The opposite is true: inherited characteristics are not necessarily fixed, and environmentally determined features are not necessarily changeable.

c, d. Neither of these statements is true. Both genetics and the environment have a large impact on the development of intelligence.

14. *b* is the answer. Devon is taking a test that does not rely heavily on education and verbal abilities. This test is attempting to measure intelligence instead of the effect of cultural advantages, such as an education. (pp. 312–313)

a. Many normal children—not just those who are mentally retarded—take IQ tests.

c. There is no such thing as a culture-free test.

d. Devon is being asked to match patterns, not to do mathematical tasks. Additionally, an achievement test measures what has already been learned; Devon is taking an IQ test, which attempts to measure intelligence, not knowledge.

15. *a* is the answer. Cattell argued that there are two types of g-factor: fluid intelligence and crystallized intelligence. Fluid intelligence is the basic power of reasoning and problem solving. It produces induction, deduction, reasoning, and understanding of relationships between different ideas. (p. 322)

b. Cognitive style is the manner or style of performing cognitive tasks. Cognitive complexity, field dependence versus independence, and impulsive versus reflective styles are all dimensions of cognitive style.

c. Crystallized intelligence involves the specific knowledge gained from past experiences as a result of applying fluid intelligence.

d. *a* is the answer.

16. *b* is the answer. Within the information-processing model, effective intellectual functioning is related to competence in basic mental processes. An educator would look at these skills to explain poor performance on an aptitude test. (pp. 322–323)

a. The analysis of a general intelligence, or g-factor, centers on the correlations among various measures of mental abilities. The information-processing approach is not concerned with final scores, but with the various skills involved in achieving them.

c. Because this model focuses on attentional resources, speed of access to memory, and other processes of intelligent behavior, the product of that intelligence (one test score) would not explain poor performance on another measure.

d. Examining the influence of environmental factors on intelligence is not a component of the information-processing approach.

17. *c* is the answer. The psychometric approach looks for a general factor of intelligence by using tests. (p. 321)

a. The information-processing approach emphasizes the influence of attention skills and processes of sensation, perception, and memory.

b. Multiple intelligences is the approach emphasizing that people could have a high level of one ability (musical intelligence) and a low level of another (logical-mathematical intelligence).

d. The triarchical theory focuses on components and adaptation to the environment.

18. *b* is the answer. The multiple intelligences theory focuses on abilities not measured by standard IQ tests. It states that a person could be high in one type of intelligence and low in others. (p. 324)

a. The information-processing approach believes that attention, perception, and memory influence our level of intelligence.

c. The psychometric approach has an interest in more standard IQ testing. Verbal comprehension and numerical ability, for example, are important to the psychometric approach.

d. The triarchical theory focuses on components and adaptation to the environment.

19. *a* is the answer. Shlomo is thinking convergently, but Jaime, by imagining all the possible ways to open the box, is thinking divergently. (pp. 326–328)

20. *c* is the answer. Mary Beth has trouble with writing that may be due to the learning disability dysgraphia. People with learning disabilities do not perform as well as their IQ test scores would suggest. (p. 330)

a. Cognitive complexity assists people in thinking about many aspects of a problem.

b. Dysphasia is a learning disability in which people have trouble understanding spoken words or recalling the words needed for effective speech.

d. Familial retardation is usually mild and results from an interaction of genetic and environmental influences. Mary Beth is of average or slightly above average intelligence; she is not retarded.

Now turn to the quiz analysis table at the end of this chapter to find which areas you know well and which areas you need to work on. Circle the numbers in the table for items on Quiz 1 that you answered correctly.

ANSWERS TO MULTIPLE-CHOICE QUESTIONS

Circle the question numbers you answered correctly.

Sample Quiz 2

1. *b* is the answer. Binet's original test was designed to identify those children who would benefit from or need special instruction. (pp. 304–305)

a. Binet did not try to create an intelligence test. He only wanted to identify those children who would benefit from special instruction.

c, d. Psychologists in the United States revised Binet's test and used it to assess the intellectual capacity of immigrants and army recruits.

2. *c* is the answer. Terman developed the first IQ quotient. If the increase in mental abilities levels off during the mid-twenties, then as people get older their IQs will decrease. (pp. 305–306)

a. Binet did not use IQ scores.

b. Spearman did not create a scoring method. He used IQ test scores to study the structure of intelligence.

d. Wechsler's IQ scores are relative scores comparing you to others of your age.

3. *d* is the answer. Although math skills in general do not require a great deal of language ability, mathematical word problems do. The test taker must be able to read, interpret, and set up the problem using language skills as well as mathematical reasoning in order to arrive at the solution. (pp. 306–307)
   a, b, c. Block design, mazes, and picture completion are all problems that require no verbal skills.

4. *d* is the answer. Variations in administration, scoring, or the test-taking environment could jeopardize the standardization of a test. (p. 308)

5. *a* is the answer. A reliable test is one that gives stable and consistent answers. If a test is given twice and yields consistent results, it is considered reliable. (pp. 308–309)
   b. Giving the same test twice is a test of reliability, not validity. To check validity, you must make sure that the content of the questions relates to the skills or knowledge being tested or that the test scores are correlated with scores on other tests relating to the same constructs or criteria.
   c. Norms are descriptions of the frequency of particular scores. In order to test for this, the same test would have to be given to a very large number of people, not the same people twice.
   d. *a* is the answer.

6. *c* is the answer. Comparing the scores on one half of a test to scores on the other half is the split-half method of testing reliability. (p. 309)
   a. The test-retest method requires the same people to take the same test twice. Their scores on the first test should be very similar to those on the second test.
   b. The alternate-forms method requires giving two different but equivalent forms of the test to the same people.
   d. There is no such thing as the criterion-forms method.

7. *a* is the answer. (p. 309)
   b. Standardization refers to the use of the same methods every time the test is given.
   c. A reliable test yields consistent and stable scores over several test sessions.
   d. *a* is the answer.

8. *b* is the answer. Joel's theory about psychology knowledge is that it is related to vocabulary. To see if his theory about the construct is supported, Joel will have to compare psychology scores to vocabulary scores. (p. 309)

   a. If we assume that the psychology graduate school entrance exam is an accepted measure of psychology knowledge, then comparing it to the exam total score would be a test of criterion validity.
   c. Comparing odd items to even items might measure split-half reliability, but wouldn't tell Joel anything about the construct.
   d. Comparing midterm scores to final exam scores also wouldn't tell Joel whether his theory about vocabulary and psychology knowledge was supported. It might be a test of predictive validity, although midterms and final exams often cover different material.

9. *c* is the answer. Asking other psychology instructors about the items on his test will evaluate the content validity. (p. 309)
   a, b. Alternate-form reliability and split-half reliability all involve comparing two sets of scores (two tests or two halves of a test, respectively). Joel is only asking for opinions.
   d. Criterion validity is evaluated by comparing a new test to an accepted measure of the same construct.

10. *d* is the answer. Group scores can be affected by socioeconomic differences. Motivation of individual test-takers can affect scores. And if there is a difference in group means, the distributions of group scores may overlap. (pp. 316–318)

11. *c* is the answer. The highest correlation should be between the IQs of the identical twins. (pp. 314–315)
    a. The correlation between the IQs of male siblings is not higher than the correlation between the IQs of identical twins.
    b. Andy and Andrea are not identical twins; their IQs would probably not be as highly correlated as the IQs of the identical twins.
    c. Correlations among the IQs of all the siblings in a family are not as high as those between the IQs of identical twins.

12. *b* is the answer. Most people could answer these questions. Therefore, this test will not tell you how people differ in intelligence. (pp. 309–310)
    a. This test is very reliable. You would give exactly the same answers every time you took it.
    c. This test is standardized; it is administered and scored in exactly the same way every time for everyone.
    d. What is wrong can be determined.

13. *d* is the answer. The correlation of a test score with some other measure of the ability tested evaluates the test's criterion validity. (p. 309)

a. When test scores match what is known about the construct of interest, the test has high construct validity.

b. Using a test to predict the ability to carry out some later endeavor successfully, such as a job or major in school, requires the test to have predictive validity.

c. When a test measures the knowledge "content" it is supposed to measure, the test has content validity.

14. *a* is the answer. Psychologists who seek to understand the structure of intelligence by examining the correlations among scores on IQ tests are following the psychometric approach. (pp. 321–322)

b. The information-processing approach studies the mental processes underlying intelligent behavior, such as the speed of information transfer from short-term to long-term memory.

c. The triarchical approach involves specific knowledge components and metacomponents: the ability to know how to set up a problem in order to solve it.

d. There is no such thing as the divergent-convergent approach to studying intelligence.

15. *b* is the answer. Fluid intelligence is basic reasoning power. Hank knew little about calculators, but logically deduced that the batteries stored inside needed to be changed. (p. 322)

a. Crystallized intelligence is composed of specific knowledge. For example, vocabulary and trivia are part of crystallized intelligence.

c. Personal intelligence is part of Gardner's multiple intelligences theory. It relates to how well people know themselves and how well they relate to others.

d. Triarchical theory, by Sternberg, may be what you were thinking of. It is not a type of intelligence.

16. *d* is the answer. Outlining figures does not require knowledge of a particular culture or of English. (pp. 312–314)

a, b. Defining common words and explaining similarities between concepts rely on vocabulary, which may be influenced by culture.

c. Picture completion tasks are less biased than tests using vocabulary, but a grandfather clock may not be equally familiar to people of various cultures.

17. *c* is the answer. Convergent thinking is the ability to apply rules of logic and general knowledge of the world in order to solve problems. IQ tests measure convergent thinking. (pp. 327–328)

a. Divergent thinking is characteristic of creative people.

b. Divergent thinking is characterized by thinking of many alternative solutions to a problem.

d. Only *c* is the answer.

18. *a* is the answer. According to the multiple intelligences approach, athletic ability is body-kinesthetic intelligence. (p. 324)

b. Attention level is important to an information-processing theorist.

c. Spatial intelligence is part of the multiple intelligences approach, but it is also measured by psychometric theorists.

d. Vocabulary is not part of the multiple intelligences approach. People with a psychometric approach are interested in language comprehension; therefore, it may be an interest of theirs.

19. *c* is the answer. Metacomponents are involved in setting up problems. (p. 323)

a, b. Divergent and convergent thinking refer to <u>methods</u> of thinking, not different processes.

d. Metacognition is the knowledge of what strategies to apply, when to apply them, and how to deploy them in new situations. Generally, children with mental retardation are deficient in metacognition.

20. *d* is the answer. Tests of divergent thinking measure creativity. (p. 327)

a. The ability to learn a new language is not correlated with creativity.

b, c. IQ scores do not correlate highly with creativity.

Now turn to the quiz analysis table at the end of this chapter to find which areas you know well and which areas you need to work on. Circle the numbers in the table for items on Quiz 2 that you answered correctly.

For each question you answered correctly, circle its number. (Quiz 1 numbers are not shaded; Quiz 2 numbers are shaded.) Are there patterns in the types of questions or the topics you got wrong that could direct your further study? Did you improve from Quiz 1 to Quiz 2?

TOPIC	TYPE OF QUESTION		
	DEFINITION	COMPREHENSION	APPLICATION
Testing for Intelligence			
History	1	2	
		1	2
Current		3, 4	
		3	
Measuring Quality of Tests			
Characteristics			5
			4
Reliability	6		7, 8
			5, 6
Validity		9	10, 11, 12
	7		8, 9, 12, 13
Evaluting IQ tests		13	14
		10	11, 16
Understanding Intelligence			
Approaches	15	17	16
		14	15
Triarchical and multiple intelligences			18
	19		18
Diversity			19, 20
		17	20

TOTAL CORRECT BY QUIZ:

QUIZ 1:	
QUIZ 2:	

Chapter 11

Motivation and Emotion

Motivation can be defined as the influences that account for the initiation, direction, intensity, and persistence of behavior. Motivation influences emotion.

OUTLINE

I. CONCEPTS AND THEORIES OF MOTIVATION (pp. 337–343)

A motive, acting as an intervening variable, may provide a single reason for the occurrence of many different behaviors and may explain fluctuations in behavior over time.

A. Sources of Motivation

Four factors can serve as sources of motivation: biological, emotional, cognitive, and social.

B. Instinct Theory and Its Descendants

Instincts were once thought to be a major factor in motivation. Instinct theory, however, may provide a description, rather than an explanation, of behavior. In addition, instinct theory failed to accommodate the role of learning in human behavior.

Evolution and Mate Selection. The evolutionary approach suggests that inborn desires to pass on our genes cause women to focus on men's resource acquisition capacity and men to focus on women's reproductive capacity. Surveys have supported this hypothesis; however, mate selection patterns may reflect social and economic influences, not innate biological needs.

C. Drive Reduction Theory

Primary and secondary drives reduce biological needs caused by an imbalance in homeostasis.

D. Arousal Theory

According to arousal theory, people are motivated to maintain their optimal level of arousal, increasing arousal when it is too low and decreasing it when it is too high. Optimal arousal levels vary from person to person.

E. Incentive Theory

According to incentive theory, behavior is goal-directed; we behave in ways that allow us to attain desirable stimuli and avoid negative stimuli. The value of a goal is influenced by biological and social factors.

II. HUNGER AND EATING (pp. 343–349)

A. Biological Signals for Hunger and Satiety

1. *Signals from the Stomach.* The stomach may partially control the hunger motive, but the cues may operate primarily when people are very hungry or very full.

2. *Signals from the Blood.* The brain monitors blood content for the presence of nutrients (glucose, fatty acids, and amino acids) and hormones (cholecystokinin, insulin, and leptin) whose presence communicates hunger or satiety.

B. Hunger and the Brain

The lateral and ventromedial hypothalamus and the paraventricular nucleus (PVN) play roles in the regulation of hunger and eating. The hypothalamus may be involved in the homeostatic maintenance of a set point. Neurotransmitter activity in the PVN may selectively motivate eating of different kinds of foods.

C. Flavor, Learning, and Appetite

Flavor and variety are important in initiating eating. More food will be eaten when a variety of tastes is offered. Classical conditioning (pairing the taste with the nutritional value) influences the preference for a variety of foods. The sight of food can elicit conditioned responses (the secretion of saliva, gastric juices, and insulin) that are associated with eating. Specific hungers, the desire for certain foods at certain times, may reflect the biological need for a nutrient found in those foods. Finally, social cues tell people what and how much are appropriate to eat in certain social situations.

D. Eating Disorders

1. *Obesity.* Obesity is a condition of severe overweight that can contribute to diabetes, high blood pressure, and increased risk of heart attack. Physiological factors that may predispose people to obesity include body type, more and larger fat cells, and a higher set point. Psychological factors include maladaptive reactions to stress.

2. *Anorexia Nervosa.* This is an eating disorder characterized by a preoccupation with food and self-starvation, and dramatic weight loss. Physical causes are unknown, but psychological factors that contribute to anorexia nervosa include a preoccupation with thinness.

3. *Bulimia nervosa.* This eating disorder is characterized by binging and purging and is usually not life-threatening. The victim may be thin, normal weight, or overweight. Bulimia nervosa appears to be caused by cultural factors, emotional problems, and possibly malfunctioning biological mechanisms.

III. SEXUAL BEHAVIOR (pp. 349–357)

A. Focus on Research: A Survey of Human Sexual Behavior

The National Health and Social Life Survey used face-to-face interviews with a representative sample of people aged 18 to 59 in the United States. For especially sensitive questions, participants sealed their anonymous written responses in envelopes. The survey found that most people have sex once a week in monogamous relationships and that about a third have had sex only a few times or not at all in the past year.

B. The Biology of Sex

Masters and Johnson's in-depth study of human sexuality resulted in a description of the sexual response cycle. Although all sex hormones circulate in both males and females, some predominate in each sex: female hormones include estrogens (estradiol) and progestins (progesterone); male hormones are androgens (testosterone). Sex hormones have both brain structure organization and behavioral activation effects. Estrogen activates females' sexual interest, and androgens may activate sexual interest in both sexes.

C. Social and Cultural Factors in Sexuality

Sexual motivation and behaviors are learned as part of gender roles, early relationships with nurturing adults, and cultural expectations. Educational programs generated by concern over sexual transmission of the AIDS virus have recently influenced sexual attitudes and practices.

D. Sexual Orientation

Sexual activities can be heterosexual, bisexual, or homosexual.

E. Thinking Critically: Do Genes Determine Sexual Orientation?

What am I being asked to believe or accept?
Perhaps genes dictate sexual orientation.

What evidence is available to support the assertion?
In a study of homosexual men with brothers, 52 percent of the identical twin brothers were homosexual or bisexual; however, only 22 percent of the nonidentical and 11 percent of the adoptive brothers were homosexual or bisexual. Similar results are found for male identical twins reared apart. Prenatal hormonal influences may affect sexual orientation. Finally, the sexual orientation of children's caregivers doesn't appear to have a significant effect on the children's subsequent orientation.

Are there alternative ways of interpreting the evidence?
Remember, although a correlation exists between genetics and sexual orientation, it does not prove that one caused the other. Possibly, the shared genes determined other nonsexual behavior, which due to environmental factors resulted in homosexual or bisexual behavior. Also, almost 50 percent of the identical twins had different sexual orientations. Finally, the internal and external physical differences could be the result of their behavior and not just genetics.

What additional evidence would help to evaluate the alternatives?
Researching sexual orientation should extend beyond the study of genetic characteristics to compare and contrast personality, cognitive, social, and developmental attributes of people with different orientations.

What conclusions are most reasonable?
Sexual orientation results from the complex interplay of both genetic and nongenetic mechanisms.

F. Sexual Dysfunctions

Sexual dysfunction exists when a person's desire or ability to have sex is inhibited. The most common sexual dysfunction in males is erectile disorder and in females is arousal disorder.

IV. ACHIEVEMENT MOTIVATION (pp. 357–360)

We work because of intrinsic and extrinsic motivation. The desire for approval, admiration, and other types of positive evaluation from ourselves and others motivates our behavior.

A. Need for Achievement

People with a high <u>need achievement</u> are motivated to master tasks and take great pride in doing so.

    1. *Individual Differences*. People with a high need to achieve set challenging but realistic goals that have clear outcomes. They like feedback from competent critics. In contrast, people with low achievement needs seem to enjoy success because they have avoided failure.

    2. *Development of Achievement Motivation*. The need for achievement appears to be largely learned from parents and other cultural arenas.

B. Gender Differences in Achievement Motivation

Men and women who are equally motivated by achievement often behave differently. Women tend to display fewer behaviors that are typical of those striving for achievement. This may be due to gender-role socialization and the type of criticism and reinforcement that women have received in the classroom.

C. Achievement and Success in the Workplace

Workers tend to be more satisfied and productive if they are encouraged to participate in decision making, given problems to solve on their own, taught more than one skill, given lots of individual responsibility, given public recognition, and allowed to set and achieve goals. Effective goals are those that are personally meaningful, specific, set by the employees, and rewarded.

V. RELATIONS AND CONFLICTS AMONG MOTIVES (pp. 360–361)

A. Maslow's Hierarchy

Abraham Maslow proposed that there are five levels of motives, or needs, arranged in a hierarchy: physiological, safety, belongingness and love, esteem, and self-actualization. We must satisfy needs or motives low on the hierarchy before we are motivated to satisfy needs at the next level.

VI. LINKAGES: CONFLICTING MOTIVES AND STRESS (pp. 361–362)

Several motives that act at the same time complicate life and can be a source of stress. Four basic types of motivational conflicts are approach-approach, avoidance-avoidance, approach-avoidance, and multiple approach-avoidance.

A. Opponent Processes, Motivation, and Emotion

According to opponent-process theory, any reaction to a stimulus is automatically followed by an opposite reaction, called the opponent process. After repeated exposure to the same stimulus, the initial reaction weakens, and the opponent process becomes stronger. We are motivated to seek a pleasurable opponent process (such as relief) or to avoid a negative one by quickly repeating exposure to the initial stimulus (such as bungee jumping).

VII. WHAT IS EMOTION? (pp. 362–367)

A. Defining Characteristics

Emotions have several defining features. Emotions are transitory (not constant). They are either positive or negative. They are partially dependent on your cognitive appraisal or interpretation of a situation. They tend to alter thought processes such as attention. They create a tendency toward certain actions. However, they are passions, not actions, because you can decide to act, but passions happen whether you want them to or not. Emotions are also felt as happening to the self. The objective aspects of emotion have learned and innate expressive displays and internal bodily responses.

B. The Biology of Emotion

    1. *Brain Mechanisms*. Activity in the limbic system is important to the experience of emotion. Voluntary and involuntary facial expressions are controlled by two different areas of the brain: the pyramidal motor system and the extrapyramidal motor system, respectively. Most researchers agree that the right hemisphere is activated during emotions and contributes more to facial expressions than the left does. However, some investigators purport that the left hemisphere is more active than the right in experiencing positive emotions.

    2. *Autonomic Nervous System Mechanisms*. Signals from the autonomic nervous system (ANS) modify the ongoing activity of the organs and glands

in the body. The ANS is made up of two branches—the sympathetic and the parasympathetic nervous systems—both of which communicate with all the organs and glands in the body. Because of different neurotransmitters used at the target organs, the two branches have opposite effects. The parasympathetic system initiates activity related to the nourishment and growth of the body. The sympathetic system prepares the body for vigorous activity and stimulates the adrenal medulla to release norepinephrine and epinephrine into the bloodstream, which in turn stimulates all the target organs of the sympathetic system. The result is the fight-or-flight syndrome. Although you are unconscious of ANS activity, you can consciously alter it.

VIII. THEORIES OF EMOTION (pp. 367–375)

A. James's Theory

1. *Observing Peripheral Response*. According to this theory, people experience emotion based on observations of their own physical behavior and peripheral responses.

2. *Evaluating James's Theory*. If the James theory is correct, there should be a unique peripheral physiological response for every emotion, and people who cannot feel their peripheral responses should not experience emotion. According to the facial-feedback hypothesis, those incapable of feeling peripheral responses can get all the physiological information necessary to perceive an emotion from facial expressions.

3. *Lie Detection*. The use of a polygraph as a lie detector is based upon the assumption that there is a link between lying and emotions and that patterns of physiological arousal will distinguish true from false statements. However, polygraph results are not 100 percent accurate.

B. Schachter's Cognitive Labeling Theory

According to this theory, emotions are produced by both feedback from peripheral responses and a cognitive appraisal of what caused those responses.

1. *Labeling Arousal*. Cognitively appraising, or attributing, the source of arousal to a specific cause dictates the specific emotion you experience.

2. *Evaluating Schachter's Theory*. First, if Schachter is correct, elimination of physiological responses should reduce the experience of emotion.

Second, if you attribute physiological arousal to a nonemotional cause, your experience of emotion should be reduced. Finally, if you experience artificially produced arousal, you should experience emotion and attribute it to the situation at hand.

3. *Transfer of Excitation*. When arousal from one experience carries over to an independent emotional situation, it is transferred excitation. People sometimes attribute prior arousal to the new situation at hand, thereby intensifying their present emotion.

C. Cannon's Theory

According to this theory, emotion starts in the thalamus and is then passed simultaneously to the cerebral cortex, where it becomes conscious, and to the autonomic nervous system.

1. *Updating Cannon's Theory*. Recent evidence suggests that the thalamus does not produce the direct central experience of emotion but that different parts of the central nervous system (for example, the amygdala) may be activated for different emotions and for different aspects of the total emotional experience. Specific parts involved include the locus coeruleus and other areas associated with the autonomic system. Brain areas activated by emotion-eliciting events have widespread outlets throughout the brain; emotion-related central nervous system activity may be widespread instead of localized to one or two places.

2. *Conclusions*. Emotion has both a peripheral physiological and a cognitive component. There also appears to be some direct experiencing of emotion by the central nervous system, independent of physiological arousal. It is not yet known which component is primarily responsible for emotion.

IX. COMMUNICATING EMOTIONS (pp. 375–378)

Facial movements and expressions play the primary role in communicating human emotions.

A. Innate Expressions of Emotion

Two types of evidence support a Darwinian proposal that states that certain emotions are innate: Infants show facial expressions appropriate to their current state, and people of all cultures show similar facial responses to show certain similar emotional stimuli.

B. Social and Cultural Influences on Emotional Expression

Culture impacts the ways in which emotions are expressed.

1. *Learning About Emotions.* People begin to communicate some emotions by learning emotion cultures and by undergoing operant shaping.

2. *Social Referencing.* People use <u>social referencing</u> in an ambiguous situation to determine how to react.

KEY TERMS

1. **Motivation** is defined as those influences that account for the initiation, direction, intensity, and persistence of behavior. (p. 337)

Example: What causes us to initiate the movements necessary to get up from the couch and get something to drink? What causes us to persist in our work, sometimes to the point of staying up all night? Why do some people exert intense effort and others no effort at all? These are the kinds of questions asked by people studying motivation.

2. **A motive** is a reason or purpose for behavior. One motive can often account for many behaviors. (pp. 337–338)

Example: A woman drives a Jaguar, wears expensive sports clothes, and joins a country club. Her motive is to demonstrate that she belongs to a specific group of people who are quite wealthy.

3. **Intervening variables** cannot be directly observed, but they help explain the relationship between a stimulus and a response. A motive is an example of an intervening variable. (p. 338)

Example: Jay is very generous with his money and time when it comes to his friends. His motive (an intervening variable) for this behavior is a desire to be liked and admired.

4. **Instincts** are automatic, involuntary, and unlearned behavior patterns that are consistently displayed in the presence of specific stimuli. (p. 339)

Example: In some species of birds, baby birds instinctively respond to the striped beak of the adult birds by opening their mouths.

5. **Instinct theory** proposed that human behavior is caused by instincts. (p. 339)

Example: An instinct theorist would say that Nancy wants to have children because she has a reproductive instinct.

6. **Homeostasis** is the tendency of an organism to maintain its physiological systems at a stable, steady level, or equilibrium, by constantly adjusting to changes in internal or external stimuli. (p. 340)

Example: Suppose that you had to walk outside in bitterly cold weather. Your body would sense this change in an external stimulus (the cold) and would begin taking action to maintain your temperature. Shivering, an adjustment that generates body heat, would help keep your temperature from dropping.

7. **Drive reduction theory** states that biological needs, which are created by imbalances in homeostasis, produce drives. (p. 340)

Example: Oscar hasn't had anything to drink for hours. He has a need for fluids, which has caused a drive to find something to drink.

8. **A need** is a biological requirement for well-being. (p. 340)

Example: Because we cannot live without food and water, they are excellent examples of needs.

9. **A drive** is a psychological state of arousal that compels us to take action to restore our homeostatic balance. When balance is restored, the drive is reduced. Examples are primary and secondary drives. (p. 340)

10. **Primary drives** are drives that arise from biological needs. (p. 340)

Example: You have primary drives for obtaining food, water, and warmth. These are basic biological needs.

11. **Secondary drives** are learned through operant or classical conditioning. We learn drives that prompt us to obtain objects that are associated with the reduction of a primary drive. (p. 340)

Example: Joseph lives in Alaska. He has learned that it is necessary to pay his power bill on time (secondary drive) in order to stay warm (primary drive) during the winter.

12. **Arousal** is a general internal level of activation reflected in the state of several physiological systems. (pp. 341–342)

> *Example:* After the announcement about the pop quiz, Paola's heart rate, muscle tension, and brain activity increased.

13. **Arousal theory** states that people are motivated to behave in ways that maintain an optimal level of arousal. The level of arousal considered optimal varies from person to person. (p. 342)

> *Example:* Jorge is sitting in his office after a twelve-hour day, unhappy and bored. His level of arousal is too low. He decides to take a vacation in a country he has never visited. Toward the end of his vacation, he begins to look forward to getting back to work. Now Jorge's level of arousal is too high. He wants to go back to a well-known environment where his arousal level will decrease.

14. **Incentive theory** states that human behavior is goal directed; we act to obtain positive stimuli and avoid negative stimuli. Positive stimuli or incentives vary from person to person and can change over time. (p. 342)

> *Example:* When Joanna and David were first married, they saved money to buy a house (incentive). Now their mortgage is paid, and buying a house is no longer an incentive that guides their behavior. Instead, they save money to take vacations in Europe.

15. **Hunger** is the state of wanting to eat. Stomach cues, signals carried by the blood, and hypothalamus activity indicate when we should eat. (p. 343)

16. **Satiety** is the state of no longer wanting to eat. It is triggered by the brain recognizing nutrients and hormones in the bloodstream. (p. 343)

17. **Obesity** is a condition of severe overweight and can contribute to diabetes, high blood pressure, and increased risk of heart attack. (p. 347)

18. **Anorexia nervosa** is an eating disorder characterized by an obsession with eating and self-starvation, sometimes to the point of death. Psychological factors associated with anorexia include a preoccupation with thinness and a distorted body image. (p. 348)

19. **Bulimia nervosa** is an eating disorder in which a person consumes large quantities of food (binges) and then attempts to eliminate the food (purges) through vomiting or laxatives. (p. 348)

20. The **sexual response cycle** is the pattern of arousal during and after sexual activity. (p. 351)

21. **Sex hormones** influence our motivation to participate in sex activity. Examples are estrogens, progestins, and androgens. (p. 351)

22. **Estrogens** are female hormones. (p. 351)

23. **Progestins** are female hormones. (p. 351)

24. **Androgens** are male hormones. Androgens are found in both males and females and play a role in sexual motivation. Testosterone is the principal androgen. (p. 351)

25. **Heterosexual** activity is sexual interaction with people of the opposite sex. (p. 353)

26. **Homosexual** activity is sexual interaction with people of the same sex. (p. 353)

27. **Bisexual** activity is sexual interaction with people of both sexes. (p. 353)

28. **Sexual dysfunctions** are conditions in which a person's ability or desire to have sex is diminished or gone. The most common sexual dysfunctions in men and women are, respectively, the erectile disorder and arousal disorder. (p. 356)

29. **Need achievement** is reflected in the degree to which people establish specific goals, care about meeting those goals with competence, and experience feelings of satisfaction in doing so. People with a high need for achievement prefer honest, even if harsh, criticism from a competent critic over unconstructive but pleasant comments. The development of this need is affected by parents, culture, and school experiences. (pp. 357–358)

> *Example:* During grade school Kelly chose to join an after-school math activity program that had regular tests in addition to projects. Kelly knew that she was good in math and wanted something new to challenge her.

30. An **emotion** is either a positive or a negative experience that is felt with some intensity as happening to the self, is generated in part by a cognitive appraisal of situations, and is accompanied by both learned and innate physical responses. (p. 363)

> *Example:* Imagine that your boss unjustly says your work is worthless. Rage wells up inside you because you have worked very hard. The involuntary experi-

ence of negative emotion just happens; you do not make it happen. Your cognitive appraisal of the situation is also important. You have determined that your boss is not kidding but is very serious. When in a rage, you may feel your face flush and your heart rate increase (reflexive physical responses).

31. The **parasympathetic** nervous system, a subdivision of the autonomic nervous system, is involved in activities relating to the growth and nourishment of the body. (p. 367)

Example: Coleman is happily relaxing after a long day of classes. As he watches a comedy on TV, his heart rate slows, but digestion activity increases.

32. The **sympathetic** nervous system, a subdivision of the autonomic nervous system, prepares the body for vigorous activity, such as the fight-or-flight syndrome. (p. 367)

33. The **fight-or-flight syndrome** is a series of physiological changes in activity, controlled by the sympathetic nervous system, which prepares the body for combat (fight) or escape (flight) from threatening situations. (p. 367)

Example: A fire alarm startles Coleman. In the fight-or-flight response activated by the sympathetic nervous system, his heart rate and breathing increase. Although he can't feel the difference as he walks to the stairway, his digestive activity has slowed and his blood sugar has increased.

34. **James's theory** of emotion states that we experience emotions only by perceiving our physiological response to an event. (pp. 367–368)

Example: As he backed away from the coiled rattlesnake, Rick didn't need to think about the situation to know that he was afraid. He could perceive that his heart was racing and that he was moving away from the danger.

35. **Attribution** is the process of identifying the cause of an event through cognitive appraisal. (p. 372)

Example: Felicia was smiling as she studied. When she noticed it, she attributed it to her happiness about a trip she was planning for the weekend.

36. **Schachter's cognitive labeling theory** of emotion suggests that after we perceive our physiological responses, we must interpret their source. According to Schachter, people may attribute the same physiological

arousal to different emotions, depending on the information available about the situation. (pp. 371–372)

Example: As Mike drove home, a car pulled out in front of him. Mike barely avoided hitting the car by swerving onto the curb. When he continued driving, his heart was racing and he was breathing heavily, sweating, and trembling. When Mike thought about the unsafe driving of the other person, he decided he was angry, not fearful.

37. **Transferred excitation** occurs when arousal from one experience carries over to a different situation. People stay aroused longer than they think they do. If people have been aroused and then encounter a new situation, they may interpret their arousal as an emotional reaction to the new situation. (p. 372)

Example: You have just run to class. Just outside the door of the classroom, one of the people working on your group project tells you that she could not finish her part of the paper that is due this period. Normally you would be angry, but your increased arousal from the run intensifies your emotion. You are not just angry; you are furious.

38. **Cannon's theory** of emotion proposes that sensory information about an event goes to the thalamus, which simultaneously causes a physiological reaction and an emotion. In other words, an emotion label is activated in the cortex at the same time as our physiological reaction. Researchers now believe that the locus coeruleus, not the thalamus, may be the brain area responsible. (pp. 373–374)

Example: Anthony wrote a play about a futuristic society that controlled the emotions of its citizens by means of electrodes that stimulated parts of their brains while they were at work. This stimulation automatically created a positive emotion and a physiological reaction, regardless of their opinions about their job.

39. **Social referencing** occurs in ambiguous social situations. People use other's body language, including posture and facial expressions, to determine appropriate choices for their behavior. (p. 377)

FILL-IN-THE-BLANKS KEY TERMS

This section will help you check your factual knowledge of the key terms introduced in this chapter. Fill in each blank with the appropriate term from the list of key terms above.

1. _____ theory holds that motivation arises out of an imbalance in homeostasis.

2. A purpose for behavior is called a(n) _____.

3. _____ are drives arising from physical needs.

4. Drives that develop because of learned associations are called _____.

5. _____ theory proposes that people behave in ways that are necessary to maintain a certain internal activation level.

6. _____ is an eating disorder characterized by a preoccupation with thinness and self-starvation.

7. In _____, a person consumes large quantities of food and then attempts to remove the food by vomiting or using laxatives.

8. _____ are a general name for male hormones.

9. A _____ is a person who is sexually active with persons of both sexes.

10. Female hormones are _____ and _____.

11. A _____ is a person who is sexually active with people of the same sex.

12. When people label their physiological arousal based on various information in their environment, this is called _____.

13. When physiological arousal carried over from one situation influences one's interpretation of a new situation, this is called _____.

14. Experiences that include both learned and reflexive physical responses that are generated by a person's appraisal of a situation are _____.

15. The _____ theory of emotion states that we experience emotion by perceiving our physiological response to an event.

Total Correct (See answer key) _____

LEARNING OBJECTIVES

1. Define motivation. Discuss the types of behaviors that motivation may help to explain. (p. 337)

2. Define motive and intervening variables, and explain the latter's role in understanding motivation. (pp. 337–338)

3. Describe the sources of motivation. (pp. 338–339)

4. Define instinct. Discuss how instinct theory explains behavior. Explain why instinct theory failed. Describe the evolutionary approach and its views of mate selection. (pp. 339–340)

5. Define homeostasis, drive, and drive reduction theory. Define primary and secondary drive and discuss their role in motivation. Explain what behaviors drive theory can and cannot account for. (pp. 340–341)

6. Define arousal. Describe the arousal theory of motivation. Discuss the role of an optimal level of arousal in motivation and the impact of more or less than an optimal level of arousal on performance. (pp. 341–342)

7. Define incentive. Describe incentive theory's attempt to explain behavior. (pp. 342–343)

8. Define hunger and satiety. List the nutrients and hormones that the brain monitors in the bloodstream as it regulates hunger and eating. Explain the role of the ventromedial nucleus, lateral hypothalamus, and paraventricular nucleus in hunger and eating. Define set point. (pp. 343–345)

9. Specify the role of flavor and learning in the regulation of eating. Define appetite. Describe the mechanisms controlling specific hungers. Give examples of the effects of a food culture. (pp. 345–346)

10. Define obesity, anorexia nervosa, and bulimia nervosa. Describe behavior associated with each of these eating disorders. (pp. 347–349)

11. Describe the survey of human sexual behavior and discuss its findings. Describe the sexual response cycle. Name the male and female hormones. Explain their organizational and activational effects. (pp. 349–353)

12. Discuss the social and cultural influences on sexual motivation. Define heterosexual, homosexual, and bisexual orientation. Describe the evidence on the extent to which genes may determine sexual orientation. Define sexual dysfunction and give examples. (pp. 353–357)

13. Define need achievement. Describe the characteristics of achievement motivation and the factors that can affect its development. Explain the possible reasons for the differences in behavior of males and females who are equally motivated to achieve. (pp. 357–359)

14. Describe the extrinsic and intrinsic factors that affect job satisfaction and dissatisfaction. Give an example of a job that has been designed to increase satisfaction and motivation. (pp. 359–360)

15. Describe Maslow's hierarchy of needs. Give examples of each kind of need. (pp. 360–361)

16. Describe the four types of motivational conflicts, and explain the relationships between motivation and stress. (pp. 361–362)

17. Discuss the opponent-process theory of motivation. Give an example of the kinds of behavior it explains. (p. 362)

18. Describe the defining characteristics of the subjective experience of emotion. (pp. 362–363)

19. Describe the role of the brain in emotion and facial expressions. Describe how the parasympathetic and sympathetic systems are involved in emotional experience, including the fight-or-flight syndrome. (pp. 363–367)

20. Discuss James's theory of emotion. Give an example of how an emotion would occur, according to this theory. (pp. 367–368)

21. Discuss the research that evaluates James's theory. Describe the facial feedback hypothesis. Discuss the assumptions upon which a lie detector test is based. (pp. 368–371)

22. Describe Schachter's cognitive labeling theory of emotion. Define attribution and give an example. (pp. 371–372)

23. Discuss the research that evaluates Schachter's theory. Define transferred excitation and give an example of its effects. (pp. 372–373)

24. Describe Cannon's theory of emotion. Discuss the updates to Cannon's theory. (pp. 373–374)

25. Compare and contrast James's, Schachter's, and Cannon's theories of emotion. (pp. 367–375)

26. Discuss the role of facial movements in expressing human emotion. Describe Darwin's theory of innate basic facial expressions. Discuss the research that supports this theory. (pp. 375–376)

27. Describe the social and cultural factors involved in communicating emotion. Describe the role and sources of learning in human emotional expression. Define emotion culture and social referencing. (pp. 376–378)

CONCEPTS AND EXERCISES

No. 1: Theories of Motivation

Completing this exercise should help you to achieve Learning Objectives 4, 5, 6, and 7.

Below is a list of several different behaviors. Which theory would best explain the motivation underlying each behavior?

1. Vivien has been working in a laboratory for six months. She has learned all the techniques necessary for the job and is now very bored. She wants to work for a different lab or apply to graduate school. _____

2. Diane spent the entire day working on the family farm. She and some friends went into town after work to have a cola. She realized several hours later that, although she was no longer thirsty, she was still drinking cola. _____

3. Lourdes is terrified of heights but repeatedly jumps off the high dive at the swimming pool. The lifeguards no longer pay any attention to her as she screams until she hits the water. They know she will surface with a big smile on her face.

   _____

4. Karl and Sarah got married in the middle of the Great Depression when money for food and shelter was scarce. They have spent most of their lives working very hard and investing their money. Their children would like them to take some time off or retire and enjoy the fruits of their labor, but Karl and Sarah insist on working to make more money.

   _____

No. 2: Emotions at the Prom

Completing this exercise should help you to achieve Learning Objectives 20, 21, 22, 23, 24, and 25.

Following are some of the experiences of Franklin High students at their school dance. After each description, choose from the following list of options the phenomenon or theory of emotion that best matches the experience. Each answer may be used more than once or not at all.

1. Joya, after dancing a slow dance with Ted, walks back to where her friends are standing. She is smiling, a little breathless, and has a quickened heartbeat and shaky knees. Joya realizes that these responses indicate that she is happy. _____

2. Helen arrived at the dance twenty minutes late. She ran all the way from the parking lot to the school. She spent several minutes talking with her friends in the bathroom, brushing her hair, and putting on new lipstick. Just as she steps into the gym to survey the crowd, she trips and falls, ripping her dress. Absolutely furious, she yells at the boy who tries to help her up, "You idiot, look what you made me do!" What could explain her intense emotional reaction? _____

3. Cecelia is dancing with her boyfriend. She simultaneously realizes how much she loves him and notices how fast her heart is beating and that she has butterflies in her stomach. _____

   ° James's theory
   ° Schachter's theory
   ° Cannon's theory
   ° Transferred excitation

CRITICAL THINKING

Sam and Martina and another friend of theirs, Pete, are arguing about the reasons for a crime. A mobster named Joey killed Tony, a member of a rival family.

Sam starts the conversation by saying, "Look, Martina, Joey has been part of the mob for years. He probably thought he had to knock Tony off before Tony killed him. The guy had a plain and simple goal—to live."

Martina returns, "You have to wonder why some guys become 'soldiers' in the mob in the first place. Lots of people think these guys are violent by nature. But sometimes I think maybe they just want the security of being part of a group. They were probably really scared the first time they killed someone and only felt relief when it was over and everyone in the group was being supportive. Now I'll bet the fear is short-lived and they feel more elation at their accomplishment. Every time they kill someone, they are 'worthy' of even more protection from the group."

Pete rubs his jaw and says, "I think he was just bored. There hasn't been a lot happening in the streets lately. I bet he just wanted a little fun. That's why he killed Tony."

Using the five critical thinking questions in the text, the clues in the story, and what you have learned about motivation, answer the following.

1. What is Sam's hypothesis? What theory of motivation would support his hypothesis?

2. What is Martina's hypothesis? What theory of motivation would support her hypothesis?

3. What is Pete's hypothesis? What theory of motivation would support his hypothesis?

PERSONAL LEARNING ACTIVITIES

1. Why do you study psychology? List the reasons you study this subject. Try to identify whether your explanations fit with a particular theory of motivation. For example, if you wrote "curiosity," which theory would be best at explaining this motive? Which reasons would incentive theory explain? Is need for achievement a factor? (Learning Objectives 5, 6, 7, and 13)

2. Try to keep track of everything you ate in one day and where and when you ate it. Were you surprised by the results? What did you notice about where and when you were eating? Did you skip a meal or snack while doing something else? What influence did the flavor of the food or the presence of other people have on you? (Learning Objective 9)

3. If there were a drug which would make everyone crave only healthy foods, would you be in favor of it? Why or why not? (Learning Objective 9)

4. Think about the times you experienced motivational conflicts—for example, when you had to decide whether to participate in an activity that had positive and negative aspects. Was it an approach-approach, approach-avoidance, avoidance-avoidance, or multiple approach-avoidance conflict? After you decided to participate (or not), did the positive or the negative features become more prominent? (Learning Objective 16)

5. Describe the way your family usually communicates emotions. For example, does your family approve of expressions of joy, anger, jealousy, love, guilt, and so on, or are some expressions discouraged? Is happiness more often expressed by a broad smile, laughter, or screams of delight and jumping around? Some of these rules may stem from the emotion culture in which you live. Can you think of examples of differences between your family's emotion communication and the larger emotion culture in which you live? (Learning Objective 27)

MULTIPLE-CHOICE QUESTIONS

SAMPLE QUIZ 1

1. Motivation is considered an intervening variable because
   a. it is a stimulus that causes a response.
   b. motives or needs are causes of behavior.
   c. it helps explain the relationship between stimuli and responses.
   d. motives or needs are responses to external stimuli.

2. Drive theory cannot explain which of the following behaviors?
   a. Eating when hungry
   b. Drinking when thirsty
   c. Putting on warm clothes when cold
   d. Exploring a new environment

3. Stewart desperately wants a job in the computer field. He has just finished an interview during which he was aggressive about his thoughts and ideas. An incentive theorist would say that Stewart
   a. has a strong aggressive instinct.
   b. thinks that being aggressive will land him the job.
   c. has a very high optimal level of arousal.
   d. is worried about having enough money to live on.

4. Which of the following is the best evidence that differences in what men and women look for in mates are more cultural than biological?
   a. Men in the United States are more ambitious than men in Canada.
   b. Most men look for an attractive mate.
   c. Most women try to look younger.
   d. Zulu women are expected to be physically strong, ambitious, and mature.

5. Dwayne enjoys spending quiet evenings at home, watching old movies. To best explain his motivation for this behavior using the arousal theory, we should say that Dwayne
   a. is rewarded by his enjoyment of the movies.
   b. has hectic, busy days and wants some peace and quiet in the evenings.
   c. has an emotional need fulfilled by watching the movies.
   d. has met his physiological needs and therefore can seek arousal.

6. Cholecystokinin is involved in the regulation of
   a. eating.
   b. thirst.
   c. sex.
   d. arousal.

7. Stefan is working a late-night shift in the emergency room. His next patient is a girl who is very dehydrated. Upon examination, Stefan finds that the girl's weight is normal but that she has nutritional imbalances and intestinal damage. Stefan's patient is probably suffering from
   a. anorexia nervosa.
   b. bulimia nervosa.
   c. obesity.
   d. none of the above.

8. Charlene is having sexual intercourse. After an orgasm, which of the following phases or periods will Charlene be *least* likely to experience?
   a. Orgasm
   b. Plateau
   c. Refractory
   d. Resolution

9. Kate has a high need for achievement. Kate's parents most likely
   a. encouraged her to try new challenges and rewarded her successes.
   b. always got involved with her work and even helped her finish assignments.
   c. told her to quit torturing herself and give up when things got tough.
   d. did not praise Kate very much because they did not want her to become satisfied and quit trying new things.

10. According to Maslow, if you were shipwrecked on a desert island, which of the following would you most likely do first?
    a. Look for dinner and fresh water
    b. Look for inhabitants
    c. Establish a form of self-government
    d. Build a place to live

11. The first time Claire eats a chili pepper it is an extremely negative experience, but after a glass of milk she feels relief. Claire eats chili peppers now because her experience initially is mild discomfort then great amounts of enjoyment. Which theory of motivation best explains Claire's current behavior?
    a. Arousal
    b. Drive
    c. Incentive
    d. Opponent-process

12. Jeff is unsure of what to do. A woman whom he doesn't like at all has invited him to go to a really great concert. She has offered to pay, but he still thinks she's egotistical and irritating. Jeff is experiencing a(n) _____ conflict.
    a. approach-approach
    b. approach-avoidance
    c. avoidance-avoidance
    d. multiple approach-avoidance

13. According to the textbook, which of the following would not be part of an emotional experience?
    a. An increase in heart rate
    b. Cognitive appraisal of a situation
    c. Pupil dilation
    d. All of the above are part of an emotional experience.

14. Kurt, who is about to take a lie detector test, has sneakily put a tack in his shoe. Kurt should jam the tack into his toe to show an increase in physiological response after
    a. questions about his alibi.
    b. control questions.
    c. relevant questions.
    d. questions about his age, education, and income.

15. Matt is very interested in a woman he met at the gym. When would be the best time for him to approach her to talk?
    a. As she is warming up before her workout
    b. During her workout
    c. When she is toweling off right after her workout
    d. In the parking lot after a shower

16. When people are scared to do something, they are said to have cold feet. Fear really is associated with a decrease in blood flow to the feet and hands, which supports the _____ theory of emotion.
    a. Cannon
    b. James
    c. Incentive
    d. Schachter

17. According to the Cannon theory of emotion, the _____ is the core, or base, of the emotional experience.
    a. adrenal medulla
    b. adrenal cortex
    c. hypothalamus
    d. thalamus

18. Gloria went to the doctor for her usual antiallergy shots. The nurse mistakenly gave her a shot of epinephrine, which caused a great deal of physiological arousal. As Gloria sailed out of the office, she decided that she was feeling shaky from drinking too much caffeinated coffee. Her lack of emotion despite physiological arousal can be explained by which theory of emotion?
    a. Darwin's
    b. James's
    c. Schachter's
    d. Cannon's

19. When Michele heard someone trying to open her car door while she was stopped at a light, she felt her heart race. A few seconds later, without consciously considering her situation, she knew her physical response was fear. Michele's experience supports the _____ theory of emotion.
    a. arousal
    b. Cannon
    c. James
    d. Schachter

20. Sam is unsure of the proper response to make to a comment from one of his friends, so he glances at Diane, his girlfriend, to see what her reaction is. He is using
    a. facial feedback.
    b. social referencing.
    c. attribution.
    d. transferred excitation.

Total Correct (See answer key) _____

SAMPLE QUIZ 2

Use this quiz to reassess your learning after taking Quiz 1 and reviewing the chapter.

1. Which of the following is the best illustration of motivation as an intervening variable?
   a. A bell causes a rat to salivate.
   b. When a person passes a candy machine, she doesn't get candy unless she is hungry.
   c. A relative calls you "amazing" and a "genius."
   d. A person tries to smile although he feels depressed.

2. Homeostasis is a key concept in which theory of motivation?
   a. Instinct theory
   b. Arousal theory
   c. Incentive theory
   d. Drive theory

3. Drew thinks that the concept of learning is vital to understanding motivation. Which of the following theories of motivation would he be least likely to agree with?
   a. Opponent-process theory
   b. Drive theory
   c. Instinct theory
   d. Incentive theory

4. Allison is a 25-year-old woman who is interested in a long-term romantic relationship. According to the evolutionary approach, to which of the following people would Allison most likely be attracted?
   a. Susan, a 25-year-old graduate student nearing completion of her degree
   b. Tom, a 25-year-old artist who has a secretarial day job
   c. Vic, a 33-year-old banker with a good salary and an interest in having children
   d. Wally, an 18-year-old, good-looking waiter who likes movies, fast cars, and having fun at parties

5. Anorexia nervosa is characterized by
   a. the eating of more calories than are necessary for body maintenance.
   b. self-starvation and weight loss.
   c. overeating and self-induced vomiting.
   d. none of the above.

6. Dr. Banner is electrically stimulating a rat's ventromedial nucleus. What will this cause the rat to do?
   a. Begin eating.
   b. Stop eating.
   c. Begin moving.
   d. Stop moving.

7. Liz was sweaty, uncomfortable, and unable to work because of the heat. Liz wants to buy an air conditioner to help her cool off; therefore, Liz is experiencing a(n) _____ drive.
   a. cognitive
   b. emotional
   c. primary
   d. secondary

8. Keenan is an adult male; therefore, which of the following statements are true of him?
   a. He has no estrogens.
   b. More progestins and estrogens circulate than androgens.
   c. More androgens circulate than progestins and estrogens.
   d. He has no androgens.

9. Julie, who has a high need for achievement, is trying to decide where to work. Which job should she take?
   a. Company 1: high pay, little responsibility, great boss
   b. Company 2: low pay, lots of responsibility, mediocre boss
   c. Company 3: medium pay, lots of responsibility, chances for advancement, demanding boss
   d. Company 4: very high pay, easy work, not much chance for advancement, great boss

10. Which of the following orders of Maslow's hierarchy of needs is correct?
    a. Safety, physiological, belongingness, self-actualization, esteem
    b. Belongingness, esteem, physiological, safety, self-actualization
    c. Physiological, belongingness, safety, esteem, self-actualization
    d. Physiological, safety, belongingness, esteem, self-actualization

11. Paula is lonely. She chose a school that is far away from home, and all her friends are at different universities. She really misses being able to tell her best friend about her day. According to Maslow, Paula is not able to fulfill which need at this point in her life?
    a. Physiological
    b. Safety
    c. Belonging
    d. Esteem

12. Lisa, a waitress, feels like screaming. One of her customers ordered steak and shrimp, but when she brought it to him, he said he had ordered steak and lobster. If she tells him that he is wrong, she could lose a big tip. If she takes the food back to the cook, he might get angry and make mistakes with her orders all night long, which would also ruin her tips. This is an example of which kind of motivational conflict?
    a. Approach-approach
    b. Approach-avoidance
    c. Avoidance-avoidance
    d. Multiple approach-avoidance

13. Jill wants to buy a new stereo, but doing so might be a financial hardship. What kind of motivational conflict is this?
    a. Approach-approach
    b. Approach-avoidance
    c. Avoidance-avoidance
    d. Multiple approach-avoidance

14. When Harley received a letter from her fiance that contained bad news, she experienced the fight-or-flight syndrome. This means Harley's
    a. parasympathetic nervous system was activated.
    b. sympathetic nervous system was activated.
    c. digestion and salivation were stimulated.
    d. respiration and heart rate slowed.

15. Janet and Joan are experiencing identical patterns of physiological arousal: increased heart rate, sweaty palms, pupil dilation, and increased breathing rate. Janet feels happy, and Joan is very scared. Which theory of emotion can explain the differences in their emotions?
    a. James's
    b. Schachter's
    c. Darwin's
    d. Cannon's

16. Which theory requires the existence of unique physiological states for every emotion?
    a. James's
    b. Cannon's
    c. Schachter's
    d. Darwin's

17. Lori and Carol are discussing the places in town where they have met the best-looking men. Based on your knowledge of transferred excitation, which place do you think would be at the top of their list?
    a. A men's clothing store
    b. A laundromat
    c. A local dance bar
    d. A restaurant

18. Which of the following is the best example of facial feedback?
    a. Jill notices that Lani grimaces as Jill steps into her apartment without wiping her feet, so Jill stops to wipe them.
    b. Someone comments that you are looking especially wonderful.
    c. You notice that you are smiling as you study and conclude you must be in a good mood.
    d. You look for evidence that your roommate is lying by scanning your roommate's face carefully.

19. People from many different cultures can recognize a smile as an indication of positive emotion. This suggests that at least some expressions of emotion are
    a. innate.
    b. culturally determined.
    c. learned.
    d. lateralized.

20. A team of alien psychologists has landed in your backyard. They want to learn how to communicate emotions to humans. You would probably spend most of your time teaching them about
    a. body postures.
    b. facial movements.
    c. hand gestures.
    d. voice inflections.

Total Correct (See answer key) _____

ANSWERS TO FILL-IN-THE-BLANKS KEY TERMS

1. Drive reduction (p. 340)
2. motive (pp. 337–338)
3. Primary drives (p. 340)
4. secondary drives (p. 340)
5. Arousal (p. 342)
6. Anorexia nervosa (p. 348)
7. bulimia nervosa (p. 348)
8. Androgens (p. 351)
9. bisexual (p. 353)
10. estrogen; progestins (p. 351)
11. homosexual (p. 353)
12. attribution (p. 372)
13. transferred excitation (p. 372)
14. emotions (p. 363)
15. James (p. 367)

ANSWERS TO CONCEPTS AND EXERCISES

No. 1: Theories of Motivation

1. *Arousal theory.* Boredom put Vivian below her optimal level of arousal. Her attempts to reach her new goals will raise her arousal to its optimal level. (pp. 341–342)

2. *Incentive theory.* Diane has been drinking cola for positive incentives—its taste and the way she feels—not because she is thirsty. (pp. 342–343)

3. *Opponent-process theory.* When Lourdes first jumped off the high dive, her initial reaction was fear followed by the relief of landing safely in the water. As time passed, the relief increased (opponent process), and the fear decreased. (p. 362)

4. *Drive theory.* Karl and Sarah have learned a secondary drive of making money. They probably learned during the Depression that a lack of money pre-

vented them from eating as much as they wanted. Therefore, they learned that making money, a secondary drive, was essential to reducing the primary drive of hunger. (p. 340)

No. 2: Emotions at the Prom

1. *James's theory.* This theory could explain Joya's emotional reaction since it is based solely on her physiological responses. She has decided that she is happy because she is experiencing all the physiological responses that occur with happiness. (pp. 367–368)

2. *Transferred excitation.* Helen was probably still physiologically aroused from running into the school from the parking lot. She transferred this excitation to the anger she felt when she ripped her dress. This intensified her emotional reaction. (pp. 372–373)

3. *Cannon's theory.* Cecelia is simultaneously experiencing the conscious emotion of being in love and a heightened physiological arousal. According to the Cannon theory, cognition and physiological reactions to emotion occur at the same time. (pp. 373–374)

ANSWERS TO CRITICAL THINKING

1. Sam hypothesizes that Joey was motivated to kill Tony in order to avoid being killed himself. The incentive theory of motivation would support this hypothesis.

2. Martina hypothesizes that Joey was originally very fearful when killing someone but immediately felt the support and concern of the rest of the mob. Now Joey is motivated to place himself in danger by killing someone, because the fear doesn't last long and it elicits the more important opposing reaction of relief and support from the group. The opponent-process theory of motivation would support this hypothesis.

3. Peter hypothesizes that since nothing was happening in the neighborhood, Joey killed Tony to increase his own level of arousal to an optimal level. The arousal theory of motivation would support this hypothesis.

ANSWERS TO MULTIPLE-CHOICE QUESTIONS

Circle the question numbers you answered correctly.

Sample Quiz 1

1. *c* is the answer. Intervening variables help us understand why a given stimulus caused a given response. For example, hunger helps explain why someone ordered a pizza after hearing a pizza advertisement. The ad is the stimulus, and ordering the pizza is the response. The motive of hunger also explains why the person did not display some other response, such as ignoring the ad. (p. 338)
   a, b, d. Motivation, motives, and needs are neither stimuli nor responses but can affect the responses made to stimuli.

2. *d* is the answer. Drives cause us to do things that will reduce needs such as hunger and thirst. Exploring a new environment doesn't reduce any known drive. (pp. 340–341)
   a, b, c. Eating when hungry, drinking when thirsty, and making oneself warm are all behaviors that reduce drives.

3. *b* is the answer. An incentive theorist would say that Stewart was behaving in a way that he thought would bring him closer to a goal or an incentive. (pp. 342–343)
   a. An instinct theorist would say that Stewart has an aggressive instinct.
   c. An arousal theorist would say that Stewart has a very high level of optimal arousal.
   d. A drive theorist would say that Stewart wants the job so that he will have enough money to buy food.

4. *d* is the answer. Although it is generally found that women prefer men who are mature and wealthy while men prefer women who are young and healthy, this is not true of the Zulu. Among the Zulu, who have different gender roles, men value maturity and ambition in a mate more than women do. (p. 340)
   a. No research has shown that men in the United States are more ambitious than men in Canada. Even if this were true, this evidence would not be as strong as that from the Zulu.
   b, c. These behaviors both fit with the evolutionary view that men look for women who are able to bear children and women try to look like they can do so.

5. *b* is the answer. Arousal theory states that people try to maintain an optimal level of arousal. According to arousal theory, Dwayne will seek relaxation when overaroused. (pp. 341–342)
   a. This would fit with incentive theory.
   c, d. These sound similar to Maslow's views; however, he did not directly address arousal in his hierarchy of needs.

6. *a* is the answer. Cholecystokinin is a chemical that is involved in the cessation of eating. (p. 344)
   b, c, d. Cholecystokinin is not involved in the regulation of thirst, sex, or arousal.

7. *b* is the answer. Bulimics can maintain a normal weight. However, due to frequent vomiting, they experience dehydration, nutritional imbalances, and intestinal damage. (pp. 348–349)
   a. Anorexics do have nutritional imbalances but do not maintain a normal weight. They starve themselves, causing a severe drop in weight.
   c. Obese people are much heavier than they should be. They are at a higher risk for diabetes, heart attack, and high blood pressure.
   d. *b* is the answer.

8. *c* is the answer. Men experience a refractory period, but women do not. (p. 351)
   a. Charlene could experience a second orgasm.
   b. Charlene could enter the plateau phase.
   d. Charlene could enter the resolution phase.

9. *a* is the answer. Children whose parents encourage them to try new things and reward them for their successes develop a high need for achievement. (pp. 357–358)
   b. Children with parents who interfered in their work would not develop a high need for achievement.
   c. Children with parents who let them give up would not develop a high need for achievement.
   d. A lack of praise would *not* encourage development of a high need for achievement.

10. *a* is the answer. Physiological needs include food, water, oxygen, activity, and sleep. These are lowest on the hierarchy and, according to Maslow, are satisfied first. (p. 360)
    b. Looking for natives might satisfy belongingness needs but would probably be done after food and water had been found.
    c. Establishing a form of self-government might satisfy belonging or esteem needs but would probably be done after food and water had been found.

d. Shelter is a safety need and would be satisfied after physiological needs.

11. *d* is the answer. According to the opponent-process theory, an opposing reaction can eventually motivate a behavior. Claire's initial reaction was extreme discomfort from the burning chili pepper, and her opposing reaction was relief. Eventually, however, her initial reaction became weaker and weaker and her opponent reaction of enjoyment took over the motivation. (p. 362)
    a. Arousal theory focuses on physiological arousal, which is not described in the item. Even if we assume that Claire ate a chili pepper because of the large amount of arousal she experienced in reaction to the first one, according to the story her "arousal" lessened with each one. Thus, she would eventually stop eating them when they stopped giving her the arousal she sought.
    b. Drive reduction theory says we seek to satisfy a need created when we experience an imbalance in homeostasis. The chili peppers are not a biological need, nor are they described as being associated with a primary drive.
    c. Incentive theory doesn't explain why Claire would continue to eat chili peppers after an initial experience that was so negative. She wouldn't have an incentive to continue something that caused her pain.

12. *b* is the answer. The situation of going to the concert has positive and negative features. (p. 361)
    a. Approach-approach conflicts occur when a person tries to decide between two things, both of which have only positive features. The concert had negative as well as positive features.
    c. Avoidance-avoidance conflicts are those in which a person must choose between two negative alternatives.
    d. A multiple approach-avoidance conflict involves two situations, each of which has positive and negative features.

13. *d* is the answer. Physiological changes, cognitive appraisal, and interpretation of one's environment are all part of an emotional experience. (pp. 362–363)

14. *b* is the answer. Innocent people usually react more strongly to control questions such as, "Have you ever tried to hurt someone?" Therefore, Kurt should jam the tack in his toe after control questions, in order to produce physiological arousal. (pp. 370–371)

a. Questions about an alibi would not be good questions to seem upset about. Like questions that specifically refer to a crime, innocent people shouldn't react very strongly when asked about their whereabouts.

c. Relevant questions are those that specifically refer to the crime. Guilty people react more strongly to relevant questions than to control questions.

d. Reactions to relevant and control questions are compared in order to determine guilt or innocence. Questions about age, education, and income are neither control nor relevant questions.

15. c is the answer. People remain physiologically aroused longer than they think they do. The woman at the gym will feel calm by the time she is toweling off, even though she will still be somewhat aroused. If Matt approaches her at this point, she will probably attribute any leftover arousal to him instead of to the exercise. (pp. 372–373)

a. The woman at the gym will experience very little physiological arousal while she is warming up. If she does experience any arousal, she will attribute it to exercising, not to Matt.

b. Weightlifting and aerobics will cause physiological arousal. However, the woman will probably attribute her arousal to these activities instead of to Matt.

d. By the time the woman has showered and gone to the parking lot, she will no longer be aroused.

16. b is the answer. According to the James theory, there are unique changes in physiological arousal associated with each emotion. Frightened people do have cold feet because of decreased blood flow; therefore, fear may have a unique physiological response. (pp. 367–369)

a. According to the Cannon theory of emotion, physiological reactions do not play a role in the labeling of emotion, because they occur at the same time as the emotion.

c. Incentive theory is a theory of motivation.

d. Schachter believes that a physiological reaction can be labeled with different emotions depending on a cognitive appraisal of the situation. Therefore, a unique physiological reaction is not necessary for each emotion.

17. d is the answer. According to the Cannon theory, emotion originates in the thalamus. Theoretically, the thalamus then sends information to the cortex, where the emotion becomes conscious. Signals are also sent from the thalamus to the autonomic nervous system. However, researchers today believe the center may be the locus coeruleus rather than the thalamus. (pp. 373–374)

a, b. The adrenal medulla and the adrenal cortex are in the adrenal glands, which are part of the peripheral nervous system. According to Cannon, the thalamus, part of the central nervous system, is the core of emotion.

c. The hypothalamus is located just below the thalamus but does not play a primary role in emotion, according to the Cannon theory.

18. c is the answer. According to the Schachter theory, if we attribute arousal to a nonemotional cause (for example, caffeine), then the experience of emotion should be reduced. Gloria was not experiencing any emotion. She simply thought she had too much coffee that morning. (pp. 371–372)

a. Darwin did not propose a theory of how we experience emotion.

b. According to the James theory, Gloria should have interpreted her physiological arousal as resulting from an emotion.

d. According to the Cannon theory, Gloria should have cognitively experienced an emotion when she felt the physiological arousal. This cannot be the answer since Gloria felt the arousal but no emotion.

19. c is the answer. James's theory suggests that we feel a physiological change and then perceive it as a specific emotion without considering the situation. (pp. 367–368)

a. Arousal is a theory of motivation.

b. Cannon's theory states that the physiological reaction and emotion label will occur at the same time.

d. Schachter's theory proposes that we make an attribution about the situation before experiencing the emotion.

20. b is the answer. Looking at another person to judge their emotional state as a guide for ours is social referencing. (pp. 377–378)

a. The facial feedback hypothesis says that our own facial muscles give us information about our emotional state.

c. Attributions are the labeling of physiological arousal, according to the Schachter theory of emotion.

d. Transferred excitation occurs when physiological arousal is unknowingly carried over into an unrelated situation.

Now turn to the quiz analysis table at the end of this chapter to find which areas you know well and which areas you need to work on. Circle the numbers in the table for items on Quiz 1 that you answered correctly.

ANSWERS TO MULTIPLE-CHOICE QUESTIONS

Circle the question numbers you answered correctly.

Sample Quiz 2

1. *b* is the answer. Motivation is an intervening variable that explains the relationship between a stimulus and a response. Upon seeing a candy machine, a person makes one response if hungry and another if not hungry. Hunger is the intervening variable that explains the relationship between seeing the candy and buying it. (p. 338)
   a. Salivation following the sound of a bell could be caused by classical conditioning. The rat was not necessarily motivated to salivate; it was just a reflex.
   c, d. It isn't clear what the stimuli and responses are in either of these choices. A compliment or an attempt at cheerfulness may be motivated behavior, but it is unclear what the intervening variables would be.

2. *d* is the answer. Homeostasis is the process of maintaining an equilibrium in our physiological systems. Drives prompt us to behave in ways that maintain this balance or equilibrium. (p. 340)
   a. Instinct theorists said that our behavior occurs in response to specific stimuli rather than as a means of maintaining a balance in our systems.
   b. Arousal theorists said that we behave in a certain way to maintain an optimal level of arousal, not to maintain a balance in our systems.
   c. Incentive theorists said that we behave in ways that allow us to reach our goals of obtaining positive incentives and avoiding negative incentives.

3. *c* is the answer. Instincts are unlearned, automatic, innate responses to specific stimuli. (p. 339)
   a. According to arousal theory, we behave in ways that maintain our optimal level of arousal. Some of the activities that increase or decrease the level of arousal are probably learned.
   b. According to drive theory, we learn secondary drives.
   d. According to incentive theory, we behave in ways that allow us to reach certain goals. Some of the behaviors that allow us to reach certain goals are learned—for example, learning how to study in order to get good grades.

4. *c* is the answer. Vic is the wealthier, more mature male among the choices. (p. 340)
   a. The evolutionary approach emphasizes procreation. It hypothesizes that women seek a man with the ability to support children; therefore, a homosexual relationship would not be the best fit with this approach.
   b, d. Tom and Wally do not have Vic's wealth and maturity; therefore, Tom and Wally are not as good a fit with the evolutionary approach to attraction and mating.

5. *b* is the answer. Anorexics starve themselves and lose weight, in some cases to the point of death. (p. 348)
   a. Obesity is characterized by eating more calories than necessary for body maintenance.
   c. Bulimia nervosa is characterized by overeating and then inducing vomiting.
   d. *b* is the answer.

6. *b* is the answer. The ventromedial nucleus of the hypothalamus is a "stop-eating" center. If stimulated, it will cause the animal to stop eating. If destroyed, the animal will overeat. (p. 344)
   a. Stimulation of the lateral area of the hypothalamus would cause a rat to start eating.
   c, d. Movement is unrelated to the hypothalamus.

7. *c* is the answer. Feeling too hot is an unlearned need that will cause psychological arousal or a drive to motivate behavior to find some way of cooling off. (p. 340)
   a. Primary and secondary drives are addressed by the drive reduction theory. It does not describe cognitive drives.
   b. The drive reduction theory doesn't include emotional drives; this is a made-up term.
   d. Secondary drives are learned needs. If the question had said that Liz needed an extra job so that she could always have enough money to satisfy any primary drives, this would have been the correct alternative.

8. *c* is the answer. Men have more androgens than female hormones like progestin and estrogen. (pp. 351–352)
   a. Men do have female hormones like estrogen.

b. Men do not have more female than male hormones.

d. Men do have androgen; it is a male hormone.

9. *c* is the answer. It is important that Julie take the job that will yield the most satisfaction, which she will find in jobs that provide opportunities for advancement and individual responsibility. She should also take the job with the fewest dissatisfying characteristics, such as low pay and a mediocre boss. (pp. 359–360)

a. Company 1 has very few dissatisfying characteristics but no satisfying characteristics either.

b. Company 2 offers a large amount of responsibility but several dissatisfying characteristics as well, such as low pay and a mediocre boss.

d. Company 4 has very few dissatisfying characteristics but no satisfying characteristics. The job carries no responsibility and does not provide any chances for advancement.

10. *d* is the answer. (pp. 360–361)

a, b, c. The order of needs in Maslow's hierarchy is as follows: physiological, safety, belongingness and love, esteem, and self-actualization.

11. *c* is the answer. Paula's need for belongingness and love (on Maslow's hierarchy) is not being fulfilled. (pp. 360–361)

a. We have physiological needs for things that are basic to survival, such as food and water.

b. Safety needs refer to physical and emotional support from a primary caregiver.

d. Our needs for esteem are met when we gain approval, admiration, and other types of positive evaluation from ourselves or others. Paula can give those to herself and does not necessarily need to have these needs fulfilled by others.

12. *c* is the answer. Lisa is in a situation in which she faces two negative outcomes: the cook will probably be angry, and the customer will probably be irritated. This is characteristic of an avoidance-avoidance situation. (p. 361)

a. An approach-approach situation is a choice between two equally positive alternatives.

b. An approach-avoidance situation is a choice that has both a positive and a negative aspect.

d. A multiple approach-avoidance situation is a choice between two situations, each of which has a positive and a negative aspect.

13. *b* is the answer. Buying the stereo will provide entertainment (positive aspect) but will also involve financial hardship (negative aspect). This is characteristic of an approach-avoidance situation. (p. 361)

a. An approach-approach situation is a choice between two equally positive alternatives.

c. An avoidance-avoidance situation is a choice between two equally negative alternatives.

d. A multiple approach-avoidance decision is a choice between two situations, each of which has a positive and a negative aspect.

14. *b* is the answer. The fight-or-flight syndrome is a pattern of increased blood pressure and heart rate, rapid breathing, and dry mouth, among other symptoms, that comes when the sympathetic nervous system has been activated. (p. 367)

a. The parasympathetic nervous system is responsible for calming the body. Its activity decreases during the fight-or-flight response.

c, d. When the sympathetic nervous system is activated, digestion and salivation decrease while respiration and heart rate increase.

15. *b* is the answer. According to the Schachter theory, our cognitive appraisals of situations can cause us to label identical physiological responses in several different ways. (pp. 371–372)

a. According to the James theory, every emotion is associated with a unique physiological response.

c. Darwin did not address the mechanism that labels emotions. He said that emotional expressions are inherited.

d. Cannon thought the perception of and the experience of the emotion were simultaneous. He did not discuss cognitive appraisal.

16. *a* is the answer. The James theory of emotion states that we experience emotion based on our physiological responses. If this is true, every emotion should be associated with a unique pattern of physiological arousal. (pp. 367–369)

b. According to the Cannon theory, the thalamus is the core of emotion. Peripheral responses do not determine which emotion we are feeling.

c. According to Schachter's theory, the same pattern of physiological arousal can be attributed to different emotions based on our cognitive appraisal of the environment. Therefore, it is not necessary to have unique patterns of physiological arousal for every emotion.

d. Darwin discussed the functions that emotion serves in survival.

17. *c* is the answer. Research has shown that, compared with people at rest, exercise-aroused people experi-

ence stronger feelings of attraction when they meet people of the opposite sex. When Lori and Carol get off the dance floor, they will transfer the excitation caused by dancing to the attractive men they see in the bar. (p. 372)

a, b, d. A clothing store, laundromat, and restaurant do not offer any activity that causes an increase in physiological arousal.

18. c is the answer. The facial feedback hypothesis is a variation on James's theory. It suggests that facial movements are information we interpret as part of our physiological response. According to James, we have a different set of facial expressions and bodily responses for each emotion. Some evidence shows that smiling will make a person feel happier. (p. 370)

a. This is an example in which Jill has used social referencing to adjust her behavior.

b. A compliment may be feedback that you look nice, but it is not part of the facial feedback hypothesis.

d. The facial feedback hypothesis proposes that feedback from our own faces informs us of our emotions. It does not deal with looking at other people's faces for evidence of emotion or lies.

19. a is the answer. Something innate should not be affected to any great degree by cultural influence. People from many different cultures all relate smiles to positive emotions. (pp. 375–376)

b, c. Events that are culturally determined or only learned are usually different in every culture. If expressions of happiness were culturally determined or learned, every culture would interpret a smile in a different way. However, this is not the case. All cultures relate smiling to positive emotion.

d. There is no casual relationship between universal recognition of emotion and the particular structure of the nervous system responsible for emotional recognition.

20. b is the answer. In humans, the face communicates emotions better than any other part of the body. (p. 375)

a, c, d. Body posture, hand movements, and voice inflection communicate emotions, but facial expressions are more important.

Now turn to the quiz analysis table at the end of this chapter to find which areas you know well and which areas you need to work on. Circle the numbers in the table for items on Quiz 2 that you answered correctly.

For each question you answered correctly, circle its number. (Quiz 1 numbers are not shaded; Quiz 2 numbers are shaded.) Are there patterns in the types of questions or the topics you got wrong that could direct your further study? Did you improve from Quiz 1 to Quiz 2?

TOPIC	TYPE OF QUESTION		
	DEFINITION	COMPREHENSION	APPLICATION
Motivation			
Concepts		1	
			1
Theories		2	3, 4, 5
		2	3, 4, 7
Hunger and eating		6	7
	5		6
Sexual behavior			8
		8	
Achievement			9
			9
Relations			10
		10	11
Conflicts			11, 12
			12, 13
Emotion			
Nature	13		
		14	
Theories		17	14, 15, 16, 18, 19
		16	15, 17, 18
Communication			20
		19	20

TOTAL CORRECT BY QUIZ:

QUIZ 1:	
QUIZ 2:	

Chapter 12

Human Development

Developmental psychology is the psychological subfield that documents the course and causes of people's physical, social, emotional, moral, and intellectual development throughout the life span.

OUTLINE

I. EXPLORING HUMAN DEVELOPMENT (pp. 383–385)

Historically, researchers and scientists have argued about which governs development: nature or nurture. Is a person's development simply a process of maturation (nature)? Or are we shaped and molded by our surroundings (nurture)? Today, psychologists recognize that both nature and nurture interact to influence the developmental process. The environment (nurture) can determine whether a genetic tendency (nature) is expressed, and genetic tendencies (nature) can evoke particular responses from the environment (nurture). Heredity and environment are correlated, as seen in cases where parents with special talents also nurture those talents in their children.

II. BEGINNINGS (pp. 385–389)

A. Prenatal Development

1. *Stages of Development.* During the first and second weeks after fertilization, the cells divide to become the embryo. During the embryonic stage, all the organs form and cells differentiate into specialized functions. During the fetal stage, which lasts until birth, the organs of the fetus grow and function more efficiently.

2. *Prenatal Risks.* Severe damage can occur if the mother takes certain drugs or contracts certain illnesses (such as rubella) during pregnancy. Teratogens, harmful external substances that result in birth defects, are especially dangerous during critical periods such as the embryonic stage. Fetal alcohol syndrome is a pattern of defects that can occur as a result of maternal ingestion of even moderate amounts of alcohol. Babies whose mothers used cocaine are born premature, underweight, and fussy, and are at greater risk for learning and other severe developmental disabilities. The effects that adverse substances will have depend upon genetic inheritance, their intensity, and the prenatal stage in which they occur.

B. The Newborn

The study of newborns is extremely difficult due to their immature motor and language abilities. Researchers commonly design studies that record infants' eye movements; they measure where infants look and for how long.

1. *Vision and Other Senses.* Newborns have 20:600 sight. They prefer to look at objects that have contour, contrast, complexity, and movement. Within two to three days after birth, infants can hear soft voices and differentiate tones. They prefer to hear speech, especially speech that is high-pitched, exaggerated, and expressive. Newborns have a good sense of smell and taste. They show a preference for the smell of their own mother's milk and can distinguish among water, sugar water, and milk.

2. *Reflexes and Motor Skills.* These are swift and automatic movements that occur in response to external stimuli. Infants have more than twenty reflexes, including the grasping, rooting, and sucking reflexes. As muscle strength increases, infants try out various methods of crawling until they find the most efficient one.

III. INFANCY AND CHILDHOOD: COGNITIVE DEVELOPMENT (pp. 389–401)

A. The Development of Knowledge: Piaget's Theory

According to Piaget, development proceeds in a series of distinct stages that occur in a specific order; each stage is qualitatively different from the next.

1. *Building Blocks of Development.* The movement through stages progresses as children develop

schemas through their interaction with the environment. Schemas are elaborated through assimilation, during which information is added to existing schemas, and accommodation, during which existing schemas are modified according to new environmental information.

2. *Sensorimotor Development.* During Piaget's first cognitive development stage, the sensorimotor period, infants' mental activity is confined to sensory and motor functions. As infants progress through this stage, they begin to learn object permanence: they become able to mentally represent objects in their minds even when they cannot see or touch them.

3. *New Views of Infants.* Psychologists using new research methods find that infants develop some mental representations earlier than Piaget suggested. (See the Focus on Research Methods section for more information.)

4. *Preoperational Development.* Lasting from two to seven years, the preoperational period is characterized by intuitive guesses. Symbol usage appears. Children in this stage do not have conservation skills.

5. *Concrete Operational Thought.* The concrete operations stage, from age seven to adolescence, is marked by the ability to conserve number and amount. However, children cannot think logically about abstract concepts during this stage. Abstract thinking occurs during Piaget's final development stage: formal operational thought.

B. Focus on Research Methods: Experiments on Developing Minds

Renee Baillargeon tested infants' knowledge about objects by measuring the amount of time they spend looking at an event. The independent variable was how much support the objects had. When infants observed an event that was physically impossible (such as a box that appeared to float), they looked longer. Baillargeon proposes that older infants know more about objects because of their increased experience with them rather than because of innate knowledge.

C. Modifying Piaget's Theory

Studies show that children are capable of many tasks, such as mental representation, conservation, and nonegocentric thinking, at earlier ages than Piaget predicted. Current psychologists view cognitive development in terms of rising and falling "waves," not fixed stages.

D. Information Processing During Childhood

From an information-processing approach, children are viewed as better able to absorb, remember, and store information in more organized ways as they grow older. Memory improves as children learn memory strategies, increase memory storage, and expand their knowledge.

E. Linkages: Development and Memory

We may be unable to recall memories from before age three because of poor encoding and storage or because the memories are implicit rather than explicit. Another possibility is that such early experiences are joined into generalized event representations, like "going to the park."

F. Culture and Cognitive Development

Children's interaction with their culture and language has significant effects on their development. Children form scripts, or mental representations of common cultural activities. A child will be much better able to perform a given task if it is presented in a familiar "script." The influence of language, teaching methods, and parental emphasis on education all contribute to cultural differences in cognitive development.

G. Individual Variations in Cognitive Development

Cognitive development can be influenced to some degree by the environment. Stimulating surroundings and positive experiences tend to enhance a child's cognitive development.

IV. INFANCY AND CHILDHOOD: SOCIAL AND EMOTIONAL DEVELOPMENT (pp. 402–414)

Infants and parents bond during the first few months of life; infants respond to parental behavior, and parents respond to the infant.

A. Individual Temperament

Temperament, an individual's style and frequency of expressing emotions, is genetically influenced and obvious at birth. If the child's temperament matches the parents' expectations, the parent-child interaction will most likely be positive. Culture and innate tendencies interact in the development of temperament throughout childhood.

B. The Infant Grows Attached

During the first year of life, infants form an <u>attachment</u> to their parents.

    1. *Motherless Monkeys.* The Harlow attachment studies demonstrate that infant monkeys are motivated by contact comfort needs. Monkeys raised in isolation exhibit severe deficits in social and emotional development.

    2. *Forming an Attachment.* In most cultures the mother is the first person to whom the baby becomes attached. Infants also become attached to fathers. Fathers are more likely to play with infants, while mothers are more likely to feed, cuddle, and talk with them.

    3. *Variations in Attachment.* Many factors, including the infant's temperament, the caretaker's responsiveness, and cultural variability, can influence the development of attachments. Securely attached children tend to be more socially and emotionally competent; more cooperative, enthusiastic, and persistent; better problem solvers; more compliant and controlled; and more playful and popular.

C. Thinking Critically: Does Day Care Harm the Emotional Development of Infants?

What am I being asked to believe or accept?
Separation created by day care can damage the mother-infant attachment and harm the child's emotional development.

What evidence is available to support the assertion?
While children who attend day care do form attachments and prefer the company of their mothers, research suggests that these children have a greater tendency to be insecurely attached.

Are there alternative ways of interpreting the evidence?
Infants in day care may be more independent than those children who stay at home. In addition, mothers who work may reward more independent behavior in their children.

What additional evidence would help to evaluate the alternatives?
Research must measure aspects of emotional adjustment other than secure attachments. In addition, researchers must demonstrate that all other variables are equal before interpreting their results. In other words, both sets of "parents" (day care and non–day care) must be comparable in every measurable way before a meaningful relationship between day care and emotional development can be identified.

What conclusions are reasonable?
Psychologists cannot conclude, at this time, that day care has an impact on emotional development.

D. Relationships with Parents and Peers

According to Erik Erikson's theory of social development, individuals pass through eight qualitatively different stages, each one associated with an issue that the individual must resolve. Positive resolution provides the basis for developing trust, autonomy, and initiative, whereas negative resolutions may leave a person psychologically troubled and less able to cope effectively with future situations.

    1. *Socialization Styles.* <u>Socialization</u> is the method by which authority figures teach children the skills and rules; socialization is shaped by cultural values.

    ° <u>Authoritarian</u> parents are firm, punitive, and unsympathetic. <u>Permissive</u> parents give children complete freedom and use lax discipline. <u>Authoritative</u> parents are firm but understanding, increase children's responsibility as they grow older, and reason with their children.

    ° Authoritarian parents tend to have children who are unfriendly, distrustful, and withdrawn. Permissive parents tend to have children who are immature, dependent, and unhappy, and who exhibit little self-control. Authoritative parents tend to have children who are friendly, cooperative, self-reliant, and socially responsible.

    ° However, correlational socialization studies do not show causation, and their results are not strong. Hence researchers cannot conclude that parental behavior *causes* a particular social outcome. Children's temperaments, physical health, and cultural environment influence social and scholastic development.

    2. *Relationships with Peers.* Two-year-olds play with the same toys that their playmates do but do not interact with one another. By age four, children begin to interact socially through play. In the final stages of the preschool years, children learn to cooperate. Schoolchildren develop friendships based on feelings, and their loyalty is long-lasting. Children who do not develop friendships have problems later in life.

E. Social Skills and Understanding

Social competence increases with the ability to detect and interpret emotional signals, to understand the concept of personal disposition, and to learn rules governing objects and emotions.

F. Gender Roles

Through socialization, children learn the norms governing gender roles in their culture. Differences between boys and girls have some roots in biological makeup, but these differences are amplified as adults and peers teach "appropriate" behaviors for boys and girls through modeling and encouragement.

V. ADOLESCENCE (pp. 414–420)

Owing to the interplay of nature and nurture, adolescents experience changes in physical size, shape, and capacity. Changes also occur in social life, reasoning ability, and self-perception.

A. The Challenges of Change

1. With the onset of puberty, sudden growth spurts occur, sexual characteristics develop, sexual interest stirs, and opportunities to experience drugs arise. Self-esteem, highly dependent on self-perceptions of physical maturation rate, is challenged.

2. Conflicts between parents and teens develop as a result of the adolescent's attempt to become independent and cope with the challenges brought on by puberty. Friends become more important than family as teens develop closer friendships and as family conflicts increase.

3. Early sexual activity is often correlated with an increase in negative or unhealthy behavior and attitudes: smoking, drinking, drug use, less open communication with parents, lower scholastic achievement, sexually transmitted diseases, and unplanned, unwanted pregnancies.

B. Identity and Development of the Self

In many Third World cultures, adulthood begins at approximately sixteen years of age. In North America, however, many people don't make the transition into adulthood until their early twenties. Lengthened adolescence has created difficulties in identity formation.

1. *Forming a Personal and Ethnic Identity.* A person's sense of self develops throughout middle childhood, then erupts during adolescence through self-consciousness and self-awareness. The self-concept also includes a social identity, which is the feeling of belonging to one or more groups. Children are aware of skin-color differences at an early age. High schoolers tend to spend most of their time with their ethnic group and do not socialize with other groups.

2. *Facing the Identity Crisis.* Identity formation is the adolescent's central task, according to Erikson's psychosocial development theory. If the individual has developed trust, autonomy, and initiative in early childhood, the identity crisis will be positively resolved.

C. Abstract Thought and Moral Reasoning

Piaget's formal operational period first occurs during adolescence. Hypothetical thinking, hypothesis generation, and abstract conceptual thinking are now possible. However, only half of Western cultural populations reach the formal operational period; the failure to reach this stage is highly correlated with a lack of education.

1. *Kohlberg's Stages of Moral Reasoning.* Kohlberg proposed that moral reasoning develops in six stages that progress from avoiding punishment and attaining pleasure (preconventional), to following rules as part of social duty (conventional), and finally to principles of justice, equality, and respect for human life (postconventional).

2. *Limitations of Kohlberg's Stages.* Research generally supports the sequence of Kohlberg's stages. In addition, however, culture and gender influence people's definition of the moral "ideal."

3. *Moral Reasoning and Moral Action.* The relationship between level of moral reasoning and behavior is complex, in part because the situation or context may be a large determinant of behavior. The development of moral behavior requires more than just cognitive knowledge; children also require experience, role models, and authoritative socialization.

VI. ADULTHOOD (pp. 420–426)

Development is a lifelong process. Adults, too, experience physical and cognitive transitions.

A. Physical Changes

The body begins to show signs of aging in middle adulthood. Shoulder width, height, and chest size decrease. Skin changes occur and flabbiness increases. In addition, sensory acuity begins to decrease, fertility declines, and susceptibility to disease is heightened.

B. Cognitive Changes

Cognitive abilities continue to improve until late adulthood. An older adult may be better able to handle complex situations than a younger adult, because of years of experience and information accumulation.

1. *Early and Middle Adulthood.* Cognitive abilities improve as young and middle-aged adults get new information, learn new skills, and refine old skills. Adults become more adept at problem solving and decision making; adult thought is more complex and adaptive than adolescent thought.

2. *Late Adulthood.* After age sixty-five, the speed of information absorption slows and memory declines. Unfamiliar tasks, complex problems, and tasks that require divided attention are more difficult for older than for younger people. However, if mental faculties are used throughout the life span, these skills are less apt to diminish.

C. Social Changes

1. *Early Adulthood* (ages twenty to forty). Many people marry during this period and become concerned with the crisis of generativity—that is, producing something that will outlast them, usually children or job achievements.

2. *Middle Adulthood* (ages forty to sixty-five). Around age forty, people may experience a mid-life transition, when they feel compelled to reappraise or modify their lives in some way. The divorce rate, which in the United States has reached 50 percent, is not linked to the ages or income of spouses. Divorce leads to problems, at least in the short term, for both spouses and children.

3. *Late Adulthood* (ages sixty-five to seventy-five). Most people in this age group consider themselves to be middle-aged. Retirement usually occurs and is a positive experience if viewed as a choice. In late adulthood, people become more reflective, cautious, conforming, and androgynous.

D. Death and Dying

A few years or months before dying, many people experience a sharp decline in mental functioning known as terminal drop. The awareness of impending death, according to Erikson, brings about the last social crisis. People reminisce and evaluate the meaningfulness of their lives.

KEY TERMS

1. **Developmental psychology** is the area of specialization that documents the course and causes of people's social, emotional, moral, and intellectual development throughout the life span. (p. 382)

Example: How do children learn to use language? Do infants respond to parents' emotional cues? Do cognitive changes occur during old age?

2. **Maturation** refers to any development process (such as walking) that is guided by biological or genetic factors (nature). These processes occur in a fixed sequence and are usually unaffected by environmental conditions (nurture). (p. 383)

Example: The development of secondary sexual characteristics occurs in a fixed sequence and is rarely affected by environmental conditions.

3. An **embryo** is that part of the zygote that will mature into an infant. (p. 385)

4. The embryo becomes a **fetus** in the third prenatal stage, which lasts from the third month of pregnancy until birth. (pp. 385–386)

5. **Teratogens** are external substances that cause defects in the developing baby when introduced into the womb. (p. 386)

6. **Critical period** refers to any time period during which some developmental process must occur; if it doesn't occur then, it never will. (p. 386)

Example: If the heart, eyes, ears, hands, and feet do not appear during the embryonic period, they will not be formed at all.

7. **Fetal alcohol syndrome** occurs in infants born to mothers who consumed heavy—sometimes even moderate—amounts of alcohol during pregnancy. The resulting defects include physical malformations of the face and mental retardation. (p. 387)

8. **Reflexes** control the majority of movement in the first weeks and months of life. They are quick, unlearned responses to external stimuli. (p. 388)

Example: The **rooting reflex** causes an infant to turn its mouth toward any object that touches its cheek. The **sucking reflex** causes the newborn to suck on any object that touches its lips.

9. A **schema** is a basic unit of knowledge that takes the form of a pattern of action, an image of an object, or a complex idea. (p. 389)

Example: Sucking on a pacifier is a schema consisting of a pattern of action.

10. **Assimilation** is the process of taking in information that adds to an existing schema. (p. 389)

Example: An infant who has learned to suck milk from a bottle will use the same sucking motion or schema when a pacifier is put in its mouth for the first time.

11. **Accommodation** is the process of taking in information that causes a person to modify an existing schema. (p. 390)

Example: Infants who have become very good at sucking milk from a bottle and are given a cup must learn new patterns of motor behavior (modify the old sucking schema) to get the liquid out of the cup and into their mouth. Watch small children just learning how to drink from a cup. They suck and slurp the liquid instead of pouring it into their mouth and swallowing.

12. The **sensorimotor period** is Piaget's first stage of cognitive development. The infant's mental activity is confined to sensory and motor functions such as looking and reaching. (pp. 390–391)

REMEMBER: Sensori means "sensory": vision, hearing, tasting, and so on. Motor means "movement": reaching, grasping, and pulling.

13. **Object permanence** is acquired during the sensorimotor period. Because children form mental representations of objects and actions, they do not have to rely on sensory information to know that an object exists even when they cannot see or touch it. (p. 391)

Example: A child knows that a rattle exists when you put it behind your back, out of sight.

14. The **preoperational period** is Piaget's second stage of cognitive development, lasting from age two to age seven. Children learn to use symbols allowing them to talk, pretend, and draw. Thinking during this time is intuitive. (p. 395)

Example: Elise likes to put on her big sister's dresses and makeup and pretend that she is going out shopping.

15. **Conservation** is the knowledge that a substance's number or amount does not change even when its shape or form does. This skill is first accomplished during the concrete operational stage. (p. 395)

Example: Ellen, who is babysitting for a nine-year-old and a four-year-old, pours each child a glass of lemonade. She gives the older child a tall skinny glass and the younger child a short fat glass. The four-year-old insists that the short fat glass does not contain as much lemonade as the tall skinny glass

(that is, she does not understand the logic of complementarity), even after Ellen has poured the contents of the tall skinny glass into the short glass and back again (reversibility). The younger child, still in the preoperational period, cannot conserve.

16. **Concrete operations** is Piaget's third stage of cognitive development, occurring approximately between the ages of seven and eleven. During this stage, children can perform such operations as addition, subtraction, and conservation (reversibility, complementarity), and visual appearances no longer dominate thinking. (p. 396)

17. **Information processing** is a cognitive approach to studying cognitive development, concerning such matters as how information is taken in, how it is remembered or forgotten, and how it is used. This approach differs from Piaget's in that it focuses on the quantitative changes that take place in the child's mental abilities, not on the qualitative changes that occur at different stages. (p. 397)

18. **Scripts** are people's mental representations of any activity or scenario in their environments. Children use scripts to take in information about the world and to solve problems. (p. 400)

Example: Mindy knows that people sit in a waiting area to see a doctor until their name is called. Then people sit in another room until a doctor comes. The doctor listens to people's hearts and tells them to cough and then tells them what medicine to buy.

19. **Temperament** is the style of emotional reactivity that an infant displays in response to the environment. It is the basic, natural disposition of an individual. (p. 403)

Example: When Sarah takes a bath, she squeals with delight, splashes in the water, and eagerly reaches for new toys. She has a very predictable schedule of eating and sleeping. Sarah is an easy baby. Franny, on the other hand, fusses all the time, cries very loudly whenever she encounters a new situation, person, or toy, and does not have a set schedule. Franny is a difficult baby.

20. **Attachment** is the close emotional relationship between an infant and his or her caregiver. For a secure attachment to develop, the caregiver must not only provide adequate, consistent care, but must also be loving, supportive, helpful, sensitive, and responsive. If the care is inadequate or the relationship is distant, the child may develop an anxious insecure attachment. (pp. 404–406)

Example: Johnny has an anxious insecure attachment; he is upset when his mother leaves but ignores or avoids her when she returns after a brief separation. Carl's attachment is secure; he may or may not protest when she leaves, but he greets her enthusiastically when she returns.

21. **Socialization** is a process of teaching children society's rules and the skills they need. Examples of socialization patterns are authoritarian, permissive, and authoritative parenting. (p. 409)

22. **Authoritarian parents** are firm, punitive, and unsympathetic. They demand children's obedience and value being authority figures. They do not encourage independence and seldom offer praise. (p. 410)

Example: Armand told his father he wanted to study hair design at the local beauty college. Rather than discuss the advantages and disadvantages of the choice with Armand, his father forbade him to apply to that college and ordered him to work over the summer mowing lawns.

23. **Permissive parents** give their children complete freedom, and their use of discipline is lax. (p. 410)

Example: Penny's parents often do not know where she is at night. She could stay overnight at a friend's house without needing to ask permission.

24. **Authoritative parents** reason with their children, are firm but understanding, and encourage give-and-take. As the children get older, the parents allow them increasing responsibility. These parents set limits, but they also encourage independence. (p. 410)

Example: Kiersten's mother is affectionate and encourages her to come to her to talk about anything. They have an agreement about what behaviors are acceptable, and recently they compromised on a later curfew.

25. **Gender roles** are the general patterns of work, appearance, and behavior associated with being male or female. (pp. 412–414)

Example: In our society some occupations have traditionally been considered more appropriate for men, others more appropriate for women. Men have been encouraged to become doctors and women to become nurses; men have been encouraged to become police officers, and women have not.

26. **Puberty** is the condition of being able for the first time to reproduce. Its onset is characterized by menstruation in females and sperm production in males. (p. 414)

27. An **identity crisis** usually occurs during adolescence. By combining bits and pieces of self-knowledge learned in childhood, the individual must develop an integrated image of himself or herself as a unique person. (p. 416)

Example: When Ray began college, he was rebellious and irresponsible at first. Eventually he settled down, chose a major, and became more conscientious again.

28. The **formal operational period** is Piaget's fourth stage of cognitive development; on average, it begins at age eleven. During this stage, children can think and reason about abstract concepts, generate hypotheses, and think logically. (p. 417)

Example: Children can think about abstract moral issues such as whether animals should be killed for fur or what the consequences of nuclear war might be.

29. **Preconventional moral reasoning**, according to Kohlberg's theory, is typical of children younger than nine years of age. Moral reasoning during this period is directed toward avoiding punishment and following rules to one's own advantage. (pp. 417–418)

Example: Morgan doesn't take cookies from the jar when she isn't supposed to because she doesn't want to get grounded.

30. **Conventional moral reasoning**, according to Kohlberg's theory, is characterized by concern for other people due to social obligations such as caring for one's spouse and family. (p. 418)

Example: Tristan doesn't take cookies from the jar when he isn't supposed to because it would disappoint his parents if he disobeyed them.

31. **Postconventional moral reasoning**, according to Kohlberg, is the highest level of moral reasoning; it is based upon personal standards or on universal principles of justice, equality, and respect for human life. (p. 418)

Example: Underground resistance fighters during World War II disobeyed local and German laws in order to preserve the lives of fellow countrymen.

32. A crisis of **generativity** usually occurs during a person's thirties. People become concerned with produc-

ing something that they consider worthwhile. To resolve this crisis, people usually have children or decide to achieve an occupational goal. (pp. 422–423)

Example: David is undergoing a change in perspective. He has found a partner in life, and now he is concerned with having children.

33. A mid-life transition often occurs during a person's forties, at which time the individual reevaluates the decisions he or she has made concerning goals and social relationships. (p. 423)

Example: Lynne recently divorced and moved to a new state to become an occupational therapist.

34. Terminal drop is the decline in mental functioning that occurs in the months or years preceding death. (p. 425)

FILL-IN-THE-BLANKS KEY TERMS

This section will help you check your factual knowledge of the key terms introduced in this chapter. Fill in each blank with the appropriate term from the list of key terms above.

1. A _____ is a substance that causes damage to the unborn child if it penetrates the womb.

2. A _____ is the time within which a developmental process must occur if it is to occur at all.

3. The _____ is Piaget's first stage of cognitive development.

4. When children do not have to rely on sensory information to know that an object exists, they have developed _____.

5. When children first become able to solve basic math problems, they have reached the stage of _____.

6. _____ parents discourage independence and are harsh, demanding, and punitive.

7. The ability to use abstract reasoning and logic is a development of the _____.

8. _____ is the ability to know that when the shape of a given substance changes, its quantity remains the same.

9. Adults in their thirties who are concerned about being productive and contributing something they consider valuable are experiencing a _____.

10. The pattern of emotions that a newborn displays in response to the environment is called _____.

11. Object permanence is acquired during the _____ period.

12. According to Piaget, the basic units of knowledge are _____.

13. The process in which existing schemas are changed to fit new information is called _____.

14. When an infant turns its head toward anything that brushes its cheek, it is exhibiting the _____.

15. Any developmental process that is entirely under genetic control is considered part of the _____ process.

Total Correct (See answer key) _____

LEARNING OBJECTIVES

1. Define developmental psychology. (p. 382)

2. Describe the history of the nature-nurture debate. (pp. 383–385)

3. Discuss the differences among Gesell's, Watson's, and Piaget's views of development. Define maturation. (pp. 383–385)

4. Describe the contributions of nature and nurture to development. Explain why heredity and environment are correlated and mutually influential. (p. 385)

5. Describe the process of development in each of the prenatal stages. (pp. 385–386)

6. Define teratogen. Define critical period and know the stage associated with it. Define fetal alcohol syndrome. (pp. 386–387)

7. Describe the capacities of a newborn's senses. Define reflex, and name three reflexes exhibited by newborns. Discuss how motor development is influenced by experimentation. (pp. 387–389)

8. Describe Piaget's theory of knowledge development. Explain why it incorporates both nature and nurture. Define schemas, assimilation, and accommodation. (pp. 389–390)

9. Describe the development of mental abilities during the sensorimotor period. Define object permanence. (pp. 390–391)

10. Explain how research has modified Piaget's description of infants in the sensorimotor period. Discuss the experiments on object permanence and the role of experience in developing knowledge during infancy. (pp. 392–394)

11. Describe the changes in cognition that occur during the preoperational period. Discuss the importance of symbol usage during this period. Describe the impact of visual perception on a preoperational child's thinking. (pp. 395–396)

12. Define conservation. Describe the changes in cognition that occur during Piaget's concrete operational stage. (p. 396)

13. Discuss the criticisms of and alternatives to Piaget's theory of cognitive development. (pp. 396–397)

14. Describe cognitive development from an information-processing approach. (pp. 397–398)

15. Discuss the research on memory in early childhood. (p. 379)

16. Describe the impact of culture on cognitive development. Define scripts. Distinguish between the learning of primary and secondary abilities. (pp. 399–400)

17. Describe the potential impact of the environment on cognitive development. (pp. 400–401)

18. Define temperament. Describe the three main temperament patterns discussed in your text. (pp. 402–403)

19. Define attachment. Describe the studies of motherless monkeys. Discuss the development of attachment and describe the three types of attachment. (pp. 404–407)

20. Discuss the question of whether day care damages the formation of a healthy mother-infant attachment. (pp. 407–408)

21. Define socialization. Describe the three parental socialization styles discussed in the text. Discuss the characteristics of children who have grown up under each of these styles. Explain the impact of the parents' culture and environment on the development of their socialization styles. (pp. 408–411)

22. Describe the different kinds of social relationships and the development of social skills in children. (pp. 411–412)

23. Describe the development of gender roles. (pp. 412–414)

24. Define puberty, and discuss the physical and psychological changes and problems that occur during adolescence. Describe the relationship adolescents have with their parents and peers. (pp. 414–415)

25. Describe the development of both the personal and the social identity. Define identity crisis. (pp. 416–417)

26. Describe the changes in cognition that occur during the formal operational period. (p. 417)

27. Describe the stages of moral reasoning suggested by Kohlberg. Define preconventional, conventional, and postconventional moral reasoning. Be able to discuss the cultural limitations of Kohlberg's stages. (pp. 417–419)

28. Describe the relationship between moral reasoning and moral action. (pp. 419–420)

29. Describe the physical, cognitive, and social changes that occur during adulthood. (pp. 420–425)

30. Define generativity, mid-life transition, and terminal drop. (pp. 422–426)

CONCEPTS AND EXERCISES

No. 1: Nature or Nurture

Completing this exercise should help you to achieve Learning Objectives 2, 3, and 4.

Today, developmental psychologists think that nature (genetic factors) and nurture (environmental factors) interact to produce an individual's characteristics. Below is a list of situations. After each description, decide whether nature or nurture had more influence on the final characteristics.

1. Even though Pauline and Beth have spent just about the same amount of time lying in the sun, Pauline's tan is very dark and Beth's is a light brown. Pauline's ability to tan so darkly is probably a result of _____.

2. Piano majors Jane and Isabelle are very dedicated to practicing, and both work at it eight hours a day. Isabelle is very frustrated because her playing is not as musical as Jane's, despite her long hours at the piano. Jane's ability to play so musically is probably a result of _____.

3. Tom and Jim are identical twins. Their parents died in a car accident when they were nine weeks old. They had no other relatives, and separate adoptions were arranged. Tom's adoptive parents are language professors at the local university, and Jim's are

advertising executives. At age twelve, Tom can speak three languages other than English; Jim is getting a D in English. The difference in their language abilities is probably due to _____.

4. Tony was slight of build in high school. When he entered college, he started working out. The first time he returned home for the summer, his mother was surprised to see his well-developed muscles. Tony's new physique is probably due to _____.

No. 2: The Toy Industry

Completing this exercise should help you to achieve Learning Objectives 8, 9, 11, 12, 13, and 26.

Bill has just landed a job with a large toy company. His first assignment is to develop a new line of toys designed for children in each of Piaget's stages of cognitive development. Match each of Bill's ideas (listed below) to the appropriate stage of cognitive development.

1. *A simple board game.* The winner is the first player to move a token completely around the board. The board itself is made of squares with pictures of animals, foods, family members (grandma, uncle, sister), and toys. Some of the squares have instructions to move ahead or fall back to the nearest square containing a picture of a certain animal, food, relative, or toy. For example, one square might instruct the player to move ahead to the nearest picture of a horn; and another, to move back to the nearest picture of a cow. To start, players roll a die and move the appropriate number of squares. A player's turn ends if he or she lands on a square with a picture. If the player lands on a square with instructions, he or she must follow them. The game is designed so that the players practice counting and recognizing different classes of objects. _____

2. *A set of edible paints.* The paints come with a set of canvases that will not absorb paint. However, paint will adhere to the surface enough to remain in place. Each canvas contains an outline of a picture. The idea is for the child to paint a picture, then peel it off the board and eat it. _____

3. *A clown-face mobile painted in vibrant primary colors.* Each battery-operated clown face will, when pulled, emit a different melody or laugh, and the eyes in each face will light up. _____

4. *A board game called Planet Wars.* Each player receives a game piece in the shape of a planet. Some planets are more desirable than others, and a roll of the dice decides who gets which. Each planet comes with an army, several nearby star systems equipped with arsenals, an assortment of special weapons, and spy devices. The winner is the player who conquers the most planets. The players must generate hypotheses to help them form strategies for attack and must be able to logically anticipate the consequences of their own moves as well as those of their opponents. _____

CRITICAL THINKING

Sam and Martina are working on a kidnapping case. Curiously, the biological mother has no pictures of the child to give to the two detectives. She has described her child, however, as five years old, male, blond, blue-eyed, smiley, and very healthy. The child has been missing for over a week now. Sam and Martina feel sorry for the child; being kidnapped is a horrible ordeal. But since the mother is an alcoholic, they know that even if they find the boy, he won't come home to a very healthy situation.

Sam and Martina get a break. They receive a report from a homemaker, Ted, in a neighboring town. Ted says that a new child, Richie—five years old with blond hair and blue eyes—has suddenly appeared on the block and is living with a long-time neighbor of Ted's, whom he dislikes. The child doesn't seem to know his own name. Ted also mentions that he looks a little "funny" and appears to be mentally retarded. Ted knows that the neighbor is unable to have children and has wanted a child for quite some time. Also, as far as he knows, she doesn't have any relatives. In addition, she became extremely flustered when Ted asked her about Richie's origins. So where had the little boy come from?

Sam decides that Richie is not the child they are looking for. Richie fits the physical description given by the mother whose child had been kidnapped, but she specifically said the boy was healthy. She also didn't mention anything odd about his looks. However, Martina is sure they have found the child.

Using the five critical thinking questions in your text, state Sam's original hypothesis and his evidence. Based on the clues in the story, what do you think Martina's alternative hypothesis is? What evidence does she have?

1. What is Sam's hypothesis upon hearing about the "new kid on the block"?

2. What evidence supports Sam's hypothesis?

3. What is Martina's alternative hypothesis?

4. What evidence supports Martina's alternative hypothesis?

5. What conclusions can Sam and Martina draw?

PERSONAL LEARNING ACTIVITIES

1. At which of Piaget's stages of cognitive development are you? What supports the classification you have given yourself? (Learning Objectives 8, 11, 12, and 26)

2. Describe the rules in your family when you were growing up and what happened when you broke a rule. Write whether you think your parent(s)/guardian(s) had an authoritarian, permissive, or authoritative parenting style and why. Mention which part of the descriptions in the text fit and which parts don't. (Learning Objective 21)

3. Watch an hour or so of children-oriented television, such as cartoons, and pay particular attention to the commercials. Take notes on what product is being sold, who is included (boys, girls, or both?), and their roles. For example, are both boys and girls shown flying toy fighter planes, or are the boys playing with planes and the girls looking on? Are the girls in the commercials giggling and brushing their doll's hair? Are boys giggling? Describe the implication of the commercial for gender roles. For example, the implication of both boys and girls washing dishes at a toy sink might be that both boys and girls help with cleaning. (Learning Objective 23)

4. Think back to a recent moral decision when you considered the reasons for and against doing something. List the reasons you gave at the time for the choice you made. What sorts of reasons did you give? Were they related to how other people would react, to what was legal, or to whether you might get punished, for example? At what stage of moral reasoning would Kohlberg place you based on this decision? Can you think of other decisions that would place you at a different level? (Learning Objective 27)

5. Consider how you have aged over the last four years. How have your thoughts, feelings, and actions changed? Imagine yourself after another four years and describe your expectations about your lifestyle, relationships, ideas, emotional reactions, and behaviors. Does your description fit well with the text's description of the average person of that age? (Learning Objectives 29 and 30)

MULTIPLE-CHOICE QUESTIONS

SAMPLE QUIZ 1

1. Jane is pregnant and has been reading about various activities that she can do with her new baby to improve the infant's intellectual skills. Jane is behaving according to what viewpoint?
   a. Nature
   b. Maturational
   c. Psychodynamic
   d. Nurture

2. A behaviorist believes that development is a result of
   a. maturational processes.
   b. natural growth guided by genetic factors.
   c. sexual impulses.
   d. the influence of external conditions.

3. Colleen is five years old. She is mentally retarded and her face is malformed. Her mother most likely
   a. took thalidomide during pregnancy.
   b. is a heroin addict.
   c. consumed alcohol during pregnancy.
   d. experienced severe stress during pregnancy.

4. Penny is going to decorate her newborn's room and wants the baby to enjoy looking all around it. Which of the following will meet her decorating needs?
   a. Wallpaper covered with very small blue flowers
   b. A mobile with very small butterflies for the far end of the room
   c. Curtains with large smiling clown faces for the window right next to the baby's bed
   d. A wall hanging of gray and white checked fabric

5. The development of the cardiovascular and nervous systems and the organs begins during which stage of prenatal development?
   a. Germinal
   b. Embryonic
   c. Fertile
   d. Fetal

6. Object permanence is acquired during Piaget's _____ period of cognitive development.
   a. formal operations
   b. concrete operations
   c. preoperational
   d. sensorimotor

7. Gary's parents are constantly amazed at how their son has changed over the past year. Suddenly, he loves to study science, is a feminist, and wants to participate in an antinuclear power demonstration. Gary has moved into the _____ stage of cognitive development.
   a. sensorimotor
   b. preoperational
   c. concrete operations
   d. formal operations

8. Jeffrey learned to pick up bits of cereal and push his fingers and the cereal into his mouth. Jeffrey discovered, however, that this method did not work for yogurt and eventually learned that yogurt is eaten with a spoon. Jeffrey's modified behavior shows
   a. accommodation.
   b. assimilation.
   c. conservation.
   d. object permanence.

9. The thinking of children who cannot yet conserve is dominated by
   a. auditory cues (hearing).
   b. visual cues.
   c. behavioral cues.
   d. verbal cues.

10. Claude enjoys pretending that he is baking cookies when he plays in sand. Claude made a ball of sand, flattened it, and exclaimed, "Wow, look how much bigger I made it!" According to Piaget, Claude is in the _____ stage of cognitive development.
    a. concrete operations
    b. formal operations
    c. preoperational
    d. sensorimotor

11. In assimilation,
    a. information is added to existing schemas.
    b. old schemas are modified.
    c. schemas don't change.
    d. none of the above

12. An authoritative parent is
    a. firm, punitive, and unsympathetic.
    b. very lax about discipline and gives the child complete freedom.
    c. firm but reasonable and explains why a child's behavior is incorrect.
    d. one who demands obedience to authority.

13. It is interesting to watch nine-month-old P.J. react to a new object. He holds onto his mother very tightly for several long moments and then, using the furniture to steady himself, walks toward the object and warily checks it out. P.J. has a temperament that is typical of
    a. easy babies.
    b. difficult babies.
    c. slow-to-warm-up babies.
    d. exploratory babies.

14. Woody's parents gave him a strict curfew, never allowed him to visit with friends until homework was finished, and did not discuss their reasons for the rules. When Woody wrote his first play, they punished him for wasting his time when he should have been studying. Woody's parents have which parenting style, according to Baumrind?
    a. authoritarian
    b. authoritative
    c. insecure
    d. permissive

15. Gloria, who is thirty years old, wants to have children, but feels she is just getting her career on track. Gloria is feeling a(n) _____ crisis, according to Erikson.
    a. intimacy
    b. integrity
    c. generativity
    d. autonomy

16. Since he graduated from college and began work in advertising, Jens has begun to feel lonely and abandoned. Most of his friends live out-of-state and those who live nearby are married, so even when he sees them he feels left out. Erikson would say that Jens is struggling with the crisis of
    a. identity versus role confusion.
    b. industry versus inferiority.
    c. integrity versus despair.
    d. intimacy versus isolation.

17. Tenita is an infant who is learning that she will be fed, clothed, and kept warm and dry. Tenita is most likely in Erikson's _____ stage of psychosocial development.
    a. intimacy versus isolation
    b. integrity versus despair
    c. generativity versus stagnation
    d. trust versus mistrust

18. During Kohlberg's second stage of moral reasoning, children
    a. consider what they will gain by the moral decision.
    b. choose an action that will bring approval.
    c. make decisions from a human rights perspective.
    d. make decisions based on their personal standards.

19. Steve has grown five inches in the past year and gained twenty pounds. One moment he is depressed over the sudden appearance of acne on his face; a moment later he is elated as he runs out the door to play a game of football with his buddies. How old is he?
   a. Eight to ten years old
   b. Ten to twelve years old
   c. Twelve to fifteen years old
   d. Eighteen to twenty years old

20. Which of the following is characteristic of the thinking of an adult over the age of sixty-five?
   a. Information is registered at a slower pace.
   b. Mathematical ability increases.
   c. Reasoning capabilities increase due to years of practice.
   d. Verbal comprehension increases as a result of a larger vocabulary.

Total Correct (See answer key) _____

SAMPLE QUIZ 2

Use this quiz to reassess your learning after taking Quiz 1 and reviewing the chapter.

1. In the context of the nature-nurture debate, nurture could be defined as
   a. a child's education.
   b. the sensitivity of the parent's care.
   c. a healthy diet.
   d. all of the above.

2. Karen, who is pregnant, drinks heavily and smokes almost two packs of cigarettes a day. Her doctor has told her that she must abstain from these activities at least during the _____ stage of her baby's prenatal development.
   a. germane
   b. embryonic
   c. fetal
   d. gestation

3. Touching an infant's _____ results in a rooting reflex.
   a. nose
   b. lips
   c. cheek
   d. palm

4. What types of sounds do infants prefer?
   a. Soothing descending tones
   b. Low pitches
   c. Monotones
   d. Female voices

5. A teratogen is a
   a. genetic abnormality.
   b. period during which the fetus is susceptible to birth defects.
   c. substance that can cause birth defects.
   d. person whose characteristics are caused by fetal alcohol syndrome.

6. Joey is six months old and loves to play "tug-of-war." When his dad leans over the crib with a toy in his hand, Joey grasps it and pulls on it. Joey's mom just got him a new toy—a little string of colored animals—to hang across his crib. She does not understand why Joey always reaches up and pulls down the string of colored animals. Joey is elaborating his schema of grasping and pulling through
   a. accommodation.
   b. integration.
   c. assimilation.
   d. anticipation.

7. Stasha enjoys putting all kinds of objects, including bugs and dirt, in her mouth. She loses interest in playing with her toy train, however, when her babysitter hides it. Stasha is most likely in Piaget's _____ stage of cognitive development.
   a. concrete operations
   b. formal operations
   c. preoperational
   d. sensorimotor

8. Susie is crying because her teddy bear, Boyd, has fallen off the kitchen table and landed on its face. She insists that her mother should put a bandage on Boyd's nose. Susie is in Piaget's _____ stage of cognitive development.
   a. sensorimotor
   b. preoperational
   c. formal operations
   d. concrete operations

9. Understanding that a substance's quantity doesn't change, even when its form does, occurs during which of Piaget's developmental stages?
   a. Sensorimotor
   b. Preoperational
   c. Concrete
   d. Formal

10. The development of the ability to use symbols occurs during the
    a. sensorimotor period.
    b. preoperational period.
    c. concrete operational period.
    d. formal operational period.

11. Temperament is first recognizable at what stage of development?
    a. birth
    b. preoperational period
    c. adolescence
    d. middle childhood

12. Two mothers are assessing their children's abilities. One turns to the other and says, "Of course Johnny is doing better at math. Now that he is older, his concentration is better and he can hold more chunks of information in his memory at the same time." _____ would agree with Johnny's mom.
    a. Piaget
    b. Erikson
    c. An information-processing theorist
    d. Kohlberg

13. Sherri babysits for Peter every afternoon and has noticed that he cries and fusses when his mother leaves. When his mother returns, Peter squirms and refuses to be held by her. Peter most likely has
    a. a secure attachment.
    b. an anxious insecure attachment.
    c. a secure avoidant attachment.
    d. a secure ambivalent attachment.

14. Child X is between five and seven years old. The parents of Child X, in accordance with the *typical* socialization behavior of most American parents, are encouraging X to achieve, act independently, explore, and assume personal responsibility. What sex is Child X?
    a. Male
    b. Female
    c. These traits are encouraged in both sexes.
    d. Cannot be determined from the information given

15. Sam and Alex want to attend a rock concert in New York City on July 4th. Sam's parents have told him that, although they understand his frustration, it is too dangerous for a fourteen-year-old to travel to the city by himself on a big holiday. Meanwhile, Alex's parents have decided that he may go to the concert. Sam's parents are _____ and Alex's parents are _____.
    a. permissive, authoritative
    b. authoritarian, permissive
    c. authoritative, authoritarian
    d. authoritative, permissive

16. Martha feels that her life has been meaningful and worthwhile, and she is not afraid of dying. Erik Erikson most likely would say that she has
    a. integrity.
    b. generativity.
    c. identity.
    d. autonomy.

17. Misha recently graduated from high school and is unsure about going to college. She hasn't picked out a career, but wonders if taking courses would help her to decide. Erikson most likely would say Misha is in the _____ stage of psychosocial development.
    a. initiative vs. guilt
    b. autonomy vs. shame and doubt
    c. integrity vs. despair
    d. identity vs. role confusion

18. Jeanine and Helen are in a drugstore spending several weeks' worth of allowance on candy. Helen decides she wants to steal the candy, but Jeanine argues that they might get caught and put in jail. According to Kohlberg, Jeanine is at which stage of moral reasoning?
    a. 1
    b. 3
    c. 4
    d. 5

19. Gunter is trying to decide whether to become an exotic dancer in a nightclub. At first, he isn't sure about whether such dancing would be immoral, but he finally decides he shouldn't take the dancing job, because others will think he is a sleaze. Gunter says, "My family wouldn't want me to support them by being exploited; therefore, it wouldn't be right to take the job." According to Kohlberg, Gunter has _____ moral reasoning.
    a. conservational
    b. conventional
    c. preconventional
    d. postconventional

20. In the past ten years, Vernon has gained weight, especially around his middle. He has a slight hearing loss and has just found out that he needs glasses. What stage of development has Vernon reached?
    a. Adolescence
    b. Early adulthood
    c. Middle adulthood
    d. Old age

Total Correct (See answer key) _____

ANSWERS TO FILL-IN-THE-BLANKS KEY TERMS

1. teratogen (p. 386)
2. critical period (p. 396)
3. sensorimotor period (pp. 390–391)
4. object permanence (p. 391)
5. concrete operations (p. 396)
6. Authoritarian (p. 410)
7. formal operational period (p. 417)
8. Conservation (p. 395)
9. crisis of generativity (pp. 422–423)
10. temperament (p. 403)
11. sensorimotor (pp. 390–391)
12. schemas (p. 389)
13. accommodation (p. 390)
14. rooting reflex (p. 388)
15. maturation (p. 383)

ANSWERS TO CONCEPTS AND EXERCISES

No. 1: Nature or Nurture

1. *Nature.* Pauline tans more easily than Beth, despite their spending the same amount of time in the sun, because Pauline's inheritance predisposes her pigmentation to be more reactive to the sun. (pp. 382–385)

2. *Nature.* Jane plays well because she has a genetic inheritance that predisposes her to be musical. (pp. 382–385)

3. *Nurture.* Jim may not have been exposed to other languages in school or at home, but his poor performance in English indicates that he does not have a natural talent for languages. Tom's parents have provided a multilingual environment for him, and this factor, rather than a genetic predisposition, is the likely reason why he can speak three languages. (pp. 382–385)

4. *Nurture.* Tony's genetic inheritance guided his physical development throughout high school. However, working out in the gym (an environmental factor, or nurture) was responsible for the changes in his muscles. (pp. 382–385)

No. 2: The Toy Industry

1. *Concrete operations.* During this stage of cognitive development, children learn how to do simple operations such as addition, subtraction, and conservation and to group objects into classes. (For example, cows, dogs, and rabbits are grouped as animals.) The board game encourages the child to practice counting and grouping objects into classes. (p. 396)

2. *Preoperational.* The ability to use symbols introduces the child to many new activities during this stage. Drawing involves creating a symbol of something in the real world. (pp. 395–396)

3. *Sensorimotor.* During this stage, an infant loves to look at large objects that move and that feature lots of contrast and complexity—especially smiling faces. The mobile is perfect for this age: it moves, it consists of faces, and its colors, lights, and sounds provide contrast. (pp. 387–388, 390–391)

4. *Formal operations.* During this stage, adolescents learn to generate hypotheses and think logically about the outcome of events. To develop a strategy for the Planet Wars game, each player must create a plan (hypothesis) and think logically about the consequences of the plan's moves. (p. 417)

ANSWERS TO CRITICAL THINKING

1. Sam doesn't think they have solved the crime. His hypothesis is that Richie can't be the child they are looking for.

2. The evidence in support of Sam's hypothesis: Ted specifically said that Richie looked "funny" and appeared to be retarded, but the biological mother had described the child as very healthy.

3. Martina's alternative hypothesis: Richie is the little boy they are looking for.

4. The evidence in support of Martina's alternative hypothesis: The biological mother is an alcoholic and her son may have fetal alcohol syndrome. That would explain Ted's description of odd-looking facial features and mental retardation. She thinks it's possible that, due to guilt, the biological mother didn't tell them about the fetal alcohol syndrome. Martina will want to collect additional evidence. She will want to know whether the mother was an alcoholic during her son's pregnancy and whether there are any medical records that discuss his health.

5. Martina thinks it may be reasonable at this point to conclude that they have the right child. (NOTE: Critical thinking is a constant process of hypothesizing, examining evidence, rehypothesizing, collecting more evidence, and so on. Martina may not be correct. Can you think of any other hypotheses that could explain these data?)

ANSWERS TO MULTIPLE-CHOICE QUESTIONS

Circle the question numbers you answered correctly.

Sample Quiz 1

1. *d* is the answer. Jane's behavior implies that she believes her infant's environment will affect his intellectual development. This belief is in accordance with a nurture viewpoint. (p. 382)
   a, b. A maturationalist would say that the development of characteristics (how the individual looks and acts) is guided by biological or genetic factors (nature), which are not generally altered by changes in the environment.
   c. From a psychodynamic viewpoint, development is the product of an individual's sexual impulses and the parents' reactions to them.

2. *d* is the answer. A behaviorist believes that external conditions are responsible for the developmental process. For example, transferring to a better educational setting will alter the development of cognitive ability. (p. 384)
   a, b. A maturationalist believes that abilities unfold with age in a fixed sequence and are determined by nature—in short, that genetics controls development.
   c. A psychodynamic theorist believes that a child's natural sexual impulses and the parental reaction to those impulses guide development.

3. *c* is the answer. Mental retardation and facial malformations are symptoms of the fetal alcohol syndrome, which occurs in infants born to mothers who drink too much alcohol while pregnant. (p. 387)
   a, b, d. Drug use of any kind (whether recreational or medicinal) and stress levels can affect prenatal development. However, the combination of symptoms listed can be linked to one specific abuse: drinking alcohol.

4. *c* is the answer. Infants can see large objects featuring lots of contrast, contour, complexity, and movement. They enjoy looking at faces. The clown faces are large and smiling and may move with the breeze. (pp. 387–388)
   a. This wallpaper design may appeal to Penny, but her infant will not have the visual capability to see the small pattern.
   b. A mobile is a good idea because the parts move, but the infant will be unable to see it in the far corner.
   d. A wall hanging of brightly colored checks may provide enough contrast for the infant to see it. However, grey and white are not as contrasting as, say, blue and red.

5. *b* is the answer. Cardiovascular and nervous systems develop during the embryonic stage. A critical period exists: If certain systems and organs do not develop properly at this time, they never will. (p. 385)
   a. The germinal stage begins with fertilization and lasts for two weeks. The zygote divides rapidly, travels down the Fallopian tubes, and attaches to the uterine wall.
   c, d. There is no such thing as the fertile stage in prenatal development. You may be thinking of the fetal stage. During this stage, systems integrate and the organs grow and begin to function more efficiently.

6. *d* is the answer. Object permanence is the ability to know that an object exists even when it is out of sight. Children acquire this ability during the sensorimotor period, the first stage of cognitive development. (p. 391)
   a. An adolescent acquires the ability to think hypothetically and to imagine logical consequences of events in the formal operational period.
   b. A child learns to perform simple operations—subtraction, addition, classification, seriation, and conservation—during the concrete operational period.
   c. A child acquires the ability to use symbols during the preoperational period.

7. *d* is the answer. Studying science involves thinking logically and being able to generate hypotheses. Being involved with feminist movements and nuclear demonstrations requires the ability to question social institutions and to think about the world as it might be or as it ought to be. (p. 417)
   a, b. Children in the sensorimotor or preoperational periods do not have the ability to question

social institutions. They may have some knowledge of feminism or nuclear power plants, but they cannot think about or accurately imagine the consequences of nuclear war or the treatment of women as inferior.

c. During the concrete operations period, children can think logically about objects they directly experience.

8. *a* is the answer. In accommodation, new information changes a schema. (p. 390)

   b. Assimilation is when new information is added to an unchanged schema.

   c. Conservation is the ability to realize that the size, quantity, or mass of an object is the same although it looks different.

   d. Children with object permanence know that an object exists even when it is hidden from view.

9. *b* is the answer. The ability to conserve involves realizing that a substance does not change in amount or number when its form changes. Thinking dominated by visual appearances makes conservation impossible. A child incapable of conserving would say that a tall skinny glass contains more liquid than a short fat glass, even when both glasses contain the same amount of liquid. (p. 395)

10. *c* is the answer. Children who cannot conserve amounts are not yet in the concrete operations stage. (p. 395)

   a. Concrete operations requires the ability to conserve.

   b. Formal operations requires the ability to think about abstract concepts.

   d. Infants in the sensorimotor period explore the world through their senses. They do not have object permanence until the end of the sensorimotor period and cannot conserve amounts. Because Claude is pretending, however, we know that he has moved beyond the sensorimotor stage.

11. *a* is the answer. (p. 389)

   b. In accommodation, old schemas are modified with new information.

   c. In assimilation, schemas may be added to, but are not significantly changed.

   d. *a* is the answer.

12. *c* is the answer. Authoritative parents are firm but reasonable and provide explanations when a child's behavior is incorrect. They encourage the child to take responsibility and to be independent. (p. 410)

   a. Authoritarian parents are firm, punitive, and unsympathetic.

   b. Permissive parents are very lax about discipline and give their children complete freedom.

   d. Authoritarian parents demand obedience to authority figures.

13. *c* is the answer. (p. 403)

   a. An easy baby has predictable cycles of eating and sleeping, reacts cheerfully to a new situation, and seldom fusses.

   b. A difficult baby is irritable and irregular.

   d. Although some infants are more exploratory than others, there is no category or classification termed "exploratory."

14. *a* is the answer. Authoritarian parents are strict and unyielding disciplinarians. (p. 410)

   b. Authoritative parents discuss rules and are more affectionate.

   c. Baumrind did not use the term insecure to describe parents.

   d. Permissive parents are less informed about their children's activities. They set few rules and rarely use discipline.

15. *c* is the answer. The tension between career and children is a conflict between two types of generativity. People experiencing the generativity versus stagnation crisis often think about leaving their mark on the world. (pp. 422–423)

   a. Erikson suggested that after the identity crisis, young adults seek intimacy. Secure love relationships are the focus, not children or career aspirations.

   b. Integrity versus despair is a crisis of old age in which people reflect on their lives. They may feel that their lives have been meaningful or they may feel despair at unaccomplished goals.

   d. Autonomy versus shame and doubt occurs at about age two when children try to control themselves and make decisions.

16. *d* is the answer. Jens is beginning to feel isolated, because he has not successfully resolved the crisis of intimacy versus isolation. (p. 409)

   a. Identity versus role confusion is a crisis Jens resolved when he went into advertising.

   b. Industry versus inferiority is a crisis experienced by children ages 6 through adolescence. They either feel curiosity or lose interest in schoolwork and other activities.

   c. Integrity versus despair is a crisis during which older people look back on their lives and decide if they accomplished what they wanted to.

17. *d* is the answer. Infants learn whether the world is a predictable place during the trust versus mistrust crisis. If their needs are met, they will most likely resolve the crisis successfully. (pp. 408–409)
   a. Intimacy versus isolation occurs in early adulthood.
   b. Integrity versus despair occurs in late adulthood.
   c. Generativity versus stagnation occurs in middle adulthood.

18. *a* is the answer. Stage 2 of moral reasoning is basically characterized by selfishness. Decisions are based on the potential for personal gain. (pp. 417–418)
   b. Children in Stage 3 make moral decisions based on the potential for others' approval.
   c. Adults in Stage 6 consider human rights or other universal ethical principles when making their moral decisions.
   d. Adolescents in Stage 5 make moral decisions based on their own personal standards.

19. *c* is the answer. (pp. 414–415)
   a, b, d. None of the other age groups corresponds to the beginning or middle of the adolescent period.

20. *a* is the answer. (p. 421)
   b, c, d. Studies have shown that verbal comprehension, mathematical ability, and reasoning begin to decline after age sixty-seven.

Now turn to the quiz analysis table at the end of this chapter to find which areas you know well and which areas you need to work on. Circle the numbers in the table for items on Quiz 1 that you answered correctly.

ANSWERS TO MULTIPLE-CHOICE QUESTIONS

Circle the question numbers you answered correctly.

Sample Quiz 2

1. *d* is the answer. <u>Nurture</u> is anything in the environment that influences an organism, including education, parents' care, physical exercise, and diet. <u>Nature</u> is any characteristic resulting from inherited genetic material, such as eye color or a physical predisposition toward a disease, body type, or temperament. (p. 382)

2. *b* is the answer. There is a critical period in the embryonic stage during which systems and organs must develop or they never will. Drugs such as nicotine and alcohol negatively affect this process. (p. 386)
   a, d. There is no such thing as the "germane" stage (you may have been thinking of the germinal stage) or the gestation stage.
   c. Alcohol and nicotine in the mother's system do affect development during the fetal stage, but not as severely as during the embryonic stage.

3. *c* is the answer. If you touch an infant's cheek, the infant will automatically turn his or her head toward your hand. This is called the rooting reflex. (p. 388)
   a. There is no reflex associated with touching an infant's nose.
   b. If you put an object, such as a nipple or your finger, to an infant's lips, the infant will automatically try to suck on it. However, this is called the sucking reflex, not the rooting reflex.
   d. Brushing an infant's palm or ball of the foot results in a grasping motion with the hands or a curling of the toes. However, this is called the grasping reflex, not the rooting reflex.

4. *d* is the answer. (p. 388)
   a, b, c. Infants prefer ascending tones, spoken by a woman or a child. They like speech that is friendly, high-pitched, exaggerated, and expressive.

5. *c* is the answer. Teratogens are external substances that can cause birth defects when taken into the womb during pregnancy. (p. 386)
   a. Teratogens are external causes of problems; they are not genetic defects.
   b. The critical period is during the embryonic stage. Teratogens are especially dangerous then.
   d. A baby with fetal alcohol syndrome is not called a teratogen. Alcohol is the teratogen.

6. *c* is the answer. Joey is assimilating because he is using the *same* schema of reaching and grasping to investigate a new object. (p. 389)
   a. Accommodation occurs when a schema is <u>modified</u> or <u>changed</u> in response to acquiring new information. If the question stated that Joey learned to push the animals back and forth in the air instead of always reaching, grasping, and pulling them down, <u>accommodation</u> would have been the answer.
   b. Integration is the process of putting two schemas together. If the question stated that Joey learned that reaching and grasping can

become a sequence of movements, this would be the correct answer.

d. There is no anticipatory process in the elaboration of schemas.

7. *d* is the answer. Children in the sensorimotor period, according to Piaget, are still acquiring object permanence. They often put things in their mouths to see how they feel. (pp. 390–391)

a. Concrete operational children have acquired object permanence and do not explore the world by putting objects in their mouths.

b. Adolescents or adults in formal operations think abstractly.

c. Preoperational children have object permanence.

8. *b* is the answer. Susie is probably between the ages of four and six and thinks that her bear, an inanimate (nonliving) object, is alive and feels pain because he fell on his face. Mom typically puts a bandage on Susie's cuts and bruises, and Susie wants the same treatment for Boyd. This behavior is characteristic of the preoperational stage. (p. 395)

a. Children in the sensorimotor stage do not recognize or label their own emotions, and therefore cannot assume that their toys have emotions.

c. Adolescents in the formal operational stage realize that inanimate (nonliving) objects do not feel pain.

d. Children in the concrete operational stage realize that inanimate (nonliving) objects do not feel pain.

9. *c* is the answer. (pp. 395–396)

a. The sensorimotor period starts with birth and extends through two years of age.

b. Conservation—understanding that substances don't change in quantity even when their shape does—is an "operation." In the *pre*operational period, children cannot perform this "operation."

d. Adolescents in the formal operational period already understand concrete operations.

10. *b* is the answer. The ability to use symbols is a cognitive development that occurs during the preoperational stage. (p. 395)

a. Object permanence is one of the principle cognitive developments that occur during the sensorimotor period.

c. A child in the period of concrete operations not only can use symbols as mental representations but can also manipulate those symbols in simple logical operations.

d. When an adolescent reaches the stage of formal operations, he or she is capable of abstract reasoning, far beyond the simple use of symbols.

11. *a* is the answer. (pp. 390–391, 403)

b, c, d. While temperament is recognizable during the preoperational period, adolescence, and middle childhood, it *first* appears at birth.

12. *c* is the answer. Developmental research based on information-processing theory focuses on the *quantitative* changes in children's mental capacities, rather than looking for qualitative advances or changes as Piaget did. A *bigger* vocabulary, *better* concentration, and retention of *more* chunks of information in memory at one time are all quantitative changes. Therefore, Johnny's mother is explaining her son's improvement as an information-processing theorist would. (NOTE: This approach focuses on quantitative changes. *Quantitative* pertains to number or amounts; so *bigger* or *more* ability accounts for a change, according to this view of cognitive development.) (pp. 397–398)

a. Piaget explained that cognitive development pertains to a *different* kind of mental ability, not just an improved ability for the same cognitive skill. The use of symbols (acquired during the preoperational period) is different from the ability to generate hypotheses (acquired during the formal operation period). (NOTE: *Quality* is defined as "a distinguishing element or characteristic." And each stage of Piaget's cognitive development theory is distinguished by a *unique* characteristic or type of thinking.)

b. Erikson studied the stages of emotional development.

d. Kohlberg was interested in moral decision making—only one type of cognitive activity. His work does not provide a general theory about the development of cognitive abilities.

13. *b* is the answer. (p. 406)

a. A child who can tolerate brief separation from his or her mother, but who welcomes contact with the mother when she returns, has a secure attachment.

c. There is no such thing as a secure avoidant attachment.

d. There is no such thing as a secure ambivalent attachment.

14. *a* is the answer. Boys are encouraged to achieve, act independently, explore, and assume personal responsibility. (pp. 412–413)

b. Girls are encouraged to be expressive, nurturant, reflective, dependent, obedient, helpful, and kind.

c. The traits listed in this question are typically encouraged only in males.

d. Research has shown that boys are encouraged to achieve, act independently, explore, and assume personal responsibility. Therefore, *a* is the answer.

15. *d* is the answer. Authoritative parents would be sympathetic (sorry that Sam has to miss the concert) but their decision would stand firm. Alex's parents give him complete freedom and are therefore permissive. Neither set of parents is authoritarian in the sense of firmly upholding rules with no explanation. (p. 410)

16. *a* is the answer. If older people reflect on their lives and are content, they have successfully resolved the crisis of integrity versus despair. (p. 425)

b. Generativity is a crisis in which people want to create something lasting to leave behind.

c. Identity versus role confusion is a crisis during adolescence when people are not sure what role they should take.

d. Autonomy is a crisis of two-year-olds, not adults.

17. *d* is the answer. Misha doesn't have the feeling that she is a unique person; she is still confused about her role. (p. 416)

a, b. Initiative versus guilt and autonomy versus shame and doubt both occur in early childhood.

c. Integrity versus despair is a crisis of late adulthood.

18. *a* is the answer. Jeanine is thinking about the painful experience of going to jail. That is why she decides against stealing the candy. This decision is characteristic of Stage 1 moral reasoning. (pp. 417–418)

b. Stage 3 moral reasoning is characterized by concern for pleasing others. If Jeanine had said that she did not want her mother to think badly of her, this would have been the correct answer.

c. Stage 4 moral reasoning is characterized by a concern for following rules and regulations. If Jeanine had said that it would be breaking the law to steal the candy, this would have been the correct answer.

d. Stage 5 moral reasoning is characterized by following one's own personal standards. If Jeanine had said that *she* does not think it is right to steal from someone, this would have been the correct answer.

19. *b* is the answer. Gunter is concerned with the approval of others (Stage 3). (pp. 417–418)

a. Conservational is not a stage of moral development.

c. Preconventional children base their decisions on the likelihood of punishment or of getting something in return.

d. The postconventional stage is characterized by recognizing the limits of laws and eventually basing decisions on universal ethical principles.

20. *c* is the answer. Adolescents are still growing. Physical signs of aging do not occur in early adulthood. And by old age, Vernon should be experiencing other physical changes, such as shrinking in height. (p. 420)

Now turn to the quiz analysis table at the end of this chapter to find which areas you know well and which areas you need to work on. Circle the numbers in the table for items on Quiz 2 that you answered correctly.

For each question you answered correctly, circle its number. (Quiz 1 numbers are not shaded; Quiz 2 numbers are shaded.) Are there patterns in the types of questions or the topics you got wrong that could direct your further study? Did you improve from Quiz 1 to Quiz 2?

TOPIC	TYPE OF QUESTION		
	DEFINITION	COMPREHENSION	APPLICATION
Exploring development		2	1
	1		
Beginnings		5	3, 4
	5	3, 4	2
Infancy and Childhood			
Cognitive development	11	6, 9	7, 8, 10
		9, 10	6, 7, 8, 12
Social and emotional development	12		13, 14, 16, 17
		11	13, 14, 15, 16, 17
Adolescence		18	19
			18, 19
Adulthood		20	15
			20

TOTAL CORRECT BY QUIZ:

QUIZ 1:
QUIZ 2:

Chapter 13

Health, Stress, and Coping

OUTLINE

I. HEALTH PSYCHOLOGY (pp. 430–431)

The field of health psychology investigates the relationship between psychological, behavioral, and social processes and physical health. A goal of health psychologists is to apply their research to prevent illness and promote better health.

II. UNDERSTANDING STRESS (pp. 431–445)

Stress is the negative physical and psychological adjustment to circumstances that disrupt, or threaten to disrupt, a person's functioning. Stress always involves a relationship between people (stress reactions) and their environments (stressors). Mediating factors affect the severity of stress reactions. Examples of mediating factors include perceived control over stressors, available social support, and quality of stress-coping skills.

A. Stressors

1. *Psychological Stressors.* Both pleasant and unpleasant events or situations can cause stress. Catastrophic events that are life-threatening, such as assault, combat, fire, and tornadoes, can lead to serious psychological disorders. Life changes and strains can be stressors, especially if they force a person to adapt. Examples of such changes include divorce, marriage, bad grades, graduation, a new job, a promotion, and death. Daily hassles, such as minor irritations, pressures, and annoyances, when experienced regularly, can act as stressors.

2. *Measuring Stressors.* Several ways of measuring stress have been developed based on the premise that stress is a process that requires a person to make some sort of life adjustment. One instrument, called the Social Readjustment Rating Scale, measures stress in terms of life-change units (LCUs). Research suggests that people who experience a greater number of LCUs are more likely to suffer physical and mental illness. The Life Experiences Survey (LES), another instrument for measuring stress, also considers an individual's perceptions of the positive or negative impact of a given stressor. By examining perceptions of stress, the LES is able to measure the role that gender and cultural differences play in experiences of stress.

B. Stress Responses

1. *Physical Stress Responses: The GAS.* The general adaptation syndrome (GAS) is a stress response composed of three stages. The fight-or-flight syndrome (FFS), or alarm reaction, is the first stage. The sequence of events causing the FFS is controlled by the sympatho-adreno-medullary system (SAM); the hypothalamus triggers the sympathetic ANS, which stimulates the adrenal medulla, which in turn secretes catecholamines into the bloodstream. Catecholamines stimulate the heart, liver, kidneys, and lungs, thereby causing rapid breathing and increases in heart rate, blood pressure, blood sugar level, and muscle tension.

° Persistent stressors initiate the resistance, or second, stage, which is controlled by the hypothalamic-pituitary-adrenocortical (HPA) system. The hypothalamus triggers the pituitary to secrete adrenocorticotropic hormone (ACTH), which stimulates adrenal cortex corticosteroid secretion. Corticosteroids generate the emergency energy needed to handle stress.

° A continual depletion of energy eventually causes exhaustion, the third stage. The body eventually succumbs to diseases of adaptation caused by damaged heart and blood vessels, suppressed immune system functioning, and prolonged strain on systems that were weak even prior to the onset of the stressor.

° Psychobiological models have expanded Selye's theory of the general adaptation syndrome to include an individual's emotional state and perceptions of the stressor.

2. *Emotional Stress Responses.* Most physical stress responses are accompanied by emotional stress responses. Emotional responses come and go with

the onset and termination of stressors. Prolonged stress causes tension, irritability, short-temperedness, and increased anxiety.

3. *Cognitive Stress Responses.* An inability to concentrate, think clearly, or remember information accurately is a common cognitive reaction to stress. Ruminative thinking, the persistent interruption of thoughts about stressful events, is a cause of the reduction in thinking ability. When catastrophizing, a person tends to dwell on and overemphasize the potentially negative consequences of events. Over-arousal causes the normal range of attention to narrow. People under stress are more likely to use mental sets and experience functional fixedness.

4. *Behavioral Stress Responses.* Behavioral stress responses such as a shaky voice, changed body posture, and facial expressions provide clues about physiological and emotional stress responses. Escape and aggression are common behavioral stress responses.

C. Linkages: Stress and Psychological Disorders

1. *Burnout and Posttraumatic Stress Disorder.* Burnout is a gradually intensifying pattern of physical, psychological, and behavioral dysfunction in response to a continual flow of stressors. Those experiencing burnout may become indifferent, impulsive, accident-prone, drug-abusing, suspicious, depressed, and withdrawn. Posttraumatic stress disorder is a pattern of adverse reactions following a traumatic event. The disorder may appear immediately or weeks to years after the event. Symptoms include anxiety, irritability, jumpiness, inability to concentrate or work, sexual dysfunction, and difficulty in interpersonal relationships. In rare cases, flashbacks may occur.

D. Stress Mediators: Interactions Between People and Stressors

Mediating factors include individual and stressor characteristics and the circumstances under which stressors occur.

1. *How Stressors Are Appraised.* Those who perceive a stressor as a challenge rather than a threat experience fewer and less intense negative stress consequences. Cognitive factors are less effective as the intensity of a stressor increases.

2. *Predictability and Control.* Intense but short stressors have a smaller negative impact if people perceive them as predictable and controllable.

3. *Coping Resources and Coping Methods.* Coping resources include time and money. Coping methods are either problem-focused or emotion-focused.

4. *Social Support.* A social support network—friends and family who lend support during stress—can greatly reduce the impact of stressors. Too much support, however, can inhibit a person's attempt to cope with stress.

5. *Stress and Personality.* Dispositional optimism, or the expectation that things will work out well, is associated with fewer illnesses and faster healing. People who do not blame themselves and who think of stressors as temporary tend to suffer fewer stress-related problems.

E. Focus on Research Methods: Mining Longitudinal Research for Insights into Personality and Health

A study that followed gifted children for seventy years showed a relationship between social dependability and longer life. People whose parents had divorced or who had unstable marriages themselves died an average of four years earlier than those whose parents hadn't divorced or who had stable marriages.

III. THE PHYSIOLOGY AND PSYCHOLOGY OF HEALTH AND ILLNESS (pp. 445–450)

A. Stress, the Immune System, and Illness

Psychoneuroimmunology is the field that studies the interaction of the psychological and physiological processes that affect the body's ability to defend itself against disease.

1. *The Immune System and Illness.* The immune system defends the body against foreign substances and microorganisms. An active immune system has many components: the leukocytes, called B-cells and T-cells; the antibodies produced by B-cells; the natural killer cells; and macrophages. Stress-related psychological and emotional factors affect the immune system through the central and autonomic nervous systems and through the endocrine system.

2. *The Immune System and Stress.* People who are stressed are more likely to develop infectious diseases and to show reactivation of latent viruses (such as AIDS) because of immune system suppression.

3. *Moderators of Immune Function.* Social support can reduce the impact of stress. Some research suggests that stress is attenuated when a person with adequate or better social support has an opportunity to express pent-up thoughts and emotions. Even

anonymous disclosure is associated with fewer health center visits.

B. Heart Disease and Behavior Patterns

People exhibiting the response pattern of cynical hostility are suspicious, resentful, frequently angry, antagonistic, and distrustful of others. Cynical hostility is a risk factor for coronary heart disease and myocardial infarction (heart attack).

C. Thinking Critically: Does Cynical Hostility Increase the Risk of Heart Disease?

What am I being asked to believe or accept?
People with cynical hostility are more at risk for coronary heart disease and heart attack.

What evidence is available to support the assertion?
Cynical hostility is associated with an increase in the time needed to return to a resting level of sympatho-adreno-medullary (SAM). Increased sympathetic nervous system activity causes the release of stress-related hormones that are damaging to the heart.

Are there alternative ways of interpreting the evidence?
Genetically determined autonomic reactivity may make both hostility and heart disease more likely.

What additional evidence would help to evaluate the alternatives?
Studies that demonstrate varying strength in the relationship between cynical hostility and heart disease across cultures would suggest that the biological link is weak.

What conclusions are most reasonable?
Research suggests that there is a strong relationship between cynical hostility and increased risk of heart attack and disease. However, any explanation of this phenomenon must take into account the possibility that biological predisposition may lead to oversensitive reactions to stress, which lead to heart disease. Also, hostile behavior may cause people with cynical hostility to encounter more stress; hostile people are more likely to smoke, drink, overeat, and not exercise. Finally, cultural factors play a role in the relationship between cynical hostility and heart disease.

D. Risking Your Life: Health-Endangering Behaviors

Many of the major health problems in Western culture are either caused or increased by behaviors that can be changed.

1. *Smoking.* Smoking accounts for more deaths than drugs, car accidents, suicides, homicides, and fires combined.

2. *Alcohol.* Abuse of alcohol contributes to irreversible brain damage and gastrointestinal illnesses as well as to heart disease, stroke, cancer, and liver disease.

3. *Unsafe Sex.* Practicing unsafe sex greatly increases the risk of contracting HIV.

IV. PROMOTING HEALTHY BEHAVIOR (pp. 450–455)

Health promotion is the process of altering or eliminating behaviors that pose health risks and at the same time encouraging healthy behavior patterns.

A. Health Beliefs and Health Behaviors

Irwin Rosenstock's health-belief model is based on the assumption that people's decisions about health-related behavior are guided by four main factors: perceived personal threat of illness; perceived seriousness of illness; belief that a particular behavior or health practice will reduce the threat; and balance between health practice cost and perceived benefits. In addition, people need to believe that they can change their behavior, which is known as self-efficacy.

B. Changing Health Behaviors: Stages of Readiness

Successful adoption of health practices involves five stages: precontemplation, contemplation, preparation, action, and maintenance. A smooth transition from one stage to another is enhanced when a decisional balance is achieved—that is, when the pros outweigh the cons of the decision.

C. Programs for Coping with Stress and Promoting Health

1. *Planning to Cope.* People who are able to adopt problem-focused coping skills and recognize which stressors can and can't be changed are better equipped to cope with stress and are more likely to escape its negative consequences. Those able to adjust their coping strategies to the stressor are most successful.

2. *Developing Coping Strategies.* Strategies for coping with stress can be cognitive (cognitive restructuring), emotional (social support), behavioral (such as time management), and physical (biofeedback and progressive relaxation training).

3. *Preventing or Coping with AIDS.* Health psychologists are educating people about safe sex and ways to minimize stress.

KEY TERMS

1. **Health psychology** is a field within psychology that does research to understand the psychological and behavior processes associated with achieving and maintaining health, treating illness, and preventing it. (p. 429)

2. **Stress** is the process of adjusting to circumstances that disrupt, or threaten to disrupt, a person's physical or psychological functioning. (p. 431)

> *Example:* Marcus is five years old. He has just started day care and has been exposed to many childhood diseases. He is under stress because his body must adjust to fighting off these diseases.

3. **Stressors** are events and situations to which people must adjust. Almost any event or situation that causes change is a stressor. Other common factors that are considered stressors include trauma, conflict, and daily hassles. (p. 431)

> *Example:* Sharon has just been offered a new job. After graduation, she will move from a small town to a large city, have new responsibilities, and want to make new friends. Although these events are positive, they will involve big changes and therefore will be stressors.

4. **Stress reactions** are the physical, psychological, and behavioral responses people display when stressors appear. (p. 431)

> *Example:* Linda gets a rash (physical response) every time she has to study for an important exam. Marsha gets nervous (emotional response) in the middle of every exam. If Marsha cannot answer the first few questions immediately, she begins talking to herself (cognitive response), saying, "I am going to flunk this exam, which will make my grade point average go down. I will never get into law school. I'll probably have to work at minimum wage for the rest of my life. I'll hate it and probably get fired for my bad attitude. Face it, I am going to be a bag lady." When Jean started her new job, she was under a great deal of pressure. Her voice shook and she frowned more (behavioral responses).

5. The **general adaptation syndrome (GAS)** is Hans Selye's name for a series of physical reactions to stress. There are three stages: the alarm reaction, the resistance stage, and the exhaustion stage. (p. 433)

> *Example:* To satisfy his intellectual curiosity, Bill is taking a full load of classes, teaching undergraduates, writing a book, and doing research for a professor in his department. At the beginning of the semester, Bill can feel his heart race as he hurries to make an appointment here or there on campus (alarm). During midterm exams, he is in a constant state of arousal but does not notice it. He is used to being busy all day (resistance). By the end of the semester, he has a constant cold, feels tired, and has high blood pressure (exhaustion). Bill's doctor tells him that he needs to take time to relax over term break. His body must have time to recuperate from trying to adjust to such an extraordinary level of stress.

6. **Diseases of adaptation** are illnesses promoted or caused by stressors. These can include colds and flu, arthritis, coronary disease, and high blood pressure. (p. 434)

> *REMEMBER:* Diseases of adaptation are due to the body's efforts to adapt to stress.

7. **Catastrophizing**, a cognitive reaction to stress, occurs when negative events are dwelt on or overemphasized. (p. 436)

> *Example:* Joaquin is waiting to interview for a job. Any minute now the interviewer will enter the room. Joaquin says to himself, "I know I look awful. The three pounds I gained on vacation are hanging over the waistband of my pants. I'll probably say something really stupid. I'll never get a job. I'll have to move home and live, in utter humiliation, with my parents."

> *REMEMBER:* <u>Catastrophe</u> means "disaster." Catastrophizing is creating a mental disaster by thinking about the negative side of events or situations.

8. **Burnout** (also called gradual mental stress) occurs in some people as a response to a continual series of stressors. Burnout is characterized by an intensifying pattern of physical, psychological, and behavioral problems that are severe enough to interfere with normal day-to-day functioning. (p. 437)

> *Example:* After years as an emergency room doctor, Coralette seems detached from her friends. She is increasingly irritable, depressed, and impulsive. Although Coralette has always been reliable, she now often oversleeps and misses the beginning of her shift.

9. **Posttraumatic stress disorder** is a stress response to a traumatic experience characterized by anxiety, irritability, jumpiness, inability to concentrate or work productively, sexual dysfunction, emotional numbness, and difficulty getting along with others. (p. 438)

Example: After witnessing the murder of a close friend, Charles has recurring nightmares and trouble sleeping. Charles is uncharacteristically rude, nervous, and distracted at work.

10. A **social support network** is a group of friends or other social contacts who can be relied upon to help during stressful situations. (p. 440)

Example: Betty and Tess are sisters and best friends. Whenever they have a problem, they know they can count on each other or other family members to lend an ear or help in any way they can.

11. **Psychoneuroimmunology** is a field that studies the interaction between psychological and physiological processes that affect the body's ability to defend itself against disease. (p. 445)

12. The **immune system** defends the body against invading substances and microorganisms. It contains special cells that attack and kill invaders, such as viruses, bacteria, and cancer cells. (p. 445)

Example: The stressful semester left Miguel's immune system compromised. Miguel contracted mononucleosis and had to postpone his final exams until after the semester break.

13. **Health promotion** is the process of learning healthy behavior patterns and eliminating behaviors that increase the risk of illness. (p. 450)

14. **Cognitive restructuring** is a cognitive coping strategy. Changing or restructuring thoughts can help reduce either the stress or the stress reaction. (p. 453)

Example: Latifeh is a perfectionist. Whenever she has to give a presentation at work, she worries about every detail and every word she is going to say. This causes her to feel extremely anxious most of the time. Cognitive restructuring would entail changing her thoughts. Instead of expecting perfection at every presentation, she might say to herself, "I am going to do the best that I can, and my best is usually more than satisfactory."

REMEMBER: Cognition means "thought." Restructuring means "altering a form." Cognitive restructuring is altering the form of thoughts in order to remove a stressor or reduce a stress reaction.

15. **Biofeedback training**, a physical coping strategy, is a technique designed to help people learn to achieve a relaxed, stress-reduced state by providing them with feedback from their bodies. Feedback is produced with equipment that reads stress-affected physiological activity such as muscle tension, heart rate, and blood pressure. With practice, people can learn to reduce the bodily effects of stress. (p. 453)

16. **Progressive relaxation training**, a physical coping strategy, teaches an individual to relax voluntary muscles. This leads to heart rate and blood pressure reduction and creates mental and emotional calmness. (p. 454)

FILL-IN-THE-BLANKS KEY TERMS

This section will help you check your factual knowledge of the key terms introduced in this chapter. Fill in each blank with the appropriate term from the list of key terms above.

1. The term for the stress reaction pattern that includes the alarm reaction is _____.

2. _____ work to understand the psychological and behavioral processes associated with achieving and maintaining health.

3. Illnesses caused, in part, by stressors are called _____.

4. _____ is the process of adapting to circumstances that threaten to disrupt one's physical or psychological functioning.

5. A person who is stressed to the point of not being able to function at work could be experiencing _____.

6. A coping method in which one seeks to reduce heart rate and blood pressure by training voluntary muscles to relax is called _____.

7. _____ is a technique in which a person learns to relax through monitoring changes in his or her physiological state.

8. The _____ defends the body against invading substances and microorganisms.

9. Anyone who dwells on or overemphasizes the negative side or potential consequence of an event or situation is _____.

10. The physical, psychological, and behavioral reactions people display when stressors appear are called _____.

11. Changing the way one thinks about stressful situations is a coping strategy known as _____.

12. Your group of friends or other social contacts who can be relied upon to help during stressful situations are your _____.

13. The field that studies the interaction between psychological and physiological processes that affect the body's ability to defend itself against disease is _____.

14. _____ are situations or events that require adjustment.

15. After a devastating event, some people will experience a reaction characterized by lack of sleep, anxiety, irritability, and behavioral dysfunction called _____.

Total Correct (See answer key) _____

LEARNING OBJECTIVES

1. Define health psychology. List the objectives of health psychologists. (pp. 429–431)

2. Define stress, stressors, and stress reactions. Give examples of stressors. Be sure to include a catastrophic event, a life change or strain, chronic stress, and a daily hassle. (pp. 431–432)

3. Describe the Social Readjustment Rating Scale and the Life Experience Survey. Explain how they are used to measure stress. (pp. 432–433)

4. Define general adaptation syndrome. Describe the three stages in this syndrome, and discuss the physiological processes underlying it. Define disease of adaptation. (pp. 433–434)

5. Discuss the major criticisms of Selye's model. (pp. 434–435)

6. Describe some common emotional, cognitive, and behavioral stress responses. Explain how ruminative thinking, catastrophizing, mental sets, and functional fixedness are linked to stress. (pp. 435–437)

7. Define burnout and posttraumatic stress disorder, and describe the conditions that can lead to both. (pp. 437–438)

8. Explain why the appraisal of stressors, their predictability, and a feeling of control can reduce the impact of stressors. (pp. 438–440)

9. Discuss the role of coping resources and methods in combating stress. Give examples of problem-focused and emotion-focused coping strategies. (p. 440)

10. Describe the effects of social support networks on the impact of stressful events. (pp. 440–442)

11. Describe disease-resistant and disease-prone personalities. Define dispositional optimism. Discuss the quasi-experimental research on the relationship between personality and health. (pp. 442–445)

12. Define psychoneuroimmunology. (p. 445)

13. Describe the components of the immune system. Discuss the relationship among the immune system, the nervous system, the endocrine system, and stress. (pp. 445–447)

14. Define cynical hostility and outline the evidence relating hostility to heart disease. (pp. 447–449)

15. List the health-endangering behaviors described in your textbook. (pp. 449–450)

16. Define health promotion. Describe the four factors in Rosenstock's health-belief model. Explain the role of self-efficacy in altering behavioral health risks. (pp. 450–451)

17. Describe the five stages in changing behavioral health risks. (p. 451)

18. List the steps in a stress-coping program. Explain the importance of being able to recognize the difference between a changeable and a nonchangeable stressor. (pp. 451–453)

19. Describe cognitive coping strategies. Define cognitive restructuring. (p. 453)

20. Describe some emotional and behavioral coping strategies. (p. 453)

21. Describe physical coping strategies. Explain the possible problems of using drugs to alter stress or stress responses. Explain how biofeedback training and progressive relaxation training can help people cope. (pp. 453–454)

22. Describe programs that promote healthier lifestyles for people at risk of AIDS. (pp. 454–455)

CONCEPTS AND EXERCISES

No. 1: Recognizing Stressors

Completing this exercise should help you to achieve Learning Objectives 2, 3, and 8.

Following are several descriptions of people's daily lives. Underline all the stressors that you can find.

1. Michelle and Ned have been married for ten years and have two children. This morning Michelle got a run in her nylons just as she was on her way out the door to take the children to school. She was going to go up and change but remembered that she had to come back to the house anyway to pick up the dog for his veterinary appointment. When Michelle did get back home, she started cleaning the house, only to find that the vacuum cleaner was broken. Sighing, she decided to scrub the bathrooms instead. By the time Ned came home, she had a headache from the children screaming, the dog whimpering, having to face dirty floors yet again, and struggling with dinner for the family.

2. Lee is trying to finish writing a grant proposal in the hopes of getting funding. The deadline for submitting the grant is in one week. Lee must also face a new crisis of some sort daily at work. His wife is starting to complain that he never spends time with her. Recently, he has started to have dizzy spells and can feel his heart pounding.

3. Jenny is five years old. Today is the first day of first grade. Jenny is horrified because she has to sit next to the neighborhood bully. He is always ramming his tricycle into hers or grabbing her swing on the playground and pushing it too high into the air. Jenny is spending the entire day imagining what he will do now that he sits next to her in class.

4. Jerry has just met his new roommate and cannot believe his bad luck. His roommate has told him that he goes to bed at 8:00 P.M., wants to study in the room every night until 7:45 P.M., must have complete quiet while he studies, and has some great posters of Bambi to hang on the walls. Jerry wants to do well in school; he was first in his high school class and wants to keep his ranking in college, but he is also worried about his social life.

No. 2: Recognizing Stress Reactions

Completing this exercise should help you to achieve Learning Objectives 4, 6, 7, and 21.

Following are several descriptions of stress reactions. Choose the name of the reaction from the list after the descriptions.

1. Boris's doctor has told him that he has an elevated level of corticosteroids. _____

2. Rosa's mother tells her that she constantly makes a mountain out of a molehill. _____

3. Lois, recently divorced, has been working three jobs for the past year to support her children. She is tired, irritable, and depressed. Her bosses are concerned because the quality of her work has gradually decreased. _____

4. Nancy knows that her husband is drinking too much. His behavior bothers her so much that she has begun taking Valium daily. _____

   ° Burnout
   ° Physical coping strategy
   ° Behavioral coping strategy
   ° Catastrophizing
   ° Resistance stage of GAS

CRITICAL THINKING

Sam and Martina are at the gym working out. Pete, an ex-cop who retired from the force when he won the lottery, still works out with them. Pete was telling them stories about the people in his new, very expensive neighborhood.

Pete says, "So this lady down the street, her name is Jenny, dies last week. A buddy of mine checked the pathologist's report; she had a massive heart attack. It's too bad. She was really nice. She was a high-priced lawyer, and her husband stayed home to take care of the kids. Now he can afford to hire a new live-in nanny for each day of the week. I hear she was loaded and had a huge insurance policy. She had such a lousy life, though. Her husband, Jeff, treated her badly, even when he knew she had a heart condition."

Sam asks, "What do you mean, really badly?"

"Well," Pete responds, "the team that cleans my house, Martha and Ed, also cleaned hers. Martha used to tell me all these stories about what Jeff used to do."

"Like what?" asks Martina.

"The usual stuff. He was having affairs. She knew because she would find women's things in the house. But Martha said he also did little things to drive her nuts all the time. For example, he would steal the papers out of her briefcase when he knew she had a big court case the next day. Martha said she heard him call her office one day, and pretending to be drunk, he made up stories about how she mistreated the kids. He would ruin her favorite clothes or 'forget' to pick up her clothes from the dry cleaners. He actually called her up once and told her that one of the kids had died in an accident and then told her he was kidding. Martha said it had been going on for two years. The guy's a sicko."

Sam says, "Yeah, if she had to die, it's too bad he didn't kill her. We could have at least put him in jail."

Martina speaks up and says, "Maybe he did kill her."

Using the five critical thinking questions in your text, the clues in the story, and what you have just learned about stress, answer the following.

1. What is Sam's hypothesis?
2. What evidence supports Sam's hypothesis?
3. What is Martina's alternative hypothesis?
4. What evidence supports Martina's hypothesis?

PERSONAL LEARNING ACTIVITIES

1. Write down a list of the stressors you have experienced in the last week. Which was the most stressful for you? Next to each item write a label for the type of stressor—catastrophic event, life change or strain, chronic stressor, or daily hassle. (Learning Objective 2)

2. Recall the last time you experienced the alarm reaction stage of the general adaptation syndrome. What was the cause? How did your body respond? How did you manage to calm yourself? (Learning Objective 4)

3. Think of a stressful situation in which you might be likely to catastrophize. List positive, constructive comments you could make to yourself instead. (Learning Objectives 6 and 19)

4. Read through the list of stressors you wrote for Personal Learning Activity 1. How did you cope with the most stressful item on the list? Would your coping method be categorized as problem-focused or emotion-focused? (Learning Objective 9)

5. Describe some of your behaviors that are risks to, or good for, your health. For example, do you smoke or exercise regularly? Have you tried to change any of the health-related behaviors you listed? If so, at which of the five stages of readiness are you for each behavior? For example, if you recently began walking two miles a day, four days a week, you are in the action stage of readiness. If it's a behavior that you want to change, but you are at the contemplation stage, perhaps you could try making specific plans and take the first step toward change (preparation stage). (Learning Objectives 15, 16, and 17)

MULTIPLE-CHOICE QUESTIONS

SAMPLE QUIZ 1

1. Which of the following is true of stress measurement?
   a. Stressors always involve major life events.
   b. Major stressors have a greater impact than several minor stressors.
   c. Sometimes consistent daily hassles cause severe stress reactions.
   d. Only a combination of major and minor stressors causes a severe stress reaction.

2. Which of the following would *not* be considered a stressor?
   a. Taking a three-week vacation
   b. Planning a wedding reception for five-hundred guests
   c. Being able to hear the neighbor's baby cry
   d. All of the above are stressors.

3. The fight-or-flight syndrome is part of the _____ stage of the GAS.
   a. resistance
   b. alarm
   c. exhaustion
   d. adaptation

4. Mario has been working two jobs for the past year and is taking a full load of classes. Mario is tired, irritable, and depressed. His bosses and teachers are concerned because the quality of his work has gradually decreased. Which of the following is Mario most likely experiencing?
   a. a behavioral stress response
   b. burnout
   c. a disease of adaptation
   d. posttraumatic stress disorder

5. Overarousal can cause
   a. increased performance on nonpracticed tasks.
   b. thinking to become clear and less muddled.
   c. a reliance on mental sets.
   d. enhanced information processing.

6. Which of the following describes a person at the resistance stage of the general adaptation syndrome (GAS)?
   a. Abel feels fine, but has a high level of corticosteroids.
   b. Belle gets one head cold after another during an entire semester.
   c. Elle's muscles are tense, her heart rate is increasing, and she is breathing hard.
   d. Lee has an ulcer, but is treating it with prescription medicines.

7. Which of the following has been said of Selye's general adaptation syndrome?
   a. It underemphasizes the biological processes involved in stress response.
   b. It adequately explains the contribution of psychological factors in reactions to stress.

c. It overemphasizes the contribution of psychological factors in the determination of stress responses.

d. It overemphasizes the biological processes involved in stress responses.

8. Melissa and Randy both have mountains of work on their desks. Melissa rolls up her sleeves in eager anticipation. She knows the project in front of her will earn her a promotion. Randy cringes every time he walks into his office and surveys the mess. He can think only of how long it is going to take him to finish. Which of them will experience the most stress?
   a. Melissa, because she is worried about getting promoted
   b. Randy, because he interprets the work as a stressor
   c. Melissa, because women are more prone to stress than men
   d. Randy and Melissa, because they both experience an equally large amount of stress

9. Julie is feeling stress while completing a midterm exam. According to your text, which of the following would most likely reduce the amount of stress Julie is feeling?
   a. The teacher said the test would be true-false questions, but it is essay format.
   b. She thinks she is going to flunk the test.
   c. She knew that the test would be hard.
   d. She doesn't know anyone else in the class.

10. Badly managed problem-focused coping strategies include
    a. imagining a positive situation.
    b. trying to eliminate a stressor that can't be changed.
    c. accepting responsibility for the problem.
    d. both (a) and (c).

11. X, the proteinaceous immune system cell, has had quite the busy day. It has been speeding through the body's war zone attacking the foreign substances it has been assigned to and is initiating their inactivation. What kind of cell is X?
    a. Natural killer
    b. T-cell
    c. Macrophage
    d. Antibody

12. Cynical hostility is characterized by
    a. patience.
    b. low levels of aggression.
    c. distrust of others.
    d. very few emotional stress reactions.

13. According to your text, the most preventable risk factor for fatal illnesses in the United States is
    a. alcohol use.
    b. diet.
    c. smoking.
    d. unsafe sex.

14. Eduardo is learning a coping technique. His instructor has told him to alternate between tensing and relaxing his muscles. Which method is he learning?
    a. Biofeedback training
    b. A behavioral coping method
    c. Progressive relaxation training
    d. Stress reaction restructuring

15. The longitudinal quasi-experiment on the relationship between personality and health showed that participants who
    a. were impulsive were more likely to die from accidents.
    b. acted conscientiously were more likely to die of heart disease.
    c. ate more healthily were more likely to get divorced.
    d. stayed married were more likely to die young.

16. Doug is learning to recognize and influence his muscle tension, heart rate, and blood pressure. He is probably learning
    a. biofeedback training.
    b. behavioral coping skills.
    c. problem-focused coping skills.
    d. emotion-focused coping skills.

17. Willy is taking sedatives in order to reduce his stress reactions. His family is trying to convince him to use another coping method. What might their reason be?
    a. Chemical coping methods provide only temporary relief from stress.
    b. Chemical coping methods can lead to addiction.
    c. Chemical coping methods will not help Willy feel that he has control over the stressors in his life.
    d. All of the above

18. A good stress-management program includes
    a. systematic stress assessment.
    b. goal setting.
    c. effective plans for coping with stressors.
    d. all of the above.

19. Cognitive restructuring is a(n)
    a. emotional reaction to stress.

b. attempt to change stress-producing thought patterns.

c. plan to restructure the use of one's time.

d. process of systematic relaxation.

20. An example of a person using a behavioral coping strategy is
   a. Bette, who exercises daily.
   b. Liang, who uses time management to ensure work is completed.
   c. Pollyanna, who says to herself, "Everything will be fine."
   d. Winston, who uses meditation to reduce his need for cigarettes.

Total Correct (See answer key) _____

SAMPLE QUIZ 2

Use this quiz to reassess your learning after taking Quiz 1 and reviewing the chapter.

1. Andy has decided to switch careers. He used to be a lawyer but has decided to become an actor. Andy cannot wait to begin his new career. This is an illustration of what kind of situation commonly associated with stress?
   a. Major life change
   b. Catastrophic event
   c. Chronic stress
   d. Daily hassles

2. Glenda feels that she has had a rotten day. She got a run in her stocking before she left the house, slammed her finger in the car door, forgot to buy cat litter at the grocery store, and just missed a phone call from her boyfriend. Based on this information, what would be her score on the Social Readjustment Rating Scale?
   a. Low
   b. Moderate
   c. High
   d. Extremely high

3. Caitlin has just broken her mother's favorite vase. She says to herself, "Boy, is Mom going to be angry. She'll ground me for a month! I'll never get to meet that cute new guy at school, which means I won't get a date for the prom. People who don't go to the prom aren't cool—no guy is going to ask me out again. I'll never get married—I'll die without ever having loved." This is an example of

a. cognitive restructuring.

b. catastrophizing.

c. trauma.

d. fight or flight.

4. It is 2:00 A.M. and Aaron is lost in New York City with no money. His sympathetic nervous system has initiated the fight-or-flight syndrome. What stage of the general adaptation syndrome (GAS) is he in?
   a. Alarm
   b. Resistance
   c. Exhaustion
   d. The fight-or-flight syndrome is not part of the GAS.

5. Cortisol, which is released from the adrenal cortex,
   a. indirectly decreases the chance of developing arthritis.
   b. can damage heart and blood vessels.
   c. increases the responsiveness of the immune system.
   d. reduces activation of the sympathetic nervous system.

6. Shane, a veteran, occasionally has flashbacks that are recollections of his experiences in Vietnam. This is a symptom of
   a. generalized anxiety disorder.
   b. posttraumatic stress disorder.
   c. the general adaptation syndrome.
   d. the fight-or-flight syndrome.

7. Oscar has an ulcer and high blood pressure. Oscar is in the _____ stage of Selye's general adaptation syndrome (GAS).
   a. acceptance
   b. alarm reaction
   c. resistance
   d. exhaustion

8. When Dr. Crusher went to the computer to explore ideas about the causes of an epidemic, she suddenly could not think. She stared at the computer screen unable to formulate any ideas or even remember information about the illness. Dr. Crusher is experiencing a(n) _____ stress response.
   a. behavioral
   b. cognitive
   c. emotional
   d. problem-focused

9. Which of the following could reduce the impact of a stressor?
   a. Interpreting it as a threat
   b. Having a social support network
   c. Feeling an inability to control it
   d. All of the above

10. Behavioral stress responses include
    a. a change in facial expression.
    b. feeling nervous.
    c. ruminative thinking.
    d. sweating.

11. Which of the following would cause the least stress?
    a. Pop quizzes scheduled by the teacher
    b. Quizzes prescheduled by the students' unanimous vote
    c. Quizzes given every Friday
    d. One quiz per month at an unannounced time

12. Layton Sepor is the head of personnel at his company. He knows that the employees have very stressful jobs. One Friday each month he invites several employees who do not know one another to go to a local bar together from lunchtime until after dinner. Sepor has
    a. engaged his employees in cognitive restructuring.
    b. set up a social support network for his employees.
    c. provided his employees with a sense of control over their stress.
    d. all of the above.

13. _____ is the field that examines the interaction of psychological and physiological processes that affect the body's ability to defend itself against disease.
    a. Neurology
    b. Psychobiology
    c. Immunology
    d. Psychoneuroimmunology

14. John hasn't declared his major yet and feels like he has no time to think about it because he is overwhelmed by the workload of his general education courses. To cope with the stress and uncertainty, he begins a diary in which he writes quick notes about events, stress, and his reactions. According to your text, John will most likely _____ as a result of his _____.
    a. improve his immune system functioning; disclosure

    b. improve his immune system functioning; behavioral stress response
    c. have no effect on his immune system; cognitive stress response
    d. have no effect on his immune system; physical coping strategy

15. According to Rosenstock's health-belief model, which of the following would help Birgit quit smoking?
    a. Perceiving a personal threat from her smoking behavior
    b. Realizing that smoking can cause lung cancer
    c. Believing that if she quits, she won't get lung cancer
    d. All of the above

16. Dr. Porter studies immune system cells called leukocytes, which mature in the bone marrow and produce antibodies. What type of cell does Dr. Porter study?
    a. B-cell
    b. T-cell
    c. natural killer cell
    d. macrophage

17. The technique that helps people monitor and control stress-affected physiological activity is
    a. health promotion.
    b. problem-focused coping.
    c. biofeedback training.
    d. physiological restructuring.

18. Amanda loves chocolate chip cookies. She knows that they aren't healthy foods, and often thinks about limiting her intake of them or giving them up. However, Amanda has made no plans to change how often she eats them. Amanda is at the _____ stage of readiness.
    a. precontemplation
    b. contemplation
    c. preparation
    d. maintenance

19. Progressive relaxation training is a _____ coping method.
    a. cognitive
    b. behavioral
    c. physical
    d. chemical

20. Sayumi is attempting to change her lifestyle to reduce her health risks from her cynical hostility; therefore, Sayumi thinks to herself, "Don't jump to conclusions; they probably didn't mean it like it

sounded" instead of, "Those jerks! Who do they think they are?" Sayumi is trying the _____ coping strategy.
    a. cognitive restructuring
    b. emotional
    c. physical
    d. precontemplation

Total Correct (See answer key) _____

ANSWERS TO FILL-IN-THE-BLANKS KEY TERMS

1. general adaptation syndrome (p. 433)
2. Health psychologists (p. 429)
3. diseases of adaptation (p. 434)
4. Stress (p. 431)
5. burnout (p. 437)
6. progressive relaxation training (p. 454)
7. Biofeedback (p. 453)
8. immune system (p. 445)
9. catastrophizing (p. 436)
10. stress reactions (p. 431)
11. cognitive restructuring (p. 453)
12. social support network (p. 440)
13. psychoneuroimmunology (p. 445)
14. Stressors (p. 431)
15. posttraumatic stress disorder (p. 438)

ANSWERS TO CONCEPTS AND EXERCISES

No. 1: Recognizing Stressors (p. 431)

1. Got a run in her nylons, picking up dog for his veterinary appointment, vacuum cleaner broken, children screaming, dog whimpering, dirty floors, struggling with dinner.

2. Deadline, new crisis, wife starting to complain.

3. First day of first grade, sit next to the neighborhood bully, ramming his tricycle into hers, grabbing her swing, pushing it too high, imagining what he will do.

4. New roommate, he goes to bed at 8 P.M., wants to study in the room every night until 7:45 P.M., must have complete quiet, has some great posters of Bambi, wants to keep his ranking in college, worried about his social life.

No. 2: Recognizing Stress Reactions

1. *Resistance stage of GAS.* Elevated levels of corticosteroids are associated with the resistance stage of the GAS. During this stage a person may be unaware of the wear and tear their body is experiencing. (p. 434)

2. *Catastrophizing.* A person who makes a mountain out of a molehill is overemphasizing the negative consequences of an event. (p. 436)

3. *Burnout.* The stress caused by a divorce and working three jobs has led to burnout for Lois. Burnout causes people to become less reliable workers and to become withdrawn, depressed, or accident prone. (p. 437)

4. *Physical coping strategy.* Nancy is not making a logical response to her distress over her husband's use of a drug. Use of a drug is a physical coping strategy, but it can have extremely negative consequences. A person may become addicted to the drug and be unable to use other methods of coping. (p. 453)

ANSWERS TO CRITICAL THINKING

1. Sam's hypothesis is that Jenny died of a heart attack.

2. Sam is using the pathologist's report as evidence to support his hypothesis.

3. Martina hypothesizes that the husband, knowing his wife had a bad heart, behaved in ways that would expose her to very consistent and sometimes high levels of stress. Martina may think Jeff wants the insurance money all to himself.

4. Martina knows that ongoing little daily hassles can be just as stressful as major catastrophes. She also knows that consistent stress can lead to diseases of adaptation. The stress induced by Jenny's husband may have caused her health to deteriorate to the point of her having a heart attack. (*NOTE:* Critical thinking is a constant process of hypothesizing, examining evidence, rehypothesizing, and collecting more evidence. Martina may not be correct.)

ANSWERS TO MULTIPLE-CHOICE QUESTIONS

Circle the question numbers you answered correctly.

Sample Quiz 1

1. *c* is the answer. Often minor daily hassles have a larger impact than one or two major stressors. (p. 433)
   a. Major life events, either positive or negative, are stressful, but small daily hassles are also stressful.
   b. Sometimes the cumulative effect of small but consistent stressors is larger than the effect of one or two major stressors.
   d. Even minor stressors alone can add up to major stress reactions.

2. *d* is the answer. Positive life events (marriage), any type of change (vacation), and consistent daily hassles (listening to a baby cry) are all stressors. (p. 432)

3. *b* is the answer. (p. 433)
   a. Resistance is the second stage of the general adaptation syndrome.
   c. Exhaustion is the third stage of the general adaptation syndrome.
   d. There is no such thing as the adaptation stage.

4. *b* is the answer. Burnout is a response to chronic stress in which a person becomes more and more irritable, indifferent, and unreliable. (p. 437)
   a. Behavioral stress responses are changes in the way people look, act, or talk. Aggression, dropping out of school, and strained facial expressions are examples. Mario is experiencing burnout, which is a pattern of physical, psychological, and behavioral stress responses.
   c. A disease of adaptation is an illness that occurs in the exhaustion stage of the general adaptation syndrome.
   d. Posttraumatic stress disorder is also a combination of physical, psychological, and behavioral stress responses, but it happens after a catastrophic event.

5. *c* is the answer. Overarousal can reduce creative problem solving, thereby creating a tendency to rely on mental sets and well-rehearsed behaviors. (pp. 436–437)
   a. Overarousal decreases performance on nonpracticed tasks.
   b. Overarousal can cause thinking to become fuzzy.
   d. Overarousal can disrupt information processing.

6. *a* is the answer. During the resistance stage of the GAS, the symptoms of the alarm reaction subside, but the body's energy is being drained and the immune system compromised. (p. 434)
   b, d. These are diseases of adaptation indicative of the exhaustion stage of the GAS.
   c. Changes in heart rate, respiration, and muscle tension are part of the alarm reaction stage of the GAS.

7. *d* is the answer. (p. 434)
   a. Selye has been criticized for overemphasizing the role of biological factors in the determination of stress responses.
   b, c. People have commented that Selye did not focus on the role of psychological factors in the determination of stress responses.

8. *b* is the answer. The way that people interpret their stress affects the impact of their stressors. Randy is interpreting his work as a stressor instead of as an opportunity. Melissa is thinking of her work as a vehicle for furthering her career. (p. 439)
   a. Melissa sees her workload in a positive way, so she will not experience as much stress.
   c. Women are no more prone to stress than men are.
   d. Randy will experience more stress than Melissa.

9. *c* is the answer. If Julie knows the test will be hard, then she should be better able to deal with it. According to your text, stressors that are predictable have less impact than those that are unpredictable. (pp. 439–440)
   a. If Julie is surprised by the format of the test, she will most likely experience more stress.
   b. If Julie believes she will fail the test, she may feel more stress.
   d. If Julie doesn't know anyone in the class, she may receive less social support at the time of the test.

10. *b* is the answer. Trying to eliminate a stressor that can't be changed will probably produce even more stress than the original stressor. (p. 440)
    a. Imagining a positive situation is an emotion-focused coping skill.
    c. Accepting responsibility for the problem is an emotion-focused coping skill.
    d. *b* is the answer.

11. *d* is the answer. (p. 446)
    a. A natural killer cell is a type of leukocyte that is especially good at antiviral and antitumor functions.

b. A T-cell is a type of leukocyte that matures in the thymus gland.

c. Macrophages engulf foreign cells and digest them.

12. *c* is the answer. People who exhibit cynical hostility are suspicious, resentful, antagonistic, and distrustful of others. Cynical hostility is a risk factor in heart disease. (p. 447)

a, b. People with cynical hostility are unlikely to be patient and nonaggressive.

d. People who exhibit cynical hostility are frequently angry.

13. *c* is the answer. (p. 449)

a, d. Alcohol abuse and unsafe sex can also lead to major health problems, but neither of these is the most preventable risk factor.

b. Diet is important to health, but smoking, alcohol abuse, and unsafe sex are greater risks to health.

14. *c* is the answer. Progressive relaxation training is a physiological coping method in which people learn to completely relax their muscles, thus reducing heart rate and blood pressure. To learn this technique, people are told to alternately tense and relax their muscles in order to better recognize the feelings of relaxation. (p. 454)

a. Biofeedback training is also a physiological coping method. People are hooked up to machines that tell them about the physiological changes occurring in their bodies. Many people, once they recognize these changes, can learn to control them.

b. Behavioral coping methods might involve taking a time-management course. Progressive relaxation training is a physiological coping method.

d. There is no such method as stress reaction restructuring.

15. *a* is the answer. People who were impulsive or low on conscientiousness were more likely to die from accidents or violence. (pp. 443–444)

b, c, d. Those who were conscientious were more likely to stay married, eat healthily, and live longer.

16. *a* is the answer. (p. 453)

b, c, d. Doug is learning a physical coping skill. None of the other responses has to do with changing one's physiological reaction to stress.

17. *d* is the answer. Chemical methods of coping provide only temporary relief from stressors, they can be addictive, and they do not provide a sense of control over stressors. People attribute their enhanced sense of well-being to the drug instead of to their own behavior. (p. 453)

18. *d* is the answer. An effective stress-management program includes a systematic stress assessment. You have to know what the problem is before you can solve it. Setting goals helps you decide whether to eliminate the stressor or attempt to reduce the impact of that stressor. Finally, an effective plan must be made in order to deal with the stressors you face. (p. 452)

19. *b* is the answer. Cognitive restructuring involves substituting constructive thoughts for stressful, destructive thoughts. (p. 453)

a. Emotional stress reactions include frustration, anger, and depression.

c. Time management is important in reducing the stress caused by a tight schedule, but this coping method is behavioral, not cognitive.

d. Progressive relaxation is the physiological coping method in which people are taught to completely relax their bodies.

20. *b* is the answer. Time management is an example of a behavioral coping strategy. (p. 453)

a. Bette is engaging in a physical coping strategy.

c. Pollyanna is engaging in a cognitive coping strategy.

d. Winston is using a physical coping strategy.

Now turn to the quiz analysis table at the end of this chapter to find which areas you know well and which areas you need to work on. Circle the numbers in the table for items on Quiz 1 that you answered correctly.

ANSWERS TO MULTIPLE-CHOICE QUESTIONS

Circle the question numbers you answered correctly.

Sample Quiz 2

1. *a* is the answer. A career switch is a major life event filled with change. Even though Andy is happy, he will have to adjust to his new lifestyle. Changes require adjustment, which is stressful. (p. 432)

b. Catastrophic events are major and shocking physical or emotional events. Traumatic incidents such as assault and natural disasters fall under this category.

   c. Andy may eventually experience chronic stress as an actor, but we can't tell that from the story; all we are told is that he is changing careers.

   d. Andy, like most people, probably experiences daily hassles, but the story illustrates a major life change, not a daily hassle.

2. *a* is the answer. Glenda's day has been filled with small daily hassles. The Social Readjustment Rating Scale measures the stress resulting from *major* life events. Glenda's rating would be low. But remember that small daily hassles can be just as stressful in some cases as major life events. (pp. 432–433)

   b, c, d. The SRRS measures stress resulting from major life events. Glenda has not experienced a major life event, so she has a low score. However, she still has experienced stress.

3. *b* is the answer. Catastrophizing is an overemphasis of the negative consequences of an event. Although Caitlin has only broken a vase, she has inflated the negative consequences of that event until she thinks she will never get married. (p. 436)

   a. Cognitive restructuring is a cognitive coping method. Positive, constructive thoughts are substituted for negative, destructive thoughts.

   c. Trauma is a major and shocking physical or emotional experience. Breaking a vase is not.

   d. Fight or flight is a term associated with the alarm reaction of the GAS.

4. *a* is the answer. The fight-or-flight syndrome is associated with the alarm reaction of the general adaptation syndrome. (p. 433)

   b, c. The resistance and exhaustion stages of the GAS are not associated with the fight-or-flight syndrome.

   d. The fight-or-flight syndrome is part of the alarm reaction of the general adaptation syndrome.

5. *b* is the answer. High levels of cortisol are associated with increases in fatty substances that are deposited in arteries and that contribute to coronary heart disease. (p. 434)

   a, c. Cortisol suppresses the functioning of the immune system, thereby promoting illnesses like heart disease, high blood pressure, and arthritis.

   d. When the sympathetic nervous system is activated, it causes surges of cortisol and catecholamines. Cortisol does not reduce the activation of the sympathetic nervous system.

6. *b* is the answer. Posttraumatic stress disorder is a pattern of adverse and disruptive reactions following a traumatic event. In rare cases, flashbacks occur. (p. 438)

   a. Generalized anxiety disorder occurs when a person experiences constant emotional arousal with no identifiable cause.

   c. The general adaptation syndrome is a series of physiological adaptations to stress.

   d. The fight-or-flight syndrome is caused by an increase in adrenaline in response to a stressor. It prepares the body to either fight or flee.

7. *d* is the answer. Oscar's ulcer and high blood pressure are diseases of adaptation, according to the GAS. He is in the exhaustion stage. (p. 434)

   a. Acceptance is not one of the stages of the GAS.

   b. The alarm reaction stage is characterized by the fight-or-flight response.

   c. Resistance is the stage in which a person isn't feeling physical symptoms of stress. The body's energy is being drained and levels of cortisol are high.

8. *b* is the answer. (p. 436)

   a. Behavioral stress responses are changes in appearance such as shakiness or aggressive actions.

   c. Emotional stress responses are changes in emotional state such as fear, anger, irritability, and so on.

   d. You may have been thinking of problem-focused coping; it is not a stress response, but an emphasis on changing or getting rid of a stressor.

9. *b* is the answer. The existence of a social support network can reduce the impact of a stressor. (pp. 439–441)

   a. Perceiving a stressor as a threat increases the negative impact of a stressor.

   c. People who believe that they have the ability to control stressors generally experience less stress, even if they cannot control the stressor.

   d. Only *b* is the answer.

10. *a* is the answer. Facial expressions, shaking hands, and stuttering are examples of behavioral stress responses. (p. 437)

   b. Feeling nervous is an emotional stress response.

   c. Ruminative thinking is a cognitive stress response.

   d. Sweating is a physical stress response.

11. *b* is the answer. When one can predict and control the presence of a stressor, the impact of that stressor is usually reduced. To students, being able to control and predict the occurrence of a quiz is much less stressful than any of the other alternatives. (pp. 439–440)
   a. Pop quizzes are not predictable and are therefore more stressful.
   c. Even though quizzes given every Friday are predictable, students have no control over the scheduling of such quizzes.
   d. One unannounced quiz per month is neither predictable nor controllable.

12. *b* is the answer. By arranging for employees to get together and socialize, Sepor has created the potential for a social support network at work. (pp. 440–441)
   a. Cognitive restructuring involves substituting constructive thoughts for negative, debilitating thoughts.
   c. Sepor has not been able to give employees a sense of control over the stressful events at work. But he has provided employees with the beginnings of a social support network.
   d. *b* is the answer.

13. *d* is the answer. Psychoneuroimmunology is the study of the interaction of psychological and physiological processes that affect the body's ability to defend itself against disease. (p. 445)
   a. Neurology is the study of the nervous system.
   b. Psychobiology is the study of the biological factors that underlie mental processes and behavior.
   c. Immunology is the study of the physiological processes that affect the body's ability to defend itself against disease.

14. *a* is the answer. Disclosure, even anonymously, was shown to improve immune system functioning. (p. 447)
   b. John is expressing pent-up thoughts and feelings, which is disclosure. A behavioral stress response is a reaction like aggression, alcohol abuse, or avoidance of the stressful situation.
   c, d. John is disclosing and it is likely to have a positive effect on his immune system.

15. *d* is the answer. (pp. 450–451)

16. *a* is the answer. B-cells are leukocytes formed and matured in the bone marrow. (p. 446)

   b. T-cells are also leukocytes, but they mature in the thymus and kill other cells.
   c. Natural killer cells are leukocytes with anti-tumor and antiviral effects.
   d. Macrophages surround and digest foreign cells.

17. *c* is the answer. (p. 453)
   a. Health promotion is the process of learning health-giving behavior patterns and eliminating behaviors that increase the risk of illness.
   b. Problem-focused coping attempts to change a stressor, not a stress response.
   d. There is no such thing as physiological restructuring. (You may be thinking of cognitive restructuring.)

18. *b* is the answer. Being aware of a problem behavior and thinking of changing are part of the contemplation stage of readiness. (p. 451)
   a. Precontemplation is the stage when a person does not perceive a problem and isn't considering change.
   c. Preparation involves making plans.
   d. Maintenance occurs after a person has successfully made a behavior change and kept it up for more than a few months.

19. *c* is the answer. Progressive relaxation is a technique used to relax the muscles, leading to reduced heart rate and blood pressure. (p. 454)
   a. Cognitive coping methods include cognitive restructuring.
   b. Behavioral coping methods include time-management improvements.
   d. Chemical coping methods fall under the physical coping strategy category and include the use of sedatives.

20. *a* is the answer. Sayumi is replacing unconstructive thoughts with more constructive ones. (p. 453)
   b. Social support is an example of an emotional coping strategy.
   c. Physical coping strategies change bodily processes through drugs, exercise, meditation, and other means.
   d. Precontemplation is a stage of readiness, not a coping strategy.

Now turn to the quiz analysis table at the end of this chapter to find which areas you know well and which areas you need to work on. Circle the numbers in the table for items on Quiz 2 that you answered correctly.

For each question you answered correctly, circle its number. (Quiz 1 numbers are not shaded; Quiz 2 numbers are shaded.) Are there patterns in the types of questions or the topics you got wrong that could direct your further study? Did you improve from Quiz 1 to Quiz 2?

TOPIC	TYPE OF QUESTION		
	DEFINITION	COMPREHENSION	APPLICATION
Understanding Stress			
Stressors		1	2
			1, 2
Responses	3	5, 7	4, 6
		5, 10	3, 4, 6, 7, 8
Mediators		10, 15	8, 9
		9	11, 12
Physiology and Psychology of Health and Illness			
Immune system		11	
	13	16	14
Heart disease	12		
Risks		13	
Promoting healthy behavior	19	18	14, 16, 17, 20
	17	19	15, 18, 20

TOTAL CORRECT BY QUIZ:

QUIZ 1:

QUIZ 2:

Chapter 14

Personality

Personality is the pattern of enduring psychological and behavioral characteristics by which each person can be compared and contrasted with other people.

OUTLINE

I. THE PSYCHODYNAMIC APPROACH (pp. 460–464)

The psychodynamic approach, developed by Freud, emphasizes the interplay of unconscious psychological processes in determining human thought, feelings, and behavior. The basis of this approach is psychic determinism, the idea that psychological factors play a major role in determining behavior and shaping personality.

A. The Structure and Development of Personality

According to Freud, personality develops out of each person's struggle to satisfy needs for food, water, air, sex, and aggression. Personality is reflected in how each person goes about satisfying these needs.

1. *Id, Ego, and Superego*. Personality is composed of three structures: the id, the ego, and the superego. The id, which operates according to the pleasure principle, contains the life instincts, called Eros, and death instincts, called Thanatos. Libido, or psychic energy, is a product of the life instincts. The ego, which operates according to the reality principle, attempts to satisfy id impulses while obeying society's rules. As we internalize parents' and society's rules, the superego forms to tell us right from wrong.

2. *Conflicts and Defenses*. The ego uses defense mechanisms to protect the individual from feeling anxious about id impulses. (See Table 14.1 for a list of defense mechanisms.)

3. *Stages in Personality Development*. Freud believed that personality develops in psychosexual stages; in each stage a part of the body becomes the child's main source of pleasure. Failure to resolve conflicts at any stage can cause fixation, an unconscious preoccupation with the pleasure area associated with that stage. Personality characteristics are a reflection of each person's fixation(s).

° The oral stage occurs during the first year of life because the mouth is the center of pleasure. The anal stage occurs during the second year when toilet training begins. The ego evolves during this stage as the child vacillates between id impulses (defecation at will) and parental demands (only on the toilet). The phallic stage emerges at three and lasts until age five. The boy experiences the Oedipus complex; he sexually desires his mother and wants to kill his father out of jealousy. The girl develops penis envy and begins to hate her mother for not providing a penis. The girl then transfers her love to her father, which is known as the Electra complex. After age five, the latency period ensues, during which sexual impulses lie dormant. During the genital stage, which begins at adolescence and lasts until death, sexual desires reappear.

B. Variations on Freudian Personality Theory

1. *Adler's Individual Psychology*. According to Adler, people strive for superiority in order to become fulfilled as persons (not to be better than others). The manner in which each person attempts to reach personal and social fulfillment constitutes personality. Adler thought that personality was directed by guiding fictions as opposed to the unconscious.

2. *Jung's Analytic Psychology*. Jung viewed the libido as a general life force that included a productive blending of basic impulses and real-world demands, of creativity and growth-oriented resolution of conflicts. Personality develops as the person tends toward introversion or extraversion and toward reliance on specific psychological functions (such as thinking versus feeling or vice versa).

3. *Other Neo-Freudian Theorists*. Several neo-Freudians, including Erik Erikson, Erich Fromm, and Henry Stack Sullivan, proposed that personality was determined by how social needs were met. Karen Horney proposed that the inferiority that women may feel is caused by restrictions imposed by men, not

penis envy, and that it is actually men who feel inferior when they experience womb envy.

C. Contemporary Psychodynamic Theories

Object relations theorists believe that the early relationships between infants and significant objects (such as primary caregivers) shape personality.

D. Evaluation of the Psychodynamic Approach

° Freud developed one of the most influential personality theories ever proposed; his ideas shaped Western thinking from medicine to religion. Psychodynamic therapies introduced the use of personality assessments, including projective tests.

° Freud's theory is criticized for being based on an unrepresentative sample: his own patients, who were predominantly upper-class Viennese women with mental problems. Freud never examined patients from, or his theory with regards to, other cultures.

° Freudian scholars acknowledge that Freud may have modified reports of therapy to fit his theory and that he may have asked leading questions during therapy. Finally, his belief that humans are driven mainly by instincts and the unconscious ignores the role of conscious drives and learning as important behavior determinants.

II. THE TRAIT APPROACH (pp. 464–471)

The trait approach has three basic assumptions: personality traits are relatively stable and therefore predictable, personality traits are consistent in diverse situations, and each person has a different set or degree of particular traits. The trait approach views personality as the combination of stable internal characteristics that people display consistently across time and across situations.

A. Traits vs. Types

Hippocrates suggested that a temperament, or personality type, is associated with a bodily fluid: blood, phlegm, black bile, or yellow bile. Physiognomy is the study of the relationship between personality type and physique type. However, research has shown that personalities are much too varied to fit into type theories.

B. Prominent Trait Theories

Personality can be seen as the combination of varying strengths of many qualities or traits.

1. *Allport's Trait Theory*. Gordon Allport believed that there are usually about seven basic or central traits. Secondary traits are more specific to certain situations and have less control over behavior.

2. *Cattell's Factor-Analytic Approach*. Using a statistical technique called factor analysis, which identifies traits that are correlated to each other, Raymond Cattell identified sixteen personality factors including shy vs. bold, trusting vs. suspicious, and relaxed vs. tense. Cattell measured the strength of these common traits through the Sixteen Personality Factor Questionnaire, or 16PF.

3. *Eysenck's Biological Trait Theory*. Hans Eysenck also utilized factor analysis to identify three basic personality factors: psychoticism, introversion-extraversion, and emotionality-stability (also often termed neuroticism). Eysenck proposed that the ease with which the nervous system can be aroused relates to positions on these personality dimensions.

C. The "Big Five" Model of Personality

More recently, trait theorists have identified five cross-cultural factors (big five or five-factor model)—Openness, Conscientiousness, Extraversion, Agreeableness, and Neuroticism—that make up personality. The big five model is supported by both Western culture and cross-cultural research.

D. Thinking Critically: Are Personality Traits Inherited?

What am I being asked to believe or accept?
Core aspects of personality may be partly inherited.

What evidence is available to support the assertion?
Data from studies of twins and adoptive children show genetic basis for general predisposition and a few traits, including activity level, sociability, anxiety, and emotionality. An estimated 30 to 60 percent of variability in personality traits is due to genetics.

Are there alternative ways of interpreting the evidence?
A child's similarities to a parent could be due to social influence. For example, the child could model the parent and siblings. Other factors, such as birth order, accidents, and illness, could have an impact on personality.

What additional evidence would help to evaluate the alternatives?
Psychologists have studied infants, a time period in which the environment hasn't yet had a chance to have an impact, and have found differences in temperament. This suggests biological and genetic influences. Studies examining adopted children have also supported the role of

biology and genetics in the formation of personality. However, more research is needed.

What conclusions are most reasonable?
The evidence does suggest that genetic influences have a significant impact on personality. However, genetic makeup probably provides only a predisposition toward certain levels of activity, emotionality, and sociability. These factors then interact with the environment to produce specific personality features.

E. Evaluation of the Trait Approach

Trait theories are better at describing behavior than at explaining it. Also, trait theories do not create a unique description of every individual. Nor can they reflect changes in a person's behavior in different environments or situations.

III. THE COGNITIVE-BEHAVIORAL APPROACH (pp. 471–475)

The cognitive-behavioral approach to personality, sometimes called the social-learning approach, equates personality with behavior. Some theorists rely solely on operant and classical conditioning for explanations of behavior. Others believe that learned thought patterns play a role in behavior and that personality is learned in social situations.

A. Roots of the Cognitive-Behavioral Approach

B. F. Skinner employed functional analysis to understand behavior in terms of its function in obtaining rewards or avoiding punishment.

B. Prominent Cognitive-Behavioral Theories

1. *Rotter's Expectancy Theory.* Julian Rotter suggested that behavior is determined by cognitive expectation—that is, what a person expects to happen following behavior and the value the person places on the outcome. Rotter developed a test that measures the degree to which people expect events to be controlled by their own internal efforts or by external forces over which they have no influence.

2. *Bandura and Reciprocal Determinism.* Personality evolves as a result of the interaction among cognitive patterns, the environment, and behavior through a process called reciprocal determinism. For example, Albert Bandura concludes that people's beliefs about the impact they have on the world and their self-efficacy (belief they will succeed) will determine emotions and behaviors.

3. *Mischel's Person-Situation Theory.* According to Walter Mischel, person variables as well as situation variables are important in explaining behavior. The most important person variables are competencies, perceptions, expectations, subjective values, and self-regulation and plans.

° Mischel's views sparked a debate that led to several conclusions (note the similarity to reciprocal determinism). First, traits influence behavior only in relevant situations. Second, traits can lead to behaviors that alter situations that, in turn, promote other behaviors. Third, people with different traits choose to be in different situations. Fourth, traits are more influential in some situations than in others.

C. Evaluation of the Cognitive-Behavioral Approach

In its favor, this approach is objective, experimentally oriented, defined by operational concepts, and based on empirical data. However, some psychologists think that behaviorists' narrow focus on behavior, the environment, and even cognitive factors still ignores other potential influences on behavior (subjective experiences, genetic and physiological factors).

IV. THE PHENOMENOLOGICAL APPROACH (pp. 475–478)

The phenomenological, or humanistic, approach defines personality as the unique way in which each individual perceives and interprets the world. The primary human motivator is an innate drive toward growth that prompts people to fulfill their unique and natural potential.

A. Prominent Phenomenological Theories

1. *Rogers' Self Theory.* Carl Rogers emphasized the concept of self-actualization, the innate tendency toward growth that motives all human behavior. The self is what people come to identify as I or me. According to Rogers, the development of self-concept depends on self-evaluations and the positive regard shown by others. Incongruities between self-evaluations and others' evaluations cause anxiety and other problems. Whenever people, instead of their behaviors, are evaluated, conditions of worth are created. People come to believe that they are worthy only under certain conditions—those in which rewarded behaviors are displayed.

2. *Maslow's Humanistic Psychology.* Abraham Maslow saw personality as the tendency to grow toward self-actualization. People can approach the

satisfaction of their needs with a deficiency orientation or growth orientation.

B. Evaluation of the Phenomenological Approach

The phenomenological approach has been instrumental in the development of many types of psychotherapy, short-term group experiences (such as encounter groups), and child-rearing practices. However, the belief that all humans are driven by a positive and innate growth potential may be naive. Also, this approach ignores potential genetic, biological, learning, social, and unconscious motivational influences on personality. Most phenomenological assessment methods are better at describing behavior than explaining it. Also, many phenomenological concepts are difficult to scientifically measure and define. The phenomenological approach is culturally confined to North America and other Western cultures. The definition of self is very different in Japan, Africa, and other parts of the world.

V. LINKAGES: PERSONALITY, CULTURE, AND HUMAN DEVELOPMENT (pp. 478–480)

Recognition of the role of cultural factors in establishing ideals of personality development requires that various approaches to personality and to the achievement of self-esteem be evaluated in terms of the extent to which they apply to cultures different from the one in which they were developed. Gender-role differences must also be considered.

VI. FOCUS ON RESEARCH METHODS: LONGITUDINAL STUDIES OF PERSONALITY (pp. 480–481)

Continuity from childhood to adulthood was noted for ill-temperedness in approximately 180 participants who were studied from 1928 to 1971. Men who were ill-tempered as children tended to have lower-status jobs and were more likely to lose their jobs and to be divorced than men who were not ill-tempered as children. Women who were ill-tempered as children tended to marry men with lower-status occupations and were more likely to be divorced.

VII. ASSESSING PERSONALITY (pp. 481–486)

Aspects of behavior can be assessed by observational methods, interviews, and personality tests. Personality tests are more standardized and economical than either observations or interviews. A test must be reliable and valid.

A. Objective Tests

The typical objective test is a paper-and-pencil form containing clear, specific questions, statements, or concepts to which a person is asked to give yes-no, true-false, or multiple-choice answers. Scores can be compared mathematically. A widely used test for diagnosing disorders is the Minnesota Multiphasic Personality Inventory (MMPI). The Neuroticism Extraversion Openness Personality Inventory, Revised (NEO-PI-R) is given to measure personality variables in normal populations.

B. Projective Tests

Tests consisting of unstructured stimuli that can be perceived and responded to in many ways are called projective tests. The Thematic Apperception Test (TAT) and the Rorschach Inkblot Test are examples of this format. Responses to projective tests reflect many aspects of an individual's personality. These tests are relatively difficult to score and tend to be less reliable and valid than objective tests.

C. Personality Tests and Employee Selection

Personality tests do seem to be useful in screening prospective employees; however, the tests can lead to incorrect predictions. Some employees believe that utilizing personality tests in the selection process is a violation of their privacy.

KEY TERMS

1. **Personality** is the unique pattern of enduring psychological and behavioral characteristics by which each person can be compared and contrasted to others. (p. 458)

   REMEMBER: Those who study personality are interested in what makes each person unique.

2. The **psychodynamic approach** to personality, developed by Freud, emphasizes the role of unconscious mental processes in determining thoughts, feelings, and behavior. (p. 460)

   REMEMBER: Freud introduced the idea that psychological activity plays a major role in behavior, mental processes, and personality. Psych refers to "mental," and dynamic pertains to "energy," "motion," and "forcefulness." Psychological factors have energy and play a forceful role in the determination of personality, behavior, and mental processes.

3. The **id**, one of the structures of personality, contains the basic instincts, desires, and impulses with which

people are born. It operates on the pleasure principle. Eros is the instinct for pleasure and sex. Thanatos is the death instinct, which can motivate aggressive and destructive behavior. The id seeks immediate gratification, regardless of society's rules or the rights and feelings of others. (p. 460)

Example: Freud might say that an infant cries whenever hungry, wet, bored, or frustrated because the infant's id wants instant fulfillment of every wish.

4. **Libido** is the unconscious psychic energy that is contained in the id. (p. 460)

5. The **pleasure principle** is the operating principle by which the wants and desires of the id push people to do whatever feels good. (p. 460)

REMEMBER: The id operates on the pleasure principle, guiding people to do whatever gives them pleasure.

6. The **ego** evolves from the id and attempts to satisfy the id's demands without breaking society's rules. The ego operates according to the reality principle. (p. 460)

Example: Suppose Thanatos (part of the id) creates a desire to cut people with knives. The ego would consider society's rules and laws about this type of activity, which say that cutting other people is wrong. But a person can become a surgeon and cut people on a daily basis. Being a physician who cuts people does not violate society's rules and may symbolically satisfy the id's demands.

7. The **reality principle** is the operating principle of the ego because the ego must find compromises between irrational id impulses and the demands of the real world. (p. 460)

Example: Naomi's id wants her to eat an entire plate of donuts, but the ego suggests a more moderate response, which may partially satisfy the id. Naomi decides to have one donut (or two).

8. The **superego** is formed from internalized values and dictates what people should do (the ego ideal) and what people should not do (the conscience). The superego can be thought of as operating on the morality principle. (p. 460)

Example: Suppose you are a small child in a candy store. Your id is "screaming" for candy. The conscience (part of the superego) is saying, "You know it is wrong to steal candy." The ego decides that the best way to handle this dilemma is for you to go

home and ask your mother for your allowance. Then you can go back and buy the candy, satisfying both the id and the superego.

9. **Defense mechanisms** are unconscious psychological and behavioral tactics that help protect a person from anxiety by preventing conscious awareness of unacceptable id impulses and other unconscious material. (p. 460)

Example: Jansen has a new baby brother whom he dislikes for taking away his parents' attention. Jansen would be very upset about his intense dislike of his sibling if he were consciously aware of it; therefore, his ego employs a defense mechanism, reaction formation, to push the negative feelings into the unconscious. Now Jansen is overly attentive and affectionate with his brother.

10. The **psychosexual stages** of development are part of Freud's psychodynamic theory of personality. Each stage is distinguished by the part of the body from which a person derives dominant pleasure. The five stages are, in their respective order, oral, anal, phallic, latent, and genital. Failure to resolve the problems that occur during the oral, anal, or phallic stages can lead to fixation. (p. 461)

11. The **oral stage** occurs during the first year of life, when the child derives pleasure from the mouth. If a child is weaned too early or too late, problems that can lead to fixation may arise. (p. 461)

Example: Bill was weaned too early, thus depriving him of pleasure during the oral stage of personality development. As an adult, he talks quite a bit, is a heavy smoker, and loves to eat.

12. The **anal stage** occurs during the second year of life, when pleasure is derived from the anal area. If toilet training is too demanding or is begun too early or too late, problems that can lead to fixation may arise. (p. 461)

Example: Art was toilet trained at a very young age and is fixated at the anal stage. As an adult, he is very neat, orderly, and extremely organized.

13. The **phallic stage** occurs from three to five years of age, when pleasure is derived from the genital area. During this stage, boys experience the Oedipus complex and girls experience the Electra complex. A fixation at the phallic stage could lead to problems with authority or difficulties maintaining love relationships. (p. 461)

Example: Eve hasn't had a long-term romantic relationship, because she finds fault with each person she dates. Although Eve doesn't realize it, she wants people to match her unreasonably high expectations and becomes irritated when they don't.

14. The **Oedipus complex** is a constellation of impulses that occur during the phallic stage. A boy's id impulses involve sexual desire for the mother and a desire to eliminate the father, with whom the boy must compete for the mother's affection. However, the fear of retaliation causes boys to identify with their fathers and acquire male gender-role behaviors. (p. 461)

15. The **Electra complex** occurs during the phallic stage when girls experience penis envy and transfer their love from their mothers to their fathers. To resolve this stage, girls identify with their mothers and acquire female gender-role behaviors. (p. 462)

16. The **latency period** occurs after the phallic stage and lasts until puberty. Sexual impulses lie dormant during the latency period. (p. 462)

Example: Will is excited about playing soccer on his grade school team and works hard to do his homework well and on time.

17. The **genital stage** occurs from puberty onward. The genitals are once again the primary source of sexual pleasure. The satisfaction obtained during this stage is dependent upon the resolution of conflicts experienced in the earlier stages. (p. 462)

Example: Penny began college this year and has made many new friends. Although she is not sexually active, Penny believes that her current romantic relationship is secure enough that it may eventually lead to a sexual relationship.

18. The **trait approach** views personality as a unique combination of dispositions or tendencies to think and behave in certain ways. The three basic assumptions of this approach are that dispositions are stable and consistent over time, that the tendency to think and behave in certain ways is consistent in diverse situations, and that each person has a unique combination of dispositions. (p. 465)

Example: When people say that their friend is sociable, understanding, and generous, they are using the trait approach to describing personality.

19. The **big five** (or five-factor model) are the five factors that trait theorists believe best define the basic organization of personality. These factors are neuroticism, extraversion, openness, agreeableness, and conscientiousness. (p. 468)

20. The **cognitive-behavioral approach** views personality as the array of behaviors that a person acquires through learning. Also important are the roles of learned thought patterns and the influence of social situations. (p. 471)

Example: Devorah explains that her friend has learned to be obnoxious at parties. Devorah believes they could shape her friend's behavior to be less obnoxious by rewarding her for more appropriate behavior.

21. The **functional analysis of behavior** was employed by Skinner to better understand behavior. Skinner wanted to know how behavior is <u>functional</u> in obtaining rewards and avoiding punishment. (p. 472)

Example: Brian, a seventeen-year-old, usually ends up denting or slightly damaging the family car whenever he drives it. Skinner would look for environmental consistencies every time this behavior appeared. As it turns out, Brian only takes the car when his usually inattentive father has gone out of town on business. When the father returns, he always spends time talking with Brian about his irresponsible behavior. Skinner might suggest that his father's attention is so reinforcing that Brian will even ruin the car to get it.

22. **Self-efficacy**, a term used by Bandura, is the expectation of success in a given situation. These cognitive expectations may play a major role in determining behavior in that situation. (p. 473)

Example: Jessica has low self-efficacy in interviewing situations and expects to do poorly. She can never think of answers to questions or creative solutions to the problems posed by the interviewer. Sandra, in contrast, has high self-efficacy in interviewing situations. Because she expects to do well, she is confident and approachable. Interviewers enjoy talking with Sandra because she is enthusiastic and energetic. The interviewers' responses further enhance Sandra's self-efficacy.

23. The **phenomenological approach** (also called the humanistic approach) to personality focuses on the individual's unique perception, interpretation, and experience of reality. Phenomenological theorists assume that humans have an innate drive to grow and to fulfill their own unique potentials. (p. 475)

Example: Perry tells the jury that his client did not take her ill daughter, Sarah, to the hospital because she firmly believed that prayer would heal her and that taking Sarah to the hospital would show that she had no faith. In his summation, Perry argues that his client perceived that western medicine would not cure Sarah and might cause her death, because prayers from nonbelievers are not answered. Perry took a phenomenological approach to explain that his client's view of reality influenced her behavior.

24. **Self-actualization** is an innate tendency toward realizing ones's potential. This concept is important in many phenomenological personality theories. If growth toward self-actualization is not impeded, a person will tend to be happy and comfortable. (p. 476)

> *Example:* Adam wanted to be a nurse ever since kindergarten, when his younger sister was sick. In his nursing classes, Adam feels a sense of accomplishment and of motivation to learn more.

25. **Self-concept** is the way one thinks about oneself. It is influenced by self-actualizing tendencies and others' evaluations. (p. 476)

> *Example:* Lucy loves to bake in her play oven. Her whole family raves over how tasty her creations are, although Lucy's apple pie was a little chewy. Now Lucy thinks that she's a fine baker and a nice person for treating her family to new desserts every day.

26. **Conditions of worth** are the beliefs that a person's worth depends on displaying the "right" attitudes, behaviors, and values. These conditions are created whenever people, instead of their behaviors, are evaluated. (p. 476)

> *Example:* Bruce sat on the desk folding all the papers into little squares, thinking that his mom would think it looked very neat. "No! Bad boy! Get down from there this instant!" yells Bruce's mom. Suddenly, he doesn't feel like his ideas are good ones. If this happens often enough, Bruce might come to believe that he is a bad person.

27. A **growth orientation** occurs when people focus on deriving satisfaction from what they have. (p. 477)

> *Example:* Pedro is a developmental psychologist. He does not get paid as much as some people, but he loves his research. He also has a supportive family and a few very close friends. Pedro concentrates most of his effort on working and on enjoying his family to the fullest. He does not worry about what he cannot have. Instead, he derives a great deal of pleasure—indeed, joy—from what he does have.

28. A **deficiency orientation** occurs when people are preoccupied with meeting needs for what they do not have. In other words, people focus on what is missing from their lives instead of what they have. (p. 477)

> *Example:* Jacqueline is the chief executive officer of a major corporation. She has a beautiful house, a membership in the "right" country club, and a large salary. However, instead of being satisfied, Jacqueline is constantly worrying about what she does not have enough money to buy.

29. **Objective tests**, one type of personality test, are paper-and-pencil tests containing clear, specific questions, statements, or concepts to which a person writes responses. (p. 482)

> *Example:* The multiple choice tests that you take in your classes are called objective tests because they can be graded objectively. Your score on an objective test can be compared mathematically with other students' scores.
>
> *REMEMBER:* Objective tests are scored objectively. The scorer has a key that shows how to assign scores, rather than each scorer choosing a way of interpreting responses.

30. **Projective tests** are composed of unstructured stimuli that can be perceived and responded to in many ways. People who use these kinds of tests assume that responses will reflect aspects of personality. It is relatively difficult to transform these tests' responses into numerical scores. (p. 484)

> *Example:* The TAT is a projective test that involves showing people pictures and asking them to tell a story about each picture.

FILL-IN-THE-BLANKS KEY TERMS

This section will help you check your factual knowledge of the key terms introduced in this chapter. Fill in each blank with the appropriate term from the list of key terms above.

1. _____ personality tests are written tests that contain clear, specific questions.

2. According to Freud, the _____ stage occurs during the second year of life, when children go through toilet training.

3. According to Freud, the basic instincts, desires, and impulses with which people are born are contained in the _____.

4. According to the psychodynamic approach, the _____ is the part of the personality that contains the conscience and that seeks to have the person behave in ways that are acceptable in society.

5. In psychodynamic theory, the ego seeks to meet the desires of the id by carefully balancing those desires with situations in the real world. This is called the _____ principle.

6. The _____ model of personality suggests that personality is based on five traits: neuroticism, extraversion, openness, agreeableness, and conscientiousness.

7. The psychoanalytical stage associated with dormant sexual impulses is called the _____ stage.

8. The _____ approach proposes that personality is a set of behaviors that a person acquires through learning.

9. People who, regardless of their success, focus on what they don't have follow a _____.

10. The phenomenological belief that all people are innately motivated to achieve their fullest potential is called _____.

11. The _____ approach views personality as a unique combination of dispositions.

12. The focus of the _____ approach is on the person's unique view of self and world.

13. Tests of personality that contain ambiguous stimuli that allow the test taker to respond in many different ways are called _____.

14. _____ is a phenomenological concept that describes people who derive satisfaction in life by focusing on enjoying the situations they are in and the possessions they have.

15. Rogers defined the term _____ as the way in which one thinks about oneself.

Total Correct (See answer key) _____

LEARNING OBJECTIVES

1. Define personality. (p. 458)

2. Describe the assumptions of Freud's psychodynamic approach to personality. (p. 460)

3. Define and describe the nature and function of the id, ego, and superego. Define libido, the pleasure principle, and the reality principle. (p. 460)

4. Define defense mechanism. Explain the purpose and give examples of defense mechanisms. (p. 460)

5. Name, define, and describe the psychosexual stages of personality development. Compare and contrast the Oedipus and Electra complexes. (p. 461)

6. Compare and contrast Adler's, Jung's, and the neo-Freudians' approaches to personality. (p. 462)

7. Define object relations. Describe contemporary psychodynamic theory's emphasis on object relations to help explain personality development. (p. 463)

8. Describe some applications and criticisms of the psychodynamic approach to personality. (pp. 463–464)

9. Describe the three basic assumptions of the trait approach to personality. (p. 464)

10. Distinguish between a trait and a type. (p. 465)

11. Compare and contrast Allport's trait theory, Cattell's factor-analytic approach, and Eysenck's biological trait theory to personality. Define the big five model. (pp. 465–468)

12. Explain the controversy surrounding the role of heredity in personality development. Discuss the twin and adoptive children research. (pp. 468–471)

13. Describe some criticisms of the trait approach to personality. (p. 471)

14. Describe the basic assumption of the cognitive-behavioral approach to personality. Define functional analysis. (pp. 471–472)

15. Compare and contrast the operant approach (Skinner) and cognitive-behavioral theories of personality. (pp. 472–475)

16. Decribe Rotter's expectancy theory, Bandura's reciprocal determinism and self-efficacy, and Mischel's person variables. (pp. 472–475)

17. Describe some applications and criticisms of the cognitive-behavioral approach to personality. (p. 475)

18. Describe the phenomenological approach to personality. (pp. 475–476)

19. Compare and contrast Rogers's self theory and Maslow's humanistic psychology. Define self-actualization, self-concept, conditions of worth, and deficiency versus growth orientation. (pp. 476–477)

20. Describe some applications and criticisms of the phenomenological approach. (p. 478)

21. Describe cultural differences in the concept of self. Explain how these differences shape the development of personality. (pp. 478–480)

22. Discuss the longitudinal studies of personality and their conclusions about the continuity of personality across the lifespan. (pp. 480–481)

23. Describe the three general methods of personality assessment. (pp. 481–482)

24. Discuss the difference between <u>objective</u> and <u>projective</u> tests and give an example of each. (pp. 482–485)

25. Describe some of the applications of personality tests. (p. 486)

CONCEPTS AND EXERCISES

No. 1: Explaining Behavior

Completing this exercise should help you to achieve Learning Objectives 2, 3, 5, 9, 10, 11, 14, 15, 18, and 19.

Jan's office is extremely neat and organized. His books are arranged alphabetically, and there is not a stray paper on the desk. His pencils, neatly arranged from shortest to longest, are so sharp that he could use them as weapons. Jan is a meticulous dresser. His clothes are never wrinkled, spotted, or torn. Match the following explanations of his behavior with the appropriate theorist or approach.

1. Jan has learned that being organized and well dressed will further his career. _____

2. Jan is fixated at the anal stage. _____

3. Being organized is one of the central traits of Jan's personality. _____

4. Jan has a personality in which he finds fulfillment in being neat and organized. _____

5. Jan may believe that he is worthwhile only if he displays neat and tidy behaviors. _____

   ° Roger
   ° Cognitive-Behavioral
   ° Allport
   ° Adler
   ° Freud

No. 2: Treatment Goals

Completing this exercise should help you to achieve Learning Objectives 2, 9, 10, 11, 13, 15, 18, and 19.

Bobbie is extremely anxious and unhappy. Match the following goals with the appropriate approach to personality listed subsequently.

1. Bobbie should become aware of her unconscious conflicts and work to resolve them. _____

2. Bobbie should become aware of her real feelings and beliefs instead of trying to fulfill the conditions of worth that her parents and others impose on her. _____

3. Bobbie should learn to think positively and realize that she controls what happens to her. _____

4. Bobbie should take some tests to assess her personality traits. If the tests show she has a disorder, she should go through some form of treatment. She can take the tests again later to monitor her progress. _____

   ° Phenomenological
   ° Cognitive-Behavioral
   ° Psychodynamic
   ° Trait

CRITICAL THINKING

Sam and Martina are discussing the use of character witnesses in violent crime court cases. Sam believes that people's personalities are very stable across diverse situations. Therefore, character witnesses who can describe personality traits should give a good indication of whether a person is capable of doing a violent crime. Martina says that people can act very differently when provoked by a situation, so character witnesses may not know everything about how likely a person is to behave in a violent manner.

Using the five critical thinking questions in your text, the clues in the story, and what you have learned about personality, answer the following.

1. What is Sam's hypothesis?

2. What is Martina's alternative hypothesis?

3. In any given case, what kinds of evidence do you think Martina would collect to support her alternative hypothesis?

PERSONAL LEARNING ACTIVITIES

1. Pick a behavior that you engage in often. Describe that behavior using the psychodynamic, trait, cognitive-behavioral, and phenomenological approaches. What are the differences in the conclusions of the four approaches? For example, procras-

tination could be explained as merely a personality characteristic or as an action rewarded in its early stages by the extra relaxation time it provides. (Learning Objectives 2, 9, 14, and 18)

2. Imagine a situation in which you have to decide whether to do something that is fun but risky. What are the id, ego, and superego saying about the proposed behavior? Many people who want to lose weight may see candy and want to eat it, for instance. What are the id, ego, and superego saying about eating something that isn't nutritious? (Learning Objective 3)

3. Locate a news report that talks about the personality of someone in the story. What approach to personality is being taken in the story? Often when criminals, heroes, political candidates, and other people are discussed, people draw conclusions about why they acted as they did. Those conclusions may focus more on the influence of the situation, the person's family background, or the person's views. What does the report assume about the chances that the person will change? (Learning Objectives 2, 9, 14, and 18)

4. Describe your personality. How much do you think was inherited and how much was influenced by the environment? (Learning Objective 12)

5. Use magazine or newspaper photos, drawings, and advertisements to make your own projective test. Cut off any identifying information such as captions or product names and then present them to friends and have them tell a story about what is going on in the pictures. Do you see any differences in their responses? For example, does one friend consistently see conflict between people in the photos while another always tells a story with a happy ending? (Learning Objective 24)

MULTIPLE-CHOICE QUESTIONS

SAMPLE QUIZ 1

1. The _____ approach to personality assumes that the unconscious plays a major role in determining behavior.
   a. trait
   b. cognitive-behavioral
   c. psychodynamic
   d. phenomenological

2. The following is a conversation going on in someone's head:

X: I am so mad that I could bash that person's skull in. I cannot believe he did that.
Y: You know you are not supposed to hurt other people.
Z: Why not tell him that his behavior is inappropriate so that he won't repeat it?
X is the _____, Y is the _____, and Z is the _____.
   a. id; ego; superego
   b. ego; id; superego
   c. superego; id; ego
   d. id; superego; ego

3. Tom finds his wife stupid and sexually unattractive, but doesn't tell her about these feelings. Instead, he criticizes his secretary for making mistakes and makes derogatory remarks about *her* appearance. This is an example of which defense mechanism?
   a. Rationalization
   b. Displacement
   c. Reaction-formation
   d. Projection

4. Antonia loves to chew on her fingernails, smokes one pack of cigarettes a day, loves to chew gum, and has always been a little overweight. Antonia is most likely fixated at which psychosexual stage of development?
   a. Oral
   b. Anal
   c. Phallic
   d. Latency

5. The Oedipus complex is part of the _____ stage of psychosexual development.
   a. oral
   b. anal
   c. phallic
   d. genital

6. Object relations are part of _____ theory.
   a. contemporary psychodynamic
   b. trait
   c. phenomenological
   d. cognitive-behavioral

7. Central traits
   a. were suggested by a behaviorist to explain behavior.
   b. organize and control behavior across many situations.
   c. are more situation-specific than are secondary traits.
   d. are seen in growth-oriented individuals.

8. Toni describes her best friend as intelligent, caring, extroverted, and lots of fun to be with. Which type of theorist would use the same type of description that Toni does?
   a. Trait
   b. Cognitive-behavioral
   c. Psychodynamic
   d. Phenomenological

9. Which of the following is an example of a person exhibiting a secondary trait?
   a. Amy, who is obnoxious and opinionated only in seminar classes
   b. Arnold, whose entire life is devoted to ridding the world of thieves, murderers, and drug dealers
   c. Cathy, who usually sees the positive side of events
   d. Dave, who loves to help those less fortunate than himself

10. LaRhonda says that she once enjoyed driving fast and took a trip every weekend. Now, however, she says she would rather get together with friends, because all that driving was really a waste of money and harmful to the environment. A phenomenological theorist would describe LaRhonda's personality in terms of the
    a. change in her self-efficacy.
    b. change in her perceptions of driving.
    c. level of extraversion she is exhibiting.
    d. level of psychoticism she is exhibiting.

11. A big five theorist would most likely describe LaRhonda's personality in terms of her
    a. level of the five psychic conflicts.
    b. perception of the benefits and costs of speeding, the value of friendship, and the positive and negative aspects of staying home.
    c. level of extraversion.
    d. level of psychoticism.

12. The belief that behavior can be situation-specific is a main argument *against* which approach to personality?
    a. Psychodynamic
    b. Cognitive-behavioral
    c. Phenomenological
    d. Trait

13. Self-efficacy is
    a. our collection of learned expectancies for success in given situations.
    b. the efficiency with which we resolve unconscious conflicts.
    c. a secondary trait.
    d. a role of the ego.

14. Rotter's expectancy theory is part of the _____ approach to personality.
    a. trait
    b. phenomenological
    c. cognitive-behavioral
    d. psychodynamic

15. At home, Rebecca's daughter is very polite. Rebecca is horrified when she finds out that her daughter is rude at school. She suggests that the teacher begin rewarding her daughter for being polite. Rebecca is taking which approach to personality?
    a. Psychodynamic
    b. Cognitive-behavioral
    c. Phenomenological
    d. Trait

16. A deficiency orientation occurs when people
    a. make do with less than perfect conditions.
    b. focus on things they do not have.
    c. attempt to fulfill their potentials.
    d. have a trait missing from their personality.

17. Kareem and Burke are having a heated argument over which theory of personality is correct. Kareem says that Burke's theory reduces humans to machines and ignores their perceptions, values, and beliefs. Kareem is probably a _____ theorist, and Burke is a _____ theorist.
    a. behavioral; psychodynamic
    b. phenomenological; psychodynamic
    c. trait; behavioral
    d. phenomenological; behavioral

18. Ed was an ill-tempered boy who had tantrums regularly. According to the longitudinal study described in your text, Ed is likely to
    a. move up to a high rank if he joins the military.
    b. grow out of his ill-temperedness by adulthood.
    c. have a lower-status job as an adult than many good-tempered men.
    d. keep his job longer than most good-tempered men do.

19. Which of the following would a phenomenological psychologist use most frequently to assess personality?
    a. Behavioral observations
    b. Objective tests
    c. Assessments of physiological activity
    d. Personal interviews

20. Tameka shows her clients a series of ambiguous pictures she painted and asks them to tell a story about each picture. Tameka hopes that her _____ personality test will uncover some of the unconscious thoughts of her clients.
    a. multiphasic
    b. objective
    c. projective
    d. cognitive-behavioral

Total Correct (See answer key) _____

SAMPLE QUIZ 2

Use this quiz to reassess your learning after taking Quiz 1 and reviewing the chapter.

1. Lydia, a married woman, is incredibly attracted to her physician. Her _____ decides that the only way to see her doctor more often is to have more frequent physicals and have even the slightest symptom investigated immediately.
    a. id
    b. ego
    c. superego
    d. eros

2. Oliver thinks that everyone in all his lecture courses is cheating. Oliver probably feels like cheating himself. This is an example of which defense mechanism?
    a. Creativity
    b. Reaction-formation
    c. Rationalization
    d. Projection

3. Fixation occurs when
    a. psychosexual conflicts are not resolved.
    b. we use defense mechanisms to relieve anxiety.
    c. the rewards in a given situation fix our behaviors.
    d. our progress toward self-actualization is blocked at some stage.

Use the following conversation to answer questions 4 and 5.

Joe: I don't think we should hire him. I saw him in a barroom brawl a few months ago. Why hire someone who is going to be aggressive in any given situation?

Kim: His MMPI scores indicate that he isn't prone to violence.

Richard: His self-concept may not include violence.

Erika: Joe, how do you know that he's always going to be aggressive? Maybe the guy was just under stress at the time. Maybe he knows from past experience that a good fist fight relieves tension.

4. Which of the following approaches is *not* represented in the above conversation?
    a. Cognitive-Behavioral
    b. Psychodynamic
    c. Phenomenological
    d. Trait

5. Which two speakers agree with the trait approach to personality?
    a. Joe and Richard
    b. Erika and Kim
    c. Joe and Kim
    d. Richard and Erika

6. Nine-year-old Cass has just bounded into the room with her latest artistic creation. She bubbles on and on about her friends at school and how much she likes her teacher. Which psychosexual stage of development is she most likely in?
    a. Oral
    b. Anal
    c. Phallic
    d. Latency

7. Dr. Lebryk believes Jack's romantic relationships are brief and unhappy because Jack had an anxious insecure attachment to his mother. Dr. Lebryk is most likely a(n) _____ theorist.
    a. big five
    b. cognitive-behavioral
    c. phenomenological
    d. object relations

8. You describe your friend as outgoing, eccentric, generous, emotional, talkative, impulsive, and easygoing. Gordon Allport would say you have listed your friend's
    a. central traits.
    b. secondary traits.
    c. level of self-efficacy.
    d. level of externality.

9. Harry believes that personality is related to the amount of hair on one's body. His personality theory is similar to what other personality theory?
    a. Psychodynamic
    b. Physiognomic
    c. Cognitive-behavioral
    d. Phenomenological

10. An author said that all people could be categorized as either believers, competitors, or rebels. This author is using a
    a. type theory.
    b. trait theory.
    c. phenomenological approach
    d. psychodynamic approach.

11. Darrell agrees with the Big Five approach to personality; therefore, he is likely to be interested in a person's level of _____, but *not* in a person's level of _____.
    a. agreeableness; extraversion
    b. agreeableness; psychoticism
    c. neuroticism; conscientiousness
    d. neuroticism; openness

12. Which of the following is *not* a criticism of the trait theories of personality?
    a. They describe behavior better than they explain it.
    b. They create descriptions that may be too general.
    c. They ignore situational influences on behavior.
    d. They place too much emphasis on the unconscious.

13. The learning process is most central to which personality theory?
    a. Psychodynamic
    b. Trait
    c. Cognitive-behavioral
    d. Big five

14. Joe is an internal, according to Rotter's expectancy theory of personality. Therefore, you would expect Joe to
    a. ignore physical symptoms of illness.
    b. work on a factory assembly line.
    c. take a self-paced course at school.
    d. all of the above

15. According to Bandura, a child could _____ through observational learning.
    a. learn to be truthful
    b. learn how to con Dad into giving up the car
    c. learn how to be assertive
    d. all of the above

16. Lontica is happily taping pages of her coloring book to the walls in her room when her father enters. "What are you—stupid?" her father bellows. "How many times have I told you that tape takes the paint off the walls and you should use your bulletin board?" Lontica's father may be creating a(n) _____, according to Rogers.
    a. deficiency orientation
    b. fixation
    c. interdependent self-system
    d. condition of worth

17. Grace tries not to stand out from the crowd. Not only does she describe herself in terms of her place in her family and work groups, but she also feels happiest when her interactions with her groups have gone well. Grace most likely
    a. has an independent self-system.
    b. has an interdependent self-system.
    c. is an internal.
    d. is an external.

18. A projective test is usually
    a. reliable.
    b. valid.
    c. easy to score.
    d. none of the above.

19. Mark has just looked through a series of pictures and described what he thinks are the stories underlying the scenes. Mark has just
    a. taken an objective test.
    b. taken the MMPI.
    c. taken a projective test.
    d. been interviewed.

20. Mimi wants to determine her client's level of depression using an objective test. Which of the following should be true of the measure?
    a. The stimuli should be ambiguous.
    b. The tester should interpret the numerical score based on norms.
    c. The unstructured format will allow for reflection of an individual's level of depression.
    d. All of the above.

Total Correct (See answer key) _____

ANSWERS TO FILL-IN-THE-BLANKS KEY TERMS

1. Objective (p. 482)
2. anal (p. 461)
3. id (p. 460)
4. superego (p. 460)
5. reality (p. 460)
6. big five (p. 468)
7. latency (p. 462)

8. cognitive-behavioral (p. 471)
9. deficiency orientation (p. 477)
10. self-actualization (p. 476)
11. trait (p. 465)
12. phenomenological or humanistic (pp. 475–476)
13. projective (p. 484)
14. Growth orientation (p. 477)
15. self-concept (p. 476)

ANSWERS TO CONCEPTS AND EXERCISES

No. 1: Explaining Behavior

1. *Cognitive-behavioral.* A behaviorist would explain Jan's behavior by finding out what behaviors were rewarded in the past. (p. 471)

2. *Freud or Psychodynamic.* Freud believed that an unresolved crisis during the psychosexual development would lead to fixation. Adults who are fixated at the anal stage are extremely neat and tidy. (pp. 460–461)

3. *Allport.* Allport was a trait theorist. He believed that people have about seven central traits. (p. 465)

4. *Adler.* Adler was a neoanalytic who believed that people adopt personalities in their quest to find fulfillment by attaining superiority. (p. 462)

5. *Rogers.* Rogers was a phenomenological theorist. He said that many people display behaviors because they believe these are the only ways in which to gain approval and thus positive self-evaluation. (p. 476)

No. 2: Treatment Goals

1. *Psychodynamic.* Freud said that unconscious conflicts are the primary root of all mental disorders. In order to eliminate the anxiety these conflicts produce, patients should be made aware of them and work to resolve them. (p. 460)

2. *Phenomenological.* Rogers said that unhappy people are out of touch with their true feelings. They are probably behaving according to others' values instead of according to their own feelings and values. (pp. 475–476)

3. *Cognitive-behavioral.* A cognitive-behavioral approach suggests that Bobbie learn and practice more positive ways of thinking and behaving. (p. 471)

4. Trait. A trait theorist might suggest that Bobbie take objective tests, such as the MMPI, to describe her personality and identify any type of possible personality disorders. (p. 465)

ANSWERS TO CRITICAL THINKING

1. Sam hypothesizes that if someone doesn't usually exhibit tendencies toward violence, then he or she probably didn't commit a violent crime.

2. Martina knows that trait theories have been criticized because they tend to ignore situational influences on behavior. She would therefore hypothesize that someone who is generally not violent could be provoked into violence by a particular situation.

3. Martina would probably want to investigate both the person's general personality traits and aspects of the situation that could explain the onset of violent behavior.

ANSWERS TO MULTIPLE-CHOICE QUESTIONS

Circle the question numbers you answered correctly.

Sample Quiz 1

1. *c* is the answer. The psychodynamic approach assumes that personality is determined by unconscious mental processes. (p. 460)
   a. The trait approach assumes that personality is a stable combination of traits or type characteristics.
   b. The cognitive-behavioral approach assumes that personality is essentially the same thing as behavior. The cognitive-behavioral approach would also say that we have expectancies based on previous experience.
   d. The phenomenological approach assumes that personality is a product of each person's values, beliefs, and perceptions.

2. *d* is the answer. X wants to be aggressive. Y knows all the rules about what behaviors one should and should not display. Z will try to obey the rules of society as well as satisfy the id and superego. (p. 460)

3. *b* is the answer. Tom is displacing his feelings from the original source to an alternate source, his secretary. (p. 461)

a. Rationalization is an attempt to explain away behavior. If this were the case, Tom might tell himself that all marriages have their low spots.

c. Reaction-formation guides behavior in the direction opposite that of the unwanted impulse. If this were the case, Tom would shower his wife with attention and affection, telling her how intelligent and beautiful he thought she was.

d. Projection is seeing unwanted impulses and desires in others. If this were the case, Tom might start noticing that his friends treat their wives very badly.

4. *a* is the answer. People fixated at the oral stage are likely to smoke, overeat, or use "biting" sarcasm. (p. 461)

b. The adult behavior of people fixated at the anal stage is characterized by excessive neatness and organization.

c. People fixated at the phallic stage will have sexual desires for people or objects other than the opposite sex and may have problems with authority.

d. People do not become fixated at the latency stage. There are no unconscious conflicts to resolve at this stage.

5. *c* is the answer. The Oedipus complex occurs during the phallic stage. According to Freud, boys desire their mothers and wish to kill their fathers. This is similar to the plot of the Greek tragedy *Oedipus Rex.* (p. 461)

a. The oral stage occurs during the first year of life, when a child derives pleasure mainly from the mouth.

b. The anal stage occurs during the second year of life, when a child derives sexual pleasure mainly from the anal area.

d. The genital stage lasts from puberty onward. The pleasure found in relationships during this stage is dependent upon the resolution of conflicts at earlier stages.

6. *a* is the answer. Object relations theorists study the relationship between people and significant objects. (p. 463)

b. Trait theorists study dispositions.

c. Phenomenological theorists focus on people's perceptions of the world and their tendency toward reaching their potential.

d. Cognitive-behavioral theorists focus on behaviors and learned thought patterns, which they believe influence personality.

7. *b* is the answer. According to Allport's trait theory, about seven central traits guide our behavior in many situations. (p. 465)

a. Central traits were proposed by Allport, who was a trait, not a cognitive-behavioral, theorist.

c. Secondary traits are more situation-specific than are central traits.

d. Growth orientation is a phenomenological concept proposed by Maslow.

8. *a* is the answer. A trait theorist would describe a person in terms of such stable characteristics. (p. 465)

b. A cognitive-behavioral theorist would describe a person in terms of behaviors and thought patterns.

c. A psychodynamic theorist would discuss the underlying unconscious conflicts that are responsible for a person's behavior.

d. A phenomenological theorist would describe a person's perception of reality, values, and beliefs.

9. *a* is the answer. A secondary trait, according to Allport, is one that is specific to certain situations. (p. 465)

b. Arnold has a trait that affects his whole life; this would not be a secondary trait, but a central trait.

c, d. Cathy sounds like she is optimistic in most situations and Dave sounds like he is often helpful; therefore, these are not secondary traits.

10. *b* is the answer. Phenomenological theorists focus on perceptions (p. 475)

a. Self-efficacy is a concept created by a cognitive-behavioral theorist, Bandura.

c, d. These are traits.

11. *c* is the answer. A big five theorist believes in five basic traits: openness, conscientiousness, extraversion, agreeableness, and neuroticism. (p. 468)

a. A psychic conflict would be the interest of a psychodynamic theorist, but none of them proposed five main conflicts.

b. Perceptions are of interest to phenomenological theorists.

d. Psychoticism is a trait, but not one of the big five. Psychoticism was proposed by Eysenck as one of three basic factors.

12. *d* is the answer. Trait theorists argue that behavior is a reflection of consistent and stable traits and that environmental or situational factors do not determine behavior. (p. 471)

a. Psychodynamic theorists have been criticized for adhering to Freud's emphasis on the unconscious and his use of patients' reports as a basis for psychosexual development theory. Freud was also accused of being sexist. But the belief in situation-specific behavior does not detract from the psychodynamic theory.

b. Cognitive-behavioral theorists have been accused of overemphasizing overt behavior and the environmental factors of reward and punishment and not attending enough to the individual's perceptions, feelings, and thoughts.

c. Phenomenological concepts are difficult to measure, more descriptive than explanatory, and naive since they are so optimistic about the nature of men and women.

13. *a* is the answer. According to Bandura, a cognitive-behavioral theorist, our learned expectations for success can influence our behavior. (p. 473)

b. Psychodynamic theorists, not cognitive behavioral theorists, focus on unconscious mental processes.

c. Self-efficacy is a cognitive-behavioral phenomenon, not a trait or secondary trait.

d. The ego is a psychodynamic concept, not a cognitive-behavioral concept.

14. *c* is the answer. Rotter's expectancy theory is part of the cognitive-behavioral approach. Rotter proposed that internals believe they control events and that externals believe that others (fate, other people, luck) control events. (pp. 472–473)

a. Expectancies are not a trait or type, both of which are the foundation of the trait approach.

b. The phenomenological approach doesn't emphasize expectancies in the development of personality.

d. Psychodynamic theories do not emphasize expectancies; they tend to focus on unconscious mental processes.

15. *b* is the answer. Rebecca is probably a behaviorist or cognitive-behaviorist. She believes that behavior is shaped by the presence of rewards and punishments in the environment. (pp. 471–472)

a. A psychodynamic theorist would want to find out what the daughter's unconscious thoughts and feelings were before suggesting a corrective measure.

c. A phenomenological theorist would probably want to know how the daughter perceives the situation at school.

d. A trait theorist would not believe that rewards and punishments would be effective, and might

think that Rebecca's daughter had a secondary trait to be impolite at school.

16. *b* is the answer. A deficiency orientation, according to Maslow, occurs when individuals focus on what they do not have instead of on what they do have. (p. 477)

a. If people focus on or derive satisfaction from what they have, they have a growth orientation.

c. Phenomenological theorists assume that we all attempt to fulfill our potentials.

d. A deficiency orientation is a phenomenological concept that is not related to traits.

17. *d* is the answer. Kareem is a phenomenological theorist because he thinks that values, beliefs, and perceptions of reality influence personality. Burke is a behaviorist; behaviorists have been accused of viewing people as machines that can be programmed using only rewards and punishments. (pp. 471–472, 475–476)

a, b, c. Behavioral theorists tend not to focus on people's values, beliefs, or perceptions of the world. Psychodynamic and trait theorists have not been accused of ignoring people's values or beliefs, nor do they view people as machines controlled by rewards and punishments.

18. *c* is the answer. The longitudinal study found that men and women who were ill-tempered children were also ill-tempered adults. The ill-tempered adults were more likely to lose their jobs and get divorced than the non-ill-tempered adults. (pp. 480–481)

a, b, d. In this longitudinal study, the men who were ill-tempered as boys tended to have lower military rank, remain ill-tempered, and lose their jobs.

19. *d* is the answer. Those who take a phenomenological view of personality believe that everyone sees a reality that is unique. Therefore, interviews, during which people can explain their points of view, would be the best method of assessment. (pp. 475–478)

a. A phenomenological theorist would say that one cannot interpret someone's behavior without knowing that person's interpretation or perception of reality.

b. An objective test assumes that people have the same general interpretation of the questions on it. If this was not the case, the questions could not be used to compare one person to another. Phenomenological views assume that each person's view of anything, including a true-false or multiple-choice question, is unique.

c. Phenomenological theorists do not depend on physiological data in personality assessment; they are more interested in conscious experience.

20. *c* is the answer. A projective test uses ambiguous stimuli to allow the taker to project unconscious conflicts and desires onto the test. If the picture of two people is unclear enough, for example, a person who has trouble with authority might make up a story about a person getting a reprimand. (p. 484)

   a. You may have been thinking of the Minnesota Multiphasic Personality Inventory (MMPI), which is an objective test.

   b. Objective tests have specific statements or questions to be read and responded to by the test taker.

   d. A cognitive-behavioral theorist would not use ambiguous stimuli to test for personality. If they used a personality test at all, it would look for generalized expectancies or ideas about the self.

Now turn to the quiz analysis table at the end of this chapter to find which areas you know well and which areas you need to work on. Circle the numbers in the table for items on Quiz 1 that you answered correctly.

ANSWERS TO MULTIPLE-CHOICE QUESTIONS

Circle the question numbers you answered correctly.

Sample Quiz 2

1. *b* is the answer. Lydia's ego has devised a solution that will let her spend more time with a man she is attracted to (thereby satisfying the id) without breaking the rules of society or doing something that the superego would disapprove of. (p. 460)

   a. The id wants to have sex with the doctor and does not particularly care what rules are broken.

   c. The superego would tell Lydia that she is married and cannot have sex with anyone but her husband.

   d. Eros is the aggregate of life instincts.

2. *d* is the answer. Oliver is projecting his unwanted impulses onto other people. (p. 461)

   a. Creativity is not a psychodynamic defense mechanism.

   b. Reaction-formation guides behavior in the direction opposite to that of the unwanted impulse. If Oliver made sure that he was extremely honest in all situations, this would be the correct answer.

   c. Rationalization is an attempt to make your own behavioral actions or mistakes seem reasonable.

3. *a* is the answer. Fixation occurs when we do not resolve psychosexual conflicts during development. For example, according to Freud, those who are weaned too early may engage in oral activities such as smoking, excessive talking, or overeating. (p. 461)

   b. We use defense mechanisms to relieve anxiety, but this is not a fixation.

   c. Fixation is not a part of behavioral theory.

   d. Fixation is not part of phenomenological theory.

4. *b* is the answer. Psychodynamic views of personality are not represented by anyone. (p. 460)

5. *c* is the answer. Joe assumes that the man in question will always be aggressive. Trait theorists assume that people have several traits that will be present in many different situations. Kim is talking about the MMPI, a personality test developed by trait theorists. (pp. 464–465, 482–483)

   a. Richard agrees with phenomenological theorists.

   b. Erika agrees with cognitive-behavioral theorists.

   d. Richard agrees with phenomenological theorists, while Erika agrees with cognitive-behavioral theorists.

6. *d* is the answer. The latency period lasts from about age five until puberty. During this time, a child focuses on education and social development. (p. 462)

   a. The oral stage occurs during the first year or so of life.

   b. The anal stage occurs during the second year or so of life.

   c. The phallic stage occurs during the third to fifth years of life.

7. *d* is the answer. Many current psychodynamic psychologists focus on object relations. Object relations theory suggests that people's relations to the mother or other primary caregivers shape a person's thoughts about social relationships later in life. Some research shows that early attachment styles are related to current relationship quality. (p. 463)

   a. A big five theorist would suggest that one of five traits is influencing Jack's troubles.

b. A cognitive-behaviorist would probably hypothesize that Jack expects to fail or that Jack is being rewarded somehow for his present behavior.

c. A phenomenological theorist would emphasize Jack's perceptions, not his attachment to his mother.

8. *a* is the answer. Most people can describe someone using about seven labels. Allport called these central traits. (p. 465)

b. Allport also thought we had secondary traits, which are more tied to a situation. For example, a person who bluffs when playing cards might not bluff in other social situations.

c, d. Self-efficacy and expectancies (internal versus external) are cognitive-behavioral concepts.

9. *b* is the answer. Physiognomic studies focus on the relationship between physical characteristics and personality. (p. 465)

a. Psychodynamic theories focus on the struggle between unconscious impulses and society's rules.

c. Cognitive-behavioral theories focus on learned patterns of behavior and mental thought processes.

d. Phenomenological theories focus on each person's perception of the world and attempts to reach her or his potential.

10. *a* is the answer. When people fit into one class or another, they are typed. (p. 465)

b. A person may have more or fewer traits than someone else, but the author said people could be placed in categories.

c, d. The phenomenological and psychodynamic approaches do not categorize people into types.

11. *b* is the answer. The big five approach believes that the basic personality dimensions are openness, conscientiousness, extraversion, agreeableness, and neuroticism, but not psychoticism. (pp. 468–469)

a, c, d. All of the traits listed are part of the big five.

12. *d* is the answer. Trait theories do not emphasize the unconscious as psychodynamic theories do. (p. 471)

a. Traits are much better at describing than explaining behavior.

b. Many trait descriptions seem to fit a large number of people, thus reducing their value for describing a given person.

c. Trait descriptions do not explain situational influences on behavior. Trait theories imply stable behavior, driven by traits, in any situation.

13. *c* is the answer. The cognitive-behavioral approach is based on the assumption that people learn how to think and act. (p. 471)

a. The psychodynamic approach focuses on the influence of unconscious mental processes on personality.

b. The trait approach attributes much of personality to inherent characteristics; it does not emphasize learning as much as the cognitive-behavioral approach does.

d. The big five model is an example of a trait theory.

14. *c* is the answer. Joe would be most likely to take a self-paced course because he would prefer being in control of his work pace. (pp. 472–473)

a, b. Joe would probably not ignore physical symptoms of illness or work very well on an assembly line. Externals would be more likely to exhibit these types of behavior.

d. *c* is the answer.

15. *d* is the answer. According to Bandura, we can learn new behaviors, learn to inhibit behaviors, and learn how to prompt or facilitate behaviors through observational learning. (p. 473)

16. *d* is the answer. According to Rogers, when one person criticizes another, rather than only correcting the behavior, a condition of worth may be created. In a condition of worth, the criticized person believes that (s)he is not worthwhile because s(he) behaved in a disapproved of way. If Lontica's father had tried to emphasize that the behavior was not correct, but that he still loved Lontica, she might not feel that her worth depended upon her behavior. (pp. 476–477)

a. A deficiency orientation is another phenomenological concept, but it occurs when a person focuses on what is missing instead of on growth or satisfaction with current possessions.

b. A fixation will occur, according to Freud, if a person does not resolve conflicts at each stage of psychosexual development. Fixations are basically unrelated to parental reprimands.

c. Interdependent self-systems are more common in collectivist cultures, where one's place in groups is emphasized.

17. *b* is the answer. People with an interdependent self-system see themselves as a fraction of a whole. They tend not to be happy when singled out for

attention, even if it is for personal achievement. (pp. 479–480)

 a. People with an independent self-system emphasize personal achievement rather than their place in a group.

 c. This relates to Rotter's expectancy theory. Internals believe that they control events through their own efforts.

 d. This is part of Rotter's expectancy theory. Externals believe that external forces control events.

18. *d* is the answer. Projective tests involve presenting a subject with an unstructured and ambiguous stimulus. Personality is supposedly reflected in the subject's response. Because the tasks are unstructured, they tend to be relatively difficult to score, unreliable, and not as valid as objective tests. (pp. 484–485)

19. *c* is the answer. Mark has just taken a projective test, most likely the Thematic Apperception Test. (p. 484)

 a, b. An objective test is a paper-and-pencil test. Answers are written, not explained aloud, by the respondent. The MMPI is an objective test.

 d. Interviews usually revolve around either structured or unstructured questions, not around ambiguous stimuli such as pictures and inkblots.

20. *b* is the answer. A person's score on an objective test is more meaningful if it can be compared to the average person. If a person receives a 9, for example, on a test of depression, we don't know if that is cause for concern unless we know that a 5 is an average score. (p. 482)

 a, c. Ambiguous stimuli and an unstructured format are part of a projective test.

 d. Only *b* is the answer.

Now turn to the quiz analysis table at the end of this chapter to find which areas you know well and which areas you need to work on. Circle the numbers in the table for items on Quiz 2 that you answered correctly.

For each question you answered correctly, circle its number. (Quiz 1 numbers are not shaded; Quiz 2 numbers are shaded.) Are there patterns in the types of questions or the topics you got wrong that could direct your further study? Did you improve from Quiz 1 to Quiz 2?

TOPIC	TYPE OF QUESTION		
	DEFINITION	COMPREHENSION	APPLICATION
Psychodynamic			
Structures	1		2, 3
			1, 2, 4
Development		5	4
	3		6
Variations and evaluation		6	
			7
Trait			
Theories	7		8, 9
			5, 8, 9, 10
Big Five			11
		11	
Evaluation		12	
		12	
Cognitive-Behavioral	13	14	15
	13		14, 15
Phenomenological	16		10, 17
			16
Culture			
			17
Longitudinal studies			18
Assessment			19, 20
		18	19, 20

TOTAL CORRECT BY QUIZ:

QUIZ 1:
QUIZ 2:

Chapter 15

Psychological Disorders

Psychopathology involves patterns of thinking and behaving that are maladaptive, disruptive, or uncomfortable either for the person affected or for others.

OUTLINE

I. UNDERSTANDING PSYCHOLOGICAL DISORDERS: SOME BASIC ISSUES (pp. 491–496)

A. What Is Abnormal?

There are several approaches to defining normality, but none is perfect. No behavior is universally abnormal.

1. *Infrequency.* Those behaviors displayed by the greatest number of people are considered normal. Statistical infrequency considers behavior that is atypical or rare to be abnormal. However, some behavior that is rare, such as creative genius, extraordinary language skills, or world-class athletic ability, is valued; therefore, statistical infrequency alone is not an adequate criterion.

2. *Personal Suffering.* Psychological problems causing distress require treatment. Because some people with disorders may not experience distress, personal suffering cannot be the only criterion for abnormality.

3. *Norm Violation.* People who behave in ways that are bizarre, unusual, or disturbing enough to violate social norms or cultural rules are termed abnormal.

4. *Behavior in Context: A Practical Approach.* The content of behavior (whether behavior is bizarre, dysfunctional, or harmful), the sociocultural context in which the behavior occurs (where and when behavior occurs), and the consequences of behavior are all taken into consideration when judging whether behavior is abnormal. A practical approach also considers whether behavior causes impaired functioning. Cultures and subcultures determine which behaviors are appropriate for a given situation.

B. Explaining Psychological Disorders

1. *Supernatural Influences.* According to supernatural or demonological principles, abnormal behavior is caused by the action of gods or demons.

2. *Biological Factors.* The ancient Greek physician Hippocrates introduced the medical model, in which he explained that psychological disorders resulted from imbalances among four humors. The medical model eventually evolved into the concept of mental illness. The medical model is now termed the neurobiological model because it looks at problems in anatomy and physiology of the brain and other areas.

3. *Psychological Processes.* Mental disorders are caused by inner turmoil or other psychological events. Psychological models include the psychodynamic, cognitive-behavioral, and phenomenological approaches.

4. *Sociocultural Context.* Sociocultural explanations rely on factors such as gender and age, physical and social situations, cultural values and expectations, and historical eras. Culture-general disorders appear in most societies, while culture-specific forms appear only in certain ones.

5. *Diathesis-Stress as an Integrative Approach.* According to the diathesis-stress model, genetics, early learning, and biological processes may all contribute to psychological disorders.

II. CLASSIFYING PSYCHOLOGICAL DISORDERS (pp. 496–501)

A. A Classification System: DSM-IV

The Diagnostic and Statistical Manual of Mental Disorders (DSM-IV) describes each form of disorder and provides criteria for diagnosis. DSM-IV consists of a series of evaluations on five dimensions called axes. Every person is rated on each axis. Axis I comprises descriptive criteria of sixteen major mental disorders. Axis II contains personality disorders and mental retardation. Axis III comprises physical conditions or disorders. Axis

IV has types and levels of stress. Axis V has a rating of the highest level of functioning. (Neurosis, characterized by anxiety, and psychosis, whose symptoms include a break with reality, are no longer major diagnostic categories in DSM.)

B. Purposes and Problems of Diagnosis

The major goals of diagnosis are to help identify appropriate treatment for clients and to accurately and consistently group patients with similar disorders so that research efforts can more easily identify underlying causes of mental illness. Two limitations of diagnosis are validity and interrater reliability. Interrater reliability is the degree to which different diagnosticians give the same label to one patient.

C. Thinking Critically: Is Psychodiagnosis Biased?

What am I being asked to believe or accept?
Clinicians's diagnoses are biased by, for example, racial stereotypes.

What evidence is available to support the assertion?
African-American people are more frequently diagnosed as schizophrenic than are European-Americans. In addition, African-Americans are overrepresented in facilities noted for higher incidences of more serious disorders (public mental health hospitals).

Are there alternative ways of interpreting the evidence?
Diagnostic differences by race may not reflect bias. There could very well be physiological or cultural differences that cause mental illness.

What additional evidence would help to evaluate the alternatives?
Studies that ask physicians to diagnose pairs of potentially mentally ill people with identical symptoms but different races could detect bias in diagnoses. Other studies that have examined diagnostic practices (examining notes and interviews) and controlled the research for the type and severity of symptoms have shown that African-Americans are more frequently diagnosed as schizophrenic. Therefore, ethnic bias is a factor in some diagnoses.

What conclusions are most reasonable?
Clinicians, because they are human, are prone to bias when diagnosing the mentally ill. However, bias can be minimized by becoming educated about a prospective patient's cultural background and its effect on behavior and mental processes.

III. ANXIETY DISORDERS (pp. 501–504)

A. Types of Anxiety Disorders

1. *Phobia.* A phobia is an anxiety disorder involving a strong, irrational fear of an object or situation that should not cause such a reaction. Specific phobias involve fear of specific physical objects, places, or activities. Social phobias involve fear of being negatively evaluated by others or publicly embarrassed by doing something impulsive, outrageous, or humiliating. Agoraphobia is a strong fear of being separated from a safe place like home or of being trapped in a place from which escape might be difficult.

2. *Generalized Anxiety Disorder.* The condition called generalized anxiety disorder involves milder but long-lasting feelings of anxiety, worry, dread, or apprehension that are not focused on any particular object or situation. Free-floating anxiety is a term sometimes used to describe the nonspecific nature of this anxiety.

3. *Panic Disorder.* Periodic episodes of extreme terror (panic attacks) without warning or obvious cause are characteristic of people with panic disorder.

4. *Obsessive-Compulsive Disorder.* The persistent intrusion of thoughts or images or a compulsive need to perform certain behavior patterns are symptoms of obsessive-compulsive disorder (OCD). When the obsessive thinking or compulsive behaviors are interrupted, severe anxiety results.

B. Causes of Anxiety Disorders

1. *Biological Factors.* Biological explanations of anxiety disorders include abnormal levels of particular neurotransmitters and oversensitive brainstem mechanisms.

2. *Cognitive Factors.* A person suffering from an anxiety disorder may exaggerate the danger associated with certain stimuli and underestimate his or her coping skills, causing anxiety and depression.

IV. LINKAGES: PSYCHOLOGICAL DISORDERS AND LEARNING (pp. 504–506)

Phobias start with distressing thoughts followed by operantly rewarded behaviors. Phobias can also be explained by classical conditioning. People may be biologically prepared to learn certain fears and avoid stimuli that had potential for harm to our evolutionary ancestors. Rare phobias may be a product of classical conditioning, but common ones such as snakes, fire, height, and insects may be due to a biological preparedness to react negatively to certain potentially hazardous things.

V. SOMATOFORM DISORDERS (pp. 506–507)

Somatoform disorders are characterized by physical symptoms with no physical cause. In conversion disorder, a person appears to be, but is actually not, functionally impaired (for example, blind, deaf, or paralyzed). The physical symptoms often help reduce stress, and the person may seem unconcerned about them. Hypochondriasis involves strong fears of a specific severe illness that are usually accompanied by complaints of many vague symptoms. In somatization disorder, a person makes dramatic but vague reports about a multitude of physical problems rather than any specific illness. Pain disorder is characterized by severe, often constant, pain with no apparent physical cause.

VI. DISSOCIATIVE DISORDERS (pp. 507–509)

° Dissociative disorders are characterized by a sudden, usually temporary, disruption in memory, consciousness, or identity. Dissociative fugue is characterized by sudden memory loss and the assumption of a new identity in a new locale. In dissociative amnesia, a person has sudden memory loss without leaving home and creating a new identity. The most dramatic and least common dissociative disorder is dissociative identity disorder (DID), formerly known as multiple personality disorder (MPD), which involves having more than one identity, each of which speaks, acts, and writes differently. Psychodynamic theorists believe that dissociative disorders are methods of repressing (forgetting) unwanted impulses or memories. Behavioral theorists believe that dissociative disorders are examples of learned behavior patterns that have become so discrepant that a person may feel like and be perceived as a different person from time to time.

° Dissociative identity disorders are currently appearing more frequently in society. Recent studies have drawn several conclusions about people displaying multiple personalities: Many have experiences they would like to forget or avoid (such as child abuse), many are skilled at self-hypnosis, and most can escape trauma by creating "new personalities" to deal with the stress.

VII. MOOD DISORDERS (pp. 509–514)

Mood disorders, or affective disorders, are characterized by persistent extreme mood swings that are inconsistent with environmental events.

A. Depressive Disorders

Major depressive disorder involves feelings of sadness, hopelessness, inadequacy, worthlessness, and guilt that persist for long periods. Also common are changes or disturbances in eating habits, sleep, decision making, and concentration. In extreme cases, depressed people exhibit delusions. A more common pattern of depression is dysthymic disorder, which involves symptoms similar to those of major depressive disorder but to a lesser degree and spread out over a longer time period.

   1. *Suicide and Depression.* Repeated bouts of depression and suicide are closely linked. Interpersonal crises, intense feelings of frustration, anger or self-hatred, the absence of meaningful life goals, and constant exposure to stress are associated with suicide and depression. Student populations, the elderly, and females have a higher incidence of suicide than the general population. Those who say they are thinking about suicide are much more likely to attempt it than the general population.

B. Bipolar Disorder

Bipolar disorder is characterized by alternating feelings of extreme depression and mania over a period of days, weeks, or years. Bipolar disorder is relatively rare in comparison to major depressive disorder. Cyclothymic disorder is a slightly more common pattern of less extreme mood swings.

C. Causes of Mood Disorders

   1. *Biological Factors.* Altered levels and possibly dysregulation of norepinephrine and serotonin (neurotransmitters), changes in the control of the stress-related hormone cortisol, abnormal biological rhythms, and genetic influences are causative factors in affective disorders. There is strong evidence that bipolar disorder may be inherited.

   2. *Psychological Theories.* Traditional psychodynamic theorists believe that people with strong dependency needs turn inward the feelings of worthlessness, guilt, and blame that are really meant for others. Behavioral theorists believe that people become depressed when they lose important reinforcements. Learned helplessness can also play a

causative factor in depression. Cognitive theorists believe that negative mental habits (such as focusing on and exaggerating the dark side of events and being generally pessimistic) and attributional style can lead to depression.

VIII. SCHIZOPHRENIA (pp. 514–520)

Schizophrenic symptoms include severely disturbed thinking, emotion, perception, and behavior, which impair a person's ability to communicate and function on a daily basis. Schizophrenia is rare, occurring in only about 1 percent of the population. Improvement is more likely if a person had achieved a higher level of functioning before the symptoms appeared.

A. Symptoms of Schizophrenia

° People with schizophrenia often display incoherent forms of thought; for example, neologisms, word salads, clang associations, and loose associations are common symptoms. Schizophrenics' thought content is equally disturbed; common symptoms include ideas of reference and thought broadcasting, blocking, and insertion.

° Symptoms of schizophrenia include an inability to focus attention or concentrate. Changes in perception of body parts or of other people may also occur. Many schizophrenics report hallucinations or false perceptions. Often, emotions are either absent ("flat affect") or inappropriate for a given situation. Movements may range from constant agitation to almost total immobility. Lack of motivation and social skills, deterioration in personal hygiene, and an inability to function from day to day are other common characteristics of schizophrenia.

B. Types of Schizophrenia

The most prominent features of paranoid schizophrenia are delusions of persecution or grandeur accompanied by anxiety, anger, superiority, argumentativeness, or jealousy. The main features of disorganized schizophrenia include delusions and hallucinations, poor communication, flat or inappropriate affect, and poor personal hygiene. The most significant characteristic of catatonic schizophrenia is movement disorder. People who experience patterns of disordered behavior, thought, and emotions and who do not fit into the other categories are diagnosed as undifferentiated schizophrenics. Finally, residual schizophrenia is a diagnosis used for those who have had a prior episode of schizophrenia but are not currently displaying symptoms.

C. Causes of Schizophrenia

1. *Biological Factors.* Possible biological causes of schizophrenia include inherited predispositions; oversensitivity to dopamine; loss, deterioration, or disorganization of certain brain cells; enlarged brain ventricles; reduced blood flow in certain parts of the brain; and abnormal brain lateralization. Not all persons with schizophrenia have all the biological problems listed here. Evidence suggests that specific symptoms are correlated with specific biological problems: positive symptoms are associated with increased dopamine activity; negative symptoms are associated with decreased dopamine activity and abnormal brain structures.

2. *Psychological Factors.* Psychodynamic theory suggests that schizophrenic symptoms represent a regression to early childhood. Behaviorists believe that schizophrenic symptoms are learned methods of trying to cope with anxiety. They may also be the product of patterns of reinforcement and punishment in early life.

3. *The Vulnerability Model: An Integrative View.* The vulnerability model takes a diathesis-stress approach. The vulnerability can be biological or psychological in nature.

IX. PERSONALITY DISORDERS (pp. 520–523)

Personality disorders, which are less severe than psychological disorders, are lifestyles or ways of behaving that begin in childhood or adolescence and create problems, usually for others. In schizotypal personality disorder, a person displays some of the peculiarities of schizophrenia but not severely enough to be diagnosed as a schizophrenic. In avoidant personality disorder, a person tends to be a loner and avoids social situations. The main characteristic of narcissistic personality disorder is an exaggerated sense of importance and abilities coupled with extreme sensitivity to criticism. The person needs to be the center of attention at all times and has few real friends. A person with antisocial personality disorder displays a long-term, persistent pattern of impulsive, selfish, unscrupulous, and even criminal behavior. The individual is intelligent and charming but does not feel guilty after causing harm or discomfort to others. Possible causes include an underarousal of the autonomic and central nervous systems, low sensitivity to physical punishment, and childhood problems.

A. Focus on Research Methods: Searching for Links between Child Abuse and Antisocial Personality Disorder

Cathy Widom used a prospective quasi-experimental design in which she first found adults who had been abused before age eleven and then interviewed them and studied their school and police records. Her comparison group was matched in terms of age, gender, ethnicity, hospital of birth, schools attended, and area of residence. Widom found that the abused group was significantly more likely to be diagnosed with antisocial personality disorder. Although a firm conclusion cannot be made that childhood abuse causes antisocial personality disorder, this study adds support to that hypothesis.

X. A SAMPLING OF OTHER PSYCHOLOGICAL DISORDERS (p. 523–527)

A. Substance-Related Disorders

Substance-related disorder is the result of the prolonged use of, or addiction to, psychoactive drugs, which can cause physical or psychological harm to the user and consequently to others around her or him.

1. *Alcohol Use Disorders.* Alcoholism afflicts 13 percent of American adults. It is a pattern of continual or intermittent drinking that may lead to addiction and almost always causes severe social, physical, and other problems. The psychoanalytic approach suggests that alcoholism results from dependency needs that were never satisfied in infancy. Behavioral theory suggests that people learn to use alcohol because it helps them cope with stressors and reduce stress reactions. Biological evidence suggests that alcoholism may be due to an inherited predisposition, especially in males.

2. *Heroin and Cocaine Dependence.* Addiction to heroin and similar drugs is largely a biological process. One million Americans are addicted to cocaine (estimate), and millions more use it. Continued cocaine use or overdose can produce a range of symptoms: nausea, hyperactivity, paranoid thinking, sudden depressive "crashes," and even death.

B. Psychological Disorders of Childhood

Childhood disorders are unique because of the incomplete nature of children's development and their limited coping skills. The majority of childhood behavior problems can be categorized as either externalizing or internalizing disorders. Common externalizing (lack of control) disorders include conduct disorders and attention-deficit hyperactivity disorder (ADHD). Internalizing (over-control) disorders include separation anxiety disorder. Autistic disorder is an example of a disorder that does not fall into either category. Autism usually appears in the first thirty months of life; these children do not like to be held, have severe difficulties with language, and play endlessly with inanimate objects in their own worlds. Although the causes of autism are unknown, several hypotheses exist, including oversensitivity to stimulation, abnormally high levels of natural opiates, and difficulty in neuronal cell communication in language areas of the brain.

XI. MENTAL ILLNESS AND THE LAW (pp. 527–528)

The mentally ill are protected in two ways when accused of committing crimes. If, at the time of trial, a person can't understand the charges or assist in the defense, she or he is said to be mentally incompetent. A person can be found not guilty by reason of insanity if, at the time of the crime, mental illness prevented her or him from understanding what she or he was doing or that the act was wrong, or if it prevented the person from resisting the impulse to do wrong. These laws were designed to protect the mentally ill, but critics question the idea of protection. Those who think that mental illness does not exist feel that these laws allow people to escape from responsibility for criminal acts.

Some states have abolished the insanity defense. Other states now permit a verdict of guilty but mentally ill. The irresistible-impulse criterion has been eliminated from the definition of insanity in federal courts, and the defense is now required to prove the defendant was insane at the time of the crime (the latter is also the case in some states).

KEY TERMS

1. **Psychopathology** involves patterns of thinking and behavior that are maladaptive, disruptive, or uncomfortable either for the person affected or for those with whom he or she associates. (p. 490)

REMEMBER: Psych refers to "mental" or "psychological," and pathos refers to "illness" or "sickness." Psychopathology means the study of mental illness or disorder.

2. The criterion of **statistical infrequency**, a method of defining abnormality, states that behaviors that commonly occur within a population are normal and those that rarely occur are abnormal. This approach is limited because some valuable behaviors are desirable but statistically rare. In addition, this approach encourages conformity, which would label inventors as eccentrics, and many entrepreneurs as abnormal. (p. 492)

Example: Very few people in the population would murder a stranger in cold blood; this behavior is considered abnormal by the infrequency criterion. (However, because few people give 30 percent of their incomes to charity, such generosity would also be considered abnormal by the infrequency approach.)

3. **Personal suffering** is the criterion for determining abnormality that is based on how much distress a person experiences. (p. 492)

Example: Sara washes her hands about once every five minutes in an attempt to remove the contamination of the world. Sara suffers greatly because of the persistent upsetting thoughts and severely dry skin.

4. The **norm violation** criterion is based on society's rules—a combination of social rules and cultural values. Defining abnormal behavior solely with this approach is problematic. Society's rules vary from culture to culture and, within a culture, evolve over time. (p. 492)

Example: Gladys usually talks to herself as she walks down the street. Because her behavior violates a norm in this culture, it is considered abnormal.

5. The **practical approach** defines abnormality based on the content, context, and consequences of behavior. To analyze the content of behavior, the following questions may be asked: Does the behavior cause impaired functioning? Is the behavior displayed at the wrong time or in an inappropriate situation? If the answers to these questions are yes, the behavior or thinking may be considered abnormal. (p. 492)

Example: Nick, a marketing executive, loves to take all his clothes off at home, turn his radio up, and sing and dance to the music. This is hardly abnormal. However, if Nick decided to do his song and dance in the middle of a client meeting, his behavior would be considered abnormal because it was being displayed at an inappropriate time.

6. **Impaired functioning** occurs when people cannot meet obligations appropriate to their social roles. (p. 492)

Example: Nora is too depressed to get out of bed and attend classes. Her friends are very worried because Nora hasn't felt like studying, eating, or even talking lately.

7. The **supernatural**, or **demonological**, **model**, the earliest model of abnormal behavior, attributes behavioral disorders to the supernatural powers of demons or gods. (p. 493)

Example: Troy experiences anxiety that is not linked to a particular situation. Troy's family believes his ancestors are angered by his current lifestyle and are taking their revenge by disturbing his peace.

8. The **medical model**, also called the **neurobiological model**, attributes abnormal behavior to the presence of biochemical, genetic, or other physical problems. (pp. 493–494)

Example: Nora's doctor believes that her depression is caused by an imbalance of some neurotransmitter levels. Nora is taking an antidepressant to correct this physical problem.

9. The **psychological model** views abnormal behavior as caused by mental processes. The psychodynamic, cognitive-behavioral, and phenomenological approaches are examples. (pp. 494–495)

10. A **sociocultural explanation** of abnormal behavior looks for the influence of factors such as gender, social situations, cultural expectations, and historical eras on behavior. (p. 495)

Example: The greater tolerance for excessive drinking in men may make alcohol abuse more likely in men than in women.

11. The **diathesis-stress model** attributes abnormal behavior to more than one cause; the model recognizes the integration of a person's biological predisposition, environmental surroundings, and psychological factors in mental illness. (p. 496)

Example: Frank has a biological susceptibility to stress. Entering the combined medical and doctoral program put him under a lot of stress. He was very depressed by the end of his first semester. Jill tends to be less stress-sensitive and is handling the same program with much less trouble.

12. **Anxiety disorders** are characterized by fear that causes a disruption in a person's life. Anxiety disorders include phobias, generalized anxiety disorders, panic dis-

order, obsessive-compulsive disorders, and posttraumatic stress disorder. (p. 501)

13. **Phobias** are strong, irrational fears of an object or situation that should not cause such a reaction. Examples are specific and social phobias. (p. 501)

14. A **specific phobia** is a fear of something specific, such as heights, animals, or air travel. (p. 501)

> *Example:* Claustrophobia is the fear of being in closed places.

15. A **social phobia** is a fear of being negatively evaluated by others or of doing something so impulsive or outrageous that public humiliation will result. (p. 502)

> *Example:* Rosa is terrified of giving a speech to her class (social situation). She is afraid that she will be completely unable to speak and will embarrass herself by stammering until she blushes and has to run away.

16. **Agoraphobia** is the fear of being alone or away from the security of home. (p. 502)

> *Example:* Eliza is afraid to leave her house. She cannot go shopping or out for an evening. She cannot hold a job or visit her friends and family. She cannot take her children to the doctor or drive them anywhere. Although she is less fearful when accompanied by her husband, she is still uncomfortable in any situation outside her home.

17. **Generalized anxiety disorder** involves relatively mild but long-lasting anxiety that is not focused on any object or situation. (p. 503)

> *Example:* Leslie has had a feeling of vague apprehension for about six weeks and always feels as though something bad is going to happen to her. She cannot sleep and is constantly tired and irritable.

18. **Panic disorder** consists of attacks of extreme fear and panic that occur with no warning and no obvious cause. Symptoms include heart palpitations, chest pain or pressure, dizziness, sweating, and a feeling of faintness. (p. 503)

> *Example:* Elise, a university professor, often experiences panic attacks. She can be in the middle of lecturing, driving her car, or browsing in a bookstore when she suddenly becomes terrified for no specific reason. She also experiences chest pain and dizziness during these episodes.

19. **Obsessive-compulsive disorder** (OCD) involves an obsession with particular thoughts or images, which motivates repetitive, uncontrollable behaviors. (p. 503)

> *Example:* Jenn cannot enter a room and feel comfortable unless she touches all the walls first. If she cannot do this, she becomes very anxious and highly agitated.

20. **Somatoform disorders** are characterized by the presence of physical symptoms of illness in the absence of a physical cause. They include conversion disorder, hypochondriasis, somatization disorder, and pain disorder. (p. 506)

> *REMEMBER:* Soma means "body." Somatoform disorders are characterized by perceived body illnesses in the absence of an actual physical problem.

21. A **conversion disorder** is a condition in which a person reports being blind, deaf, paralyzed, insensitive to pain, or even pregnant, but is not. The imagined physical disabilities often help the person be removed from the stressful situation. (p. 506)

> *REMEMBER:* Conversion means a "change from one state to another." Think of a person experiencing a changed physical state (blindness, deafness) but without physical explanation.
>
> *Example:* Joanie is a volunteer nurse on a cancer ward. She calls the hospital and calmly tells them that she cannot come to work because she cannot move her legs. There is nothing physically wrong, but the problem allows her to avoid dealing with patients who are in great pain and near death.

22. **Hypochondriasis** is an unjustified concern that one has a serious illness. The hypochondriac makes frequent visits to doctors and will not be convinced that he or she is healthy. (p. 507)

23. **Somatization disorder** is similar to hypochondriasis. People frequently go to the doctor with vague complaints about a multitude of physical problems rather than any specific disease. (p. 507)

24. **Pain disorder** involves the experience of sometimes extreme pain in the absence of a physical cause. (p. 507)

25. **Dissociative disorders** involve a sudden and usually temporary disruption in a person's memory, consciousness, or identity. (p. 507)

Example: Bill, lost in New York City, does not remember his name, home address, or workplace. He cannot remember anything that will give him a clue to his identity. Bill is suffering from a dissociative disorder.

REMEMBER: Dissociate means to "break a connection" or "disunite." Bill is disconnected from his past.

26. **Dissociative fugue** is a disorder in which a person experiences sudden memory loss, adopts a new identity, and moves to a new place. (p. 508)

27. **Dissociative amnesia** involves sudden loss of memory for personal information, but the person does not adopt a new identity and move to a new locale. (p. 508)

28. **Dissociative identity disorder** (the least common dissociative disorder) is a condition in which a person reports having more than one identity, each of which speaks, acts, and writes in a very different way. (p. 508)

29. **Mood disorders** (also called affective disorders) are extreme changes in mood, lasting for extended periods of time, that are inconsistent with the happy or sad events in a person's life. They include major depressive disorder, dysthymic disorder, mania, and bipolar disorder. (pp. 509–512)

30. **Major depressive disorder** is a mood disorder typified by feelings of sadness and hopelessness and an inability to enjoy oneself or take pleasure in anything. Simple tasks seem to require enormous effort, and concentration is impaired. (p. 510)

Example: Shelly is depressed. She sits on the couch and watches television without enjoying the shows. She lacks the energy to clean the house or to care for the children. She cries frequently for no apparent reason other than that she feels life is pointless.

31. **Delusions** are false beliefs. There are several types of delusions. (p. 510)

Example: Regina believes that she has been selected by the government to take over the moon once it is colonized. She anxiously checks the mail each day to see if her instructions have arrived from the president.

32. **Dysthymic disorder** is a form of mood disorder that is similar to depression but is less severe and lasts for a longer time. (p. 510)

33. **Mania** is an elated, very active emotional state. (p. 512)

Example: Lenny is a carpenter. While in a manic state, he decided to build a copy of the Empire State Building in his backyard. He called his office and quit his job, ordered supplies, and asked his neighbors to help him. When the people down the street tried to tell Lenny that he should check the city building codes before undertaking such an enormous task, he became belligerent. He stormed out of their house, accusing them of having no faith in the will, determination, and ability of American neighborhoods.

34. **Bipolar disorder** (manic-depression) is a form of mood disorder that involves extreme mood changes in which feelings of mania are followed by severe depression. (p. 512)

REMEMBER: Bi means "two," and polar means "extreme." A bipolar disorder is an affective disorder in which mood alternates between two opposite feelings: elation (mania) and extreme sadness (depression).

35. **Cyclothymic disorder** is a less severe form of bipolar disorder in which mood swings are not as extreme. (p. 512)

REMEMBER: A person's moods cycle between happiness and sadness in cyclothymic disorder.

36. **Schizophrenia** is characterized by several types of abnormal behaviors or disorders, including abnormalities in thinking, perception and attention, affect, motor behavior, personal identity, motivation, and day-to-day functioning. There are five types of schizophrenia: paranoid, disorganized, catatonic, undifferentiated, and residual. (pp. 515–517)

Example: Neologisms, an abnormality seen in schizophrenics' thinking, speaking, and writing, are words that have meaning only to the person speaking them. For example, the word teardom in "I hereby teardom your happiness" is a neologism. There is no such word.

37. **Hallucinations** are false perceptions that occur in schizophrenics. (p. 516)

Example: Many schizophrenics hear "voices" talking to them inside their heads. They may also report seeing things that don't really exist.

38. **Paranoid** schizophrenia accounts for about 40 percent of all schizophrenia diagnoses. The most common symptoms include delusions of grandeur or persecution, which can be accompanied by anger, argumentativeness, anxiety, or jealousy. (p. 517)

39. Disorganized schizophrenia includes symptoms of delusions and hallucinations, ritualistic movements, flat affect, and possible loss of bladder and bowel control. (p. 517)

40. Catatonic schizophrenia is usually diagnosed when movement disorders are present. An individual can alternate between total immobility and wild agitation. (p. 517)

41. Undifferentiated schizophrenia accounts for about 40 percent of schizophrenia diagnoses. People whose schizophrenic symptoms fit none of the above patterns are diagnosed as undifferentiated schizophrenics. (p. 517)

42. Residual schizophrenia describes a person who had an episode of schizophrenia in the past but exhibits no current symptoms. (p. 517)

43. Personality disorders are long-standing behavior patterns that create problems, usually for others, and are not as severe as mental disorders. There are several types of personality disorders, including schizotypal, avoidant, narcissistic, and antisocial. (p. 520)

44. Schizotypal personality disorder occurs in a person who exhibits symptoms similar to but less severe than schizophrenia. (p. 521)

45. Avoidant personality disorder is characterized by a long-term pattern of avoiding social interaction or situations. People with this disorder tend to be loners and extremely sensitive to criticism. (p. 521)

46. Narcissistic personality disorders are diagnosed when people have an exaggerated sense of self-importance, have to be the center of attention, have severe feelings of self-doubt, and have very few true friends. (p. 521)

Example: Tom is inconsiderate of everyone, especially the people who work for him. He borrows money from them, stops at their homes all night, and demands that they run their lives around his schedule. If one of his workers approaches him with a problem, Tom always ends up talking about himself instead of focusing on the person who has asked him for help. Tom's primary goal in life is to become famous, and he tells everyone how brilliant his ideas are. But deep down he has a very strong fear that he is not very good at his job.

47. Antisocial personality disorder involves a long-term persistent pattern of impulsive, selfish, unscrupulous, even criminal behavior. People with antiso-

cial personalities appear to have no morals and can be dangerous to the public because they very rarely experience deep feelings for anyone. Typically, they are smooth-talking, intelligent, charming liars who have no sense of responsibility. (p. 521)

Example: Andre, although quite charming, has been in trouble since his early teens. He has stolen cars, broken into people's homes, terrorized small children, and conned elderly people out of their social security checks. His parents and social worker have tried all sorts of remedies from punishment to counseling to no avail. Andre is now thirty and in prison for raping and murdering a teenage girl. The prison psychiatrist noted that Andre expresses no regret or remorse for his behavior.

48. Substance-related disorders are characterized by long-term drug use that causes physical or psychological harm to the user or others. Alcoholism is one example. (p. 523)

49. Addiction is a physiological need for a substance. It is evident when a person needs more and more of a substance to achieve the desired effect. (p. 523)

50. Alcoholism is characterized by frequent and extreme consumption of alcoholic beverages. (p. 523)

Example: Nancy has been an alcoholic for twenty years. She began drinking socially when she moved to the suburbs. Eventually, she drank every day to the point of being drunk, and she finally lost her job. Her children have suffered because they do not have regular meals, cannot bring their friends home, and often hear their parents argue about their mother's drinking.

FILL-IN-THE-BLANKS KEY TERMS

This section will help you check your factual knowledge of the key terms introduced in this chapter. Fill in each blank with the appropriate term from the list of key terms above.

1. The _____ criterion labels behavior as abnormal if it doesn't conform to society's rules.

2. Abnormal behavior is defined as anything that is uncommon, according to the _____ criterion.

3. The _____ model attributes abnormal behavior to the interaction between a person's genetic predisposition and the environment.

4. A person with an intense fear of objects has a _____ phobia.

5. A person who becomes anxious when leaving her or his home has _____.

6. A person who suffers from constant but mild depression may have _____.

7. A person who appears to be paralyzed but really isn't may suffer from _____.

8. A person plagued by particular thoughts suffers from _____.

9. _____ are sure they are sick and report a variety of unrelated symptoms during frequent visits to the doctor.

10. Sudden and usually temporary disruptions in a person's memory, consciousness, or identity are symptoms of _____.

11. A person plagued by attacks of extreme fear could be diagnosed as having a _____.

12. A person who suffers from frequent and violent mood swings (extreme depression to mania) has _____.

13. Abnormalities in thought, perception, affect, motivation, and motor behavior are characteristic of _____.

14. People who evade social situations and interactions, like to be alone, and are overly sensitive to criticism may be experiencing _____.

15. _____ is a physiological need for a drug.

Total Correct (See answer key) _____

LEARNING OBJECTIVES

1. Define psychopathology. Explain why psychopathology is a social as well as a personal matter. (pp. 490–491)

2. Describe four criteria for abnormality. Discuss the advantages and disadvantages of using each criteria. Describe the practical approach and impaired functioning. (p. 492)

3. Describe the four main explanations for psychological disorders: supernatural influences, biological factors, psychological processes, and sociocultural context. (pp. 493–496)

4. Give an example of how the medical or neurobiological model would explain disorders. (pp. 493–494)

5. Describe the approaches that are part of the psychological model. (pp. 494–495)

6. List and give examples of sociocultural explanations for psychological disorders. (p. 495)

7. Define diathesis-stress model. (p. 496)

8. Describe the contents of the Diagnostic and Statistical Manual of Mental Disorders (DSM-IV). List the five axes used in diagnosis based on DSM-IV. (pp. 496–497)

9. Explain why accurate and reliable diagnosis is important. Define interrater reliability, and discuss its relationship to diagnosis. (p. 499)

10. Define anxiety disorder. Specify what disorders are classified as anxiety disorders. (p. 501)

11. Define phobia, and give a brief description of specific phobia, social phobia, and agoraphobia. (pp. 501–502)

12. Define generalized anxiety disorder, panic disorders, and obsessive-compulsive disorders. Explain the difference between obsessions and compulsions. (p. 503)

13. State the causes, according to the various theoretical models, of anxiety disorders. (pp. 503–504)

14. Discuss how we are biologically prepared to learn certain phobias. (p. 505)

15. Define somatoform disorder. Give a brief description of conversion disorder, hypochondriasis, somatization disorder, and pain disorder. (pp. 506–507)

16. State the causes, according to various theoretical models, of somatoform disorders. (p. 507)

17. Define dissociative disorder. Compare and contrast dissociative fugue and dissociative amnesia. Describe dissociative identity disorder. (pp. 507–508)

18. State the causes, according to the various theoretical models, of dissociative disorders. (pp. 508–509)

19. Define mood disorders. Give a brief description of major depressive disorder, dysthymic disorder, bipolar disorder, mania, and cyclothymic disorder. (pp. 509–512)

20. Describe the relationship between depression and suicide. List the general guidelines for determining if a person might commit suicide. (pp. 510–511)

21. State the biological and psychological causes, according to various theoretical models, of mood disorders. Describe how learned helplessness and attributional style may contribute to depression. (pp. 512–514)

22. Define schizophrenia. Describe the disorganized thought and language characteristic of schizophrenia. Give examples of neologisms, loose associations, clang associations, and word salad. (pp. 514–515)

23. Describe ideas of reference, thought broadcasting, thought blocking, thought withdrawal, thought insertions, and hallucinations. (pp. 515–516)

24. Compare and contrast paranoid, disorganized, catatonic, undifferentiated, and residual schizophrenia. List the percentage of the total schizophrenic population each type represents. (p. 517)

25. State the possible causes of schizophrenia, according to various theoretical models. (pp. 517–520)

26. Define personality disorder. Give a brief description of schizotypal, avoidant, narcissistic, and antisocial personality disorders. (pp. 520–521)

27. State the possible causes of personality disorders. Discuss the quasi-experimental research on the link between child abuse and antisocial personality disorder (pp. 521–523)

28. Define substance-related disorder and addiction. (p. 523)

29. Describe the problems associated with and the theoretical explanations for the development of alcohol, heroin, and cocaine dependence. (pp. 524–526)

30. Describe the differences between externalizing and internalizing disorders of childhood. Define conduct disorders, attention-deficit hyperactivity disorder, separation anxiety disorder, and autistic disorder. (pp. 526–527)

31. Discuss the laws designed to protect the rights of people with severe psychological disorders who are accused of a crime. (pp. 527–528)

32. Describe the legal reform procedures regarding mental illness. (p. 528)

CONCEPTS AND EXERCISES

No. 1: Choosing a Jury

Completing this exercise should help you to achieve Learning Objective 2.

Connie, a fifty-year-old woman, has killed her husband. She has pleaded not guilty and will stand trial. The prosecution and the defense lawyer are now in the process of selecting jurors. Connie's lawyer will attempt to convince the jury that, although she has committed a crime, the long-standing physical and mental abuse that she and her children endured makes her behavior understandable. She should, therefore, receive a lesser sentence.

Connie's lawyer will want jurors with a particular approach to defining abnormality. Each juror will be presented with the following list of behaviors and asked if he or she thinks that the behaviors are abnormal and why.

- ° Getting drunk and singing at the top of your lungs
- ° Leading a hunger strike outside the White House
- ° Having a very high IQ
- ° Owning one hundred cats

If you were Connie's lawyer, which of the following two prospective jurors would you choose?

Prospective juror one: I think there are times when the situation calls for a little celebration. I remember when my first grandchild was born. I whooped it up a little myself. As for a hunger strike, well, I think that some people, because of the circumstances in their lives, have been mistreated in this society. Someone should protest for them.

I knew this fella who is powerful smart, and he is a bit strange, but heck, if we didn't have people who were a little bit different, the world would be an awful boring place.

'Bout them cats. Hmmm. I had an aunt who had more cats than she did hairs on her head. She loved those varmints as if they were kids. She wasn't any stranger than the other folk that I knew. She just didn't have anybody living at home anymore, and the cats gave her something to care for and love. Everybody needs something to love.

Prospective juror two: The law strictly forbids drinking where I live, and based on that, I think people should not do it. Furthermore, if people want to change the system, they should do it through the proper channels. Holding a hunger strike is not the way to make a difference. People will only think you are a little weird if you sit on some steps and don't eat. I don't like very smart people. All the brainy people I knew in school were either uppity or nerds, not like everybody else. There are laws about the number of pets one is allowed to own, and I think that the law should be upheld at all times.

No. 2: The Who's Who of Psychological Disorders

Completing this exercise should help you to achieve Learning Objectives 10–19 and 21–25.

Ron, a hospital receptionist, is in trouble. He has several patients sitting in the reception room, and he has misplaced all the morning files. He does not know which patient is supposed to see which doctor. He has written a list of everything he can remember in order to get each patient to the right doctor. See if you can help him with the rest of his list.

° Doctor 1 has ordered a brain scan that would provide a view of the patient's ventricles.
° Doctor 2 is trying to find out what types of childhood abuse this patient was exposed to.
° Doctor 3 talked to his patient last week for an hour or so. The discussion revolved around ways in which the person could take control over his life and not feel so helpless.
° Doctor 4 has been investigating the presence of mood disorders in the family history of her patient.
° Doctor 5 is trying to discover what has made his patient so afraid of flying.

° Patient A has been standing alone in a corner for over an hour with one foot off the floor and her arms outstretched.
° Patient B is sitting next to the window, sobbing. Ron remembers that last week this man was trying to get all the people in the office to help him run for president.
° Patient C is trying to console patient B.
° Patient D is sobbing silently to herself. Her hair and clothing are dirty. Ron knows this woman lost her job after staying home and sleeping for two weeks.
° Patient E, when paying the bill for each office visit, gives Ron a check with a different name and handwriting each time.

Doctor 1 is probably seeing patient _____.

Doctor 2 is probably seeing patient _____.

Doctor 3 is probably seeing patient _____.

Doctor 4 is probably seeing patient _____.

Doctor 5 is probably seeing patient _____.

CRITICAL THINKING

Centuries ago, people with abnormal behavior were thought to be witches possessed by demons. One of the standard methods for determining whether someone was a witch was to bind the suspect's hands and feet and then throw her into a lake. If she drowned, she was normal and therefore innocent. If she didn't drown and survived the ordeal, she was judged guilty and put to death.

Using your critical thinking skills, explain what is wrong with this thinking.

PERSONAL LEARNING ACTIVITIES

1. Write descriptions of behaviors you observed in the last month that you think are unusual. Evaluate them using each of the criteria (statistical infrequency, personal suffering, norm violation). Was one criterion more likely than the others to be labeled abnormal? According to the practical approach, are the behaviors abnormal? (Learning Objective 2)

2. Use your list of unusual behaviors from Personal Learning Activity 1 to think about the causes of behavior. Describe supernatural, neurobiological, and sociocultural explanations of the cause of the behaviors. (Learning Objective 3)

3. Imagine you have a major psychological disorder. Although it is difficult to know what someone else experiences, try to use the information in your text to identify the symptoms you might display. Give the details of how your current life would be different if you had this disorder. What behaviors would you exhibit if you went to class, to dinner, or were alone in your home? How would the disorder, and others' reactions to it, make you feel? For example, if you experienced dysthymia, how would you view course work, recreation, and relationships? What would your friends notice about you? How would you interpret their concern? (Learning Objectives 10–12, 15, 17, 19, and 22–24)

4. Choose a disorder—perhaps the one you described in Personal Learning Activity 3—and describe what a psychodynamic, a cognitive-behavioral, a biological, and a phenomenological theorist would believe caused the disorder. (Learning Objectives 4 and 5)

5. What is your opinion of the not-guilty-by-reason-of-insanity defense and the guilty-but-mentally-ill verdict? Do you think that courts should require defendants to prove they were insane rather than require the prosecution to prove the defendant was sane? If not, why not? If so, why? (Learning Objectives 31 and 32)

MULTIPLE-CHOICE QUESTIONS

SAMPLE QUIZ 1

1. The impaired functioning criterion is most associated with which approach to defining abnormality?
   a. Statistical infrequency
   b. Psychopathological
   c. Norm violation
   d. Practical

2. Encouraging conformity is associated with which approach to defining normality?
   a. Practical
   b. Norm violation
   c. Statistical infrequency
   d. Both (b) and (c)

3. According to the _____ model, disorders are evidence of an obstruction in the self-actualization process.
   a. phenomenological
   b. supernatural
   c. psychopathological
   d. perceptual

4. Zelda is depressed. She is sitting in her cell after being condemned as a witch, according to the criteria set by the church. What century is she living in, and what model of abnormal behavior do her prosecutors believe in?
   a. Twentieth; supernatural
   b. Twentieth; medical
   c. Twelfth; supernatural
   d. Twelfth; phenomenological

5. The DSM-IV lists five axes for diagnosticians to use in evaluating people. Which of the following is *not* covered in one of the axes?
   a. Major psychological disorder description
   b. Physical condition
   c. Stress level
   d. Social status

6. Kat has dropped out of school. She cannot attend class because the thought of leaving her apartment leaves her feeling nauseated, anxious, and faint. Her symptoms suggest that she
   a. suffers from agoraphobia.
   b. has a phobia about classrooms.
   c. has panic attacks.
   d. has test anxiety.

7. Laurence is a psychotherapist. One of his patients, Heidi, complains of being very shy and lonely. She also says that she has a very intense need to touch repeatedly all four walls of any room she has never been in before. Laurence tells Heidi that she learned this compulsive behavior so that she could delay immediate social contact with anyone in the room, thereby avoiding the anxiety caused by her extreme shyness. Laurence adheres to the _____ model of abnormal behavior.
   a. psychodynamic
   b. phenomenological
   c. cognitive-behavioral
   d. neurobiological

8. Sergio, a psychiatric intern, has just completed an evaluation of his new patient by using DSM-IV. Read his evaluation and find what is missing: The patient is experiencing major depressive disorder, has a dependent personality, has had very minor stress in the past few months, and is in good physical health.
   a. Axis I
   b. Axis II
   c. Axis IV
   d. Axis V

9. An excessive and unwarranted fear of doorways would be considered
   a. a specific phobia.
   b. a social phobia.
   c. agoraphobia.
   d. panic disorder.

10. A conversion disorder is characterized by
    a. functional impairment of a limb or sensory ability with no apparent physical cause.
    b. severe pain with no apparent cause.
    c. a constant fear of becoming seriously ill.
    d. frequent vague complaints of physical symptoms.

11. Tomas has been suffering from severe chest pain for the past few weeks. His doctor has run extensive tests but can find no physical problem. Tomas
    a. may have a pain disorder.
    b. is a hypochondriac.
    c. is paranoid.
    d. suffers from somatization disorder.

12. "Massive repression of unwanted impulses or memories is responsible for dissociative disorders," is most likely a quote from a _____ theorist.
    a. cognitive-behavioral
    b. phenomenological
    c. psychodynamic
    d. sociocultural

13. Nuwanda and a classmate are talking when Mary approaches and calls Nuwanda "Paul." Although Nuwanda explains that he's from Dallas, Mary convincingly argues that he is Paul, her next-door neighbor in Chicago for twenty years. Nuwanda's identification card confirms that his name is Paul, but he insists that he has no memory of living in Chicago or of being called Paul. Nuwanda/Paul most likely has
    a. dissociative amnesia.
    b. dissociative fugue.
    c. a conversion disorder.
    d. schizophrenia.

14. For the past three months, Beth has been sleeping twelve to sixteen hours a day and has gained thirty pounds. Gail can barely sleep at all and has lost fifteen pounds without trying; she just does not want to eat. Both women could be suffering from
    a. obsessive-compulsive disorder.
    b. major depressive disorder.
    c. hyperchondriasis.
    d. hypochondriasis.

15. Pam noticed during their daily tutoring sessions that Enya seemed unhappy for about a week, then happy for the next week. Sometimes the moods lasted longer, but Enya never settled into sadness or happiness for more than a few weeks at a time. Enya consulted a therapist, who suggested that since her mood swings were neither extreme nor debilitating, she most likely was experiencing
    a. depression.
    b. cyclothymic disorder.
    c. dysthymic disorder.
    d. mania.

16. Maggie's mother notices that Maggie has become much less concerned about her appearance and hygiene lately, but what concerns her even more is that Maggie seems to giggle inappropriately and has difficulty in communicating. When Maggie's mother asks her what is wrong, Maggie replies, "Nothing something bumpthing. I cannot say play day may lay." What disorder does Maggie most likely have?
    a. catatonic schizophrenia
    b. disorganized schizophrenia
    c. bipolar disorder
    d. dissociative identity disorder

17. Juan has been diagnosed as schizophrenic. He is positive that all the students sitting around him during a test are cheating by reading his thoughts. Juan is experiencing thought

a. blocking.
b. withdrawal.
c. insertion.
d. broadcasting.

18. During your first semester at college, you had a difficult time living with your roommate. He was basically insecure but bragged about his accomplishments both in the classroom and out. He used all your things as though he had a right to them, and he always had to be the center of attention at every party. Your roommate could have been diagnosed as having a(n) _____ disorder.
    a. antisocial personality
    b. narcissistic personality
    c. process
    d. sociopathic personality

19. Which of the following is a risk for substance abusers?
    a. AIDS
    b. Poor nutrition
    c. Suicide
    d. All of the above

20. Aaron is an infant who shows no signs of attachment to his parents. He doesn't like to be held and doesn't smile or laugh. Of the following, Aaron is most likely experiencing _____ disorder.
    a. infantile schizotypal
    b. autistic
    c. antisocial personality
    d. narcissistic personality

Total Correct (See answer key) _____

SAMPLE QUIZ 2

Use this quiz to reassess your learning after taking Quiz 1 and reviewing the chapter.

1. According to the infrequency criterion, behavior would be considered abnormal if it
    a. caused discomfort.
    b. was uncommon.
    c. was bizarre but situationally appropriate.
    d. impaired a person's ability to function.

2. Stephen, a college student, drinks so much every weekend that he is barely able to function on Monday. Stephen's behavior would be labeled abnormal by the _____ approach.
    a. demonological
    b. practical
    c. diathesis-stress
    d. logical

3. Supernatural explanations of abnormal behavior form the basis of what model?
   a. Cognitive-behavioral
   b. Phenomenological
   c. Neurobiological
   d. Demonological

4. Michael is reacting poorly to the news that his closest friend is dead. He is experiencing insomnia and sometimes believes he hears his friend's voice. After his condition worsens, Michael is diagnosed with schizophrenia. Ellyn maintains that Michael is having difficulties in coping because he inherited a predisposition towards schizophrenia, but she says it never would have appeared if he hadn't lost his closest friend. Ellyn is explaining Michael's abnormal behavior using the _____ model.
   a. diathesis-stress
   b. cognitive-behavioral
   c. supernatural
   d. phenomenological

5. Mary Sue, a brilliant neurosurgeon, visits the local animal shelter every morning and lectures the animals on the dangers of ingesting poisonous microbes. Although her behavior is considered a bit strange, the shelter's workers like having someone lavish attention on the animals. Afterward, Mary Sue goes to work and starts her day on time. Mary Sue's behavior would be considered abnormal according to which approach or criterion?
   a. Statistical infrequency
   b. Psychopathological
   c. Logical
   d. Practical

6. Which of the following is no longer contained in the current DSM?
   a. Bipolar disorder
   b. Neurosis disorder
   c. Generalized anxiety disorder
   d. All are contained in the current DSM.

7. Because Shantha has recurring thoughts about losing her belongings, she is continually checking the location of knickknacks and making sure her doors are locked. Shantha's strange behavior is most likely
   a. an obsession.
   b. a compulsion.
   c. due to mania.
   d. due to a conversion disorder.

8. Frank is so afraid of getting sick at the dinner table and being humiliated that he will not eat at a restaurant. Frank has
   a. a specific phobia.
   b. agoraphobia.
   c. a social phobia.
   d. an obsessive-compulsive disorder.

9. Dr. Arenas, who has a psychodynamic orientation, is seeing a client with a conversion disorder. What will Dr. Arenas most likely say is the explanation for the patient's conversion disorder?
   a. The client has been reinforced for showing fear.
   b. The client's unconscious conflicts produced anxiety, which showed itself as a physical symptom.
   c. The client's repressed memories may have caused the amnesia.
   d. The client views the world as an unfriendly place.

10. Hans, a police officer, was working the night shift when he came upon a young man who claimed that he could not remember his name, where he lived or worked, or anything else about himself. Most likely the mystery person displays
    a. dissociative disorder.
    b. antisocial personality disorder.
    c. dissociative identity disorder.
    d. schizophrenia.

11. Cognitive-behavioral theorists would probably say that people who _____ are most likely to become depressed.
    a. exaggerate the dark side of events
    b. blame themselves when things go wrong
    c. jump to overly pessimistic generalizations
    d. all of the above

12. Philip displays bipolar disorder. Which statement would best describe him?
    a. He is sometimes very depressed and sometimes in a pleasant mood.
    b. He is alternately depressed and wildly elated.
    c. He has sudden onsets of depression that last for a few hours and then he feels fine.
    d. His disorder is a very common one.

13. Mercedes has just brought home a dog from the pound. She was told that the dog's previous owners kept it on a leash and beat it daily for no reason. Mercedes notices that when the neighborhood kids bother the dog, it does not even try to run away. Mercedes' dog most likely has
    a. generalized anxiety.
    b. learned helplessness.
    c. hypersensitive brainstem mechanisms.
    d. enlarged ventricles.

14. While visiting a psychiatric ward, you overhear one of the patients deliver the following monologue: "Thereby the obfuscation incipient to redundant and undeniably factual parapsychosis is left in a state transcendental to the issue of man's inhumanity to buildings and federal income tax." This type of communication is called
    a. word salad.
    b. clang association.
    c. insertion
    d. attention association.

15. Childhood externalizing behavior problems include
    a. problems that create distress within the child.
    b. autistic disorder.
    c. attention-deficit hyperactivity disorder.
    d. all of the above.

16. Abraham is a catatonic schizophrenic. Which of the following symptoms is he most likely to exhibit?
    a. Alternation between bizarre poses and wild excitement
    b. Unorganized delusions, inappropriate giggling, and incoherent speech
    c. Delusions of grandeur and argumentativeness
    d. Strong fear of disease

17. What type of personality disorder would you expect to find among people in jail for fraud?
    a. Narcissistic
    b. Depressive
    c. Antisocial
    d. Mood

18. Which type of schizophrenia is the most common?
    a. Thought-disordered
    b. Paranoid
    c. Catatonic
    d. Disorganized

19. Victor, a ten-year-old, tells a psychologist that he first came to the court system after setting a car on fire at age eight. In the numerous police contacts since then, he has been accused of theft, assault, and willful destruction of property. Victor most likely has
    a. autistic disorder.
    b. narcissistic personality disorder.
    c. conduct disorder.
    d. schizotypal personality disorder.

20. Willis is accused of killing his parents, but he doesn't seem to understand what is going on. He continues to ask to see his parents and wants to go home with them. Willis may be declared mentally incompetent to stand trial if he

a. does not understand the charges even after treatment with psychoactive drugs.
b. shows he had an irresistible impulse to murder his parents.
c. did not know that killing his parents would be permanent.
d. is diagnosed with a major psychological disorder.

Total Correct (See answer key) _____

ANSWERS TO FILL-IN-THE-BLANKS KEY TERMS

1. norm violation (p. 492)
2. infrequency (p. 492)
3. diathesis-stress (p. 496)
4. specific (p. 501)
5. agoraphobia (p. 502)
6. dysthymic disorder (p. 510)
7. conversion disorder (p. 506)
8. obsessive-compulsive disorder (p. 503)
9. hypochondriacs (p. 507)
10. dissociative disorders (p. 507)
11. panic disorder (p. 503)
12. bipolar disorder (p. 512)
13. schizophrenia (p. 515)
14. avoidant personality disorder (p. 521)
15. Addiction (p. 523)

ANSWERS TO CONCEPTS AND EXERCISES

No. 1: Choosing a Jury

Connie's lawyer wants jurors who define abnormal behavior from the practical approach. He wants jurors who think that her behavior is understandable given the context or situation of her home life. Connie's lawyer should choose prospective juror 1. When evaluating the abnormality of each behavior listed, this person considers the context as well as the content of the behavior. Prospective juror 2 is very concerned about the frequency of behaviors (the statistical infrequency criterion) and the social rules about behaviors based on the legal system (the norm violation criterion). (pp. 492–493)

No. 2: The Who's Who of Psychological Disorders

°A. Doctor 1 is seeing a catatonic schizophrenic. This type of schizophrenia is characterized by abnormal movement, such as stupor. Recent research suggests that negative symptoms, such as catatonia, are associated with abnormal brain structures, including the ventricles. (p. 518)

°E. Doctor 2 is seeing a patient who has dissociative identity disorder. This disorder is often associated with childhood abuse, although not always. (p. 509)

°D. Doctor 3 is seeing a depressed person. Learned helplessness may lead to depression, which is why this doctor is trying to help this person realize that she does indeed have control over her life. (p. 513)

°B. Doctor 4 is seeing a person with bipolar disorder (also called manic-depression). Genetic factors seem to play a large role in this affective disorder, which is why the doctor is trying to trace the family history. (p. 512)

°C. Doctor 5 is treating a specific phobia, which is characterized by the fear of something, such as flying. She is trying to find out what learning experience caused this person to be afraid of flying. (You had to use the process of elimination to find the correct answer.) (p. 501)

ANSWERS TO CRITICAL THINKING

The hypothesis: The suspect is a witch. The evidence: Those who survive are witches and those who die are not. (NOTE: There was no attempt to formulate or test an alternative hypothesis, because the suspect was dead.)

ANSWERS TO MULTIPLE-CHOICE QUESTIONS

Circle the question numbers you answered correctly.

Sample Quiz 1

1. *d* is the answer. The impaired functioning criterion, part of the practical approach, asks whether a person can display the behavior in question and still meet the demands of everyday life. (pp. 492–493)
   a, c. The impaired functioning criterion is not part of the statistical infrequency or norm violation criteria.
   b. Psychopathology, another word for mental illness, is not an approach to defining abnormality.

2. *d* is the answer. To conform, one follows the practices of the majority. Statistically, behaviors that are displayed by the majority of people are normal. According to the norm violation criterion, society determines which social rules to follow. Both criteria are problematic because some of the world's unique (nonconforming) people might thus be considered abnormal. (p. 492)
   a. According to the practical approach, normal behavior can be unique (not seen frequently in other people) as long as the demands of everyday life are met and the behavior is situationally appropriate (approved of by others in that situation).
   b. c is also correct.
   c. b is also correct.

3. *a* is the answer. According to the phenomenological model, failure to be in touch with and express one's true feelings causes an obstruction in the self-actualization process. When this happens, the person distorts his or her perceptions of reality, which causes behavior disorders. (p. 495)
   b. According to the demonological model, supernatural forces cause abnormal behavior.
   c. Psychopathology is another word for mental illness, not an approach to defining abnormal behavior.
   d. A person's perception of reality is a cause of abnormal behavior, according to the phenomenological model, but perception is not a synonym for the name of this model.

4. *c* is the answer. From the fifth to the fifteenth centuries, supernatural explanations of behavior disorders dominated. Religious leaders played a large role in deciding who was a witch or a heretic. (p. 493)
   a, b. During the twentieth century, the medical model, which said that abnormal behavior is caused by physical problems, not sorcery, became established.
   d. The phenomenological model was not articulated in the twelfth century.

5. *d* is the answer. (pp. 496–497)
   a, b, c. The five axes comprise major disorder description, mental retardation or personality disorders, physical condition, stress level, and highest functioning level.

6. *a* is the answer. Kat becomes anxious when she thinks about leaving her home. This is a symptom of agoraphobia. (p. 502)
   b. Being unable to attend class is a consequence of Kat's fear of leaving her apartment, but it is not the object of her phobia.

  c. Panic attacks are characterized by extreme terror, racing heartbeat, and, sometimes, the feeling of going crazy. Kat did not experience any of these symptoms.

  d. There is no mention of tests or test anxiety in the question. Kat is afraid of leaving her apartment.

7. *c* is the answer. Cognitive-behavioral theorists see compulsive behaviors as learned habits that allow a person to escape or avoid anxiety-provoking situations. For Heidi, who is painfully shy, new social situations cause extreme anxiety. (p. 495)

  a. A psychodynamic therapist would look for unconscious conflicts. Laurence is focusing on the behavioral basis of Heidi's problem.

  b. A phenomenological therapist might suggest that Heidi's behavior is caused by her unique perceptions of social situations.

  d. Those who view abnormal behaviors as symptoms of neurobiological or medical problems would look for physiological irregularities.

8. *d* is the answer. Axis V evaluates the highest level of adaptive functioning over the previous year. This is not mentioned in Sergio's report. (pp. 496–497)

  a. Axis I lists descriptions of the major psychological disorders. Sergio's patient is experiencing major depressive disorder.

  b. Axis II lists mental retardation and personality disorders. Sergio's patient has a dependent personality.

  c. Axis IV rates the level of stress experienced in the recent past. Sergio's patient has experienced very minor stress in the past few months.

9. *a* is the answer. (p. 501)

  b. A social phobia is the fear of doing something that would cause embarrassment in public.

  c. Agoraphobia is the fear of leaving home or being away from a loved one.

  d. Panic disorder causes moments of terror in which the person believes he or she will die.

10. *a* is the answer. Typical conversion disorders involve functional impairment, such as blindness, paralysis, or deafness, with no apparent physical cause. (p. 506)

  b. Pain disorder is characterized by severe pain with no apparent cause.

  c. Hypochondriacs constantly fear becoming seriously ill.

  d. People with somatization disorder or hypochondriasis have a tendency to complain of vague symptoms.

11. *a* is the answer. Severe pain in the chest, neck, or back with no apparent physical cause is a classic symptom of the somatoform disorder called pain disorder. (p. 507)

  b. A hypochondriac worries about being stricken with a serious disease and often reports vague symptoms. Severe pain is not a vague symptom.

  c. A paranoid person usually worries about being persecuted by a particular person or group.

  d. Somatization disorder involves vague reports of unrelated problems, but Tomas was quite specific about his chest pain.

12. *c* is the answer. Dissociative disorders involve some degree of disruption in memory, consciousness, or personal identity. According to the psychodynamic model, psychological disorders are caused by unresolved unconscious psychological conflicts. When they threaten to become conscious and cause anxiety, the individual finds a way to keep them in the unconscious. To accomplish this, some people may forget not only unconscious material but also who they are or any of the personal bits of information that identify them. (p. 508)

  a. A cognitive-behavioral theorist would say that an individual has been rewarded in some way for dissociating. Perhaps distressing anxiety is removed when the person forgets her or his identity or escapes into another personality.

  b. A phenomenological (or humanistic) theorist would say that an individual's multiple personalities actually represent the overt expression of dramatically conflicting perceptions of the world.

  d. A sociocultural theorist would look to society, the environment, and social roles for the cause of a disorder.

13. *b* is the answer. Paul has not only forgotten about his previous life, but he has moved to a new location and assumed a new identity as a student named Nuwanda. (p. 508)

  a. Dissociative amnesia is forgetting personally relevant information, but one does not move to a new location and create a new identity.

  c. Conversion disorders are a type of somatoform disorder in which people experience physical symptoms, like paralysis, that do not have a physical cause.

  d. Schizophrenia is characterized by more disordered thoughts and perceptions.

14. *b* is the answer. Weight loss or gain and sleep changes, including oversleeping or insomnia, are typical of depression. (p. 510)

a, d. Weight loss or gain and sleeping problems do not usually occur in obsessive-compulsive disorder or hypochondriasis.

c. There is no disorder known as hyperchondriasis.

15. *b* is the answer. Cyclothymic disorder is a less severe version of bipolar disorder. Since Enya is still able to work, her swings are not as extreme as the swing from mania to depression. (p. 512)
a. Enya cycles between happiness and sadness; she is not just sad. In addition, major depressive disorder is more debilitating than what Enya is experiencing. People with major depressive disorder feel hopeless and worthless for weeks or months and lose interest in recreation, friends, and work.
c. Dysthymic disorder is a less severe form of depression in which people feel the sadness and lack of pleasure associated with depression, but less intensely and for a longer time.
d. Mania is an agitated, ecstatic, energetic state. Enya cycles between happiness and sadness.

16. *b* is the answer. Disorganized schizophrenia is characterized by unrelated delusions and hallucinations, inappropriate laughter, and neglected personal hygiene. (p. 517)
a. The most notable feature of catatonic schizophrenia is its disordered movement. A person may vary between wild excitement and total immobility.
c. Bipolar disorder is a mood disorder in which a person varies from depression to mania.
d. Dissociative identity disorder is a disorder in which a person has two or more personalities that speak, write, think, and act in different ways.

17. *d* is the answer. Juan believes that other people can hear his thoughts. This is called thought broadcasting. (p. 516)
a, b. The belief that a person's thoughts are being prevented or that thoughts are being "stolen" as soon as they appear is called thought blocking or thought withdrawal.
c. The belief that other people's thoughts are being put into a person's mind is called insertion.

18. *b* is the answer. Your roommate sounds self-centered, arrogant, and thirsty for attention all the time. This combination of symptoms is typical of narcissistic personality disorder. (p. 521)
a, d. Someone who coldly and calmly manipulates your feelings, time, or money would fit the de-

scription of someone with an antisocial personality disorder.
c. There is no such thing as a process disorder.

19. *d* is the answer. Heroin and cocaine users are especially at risk for AIDS, but all substance abusers can suffer poor nutrition. Alcohol and other drugs are implicated in many suicides. (p. 525)

20. *b* is the answer. Autistic disorder is a type of childhood disorder. Children with autistic disorder are not attached to caregivers, do not make eye contact, and are generally unable to be social. They may rock themselves and play with objects endlessly. (p. 527)
a. There is no such thing as infantile schizotypal disorder.
c. Antisocial personality disorder is a long-term pattern of irresponsible, rash, unprincipled behavior.
d. Narcissistic personality disorder is characterized by an exaggerated sense of self-importance and a need for attention.

Now turn to the quiz analysis table at the end of this chapter to find which areas you know well and which areas you need to work on. Circle the numbers in the table for items on Quiz 1 that you answered correctly.

ANSWERS TO MULTIPLE-CHOICE QUESTIONS

Circle the question numbers you answered correctly.

Sample Quiz 2

1. *b* is the answer. The statistical infrequency criterion says that a behavior is normal if many people in a given population display it, and abnormal if few people display the behavior. (p. 492)
a. The practical approach considers the discomfort that a particular behavior causes as a factor for defining abnormality.
c. Content and appropriateness are evaluated by the practical approach to defining abnormality.
d. Meeting the demands of everyday life is part of the impaired functioning criterion, an important feature of the practical approach.

2. *b* is the answer. Stephen's behavior prevents him from meeting the demands of his everyday life. Therefore, his behavior meets the impaired functioning criterion in the practical approach. (p. 492)

a. Demonological principles are used to explain behavior, not classify it. If the question had asked which approach would say that Stephen's behavior was caused by the devil, this would have been correct.

c. The diathesis-stress model is also used to explain behavior. It proposes that people with disorders may have had a genetic predisposition to develop the disorder, but that environmental stressors brought it on. The item doesn't say that Stephen has an inherited tendency toward alcoholism or another disorder.

d. There is no such thing as the logical approach to defining abnormality.

3. d is the answer. According to the supernatural model, demons, gods, and witches were thought to cause abnormal behavior. (p. 493)

a. According to the cognitive-behavioral model, abnormal behavior and thought is learned, usually in a social context.

b. According to the phenomenological model, distorted perceptions of the world cause abnormal behavior.

c. According to the neurobiological model, physiological problems cause abnormal behavior.

4. a is the answer. The diathesis-stress model suggests that some people inherit a tendency toward a disorder, but that it may not develop unless environmental stressors are severe. (p. 496)

b. The cognitive-behavioral approach emphasizes learning.

c. The demonological or supernatural explanation of behavior is that it is caused by spirits or demons.

d. Perceptions are emphasized by phenomenological theorists.

5. a is the answer. According to the statistical infrequency criterion, behaviors are abnormal unless displayed by a large number of people. Few, if any, neurosurgeons lecture animals on the dangers of ingesting dangerous microbes. (p. 492)

b. There is no such thing as the psychopathological approach to defining abnormality.

c. There is no such thing as the logical approach to defining abnormal behavior.

d. The practical approach evaluates behavior content in the context of a situation. Mary Sue's behavior is not harmful and does not interfere with her everyday functioning, although it is a bit bizarre. However, this approach states that if everyone in the situation approves, even a bizarre behavior may not be considered abnor-mal. The shelter's workers like to see Mary giving the animals attention every day. Her behavior is not abnormal in this context.

6. b is the answer. Neither neurosis nor psychosis is contained in the DSM-IV because they are considered too vague to be of diagnostic use. (p. 497)

7. b is the answer. Compulsions are behaviors that the person thinks will keep harm from coming to him or herself, family, or friends. (p. 503)

a. An obsession is an unwanted, persistent thought.

c, d. Mania and conversion disorder do not cause unwanted, persistent thoughts and repetitive behaviors.

8. c is the answer. Never displaying a behavior in public, such as eating or writing, for fear of humiliation is called a social phobia. Frank is afraid that he will embarrass himself by getting sick in public, so he refuses to eat at restaurants. (p. 502)

a. Specific phobias include fear of objects or situations, such as heights, dogs, or air travel, but do not include any social factors. In other words, people may have a fear of spiders and not feel worried that their fear will humiliate them.

b. Agoraphobia is a fear of leaving one's home and, sometimes, of being alone.

d. Obsessive-compulsive disorder is characterized by taking great pains to be organized, neat, clean, or particular about details or by recurring, unpleasant thoughts.

9. b is the answer. Conversion disorders are physical symptoms, like paralysis or blindness, without physical causes. A psychodynamic theorist would be likely to say that a person is translating an unacceptable unconscious desire or conflict into a symptom that excuses the person from the difficult situation. (p. 507)

a. The client may have been reinforced by getting out of an activity due to physical disability, but not for showing fear.

c. Repressed memories are a psychodynamic concept, but amnesia is not part of conversion disorder.

d. A phenomenological explanation would deal with such perceptions.

10. a is the answer. A dissociative disorder is characterized by disruptions in memory, consciousness, or identity. (pp. 507–508)

b. Someone with antisocial personality disorder usually displays a pattern of impulsive, selfish, and even criminal behavior. However, the symptoms associated with personality disorders do not usually include memory loss.

c. Symptoms of dissociative identity disorder may include blackouts or a loss of memory over a certain period of time when an alternate personality takes over, but not a loss of personal information, such as one's name.

d. A schizophrenic experiencing thought blocking or withdrawal may feel as though he or she is being prevented from remembering his or her own name, job, or family, but there are no specific symptoms of memory loss typical of schizophrenia.

11. *d* is the answer. A cognitive-behavioral theorist would say that our thinking, positive or negative, or our blaming ourselves instead of the environment can lead to depression. (p. 513)

12. *b* is the answer. A bipolar disorder belongs to the family of affective disorders because it involves changes in mood and, consequently, behavior. (p. 512)

a, c. A pleasant mood is normal, so there is only one symptom present in each answer: depression. Both mania and depression must be present before a bipolar disorder is suspected.

d. Bipolar disorders are very rare (one out of a hundred) compared with depression (thirty out of a hundred).

13. *b* is the answer. Mercedes' dog has learned helplessness; it has learned or come to believe that its actions—barking and growling—will not control its environment by scaring the children away. (p. 513)

a. Generalized anxiety is worry and fear detached from any specific cause.

c. Hypersensitive brainstem mechanisms are associated with panic disorder in humans.

d. Enlarged ventricles are associated with schizophrenia in humans.

14. *a* is the answer. Schizophrenics typically have disorders of thought, both in content and form. Problems with form include word salad—that is, communication that is just a jumble of words. (p. 515)

b. Clang associations are disorders of thought, but they usually involve words that rhyme or have double meanings.

c. Schizophrenics complaining of thought insertions (a thought content disorder) believe that other people are placing thoughts in their heads.

d. There is no such thing as attention association. (You are probably confusing two symptoms of schizophrenia: loose associations and disorders of attention.)

15. *c* is the answer. (p. 526)

a. Internalizing disorders, such as separation anxiety disorder, cause internal distress.

b. Autistic disorder fits neither the internalizing nor the externalizing categories.

d. Only *c* is the answer.

16. *a* is the answer. Catatonic schizophrenia symptoms include movement extremes from immobility to wild flailing and a rejection of efforts to communicate. People with catatonic schizophrenia may show waxy flexibility, which allows them to be posed in any position. (p. 517)

b. These are more characteristic of a disorganized schizophrenic.

c. These are more characteristic of a paranoid schizophrenic.

d. Strong fear of disease is associated with hypochondriasis.

17. *c* is the answer. People in this category, also called psychopaths or sociopaths, display a long-term, persistent pattern of impulsive, selfish, unscrupulous, and even criminal behavior. (p. 521)

a. The main characteristic of narcissistic personality disorder is an exaggerated sense of self-importance. Although these people may be annoying in their constant quest for attention from the right people, they usually are not free of guilt, nor do they tend to commit crimes.

b. Depression is a mood disorder, not a personality disorder, involving feelings of sadness and hopelessness and a loss of self-worth.

d. A mood disorder is not a personality disorder. Mood disorders, such as depression or mania, involve changes in emotions.

18. *b* is the answer. Paranoid schizophrenia accounts for about 40 percent of all diagnoses. (p. 517)

a. Thought disorders are symptoms, not a type of schizophrenia.

c. Catatonic schizophrenia accounts for 8 percent of schizophrenic diagnoses.

d. Disorganized schizophrenia accounts for 5 percent of schizophrenic diagnoses.

19. *c* is the answer. Conduct disorder falls under the externalizing category. Its primary features are aggressive, destructive, disobedient behaviors. (p. 526)

    a. Autistic disorder is neither an externalizing nor an internalizing disorder. It is a severe condition usually diagnosed in the first 30 months of life and is characterized by ritualistic play, lack of attachment to caregivers, and lack of positive emotional expressions.

    b. Narcissistic personality disorder is not a disorder of childhood and is identified when a person is egotistical, overly sensitive to criticism, and in need of attention.

    d. Schizotypal personality disorder is similar to schizophrenia, but not as severe. People with this disorder may have odd beliefs, but they do not hallucinate.

20. *a* is the answer. Mentally incompetent to stand trial is a rare outcome, because therapy or psychoactive drugs can usually produce at least temporary competence. (p. 527)

    b. The irresistible impulse test is related to judgments of not guilty by reason of insanity. Federal cases do not allow this lack-of-control criterion to be used to support a claim of insanity.

    c. If he didn't understand what he was doing, he may be not guilty by reason of insanity, but may be competent to stand trial.

    d. Diagnosis with a psychological disorder may or may not be enough to show mental incompetence; after all, many people with disorders are able to understand court proceedings.

Now turn to the quiz analysis table at the end of this chapter to find which areas you know well and which areas you need to work on. Circle the numbers in the table for items on Quiz 2 that you answered correctly.

For each question you answered correctly, circle its number. (Quiz 1 numbers are not shaded; Quiz 2 numbers are shaded.) Are there patterns in the types of questions or the topics you got wrong that could direct your further study? Did you improve from Quiz 1 to Quiz 2?

TOPIC	TYPE OF QUESTION		
	DEFINITION	COMPREHENSION	APPLICATION
Defining abnormality		1, 2	
	1		2, 5
Explaining disorders		3	4
		3	4
Classifying disorders		5	8
		6	
Anxiety			6, 7, 9
			7, 8
Somatoform	10		11
			9
Dissociative		12	13
			10
Mood			14, 15
		11	12, 13
Schizophrenia			16, 17
		18	14, 16
Personality			18
			17
Other		19	20
	15		19
Mental illness and law			
			20

TOTAL CORRECT BY QUIZ:

QUIZ 1:
QUIZ 2:

Chapter 16

Treatment of Psychological Disorders

Psychotherapy is used by those who take a psychodynamic, phenomenological, or behavioral approach to the treatment of psychological disorders. It involves treating disorders with psychological methods, such as analyzing problems, talking about possible solutions, and encouraging more adaptive ways of feeling, thinking, and acting. The biological approach uses drugs and other physical treatments. Most psychologists consider themselves to be eclectic—that is, they draw on one or more of the approaches in helping any given client.

OUTLINE

I. BASIC FEATURES OF TREATMENT (pp. 532–534)

All methods of treatment share certain basic features, including a client or patient seeking relief from problems; a person who is socially accepted as one who can help the client because of training or experience; a special social relationship between client and therapist, which helps ease the client's problems; a theoretical explanation of those problems; and a set of procedures for dealing with them.

Clients can be categorized as inpatients, outpatients, or those seeking personal growth. Psychiatrists are medical doctors who specialize in the treatment of mental disorders and can prescribe medications. Psychologists who do psychotherapy usually have a doctoral degree in clinical or counseling psychology, but currently cannot prescribe drugs. The main goal of psychotherapists is to help people change their thinking, feeling, and behavior so that they will be happier and more productive.

II. PSYCHODYNAMIC PSYCHOTHERAPY (pp. 534–537)

Freud's method of treatment, psychoanalysis, attempts to help the patient understand unconscious conflicts and wishes and work through their implications for everyday life.

A. Classical Psychoanalysis

Free association consists of asking a client to verbalize all thoughts, feelings, and memories that come to mind. The content and pattern of associations contain clues to unconscious material. In the interpretation of dreams, a patient reports the manifest content (the surface story) of a dream and works to understand its latent content (the unconscious meaning), as represented by the dream's symbols. The psychoanalyst looks for evidence that the feelings, reactions, and conflicts the client experiences toward others have been transferred onto the therapist. Transference may help the client reenact and gain insight into old conflicts.

B. Contemporary Variations on Psychoanalysis

Psychoanalysis requires much time, money, verbal skill, and abstract thinking ability; these requirements limit its use. Variations on psychoanalytic treatments, such as ego analysis, deemphasize the past and focus on helping the client use the ego to solve problems.

Object relations therapy is a contemporary psychodynamic approach to psychotherapy. Therapists using this approach believe that personality and the arising conflicts that cause problems stem from the need for supportive human relationships, such as the mother-child bond. The therapist takes an active role in therapy and tries to establish a supportive and nurturing relationship with the client so that she or he can experience what may have been missed as an infant.

Other variations on psychoanalysis include psychoanalytically oriented psychotherapy and time-limited dynamic psychotherapy.

III. PHENOMENOLOGICAL PSYCHOTHERAPY (pp. 537–540)

Phenomenologists, or humanistic psychologists, believe that behavior is shaped by an innate drive toward growth that is guided by an individual's interpretation of the world. Phenomenological treatment is based on the following assumptions: Treatment is a human encounter between equals, not a cure; clients will improve on their own, given the right conditions; an accepting and supportive relationship will support clients' growth; and clients must remain responsible for choosing how to feel and think.

A. Client-Centered Therapy

Carl Rogers' client-centered, or person-centered, therapy is based on creating a relationship characterized by unconditional positive regard, empathy, and congruence.

1. *Unconditional Positive Regard.* The therapist must show that he or she genuinely cares about and accepts the client as a person and trusts the client's ability to change.

2. *Empathy.* The therapist must appreciate how the world looks from the client's point of view. Empathy is communicated through a technique called reflection.

3. *Congruence.* The way the therapist feels is consistent with the way he or she acts toward the client. The therapist's unconditional positive regard and empathy are real, not manufactured.

B. Gestalt Therapy

The goal of Frederick S. Perls' Gestalt therapy is to help clients become more self-aware and self-accepting so that they can begin growing again in their own unique, consciously guided directions. Gestalt therapists encourage clients to become aware of real feelings that they have denied, and to discard foreign feelings, ideas, and values. Therapists are directive in helping clients focus on present, not past, feelings. Role play and imaginary dialogues are two facets of this therapy.

IV. BEHAVIOR THERAPIES (pp. 540–546)

Therapists who use behavior therapies assume that problems are learned patterns of thinking and behaving that can be changed without looking for the meanings behind them. Treatments that utilize classical conditioning principles are referred to as behavior therapy; those utilizing operant conditioning are called behavior modification. Therapies that focus on changing thinking patterns as well as overt behavior are called cognitive-behavior therapy. Basic features of behavior therapy include the development of a good client-therapist relationship, a list of behaviors and thoughts to be changed, a therapist who acts as a teacher by setting and implementing specific treatment plans, and ongoing evaluation of the effects of therapy.

A. Techniques for Modifying Behavior

1. *Systematic Desensitization.* During desensitization, a client practices progressive relaxation while imagining fear-provoking situations from an anxiety hierarchy. The process of remaining calm while thinking about something feared weakens the learned association between anxiety and the feared object or situation.

2. *Modeling.* Through participant modeling, a client can learn about or get comfortable displaying desirable behaviors. The therapist demonstrates desirable behaviors, and the client gradually practices them. The clients can learn to be more appropriately self-expressive and more comfortable in social situations through assertiveness and social skills training.

3. *Positive Reinforcement.* A therapist systematically uses positive reinforcement to alter problematic behaviors. The receipt of rewards or tokens is dependent upon a client's display of desirable behaviors. In institutions, behavior therapists sometimes establish a token economy.

4. *Extinction.* Behavior can be modified by removing reinforcers that normally follow a particular response. A procedure called flooding, which extinguishes a classically conditioned fear response, keeps a patient in a feared but harmless situation. As a result, the client who is deprived of the normally rewarding escape pattern has no reason for continued anxiety.

5. *Aversive Conditioning.* This technique uses classical conditioning to reduce undesirable behavior by associating it with some psychological or physical discomfort.

6. *Punishment.* To eliminate a dangerous or disruptive behavior, an unpleasant stimulus is presented after the behavior, which reduces its occurrence.

B. Cognitive-Behavior Therapy

Cognitive-behavior therapy can help people change negative thoughts, which can induce depression, anger, or anxiety.

1. *Rational-Emotive Therapy and Cognitive Restructuring.* Rational-emotive therapy (RET) tries to eliminate learned problem-causing thoughts. Cognitive restructuring and stress inoculation training can teach a client new and calming thoughts to help her or him cope with stressful or anxiety-provoking situations.

2. *Beck's Cognitive Therapy.* Cognitive therapy rests on the assumption that a client has formed

negative thoughts about the self and the world. Treatment involves demonstrating the inaccuracy of these thoughts by testing them.

V. GROUP, FAMILY, AND COUPLES THERAPY (pp. 546–548)

Group therapy is the simultaneous treatment of several clients by one therapist. There is no predominant theoretical approach to group therapy. Groups are organized around either one type of problem or one type of client. Group therapy has several advantages: The therapist can observe clients' personal interactions; clients realize that they aren't the only people with a particular problem; clients support one another, which increases self-esteem; and clients learn from one another.

Family therapy is based in part on the psychodynamic theory that a patient's problems stem from early family relationships and problems, that patients released from mental hospitals often relapse, and that problems are multifaceted and must be dealt with in the setting in which they are maintained. In family therapy, the entire family is the "client," and the therapist attempts to create harmony within the family by facilitating each member's understanding of the family's interactions and how they relate to problems.

Couples therapy focuses on communication between partners. Therapists and clients often set "rules for talking" to improve communication skills.

VI. EVALUATING PSYCHOTHERAPY (pp. 548–556)

A. Focus on Research Methods: Meta-Analysis of Experiments on Psychotherapy

Research using meta-analysis indicates that better designed studies of the effectiveness of psychotherapy yield larger estimates of its success, client improvement is relatively durable, and only a small percentage of clients become worse after psychotherapy. There is controversy, however, over whether the use of meta-analysis is appropriate given the diverse range of "success" definitions in therapy.

B. Thinking Critically: Is One Approach to Psychotherapy Better than the Others?

What am I being asked to believe or accept?
All methods of psychotherapy are equally effective.

What evidence is available to support the assertion?

Studies have failed to show that one method is superior to another. Also, research demonstrates that all therapies are better than no therapy.

Are there alternative ways of interpreting the evidence?
Some argue that the evidence has been collected with the wrong methodology. For example, behavior therapists argue that personality tests, interviews, and self-ratings are too vague. In addition, procedures have not been tested outside the construct of the theories with which they are associated. Finally, success may be due, not to specific therapies, but rather to their common features: therapist support, hope for improvement, and the discovery of new ways to look at old problems.

What additional evidence would help to evaluate the alternatives?
Research that focuses on which combinations of therapists, clients, and treatments produce the most successful results still needs to be conducted.

What conclusions are most reasonable?
Caution should be used when drawing conclusions about the relative superiority of different approaches to therapy.

C. Addressing the "Ultimate Question"

The client-therapist relationship, an "approach-free" factor, is extremely important in the success of any therapy. When choosing a type of therapy, a person should give careful consideration to what approach he or she finds appealing, the therapist's "track record," and the potential for forming a productive client-therapist relationship.

D. Cultural Factors in Psychotherapy

Cultural differences may lead a client and therapist to have different expectations and goals about the outcome of therapy and the approach and methods used. Currently, psychologists are working to align cultural influence and choice of a specific treatment. Also, mental health training programs are trying to recruit more students from varying cultures, and clinicians are being trained to recognize and understand cultural differences in verbal and nonverbal communication.

E. Rules and Rights in the Therapeutic Relationship

The ethical standards of the American Psychological Association forbid a sexual relationship between therapist and client. A therapist must also hold whatever the client says in complete confidentiality. Exceptions to this rule include situations in which the client's current or historical condition is used as part of a civil or criminal defense, the client is so severely disturbed or suicidal that hospitalization is required, the therapist must defend against a malpractice suit, the client reveals information about sexual or physical abuse of a child, or the therapist believes that the client may commit a violent act against another person.

Clients are also protected against being placed or kept in an institution unnecessarily. A person threatened with commitment must have written notice, a chance to prepare a defense with an attorney, a court hearing (with a jury if the client wishes), and the right to take the Fifth Amendment. Furthermore, the prosecution must prove that the client is mentally ill *and* poses a danger to himself or herself and others. Once in an institution, a client may refuse certain treatments, and states are required to review every case periodically to determine if the client should be released.

VII. BIOLOGICAL TREATMENTS (pp. 556–563)

Biological treatments for psychological disorders have been in existence since the time of Hippocrates. Methods used in the sixteenth through eighteenth centuries included laxative purges, bleeding of "excess" blood, induced vomiting, cold baths, hunger, and other physical discomforts, all of which were designed to shock the patient back to normality.

A. Electroconvulsive Therapy

Electroconvulsive therapy (ECT) was used in the 1940s and 1950s to treat schizophrenia, depression, and sometimes mania. Today, ECT is used primarily to treat severe depression in patients who don't respond to psychoactive drugs and are at risk for suicide. ECT procedures have changed; today, shock is applied to one hemisphere and patients are given a deep muscle relaxant prior to treatment. Why ECT works is unclear. ECT is one of the most controversial biological treatments.

B. Psychosurgery

Psychosurgical techniques, including prefrontal lobotomies, were once used to treat problems involving strong emotional responses, such as schizophrenia, depression, anxiety, aggressiveness, and obsessive-compulsive disorders. Today, psychosurgery is done only as a last resort and involves the destruction of only a tiny amount of brain tissue.

C. Psychoactive Drugs

Psychoactive drugs have largely replaced ECT and psychosurgery.

1. *Neuroleptics (Antipsychotics).* Neuroleptic, or antipsychotic, drugs are effective in reducing delusions, hallucinations, paranoid suspiciousness, and other severe forms of disturbed thought and behavior. Phenothiazines and haloperidol are common neuroleptics that produce improvement in 60–70 percent of patients. However, these drugs and clozapine, a new neuroleptic, produce side effects such as tardive dyskinesia and, in some cases, death.

2. *Antidepressants.* By increasing the amount of serotonin or norepinephrine available at synapses, antidepressants such as monoamine oxidase inhibitors, tricyclic antidepressants, and fluoxetine can produce a gradual lifting of depression, allowing the person to return to normal life.

3. *Lithium.* Lithium, although associated with severe side effects, is helpful in reducing and even preventing both the depression and the mania associated with bipolar disorder.

4. *Anxiolytics.* Anxiolytics (originally called tranquilizers) are the most widely used of all legal drugs. They relieve anxiety and tension. Some of them, however, are potentially addictive and, when mixed with alcohol, can have fatal consequences.

5. *Human Diversity and Drug Treatment.* Drugs can have varying effects on different ethnic groups and genders.

D. Evaluating Biological Treatments

Although drugs can at times be very useful in the treatment of mental disorders, enthusiasm about drugs is not universal. At least three limitations apply: Drugs may cover up the problem without permanently curing it; drugs carry the potential for abuse, resulting in physical or psychological dependence; and many drugs have undesirable side effects.

E. Drugs and Psychotherapy

It is unclear which is more effective in treating psychological disorders: drugs or psychotherapy. It has been suggested that, where indicated, treatment begin with some form of psychotherapy and that drug treatments be added only if psychotherapy is ineffective.

VIII. LINKAGES: BIOLOGICAL ASPECTS OF PSYCHOLOGY AND THE TREATMENT OF PSYCHOLOGICAL DISORDERS (pp. 563–564)

Therapeutic drugs alter neurotransmitter activity by enhancing or inhibiting the binding of neurotransmitters to receptors; acting as receptor antagonists by blocking neurotransmitters' receptor site and, as a result, inhibiting action potential activity; or increasing the amount of neurotransmitter available at the synapse by stimulating neurotransmitter production or blocking reuptake.

IX. COMMUNITY PSYCHOLOGY: FROM TREATMENT TO PREVENTION (pp. 564–565)

Community psychology is a movement that attempts to increase early detection of problems and minimize or prevent mental disorders by making social and environmental changes.

KEY TERMS

1. **Psychotherapy** is the treatment of psychological disorders using psychological methods, such as analyzing problems, talking about possible solutions, and encouraging more adaptive ways of thinking and acting. (p. 532)

> *Example:* Psychoanalysis, client-centered therapy, Gestalt therapy, rational-emotive therapy, and cognitive-behavior therapy are all examples of psychotherapy.

2. **Psychologists** are people who practice some form of psychotherapy. Many have Ph.D.'s in clinical or counseling psychology and advanced specialty training. Currently, psychologists cannot by law prescribe medications to their clients. (p. 533)

3. **Psychiatrists** are medical doctors who specialize in the treatment of mental disorders. Psychiatrists usually use biological treatments and some psychotherapy. (p. 533)

4. **Psychoanalysis**, a method of psychotherapy, seeks to help clients gain insight by recognizing, understanding, and dealing with the unconscious thoughts and emotions presumed to cause their problems. Psychoanalysis also aims to help clients work through the many ways in which those unconscious causes appear in everyday behavior and social relationships. (p. 534)

5. **Free association** is a psychoanalytic method in which the client is asked to report *all* feelings, thoughts, memories, and images that come to mind. The content and, especially, the pattern of these mental processes should provide clues to unconscious activity. (p. 534)

> *REMEMBER:* In free association, the pattern of thoughts is just as important as what is said. When clients stop talking or report that their minds have gone blank, Freud would say that they are trying to keep unconscious material from becoming conscious. He was most interested in the ideas just prior to these blank moments.

6. **Transference** occurs when a client relates to a therapist based on feelings, attitudes, reactions, and conflicts experienced in childhood toward parents, siblings, and other significant people. (p. 535)

> *Example:* Ramona complains that she is tired of being under severe stress. Her therapist suggests that she join an exercise class. She immediately becomes defensive and sarcastic toward the therapist, saying, "Easy for you to say. You're thin and don't have to watch what you eat. Well, I hate exercising. God, you are as bad as my sister, always telling me how to improve myself." Ramona pauses for a moment and says, "I always wanted to be like her. My mother loved her so much and always paid more attention to her." Notice that the anger and jealousy that Ramona originally directed toward the therapist are actually feelings about her sister. The therapist merely suggested that Ramona join an exercise class to improve her energy level, not to improve her outward appearance.

7. **Client-centered** (or **person-centered**) **therapy**, developed by Carl Rogers, assumes that a client has a drive toward self-actualization. This therapy is based on a relationship between client and therapist that is characterized by unconditional positive regard, empathy, and congruence. Wanting the client to learn to solve his or her own problems, the therapist is nondirective and does not give advice. (p. 538)

8. **Unconditional positive regard** refers to an attitude of total acceptance and respect that a therapist must have toward a client to create a therapeutic environment. If a therapist does not express unconditional positive regard to the client, therapy will not enable the person to overcome his or her barriers to self-actualization. (p. 539)

> *REMEMBER:* The therapist communicates acceptance *without conditions;* even if the client admits to socially undesirable behaviors or views, the therapist is encouraging and respectful.

9. **Empathy**, an important feature of client-centered therapy, involves a therapist's trying to see the world as a client sees it. The therapist may show the client that understanding by not only listening attentively but also be reflecting what the client says. (p. 539)

Example: Yvonne came into therapy because she resented having to care for her younger sisters even though she knew that her mother was working three jobs. Yvonne's therapist must try to see the world from Yvonne's point of view and can accomplish this by understanding the constraints that Yvonne feels as a result of such tremendous responsibility.

10. **Reflection** is a method used in client-centered therapy. A therapist restates or paraphrases a client's responses in order to show that she or he is listening and to help the client be more in touch with feelings. (p. 539)

Example: Read the example for key term 9. The therapist might respond to Yvonne by saying, "You're tired of doing so much around the house with your sisters, which prevents you from going out and doing what you want. You're angry at your mom." The therapist has reflected what Yvonne has said, thus also demonstrating empathy.

11. **Congruence** (sometimes called genuineness) refers to a consistency in a therapist's feelings and behavior toward a client. The therapist's behavior toward the client must be a reflection of how he or she really feels; it cannot be an act. Ideally, the client will learn that openness and honesty can be the foundation of a human relationship. (p. 539)

Example: Read the examples for key terms 9 and 10. The therapist must genuinely feel empathy and unconditional positive regard for Yvonne. She cannot think to herself that Yvonne is spoiled and selfish. The therapist must actually accept Yvonne's feelings with unconditional positive regard for her worth as a person.

12. **Gestalt therapy** is a form of phenomenological treatment developed by Frederick Perls. A Gestalt therapist takes an active and directive role in helping a client become aware of denied feelings and impulses and learn how to discard foreign feelings, ideas, and values. Also, the therapist helps the client become more self-accepting. Methods used include dialogues with people, inanimate objects, and various body parts. (p. 540)

Example: When Renee describes how angry she became when her boss asked her to stay late, the therapist suggests they role-play the conversation between Renee and her boss. Renee finds that it really wasn't the request that made her the most angry; it was her perception that the boss assumed she had nothing better to do.

13. **Behavior therapy** uses the principles of classical conditioning to change behavior by helping or teaching clients to act and think differently. Usually, an incorrectly learned association between a CS and a UCS is destroyed. (p. 541)

Example: Flooding and aversive conditioning are examples of behavior therapies. (See key terms 22 and 23.)

14. **Behavior modification** uses the principles of operant conditioning to change behavior. (p. 541)

Example: Modeling is an example of behavior modification therapy. (See key term 17.)

15. **Cognitive-behavior therapy** attempts to pinpoint thought patterns that lead to depression, anger, or anxiety. Once these thoughts are recognized, they can be eliminated and replaced with more constructive thought patterns. (p. 541)

16. **Systematic desensitization** is a behavioral therapy method based on classical conditioning that is especially effective in the treatment of phobias. The technique seeks to extinguish the fear response by pairing fear-producing stimuli with calm, relaxed feelings. (p. 541)

Example: Constance is terrified of heights. Her therapist asks her to create an anxiety hierarchy. She lists several "height" experiences from the least to the most frightening.
  a. Standing on a small step stool
  b. Standing on the bottom rung of a ladder
  c. Looking out the top-floor window of a three-story building
  d. Standing on the middle rung of a ladder
  e. Standing on the top rung of a ladder
  f. Standing and peering into an empty ten-story elevator shaft
  g. Standing on the edge of Niagara Falls
  h. Standing on the edge of the lookout tower over the Grand Canyon
  i. Riding in a helicopter

Constance's therapist will gradually work through each of these scenes using systematic desensitization.

17. **Modeling** is a behavioral modification method in which a client can learn new behaviors by watching the behavior of others and then practicing these behaviors. (p. 542)

Example: Kip is afraid of snakes. Modeling therapy might include having him watch films of people handling snakes. Then he might be present in the same room while others are handling snakes. Finally, he might practice handling snakes himself.

18. **Assertiveness and social skills training** is a set of behavioral methods used to teach clients how to be more comfortable, expressive, and effective in social situations. (p. 542)

Example: Nan, a very shy woman, was constantly being taken advantage of despite her knowledge of auto mechanics. Every time she took her car to a mechanic, the garage overcharged her or did unnecessary work. She knew this but just could not bring herself to say something about it until she had gone through assertiveness training.

REMEMBER: People are taught how to be assertive, not aggressive. Nan does not have to be aggressive in order to express herself effectively in the auto shop. Instead, she simply needs to be direct in her demand for fair service.

19. **Positive reinforcement** is anything that, when received by a person, increases the likelihood that the person will repeat the behavior that elicited the positive consequence. Positive rewards are contingent upon the performance or display of the desired behavior. (pp. 542–543)

Example: A therapist who is assisting a client with a weight problem may give the client lots of praise (positive reinforcement) when the client loses one pound in the hopes that the praise will motivate the client to continue to follow the program. Praise is contingent upon weight loss; that is, if the client loses no weight, no praise is given.

20. A **token economy**, based on principles of operant conditioning, is used by behavior therapists, mainly in institutional settings. A system is implemented in which a client must display certain behaviors in order to receive tokens. These tokens can then be exchanged for extended privileges, such as snacks, movies, and field trips. (p. 543)

Example: Tony and his therapist have decided that he should be able to complete his daily homework and keep his room neat. For every completed homework assignment, he receives two tokens. When he makes his bed, picks up his clothes, and keeps his dresser organized, he receives three tokens. Tony exchanges his tokens for field trips to local museums or for dinner in town.

REMEMBER: Eventually social reinforcements, such as smiles of approval and encouragement, come to replace tokens.

21. **Extinction** occurs when stimuli that previously elicited a conditioned response no longer cause that response. Extinction is a result of the breakdown of the relationship on which the original conditioning was based. Flooding is a behavioral technique based on extinction. (p. 543)

22. **Flooding** is a behavior therapy technique used to treat phobias. A client is placed in a feared but harmless situation. Prevented from escaping, the client has the opportunity to realize that she or he has no reason to be afraid. In classical conditioning terms, the client realizes that the feared thing (CS) doesn't really predict a terrifying or harmful problem (UCS). (p. 543)

Example: Clint was extremely afraid of riding on buses. He and his therapist rode a city bus for an hour. Clint was very frightened at first, but then he calmed down, and eventually he lost his fear. Clint realized that the bus ride (CS) did not predict any catastrophic event (UCS).

23. **Aversive conditioning** is a behavior therapy based on classical conditioning. Negative behaviors often must be eliminated, at least partially, before new behaviors can be learned. Aversive conditioning associates the undesirable behavior with an unpleasant physical feeling. People discontinue using behaviors that result in discomfort. (p. 544)

Example: In the movie *A Clockwork Orange*, the main character spends most of his time raping and beating women. Later he is forced to watch movies of these types of behaviors while experiencing the effects of a nausea-producing drug. After the treatment, the mere sight of a woman makes him violently ill.

24. **Punishment**, a behavior modification method, is a negative consequence that follows a behavior and that *decreases* the likelihood that the problem behavior will be repeated. Usually, punishment is used as a last resort to eliminate problem behaviors. (p. 544)

Example: Peter is seven years old and lives in an institution. He climbs on the roofs of the buildings in the development. He has already fallen and broken his legs and arms three times. Despite repeated attempts to stop this behavior using a token economy, Peter still climbs on the roofs. His therapist has decided that punishment is the only way to keep Peter from putting himself in an extremely dangerous situation.

25. **Rational-emotive therapy** is a form of cognitive-behavior therapy developed by Albert Ellis. A client is taught to recognize self-defeating thought patterns and to replace them with more constructive thoughts. (p. 545)

Example: Brady is a personnel administrator. He feels uncomfortable because he is often faced with disciplinary decisions that result in angry employees. His therapist has pointed out that it is unrealistic to think that everyone will like him and be happy with his decisions all the time. Brady learns to treat people fairly and not to expect them to like all of his decisions.

26. **Cognitive therapy** consists of a type of cognitive restructuring in which a client sees that her or his depression is due in part to erroneous and illogical thought patterns. The therapist helps point out those thoughts that precede anxiety and depression and then works with the client to test the logic of these thoughts. (p. 545)

Example: Leslie is convinced that she will never be successful on her new job. As a result, she is very anxious. Her therapist helps her list the skills she will need on the new job. Then Leslie and the therapist recall past jobs where Leslie performed very well using just those skills. Leslie's therapist helps her see that her anxiety-producing thoughts about her performance are wrong.

27. **Group therapy** is psychotherapy conducted with groups of about five to ten people. The therapist can observe clients interacting with one another in real social situations; clients feel less alone when they realize that other people are struggling with similar problems; and clients can learn from one another. (p. 546)

Example: Misha is in a support group for teen mothers. The group members meet with a therapist once a week to discuss how things are going and to offer each other support.

28. **Family therapy** involves two or more individuals from the same family, one of whose problems make him or her the initially identified client, but the real client is the family. The goal of family therapy is to create harmony within the family by helping each member better understand the family's interactions and the problems they create. (p. 547)

Example: Robert has been hostile and depressed lately, but he is not attending therapy alone. Robert's parents and sometimes his siblings go to sessions with him. The therapist observes how the family members interact and tries to help them see how they affect each other.

29. **Couples therapy** is similar to family therapy; its focus is on communication between partners. (p. 548)

30. **Electroconvulsive therapy (ECT)** involves passing electric current through the brain. Today, shock is applied to only one brain hemisphere, and patients are given a deep muscle relaxant prior to treatment to prevent injury. ECT is used to treat depression when other treatments have failed. (p. 557)

31. **Psychosurgery** involves destroying a very small amount of brain tissue in order to alleviate psychological disorders. This treatment is used as a last resort in treating problems involving strong emotional reactions. (p. 558)

REMEMBER: Psychosurgery treats <u>psychological</u> problems through <u>surgical</u> techniques.

32. **Prefrontal lobotomy** was an early form of psychosurgery that involved drilling holes in the skull, inserting a sharp instrument, and moving it from side to side to destroy brain tissue. (p. 558)

33. **Neuroleptic (Antipsychotic)** drugs are used to treat severe psychopathology. These drugs are effective in reducing hallucinations, delusions, paranoid suspiciousness, and incoherence. Unfortunately, neuroleptics such as chlorpromazine and haloperidol can cause severe side effects such as tardive dyskinesia. (p. 558)

34. **Antidepressants**, which increase levels of serotonin and norepinephrine, are useful in treating depression. This class of drugs includes monoamine oxidase inhibitors, tricyclic antidepressants, and fluoxetine. (p. 560)

35. **Lithium** calms manic patients and can prevent the depression and mania of bipolar disorder. (p. 560)

36. **Anxiolytics (tranquilizers)**, such as Librium and Valium, are used to reduce anxiety, tension, and in some cases agoraphobia (Xanax). These drugs can be addictive and should not be combined with alcohol. (pp. 560–561)

37. **Community psychology** attempts to minimize or prevent psychological disorders. Community psychologists' efforts take two forms: attempts to eliminate causative factors of underlying psychological problems (such as poverty and inadequate or crowded housing) and early recognition of psychological problems and interventions designed to prevent problems from becoming worse. (p. 564)

FILL-IN-THE-BLANKS KEY TERMS

This section will help you check your factual knowledge of the key terms introduced in this chapter. Fill in each blank with the appropriate term from the list of key terms above.

1. _____ are physicians who have received special training in the treatment of mental disorders.

2. When psychoanalysts ask their patients to _____, patients report everything that is going through their minds.

3. When a therapist communicates that he or she understands how a client feels, the therapist is showing _____.

4. In client-centered therapy, it is important that the way a therapist feels and behaves toward a client be consistent; in other words, the therapist must show _____.

5. _____ is a set of techniques designed to help clients be comfortable and effective in situations that involve other people.

6. A therapeutic technique that associates unpleasant feelings with undesirable behaviors and thereby causes a client to discontinue the undesirable behaviors is called _____.

7. Identifying and eliminating thought patterns that lead to depression, anger, or anxiety are the goal of _____.

8. _____ is a technique in which small amounts of brain tissue are destroyed in order to alleviate a psychological disorder.

9. _____ increase the amount of serotonin or norepinephrine available at synapses.

10. _____ focuses on the prevention of psychological disorders.

11. _____ block the action of dopamine and are used to treat severe mental disorders such as schizophrenia.

12. _____ occurs when a client behaves toward a therapist as if the therapist were a significant person from the client's childhood.

13. _____, developed by Carl Rogers, is based on the phenomenological approach.

14. A behavioral therapist might use _____ to increase the chances that a client will repeat a desirable behavior.

15. _____ is a cognitive-behavior therapy technique in which clients are taught to recognize self-destructive thought patterns and replace them with constructive ways of thinking.

Total Correct (See answer key) _____

LEARNING OBJECTIVES

1. Define psychotherapy. Describe the approach of an eclectic therapist. (p. 532)

2. Describe the common features of treatments. Define and distinguish between a psychiatrist and a psychologist. Describe other types of therapists. (pp. 532–534)

3. Describe the history of psychoanalysis. (p. 534)

4. Describe the goals of a psychoanalyst. (p. 534)

5. Define free association, manifest and latent contents of dreams, and transference. Discuss the ways in which these methods of psychotherapy reveal clues about unconscious mental processes. (pp. 534–535)

6. Describe the difference between Freud's original psychoanalysis and modern variations. Describe some of the methods used in contemporary psychoanalysis. Discuss the criticisms of psychoanalysis. (pp. 535–537)

7. Describe the theoretical basis of the phenomenological approach to therapy. List the four assumptions on which phenomenological therapists operate. (pp. 537–538)

8. Describe client-centered therapy. Define and discuss the importance of unconditional positive regard, empathy, reflection, and congruence in this therapy. Compare and contrast client-centered therapy with Gestalt therapy. (pp. 538–540)

9. Define behavior therapy. Describe its basic features and the assumptions on which it is based. (pp. 540–541)

10. Explain the differences among behavior therapy, behavior modification, and cognitive-behavior therapy. (p. 541)

11. Define systematic desensitization, modeling, assertiveness and social skills training, token economy, flooding, aversive conditioning, and the other behavioral methods of therapy. Give an example of each. Specify which type of learning each method is based on: classical or operant conditioning. (pp. 541–544)

12. Define cognitive-behavior therapy. Compare and contrast it with other behavior therapies. (pp. 544–546)

13. Define rational-emotive therapy, cognitive restructuring, stress inoculation training, and Beck's cognitive therapy. (pp. 545–546)

14. Define group, family, and couples therapy. Discuss the advantages and disadvantages of each. (pp. 546–548)

15. Define meta-analysis. Discuss the results of research that has attempted to evaluate psychotherapy's effectiveness. (pp. 549–551)

16. Discuss the following questions: Is there one form of psychotherapy that is best? What should a person look for when seeking psychotherapy? (pp. 551–552)

17. Discuss the cultural influences on the choice of psychotherapy, its goals, and its expectations. (pp. 552–555)

18. Describe a client's rights in a therapeutic relationship. (pp. 555–556)

19. Describe the assumptions underlying biological treatments. (pp. 556–557)

20. Describe the historical and present use of electroconvulsive therapy (ECT). (pp. 557–558)

21. Define prefrontal lobotomy. Describe the historical and present use of psychosurgery. (p. 558)

22. Define neuroleptic (antipsychotic), antidepressant, Lithium, and anxiolytic, and specify which is used for what type of psychological problem. Explain the side effects of these drugs and how each works within the nervous system. Discuss the joint use of drugs and psychotherapy. (pp. 558–563)

23. Describe the ways that psychoactive drugs affect neurotransmitters. Define receptor antagonist and reuptake. (pp. 563–564)

24. Define community psychology. Describe the types of work involved in community psychologists' attempts to treat and prevent mental illness. (pp. 564–565)

CONCEPTS AND EXERCISES

No. 1: Differentiating Approaches to Therapy

Completing this exercise should help you to achieve Learning Objectives 4, 5, 8, 9, 10, 13, and 19.

Several psychotherapists have met at a convention to have dinner. Over coffee they argue about the various causes of abnormal behavior and mental processes. Decide what type of therapy each therapist probably practices.

Patricia: Clearly, thoughts in the unconscious drive behavior. If unconscious thoughts are revealed, the client can understand and possibly change the problematic behavior. You, on the other hand, Eliot, treat only the behavior and not the cause. _____

Eliot: What does it matter if I treat only the behavior? My goal is to create new behaviors that allow people to function in their environment. If they are functional, they will probably be successful and receive positive reinforcement, making them feel good about themselves. _____

Randa: She has a point, Eliot. If you would try to alter conscious thought patterns as I do, replacing problematic ones with functional ones, then many behaviors associated with those thoughts might change as well. _____

Ida: I think you are all a bit manipulative. We are therapists, but our clients have the ability to grow and change on their own. They just need to get in touch with their feelings. All we have to do is step back, accept them as people, and show them it's okay to accept themselves just as they are. _____

Lana: Pretty soon, you folks are going to be out of a job. When we understand how the brain works, we will be able to treat most psychological problems with drugs or corrective surgery. _____

No. 2: Identifying Methods of Therapy

Completing this exercise should help you to achieve Learning Objectives 6, 8, 9, 11, 12, 14, 20, 22, 23, and 24.

Following are several descriptions of treatments given to various clients. Read each description, and then answer the question following it.

1. Clarice, a schizophrenic, takes a drug that blocks the action of dopamine in her brain. What type of drug is she taking? _____

2. Cal is afraid of writing his name in public. His therapist has taken him to a busy shopping mall and asked him to write his name until he has covered several pieces of paper. What is this behavioral method? _____

3. Layla is overweight. Her therapist has given her a drug that will make her nauseous as soon as she begins to feel the slightest bit full after eating. What is this behavioral method? _____

4. Flora has received almost every treatment available for depression. Her doctor has suggested a drastic

method as a last resort. What is this method?

5. Antero is painfully shy. His teacher has devised a new system to prompt Antero to participate in group discussions at school. Every time Antero speaks, he will receive ten points. At the end of the day, he can cash in his points for special privileges, such as going to the library or choosing what book the teacher is going to read to the class. What behavioral method is his teacher using?

CRITICAL THINKING

A concerned neighbor, Aida Schultz, calls the precinct with reports of an old man walking around the block. He appears to be slightly spastic and a bit dizzy and has odd dark spots on his arms and hands. She also says that the man keeps sticking his tongue out, whether there is someone in front of him or not. Other reports from this same neighborhood have been coming in regarding an old man who is scaring children. Sam and Martina go to check these reports out.

When they arrive at Aida Schultz's house, they ask where she last saw the man. She points down the block. Sam and Martina slowly cruise the street and then turn the corner.

"There he is!" cries Sam. "I bet he's the one who's been scaring all the kids around here. Let's go pick him up."

"Not so fast. There may be a reason for his symptoms," Martina remarks.

Using the five critical thinking questions in your text, the clues in the story, and what you have learned about psychotherapy, answer the following:

1. What is Sam's hypothesis?

2. What evidence supports Sam's hypothesis?

3. What is Martina's alternative hypothesis?

4. What evidence supports Martina's hypothesis? What other evidence might Martina need?

5. What conclusions are reasonable?

PERSONAL LEARNING ACTIVITIES

1. Do you believe in Freud's unconscious? Why or why not? What kind of impact could the unconscious have on your behavior? (Learning Objectives 4 and 5)

2. Use reflection, a client-centered technique, in your next conversation with a friend. Was it difficult to summarize what your friend said? How did your friend react? (Learning Objective 8)

3. Explore the use of role play. Meet with friends or classmates and identify a situation in which you'd like to respond differently. After you have identified a situation, choose roles and practice the response you would like to exhibit next time you are really in the situation. For example, in assertiveness and social skills training, therapists often have clients practice making conversation, expressing dissatisfaction with service, or asking for a favor. (Learning Objective 11)

4. Think of a situation in which a cognitive-behavior technique could improve your reaction. Write the thing you usually say to yourself during the event and then write an alternative reaction. For example, if you tend to get nervous during exams, you could imagine what you usually say to yourself during testing situations and try to identify self-defeating thoughts. What would a rational-emotive therapist suggest that you say to yourself instead? You could write the alternatives to your usual thinking style in your notebook and look at it before your next test begins. (Learning Objectives 12 and 13)

5. If a drug were discovered that could make anyone feel happier, would you be in favor of its development? Why or why not? Would you take it? (Learning Objective 19)

MULTIPLE-CHOICE QUESTIONS

SAMPLE QUIZ 1

1. The common features of any type of therapy include
   a. a client or patient.
   b. someone socially accepted as being able to help the client.
   c. a theoretical approach to understanding and treating the client's problems.
   d. all of the above.

2. Sayumi is a licensed psychologist. Which of the following statements is most likely true of her? Sayumi has a(n)
   a. doctoral degree in clinical psychology.
   b. psychodynamic approach to therapy.
   c. private practice.
   d. M.D. degree.

3. The focus of Freudian psychoanalysis is on
   a. getting the client in touch with his or her present feelings.
   b. helping the client gain insight into unconscious problems.
   c. replacing problematic behaviors with desirable behaviors.
   d. teaching the client new ways of thinking.

4. Carl Rogers developed
   a. client-centered therapy.
   b. rational-emotive therapy.
   c. cognitive-behavior therapy.
   d. object relations therapy.

5. Last night Christi dreamed she was running around her backyard, dropping down into a well, and resurfacing through a hole in the ground, only to run back to the well and drop down again. This describes the
   a. manifest content of her dream.
   b. transference of her dream.
   c. latent content of her dream.
   d. free association within the dream.

6. As Dwayne prepares for an exam, he comments to his friend, Rerun, "This test is gonna be a seize." Rerun says, "A seize? Don't you mean 'a breeze?'" A _____ therapist would be most likely to think that Dwayne's comment indicates that he unknowingly fears freezing up during the exam and can't admit to it consciously.
   a. behavioral
   b. community
   c. phenomenological
   d. psychodynamic

7. Vivian is tearfully telling a friend that she is depressed and does not even know why. Her friend says, "You seem to be so unhappy, a little confused, and maybe a bit scared, too." Vivian's friend is using which method associated with client-centered therapy?
   a. Sympathy
   b. Empathy
   c. Reflection
   d. Both (b) and (c)

8. Pat is afraid of using a computer. To counteract Pat's misconceptions about what could happen if she used a computer, her therapist suggests a dialogue exercise. Pat is to imagine that she is talking to a computer and fill in what the computer would "say" to her. Pat's therapist is using _____ therapy.
   a. client-centered
   b. Gestalt
   c. psychoanalysis
   d. systematic desensitization

9. A _____ therapist would use rational-emotive therapy.
   a. psychoanalytic
   b. phenomenological
   c. cognitive-behavior
   d. biological

10. In behavioral therapy, associating an unpleasant stimulus with the simultaneous occurrence of an undesirable behavior is called
    a. aversive conditioning.
    b. object relations therapy.
    c. flooding.
    d. building an anxiety hierarchy.

11. Harvey is a psychotherapist. In treating his clients, he uses systematic desensitization and participant modeling in cases of phobia. What type of therapist is Harvey?
    a. Behavioral
    b. Psychoanalytic
    c. Phenomenological
    d. Biological

12. Bonnie fears driving in the mountains. Her therapist has suggested that they take a ride into the mountains for several hours. What method is the therapist proposing?
    a. Aversive conditioning
    b. Modeling
    c. Punishment
    d. Flooding

13. As part of Karla's therapy session, she spends an evening role-playing with other members of her group. Situations such as returning faulty merchandise, sending improperly prepared food back to the cook in a restaurant, and telling her roommate when she needs quiet in the room are the topics of the evening. Karla is experiencing
    a. depression.
    b. punishment.
    c. assertiveness training.
    d. aversive conditioning.

14. Group therapy is associated with which theoretical approach?
    a. Group therapy has no particular theoretical approach.
    b. Phenomenological
    c. Behavioral
    d. Psychoanalytical

15. When Shau-Jin is angry at Wendy, he often says things like, "Why do you always criticize me?" and, "You're such a nag!" The therapy that would focus most on their communication pattern would be
    a. couples therapy.
    b. extinction.
    c. rational emotive therapy (RET).
    d. psychoanalysis.

16. According to the Ethical Standards of the American Psychological Association, a therapist may disclose information mentioned by a client during therapy when
    a. the client is applying for a job and the employer asks for information.
    b. the client ends therapy.
    c. defending herself or himself against a malpractice charge.
    d. any of the above.

17. In the past, memory loss, speech disorders, and even death have been associated with which type of treatment?
    a. Psychosurgery
    b. Lithium
    c. Electroconvulsive therapy
    d. Prefrontal lobotomy

18. Tico is talking incoherently and is experiencing so many hallucinations and delusions that her psychiatrist will most likely prescribe a(n)
    a. antidepressant.
    b. anxiolytic.
    c. depressant.
    d. neuroleptic.

19. Which of the following is *not* a criticism of drug therapy?
    a. Drug therapy may treat only symptoms, not the problem itself.
    b. Drug therapy may make patients depend on the drug, instead of on their own efforts, for improvement.
    c. Many drugs have unwanted side effects.
    d. Drug therapy is more expensive than any other kind of therapy.

20. Liesette tries to influence lawmakers to provide more help for people in poverty, because she believes such a tactic will prevent problems caused by malnutrition, overcrowding, and homelessness. Liesette most likely is a _____ psychologist.
    a. behavior
    b. community
    c. phenomenological
    d. psychodynamic

Total Correct (See answer key) _____

SAMPLE QUIZ 2

Use this quiz to reassess your learning after taking Quiz 1 and reviewing the chapter.

1. The type of therapy to be used should be based on knowledge of
    a. the approach and methods the client is comfortable with.
    b. a potential therapist's track record.
    c. the potential for a positive client-therapist relationship.
    d. all of the above.

2. Simone asks her clients to remember their childhood experiences in order to gain insight into unconscious processes and thoughts. Simone is probably a _____ therapist.
    a. behavioral
    b. Gestalt
    c. client-centered
    d. psychodynamic

3. Which of the following would a psychoanalyst be *least* likely to use in therapy?
    a. Dream interpretation
    b. Ego analysis
    c. Free association
    d. Modeling

4. Empathy in client-centered therapy is
    a. perceiving a client's view of reality.
    b. restating or paraphrasing a client's words.
    c. unconditional positive regard.
    d. congruence between a therapist's words and actions.

5. Which of the following describes flooding?
   a. A client is gradually exposed to a feared stimulus.
   b. A client is placed in a fearful situation and not allowed to escape.
   c. A client learns not to let negative thoughts overwhelm or flood the mind.
   d. A client receives a negative stimulus following an undesirable behavior.

6. Mac is a therapist who relies on his clients' natural drive toward growth. Marcia tells him that she thinks she's so ugly it is not worth it to exercise or try to dress nicely, and she asks him if he thinks she is ugly. Rather than interpreting Marcia's behavior, Mac discloses his honest reaction, saying, "Right now you think it is futile to try to improve your looks. Although I think you are attractive, what *you* think is much more important and it seems you are discouraged." Mac is exhibiting _____, which is associated with _____ therapy.
   a. analysis of transference; psychodynamic
   b. congruence; client-centered
   c. reflection; cognitive-behavioral
   d. sympathy; phenomenological

7. In psychoanalysis, transference occurs when
   a. unconscious thoughts become conscious.
   b. a client transfers feelings about a significant person onto a therapist.
   c. the manifest content of a dream is translated into latent content.
   d. free association reveals unconscious conflicts.

8. Aversive conditioning is
   a. based on operant conditioning.
   b. based on classical conditioning.
   c. used to increase a behavior's occurrence.
   d. based on reward and punishment.

9. Alec is frightened to leave his apartment. His therapist has instructed him to make a list of progressively frightening thoughts about leaving home. Alec is constructing a(n) _____ as part of _____.
   a. anxiety hierarchy; systematic desensitization
   b. fear manifest; cognitive restructuring
   c. anxiety hierarchy; flooding
   d. fear manifest; psychoanalysis

10. Amy has been sent to a camp for children with behavior disorders. On her first day, she and her counselor decide what behaviors Amy will learn to do on a daily basis. These include playing coopera-tively, speaking respectfully to the counselors, and helping clean the dining hall after dinner. Immediately following the successful display of a behavior, Amy receives a pink piece of cardboard. Each day she can trade these pieces of cardboard for special activities and privileges. This is an example of
    a. aversive conditioning.
    b. flooding.
    c. token economy.
    d. cognitive restructuring.

11. Dan is a hyperactive child who continually injures himself. His doctors have tried everything they can think of to stop this behavior. What kind of therapeutic method would probably be best for Dan?
    a. Traditional psychoanalysis
    b. Flooding
    c. Punishment, followed by rewards for approved behavior
    d. Electroconvulsive therapy

12. Jane has gone to see a therapist because she is very depressed and dislikes herself. She doesn't get perfect grades and is not the most popular person on her dorm floor. What kind of therapy do you think would be best for Jane?
    a. Antidepressant drugs
    b. Rational-emotive therapy
    c. Aversive conditioning
    d. Token economy

13. Roberto has a dog phobia. He and his therapist go for a walk, and Roberto watches from across the street as his therapist approaches people who are walking their dogs. The therapist asks the owner if the dog is friendly, lets the dog sniff his hand, and gently pats the dog. The therapist is using _____ to help Roberto.
    a. token economies
    b. modeling
    c. flooding
    d. classical conditioning

14. Alex is a young boy whose parents recently divorced. His parents want him to see that many children are making the adjustment he's making; therefore, his parents would most likely seek _____ for Alex.
    a. Gestalt therapy
    b. group therapy
    c. psychoanalysis
    d. social skills training

15. In which of the following scenarios may a therapist *not* reveal confidential information?
    a. When discussing a case with a family member
    b. When defending herself or himself against a malpractice charge
    c. When a client requires hospitalization
    d. When a therapist feels a client may physically harm another person

16. Jill's therapist has recommended electroconvulsive therapy (ECT). Jill is probably experiencing
    a. schizophrenia.
    b. depression.
    c. hallucinations.
    d. anxiety.

17. Which of the following is *not* a problem encountered in research on psychotherapy's effectiveness?
    a. Statistically significant results may not be clinically significant.
    b. The results of most studies were fabricated.
    c. Research data that indicate that the success of psychotherapy have at times been ignored.
    d. Therapists using different methods employ different measures of success.

18. Nina has been experiencing moods of extreme elation alternating with severe depression. What kind of drug will her doctor most likely prescribe?
    a. Tricyclics
    b. Phenothiazines
    c. Monoamine oxidase inhibitors
    d. Lithium

19. When Terence takes a tricyclic antidepressant, norepinephrine remains in the synapse rather than flowing back into the presynaptic terminal. The antidepressant is
    a. acting as a receptor antagonist.
    b. blocking reuptake.
    c. causing tardive dyskinesia.
    d. preventing anxiolytic action.

20. Michel has spent the morning teaching preschool teachers the early signs of psychological problems, hoping that children can be helped before their problems become severe. What kind of psychologist is Michel?
    a. Biological
    b. Rational-emotive
    c. Community
    d. None of the above

Total Correct (See answer key) _____

ANSWERS TO FILL-IN-THE-BLANKS KEY TERMS

1. Psychiatrists (p. 533)
2. free associate (p. 534)
3. empathy (p. 539)
4. congruence (p. 539)
5. Assertiveness and social skills training (p. 542)
6. aversive conditioning (p. 544)
7. cognitive behavior therapy (p. 544)
8. Psychosurgery (p. 558)
9. Antidepressants (p. 560)
10. Community psychology (p. 564)
11. Antipsychotics or neuroleptics (p. 558)
12. Transference (p. 535)
13. Client-centered therapy (p. 538)
14. positive reinforcement (p. 542)
15. Rational-emotive therapy (p. 545)

ANSWERS TO CONCEPTS AND EXERCISES

No. 1: Differentiating Approaches to Therapy

° *Psychoanalysis.* Patricia believes that unconscious mental processes cause behavior. Methods such as free association, dream analysis, transference, and analysis of everyday behaviors are designed to bring unconscious material into conscious awareness. (pp. 534–537)

° *Behavior therapy.* Eliot's goal is to change behavior, not mental processes. Methods such as token economies, flooding, and aversive conditioning are designed to change behavior. (pp. 540–544)

° *Cognitive-behavior therapy.* Randa believes that behavior can be changed by altering harmful conscious thought patterns. Cognitive restructuring and rational-emotive therapy are methods designed to alter thought patterns. (pp. 544–546)

° *Phenomenological therapy.* Ida believes that her clients have a natural tendency toward growth and change. Clients simply need to get in touch with their feelings. Empathy, reflection, congruence, and unconditional positive regard help clients achieve this goal. (pp. 537–540)

° *Biological therapy.* Lana believes that altering the nervous system's chemical activity will change behavior. (pp. 556–562)

No. 2: Identifying Methods of Therapy

1. *Phenothiazine* or *haloperidol*. These neuroleptics are used to treat severe disorders such as schizophrenia. Their antipsychotic effects are due to their receptor antagonist action. (pp. 563–564)

2. *Flooding*. Cal is being exposed to the object or event that he fears, and he will not be allowed to escape. He will eventually realize that there is nothing to fear. (p. 543)

3. *Aversive conditioning*. Layla will come to associate the feeling of being full (conditioned stimulus) with nausea (unconditioned stimulus). (p. 544)

4. *Electroconvulsive therapy*. This is a last-resort treatment for depression. (p. 557)

5. *Token economy*. The points act as tokens, which can later be exchanged for whichever positive reinforcement Antero chooses. (p. 543)

ANSWERS TO CRITICAL THINKING

1. Sam believes that this is the old man who has been scaring the neighborhood children.

2. The evidence is that the man matches the description called in by several neighbors.

3. Martina hypothesizes that the man may be suffering from tardive dyskinesia.

4. The evidence is that the old man appears to be dizzy and has odd pigmentation on his arms. He also exhibits tongue thrusting, which is also a common symptom of tardive dyskinesia. Martina may want to find where the man has been staying and ask those caring for him if he is taking neuroleptics.

5. Martina can't draw any conclusions until she obtains additional evidence.

ANSWERS TO MULTIPLE-CHOICE QUESTIONS

Circle the question numbers you answered correctly.

Sample Quiz 1

1. *d* is the answer. Therapies all involve a client, a therapist who is socially accepted as being able to help the client, and a theoretical approach (psychoanalytic, phenomenological, behavioral, biological) to understanding the client's problems and treating them. (pp. 532–533)

2. *a* is the answer. Psychologists generally have a doctoral degree in clinical or counseling psychology. (p. 533)
   b. A psychologist would not necessarily have a psychodynamic approach. Sayumi could have a phenomenological, behavior, cognitive-behavior, or eclectic approach.
   c. Many psychologists work in academic settings or in clinics or hospitals.
   d. A psychiatrist is required to have an M.D. degree, but a psychologist is not.

3. *b* is the answer. The focus of psychoanalytic therapy is to reveal and work through unconscious conflicts. (p. 534)
   a. Phenomenological therapies help clients get in touch with and express their present feelings.
   c. Behavior therapies usually focus on replacing undesirable behaviors with new ones.
   d. Cognitive-behavior therapies focus on teaching the client new and more constructive ways of thinking.

4. *a* is the answer. Carl Rogers developed the phenomenological methods of client-centered therapy (or person-centered therapy). (p. 538)
   b. Albert Ellis developed rational-emotive therapy.
   c. Rational-emotive therapy is a type of cognitive-behavior therapy.
   d. Object relations therapy is a variation on psychoanalysis.

5. *a* is the answer. A dream's plot or story line is called the manifest content. (p. 535)
   b. Transference occurs when a client projects attitudes and feelings about a person in his or her life onto a therapist.
   c. A dream's symbolic interpretation is called the latent content.
   d. The method of free association does not occur within dreams. Clients may, however, be asked to free-associate about the content of their dreams.

6. *d* is the answer. A psychodynamic therapist would be likely to find unconscious meaning in behaviors. (p. 535)
   a. A behavioral therapist would focus on learning of behaviors, not unconscious meanings.
   b. A community psychologist works to prevent disorders.
   c. Phenomenological therapists are interested in a client's viewpoint, but would be unlikely to assume that Dwayne could not become aware of his fear.

7. *d* is the answer. Paraphrasing what Vivian has said (reflection) expresses empathy; her friend seems to know just how she feels. (p. 539)
   a. Sympathy involves expressing concern for someone else but is not necessarily based on empathy, nor does sympathy involve reflection.
   b. This is only one part of the answer.
   c. This is only one part of the answer.

8. *b* is the answer. Gestalt therapy, a form of phenomenological therapy, uses more active methods to help clients become more self-accepting. Clients might carry on imaginary conversations with people, parts of themselves, or objects. (p. 540)
   a. Client-centered therapy is a type of phenomenological therapy, but it allows the client to direct the course of a session.
   c. Psychoanalysis seeks to uncover unconscious conflicts by interpreting transference, free association, and dreams.
   d. Systematic desensitization is a behavioral treatment for phobias; however, it involves visualizing progressively more frightening situations while remaining calm.

9. *c* is the answer. Rational-emotive therapy is a cognitive-behavior therapy. Clients are taught to recognize damaging thoughts and to replace them with more positive and functional thoughts. (pp. 544–545)
   a. Psychoanalysts focus on revealing a person's unconscious thoughts and conflicts.
   b. Phenomenological therapists focus on a person's feelings and drive toward growth.
   d. Biological therapists use biological treatments either alone or in conjunction with other forms of therapy to cause changes in nervous system functioning.

10. *a* is the answer. Aversive conditioning is used to decrease a behavior's occurrence. An unpleasant stimulus is experienced every time an undesirable behavior is displayed. (p. 544)
    b. Object relations therapy is a type of psychoanalytic therapy.
    c. Flooding is based on extinction. A client is exposed to the entire object, situation, or event that he or she fears. Since the client cannot escape, he or she has the chance to realize that the fear is unfounded.
    d. An anxiety hierarchy is used in systematic desensitization.

11. *a* is the answer. Harvey is a behavioral therapist because he uses methods based on learning theory. (pp. 541–542)

b. A psychoanalyst would be far more likely to use free association, dream analysis, and other methods aimed at revealing unconscious material.
c, d. A phenomenological or biological therapist would probably not use systematic desensitization.

12. *d* is the answer. To use the flooding method, a client is placed in a feared but harmless situation and not allowed to escape. The person soon realizes that he or she has nothing to fear. Exposing Bonnie to the situation she fears and not allowing her to escape may help her overcome her fear of driving in the mountains. (pp. 543–544)
    a. Aversive conditioning is also used to decrease behavior. However, a client experiences a negative stimulus when she or he engages in the undesirable behavior.
    b. Modeling involves teaching a client desirable behaviors by demonstrating those behaviors and showing the client how to behave more calmly in feared situations. However, the client is not actually in the feared situation.
    c. Punishment, a procedure used to decrease a behavior, involves presenting a negative stimulus following an undesirable behavior.

13. *c* is the answer. Karla is learning how to be assertive in social situations. Remember, being assertive is not the same thing as being aggressive. Karla can be assertive, get her food prepared the way she likes it, and not be aggressive. (p. 542)
    a. Karla may be a little bit depressed that she cannot get what she wants in social situations. However, this depression is a symptom of not being assertive.
    b, d. Punishment and aversive conditioning are used to decrease undesirable behaviors. Karla is in therapy to learn new behaviors, not to decrease old, undesirable ones.

14. *a* is the answer. Group therapy has no particular theoretical assumptions underlying it. Instead, groups are organized around a specific type of problem (such as alcoholism) or client (such as teenagers). (p. 546)
    b, c, d. Group therapies are not associated with a particular theoretical approach.

15. *a* is the answer. Therapists often recommend couples therapy if communication with a partner seems to be a major problem. In couples therapy, people practice more constructive ways of getting ideas across. Rather than calling Wendy names or over-

generalizing, for example, Shau-Jin probably would be encouraged to say something about how he feels in the present situation. (p. 548)

b. Extinction removes the reinforcers that usually follow a behavior. It is a behavior therapy that doesn't work on communication skills.

c. Rational emotive therapy would concentrate on irrational ideas, not communication.

d. Psychoanalysis would focus on unconscious conflicts rather than on communication.

16. *c* is the answer. Confidentiality is a critical aspect of therapy that is seldom violated. However, if a client brings a malpractice suit against the therapist, the records of their sessions could be important evidence of the therapist's efforts to help. (p. 555)

a. Employers do not have a right to information about confidential therapy sessions.

b. The end of therapy does not signal the end of the obligation to protect a client's right to privacy.

d. Only *c* is correct.

17. *c* is the answer. In the past, ECT had serious side effects. Among them were broken bones, memory loss, speech disorders, and, in some cases, death. (p. 557)

a, d. Psychosurgery also has serious side effects, which include memory loss but not broken bones.

b. Lithium is problematic to administer, but these side effects are not associated with this drug.

18. *d* is the answer. Neuroleptics or antipsychotics reduce the intensity of psychotic symptoms such as Tico's. (p. 558)

a. Antidepressants improve mood, but do not influence psychotic symptoms.

b. Anxiolytics or tranquilizers reduce tension and anxiety.

c. As discussed in Chapter 6, a depressant is a psychoactive drug that slows the activity of the central nervous system.

19. *d* is the answer. Drugs are not necessarily the most expensive form of therapy. Freudian psychoanalytic therapy, because it can take several years, is very expensive. (p. 562)

a, b, c. These are all problems with drug therapy.

20. *b* is the answer. Prevention of problems such as psychological disorders is the focus of community psychologists. (p. 564)

a. Behavior psychologists focus on learning.

c. Phenomenological psychologists focus on perceptions.

d. Psychodynamic psychologists focus on unconscious conflicts.

Now turn to the quiz analysis table at the end of this chapter to find which areas you know well and which areas you need to work on. Circle the numbers in the table for items on Quiz 1 that you answered correctly.

ANSWERS TO MULTIPLE-CHOICE QUESTIONS

Circle the question numbers you answered correctly.

Sample Quiz 2

1. *d* is the answer. The client should be comfortable with the methods used, should know the therapist's track record, and should feel capable of developing a positive relationship with the therapist. (p. 552)

2. *d* is the answer. Psychodynamic therapists (or psychoanalysts) believe that exploring childhood experiences and thereby gaining understanding of unconscious processes are the keys to resolving mental illness. (pp. 534–535)

a. Behavioral therapists may focus on past learning experiences, but they usually deal with current behaviors, not unconscious processes and thoughts.

b. Gestalt therapists concentrate on identifying the problematic ways in which people may be behaving so that they live according to the expectations of others, not according to their true selves. Therapists may focus on the incorrect thought patterns that clients possess and the ways in which they defend against self-exploration.

c. Client-centered therapists focus on creating a therapeutic environment in which clients can explore the reasons for their problems and get themselves back on the track toward fulfillment and self-actualization.

3. *d* is the answer. Modeling is a behavior modification technique. (p. 542)

a, c. Dream interpretation and free association are part of classical psychoanalysis.

b. Ego analysis is a neo-analytic treatment.

4. *a* is the answer. A client-centered therapist must empathize, or perceive the world from the client's point of view. (p. 539)

b. Restating or paraphrasing a client's feelings is a way of demonstrating empathy.

c. Unconditional positive regard is necessary to let a client know that a therapist cares about and accepts the client as a person.

d. Congruence is the match between a therapist's words and actions toward a client. The therapist must actually experience, not just act out, unconditional positive regard and empathy for the client.

5. b is the answer. A client is exposed to the feared situation, object, or event and is not allowed to escape. Since the person cannot escape, he or she can come to realize that there is nothing to fear. (p. 543)

a. Gradual exposure to a feared stimulus takes place in systematic desensitization or participant modeling.

c. Cognitive restructuring can teach a client to replace destructive thoughts with more effective or constructive ones.

d. Presenting an unpleasant stimulus after an undesirable behavior is called punishment.

6. b is the answer. Congruence between thoughts and actions is part of client-centered therapy. (p. 539)

a. Analysis of transference is a psychodynamic technique in which the client's reaction to the therapist is compared to conflicts with significant others in childhood.

c. Reflection is a client-centered therapy technique.

d. You may have been thinking of empathy, which is a client-centered technique.

7. b is the answer. Psychoanalysts believe that if they reveal nothing about themselves, clients will begin to transfer onto them many feelings and attitudes about conflicts experienced with significant people in their lives. (p. 535)

a, d. Free association does help reveal unconscious conflicts, making them conscious, but this process is not called transference.

c. Interpreting a dream's manifest content in order to understand its symbolic or latent content is part of psychoanalytic treatment. This process is not called transference.

8. b is the answer. Aversive conditioning is based on classical conditioning. (p. 544)

a, d. Methods such as token economies and punishment are based on operant conditioning principles.

c. Aversive conditioning is used to decrease the occurrence of a specific behavior.

9. a is the answer. An anxiety hierarchy is a list of fear-producing situations that is constructed for use in systematic desensitization. (pp. 541–542)

b, d. There is no such thing as a fear manifest. (You may have been thinking of manifest content, which is used in psychodynamic dream analysis.)

c. Alec has constructed an anxiety hierarchy, but this hierarchy is a part of systematic desensitization, not flooding. Flooding is a behavioral technique in which a person is repeatedly put into the fear-producing situation until the conditioned fear response is extinguished.

10. c is the answer. The camp has set up a type of economic system in which campers receive tokens when they display behaviors they have agreed to work on. The campers can exchange their tokens for various forms of positive reinforcement. In Amy's case, her tokens are exchanged for special activities and privileges. Token economies serve to increase the occurrence of desirable behaviors. (p. 543)

a. Aversive conditioning is used to decrease, not increase, a behavior's occurrence.

b. Flooding is used to decrease a behavior, usually avoidance.

d. Cognitive restructuring involves replacing negative and damaging thoughts with more constructive ones.

11. c is the answer. Self-injury is dangerous and needs to be corrected as soon as possible. Dan's doctors tried many forms of therapy, and each one failed. Punishment, used as a last resort, may help decrease Dan's harmful behavior, allowing more adaptive behavior to be rewarded. (p. 544)

a. Traditional psychoanalysis would be difficult for a child, who might not have adequate verbal skills or abstract thinking ability.

b. Flooding is used to decrease avoidance behavior resulting from a phobia. Dan does not appear to be phobic. He is hyperactive.

d. Electroconvulsive therapy involves passing an electric current through one side of the brain. It is used as a last resort to treat depression. Dan is hyperactive, not depressed.

12. b is the answer. Jane's ideas about having everyone like her and being a perfect student are probably at the root of her depression. Rational-emotive therapy will help her recognize and eliminate these unhealthy thoughts. (p. 545)

a. Jane's depression might be alleviated by antidepressants, but it is obvious that her thought patterns about being liked and perfect will continue to cause her problems. Changing her thinking should alleviate her depression on a long-term basis.

    c. Aversive conditioning is used to decrease a specific behavior. Jane needs to change her thought patterns, not a specific behavior.

    d. Token economies are used to increase the occurrence of desired behaviors. Jane needs to change her thought patterns, not her overt behavior.

13. *b* is the answer. Modeling involves teaching a client desirable behaviors by demonstrating those behaviors and showing the client how to behave more calmly in feared situations. (p. 542)

    a. Token economies involve receiving tokens for demonstrating desirable behaviors. The tokens can later be traded in for rewards or privileges. Roberto is not performing any behaviors; he is watching how his therapist behaves with dogs.

    c. Flooding involves placing a client in a feared but harmless situation. Once deprived of his or her normally rewarding escape pattern, the client has no reason for continued anxiety. If Roberto and his therapist had shut themselves in a small room with a gentle, friendly dog, this would have been the answer.

    d. Classical conditioning is a part of aversive conditioning and flooding. Modeling is based on operant conditioning.

14. *b* is the answer. Alex would meet other children of divorced parents in group therapy, which would make him feel less alone and allow him to learn from others. (p. 546)

    a. Gestalt therapy could be used in a group format, but it would not require a group format.

    c. Psychoanalysis is an individual therapy.

    d. Social skills training is often done in groups, but would not focus on sharing concerns about parental divorce.

15. *a* is the answer. A therapist is bound by law to keep strictly confidential any information revealed by a client. He or she can discuss a case with a client's family only if the client gives permission. (p. 555)

    b, c, d. These are all situations in which a therapist may release information given by a client.

16. *b* is the answer. ECT is currently used to treat depression that has not responded to other treatments. (p. 557)

    a, c. ECT was once used to treat schizophrenia, but isn't currently. Hallucinations are a symptom of schizophrenia and other serious psychopathologies.

    d. Drugs are used to treat anxiety.

17. *b* is the answer. Fabricated studies were not a problem mentioned in the text's discussion of the evaluative studies on psychotherapy. (pp. 548–552)

    a. Successful therapy means that a client perceives relief and is better able to function on a day-to-day basis. So, although tests may show improvement, demonstration of clinical significance is also important.

    c. Hans Eysenck, who conducted one of the first large-scale comparisons of psychotherapy effects, was accused of ignoring evidence that therapy did indeed help clients.

    d. A behavioral therapist would probably define the success of a client differently than a psychoanalyst would, making it difficult to compare the effectiveness of different types of therapy.

18. *d* is the answer. Lithium is used to treat bipolar disorders. (p. 560)

    a, c. Tricyclics and MAO inhibitors are used to treat depression.

    b. Phenothiazines are used to treat severe disorders such as schizophrenia.

19. *b* is the answer. Blocking reuptake keeps a neurotransmitter from returning to the presynaptic cell. (p. 564)

    a. A receptor antagonist does block neurotransmitters, but it blocks them from binding to a postsynaptic cell.

    c. Tardive dyskinesia is a side effect caused by neuroleptics after years of use.

    d. Anxiolytics are anti-anxiety drugs.

20. *c* is the answer. Community psychologists seek both to treat and to prevent psychological problems. Michel believes that if psychological problems are detected in their early stages, treatment will be shorter, less expensive, and possibly more effective. (p. 564)

    a, b, d. Michel could believe in a psychoanalytic, phenomenological, biological, or behavioral approach to treating psychological problems. However, those who work to reduce stressors in the environment and in public domains such as schools are called community psychologists.

Now turn to the quiz analysis table at the end of this chapter to find which areas you know well and which areas you need to work on. Circle the numbers in the table for items on Quiz 2 that you answered correctly.

For each question you answered correctly, circle its number. (Quiz 1 numbers are not shaded; Quiz 2 numbers are shaded.) Are there patterns in the types of questions or the topics you got wrong that could direct your further study? Did you improve from Quiz 1 to Quiz 2?

	TYPE OF QUESTION		
TOPIC	**DEFINITION**	**COMPREHENSION**	**APPLICATION**
Basic features		1	2
		1	
Psychodynamic	3		5, 6
	7	3	2
Phenomenological		4	7, 8
	4		6
Behavior	10	9	11, 12, 13
	5	8	9, 10, 11, 12, 13
Group, family, couples		14	15
			14
Evaluation			16
		15, 17	
Biological		17, 19	18
		19	16, 18
Community			20
			20

TOTAL CORRECT BY QUIZ:

QUIZ 1:
QUIZ 2:

Chapter 17

Social Cognition

Social psychology focuses on the effects of the social world on the behavior and mental processes of individuals. The mental processes associated with how people perceive and react to other individuals and groups are called social cognitions.

OUTLINE

I. SOCIAL CONSTRUCTION OF THE SELF (pp. 570–571)

Two important components of the self are self-concept, the beliefs we have about our characteristics, and self-esteem, our evaluation of ourselves.

A. Social Comparison

According to the theory of social comparison, people use other people as a basis of comparison for self-evaluation when no objective criteria exist. People compare themselves to groups of other people called reference groups. As changes occur over the course of life, people change reference groups. People may find their self-evaluations to be poor in comparison to others in the new group and begin to experience relative deprivation. Usually people do not compare themselves to others who are not in their immediate reference group. Chronic use of extreme reference groups can lead to depression and anxiety.

B. Social Identity Theory

Many people form a social identity (also known as group identity), which may create associations based on nationality, gender, or religion. However, social identities foster prejudice, discrimination, and intergroup conflict based on the "us versus them" phenomenon.

II. LINKAGES: SOCIAL COGNITION AND PSYCHOLOGICAL DISORDERS (p. 571)

One's mental representation of self, or self-schema, can be unified or differentiated. People with a unified self-schema interpret failure as implying incompetence in all areas of their lives, whereas those with differentiated self-schemas limit feelings of failure to just the one failed life area. Self-schemas also contain the "actual self," the "ideal self," and the "ought self." Focus on the discrepancies between the actual and ideal selves produces sadness, disappointment, dissatisfaction, and possibly depression. Discrepancies between the actual and ought selves can contribute to guilt and fear of rejection and occasionally anxiety-related disorders.

III. SOCIAL PERCEPTION (pp. 572–579)

Social perception refers to the processes through which people interpret information about others, draw inferences about them, and develop mental representations of them.

A. The Role of Schemas

People often use schemas, or mental representations, to perceive and interpret new information. Schemas influence our processing, retention, and judgment of new information.

1. *First Impressions.* Schemas allow us to quickly categorize a person we have just met. The first impression is formed quickly and is difficult to change.

2. *Forming Impressions.* Many people tend to feel that other people they meet hold similar values to their own; consequently, they form positive first impressions. However, negative information is given more weight than positive information.

3. *Lasting Impressions.* First impressions are difficult to change because they shape interpretations of new information. People tend to remember their initial general impressions better than later corrections.

4. *Self-Fulfilling Prophecies.* An initial impression can create a self-fulfilling prophecy. People behave in ways that elicit behaviors consistent with their first impression of the person.

B. Explaining Behavior: Attribution

We make attributions about a person's behavior according to the internal characteristics of a person or to the external characteristics of the situation.

1. *Sources of Attributions.* How people go about making attributions depends on consensus, consistency, and distinctiveness. An internal attribution is made if consensus is low, consistency is high, and distinctiveness is low.

2. *Focus on Research Methods: A Cross-Cultural Experiment on Attribution.* A group of U.S. students and a group of Hindu Indian students were asked to explain the reciprocal or spontaneous helping described in stories. The U.S. students explained the reciprocal helping as "repaying a favor" (an external cause) rather than "liking to help" (an internal cause). Most of them also felt that there was very little moral responsibility involved. Generally, the Hindu students thought that reciprocal helping occurred because the helper liked to help. The Hindus thought the spontaneous helpers liked to help slightly less than the reciprocal helpers, which, again, was the opposite of the Americans' point of view.

3. *The Fundamental Attribution Error.* Attributional biases are tendencies to systematically distort one's view of behavior. The fundamental attribution error is the tendency to attribute other people's behavior to internal causes.

4. *Other Attributional Biases.* The actor-observer bias is the tendency to attribute others' behavior to internal causes and our own behavior to external causes, especially when the behavior is inappropriate or involves failure. The self-serving bias is the tendency to take credit (make an internal attribution) for success and blame external causes for failures.

C. The Self-Protective Functions of Social Cognition

As in the self-serving bias, people are often motivated to think in ways that protect them from upsetting or threatening conclusions. Many people exhibit a pattern of unrealistic optimism; they believe that positive events are more likely and negative events less likely to happen to them than to others. Unique invulnerability contributes to unrealistic optimism. People often adopt a self-handicapping strategy when they anticipate a loss of self-esteem so that they can attribute the possible failure to an external cause.

IV. ATTITUDES (pp. 579–583)

A. The Structure of Attitudes

Attitudes have three components: cognitive (belief), affective (emotional), and behavioral (way of acting). These three components are not always strongly aligned. Four factors determine whether behavior will be consistent with other attitude components: attitude consistency with subjective norms, perceived control of the attitudinal behavior, direct experience with the attitude object, and how closely self-behavior is monitored.

B. Forming Attitudes

Learning plays an important role in attitude formation. Social learning is especially important; classical and operant conditioning can also produce positive or negative attitudes. The mere exposure effect plays a role in attitude formation; all else being equal, positive attitudes are positively correlated with exposure frequency.

C. Changing Attitudes

Persuasive communications can change attitudes depending on several factors.

1. *Two Routes to Attitude Change.* Attitude change depends on three things: characteristics of the communicator, message content, and audience. According to the elaboration likelihood model of attitude change, messages can change attitudes through two routes: peripheral (generally ignores content) and central (focuses on logic and content). The peripheral route is more likely when a person is busy thinking about something else.

2. *Cognitive Dissonance Theory.* Cognitive dissonance theory holds that when attitudes are inconsistent (or "dissonant"), people feel uneasy and are motivated to make them consistent. One way to do so is to change the inconsistent attitude.

3. *Self-Perception Theory.* The self-perception theory suggests that when situations occur in which people are unsure about their attitudes, they will observe their own behavior and infer what their attitudes must have been.

V. PREJUDICE AND STEREOTYPES (pp. 583–588)

Stereotypes are impressions or schemas of entire groups of people. They often lead to prejudice, a positive or negative attitude toward the group. The behavioral component of prejudice is often discrimination.

A. Theories of Prejudice

1. *Motivational Theories.* People with authoritarian personalities tend to obey anyone above them in social status and demand deference from anyone

below them in social status. To protect themselves from threats, they strongly identify with their own ethnic, cultural, or social group—known as their in-group. People with authoritarian personalities may be predisposed to develop negative stereotypes of people in their out-groups.

2. *Cognitive Theories.* Given the complexity of the world, people tend to categorize others in groups. Grouping people into social categories can result in stereotypes and illusory correlations between behavior and an ethnicity.

3. *Learning Theories.* Children often learn stereotypes from their parents, their peers, and others.

B. Reducing Prejudice

The contact hypothesis states that stereotypes and prejudices about a group should be reduced as friendly contact between members of equal standing in the two groups is increased. Research suggests that intergroup contact has positive effects when members have equal social and economic status, are in a situation that demands interdependence and cooperation, interact on a one-on-one basis, and are perceived as typical of that group.

C. Thinking Critically: Is Ethnic Prejudice Too Ingrained to Ever Be Eliminated?

What am I being asked to believe or accept?
People who deny having prejudices still have negative stereotypes about and show discrimination toward ethnic out-groups. These negative attitudes run so deep in all of us that ethnic prejudice can never be eliminated.

What evidence is available to support the assertion?
The theory of aversive racism suggests that although many European-Americans find ethnic prejudice aversive, they will still display it, especially when they don't have to admit that they are prejudiced. Several studies show that people who consider themselves unprejudiced are inclined to discriminate. Priming studies show that negative stereotypes can be activated even among people who asserted that they have none.

Are there alternative ways of interpreting the evidence?
If people are unaware of their prejudices, such views will be difficult to change. Perhaps people are more aware than they'd like to admit, however.

What additional evidence would help to evaluate the alternatives?
More research should study whether subconscious stereotype processes continue to influence people who have been told to consciously try not to let stereotypes influence them.

What conclusions are most reasonable?
Prejudice may be subconscious in some people. We should carry on the fight against conscious stereotyping, prejudice, and discrimination.

VI. INTERPERSONAL ATTRACTION (pp. 588–592)

A. Keys to Attraction

1. *The Environment.* Proximity is an important predictor of attraction. The more often people interact, the more they tend to like each other. The situation in which people meet also influences attraction. If people meet others in positive circumstances, they are more likely to be attracted to each other.

2. *Similarity.* People tend to like others who have attitudes similar to their own, especially attitudes about other people. Attitudes influence attraction, and attraction influences attitudes.

3. *Physical Attractiveness.* People tend to like attractive people. Also, according to the matching hypothesis, people tend to form committed relationships with people who are similarly attractive.

B. Intimate Relationships and Love

Interdependence, affection, emotional expressiveness, cohesiveness, and sexuality are often cited as important components of intimacy.

1. *Analyzing Love.* Sternberg's triangular theory of love suggests that love is a function of intimacy, passion, and commitment. Romantic love is characterized by intense and arousing physical attraction and feelings of closeness. Companionate love is less arousing but more committed and has a similarly high level of intimacy. The most complete and satisfying love is consummate love, which includes a high level of passion, intimacy, and commitment.

2. *Strong and Weak Marriages.* People report high levels of marital satisfaction when communication is high, the relationship is perceived as equitable, and conflict and anger are resolved effectively.

KEY TERMS

1. **Social psychology** focuses on the effects of the social world on the behavior and mental processes of individuals (p. 569)

2. **Social cognition** refers to the mental processes by which people perceive and react to others. (p. 569)

3. Our **self-concept** is the set of beliefs we have about who we are and what we're like. (p. 570)

Example: Mimi believes she is a responsible student, a caring friend, and a somewhat shy person.

4. **Self-esteem** consists of the evaluations we make about how worthy we are as human beings. (p. 570)

Example: Although Joshua recently failed a thermo-dynamics quiz, he knows that he is smart and a good person.

5. The theory of **social comparison** states that in the absence of objective criteria, people compare themselves to others for the purpose of self-evaluation. (p. 570)

Example: If you want to know how athletic you are, you might compare yourself to friends of the same sex.

6. **Reference groups** are the categories of people to which individuals see themselves as belonging and to which they habitually compare themselves. (p. 570)

Example: Jerome is an undergraduate student at a major university. He would probably consider his reference group to be other students; therefore, he would not compare his attractiveness or wardrobe to that of models he sees in magazines.

7. **Relative deprivation** occurs when a person's relative standing on any dimension is poor compared to that person's social reference group. (p. 570)

Example: Rachel has just graduated with a Ph.D. in biology and taken a new job. At the university, she was considered one of the best students in her department. At her new job, she must start over and earn the respect of her superiors and peers. She experiences relative deprivation as she begins her new job.

8. **Social identity**, a part of our self-concept, is our belief about the groups to which we belong. (p. 571)

Example: Karl says he is a German-American Lutheran farmer.

9. **Self-schemas** are the mental representations people form of themselves. They are based on social comparison and social identity. (p. 571)

Example: Sapna, who has a differentiated self-schema, thinks of herself as a capable student, but an incapable car mechanic.

10. **Social perception** refers to the processes through which people interpret information about others. Social perception influences the conclusions one makes about another person's personality style and why the person behaves in certain ways. (p. 572)

11. A **self-fulfilling prophecy** is the process by which an impression of a person, object, or event elicits behavior that confirms the impression. (pp. 573–574)

Example: Jayne believed that she would never succeed in college. During her first semester, she found that she had to study much harder than she did in high school and decided it was a sign that she was stupid. Jayne quit studying, thinking that it was of no use, and flunked out of school.

12. **Attribution** is the process of explaining the causes of people's behavior, including one's own. Internal or external causes can account for behavior. (p. 574)

Example: How would you respond to an inquiry about the causes of your grades? Would you say that you are smart and work hard (internal causes) or that you are lucky and consistently end up with easy professors (external causes)?

13. The **fundamental attribution error** is the tendency to attribute the behavior of others to internal factors. (p. 577)

Example: Latanya's brother calls and tells her that he has just flunked an algebra exam. Before he can speak another word, Latanya is telling him that he is either lazy or stupid or both. She thinks that her brother's behavior, not situational factors, caused him to flunk his algebra test.

14. The **actor-observer bias** is the tendency to attribute one's own behavior to external factors, and others' behavior to internal factors, especially when the behavior is inappropriate or involves failure. (p. 578)

Example: When John failed to stop at a stop sign, he attributed his behavior to the sun in his eyes and poor placement of the sign (external factors). When someone else runs a stop sign, however, John thinks they did so because of carelessness or lack of attention (internal factors).

15. The **self-serving bias** is the tendency to take credit for success but to blame external causes for failure. (p. 578)

Example: Jerry has noticed that whenever his company wins a big account with a new client, each person claims responsibility for the success. However, when a client decides to take its business elsewhere, everyone denies responsibility for the problems that precipitated the client's departure. People like to take credit for success but do not like to take the blame for failure.

16. An **attitude** is the tendency to think, feel, or act positively or negatively toward objects in our environment. Therefore, it has cognitive, affective, and behavioral components. (p. 579)

Example: Stephanie joins the marching band because she believes it challenges its members to become better musicians (cognitive component). She practices her clarinet nearly every day (behavioral component) and enjoys band practices and performances (affective component).

17. The **elaboration likelihood model** states that a message may change a person's attitude through a peripheral or central route. Taking a central route (such as critical thinking) to changing an attitude requires both the motivation and the ability to do so. (p. 581)

Example: Matthew chose to purchase a generic medication after reading an informational pamphlet and discussing it with his doctor (central route). Jennifer chose to buy generic medicines after seeing a television commercial with a trustworthy, confident person describing their advantages (peripheral route).

18. The **cognitive dissonance theory** states that people prefer that their cognitions about themselves and the rest of the world be consistent with one another. When cognitions are inconsistent, or dissonant, people feel uneasy and are motivated to make them more consistent. (p. 582)

Example: Jan is an advertising executive. She is working on a cigarette company's account, but she thinks that cigarettes should not be advertised to teenagers. Her attitudes and behavior are inconsistent. She will have to change her attitude about cigarette advertising or change jobs in order to reduce cognitive dissonance and the psychological tension it causes.

19. **Self-perception theory** states that we review our own behavior in order to determine what our attitudes are. (p. 583)

Example: To be initiated into his boyhood group of friends, Gabriel was required to eat a worm, a live goldfish, and the head of a bumblebee. After eating these, Gabriel liked the group even more than he did before. He inferred that he must really like the group because he was able to overcome his loathing of worms, live fish, and bugs.

20. **Stereotypes** are impressions or schemas of entire groups of people. Stereotypes operate on the false assumption that all members of a group share the same characteristics. This can lead to prejudice. (p. 583)

Example: Vance is interviewing candidates for a position in his company. He has decided not to hire anyone with a Ph.D. He has been told by his peers that people with Ph.D.'s are flaky, absent-minded, and socially inept.

21. **Prejudice** is holding a preconceived positive or negative attitude about an individual based on her or his membership in a group of people. These attitudes have cognitive, affective, and behavioral components. (p. 584)

Example: Isa, an American, went to study in Russia for a year. She met a child on the street one day who asked her why Americans wanted to destroy the world with nuclear bombs. The child had never been exposed to Americans before but had prejudged them based on information from the press, her parents, and her peers.

22. **Discrimination** is the differential treatment of various groups that can be the behavioral component of prejudice. (p. 584)

Example: Gabrielle has brought her date, an artist, to meet her parents. She is very embarrassed because her father will not even speak to him. Later, she asks her father to explain his extremely rude behavior. He remarks that all artists are shiftless and no good and forbids her to see her friend again.

23. The **contact hypothesis** states that a person's prejudices and stereotypes about a group should be reduced with repeated friendly exposure (contact) to members of equal standing in that group. This provides an opportunity for prejudiced people to learn about members of the group as individuals. (pp. 585–586)

Example: Anna grew up in the East. Her parents always told her that people who spoke with a southern accent were stupid and lazy. When Anna's company relocated her to Texas, she eventually came to enjoy interacting with other employees and found them to be competent at their jobs.

24. The theory of **aversive racism** contends that although many European-Americans are repulsed by prejudice, they will still sometimes show it, especially when they can do so without admitting, even to themselves, that they are prejudiced. (p. 587)

Example: Dawn usually locks her car door as soon as she gets in. When she forgets to do so, however, she often remembers to lock it when she stops at a stoplight and sees an African-American man. Dawn doesn't notice that she does not suddenly remember to lock her door when she is at a stoplight and sees a European-American man or woman; therefore, she is able to think of herself as unprejudiced.

25. The **matching hypothesis** states that a person is more likely to form committed relationships with others who are similar in physical attractiveness than with those who are notably more or less attractive. (p. 590)

Example: As you walk around your campus or neighborhood, look at the couples you see. They will often be about equal in attractiveness.

FILL-IN-THE-BLANKS KEY TERMS

This section will help you check your factual knowledge of the key terms introduced in this chapter. Fill in each blank with the appropriate term from the list of key terms above.

1. The mental processes with which we think about others are called _____.

2. After moving into a new reference group, a person sometimes feels inadequate; this phenomenon is called _____.

3. The mental representations people form of themselves are _____.

4. The process of explaining the causes of behavior is called _____.

5. The people to whom we compare ourselves are called a _____.

6. The tendency for people to be attracted to those of similar physical attractiveness is described in the _____.

7. A _____ can cause behavior that confirms an original hypothesis.

8. The _____ bias says that we usually attribute other people's behavior to internal factors, especially when the behavior is negative.

9. The _____ bias says that we attribute our successes to internal factors, and our failures to external factors.

10. Schemas of entire groups of people that assume that all members share the same characteristics are called _____.

11. The _____ model of attitude change states that a message may change a person's attitude through a peripheral or central route.

12. The notion that group stereotypes should be reduced by members of different groups getting to know one another is part of the _____.

13. The theory of _____ contends that although many European-Americans are repulsed by prejudice, they still sometimes show it.

14. The _____ is the tendency to see the behavior of others as a function of internal personality factors.

15. According to _____, people determine what their attitudes are by examining past behavior.

Total Correct (See answer key) _____

LEARNING OBJECTIVES

1. Define social cognition and social psychology. Compare and contrast self-concept and self-esteem. (pp. 569–570)

2. Discuss the theory of social comparison. Describe the relationship of reference groups to the process of self-evaluation. Define relative deprivation. (p. 570)

3. Define social identity. Discuss the theory of social identity. (p. 571)

4. Discuss how self-schemas affect our vulnerability to psychological disorders. (p. 571)

5. Define social perception. Describe the influences, including the role of schemas, on impression formation. Explain why impressions are difficult to change. (pp. 572–573)

6. Define self-fulfilling prophecies. Discuss the relationship between self-fulfilling prophecies and impressions. (pp. 573–574)

7. Define attribution. Describe the three criteria used in making attributions and explain how they influence whether we make an internal or external attribution. (pp. 574–575)

8. Describe the cross-cultural experiment on attribution and its outcome. (pp. 576–577)

9. Define the <u>fundamental attribution error</u>, and give an example of it. Define the <u>actor-observer bias</u> and the <u>self-serving bias</u>, and give examples of each. (pp. 577–579)

10. Define <u>attitudes</u>. Describe the cognitive, affective, and behavioral components of attitudes and give an example of each. (pp. 579–580)

11. Discuss how attitudes are formed and changed. Include the mere exposure effect and the <u>elaboration likelihood model</u> of attitude change. (pp. 580–582)

12. Define <u>cognitive dissonance</u>, and describe the process of reducing it. (pp. 582–583)

13. Define <u>self-perception</u>. Describe the influence of past behavior on attitudes, according to the self-perception theory. (p. 583)

14. Define <u>stereotype</u>, <u>prejudice</u>, and <u>discrimination</u>. (pp. 583–584)

15. Compare and contrast the <u>motivational</u>, <u>learning</u>, and <u>cognitive</u> theories of stereotypes and prejudice. Define the authoritarian personality and social categories. (pp. 584–585)

16. Describe the <u>contact hypothesis</u>. Discuss the specific conditions necessary for the contact hypothesis to hold true. (pp. 585–586)

17. Discuss the studies on the possibility of eliminating prejudice. Define <u>aversive racism</u>. (pp. 586–588)

18. Describe the influences of the environment, similarity, and physical attractiveness on attraction. Define the <u>matching hypothesis</u>. (pp. 588–590)

19. Describe the most important components of an intimate relationship. (pp. 590–591)

20. Describe Sternberg's triangular theory of love. Discuss the differences among romantic love, companionate love, and consummate love. Describe the factors which influence marital satisfaction. (pp. 591–592)

CONCEPTS AND EXERCISES

No. 1: Persuasive Advertising

Completing this exercise should help you to achieve Learning Objectives 10, 11, 12, and 13.

For each of the following advertising campaigns, use the list below to suggest a reason for the chosen method.

1. Richard Nixon spent $21 million on promotion and advertising during his presidential campaign. Many famous Americans made commercial spots for Nixon. His spokesman in the South was John Wayne, and Jackie Gleason endorsed Nixon in the East. Why would a presidential candidate seek endorsements from movie stars? _____

2. An organization that wants people to sponsor a needy child has a television commercial in which they show children in poor living conditions. While the pictures of apparently malnourished, homeless children are shown, an announcer suggests that no one would want a child to go hungry another day. "If you care," the speaker says, "you'll call now to sponsor a child." What is this advertisement trying to create in its viewers? _____

3. A drug company places advertisements in medical journals. Each is a full page and contains many details about the drug, its dosage, advantages, and side effects. Why would the company put so much information in their advertisement? _____

4. During a televised movie, a beverage company arranges to have their products advertised many times. Viewers sometimes see two or three of their commercials in one break. _____

   ° Mere exposure effect
   ° Peripheral route
   ° Central route
   ° Cognitive dissonance
   ° Self-perception

No. 2: Prejudice and Love

Completing this exercise should help you to achieve Learning Objectives 15, 16, 18, and 20.

For each of the descriptions, decide which theory or concept best fits the situation.

1. Karen is an office clerk. When students come to help for the summer, she is extremely rude and orders them around. However, when her boss tells her what to do, Karen is extremely obedient and efficient. _____

2. Carlos and Sanya are not very sexually aroused by one another, but both believe strongly that they will remain married for many years to come. Carlos and Sanya discuss their hopes and dreams as well as daily events. _____

3. Lucy and Ricky have a fiery relationship and feel that they can share much with each other, but they aren't sure how long their relationship will last.

   _____

4. When Dino's parents saw people who appeared to be from a different racial or ethnic group, they looked at each other and then watched the people as long as they were in the neighborhood. Dino noticed their behavior and now feels suspicious of anyone who appears different from him.

   _____

   ° Motivational theory of prejudice
   ° Learning theory of prejudice
   ° Cognitive theory of prejudice
   ° Contact hypothesis
   ° Romantic love
   ° Companionate love
   ° Consummate love

CRITICAL THINKING

Sam and Martina are trying to discover the motive for a murder. When questioned, the killer, a forty-year-old man named Brian Canton, said he just felt like killing the victim even though he didn't know him. Sam decides that Brian has an antisocial personality and leaves the interrogation room. Martina is not so sure and continues to talk to Brian.

Later, Sam is incredibly frustrated. "Look, Martina, the guy is admitting to a classic symptom of antisocial personality. He just *felt like it*. He hasn't shown any signs of remorse. This is an easy one. We finally have a break here."

Martina snaps, "If you had stayed in the room for a little while longer, you would have picked up some information that would have led you to an alternative hypothesis."

"Oh yeah? Like what?" asks Sam.

Martina replies, "He kept telling me how much he hated killing that guy. And he kept wanting to know if anything bad would happen to his family. Doesn't sound like an antisocial personality to me. Besides, do you know how rare antisocial personalities are? The guy would have a criminal record a mile long." Martina thinks for a minute. "I've got it. That guy was a paid assassin. I'll be right back. I need to ask some more questions. Sam, you go take care of the paperwork on this one. We'll meet later."

That afternoon Sam and Martina get together again. Sam sighs and says, "Okay, I know you've got it figured out. Let's hear the answers to those questions you always use."

Using the five critical thinking questions in your text, the clues in the story, and what you have learned about cognitive dissonance, answer the following.

1. What is Sam's hypothesis?

2. What evidence supports Sam's hypothesis?

3. What is Martina's alternative hypothesis?

4. What additional evidence supports Martina's hypothesis?

5. What conclusions are reasonable?

PERSONAL LEARNING ACTIVITIES

1. Answer the following questions. Are you attractive? Are you extremely intelligent? Do you dress well? Are you well educated? The individuals or groups of people to whom you compare yourself when answering these questions are your reference groups. Who made up your reference groups? Were the groups different for each question? Think about where you will be in ten years. How might your reference groups change? In what situations could you experience relative deprivation? (Learning Objective 2)

2. Write a description of yourself. Which parts of your description are aspects of your self-concept, self-esteem, personal identity, and social identity? (Learning Objectives 1 and 3)

3. Recall your first impression of someone you met in the last year. How did your impression of that person change as you got to know her or him better—or did it change? (Learning Objective 5)

4. Sit in a public place for about ten minutes and write notes on the behavior of people you observe. Later in the day look over your descriptions for evidence of characteristics you attributed to the people. For example, did you write only comments such as, "Saw a person wearing a backpack walk by with his head tilted down. When he turned the corner, he bumped into another person." Or did you make assumptions about motives, occupations, and personalities? The same situation, for instance, might have been described as follows: "Watched a depressed and frustrated student carelessly crash into another person." Identify instances where you may have been influenced by the fundamental attribution error or prejudices. To do so, you could get a friend to observe the same situation with you and see how your notes compare. (Learning Objectives 9 and 14)

5. Describe a couple in a romantic relationship. How do the people feel, think, and act toward each other? Identify what level of each of Sternberg's characteristics (intimacy, passion, and commitment) you think the pair exemplifies. According to Sternberg, which type of love best fits the description you gave? (Learning Objective 20)

MULTIPLE-CHOICE QUESTIONS

SAMPLE QUIZ 1

1. _____ are sets of people to whom we compare ourselves during self-evaluation.
   a. Reference groups
   b. Relative groups
   c. Career groups
   d. Outgroups

2. Cindy is preparing to switch from her public school to an exclusive private school for gifted students. Because Cindy won't be the smartest student any more, she will be more likely to experience _____ at the private school than at the public school.
   a. cognitive dissonance
   b. the fundamental attribution error
   c. relative deprivation
   d. self-fulfilling prophecies

3. Compared to those with a differentiated self-schema, people with a unified self-schema are _____ to be vulnerable to feelings of failure in many areas of life just because they failed in one area.
   a. more likely
   b. less likely
   c. equally likely
   d. cannot be determined

4. "I am a Muslim," said Alaa. Alaa described his
   a. self-esteem.
   b. self-schema.
   c. social identity.
   d. social perception.

5. On Gena's first day at work, her boss was short-tempered and gruff with her. From then on she was constantly prepared for more nasty comments. Gena's defensiveness irritated her boss further and caused her boss to be even more short-tempered. When Gena's boss gave her a negative six-month evaluation, it was most likely due to
   a. a stereotype.
   b. prejudice.
   c. a self-fulfilling prophecy.
   d. discrimination.

6. Carol goes to a party to meet people. While there, she is introduced to Rico, an attractive man about her age. During their conversation, Rico is rude several times. Based on what you know about impression formation, which of the following is likely to be her response?
   a. Carol will assume that Rico is rude because he had a bad day.
   b. Carol will assume that Rico is a rude person.
   c. Carol is experiencing a self-fulfilling prophecy.
   d. Carol will assume that Rico is similar to her and form a positive impression.

7. An attributional bias in which we attribute our failures to external causes and our successes to internal factors is called the
   a. actor-observer bias.
   b. fundamental attribution error.
   c. self-fulfilling prophecy.
   d. self-serving bias.

8. Kassandra fears that she is not capable of handling the job associated with a promotion for which she has been recommended. She is always on time for work but shows up late and poorly prepared for the interview with the head of the company. Kassandra is exhibiting
   a. a self-handicapping strategy.
   b. a self-fulfilling prophecy.
   c. the fundamental attribution error.
   d. a self-serving bias.

9. When showing the campus to a group from India, Frasier mentions that many university alumni who received scholarships now contribute money to help others complete their degrees. Frasier comments that the alumni were repaying the favor. If the tour group is similar to the Hindu Indians described in your text, most of them are likely to believe that the alumni
   a. liked to help.
   b. were repaying a favor.
   c. have helpful personalities.
   d. do not like to help, but feel forced to do so.

10. Julia is proud to be dating Vernon because he is thoughtful and considerate to everyone. He always sends her flowers and is willing to help his friends. Julia's friends are envious; none of their boyfriends is as considerate as Vernon. Vernon's behavior demonstrates _____ consensus, _____ consistency, and _____ distinctiveness. Julia

will attribute his behavior to an _____ cause.

a. high; high; high; external
b. high; low; high; internal
c. low; high; low; internal
d. high; high; low; external

11. Bridget and Jay just got into the car to go to lunch. Bridget asks Jay to wear his seatbelt, but he ignores her. Which of the following best explains Jay's behavior?
a. Cognitive dissonance
b. Unique invulnerability
c. Self-handicapping strategy
d. Self-serving bias

12. Norma loves to put cold cream on her face because she believes that it prevents wrinkles. She buys new cold cream about every two weeks. What is the affective component of Norma's attitude toward cold cream?
a. She buys a large quantity of cold cream.
b. She loves cold cream.
c. She believes that cold cream will prevent wrinkles.
d. She puts cold cream on her face.

13. Erik always says that looks are not important to him when he asks a woman out; however, recently he did not invite either of two women he liked to a dance because he didn't think they were attractive. When his friend points out the difference between what Erik said was important and what was really influencing him, Erik most likely experienced
a. the actor-observer bias.
b. cognitive dissonance.
c. deindividuation.
d. the mere exposure bias.

14. Renato says that stereotyping occurs because people group others into social categories and see all members of a category as similar. Renato agrees with the _____ theory of prejudice.
a. motivational
b. cognitive
c. contact
d. learning

15. A manufacturing plant supervisor discovers that prejudice and discrimination are creating conflict among her employees. The supervisor reorganizes the staff so that each work group has people of different ethnicities with equal status who must work together to solve problems. The supervisor agrees with the _____ theory of prejudice.

a. motivational
b. deprivational
c. aversive racism
d. learning

16. Casisi complies with the requests of teachers, elder relatives, and his boss. However, when a younger sibling or an acquaintance makes a request, he doesn't feel obligated to fulfill it. Casisi likes the security of feeling part of a group, so he'll sometimes taunt or harass people who aren't members of his ethnic group. Casisi's behavior is best explained by the _____ theory of prejudice.
a. motivational
b. cognitive
c. contact
d. learning

17. Which of the following is a good predictor of whether people will form a committed relationship?
a. Similar attitudes
b. Similar degrees of attractiveness
c. Lack of conflict and anger
d. Both (a) and (b)

18. Susan has just moved into a new dormitory. She will most likely become good friends with the women
a. on the floor above hers.
b. in the dorm next door.
c. in the room next door.
d. at the other end of the hall.

19. With whom would you be most likely to fall in love at first sight?
a. Your tour guide in the Mojave Desert in August
b. The person who fills your gas tank when you are in a hurry
c. The person you bump into on the quad on a beautiful spring day
d. There is an equal probability that you would fall in love with any of the above.

20. George and Louise share their thoughts, hopes, and daily worries and plan to stay married until death parts them. They enjoy an active and creative sex life. According to Sternberg's theory, George and Louise have _____ love.
a. consummate
b. companionate
c. fatuous
d. romantic

Total Correct (See answer key) _____

SAMPLE QUIZ 2

Use this quiz to reassess your learning after taking Quiz 1 and reviewing the chapter.

1. Jack is depressed. He took a job in the city after completing graduate school on a scholarship and graduating with honors. Now that he is in the city, it seems that everyone is older, richer, and wiser than he is. Jack is experiencing
   a. cognitive dissonance.
   b. relative deprivation.
   c. role isolation.
   d. a self-fulfilling prophecy.

2. Jack (see question 1) is depressed because he has changed his
   a. reference group.
   b. relative group.
   c. social identity.
   d. self-schema.

3. Our social identity is our
   a. desire to be like our peers.
   b. desire to be like our idols.
   c. belief about our self-worth.
   d. belief about the groups to which we belong.

4. The "ideal self" is
   a. what a person actually is.
   b. what a person wants to be.
   c. what a person feels he or she should be.
   d. none of the above.

5. Even when things aren't going well for Wenlan in school, she feels good about herself. She and her partner, Chris, have been together for two years and have many close friends. Wenlan believes her academic problems don't reflect on her overall competence; therefore, she has a(n)
   a. differentiated self-schema.
   b. unified self-schema.
   c. dissonant self-concept.
   d. consolidated self-esteem.

6. When Lance introduced himself to Nathan, he mentioned that he worked as a cashier in a supermarket. Nathan remembered all of Lance's comments about food and car repairs and remembered none of his comments about English poets and politics. Nathan's perception was most likely biased by
   a. discrimination.
   b. a schema.
   c. social comparison.
   d. the actor-observer bias.

7. According to the fundamental attribution error, we
   a. always attribute our behavior to internal causes.
   b. always make an internal attribution for our successes.
   c. usually attribute others' behavior to external causes.
   d. usually attribute others' behavior to internal causes.

8. People attribute behavior to an external cause when it has _____ consistency, _____ distinctiveness, and _____ consensus.
   a. high; low; low
   b. high; high; low
   c. high; low; high
   d. low; high; high

9. Felicia's first novel has sold over 1 million copies, but Felicia thinks it is due to luck. She thinks other best-selling novels are written by talented writers; therefore, she is demonstrating the
   a. fundamental attribution error.
   b. actor-observer bias.
   c. self-perception theory.
   d. self-serving bias.

10. While talking about her daughter Nicole, Clarissa says, "I have taught Nicole to be considerate, thoughtful, and moral, but Nicole's father is responsible for her inability to manage her money." This is an illustration of
    a. the fundamental attribution error.
    b. the self-serving bias.
    c. the actor-observer bias.
    d. relative deprivation.

11. Discrepancies between attitudes lead to
    a. prejudice.
    b. cognitive dissonance.
    c. the fundamental attribution error.
    d. relative deprivation.

12. Gladys thinks that AIDS research should be supported and is distressed that it may not make breakthroughs fast enough to save people who are currently HIV-positive. When asked for a donation to an AIDS research foundation, however, she refuses. Therefore, she will feel uncomfortable because her _____ and _____ components are not in agreement.
    a. cognitive; behavioral
    b. affective; cognitive
    c. central; peripheral
    d. peripheral; behavioral

13. When Mark sees a television commercial that shows a couple meeting and falling in love, he immediately phones the number they list to sign up for the dating service. Mark most likely used _____ to change his attitude.
   a. a central route
   b. a peripheral route
   c. "cognitive busyness"
   d. "cognitive dissonance"

14. Margie wants to reduce children's prejudices; therefore, she decides to run an after-school program in her grade school to bring together students of different backgrounds for games, study sessions, and snacks. Based on the description of successful intergroup contact given in the text, which of the following would bring Margie the most success?
   a. Allow the children to choose sides for a game of basketball.
   b. Have the different ethnic groups describe their families' customs.
   c. Design a project that will require all the children to cooperate in order to succeed.
   d. Point out the errors of the high-status children.

15. Cognitive dissonance and the self-perception theory differ in that
   a. cognitive dissonance involves attitudes, whereas self-perception involves attribution.
   b. cognitive dissonance involves attitude change, whereas self-perception involves social facilitation.
   c. cognitive dissonance involves the reduction of internal tension, whereas self-perception does not.
   d. none of the above

16. In-groups are similar to
   a. reference groups.
   b. relative deprivation groups.
   c. social facilitators.
   d. none of the above.

17. Ed thinks prejudice and discrimination could destroy society. Ed is always fairly careful with his money, but he doesn't admit that he tends to check his change more carefully when the cashier is an African-American. Ed's behavior fits best with the _____ theory of prejudice.
   a. motivational
   b. cognitive
   c. aversive racism
   d. learning

18. Claudia and Kathy are good friends. Claudia likes Elizabeth, but Kathy does not. This difference in their attitudes creates problems when they try to plan social gatherings. Claudia and Kathy's relationship is
   a. balanced.
   b. imbalanced.
   c. dissonant.
   d. distinctive.

19. According to Sternberg's triangular theory of love, the most mutually fulfilling type of love is
   a. passionate love.
   b. companionate love.
   c. consummate love.
   d. any of the above.

20. Amanda and Roger are likely to become committed to each other because they are similar in attractiveness, according to
   a. proximity effects.
   b. reciprocal causality.
   c. the matching hypothesis.
   d. the mere exposure effect.

Total Correct (See answer key) _____

ANSWERS TO FILL-IN-THE-BLANKS KEY TERMS

1. social cognition (p. 569)
2. relative deprivation (p. 570)
3. self-schemas (p. 571)
4. attribution (p. 574)
5. reference group (p. 570)
6. matching hypothesis (p. 590)
7. self-fulfilling prophecy (pp. 573–574)
8. actor-observer (p. 578)
9. self-serving (p. 578)
10. stereotypes (p. 583)
11. elaboration likelihood (p. 581)
12. contact hypothesis (p. 585)
13. aversive racism (p. 587)
14. fundamental attribution error (p. 577)
15. self-perception theory (p. 583)

ANSWERS TO CONCEPTS AND EXERCISES

No. 1: Persuasive Advertising

1. *Peripheral route.* Nixon most likely hoped that people would use the peripheral route to attitude change by focusing on their liking the famous stars

rather than on his qualifications. Different celebrities were chosen to support Nixon in different areas of the country because they were considered credible and similar to the population in that area. (p. 581)

2. *Cognitive dissonance.* The announcer's comment may be aimed at creating cognitive dissonance in the viewers. People who feel badly about the misfortunes of others might feel cognitive dissonance if they do not act to relieve a person's suffering. Although cognitive dissonance can be resolved by changing attitudes, the advertisers are probably hoping that viewers will resolve the dissonance by changing their behavior and phoning to sponsor a child. (p. 582)

3. *Central route.* By giving so much information, a company may be hoping that people will use critical thinking to consider the advantages and disadvantages of their product. (p. 581)

4. *Mere exposure effect.* People tend to like things they have seen more often. As your text notes, advertisers try to take advantage of this tendency by showing their advertisements repeatedly. (p. 581)

No. 2: Prejudice and Love

1. *Motivational theory of prejudice.* Karen orders around people she sees as having lower status, but obeys people she sees as having higher status; therefore, she may have an authoritarian personality. An authoritarian personality motivates people to identify with their in-group and dislike other groups. (p. 584)

2. *Companionate love.* Carlos and Sanya are low on passion and high on commitment and intimacy, according to Sternberg's theory. (p. 591)

3. *Romantic love.* Lucy and Ricky have a high level of passion and intimacy, but a low level of commitment. (p. 591)

4. *Learning theory of prejudice.* Dino learned discriminatory behaviors from his parents through observational learning. Although Dino may have had very little contact with the ethnic group, he now has suspicions about anyone from the group. (p. 585)

ANSWERS TO CRITICAL THINKING

1. Sam hypothesizes that Brian has an antisocial personality.

2. The evidence is Brian's remark that he just felt like killing the guy.

3. Martina hypothesizes, based on cognitive dissonance theory, that Brian got paid to do the killing but didn't really want to do it.

4. Martina probably wants to find out if Brian or any member of his family needed money.

5. What conclusions are most reasonable? If Brian answered yes, Martina could conclude that Brian was a paid assassin. But she probably shouldn't form a conclusion just yet. What else could Martina ask Brian that would support her hypothesis?

ANSWERS TO MULTIPLE-CHOICE QUESTIONS

Circle the question numbers you answered correctly.

Sample Quiz 1

1. *a* is the answer. The groups of people to which we think of ourselves as belonging and to which we compare ourselves are called reference groups. (p. 570)
   b. Our relatives may form a reference group. But we are members of many groups and compare ourselves to many groups besides our relatives. Or perhaps you were thinking of relative deprivation, in which a person feels a lack of something like money, due to a comparison with a well-off reference group.
   c. People who share the same career may form a reference group, but we also compare ourselves to many groups outside our profession.
   d. An out-group is any group of which we do not consider ourselves a member.

2. *c* is the answer. Going from being one of the best to being average can make a person feel sad for the loss of status, although an objective measure would show that Cindy is as smart as she ever was. (p. 570)
   a. Cognitive dissonance is experienced when attitudes or attitudes and behaviors are not in line with one another.
   b. The fundamental attribution error is the tendency to believe that others' behaviors are caused by their personal characteristics rather than by the environment.
   d. Self-fulfilling prophecies occur when we allow our expectations to influence our actions, which, in turn, influence those around us into behaving as we expected.

3. *a* is the answer. (p. 571)

   b, c, d. Those with a unified self-schema feel that failure in one area of life implies failure in all others. Those with an undifferentiated self-schema isolate a failure in one area of life from all other unrelated areas.

4. *c* is the answer. A social identity is our set of beliefs about the groups to which we belong. Those groups may be religions, nationalities, or ethnic groups, to name a few. (p. 571)

   a. Self-esteem is a positive or negative evaluation of how worthwhile we are. If Alaa had said, "I'm a worthless idiot" or "Gosh, I am a nice guy," he would be showing his level of self-esteem.

   b. A self-schema is a mental representation of oneself. We use social comparison and our social identity to construct our self-schema, but it can include situational factors, such as, "I'm shy at big parties, but open with my close friends."

   d. Social perception is a rather general term for how we interpret information about others and make inferences based on that information. It includes a mental representation of other people, but does not include the groups to which we personally belong.

5. *c* is the answer. Gena fulfilled her own prophecy. She was defensive because she expected her boss to be gruff. As a result, she elicited the boss's irritability and was given a negative evaluation. (p. 574)

   a. A stereotype is an impression of a group of people. Gena has formed a first impression about only one person: her boss.

   b. Prejudice is a preformed negative or positive judgment about a group of people. This would have been the correct answer only if Gena's first impression had led her to believe that all bosses were gruff and nasty.

   d. Discrimination is the differential treatment of certain groups or individuals. If Gena's boss treated her negatively because, say, she was a female or a black or a lesbian or pregnant, this example would demonstrate discrimination.

6. *b* is the answer. Negative acts such as being rude tend to heavily influence first impressions. Also, people assume that negative behavior reflects undesirable characteristics. Therefore, Carol will form a negative impression of Rico and probably assume that he is a rude person. (pp. 572–573)

   a. In forming first impressions, people tend to assume that negative acts are due to some unde-

sirable characteristic of the person being evaluated. Carol is likely to assume that Rico is rude, rather than believe his behavior is the result of a bad day.

   c. A self-fulfilling prophecy occurs when an already-formed first impression of another person elicits behavior that confirms that impression. Carol had no impression of Rico prior to their conversation at the party.

   d. All else being equal, people assume that others are similar to themselves. Since people usually evaluate themselves positively, they also evaluate others positively. However, all else is not equal in this situation. Rico is rude to Carol. Since negative acts usually carry a lot of weight and are assumed to reflect negative characteristics, Carol will form a negative impression of Rico.

7. *d* is the answer. The self-serving bias is the belief that our behavior is responsible for our successes but not for our failures. (p. 578)

   a. The actor-observer bias is the tendency to attribute our own behavior to external causes and others' behavior to internal causes.

   b. According to the fundamental attribution error, we are more likely to attribute other people's behavior to internal causes.

   c. A self-fulfilling prophecy is not an attributional bias but a situation in which one person behaves toward another in a manner that elicits a response consistent with the person's initial expectations of the other.

8. *a* is the answer. Kassandra, fearing failure, has arranged to blame the possible failure on external factors, such as being late. This arrangement is called a self-handicapping strategy. (p. 578)

   b. In a self-fulfilling prophecy, the expectations and behavior of one person influence the behavior of another person. In this scenario, only Kassandra's behavior is in question.

   c. The fundamental attribution error refers to the tendency to attribute the behavior of others to internal factors.

   d. The self-serving bias is the tendency to attribute our successes to internal factors and our failures to external factors. In this example, Kassandra is arranging for her possible failure to be caused by external factors, not making attribution about existing successes and failures.

9. *a* is the answer. The Hindu Indians in the cross-cultural experiment thought that reciprocal helpers

enjoyed helping more than spontaneous helpers did. (pp. 576–577)

b. The U.S. students were likely to see the reciprocal helping as externally caused.

c. The experimenters noted that Hindus in India tend not to distinguish between helping motivated by duty and helping motivated by personal traits.

d. Although the Hindu students believed that reciprocal helpers felt a moral responsibility to return a favor, they still thought the helpers liked to help.

10. c is the answer. Vernon's behavior has a low degree of consensus because not everyone is considerate and thoughtful. His behavior has a high degree of consistency because he is always considerate and thoughtful. His behavior has a low degree of distinctiveness because he is considerate and thoughtful toward all his friends. (pp. 574–575)

a, b, d. Vernon's behavior could be attributed to external factors only if everyone was considerate and thoughtful (high consensus), if he was considerate only in a specific situation (high distinctiveness), and if he was not consistently considerate (low consistency).

11. b is the answer. Jay is unrealistically optimistic as a result of thinking that he is invulnerable. (p. 578)

a. Cognitive dissonance occurs when components of an attitude do not match up and cause discomfort. There is nothing in the story to suggest that Jay feels uncomfortable, for example, because his cognitive component doesn't match his behavioral component.

c. People using the self-handicapping strategy behave in a less than efficient or healthy way so that they have an excuse when they fail.

d. The self-serving bias is when a person takes credit for success, but not for failure.

12. b is the answer. The affective component of an attitude is a positive or negative evaluation of an object, person, event, or situation. Norma loves (has a positive evaluation of) cold cream. (pp. 579–580)

a. Buying cold cream is the behavioral component of Norma's attitude.

c. Norma's belief that cold cream will reduce wrinkles is the cognitive component of her attitude.

d. Putting cold cream on her face is part of the behavioral component of her attitude.

13. b is the answer. When our behavior doesn't match our beliefs (cognitive component), we feel uncomfortable and motivated to change either the attitude or the behavior. (p. 582)

a. The actor-observer bias has to do with attributing behavior to external versus internal causes; it doesn't deal with disagreement between components of an attitude.

c. Deindividuation, which is discussed in Chapter 18, is the feeling of losing oneself in a crowd.

d. The mere exposure effect occurs when people who see each other often are more likely to become friends.

14. b is the answer. The cognitive theory of prejudice suggests that we use schemas and cognitive shortcuts such as social categories. (pp. 584–585)

a. The motivational theory of prejudice proposes that people with authoritarian personalities have a tendency to obey people of higher status and discriminate against people of lower status.

c. The contact hypothesis is not a theory of prejudice, but it is based on the cognitive and learning theories.

d. Learning theory emphasizes that observational learning and operant conditioning can teach children about stereotypes and prejudice.

15. d is the answer. Learning and cognitive theories of prejudice have led to the contact hypothesis, which states that stereotypes and prejudices about a group should be reduced as contact with that group increases. The supervisor has arranged for contact among ethnic groups by placing one person of equal status from each ethnicity in each work group. (pp. 585–586)

a. The motivation theories of prejudice and stereotypes focus on the personality structure of the individual. People with authoritarian personalities view the world as a strict social hierarchy. These people know whom they have to obey and from whom they can demand discipline. They often stereotype people of lower status.

b. Deprivational is not a type of prejudice theory.

c. Aversive racism theory also focuses on the person exhibiting discrimination. The theory suggests that many people who are repulsed by racism are, in fact, prejudiced.

16. a is the answer. Motivation theory suggests that people with authoritarian personalities view the world as a strict social hierarchy. These people know whom they have to obey and from whom they can demand discipline. They often stereotype people of lower status. (p. 584)

b. Cognitive theorists emphasize that the cognitive shortcuts we use to make sense of our social world can contribute to stereotypes.

c. The contact hypothesis states that prejudice will decrease as contact between groups increases.

d. Learning theory proposes that we learn stereotypes and prejudices by watching others and by being reinforced when we express prejudice.

17. *d* is the answer. Frequent contact, similar attitudes, and similar attractiveness are associated with positive relationships. (pp. 588–590)

a. *b* is also the answer.

b. *a* is also the answer.

c. Conflict and anger are part of any relationship. The successful resolution of conflict and anger is indicative of a positive relationship.

18. *c* is the answer. Research has shown that next-door neighbors are more likely to become good friends than are people who live at opposite ends of the hall or farther away. (pp. 588–589)

a, b, d. People tend to like those with whom they have the most contact. Susan will probably have more contact with the women living next door.

19. *c* is the answer. You are much more likely to be attracted to people if you meet them in a comfortable setting. (p. 589)

a. You would be hot and sticky, not comfortable, on a tour of the Mojave Desert in August.

b. If you were in a hurry, you would not have sufficient contact with a gas station attendant.

d. You would be more attracted to the person you met in comfortable physical surroundings.

20. *a* is the answer. George and Louise's relationship has a high level of intimacy, commitment, and passion. (p. 591)

b. Companionate love is low on passion, but high on intimacy and commitment.

c. Fatuous love is high on passion and commitment, but low on intimacy.

d. Romantic love is high on passion and intimacy, but low on commitment.

Now turn to the quiz analysis table at the end of this chapter to find which areas you know well and which areas you need to work on. Circle the numbers in the table for items on Quiz 1 that you answered correctly.

ANSWERS TO MULTIPLE-CHOICE QUESTIONS

Circle the question numbers you answered correctly.

Sample Quiz 2

1. *b* is the answer. Although Jack isn't truly "deprived," he is experiencing deprivation compared to what he was used to before. (p. 570)

a. Cognitive dissonance is the product of conflicting attitudes.

c. There is no such thing as role isolation.

d. A self-fulfilling prophecy is an impression that elicits behavior confirming the impression. Jack's impressions are not making him depressed. His standing in comparison to others' in his new reference group is making him unhappy.

2. *a* is the answer. Jack had a lot of status in his old reference group of students. Now that he is a member of a new group, it will take time to improve his standing in comparison to the other group members. His low status at present is making him depressed. (p. 570)

b. Our relatives may form a reference group. But we are members of many groups and compare ourselves to many groups besides our relatives.

c. He probably still considers himself a member of the same religion, nation, and ethnic group.

d. The story doesn't describe whether Jack has a differentiated or a unified self-schema and doesn't indicate that it changed.

3. *d* is the answer. Our social identity is our belief about our membership in groups. (p. 571)

a, b. We may want to be like our peers or idols, but *d* is the best answer.

c. Self-esteem is our belief about our self-worth.

4. *b* is the answer. (p. 571)

a. The "actual" self is what a person actually is.

c. The "ought" self is what a person feels she or he should be.

d. The answer is *b*.

5. *a* is the answer. Wenlan thinks of herself as having different attributes in different situations. (p. 571)

b. If Wenlan had a unified self-schema, she would feel badly about her whole life when her academic performance was poor.

c, d. There is no such thing as dissonant self-concept or consolidated self-esteem.

6. *b* is the answer. When Nathan thought about Lance's job, it most likely activated a schema for cashiers or supermarket workers that didn't include interests in poetry and politics. (p. 572)
    a. Discrimination is the behavioral component of a prejudicial attitude, but it does not bias memory.
    c. Social comparison is the process by which we compare ourselves to others. Nathan may have been comparing himself to Lance, but it was not an influence on his memory.
    d. The actor-observer bias relates to internal versus external attributions, not memory for personal information.

7. *d* is the answer. According to the fundamental attribution error, we usually attribute others' behavior to internal causes. (p. 577)
    a. According to the fundamental attribution error, we attribute others' behavior to internal causes.
    b. According to the self-serving bias, we attribute our successes to internal causes.
    c. According to the fundamental attribution error, we usually attribute others' behavior to internal, not external, causes.

8. *d* is the answer. Low consistency, high consensus, and high distinctiveness would lead to an external attribution. (pp. 574–575)
    a, b, c. High consistency means that a person always behaves in a similar manner. Low consensus means that not many people display a particular behavior. Low distinctiveness means that the behavior occurs in many situations. These features would lead one to attribute someone's behavior to an internal cause; that person often displays the behavior in many situations, whereas other people do not. The behavior is probably due to a characteristic of the person, not to an external cause.

9. *b* is the answer. The actor-observer bias occurs when we attribute our own behavior to external factors, such as luck, and others' behavior to internal factors, such as talent. (p. 578)
    a. According to the fundamental attribution error, we attribute other people's behavior to internal factors—in this case, creativity. Felicia is attributing her own behavior to an external cause, luck.
    c. Self-perception involves determining one's own attitudes. The question asks why Felicia attributes the success of her book to luck, not what her attitudes are.

    d. The self-serving bias predicts that Felicia will take personal credit for her success.

10. *b* is the answer. According to the self-serving bias, we take credit for success but blame external causes for failure. Nicole's mother is taking credit for Nicole's good habits and qualities but not for her bad ones. (p. 578)
    a. According to the fundamental attribution error, Nicole's mother should attribute Nicole's behavior to Nicole's internal characteristics. Instead, she believes that the causes of Nicole's behavior are her and her husband's style of raising their daughter (characteristics that are external to Nicole).
    c. The actor-observer bias is the tendency to attribute our own behavior to an external cause. Nicole's mother is making attributions about Nicole's behavior, not her own.
    d. People experience relative deprivation when they compare themselves to others who have a higher standard of living.

11. *b* is the answer. Cognitive dissonance is internal tension due to conflicting attitudes or components of attitudes. (pp. 582–583)
    a. Prejudice is a preformed negative or positive attitude toward an entire group of people. Stereotypes can lead to prejudice.
    c. The fundamental attribution error refers to mistakes made in explaining the causes of behavior.
    d. Relative deprivation occurs when, as a new member of a reference group, a person's standing in comparison to others is low.

12. *a* is the answer. Gladys's feelings and behavior about AIDS research do not match; therefore, she is likely to experience cognitive dissonance. (pp. 579, 582)
    b. Gladys is upset (affective) because she thinks that research should be better supported (cognitive). These components are in agreement.
    c, d. Central and peripheral are routes to attitude change; they do not explain Gladys's cognitive dissonance.

13. *b* is the answer. Mark is not thinking critically about the dating service. He is using appearances (happy couples) to make his decision. (p. 581)
    a. A central route would be one that considers the content of the message to be more important than the communicator.
    c. Cognitive "busyness" occurs when we are involved in thinking about something other than

the decision to be made. It makes a peripheral route to decision-making more likely. Mark is not described as being busy thinking about something else.

d. Cognitive dissonance occurs when thoughts, behaviors, and attitudes are inconsistent with one another.

14. c is the answer. Cooperation is an important factor in determining the success of contact in reducing prejudice. Activities like the jigsaw technique often help reduce prejudice. (pp. 585–586)

a, d. A sports competition or the singling out of a few individuals will probably not reduce prejudices, and in fact, may worsen them.

b. A presentation of information may help students understand each other, but won't be as effective as having the students cooperate.

15. c is the answer. Cognitive dissonance, unlike self-perception, involves internal tension caused by discrepant or conflicting attitudes. According to self-perception theory, people who are unsure about their attitudes examine their past behavior to determine them. This does not involve any uneasiness or internal tension. (pp. 582–583)

a. Cognitive dissonance and self-perception theory both involve attitudes.

b. Self-perception does not involve social facilitation.

d. c is the answer.

16. a is the answer. An in-group is any category of people of which we consider ourselves a member. (p. 584)

b. There is no such thing as a relative deprivation group. Relative deprivation occurs when our standing in comparison to members of a reference group is low.

c. There is no such thing as a social facilitator. Social facilitation occurs when the presence of other people improves performance.

d. a is the answer.

17. c is the answer. The theory of aversive racism suggests that even people who are disgusted by prejudice may sometimes show it. This theory supports the idea that racism is so ingrained in us that sometimes we may not even realize we are showing it. (p. 587)

a. The motivational theory emphasizes how personality can make us more or less likely to look for status differences between ourselves and others.

b. The cognitive theory of prejudice states that prejudice may result from the social-cognitive processes people use in dealing with the world.

d. Learning theory suggests that children acquire prejudice by watching others.

18. b is the answer. A relationship is imbalanced if friends disagree on their evaluation of a third person. (p. 589)

a. In a balanced relationship, friends agree on their evaluation of a third person.

c. Perhaps you were thinking of cognitive dissonance. It deals with disagreement in one person's attitudes, behaviors, and feelings.

d. Relationships are not rated on distinctiveness; behaviors are. In addition, we don't know if Claudia and Karen's behavior is distinctive without having information about their behavior toward many other people.

19. c is the answer. Consummate love, which consists of high levels of passion, intimacy, and commitment, is the most mutually satisfying type of love. (p. 591)

a. Romantic love is composed of high levels of passion and intimacy but low levels of commitment.

b. Companionate love is characterized by intimacy and commitment but lacks passion.

d. Although all types of love have their advantages, only consummate love has passion, intimacy, and commitment.

20. c is the answer. The matching hypothesis states that people tend to form committed relationships with people who are similar in physical attractiveness. (pp. 589–590)

a. Proximity makes relationships more likely to form when people see each other often.

b. Reciprocal causality is the term used when attraction is both a cause and a consequence of similarity.

d. The mere exposure effect is the reason for the effect of proximity.

Now turn to the quiz analysis table at the end of this chapter to find which areas you know well and which areas you need to work on. Circle the numbers in the table for items on Quiz 2 that you answered correctly.

For each question you answered correctly, circle its number. (Quiz 1 numbers are not shaded; Quiz 2 numbers are shaded.) Are there patterns in the types of questions or the topics you got wrong that could direct your further study? Did you improve from Quiz 1 to Quiz 2?

TOPIC	TYPE OF QUESTION		
	DEFINITION	COMPREHENSION	APPLICATION
Social construction	1	3	2, 4
	3, 4		1, 2, 5
Social Perception			
Schemas and impressions			5, 6
			6
Attribution	7		8, 9, 10, 11
	7	8	9, 10
Attitudes			12, 13
		11, 15	12, 13
Prejudice	14	16	15
		16	14, 17
Interpersonal attraction		17	18, 19, 20
		18, 19, 20	

TOTAL CORRECT BY QUIZ:

QUIZ 1:
QUIZ 2:

Chapter 18

Social Behavior and Group Influences

OUTLINE

I. SOCIAL INFLUENCE (pp. 596–598)

° Norms are learned social rules that prescribe what people should or should not do in various situations. Descriptive norms communicate what other people would do. Injunctive norms tell us what others would approve or disapprove of. The social influence exerted by norms creates orderly social behavior. We learn them from parents, teachers, clergy, peers, and other cultural agents.

° Social influences also create deindividuation, a personal loss of individuality that occurs as people become "submerged" within a group. A deindividuation experience can cause people to perform acts they normally wouldn't because personal accountability is diminished and attention shifts from internal behavioral standards to the external group standards.

II. LINKAGES: MOTIVATION AND THE PRESENCE OF OTHERS (pp. 598–599)

Social factors often influence motivation. Social facilitation occurs when the presence of another person improves performance, and social impairment occurs when another's presence harms performance. Levels of arousal, task complexity, the expectations of peer evaluation, and increased self-evaluation interact to produce these phenomena. Social loafing, where some people in a group do not participate, may occur as people's individual contribution to a group's performance becomes difficult to measure.

III. CONFORMITY AND COMPLIANCE (pp. 599–603)

Conformity results from unspoken group pressure; compliance results from spoken group pressure.

A. The Role of Norms

Group norms tend to affect people's behavior even after the people are no longer members of that group.

B. Why Do People Conform?

Groups create norms; they decide what is right, wrong, and expected in a situation. Norms determine who will be liked and disliked in a group and who will receive rewards and punishments in a given social situation.

C. When Do People Conform?

1. *Ambiguity of the Situation.* The more difficult it is to determine what is physical reality, the more people rely on the opinions of others.

2. *Unanimity and Size of the Majority.* Conformity is greatest when a group decision is unanimous. The more people in a group making independent assessments, the higher the degree of conformity by an individual.

3. *Gender.* On tasks equally familiar to men and women, no gender differences in conformity are found.

D. Inducing Compliance

People can be induced to comply with requests by starting with small requests, as in the "foot-in-the-door" technique; by starting with an unreasonable request, as in the "door-in-the-face" procedure; or by gaining verbal agreement for one request and then demonstrating the need to escalate the cost of the original commitment, as in the "low-ball" approach.

IV. OBEDIENCE (pp. 603–608)

Obedience is yielding to a demand from an authority figure because of the belief that the demand must be obeyed. Stanley Milgram created a procedure to measure obedience. He developed a situation in which subjects thought they were delivering shocks to a person, but the person was never actually shocked. When confederates complained about the pain of the shock they were supposedly receiving, Milgram demanded that the subjects continue to deliver the shocks. Despite feeling stressed, 65 percent of the subjects delivered the full 450 volts of shock possible.

A. Factors Affecting Obedience

1. *Prestige.* When the status and legitimacy of the experimenter were reduced, obedience decreased, but only from 65 to 48 percent.

2. *Presence of Others Who Disobey.* The presence of others who disobeyed decreased obedience to 10 percent.

3. *Personality Characteristics.* Although social influences are the strongest factor in obedience, people high in authoritarianism were more likely than others to shock the learner. People with an external locus of control were also more likely to obey.

B. Evaluating Milgram's Studies

1. *Ethical Questions.* Some observers say that the experiment was unethical. However, Milgram argued that his debriefing procedure and continued contact with his subjects showed that it was a positive experience. Ethical questions are difficult ones. Milgram's study would probably not be approved by today's ethics committees.

2. *Questions of Meaning.* History has supported Milgram's data. However, it has been suggested that the subjects' behavior was guided by their role and by their belief that they were not harming another person.

V. AGGRESSION (pp. 608–614)

Aggression is an act intended to harm another person. Recent research in the United States shows that a third to a half of all couples display physical aggression toward each other.

A. Why Are People Aggressive?

According to Freud, aggression is an inborn instinct that needs release in behavior. Evolutionary psychologists believe that aggression aided the survival of gene pools and was passed down through generations. However, in some societies, aggression is rare and peaceful coexistence is the norm. Aggressive behavior results from a nurture/nature interaction.

1. *Genetic and Biological Mechanisms.* Research demonstrates hereditary influences on aggressive behavior. Lesions within certain brain areas can lead to aggression, and male hormones such as testosterone are associated with higher levels of aggression. Drugs may also affect aggression.

2. *Learning and Cultural Mechanisms.* People learn to be aggressive by watching others or by being reinforced for aggressive acts.

B. When Are People Aggressive?

1. *Frustration and Aggression.* According to the modified frustration-aggression hypothesis, frustration produces a readiness to respond aggressively, but aggression is displayed only if there are environmental cues that invite or are associated with an aggressive response. Frustration creates this readiness only to the degree that it produces a negative emotion.

2. *Generalized Arousal.* In transferred excitation, an internal characteristic and environmental conditions interact to produce aggression. Generalized arousal is most likely to produce aggression when the situation contains some reason, opportunity, or target for aggression.

C. Thinking Critically: Does Pornography Cause Aggression?

What am I being asked to believe or accept?
There is a casual link between the viewing of pornographic material and several forms of antisocial behavior, including sexually related crimes.

What evidence is available to support the assertion?
Convicted rapists use pornography extensively, and often do so right before they commit a crime. Those aroused by aggressive themes are also potentially the most sexually aggressive. Experimentally induced arousal, especially negative arousal, seems to be readily transferred into aggressive acts.

Are there alternative ways of interpreting the evidence?
Convicted rapists are not credible; they may have wanted to blame pornography for their crimes. Also, preferring violence-oriented pornography doesn't prove that such materials create an impulse to rape someone. With regard to the transfer-of-excitation studies, the observation of violence, not sex, could have been the cause for increased aggression.

What additional evidence would help to evaluate the alternatives?
Research needs to examine the effects of violence and sex when presented separately. In addition, factors that affect men's reaction to pornography and that involve violence must be more clearly understood. Do men who are prone to committing rape have greater needs to dominate and control women?

What conclusions are most reasonable?
Portrayals of violence, including aggressive pornography, affect attitudes toward aggression and may make some

viewers more likely to commit sexual violence. However, for most people, sexual arousal and aggression remain quite separate.

D. Environmental Influences on Aggression

Environmental psychology is the study of how people's behavior is affected by the environment in which they live. Hot weather, air pollution, noise, and crowding can all lead to increased aggression.

VI. ALTRUISM AND HELPING BEHAVIOR (pp. 614–619)

Helping behavior is any act that is intended to benefit another person. Altruism is a desire to help another person rather than benefit oneself.

A. Why Do People Help?

1. *Arousal: Cost-Reward Theory.* The arousal: cost-reward theory suggests that people feel upset when they see a person in need and are motivated to do something to reduce the unpleasant arousal. People then compare the costs of helping versus not helping. If the costs of helping and not helping are both high, other factors come into play. The clearer the need for help, the more likely people are to help. The presence of others inhibits helping behavior due to diffusion of responsibility, a belief that someone else will help. Environmental and personality characteristics also influence helping.

2. *Empathy-Altruism Theory.* According to the empathy-altruism theory, helpfulness is seen in those who have empathy with another person in need.

3. *Evolutionary Theory.* Evolutionary theories propose that people help others to ensure the survival of their genes, at the risk of endangering themselves.

B. Focus on Research Methods: A Laboratory Analogue of Kin Selection

Researchers cannot ethically put people in danger to see who will help them; therefore, researchers used a laboratory simulation, or analogue. Participants were asked to imagine situations in which they could only help one of three people. The outcome of the experiment indicates that people describe themselves as more likely to save the life of or do a favor for a close relative than an unrelated friend in a hypothetical situation.

VII. COOPERATION, COMPETITION, AND CONFLICT (pp. 620–622)

Cooperation is any type of behavior in which several people work together to attain a goal. Competition exists whenever individuals try to attain a goal for themselves while denying that goal to others.

A. The Prisoner's Dilemma

Researchers have created a game in which cooperation guarantees the best mutual outcome but in which there are incentives to compete. Players cannot be certain that their partners will cooperate. Research shows that people tend to respond competitively because winning is rewarding and competition seems to beget more competitive behavior.

B. Social Dilemmas

Social dilemmas are situations in which an action that is most rewarding for each individual will, if adopted by all, become catastrophic for the group.

C. Fostering Cooperation

Cooperation increases when nonthreatening and relevant communications increase. Behavior that is consistently cooperative can either increase cooperation or function as an invitation to exploit. Playing tit-for-tat, or rewarding cooperative responses with cooperation, produces a high degree of overall cooperation.

D. Interpersonal Conflict

Interpersonal conflict is a social dispute in which one person believes that another stands in the way of something of value. When one person can win only at another's expense, it is a zero-sum game, which can lead to interpersonal conflict.

1. *Causes of Conflict.* There are four major causes: competition for scarce resources, revenge, attributing another's motives to unfriendliness, and faulty communication.

2. *Managing Conflict.* Conflict can lead to beneficial changes. It is much better to manage conflict than to eliminate it. Bargaining, third-party interventions, and the introduction of superordinate goals are all methods of managing conflict.

VIII. GROUP PROCESSES (pp. 622–625)

A. Group Leadership

Leaders tend to score high on whatever skills are important to the group. They tend to have good social skills and to be ambitious, enjoying their leadership positions. Leadership ability also depends on the situation and on the person's style of handling it. Both the task-oriented style and the person-oriented style of leadership are effective, depending on the structure of the group's task and the time pressure the group is under. Research has uncovered gender differences in leadership. Women are more democratic and tend to use the person-oriented style of leadership, whereas men tend to be more task-oriented.

B. Groupthink

In small, closely-knit groups, decisions can reflect a process called groupthink, a pattern of thinking that over time renders members unable to evaluate decisions realistically. Groupthink occurs when the group feels isolated from outside forces, intense stressors are experienced, and the leader has already made up his or her mind. Assigning someone a "devil's advocate" role and arranging ways to gather opinions anonymously can help avoid groupthink.

KEY TERMS

1. **Norms** are learned, socially based rules that dictate correct and incorrect behavior for various situations. Norms vary with the culture, subculture, and situation. (p. 596)

> *Example:* Many of your daily behaviors follow the social norms present in our culture. Sometimes it is easier to understand norms by thinking about what would happen if they were broken. Think, for instance, what would happen if you broke the social norm dictating that you may not go shopping wearing only your underwear.

2. **Deindividuation** occurs when people in a group temporarily lose their individuality and behave in ways that they would not otherwise. (p. 597)

> *Example:* Molly is usually a very quiet individual. However, when in the crowd at a football game, she joined others in jeering and booing the officials.

3. **Social facilitation** occurs when the presence of other people improves performance. Usually, the presence of others increases arousal because it indicates to performers that they will be evaluated. (p. 598)

> *Example:* Jon doesn't run as fast by himself as he does when in a race.

4. **Social impairment** occurs when the presence of other people hinders performance by increasing arousal. Usually, new, complex, or difficult tasks are most vulnerable to social impairment. (p. 598)

> *Example:* Tony has practiced the song "Mad Man" on his bongo drums only a few times and is now playing it for his instructor. He is making even more mistakes than he did when he practiced by himself.

5. **Social loafing** occurs when an individual working in a group exerts less effort than when working alone because the group "hides" his or her individual performance. (p. 599)

> *Example:* Helmut is a bright but lazy individual. In work groups at the office, he goes to all the meetings on his projects but exerts very little effort, knowing that nobody will really be able to measure his personal performance in the group.

6. **Conformity** occurs when people change their behavior or beliefs as a result of real or imagined unspoken group pressure. (p. 599)

> *Example:* Jill wears a suit to the office because all her coworkers wear suits.

7. **Compliance** occurs when people adjust their behavior because of the directly expressed wishes of an individual or a group. (p. 599)

> *Example:* Carlotta, Cecelia, and Carmen are sisters. Their mother tells them that if they want to go swimming, they must all clean their rooms. Carlotta and Cecelia hurry to straighten their rooms, but Carmen at first refuses to touch the mess in her bedroom. After Carlotta and Cecelia repeatedly ask Carmen to help, Carmen finally complies and cleans her room.

8. **Obedience** occurs when people comply with a demand, rather than a request, because they think they must or should do so. (p. 603)

> *Example:* Carlotta's mother tells her that she must clean her room, and Carlotta obeys.

9. **Aggression** is an act intended to harm another person. (p. 608)

> *Example:* Ned is playing in the sandbox at the playground when other children begin to insult him. He

retaliates by throwing sand in their faces with the express purpose of hurting them.

10. The **frustration-aggression hypothesis** suggests that frustration produces a readiness to act aggressively but that aggression will occur only if there are cues in the environment that invite or are associated with an aggressive response. (p. 610)

Example: After attempting nine slam dunks of the basketball and missing them all, Kimberly notices a bully shoving her brother around the park. Although not usually violent, she reacts by punching the bully in the stomach.

11. **Environmental psychology** is the study of how people's behavior is affected by the environment in which they live. (p. 613)

Example: Heat, air pollution, noise, and overcrowding are environmental factors that contribute to aggression. Bill is a paramedic in Chicago. He hates the summer because the number of violent calls his ambulance receives increases dramatically as the temperature rises in June, July, and August.

12. **Helping behavior** is any act that is intended to benefit another person. (p. 614)

Example: Sophie knows that one of her best friends is working extremely hard and has barely enough time to clean, cook, and do laundry. Sophie, an excellent cook, prepares three weeks' worth of dinners for her friend.

13. **Altruism** is a desire to help another person rather than benefit oneself. (p. 615)

Example: People who sacrifice their own lives in order to save others' are acting altruistically.

14. The **arousal: cost reward theory** explains that people help if they are distressed by someone's need and if the costs of not helping outweigh the costs of helping. (p. 615)

Example: Michael feels terrible when he sees that Mary's fall on the sidewalk has injured her and scattered her packages everywhere. He knows that he'll be late to work if he helps, but after a moment he decides that his guilt over not helping would be worse than having to explain his late arrival.

15. The **diffusion of responsibility** is the tendency to deny any personal responsibility for responding to someone who needs help when others are present. (p. 616)

Example: When Mary falls and injures herself, most of the onlookers wait for someone else to do something. Each may be thinking that a person more qualified to help may be in the crowd.

16. The **empathy-altruism theory** proposes that helping is often a result of empathy with the person in need of help. (p. 617)

Example: Sandeep knows what it feels like to be totally confused about a homework assignment, so he feels badly for his classmate Randy and stays after class to clarify the directions. Other students who don't feel empathy for Randy leave the two to work out the problem together.

17. **Evolutionary theories** explain helping behavior as the result of concern that one's genes survive in future generations. (p. 617)

Example: An evolutionary theorist would say that Tina is more likely to donate bone marrow to a close relative than to a stranger because the donation would help Tina's genetic characteristics survive.

18. **Cooperation** is any type of behavior in which several people work together to attain a goal. (p. 620)

Example: Claudia and Missy are sisters. Until they were teenagers, they could not stand each other. However, once they realized that they were interested in breaking the same parental rules, they began to cooperate and cover for each other.

19. **Competition** exists whenever individuals try to attain a goal for themselves while denying that goal to others. (p. 620)

Example: James is very intelligent. He knows that he can win a scholarship given to the highest-ranking student at the end of the year. He formulates a competitive strategy and stops tutoring his classmates.

20. The **prisoner's dilemma game** is a game that tests a person's willingness and tendency to cooperate. Pairs of subjects are presented with a choice of behaviors. One choice does nothing for either subject; another choice moderately rewards both subjects; and a third rewards one subject and does nothing for the other subject. (p. 620)

Example: Alison's video game gives the greatest number of total points when both players press the "buddies" button. Alison gets more points individually, however, when the other player presses the buddies button and Alison presses the "rivals" button. The risk is that if they both push the rivals button, they lose their points, but neither knows what the other will do. Alison thinks that getting the same number of points as the other player by pressing the buddies button is not very interesting; therefore, she decides to press the rivals button once in a while.

21. **Social dilemmas** are situations in which an action that is most rewarding for each individual will, if adopted by all, become disastrous for everyone. (p. 621)

Example: If one person in a residence hall chooses to litter the hallway with unwanted papers, the behavior may be rewarded by its ease in ridding the person of garbage. If everyone chooses to litter the hallways, however, the hallways will eventually be too full of garbage to walk through.

22. **Zero-sum games** are situations in which one person must lose so that another may gain. (p. 621)

Example: At a swim meet, one person is declared the winner of each race. The other swimmers may place second or third in a race, but they cannot win.

23. **Interpersonal conflict** is a process of social dispute in which one person believes that another stands in the way of something of value. (p. 621)

Example: Meghan and Jamila are up for the same promotion. Because the promotion can only go to one of them (a zero-sum game), Meghan and Jamila each try to make their own good points overshadow the other's.

24. **Task-oriented leaders** are those who provide close supervision, discourage group discussion, and give many directives. (p. 623)

Example: Rebecca knows that to get the construction estimate out by noon, she'll need to give each worker a job. As they work on their separate contributions, she'll track their progress to ensure that each can accomplish her or his part. Rebecca doesn't think it's necessary to get the workers' opinions, especially since there is not much time.

25. **Person-oriented leaders** are those who provide loose supervision, ask for group members' ideas and opinions, and demonstrate concern for subordinates' feelings. (p. 623)

Example: Each time his group has a new project, Lorcan first asks group members to contribute ideas without censoring them. Eventually the group works together to choose the best ideas and Lorcan tries to ensure that everyone is in agreement.

26. **Groupthink** is the deterioration over time of a small, closely knit group's ability to evaluate realistically the available options and the decisions it makes. (p. 625)

Example: The union leaders discussing the latest contract proposal tend to ignore any suggestion that it is fair. The head of the union does not believe they should accept any contract that gives them a cut in pay. The small group discussing it is unaware that some union members are willing to make that sacrifice; therefore, they keep rejecting the company's offers.

FILL-IN-THE-BLANKS KEY TERMS

This section will help you check your factual knowledge of the key terms introduced in this chapter. Fill in each blank with the appropriate term from the list of key terms above.

1. A change in behavior that occurs in response to unspoken pressure from a group is called _____.

2. _____ occurs when people comply with a demand because they think they must do so.

3. When a person changes his or her behavior in response to a spoken request, it is called _____.

4. Any act that is intended to harm another person is considered _____.

5. _____ are social rules that indicate correct and incorrect behavior in various social situations.

6. When individuals working in a group don't work as hard as they would if they were working alone, _____ has occurred.

7. The study of how a person's surroundings affect his or her behavior is part of _____.

8. Concern for another's welfare above and beyond one's own is called _____.

9. People who believe that helping behavior occurs because people are upset by a person's misfortune and think the price of helping is not too high would agree with the _____ theory.

10. When people in the presence of others see someone who needs help but assume that someone else will help, they have experienced _____.

11. Behaviors that reward each individual but would harm the group if everyone did them lead to a _____.

12. Sometimes in a crowd people do things they wouldn't normally do. They are probably experiencing _____.

13. _____ leaders provide close supervision, suggest behavior, and discourage group discussion.

14. _____ proposes that people will help others when they can relate to the problems of the person in need.

15. A person whose performance was improved by the presence of other people has experienced _____.

Total Correct (See answer key) _____

LEARNING OBJECTIVES

1. Define norms and describe their influence on social behavior. (pp. 596–598)

2. Define deindividuation and describe the factors that cause it. (pp. 597–598)

3. Define and give examples of social facilitation and social impairment. Describe the social factors that influence motivation and define social loafing. (pp. 598–599)

4. Compare and contrast conformity and compliance. Describe the role of norms in conformity and compliance. (pp. 599–601)

5. Describe the factors that lead to conformity. (pp. 601–602)

6. Explain the strategies for inducing compliance, including foot-in-the-door, door-in-the-face, and low-ball techniques. (pp. 602–603)

7. Define obedience. Describe Milgram's study and his findings on obedience. (pp. 603–605)

8. Name and describe the factors that influence obedience. (pp. 605–606)

9. Discuss the ethical considerations in carrying out an experiment like Milgram's. (pp. 606–608)

10. Define aggression. (p. 608)

11. Describe the Freudian and evolutionary theories of aggression. (p. 608)

12. Describe the genetic and biological influences on aggression. Discuss the roles of areas of the brain, hormones, and drugs in aggressive behavior. (p. 609)

13. Describe the role of learning and cultural mechanisms, including observational learning, in aggression. (pp. 609–610)

14. Define the frustration-aggression hypothesis. Describe the role of arousal and transferred excitation in aggression. (pp. 610–611)

15. Discuss the question of whether pornography causes aggression. (pp. 611–613)

16. Define environmental psychology and describe the environmental influences on aggression. (pp. 613–614)

17. Define helping behavior and altruism. Describe the development of helping behavior. (pp. 614–615)

18. Discuss how the arousal: cost-reward theory explains helping behavior. Describe the characteristics of situations in which people would or would not be likely to display helping behavior. Define diffusion of responsibility. (pp. 615–617)

19. Describe the empathy-altruism and evolutionary theories of helping. Discuss the study of helping behavior through a laboratory analogue experiment. Explain what conclusions are reasonable. (pp. 617–619)

20. Define cooperation and competition. Describe the research findings from experiments with prisoner's dilemma games. (pp. 620–621)

21. Describe the factors affecting cooperation and competition. Define social dilemmas and the tit-for-tat strategy. (p. 621)

22. Define zero-sum games and interpersonal conflict. Describe the four main causes of interpersonal conflict. Explain why managing conflict effectively is better than trying to eliminate it. (pp. 621–622)

23. Describe the personality characteristics of a good leader. Define the task-oriented and person-oriented styles of leadership. Describe the types of situations that call for the use of each style. (pp. 622–624)

24. Define groupthink. What can be done to minimize or prevent it from happening? (pp. 624–625)

CONCEPTS AND EXERCISES

No. 1: Group Decision Making

Completing this exercise should help you to achieve Learning Objectives 23 and 24.

Charlotte is the president of a major corporation. She wants to give a problem to three different groups of her top management people. Match the descriptions of each group's interaction with the appropriate term from the list following the exercise.

1. Group 1, a very tightly knit group, made a decision that surprised everyone. Consultants had even been called in, but the group disagreed with their suggestions. Finally, the leader made the decision and asked the "troops to rally 'round." _____

2. Gordon spent an hour at the beginning of the meeting gathering the opinions of all group members. At the end of four hours, the group agreed on a plan of action that incorporated many of the members' opinions. _____

3. Kathleen spent the first thirty minutes delegating jobs for individuals to carry out. At the end of four hours, each individual presented his or her results. Kathleen did not encourage group discussion. _____

   ° Groupthink
   ° Task-oriented leadership
   ° Person-oriented leadership

No. 2: Sales Training

Completing this exercise should help you to achieve Learning Objectives 1 and 6.

George fits the stereotype of a particularly sleazy used car salesman, but he sells new cars. He trains his new staff by telling them about some of the successful strategies he has used in the past. Use the list below to name the strategies that George is describing.

1. "Nobody wants to spend money on cars these days, especially not on the extras, what with the recession and all. So you gotta get 'em warmed up to the idea a little at a time. First, get them to buy the inexpensive extras, like power locks. Then you can move up to the medium-priced gadgets, like a better-than-average stereo. When they agree to buy the car and all the gadgets you've sold so far, go for the big, expensive ones, like a sunroof." _____

2. "Guys come in here all the time lookin' for a car that basically does the same thing, ya know. I mean he has to drive to work, the wife goes to the grocery store, and he takes the kids to baseball practice. Ninety percent of the guys coming in here will tell ya the same thing. But we got a problem. We have to sell a variety of cars. Sometimes it's easy 'cause this guy likes the red one and that guy likes the blue one. But if you have to move inventory, get a guy to agree to buy a moderately priced car. Get him all excited about how great that car is, how good he is going to look in it, and on and on. Then tell him, oops! you forgot; it isn't available anymore. Then show him one that is even more expensive. I guarantee you, nine times outta ten, he's gonna buy it." _____

3. "So you got a customer who is worried about spending too much money. So show him all the really expensive cars that are definitely out of his price range. When he starts to get a little fussy, tell him he's right; you shouldn't have been trying to sell him an expensive car. Then start showing him the price range he can afford. After seein' all those big price tickets on the fancy cars, the one he buys will seem small in comparison. You'll probably even be able to get an extra thousand or so outta him for the car." _____

   ° Low-ball
   ° Foot-in-the-door
   ° Door-in-the-face
   ° Reciprocity norm

CRITICAL THINKING

Several days ago, there was an assault on a woman during a huge demonstration against nuclear weapons. Those responsible for the attack ran off before the police got there. Martina and Sam have obtained a list of anti-nuclear weapons members who were supposed to be at the demonstration. They are pulling all twenty-three in for possible identification by the victim. Martina is waiting for the twenty-first individual on the list when Sam hauls a big burly guy into the office. "Martina," he says with a smug grin, "this is our guy!"

Martina looks up and says, "So this is number twenty-one, huh?"

"Nah," Sam replies. "This is number twenty-two, Bruce Robe. I checked on twenty-one, a guy named Mikey Smitt. What a loser. He's this timid little pipsqueak of a guy. No way he could have landed the punches that made the bruises on that woman's face."

Martina looks at Robe and asks, "Do you have an alibi for the date in question?" Robe, looking furious, says, "You bet I do. I've been trying to tell that to this monkey of a partner of yours ever since he yanked me away from my breakfast this morning."

Martina patiently listens to Robe's story, then makes a few phone calls and verifies his alibi. Martina looks gruffly at Sam. "Go get number twenty-one. I think he is our guy."

Sam is angry. "No way. This is our guy. He's lyin' about where he was. That other guy is this timid mouse. I bet he doesn't even know how to throw a punch, let alone have the guts to do it!"

Martina sighs. "Just go and bring Mikey Smitt in for questioning. NOW!"

Using the five critical thinking questions in your text, the clues in the story, and what you have learned about behavior, answer the following.

1. What is Sam's hypothesis?

2. What evidence supports Sam's hypothesis?

3. What is Martina's alternative hypothesis?

4. What evidence supports Martina's hypothesis?

5. What conclusions are reasonable?

PERSONAL LEARNING ACTIVITIES

1. Describe the norms you follow during a usual day. Do you stand facing forward in an elevator, walk on the right side of sidewalks, and talk quietly in a library? (Learning Objective 1)

2. Violate a norm as an experiment. (Don't do anything dangerous or illegal, of course!) Perhaps you could stand at a door and open it for each approaching person or make a paper hat and walk around in public wearing it. It would also violate a norm if you sat right next to someone when there were many empty seats on a bus. How did other people react to you? How did it make you feel? Based on your experience, outline some of the reasons people generally follow norms. (Learning Objective 1)

3. Try to get someone to comply with a request by using the foot-in-the-door, door-in-the-face, or low-ball technique. For example, you might see if someone is more likely to photocopy notes for you, help you pick up litter, or carry your backpack if you try one of the above methods rather than just asking. (Learning Objective 6)

4. How do you think our view of violence would differ if we didn't see shootings, beatings, and bombings on television or in movies? (Learning Objective 13)

5. Think of a social dilemma you could experience and identify how you would make a decision about how to behave. For instance, what would most influence your decision about putting paint, oil, or other household chemicals in the garbage? What would influence your decision about whether to recycle aluminum soda cans? It might be easier for you to throw them in the garbage than to find a special recycling bin, but if no one recycled them it would be bad for the environment. (Learning Objective 21)

MULTIPLE-CHOICE QUESTIONS

SAMPLE QUIZ 1

1. People sometimes behave with fewer inhibitions when they are in a group than when they are alone. This phenomenon is called
   a. diffusion of responsibility.
   b. deindividuation.
   c. situation ambiguity.
   d. social facilitation.

2. Everyone felt very uncomfortable when Ashley kept smiling during a funeral. Ashley's smiling defied
   a. deindividuation.
   b. social facilitation.
   c. social loafing.
   d. a norm.

3. Stacey's auto racing time has not improved in days. Although she knows the course well, she is no longer improving. To increase her speed Stacey should
   a. have someone race against her.
   b. eject her staff and race the course without anyone recording times.
   c. combat deindividuation.
   d. reduce the bystander effect.

4. Shawn's instructor doesn't observe or grade student study group behavior; therefore, Shawn sits back and listens to the other students. Shawn is exhibiting social
   a. facilitation.
   b. impairment.
   c. loafing.
   d. penalty.

5. Conformity is highest
   a. when the stimulus is unambiguous.
   b. when unanimity exists.
   c. in men.
   d. in women.

6. Perry is traveling in France. As he walks into his hotel, he notices everyone handing ten francs to the doorman. Perry also hands the doorman ten francs. This is an example of
   a. conformity.
   b. compliance.
   c. obedience.
   d. social facilitation.

7. In the foot-in-the-door technique,
   a. larger and larger requests are made.
   b. a straightforward request is made.
   c. a very large request is made, followed by a smaller one.
   d. the original commitment is devalued, and a request is made for more.

8. Ethan has just joined a new group of friends. They want to break windows at the back of the school building for fun. Ethan protests, but the group keeps saying, "Aw, why not come with us? Are you a chicken?" He finally decides to go along with the group; therefore, Ethan has
   a. conformed.
   b. complied.
   c. obeyed.
   d. competed.

9. Colleen wants to get one day off work during final exam week, but knows that her boss won't be too happy about the idea. Colleen explains that she really needs to study and asks for the whole week off. After the boss refuses, she asks for the one day off she originally wanted. Colleen has used the
   a. conformity method.
   b. door-in-the-face technique.
   c. foot-in-the-door technique.
   d. obedience method.

10. Obedience is
    a. conformity to a request.
    b. private acceptance of a suggestion.
    c. yielding to a command from an authority figure.
    d. a response to aggressive behavior.

11. Diffusion of responsibility occurs when
    a. many people are present when someone needs help.
    b. groups try to make decisions.
    c. a leader divides work equally among his or her staff.
    d. people do not take responsibility for aggressive acts.

12. Which is not true of the relationship between pornography and aggression?
    a. Portrayals of violence affect attitudes toward aggression.
    b. Men are more aggressive toward women but not toward men after viewing aggressive pornography.
    c. Some rapists become aroused after viewing aggressive pornography.
    d. All of the above are true.

13. Agatha is moving to a big city to begin her career. She wants to find a very safe apartment to live in. Which of the following should she choose?
    a. An area near the airport because her job requires her to travel quite a bit
    b. An area that has zoning laws restricting the number of occupants per building
    c. A high-rise apartment building
    d. An area near the plant where she works, despite the smell

14. According to the arousal: cost-reward theory, Darien will be most likely to help the lost child crying in the mall if she
    a. is related to the child.
    b. is very worried for the child's safety and has the time to help.
    c. has been to the mall many times.
    d. knows what it feels like to be a lost child.

15. Dean doesn't properly maintain his car's exhaust system due to the expense. If everyone behaved like Dean, the air pollution would become unbearable; therefore, Dean's situation is an example of a(n)
    a. analogue experiment.
    b. prisoner's dilemma.
    c. social dilemma.
    d. zero-sum game.

16. Brian is aggravated because he needs to discuss a group project with his classmate Kevin, who keeps ignoring him. When Brian suggests a meeting time, Kevin tells him that a meeting is impossible. Brian then pushes Kevin against a wall and rips up his appointment book. Brian's behavior best fits the _____ of aggression.
    a. biological theory
    b. deindividuation theory
    c. frustration-aggression hypothesis
    d. social dilemma hypothesis

17. Tim and Jill are medical students. At the beginning of the semester, Tim does not let Jill borrow his notes. When Tim asks Jill for her notes, she won't let him borrow them. Before the midterm exam, though, he calls her and offers his notes and assistance. Before the final exam, Jill offers her notes and assistance. Tim and Jill are employing which strategy?
    a. Tit-for-tat
    b. Low-ball
    c. Altruism
    d. Foot-in-the-door

18. Darrell's and Tomer's softball teams have a friendly rivalry. Because only one team can win, they often try to distract each other while competing. Darrell and Tomer are participating in a(n)
    a. injunctive norm.
    b. prisoner's dilemma.
    c. tit-for-tat strategy.
    d. zero-sum game.

19. Bernadette is a task-oriented leader. She would be most suited to lead in which type of job?
    a. Assigning people to duties that fit their abilities
    b. Getting a report out to the boss as quickly as possible
    c. Managing people who are not familiar with their jobs
    d. All of the above

20. Mary, the president of the student council, wants to reduce the likelihood of groupthink. In order to be successful, she should most likely
    a. isolate the group from other student groups.
    b. forcefully explain her position before allowing others to contribute ideas.
    c. suggest that everyone contribute suggestions anonymously.
    d. use task-oriented leadership.

Total Correct (See answer key) _____

SAMPLE QUIZ 2

Use this quiz to reassess your learning after taking Quiz 1 and reviewing the chapter.

1. Why do norms influence behavior to such a great degree?
    a. They allow us to predict the behavior of others.
    b. They let us know which behaviors will be rewarded.
    c. They let us know how to behave in new situations
    d. They do all of the above.

2. At the football game, Bob felt swept up in the excitement and rushed onto the field with the rest of the fans. If Bob had thought things through, he would not have helped the mob push over the goal posts, but he experienced
    a. deindividuation.
    b. diffusion of responsibility.
    c. social facilitation.
    d. compliance.

3. Claudette is a piano major. She has been practicing for her end-of-the-semester performance for four months and has the music memorized. At her lessons, however, she plays lackadaisically. Her teacher wants to prepare her for her performance and arranges to have a few faculty members come to Claudette's next lesson to hear her play. Claudette plays flawlessly. What do you think happened?
    a. Social facilitation
    b. Social impairment
    c. Social enhancement
    d. Social diffusion

4. Lori's bridesmaids like the pink, backless dress, but Lori does not. Although no one actually asks her to concede, she decides to go along with the crowd and choose that dress. Lori has exhibited
    a. conformity.
    b. compliance.
    c. consensus.
    d. none of the above.

5. Ambiguous social situations facilitate which of the following?
    a. Diffusion of responsibility
    b. Conformity
    c. Use of norms to guide behavior
    d. All of the above

6. Myron wants his secretary to stay late. He gets her to agree to stay until 7 P.M. and then tells her that it will not do him any good unless she stays until 10 P.M. This is called the _____ technique.
    a. foot-in-the-door
    b. door-in-the-face
    c. low-ball
    d. tit-for-tat

7. Sherry is in a jam. She needs a place to stay in New York while she looks for a job. Several weeks before her trip, she calls a friend and asks if she can stay for a night. Once Sherry arrives, she asks if she can stay for several days. On the second day, she asks if she can stay for an entire week. Sherry is employing which method of compliance?
   a. Zero-sum game
   b. Tit-for-tat strategy
   c. Low-ball technique
   d. Foot-in-the-door technique

8. Ken knows that because of politics, he has to fire one of his employees. He wants to get one of his subordinates, Stan, to do the dirty work. In which situation will Stan be *least* likely to obey Ken?
   a. Ken stays in the room when Stan fires the other employee.
   b. Ken lets Stan think that the employee has not done a good job.
   c. Ken calls Stan on the phone and tells him to fire the other employee.
   d. Stan can fire the employee over the phone.

9. Naomi has decided to do an experiment on obedience. She has asked confederates to stop people on the sidewalk and order them to put money in an empty parking meter close by. Which confederate will produce the highest obedience rate?
   a. An old man dressed in tattered clothes
   b. A man dressed in tennis shorts and carrying a racket
   c. A man dressed in a white air force uniform
   d. A young man dressed in jeans and a t-shirt

10. Which of the following environmental factors has been associated with aggression?
    a. Air pollution
    b. Collectivist cultures
    c. Quiet
    d. All of the above

11. Donna is angry at her two sons, because she found them in their room having a laser fight way past their bedtime. They were using their toothbrushes as laser guns. She decides not to let them watch any more violent cartoons. Donna's decision is in agreement with which approach to aggression?
    a. Biological
    b. Learning
    c. Frustration-aggression hypothesis
    d. Instinct

12. Which of the following summarizes the evolutionary view of helping behavior?
    a. People feel good when they help others.
    b. People display helping behaviors to protect the gene pool.
    c. People want to protect other individuals.
    d. People learn to be helpful.

13. Patty has just broken her leg. In which situation will she receive the most help?
    a. On the university commons during a rally
    b. In the auditorium where new students are signing up for classes
    c. On her way home for a shower in her baggy, ripped sweats
    d. If she screams that she needs help

14. One similarity between a prisoner's dilemma and a social dilemma is that
    a. both involve third-party interventions.
    b. both are caused by diffusion of responsibility.
    c. people use groupthink for each.
    d. people don't know what choices others are making.

15. The shelter for homeless people has a large number of volunteers who were once homeless. When such volunteers are asked why they contribute so much to the shelter, they often say it's because they know what it feels like to be without a home. Their explanation fits best with the _____ theory of helping.
    a. arousal: cost-reward
    b. empathy-altruism
    c. environmental
    d. evolutionary

16. The tit-for-tat strategy involves being competitive
    a. in response to competition.
    b. in response to cooperation.
    c. after initiating cooperation.
    d. after initiating competition.

17. If two community service organizations want to reduce the conflict between groups, the best course of action would be to
    a. find a common community service goal.
    b. ensure that each individual's contributions are noted and rewarded.
    c. keep members from discussing issues outside of meetings.
    d. start a contest to see which group can raise the most money for their projects.

18. A task-oriented leadership style is useful when the job to be done
    a. is structured.
    b. is unstructured.
    c. does not need to be completed rapidly.
    d. is well understood by employees.

19. Karen is the coordinator of all the psychology teachers. She asks for opinions and suggestions from all the teachers regarding any task the group must accomplish. What style of leadership is she using?
    a. Tit-for-tat
    b. Person-oriented
    c. Task-oriented
    d. Autocratic

20. The phenomenon of poor decision making in closely knit groups with strong leaders is called
    a. deindividuation.
    b. groupthink.
    c. catharsis.
    d. social impairment.

Total Correct (See answer key) _____

ANSWERS TO FILL-IN-THE-BLANKS KEY TERMS

1. conformity (p. 599)
2. Obedience (p. 603)
3. compliance (p. 599)
4. aggression (p. 608)
5. Norms (p. 596)
6. social loafing (p. 599)
7. environmental psychology (p. 613)
8. altruism (p. 615)
9. arousal: cost reward (p. 615)
10. diffusion of responsibility (p. 616)
11. social dilemma (p. 621)
12. deindividuation (p. 597)
13. Task-oriented (p. 623)
14. Empathy-altruism theory (p. 617)
15. social facilitation (p. 598)

ANSWERS TO CONCEPTS AND EXERCISES

No. 1: Group Decision Making

1. *Groupthink.* This group is very close, disregards outside counsel, and is heavily influenced by a leader who makes a surprising decision and then asks for/expects support. (p. 625)

2. *Person-oriented leadership.* This group leader is asking for the opinions of all the members, a characteristic of this style of leadership. (p. 623)

3. *Task-oriented leadership.* Kathleen is almost dictatorial. She makes a list of tasks, hands them out to the group, and does not ask for any opinions. And, she makes the final decision on her own. (p. 623)

No. 2: Sales Training

1. *Foot-in-the-door.* Once George gets a customer to buy the less expensive options, the customer has let George get his foot in the door and may be more easily convinced that more expensive options are worthwhile. (p. 602)

2. *Low-ball.* After a customer has agreed to buy a car, the customer is unlikely to back out of the deal completely when told that the car is unavailable. George used low-ball to gain compliance by getting the person to agree to buy one car, preventing the purchase, and then getting the customer to buy a more expensive car. (p. 603)

3. *Door-in-the-face.* A customer who was shown many unaffordably expensive cars may be relieved when George finally shows the affordably priced cars. After continually saying "no" to the expensive cars (like slamming the door in George's face), the customer may feel that buying a less expensive car is a compromise. (p. 603)

ANSWERS TO CRITICAL THINKING

1. Sam's hypothesis is that Robe led the assault.

2. Robe's size and Sam's stereotype of the small, timid-looking man support his hypothesis.

3. Martina hypothesizes that Mikey Smitt could have led the assault.

4. The possibility of deindividuation and the fact that compact, sinewy guys can do some damage if they want to are Martina's evidence.

5. Martina can't conclude anything at this point. She will probably ask Smitt for an alibi and put him in a line-up for identification by the victim.

ANSWERS TO MULTIPLE-CHOICE QUESTIONS

Circle the question numbers you answered correctly.

Sample Quiz 1

1. *b* is the answer. Deindividuation occurs because people feel they won't be held accountable for their actions. (p. 597)
   a. Diffusion of responsibility means that the more people there are in a crowd, the less likely each individual is to help someone in need.
   c. There is no such phenomenon as situation ambiguity.
   d. Social facilitation occurs when the presence of others increases performance.

2. *d* is the answer. When Ashley violated a norm, it made the people around her uncomfortable. Usually the person breaking the social rule also feels uneasy. (p. 596)
   a. Deindividuation is losing oneself in the group action, as in a mob.
   b. A person experiencing social facilitation performs better while people are around than when alone.
   c. Social loafing occurs when a person in a group doesn't do his or her share of the work.

3. *a* is the answer. When a task is well-rehearsed, people often perform better with others present. If Stacey knows the course well, then having someone race her may be the motivation she needs to push herself to drive her best. (pp. 598–599)
   b. A well-rehearsed activity is not usually harmed by the presence of others; therefore, such social impairment shouldn't be a factor for Stacey.
   c. Deindividuation is feeling "swept up" by the mood of a crowd.
   d. The bystander effect is related to diffusion of responsibility, which is the hesitance of people to help when others are around. Each person puts the responsibility of helping on the other bystanders.

4. *c* is the answer. Shawn is not making much of an effort because he doesn't believe his behavior in the group is being monitored. (p. 599)
   a, b. Social facilitation and social impairment relate to behaviors on which we think we might be evaluated. Social facilitation is when others' presence improves performance; social impairment is when others' presence worsens performance.
   d. Social penalty is not a term.

5. *b* is the answer. When everyone else has the same view, it is more likely that another person will conform. (p. 601)
   a. An unambiguous stimulus would be less likely to cause conformity, because people would be more sure of their decisions and not have to rely on others for cues.
   c, d. No gender differences in conformity have been found when the situations were equally familiar.

6. *a* is the answer. Perry, as a result of unspoken pressure, is conforming. (p. 599)
   b. If someone had suggested that he give the doorman ten francs, this would have been the correct alternative.
   c. If someone in authority had demanded that he give the doorman ten francs, this would have been the correct alternative.
   d. Social facilitation occurs when an activity goes better while others are present. This doesn't relate to Perry's situation.

7. *a* is the answer. (p. 602)
   b. Asking for something is a request, not a technique for inducing compliance.
   c. The door-in-the-face technique involves making a large request, having it denied, and then making a smaller request.
   d. The low-ball technique occurs when a person claims the original commitment won't work and asks for more.

8. *b* is the answer. Ethan is changing his behavior in response to expressed (spoken) social influence. (p. 599)
   a. Conformity occurs when people change their behavior in response to real or imagined unspoken peer pressure.
   c. Ethan's friends are not authority figures who demanded that he go along with them; they just applied social pressure.
   d. Ethan was not in competition with his friends; they were asking him to go with them.

9. *b* is the answer. Colleen has asked for something she knows her boss can't give her. She believes that the boss will feel badly for refusing her first request and will go along with her second, more realistic, request. (p. 603)
   a. Conformity is going along with unspoken pressure; there is no "conformity method."
   c. The foot-in-the-door technique would be the reverse of what Colleen tried. She might ask for a few hours off (make a small request), then see if the boss would be willing to give her the whole day off (a slightly larger request).
   d. Colleen's boss has more authority than she has; therefore, she is not demanding obedience. There is no such thing as "obedience method."

10. *c* is the answer. Obedience occurs when people yield to a demand, rather than a request, because they think they must. (p. 603)
    a. Conformity results from unspoken group pressure, not a request.
    b. People can and do comply without accepting or agreeing with the suggestion.
    d. Obedience is not a response to aggression.

11. *a* is the answer. When many people are present, diffusion of responsibility occurs, and helping behavior is reduced. (p. 616)
    b. Diffusion of responsibility is not related to group decision making. (You may be thinking of groupthink, the inability of a small, closely knit group to evaluate realistically the decisions it makes.)
    c. Diffusion of responsibility is related to helping behavior, not to leadership styles.
    d. Diffusion of responsibility is related to helping behavior, not to aggression.

12. *d* is the answer. Portrayals of violence do alter attitudes toward violence, arouse some rapists, and cause an increase in men's aggression toward women but not toward other men. (pp. 611–613)

13. *b* is the answer. As crowding increases, so does aggression. Living in an area where zoning laws limit crowding would be safer than living in any of the other alternatives. (pp. 613–614)
    a. Living near the airport will increase the noise in Agatha's neighborhood. Unwanted noise has been associated with increases in aggression.
    c. People who live in high-rise buildings are more likely to act aggressively.
    d. Air pollution raises levels of aggression.

14. *b* is the answer. Once a person is upset by another's misfortune, the person will weigh the costs of helping versus not helping. Darien is upset and the cost of helping is not very high. (p. 615)
    a. This would be an evolutionary view of why people help.
    c. Being familiar with an area does increase helping behavior, but this is not part of the arousal: cost-reward theory.
    d. The empathy-altruism model proposes that helping is often a result of empathy.

15. *c* is the answer. What is economically beneficial for Dean would be terrible for the environment if everyone did it. (p. 621)
    a. An analogue experiment was used to study the evolutionary approach to helping behavior. It was called analogue because the people were asked to imagine their reactions to hypothetical situations, rather than being placed in those situations. Dean is not in an analogue experiment.
    b. A prisoner's dilemma occurs when two people are differentially rewarded for cooperating or competing. The greatest number of individual wins results from one person choosing a competitive response and the other person choosing a cooperative response. The greatest number of overall wins results from cooperation. The smallest number of overall wins results from both people making a competitive response.
    d. In a zero-sum game, only one person can win. If Dean were to properly maintain his car, other people would *not* automatically have something taken away; therefore, this is not a zero-sum game.

16. *c* is the answer. Brian was frustrated by Kevin's lack of cooperation and, therefore, was more likely to behave aggressively toward Kevin. (p. 610)
    a. Biological theories of aggression would cite high testosterone levels or damage to certain brain areas as the cause of aggression. Brian's physiological state is not described.
    b. Deindividuation is the sense that one won't be held responsible for actions committed while in a crowd of people. Brian is not in a crowd; he could easily be identified as the person who assaulted Kevin. There is no such thing as deindividuation theory.
    d. A social dilemma involves making a decision about an action that will take some investment of time, effort, or money versus an action that is easier but more harmful to the society as a whole. Social dilemmas are situations, not hypotheses.

17. *a* is the answer. The tit-for-tat strategy involves punishing competitive moves with competition and rewarding cooperative moves with cooperation. (p. 621)
    b. The low-ball technique is used to increase compliance by first getting a commitment and then devaluing that commitment and making an even larger request.
    c. Altruism is the desire to help someone without an external incentive. Neither Tim nor Jill freely shares notes; they are making an exchange.
    d. The foot-in-the-door technique involves making gradually larger and larger requests.

18. *d* is the answer. In a zero-sum game, when one person wins, the other must lose. (p. 621)
   a. An injunctive norm is a guide to what a person should do. An example of following the injunctive norm of reciprocity is giving a present to someone in return for a present.
   b. In the prisoner's dilemma, a person can gain by cooperating. It is not a situation where only one can win at the others' expense.
   c. The tit-for-tat strategy may be used when cooperation is possible, unlike this game, where only one team can win.

19. *d* is the answer. The task-oriented style of leadership works best when people need to be assigned duties, when time is short, or when workers are unfamiliar with their jobs. (p. 623)

20. *c* is the answer. When people hear others all pushing for the same idea, they are more hesitant to disagree. If suggestions were made anonymously, perhaps more ideas would be proposed. (p. 625)
   a, b. Group isolation and leaders who take a firm stand contribute to groupthink.
   d. Task-oriented leadership would mean that Mary would give instructions rather than consult the group, but it would not improve the choices made, nor would it make groupthink unlikely. Mary might still feel she had the support of the group for the ideas she was directing them to carry out.

Now turn to the quiz analysis table at the end of this chapter to find which areas you know well and which areas you need to work on. Circle the numbers in the table for items on Quiz 1 that you answered correctly.

ANSWERS TO MULTIPLE-CHOICE QUESTIONS

Circle the question numbers you answered correctly.

Sample Quiz 2

1. *d* is the answer. Norms make us more comfortable because we know what to expect from others and how to behave. (pp. 596–597)

2. *a* is the answer. Much of mob behavior can be explained by the loss of personal identity that comes with getting caught up in the group mentality. (p. 597)

   b. Diffusion of responsibility is the spreading around of responsibility for helping when many people see someone in need.
   c. Social facilitation occurs when our performance benefits from the presence of other people. Bob is just going along with the mob, not improving a personal performance.
   d. Bob is not complying with a request, he is conforming to the riotous behavior of others.

3. *a* is the answer. We become aroused in the presence of others. Dominant or well-rehearsed behaviors are usually performed better under these circumstances. (pp. 598–599)
   b. If Claudette was playing a particularly difficult piece that she did not know well, this would have been the answer.
   c, d. There is no such thing as social enhancement or social diffusion.

4. *a* is the answer. Conformity occurs when people, in the face of unspoken peer pressure, change their behavior to match that of other group members. (p. 599)
   b. Compliance occurs when people change their behavior because of expressed social influence.
   c. When people's behavior is based on their beliefs and happens to match that of other people, consensus exists.
   d. *a* is the answer.

5. *d* is the answer. (p. 601)
   a, b, c. In an ambiguous situation, people let norms guide their behavior, tend to conform, and are less likely to help because they do not clearly recognize the need for help.

6. *c* is the answer. Myron first got his secretary to agree to stay late. Then he said staying late would do him no good unless she stayed very late. (p. 603)
   a. The foot-in-the-door technique involves starting out with a small request, which is complied with, and then making larger and larger ones. The secretary did not have a chance to comply with the first request; instead, it was labeled as unhelpful.
   b. The door-in-the-face technique involves first making a very large request, which is usually refused, and then making a smaller request. The smaller request is usually granted.
   d. The tit-for-tat technique rewards cooperation with cooperation, but punishes competition with competition.

7. *d* is the answer. Sherry is gradually making larger and larger requests, which represents the foot-in-the-door technique. (p. 602)

   a, b. The tit-for-tat strategy and zero-sum game are competitive. Sherry is not competing with her friend.

   c. The low-ball technique involves getting an original commitment, not allowing compliance by devaluing that commitment, and asking for more. Instead, Sherry is gradually asking for more and more after her friend has complied with previous requests.

8. *c* is the answer. As the physical distance between Stan and Ken increases, the likelihood of Stan obeying Ken decreases. This is similar to Milgram's experiment. When the proximity of the experimenter to the subject decreases, the obedience of the subject decreases as well. (pp. 605–606)

   a. The level of obedience increases when an authority figure gives the directions while in close proximity. If Ken is in the room, Stan will be much more likely to obey.

   b. If Ken can convince Stan that the employee is responsible for getting himself fired, the likelihood of Stan obeying will increase.

   d. If Stan can fire the employee over the phone (a greater distance than doing the firing in person) he will be more likely to obey Ken.

9. *c* is the answer. The uniform will communicate a prestigious and authoritative presence. Obedience increases as the prestige and authority of the person giving the orders increase. (p. 605)

   a, b, d. None of these types of clothing communicates prestige or authority.

10. *a* is the answer. Like crowding, hot weather, and noise, air pollution is stressful and makes aggression more likely. (pp. 613–614)

   b. Culture is not an environmental factor; it has an effect based on learning and values. In addition, aggression is less common in collectivist than individualist cultures.

   c. A quiet environment is not stressful and is not associated with aggression.

   d. Only *a* is correct.

11. *b* is the answer. According to the learning approach, we can learn aggression by watching others' aggressive behavior. The boys may have learned their aggressive behavior from watching violent cartoons. (pp. 609–610)

   a. According to the biological viewpoint, aggression is caused by physical factors, not by learning.

   c. According to the frustration-aggression hypothesis, aggression is displayed if a person is frustrated and there are aggressive cues in the environment.

   d. Instinct theory proposes that aggression is natural, not learned.

12. *b* is the answer. Evolutionary theorists believe that helping behavior increases the chances of survival. Consequently, the chances of one's own genes being passed on increase. (pp. 617–618)

   a, d. A learning theorist would say that people learn helping behaviors because they are rewarded for them.

   c. According to evolutionary theory, people do not help others for the sake of those individuals but rather to increase the chances of passing on their own genes.

13. *d* is the answer. Patty's screams communicate that she does in fact need help. Research has demonstrated that when people clearly understand that a person is in need of aid, the incidence of helping behavior increases. (pp. 615–617)

   a. A rally is usually well attended. When many people are present, diffusion of responsibility occurs, and helping behavior is less likely.

   b. People who are unfamiliar with their surroundings are usually less likely to help. New students are probably unfamiliar with their surroundings.

   c. An attractive, well-dressed person is much more likely to be helped. Patty probably doesn't look too attractive in her baggy, ripped sweats.

14. *d* is the answer. In a prisoner's dilemma, people often respond competitively, thinking that they may get taken advantage of by the other person if they don't. In a social dilemma, people do not know if they will be the only one behaving in a certain way. If people knew that everyone else planned to make the same choice (throwing motor oil down a storm drain, for example), it might be more of a concern. (pp. 620–621)

15. *b* is the answer. According to the empathy-altruism theory of helping behavior, if people know what the person in need feels like, they will be more likely to help. (p. 617)

   a. The arousal: cost-reward theory doesn't focus on empathy for the person in need; it focuses on the upset of the helper. If the person is upset enough by the other person's plight, he or she is likely to evaluate the price of helping.

c. There isn't an environmental theory of helping behavior, although population density and noise do influence helping.

d. The evolutionary theory states that we are more likely to help relatives. Evolutionary theorists do not take empathy or arousal into account.

16. *a* is the answer. When the tit-for-tat strategy is used, presumably to increase cooperation, competitive maneuvers are punished with competitive maneuvers. (p. 621)

b. If cooperative moves are punished with competitive moves, cooperation will decrease.

c, d. All these strategies involve responses to the other player's move. There are no strategies based on a pattern of cooperation or competition on the part of just one player.

17. *a* is the answer. When superordinate goals are emphasized, people feel like part of the same group, and usually work together better. (p. 622)

b. Recognizing individual contributions would probably create more competition and conflict.

c. Communication generally has a positive impact. Often when people discuss issues further, they can correct misperceptions or attributional errors.

d. A contest would most likely increase competition, thereby increasing conflict.

18. *b* is the answer. A task-oriented leadership style is useful when the job is unstructured or on a tight time schedule, or when employees are not very familiar with their jobs. (p. 623)

a, c, d. A person-oriented style is useful when the job is structured or on a relaxed time schedule, and when employees are very familiar with their jobs.

19. *b* is the answer. The person-oriented style is characterized by asking group members for their opinions. (p. 623)

a. The tit-for-tat method is a competitive strategy, not a leadership style.

c. A task-oriented style is characterized by giving directives without input from the group.

d. There is no such thing as an autocratic style of leadership.

20. *b* is the answer. Small, closely knit groups with strong, opinionated leaders tend to lose the ability to evaluate their decisions realistically. (p. 625)

a. Deindividuation is the tendency of people to behave in a less inhibited way when in a crowd.

c. Catharsis is the release of aggressive tendencies by the channeling of that energy into socially approved activities.

d. Social impairment occurs when a person performs more poorly while others are present.

Now turn to the quiz analysis table at the end of this chapter to find which areas you know well and which areas you need to work on. Circle the numbers in the table for items on Quiz 2 that you answered correctly.

For each question you answered correctly, circle its number. (Quiz 1 numbers are not shaded; Quiz 2 numbers are shaded.) Are there patterns in the types of questions or the topics you got wrong that could direct your further study? Did you improve from Quiz 1 to Quiz 2?

TOPIC	TYPE OF QUESTION		
	DEFINITION	COMPREHENSION	APPLICATION
Social influence	1		2
		1	2
Presence of others			3, 4
			3
Conformity		5	6
		5	4
Compliance	7		8, 9
			6, 7
Obedience	10		
			8, 9
Aggression		12	13, 16
		10	11
Altruism	11		14
	12		13, 15
Cooperation, Competition, and Conflict			
Dilemmas			15
		14	
Cooperation			17
	16		
Conflict			18
			17
Group Processes			
Leadership		19	
		18	19
Groupthink			20
	20		

TOTAL CORRECT BY QUIZ:

QUIZ 1:

QUIZ 2:

Behavioral Genetics

Behavioral genetics is the study of how genes affect behavior. Behavioral genetics researchers look at the impact of genetics and environment on behavior.

OUTLINE

I. THE BIOLOGY OF GENETICS AND HEREDITY (pp. A-1–A-2)

Genetics is the biology of inheritance. Chromosomes are long, thin structures composed of genes. Genes, which are made up of deoxyribonucleic acid (DNA), provide instructions for the synthesis of proteins, which are the basis of physical traits, such as eye color. Male sperm cells and female egg cells are formed by meiosis, which leaves them with twenty-three single chromosomes. The twenty-three single chromosomes are combined in conception to form a new cell, called a zygote. The forty-six chromosomes contain the genes, which are the individual's genotype. Many traits are polygenic—that is, influenced by many genes.

II. A BRIEF HISTORY OF GENETIC RESEARCH IN PSYCHOLOGY (p. A-3)

Sir Francis Galton first suggested family, twin, and adoption studies be used to study the link between heredity and human behavior. Galton referred to genetic influences as "nature" and environmental influences as "nurture." Although a genetic contribution to intelligence was supported by studies in 1924, research on genetic influences was inhibited by behaviorism and the association of genetics research with the views of the Nazis. The work of Arthur Jensen and Richard Herrnstein angered people because of its focus on ethnic and class differences.

III. THE FOCUS OF RESEARCH IN BEHAVIORAL GENETICS (p. A-4)

Behavioral genetics is the study of differences in a given trait in a population, not the study of the development of that trait for an individual. Average differences in height in a specific population are influenced primarily by genetics, for example; however, we cannot say that a specific person's height was influenced primarily by genetics. Genes can affect a trait without completely determining whether or not it will appear.

IV. THE ROLE OF GENETIC FACTORS IN PSYCHOLOGY (pp. A-4–A-6)

A. Genetic Influences Over the Life Span

Genetic influences on mental ability apparently increase throughout the life span. A possible reason for this is that inherited predispositions may lead people to choose environments that are favorable to the development of this ability.

B. Genes Affecting Multiple Traits

Genes that influence one trait may also influence others. Anxiety and depression may be affected by some of the same genetic factors. Mental ability and scholastic achievement may be influenced by a common set of genes.

C. Identifying Genes Related to Behavior

Huntington's disease, which leads to a loss of motor control, personality changes, and forgetfulness, is caused by a single dominant gene. Several genes have now been linked to Alzheimer's disease.

V. BEHAVIORAL GENETICS AND ENVIRONMENTAL INFLUENCES (pp. A-6–A-7)

While genetic causes of schizophrenia have been supported with evidence from behavioral genetics research, environmental factors can be just as important. Often fifty percent or more of the variance among individuals is due to nongenetic factors. One goal of psychologists is to study the "nonshared" aspects of the environment to see how the different environments of family members influence the appearance of traits. Events and others' behavior can be experienced differently by children in the same family.

A current hypothesis to be investigated is that genetic differences between siblings can contribute to differences in how they are treated. Research so far indicates that parents' responsiveness is related to children's mental ability and that children choose playmates partly based on genetically influenced traits such as temperament. Nature and nurture, therefore, are interacting to influence a person's characteristics.

KEY TERMS

1. **Behavioral genetics** explores the impact of genetics and environmental factors on differences in the behavioral tendencies of groups. (p. A-1)

   Example: Studies of people with schizophrenia show a genetic and environmental influence.

2. **Genetics** is the study of the biology of inheritance. (p. A-1)

3. **Chromosomes** are made up of genes. Each sperm and ovum contains twenty-three single chromosomes. Fertilization results in twenty-three pairs of chromosomes. (p. A-1)

4. **Genes** contain a coded message that provides the blueprint for constructing every aspect of a human or animal. Genes reside on chromosomes within most body cells. (p. A-1)

5. **Deoxyribonucleic acid (DNA)** is composed of molecules that make up a gene. The arrangement of these molecules determines which protein a gene will produce. Thus, DNA provides the individual's genetic code, a blueprint for constructing the entire human being. (p. A-1)

6. A **polygenic** characteristic is influenced by more than one gene. (p. A-2)

   Example: Height is influenced by more than one gene.
   REMEMBER: Poly means "more than one." Polygenic means "more than one gene."

7. **Genotype** is the full set of genes that individuals inherit from their parents. (p. A-2)

   REMEMBER: A genotype will tell you what type of genes someone has.

8. A **phenotype** results from the interaction between a person's genotype (nature) and the environment (nurture); it is how he or she looks and acts. (p. A-2)

REMEMBER: You can see a person's phenotype. A photograph shows you the same information as a phenotype.
Example: Rick was a calm, happy baby and became an easygoing, happy child. Part of his phenotype is his calm personality. (No one knows how much of his personality is genetically, and how much environmentally, influenced.)

FILL-IN-THE-BLANKS KEY TERMS

This section will help you check your factual knowledge of the key terms introduced in this appendix. Fill in each blank with the appropriate term from the list of key terms above.

1. _____ is the study of the biology of inheritance.

2. Characteristics that are influenced by more than one gene are called _____.

3. The study of the impact of genetics and environment on differences in the behavioral tendencies of groups is _____.

4. _____ are made up of genes.

5. The interaction of a person's genotype and the environment produces the person's _____.

Total Correct (See answer key) _____

LEARNING OBJECTIVES

1. Explain how behavioral genetics is a study of both environment and heredity. (p. A-1)

2. Define genetics. (p. A-1)

3. Define chromosomes, genes, and deoxyribonucleic acid (DNA). (p. A-1)

4. Define mitosis. Name the elements involved in meiosis and describe the process itself. (p. A-2)

5. Explain how dominant and recessive genes affect the expression of a trait. Define polygenic. (p. A-2)

6. Define genotype and phenotype. (p. A-2)

7. Discuss the history of behavioral genetics, including studies by Galton and the factors that inhibited research in behavioral genetics. (p. A-3)

8. Describe some of the misunderstandings about behavioral genetics. Define heritability. (p. A-4)

9. Describe the results of research on genetic influences over the life span and the genetic influence of

multiple traits. Discuss the studies of the genes responsible for Huntington's and Alzheimer's diseases. (p. A-5)

10. Discuss how nonshared environmental factors may explain differences between siblings. (p. A-6)

11. Discuss the influence of genetics on environmental events. (p. A-7)

CONCEPTS AND EXERCISES

Completing this exercise should help you to achieve Learning Objective 6.

A person's phenotype comes from the interaction of genetics (nature) and environment (nurture). For the situations listed below, decide whether nature or nurture had more influence on the person's phenotype.

1. Pamela and Priscilla swim together every day for the same amount of time. Although they've done the same workout for years, Pamela is still a much better swimmer than Priscilla. Pamela's higher level of swimming skill is most likely a result of _____ .

2. Ken and Ben are identical twins. Ever since their grandmother bought him an electronics set, Ken was interested in how electronic appliances ran. Ken took apart toasters, radios, and a computer to see if he could figure them out and talked with his grandmother about her job as an electrical engineer. Ben, meanwhile, was interested in becoming a drummer with a rock band. The difference in Ken and Ben's interests is most likely the result of _____ .

PERSONAL LEARNING ACTIVITIES

1. Think of an example of a way a natural ability could influence a person's environment. (Learning Objective 11)

2. If you raised dogs of different breeds in an identical environment, what differences would you expect? What does this say about the origin of the differences? For example, what types of behaviors would you expect to see from a collie, a cocker spaniel, and a rottweiler if they all experienced the same environmental conditions?

3. Suppose that researchers identified a gene associated with violent behavior and, therefore, could diagnose in childhood who would be likely to become violent. What are the advantages and disadvantages of such research? What are the ethical considerations?

MULTIPLE-CHOICE QUESTIONS

SAMPLE QUIZ 1

1. A behavioral genetics researcher would be most interested in studying
   a. genetics.
   b. environments.
   c. people's traits.
   d. all of the above.

2. A person's height is influenced by more than one pair of genes; therefore, height is a _____ characteristic.
   a. dominant
   b. recessive
   c. polygenic
   d. dizygotic

3. Althea and Karina are identical twins, but have quite different personalities. Althea is active, optimistic, outgoing, and a risk-taker; Karina is moody, shy, and cautious. From this description we can say that Althea and Karina have different
   a. genotypes.
   b. phenotypes.
   c. heritabilities.
   d. degrees of freedom.

4. Which of the following people most stimulated research in the field of behavioral genetics?
   a. Francis Galton
   b. John B. Watson
   c. Arthur Jensen
   d. Richard Herrnstein

5. A person with the single gene responsible for Huntington's disease is likely to experience _____ in adulthood.
   a. personality changes and loss of motor control
   b. an increase in intelligence
   c. a decrease in intelligence
   d. no problems or symptoms

6. Suppose a large sample twin study showed that about 40 percent of the variance in sociability can be accounted for by genetic factors. The researchers should conclude that
   a. nongenetic factors are unimportant.
   b. nongenetic factors are at least as important as genetic factors.
   c. most of the time, if one fraternal twin is sociable, the other will be too.
   d. most of the time, if one identical twin is sociable, the other will be too.

7. Thomas has a low IQ. His brother, Chris, has a relatively high IQ. Compared to Chris, Thomas tends to make friends with children with low IQs. In addition, their parents often pay more attention to Chris because he asks so many questions. Unlike Chris's experiences, Thomas's interactions with his peers and his parents do not encourage his cognitive development. Thomas and Chris's experiences are an example of how
   a. genetics may influence the environment.
   b. the environment may influence genetics.
   c. genetics determine intelligence.
   d. the environment determines intelligence.

Total Correct (See answer key) _____

SAMPLE QUIZ 2

Use this quiz to reassess your learning after taking Quiz 1 and reviewing the appendix.

1. A cell is undergoing meiosis; therefore, we know that, of the following, it is most likely
   a. a brain cell.
   b. a skin cell.
   c. an ovum.
   d. a zygote.

2. Kathleen's mom used cocaine while pregnant with her. As a result, Kathleen is small for her age, has malformed kidneys, is unable to concentrate, and is irritable. Her mom influenced Kathleen's _____ by using cocaine.
   a. genotype
   b. phenotype
   c. blood type
   d. polytype

3. Sir Francis Galton's most famous behavioral genetics study showed that
   a. personality is environmentally influenced.
   b. personality is genetically influenced.
   c. genius runs in families.
   d. the environment influences intelligence.

4. Imagine that researchers discover that activity level is highly heritable. In fact, about 75 percent of the differences among people can be explained by genetic differences. Twenty-year-old Randy is extremely active. He can't stand to sit still for long and is constantly in need of stimulation from other people, the television, or the stereo. According to your text, we can conclude that Randy
   a. inherited 75 percent of his activity level, and the environment added the other 25 percent.
   b. inherited an unusually high level of activity.

   c. is more active than average due to environmental effects.
   d. is more active than average for unknown reasons.

5. Marcus and Craig are identical twins; their sisters, Ashley and Tanya, are fraternal twins. As they age from childhood through late adulthood, we should expect the correlation between the IQs of _____ to increase.
   a. Marcus and Craig
   b. Ashley and Tanya
   c. Ashley and Marcus
   d. Craig and Tanya

6. Which of the following is most likely caused by a nongenetic factor?
   a. Huntington's disease
   b. Phenylketonuria
   c. Eye color
   d. Measles

7. Researchers reported the discovery of a gene linked to novelty-seeking behavior. If you found out you had the gene associated with high novelty-seeking, you could conclude that
   a. you are very likely to be bored when alone.
   b. you are very unlikely to be bored when alone.
   c. you may or may not show novelty-seeking behavior.
   d. your risky behaviors are genetically caused.

Total Correct (See answer key) _____

ANSWERS TO FILL-IN-THE-BLANKS KEY TERMS

1. genetics (p. A-1)
2. polygenic (p. A-2)
3. behavioral genetics (p. A-1)
4. chromosomes (p. A-1)
5. phenotype (p. A-2)

ANSWERS TO CONCEPTS AND EXERCISES

No. 1: (pp. A-1–A-3)

1. *Nature*. Pamela's higher level of swimming skill is most likely an inherited talent, because she and Priscilla have similarly practiced swimming for years.

2. *Nurture.* Because Ken and Ben are identical twins, the difference in their interests is most likely the result of environmental influence.

ANSWERS TO MULTIPLE-CHOICE QUESTIONS

Circle the question numbers you answered correctly.

Sample Quiz 1

1. *d* is the answer. The influences of genetics and environment on behavioral characteristics, and the interaction between the two, are all the focus of behavioral genetics researchers. (p. A-1)

2. *c* is the answer. A characteristic influenced by many genes is polygenic. (p. A-2)
   a. Dominant genes are phenotypically expressed when present in the genotype.
   b. Recessive genes need to be paired with a similar recessive gene in order to be expressed in the phenotype.
   d. The appendix describes monozygotic twins as being genetically identical because they come from a single fertilized egg. Dizygotic (fraternal) twins are no more similar than any other two siblings, because they come from two separate egg cells.

3. *b* is the answer. The interaction between genes and environment has produced different phenotypes for Althea and Karina. (p. A-2)
   a. Identical twins are genetically the same. In other words, they have the same genotypes.
   c. The heritability of a characteristic cannot be determined for one or two people; it is a population parameter. Heritability estimates give researchers an idea of how much of the variation of a trait in a population is due to genetic variation.
   d. Degrees of freedom is a concept relating to statistics, not behavioral genetics.

4. *a* is the answer. Francis Galton was a pioneer in the field of behavioral genetics. He suggested several types of studies for investigating the influence of genetic and environmental effects. Although Galton overstated the influence of inherited characteristics, his work did create interest in the field. (p. A-3)
   b. Watson was a behaviorist who promoted the idea that a person's capacities, temperament, and talents are due to training rather than genetics. This inhibited research on behavioral genetics.

c, d. Arthur Jensen proposed that differences between blacks and whites were caused by genetics; Richard Herrnstein thought social class differences were influenced by genetics. The publication of these views had a negative effect on research.

5. *a* is the answer. Huntington's disease is caused by a single dominant gene; therefore, the symptoms of deterioration of the central nervous system, loss of motor control, and personality changes are likely to appear in adulthood. (p. A-5)
   b, c. Huntington's disease is not characterized by a change in level of intelligence, although it can cause forgetfulness.
   d. Because the gene responsible for Huntington's disease is dominant, it will be expressed outwardly whenever present.

6. *b* is the answer. If 40 percent of variance is accounted for genetically, then 60 percent is due to environmental factors. (p. A-4)
   a. Nongenetic factors account for more of the variability in this case than do the genetic factors.
   c. Fraternal twins, like other nonidentical twin siblings, share only 50 percent of their genes; therefore, they may or may not be similar on sociability.
   d. Identical twins are genetically the same. However, only 40 percent of the variance in sociability in our hypothetical study is accounted for by genetic factors; therefore, more than half of the time, identical twins may have different levels of sociability.

7. *a* is the answer. Although Thomas and his parents may be unaware of the differences, Thomas' level of intelligence appears to be influencing his environment. He chooses less intelligent friends than Chris and gets less attention from his parents. (p. A-7)
   b. The environment is not changing Thomas's genotype.
   c. Genetics have an influence on intelligence, but do not completely determine it. The story is showing how a person's environment may or may not may encourage cognitive development.
   d. The environment has an influence on intelligence, but does not completely determine it. The story shows how a person's level of intelligence may influence his environment.

Now turn to the quiz analysis table at the end of this appendix to find which areas you know well and which areas you need to work on. Circle the numbers in the table for items on Quiz 1 that you answered correctly.

ANSWERS TO MULTIPLE-CHOICE QUESTIONS

Circle the question numbers you answered correctly.

Sample Quiz 2

1. *c* is the answer. Meiosis is the process that occurs when males' sperm cells and females' egg cells are formed. Chromosome pairs are split and recombined. (p. A-2)
   a. Brain cells do not divide.
   b. Regular body cells, like skin cells, divide by mitosis.
   d. A zygote is the result of a sperm fertilizing an egg.

2. *b* is the answer. Although Kathleen could have been genetically susceptible to harm from a foreign substance during the critical period of embryonic development, it was her phenotype that was affected by her mother's drug use. (p. A-2)
   a. Kathleen's genotype is the set of genes that she inherited from her parents. Her mother, of course, was one influence on Kathleen's genotype; however, her mother's drug use was unlikely to have affected Kathleen's genotype.
   c. Again, Kathleen's parents influenced her blood type, but her mother's drug use did not.
   d. Polytype is not a term. Perhaps you were thinking of polygenic. A trait that is polygenic is controlled by many genes.

3. *c* is the answer. Galton's family study showed that genius ran in families. Although Galton made the extreme interpretation that genetics was a much more powerful influence than the environment, his work awakened interest in the field of behavioral genetics. (p. A-3)
   a, b. Galton's most famous study did not address personality traits.
   d. Galton concluded that genetics caused genius to run in families, although intelligence is certainly influenced by the environment.

4. *d* is the answer. Even with highly heritable traits, we can make no conclusions about an individual's amount of inherited trait. Randy may be more active than average because of genetics, but knowledge of a trait's heritability allows only generalizations about people on average, not about one person. (p. A-4)
   a. In our imaginary example, 75 percent of the activity level differences between people are explained by genetics. This is not the same as saying that an individual inherited 75 percent of a characteristic.
   b. Randy may indeed have inherited an unusually high level of activity, but we cannot say for sure.
   c. The environment could have caused Randy's high activity level, but we cannot say for sure.

5. *a* is the answer. The IQ scores of identical twins become more similar over the life span. (p. A-5)
   b, c, d. We don't have any reason to expect increases in IQ correlations among siblings who are not identical twins; indeed, such correlations may actually decrease.

6. *d* is the answer. The measles is an illness caused by a virus. Even if you weren't sure what measles were or what caused them, you could have arrived at this answer through the process of elimination. (pp. A-2–A-5)
   a. Huntington's disease is caused by a single dominant gene.
   b. Phenylketonuria occurs when the two recessive genes responsible for it are inherited.
   c. Eye color is caused by more than one pair of genes.

7. *c* is the answer. Knowing that a gene is associated with a behavior does not allow us to know whether a particular person will exhibit that behavior—unless the behavior is completely determined by the gene. (pp. A-4–A-7)
   a, b. Boredom when alone may occur for a person high on the novelty-seeking trait, but we cannot predict such a specific feeling from a person's genotype.
   d. As with other traits, it is highly likely that 50 percent or more of the variance associated with novelty-seeking is environmentally caused; therefore, risky behaviors are more likely to have been influenced by the environment than by a person's genotype.

Now turn to the quiz analysis table at the end of this appendix to find which areas you know well and which areas you need to work on. Circle the numbers in the table for items on Quiz 2 that you answered correctly.

For each question you answered correctly, circle its number. (Quiz 1 numbers are not shaded; Quiz 2 numbers are shaded.) Are there patterns in the types of questions or the topics you got wrong that could direct your further study? Did you improve from Quiz 1 to Quiz 2?

TOPIC	TYPE OF QUESTION		
	DEFINITION	COMPREHENSION	APPLICATION
Biology of genetics	1, 2		3
		1	2
History		4	
			3
Research			
			4
Role of genetic factors in psychology		5	
		5	
Environmental influences			6, 7
		6	7

TOTAL CORRECT BY QUIZ:

QUIZ 1:
QUIZ 2:

Appendix

Statistics in Psychological Research

Statistics are used to understand and interpret psychological research results.

OUTLINE

I. DESCRIBING DATA (pp. A-9–A-13)

A. The Frequency Histogram

Frequency histograms, graphic descriptions of data, are useful for visualizing and better understanding the "shape" of research data.

B. Descriptive Statistics

The numbers that summarize a pool of data are called descriptive statistics. The four basic categories measure the number of observations, summarize the typical value of the data set, summarize the variability of the data set, and express the correlations.

1. *N*. The easiest statistic to compute is N, the number of observations in the data set.

2. *Measures of Central Tendency.* Three statistical measures describe the typical value of a data set. The mode is the score that occurs most often in the data set. The median is the halfway point in the data set: half of the scores fall above the median, and half fall below it. The mean is the arithmetic average of all the scores in the data set.

3. *Measures of Variability.* There are two statistical measures that indicate the dispersion of scores in a data set, or that measure variability. The range de-

scribes the distance between the highest score and the lowest score. The standard deviation measures the average difference between each score and the mean of the data set.

4. *The Normal Distribution.* When most of the scores in a data set fall in the middle of a distribution that has few extreme scores, the data resemble a bell-shaped curve called the normal distribution. The mean, median, and mode all have the same value. The normal distribution is the basis for percentiles and standard scores. A percentile indicates the percentage of subjects or observations that fall below a given score. A standard score expresses distance in standard deviations from the mean.

5. *Correlation.* The relationship between two variables is described by a correlation. The statistical measures that represent this relationship are called correlation coefficients.

II. INFERENTIAL STATISTICS (pp. A-13–A-16)

Inferential statistics provide a measure of confidence or probability that conducting the same experiment again would yield similar results.

1. *Differences Between Means: The t Test.* The t test, a type of inferential statistic, assesses whether differences between two means occurred because of chance or because of the effect of an independent variable. Results that show a low probability of chance effects are statistically significant. Performing a t test requires using (a) the difference between the means, (b) the standard deviation, and (c) the number of observations or subjects. The researcher also takes the degrees of freedom and p value into account.

2. *Beyond the t Test.* Other statistical tests are used to analyze data from experiments that are more complex than comparisons between two groups. An analysis of variance analyzes the effects of more than one variable on a dependent variable.

KEY TERMS

1. The **null-hypothesis** asserts that the independent variable manipulated by the experimenter has no effect on the dependent variable measured by the experimenter. (p. A-9)

2. A **frequency histogram** is a graphic display of data in the form of bars that tell how often different data values occur. (p. A-9)

REM EMBER: Frequency means "how often." This graph tells you how often various scores occurred.

3. *N* describes the number of observations in a data set. (p. A-10)

4. **Normal distribution** describes a data set in which the scores fall symmetrically around the mean; it is represented by a bell-shaped curve. The scores are scattered so that half are above the mean and half below. The mean, median, and mode are always equal in a normal distribution. (pp. A-11–A-12)

> *REMEMBER:* If you are having problems understanding what a normal distribution is, be sure to do the exercise "A Statistical Report Card."

5. A **percentile score** indicates the percentage of people or observations that fall below a given score in a normal distribution. (p. A-11)

> *Example:* If your psychology exam score is at the 95th percentile, you know that you did better than 95 percent of the people who took the test. It does not mean that you answered 95 percent of the questions correctly.

6. **Standard scores** express the value of a score by indicating its distance in standard deviations from the mean. (p. A-12)

> *Example:* A standard score of +1.5 means that the score is 1.5 standard deviations above the mean of the distribution.

7. The *t* **test** is one inferential statistical method used to analyze data. The outcome of this test indicates whether the differences found between two means are the result of chance factors or changes in the dependent variable produced by the independent variable. A *t* value is computed by the following formula:

$$t = \frac{M_1 - M_2}{\sqrt{\dfrac{(N_1 - 1)S_1^2 + (N_2 - 1)S_2^2}{N_1 + N_2 - 2}}}$$

(pp. A-14–A-16)

8. **Degrees of freedom** are numbers calculated for use in interpreting *t* values (and other inferential statistics procedures). (p. A-15)

FILL-IN-THE-BLANKS KEY TERMS

This section will help you check your factual knowledge of the key terms introduced in this chapter. Fill in each blank with the appropriate term from the list of key terms above.

1. A _____ _____ states that the independent measure will not affect the dependent measure.

2. A _____ _____ is a graphic display of data.

3. In a _____ _____, scores fall symmetrically around the mean.

4. The value that denotes the percentage of people or observations that fall below a given score is called a _____ _____.

5. The _____ score indicates the value of a score by measuring its distance in standard deviations from the mean.

6. A _____ is used to evaluate the differences between two means in a data set.

Total Correct (See answer key) _____

LEARNING OBJECTIVES

1. Describe the differences between descriptive and inferential statistics. (p. A-9)

2. Define null hypothesis. (p. A-9)

3. Describe a frequency histogram, and explain why it is used. (pp. A-9–A-10)

4. Name the four basic categories of descriptive statistics. (pp. A-10)

5. Define measure of central tendency, and describe the three measures of central tendency. (p. A-10)

6. Explain how to calculate the mean, median, and mode for a given data set. (p. A-10)

7. Define measure of variability, and describe the two measures of it. (pp. A-10–A-11)

8. Discuss the features of a normal distribution. (pp. A-11–A-12)

9. Define percentile score and standard score, and explain how to use each one. (pp. A-11–A-12)

10. Define correlation. Specify the formula for computing a correlation coefficient. (pp. A-12–A-13)

11. Define _t test_. Specify the formula for calculating a _t_ value as well as the procedures for interpreting it. (pp. A-14–A-16)

12. Define <u>degrees of freedom</u>. (p. A-15)

13. Define <u>analysis of variance</u>, and explain when this statistic is used. (p. A-16)

CONCEPTS AND EXERCISES

No. 1: Statistics and the Consumer

Completing this exercise should help you to achieve Learning Objectives 3 and 5.

Richard has just won the lottery and has hired you to help him spend his money. He has given you a stack of statistical documentation on the qualities of all the brand-name items he wants to buy. Because Richard knows nothing about statistics, you must choose the best brand for the money.

1. Richard wants a sports car and cares only about its maximum speed. Your information says that the mean maximum speed of car A is 180 mph; the standard deviation for all the speed trials is 32 mph. The mean maximum speed of car B is 173 mph, with a standard deviation of 5 mph. Which car should Richard buy? _____

2. Richard wants to buy and sell property to make a profit. Therefore, he needs to know which areas contain properties that will increase quickly in value. In the last five years, Brentwood Oaks has had a mean increase in value of 15 percent and a standard deviation of 2 percent. Redwood Estates has had a mean increase of 18 percent and a standard deviation of .5 percent. In which area should Richard buy? _____

3. Richard is overweight and wants to get in shape. Clients at the Body Beautiful Fitness Center have achieved a mean loss of 35 pounds with a standard deviation of 20 pounds. Clients at the Bare Bones Fitness Center have achieved a mean loss of 25 pounds with a standard deviation of 4 pounds. At which center can Richard be more sure of losing 20–25 pounds? _____

4. Richard and one of his new friends want to bet on the season performance of various football teams. Each man will pick the team that he thinks has the chance of scoring the most points in the upcoming season. Whoever picks the highest-scoring team will win. Team A has a mean point total of 355 for the past five seasons, with a standard deviation of 15 points, and team B has a mean point total of 370 for the past five seasons and a standard deviation of 5 points. Which team should Richard pick? _____

No. 2: Choosing the Correct Statistical Method

Completing this exercise should help you to achieve Learning Objectives 8, 9, and 10.

Pick the most appropriate statistical method for analyzing the data from the following three experiments.

1. A psychologist believes that environment affects the development of connections among nerve cells in the brain. She raises two groups of rats. Rats in group 1 live together in a cage filled with toys. Rats in group 2 are housed in separate steel cages with no toys. After several months, the psychologist examines the brains of the rats to see if there are differences between the two groups in the number of nerve cell connections. _____

2. Some psychologists believe that genetic factors determine intelligence. Others believe that environmental factors, such as educational opportunities, nutrition, and the quality of care received during childhood, determine intelligence. To test this hypothesis, a psychologist looks for a relationship between IQ scores and socioeconomic status. _____

3. A psychologist believes that the different types of therapy used to treat abnormal behavior are not really different from one another. To test this, he chooses three different therapies and divides his group of subjects, all of whom are suffering from severe depression, into three groups. Each group receives one type of therapy. After all the subjects have been treated for six months, their level of depression is measured. _____

No. 3: A Statistical Report Card

Completing this exercise should help you to achieve Learning Objective 8.

You have just started attending a progressive high school. Instead of grades, your report card contains a normal distribution indicating where your performance falls in relation to everybody else's. You wonder how to interpret this report of your performance, so you ask a teacher.

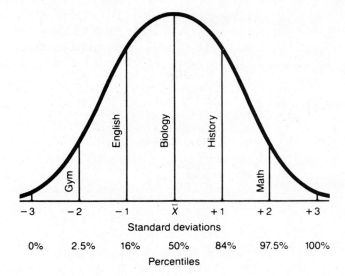

Standard deviations

| 0% | 2.5% | 16% | 50% | 84% | 97.5% | 100% |

Percentiles

The teacher explains that the graph represents a normal distribution. If your school assigned grades, the top 10 percent of the class would receive A's; the top 16 percent of the class would receive either A's or B's; 68 percent of the class would receive C's; the bottom 16 percent of the class would receive D's; and the bottom 2.5 percent would receive D's and F's.

1. What grade did you get in history? _____

2. What percentage of the students in history did better than you? _____

3. In what course did you perform both better and worse than 50 percent of the class? _____

4. What percentage of the class did better than your performance in gym? _____

5. What grade did you get in math? _____

6. You scored higher than what percentage of your class in math? _____

7. In what course is your grade equal to the median? _____

8. In what course is your grade equal to the mode? _____

PERSONAL LEARNING ACTIVITIES

1. Take a survey and compute measures of central tendency on your data. For example, you could find out at what age people first got a job, drove a car, or had a date. You might find that the modal age for a first date is higher than the mean or median age. (Learning Objectives 5 and 6)

2. For the survey data you collected in Personal Learning Activity 1, you could compute a correlation coefficient following the instructions on page A-12 in your text. For example, are people who first drove at an older age also likely to have had their first date at an older age? If this is the case, you would find a positive correlation between "drive age" and "date age." (Learning Objective 10)

MULTIPLE-CHOICE QUESTIONS

SAMPLE QUIZ 1

1. If a visual presentation of data is required, you would use a
   a. frequency histogram.
   b. normal distribution.
   c. measure of central tendency.
   d. measure of variability.

2. The _____, a measure of central tendency, is affected by extreme or unrepresentative scores.
   a. mean
   b. median
   c. standard deviation
   d. range

Donald is a high school football coach. He has kept track of the number of touchdowns his players have made during every game. Using the data that he has collected, answer the next three questions.
Data: 1, 2, 3, 3, 8, 10, 7, 6, 5

3. What is the mode?
   a. 3
   b. 4
   c. 5
   d. 6

4. What is the median?
   a. 3
   b. 4
   c. 5
   d. 6

5. What is the mean?
   a. 3
   b. 4
   c. 5
   d. 6

6. Which of the following data sets would best fit the definition of a normal distribution?
   a. 1, 1, 2, 4, 6, 7, 8, 23
   b. 1, 6, 6, 12, 100, 100, 200
   c. 1, 2, 3, 4, 5, 5, 5, 6, 7, 8, 9
   d. 2, 4, 6, 8, 10, 10, 11

7. Jean Luc completed a study of music tastes. He found a significant correlation of .51 between the amount of milk people drink and the amount of jazz they listen to. The correct interpretation of this correlation is that in Jean Luc's sample
   a. people who drink more milk tend to listen to more jazz.
   b. people who drink more milk tend to listen to less jazz.
   c. listening to jazz music causes people to drink milk.
   d. drinking milk causes people to listen to jazz music.

8. Researchers use _____ statistical methods to summarize and present their data.
   a. descriptive
   b. significant
   c. inferential
   d. standard

9. A higher t value will be obtained if
   a. the N is large.
   b. the standard deviation is small.
   c. the difference between the two means is quite large.
   d. all of the above.

10. Cheryl designed an experiment to find out how the loudness of her music affects her fans' enjoyment of her concerts. One group in Cheryl's experiment is assigned to the "ears ring for two days" condition, where the music is very loud. Another group hears the same music at a loud but nondamaging level, and a third group hears it at a low level. She then has them complete a questionnaire to rate their enjoyment. Cheryl should use _____ to determine if there is a significant difference between the three groups.
    a. an analysis of variance
    b. a correlation coefficient
    c. the median
    d. a t test

Total Correct (See answer key) _____

SAMPLE QUIZ 2

Use this quiz to reassess your learning after taking quiz 1 and reviewing the appendix.

1. In order to best illustrate the differences in the weekly sales figures for each type of fat-free cookie, the "Cookie Man" should show
   a. the median overall cookie sales.
   b. a histogram indicating the weekly sales of each variety of cookies.
   c. the range of weekly sales figures for each cookie type.
   d. the standard deviation for each cookie type.

2. N is equal to the number of
   a. subjects in an experiment.
   b. observations in a data set.
   c. independent variables in an experiment.
   d. dependent variables in a data set.

3. You have decided to buy a certain kind of car because you heard that it gets great gas mileage. According to a consumer magazine, the mean gas mileage obtained during testing was 30, the median was 26, and the mode was 25. If you purchase this kind of car, the gas mileage you are likely to get will most likely
   a. be more than 30 miles per gallon.
   b. vary from 20 to 40 miles per gallon.
   c. be less than 30 miles per gallon.
   d. be 28 miles per gallon.

4. Chitra found a strong positive correlation (r = .80) between class attendance and exam scores. Chitra should conclude that
   a. attending class more often causes students to learn more.
   b. scores tend to be higher for students who attend class more often.
   c. students who attend class less often tend to score higher on tests.
   d. high scores make students feel less of a need to attend class.

5. Maxine found that she scored at the 93rd percentile on her calculus exam. This means that
   a. she got 93 percent of the problems correct.
   b. seven other people in the class scored higher than Maxine.
   c. she scored higher than 93 percent of the calculus class on the test.
   d. she did 93 problems correctly.

6. The mean is a poor descriptive measure of central tendency when
   a. the standard deviation is very small.
   b. it is very large.
   c. the range is very small.
   d. there are extreme or unrepresentative scores in the data set.

When Vitus asked his psychology and rhetoric classmates to rate his personality on a scale from 1 (irritating) to 10 (extremely pleasant), he received the following data:

Psychology class: 1 9 4 6 3 3 9
Rhetoric class: 8 7 7 8 8 9 9

7. What are the mean and median ratings of his psychology class?
   a. 3, 6
   b. 5, 4
   c. 5, 6
   d. 6, 5

8. Which of the following statements best describes the above sets of ratings?
   a. The rhetoric class has extremely high variability.
   b. The rhetoric class has more variability than the psychology class.
   c. The psychology class has more variability than the rhetoric class.
   d. The psychology class has extremely high variability.

9. Pierre has been computing t values for statistical analysis of his data. He has discovered a mistake in his calculation of the standard deviations for his data groups. They are much higher than he originally thought. The recalculated t values will be
   a. higher, thereby increasing his chances of getting statistically significant results.
   b. higher, thereby decreasing his chances of getting statistically significant results.
   c. lower, thereby increasing his chances of getting statistically significant results.
   d. lower, thereby decreasing his chances of getting statistically significant results.

10. Chris has done an experiment that involves two independent variables. Which inferential statistical measure should she use to analyze her data?
    a. Mean
    b. Standard deviation
    c. t test
    d. Analysis of variance

Total Correct (See answer key) _____

ANSWERS TO FILL-IN-THE-BLANKS KEY TERMS

1. null hypothesis (p. A-9)
2. frequency histogram (p. A-9)
3. normal distribution (pp. A-11–A-12)
4. percentile score (p. A-11)
5. standard (p. A-12)
6. t test (p. A-14)

ANSWERS TO CONCEPTS AND EXERCISES

No. 1: Statistics and the Consumer

1. *B*. Richard wants to buy a car that is consistently fast. Car A has a higher mean speed than car B over all the time trials. However, the standard deviation is very large. This indicates that car A is fast but not consistently fast, and that there was much variation in the data from the time trials. Car B's speed is 7 miles per hour slower than car A's, but the variation is low. Therefore, Richard should buy car B since he can depend on it to be more consistently fast. (pp. A-10–A-11)

2. *Redwood Estates*. To make money quickly but with very low risk, Richard must buy property that will increase in value consistently and at a fairly fast rate. Redwood Estates has a higher mean increase in property value and a small standard deviation, which indicate that the mean is a good description of the increase in the property's value. Richard should buy land in Redwood Estates. Brentwood Oaks not only has a lower mean value increase but also a great deal of variability in the increase. (pp. A-10–A-11)

3. *Bare Bones*. If Richard wants to be sure to lose weight, he should go to the Bare Bones Fitness Center. Even though the mean weight loss there is lower by 10 pounds, the variability is low, which means that most people who have gone there have lost close to 25 pounds. The Body Beautiful Fitness Center has a higher mean weight loss but also a higher variability, which means that some people have lost a lot of weight there, while others have lost very little. (pp. A-10–A-11)

4. *B*. Team B has consistently scored close to 370 points for the past five years. Team A has a mean of 355 points but has not been consistent. This means that some years it scored well above 355 points and some years well below 355 points. Team B's mean point total is higher and more consistent than team A's mean point total. Therefore, Richard should bet on team B. (pp. A-10–A-11)

No. 2: Choosing the Correct Statistical Method

1. t *test*. This psychologist is going to compare the mean number of nerve cell connections in rats from group 1 to the mean number of nerve cell connections in rats from group 2. She will use a *t* test, which will tell her how likely it is that the differences between the means of the two groups are due to the effects of the different environments or to chance. If her results are significant, then she can conclude that the housing did indeed cause changes in the number of nerve cell connections in the brains of the rats. (p. A-14)

2. *Correlation coefficient*. This psychologist is looking at the relationship between two variables: level of intelligence and environmental conditions. Therefore, she will find the correlation coefficient that represents this relationship. Remember, even if the correlation is very high, the psychologist can conclude only that these variables are related. She cannot conclude that environmental conditions cause changes in the level of intelligence. Correlation does not imply causation. (pp. A-12–A-13)

3. *Analysis of variance*. This psychologist is interested in the effect of therapy (independent variable) on depression (dependent variable). He wants to know if there are any differences in the effectiveness of three different types of therapy. Therefore, there are three levels of the independent variable. These data require an analysis of variance. (p. A-16)

No. 3: A Statistical Report Card

1. *B*. The top 16 percent of your class would receive either A's or B's. Only the top 10 percent would receive A's. Your history total falls at the 84th percentile (100 – 16 = 84), not in the upper 10 percent. Therefore, your performance is at a B level. (pp. A-11–A-12)

2. *16 percent*. Your history performance is at the first, or +1, standard deviation, which is also the 84th percentile. Therefore, you did better than 84 percent of the history students, and 16 percent did better than you (100 – 84 = 16). (pp. A-11–A-12)

3. *Biology*. In a normal distribution, 50 percent of the scores fall above the mean, and 50 percent fall below the mean. Your biology performance is at the mean. You scored higher than 50 percent of your biology class, and 50 percent of the class scored higher than you. (pp. A-11–A-12)

4. *97.5 percent*. Your gym grade falls at –2 standard deviations. The percentile at –2 standard deviations is 2.5. You did better than 2.5 percent of the class, and 97.5 percent of the class did better than you (100 – 2.5 = 97.5) (pp. A-11–A-12)

5. *A*. Your achievement in math is at the 97.5 percentile. The upper 10 percent of your class would have received A's. You are in the upper 2.5 percent (100 – 97.5 = 2.5); therefore, your performance is at the A level. (pp. A-11–A-12)

6. *97.5 percent*. Your math total falls at +2 standard deviations, which is also the 97.5th percentile. Therefore, you did better than 97.5 percent of the class. (pp. A-11–A-12)

7, 8. *Biology*. In a normal distribution the mean, median, and mode are equal. Your biology performance falls at the mean of the distribution; hence, your biology performance is equal to the median and the mode. (pp. A-10–A-12)

ANSWERS TO MULTIPLE-CHOICE QUESTIONS

Circle the question numbers you answered correctly.

Sample Quiz 1

1. *a* is the answer. (p. A-9)
   b. A normal distribution describes a certain type of data set. It is not used to present data.
   c. A measure of central tendency is a numerical, not visual, description of data.
   d. A measure of variability is a numerical, not visual, description of data.

2. *a* is the answer. To calculate the mean, the values of all the scores in a data set are used. Therefore, if one or more of the scores differ greatly from the rest, the value of the mean changes, making it a less accurate description of central tendency. (p. A-10)
   b. The calculation of the median considers all the scores but not their values, so that each score carries the same weight. The median is always the score that splits the data in half. Therefore, scores with extremely high or low values will not affect the median.
   c. The standard deviation is a measure of variability, not a measure of central tendency.
   d. The range is a measure of variability, not a measure of central tendency.

3. *a* is the answer. The mode is the most frequently occurring score, which is 3. (p. A-10)

4. *c* is the answer. To find the median, rearrange the scores from lowest to highest and then find the score that splits the data in half. The data from lowest to highest: 1, 2, 3, 3, 5, 6, 7, 8, 10. There are nine scores, so the fifth score will split the set such that half the scores (four) are below it and half (four) are above it. The value of the fifth score is 5. (p. A-10)

5. *c* is the answer. The mean is 5. It is calculated by adding all the scores and then dividing by the number of scores. The sum of all the scores is 45, which, divided by 9 (the total number of scores), is 5. (p. A-10)

6. *c* is the answer. The mean, median, and mode are equal in a normal distribution. (pp. A-11–A-12)
   a, b, d. None of these data sets has a mean, a median, and a mode that are all equal.

7. *a* is the answer. A significant positive correlation coefficient indicates that as one variable increases the other tends to increase. As milk drinking increases, jazz listening increases. (pp. A-12–A-13)
   b. In a negative correlation, as one variable increases, the other decreases. Jean Luc found a positive correlation.
   c, d. A correlation only indicates a relationship; therefore, Jean Luc cannot conclude that either of these are true.

8. *a* is the answer. (pp. A9–A-13)
   b. There is no such thing as a "significant statistical" method. Researchers use inferential statistics to conclude from data that experimental results are statistically significant.
   c. Inferential statistics are the mathematical procedures psychologists use to draw conclusions from data and make inferences about what they mean.
   d. There is no such thing as a standard statistic.

9. *d* is the answer. Mathematical reasoning shows that any of the answers will increase the value of *t*. This conclusion can also be reached by considering the purpose of a *t* test—that is, to determine if the obtained difference between two means is due to chance or to the real effect of an independent variable. (pp. A-14–A-16)
   a. As the sample gets larger, any random factors that are present should be canceled out by the majority.

b. If the standard deviation is small, the means are more accurate descriptions of the activity in a data set. Therefore, any differences are more likely to be real, not a chance occurrence resulting from the presence of unrepresentative scores.
   c. In a worst-case situation, the difference between two means could be due to bad samples or extreme scores. However, if the difference between the means is very large, there will still be a difference after all these effects are adjusted for.

10. *a* is the answer. An analysis of variance is the inferential statistic that is used when comparing more than two groups. (p. A-16)
   b. A correlation coefficient indicates the strength and direction of the relationship between two variables. Cheryl cannot infer from a correlation coefficient whether her three groups are different.
   c. One median will not allow for comparisons between groups. Even if we found different medians for each group, it would not allow us to infer that they were significantly different.
   d. A *t* test is an inferential statistic, but it only compares two groups.

Now turn to the quiz analysis table at the end of this appendix to find which areas you know well and which areas you need to work on. Circle the numbers in the table for items on Quiz 1 that you answered correctly.

ANSWERS TO MULTIPLE-CHOICE QUESTIONS

Circle the question numbers you answered correctly.

Sample Quiz 2

1. *b* is the answer. A frequency histogram would show visually how the weekly sales figures differed. (pp. A-9–A-10)
   a. The median overall cookie sales would be one number indicating how sales generally have gone.
   c. The range of sales figures would show how large the variation in cookie sales had been each week, but would not be a good illustration of how many cookies were sold each week. After all, if 10,000 boxes of Cookie One were sold one week, and the next week it was 20,000, that would be a range of 10,000. If we compared the weekly sales of Cookie Two—50,000 and

60,000 (a range of 10,000)—we would see no difference in the figures for cookie types one and two.

d. Like the range, the standard deviation describes variability rather than general sales figures.

2. *b* is the answer. Observations or scores are numerical representations of the measurement of the dependent variable. The total number of observations is called *N*. (p. A-10)

a. If each subject gives two responses or answers in an experiment, then the total number of observations, *N*, will be equal to twice the size of the sample. Therefore, counting the number of subjects will not always give the value of *N*.

c, d. The number of independent or dependent variables will not tell you how many observations a data set has.

3. *c* is the answer. Since the mode and median are both below 30, you should suspect that the median has been artificially inflated by a few extreme, unrepresentative scores. Therefore, the gas mileage will probably be lower than 30 miles per gallon. (p. A-10)

a, b, d. The mean has been inflated by a few extreme unrepresentative scores. The car's mileage will be lower than 30 miles per gallon. However, you cannot predict on the basis of the data given just how much lower it will be, nor can you predict what the range of performance will be.

4. *b* is the answer. A positive correlation indicates that as attendance increased, exam scores increased. (pp. A-12–A-13)

a. Correlations show relationships between variables. A high correlation indicates a stronger relationship, but cannot indicate if one variable causes the other—or if a third variable causes both of them.

c. If the correlation were negative, then this would be the correct answer.

d. Even if the correlation were negative, we would need to do an experiment to find out if high scores cause students to feel less of a need to attend class.

5. *c* is the answer. A percentile score indicates the percentage of people or observations that fall below a given score in a normal distribution. Therefore, 93 percent of Maxine's calculus class received scores that were lower than hers. (pp. A-11–A-12)

a. A percentile does not show how many problems Maxine answered correctly. It does show how well Maxine did relative to the other people in her class.

b. How many people did better or worse than Maxine cannot be calculated unless the number of people in her class is known.

d. The percentile is not related to the number of problems on the test.

6. *d* is the answer. The mean is an average of the values of all the scores in a data set. Extremely low or extremely high scores can have a huge effect on the value of the mean, and it will not provide an accurate description of where most of the scores tend to fall. (p. A-10)

a. If the standard deviation is small, most of the scores in the data set cluster around the mean, and the mean accurately represents the central tendency of the data.

b. The size of the mean does not make it a better or worse measure of central tendency. A large mean could accurately indicate a predominance of large scores in the data set or the presence of very large unrepresentative scores.

c. If the range is small, there may not be much variability in the data. The less variability there is, the more accurate the mean is in conveying where the scores had a tendency to center.

7. *b* is the answer. The mean is calculated by adding the scores and dividing by the number of observations. Thirty-five divided by 7 is 5. To find the median, you must put the scores in order (1, 3, 3, 4, 6, 9, 9) and choose the middle one (4). (p. A-10)

8. *c* is the answer. Even without calculating a standard deviation, one can see that the ratings of the rhetoric class are all within one point of the mean, which is 8. The rhetoric class has a range of 2, and the psychology class has a range of 8. (pp. A-10–A-11)

a, d. Neither class has extremely high variability.

b. The ratings of Vitus's psychology classmates vary more than those of his rhetoric classmates.

9. *d* is the answer. If you look at the formula for a *t* test, you will see that increasing the standard deviation will decrease the overall value of the equation, or *t*. The lower the value of *t* is, the more likely it is to be smaller than the *t* values listed in a *t* table and, hence, statistically insignificant. (pp. A-14–A-16)

a, b. A larger standard deviation will result in a smaller *t* value.

c. A larger standard deviation will result in a smaller *t* value. But the obtained *t* value must still be equal to or larger than the *t* values listed in a *t* table for the data to be considered statistically significant.

10. *d* is the answer. In an experiment with two or more independent variables, the results may be due to either of the independent variables or the interaction between them. An analysis of variance can measure the size and source of these effects. (p. A-16)

   a, b. The mean and standard deviation are necessary to compute inferential statistics (such as the *t* test and analysis of variance), but they are descriptive statistics.

   c. A *t* test is an inferential statistic, but it is used to test the difference between two means in an experiment that uses only one independent variable.

Now go to the quiz analysis table below to find which areas you know well and which areas you need to work on. Circle the numbers in the table for items on Quiz 2 that you answered correctly.

For each question you answered correctly, circle its number. (Quiz 1 numbers are not shaded; Quiz 2 numbers are shaded.) Are there patterns in the types of questions or the topics you got wrong that could direct your further study? Did you improve from Quiz 1 to Quiz 2?

TOPIC	TYPE OF QUESTION		
	DEFINITION	COMPREHENSION	APPLICATION
Describing Data			
Frequency histogram	1		
			1
Descriptive statistics	8	2	3, 4, 5, 6, 7
	2	6	3, 4, 5, 7, 8
Inferential Statistics			
Differences between means		9	
			9
Beyond the *t* test			10
			10

TOTAL CORRECT BY QUIZ:

QUIZ 1:
QUIZ 2:

417/00

417/00